2068

Understanding Social Welfare

Understanding Social Welfare

SIXTH EDITION

Ralph Dolgoff

University of Maryland, Baltimore

Donald Feldstein

Council of Jewish Federations

Boston   New York   San Francisco
Mexico City   Montreal   Toronto   London   Madrid   Munich   Paris
Hong Kong   Singapore   Tokyo   Cape Town   Sydney

Editor in Chief: *Karen Hanson*
Series Editor: *Patricia Quinlin*
Editorial Assistant: *Annemarie Kennedy*
Marketing Manager: *Taryn Wahlquist*
Editorial Production Service: *Chestnut Hill Enterprises, Inc.*
Manufacturing Buyer: *JoAnne Sweeney*
Cover Administrator: *Linda Knowles*
Electronic Composition: *Omegatype Typography, Inc.*

For related titles and support materials, visit our online catalog at www.ablongman.com.

Between the time Website information is gathered and published, some sites may have closed. Also, the transcription of URLs can result in typographical errors. The publisher would appreciate notification where these occur so that they may be corrected in subsequent editions.

Library of Congress Cataloging-in-Publication Data

Dolgoff, Ralph.
    Understanding social welfare / Ralph Dolgoff, Donald Feldstein.—6th ed.
      p. cm
    Includes bibliographical references and index.
    ISBN 0-205-36006-8 (alk. paper)
      1. Public welfare—United States. 2. Social service—United States. 3. United States—Social policy. I. Feldstein, Donald. II. Title.

HV95.D64 2002
361.973—dc21

                                  2002018408

Printed in the United States of America

10 9 8 7 6   07 06 05

Contents

5 *America, Poverty, Two Paths: The American Experience II*   **88**

Preface

As this preface is being written, it is becoming clear that the national and international contexts confronting the United States do not support attempts to deal with issues of poverty, health, education, and social problems in general, and—unfortunately—it seems hardly likely that the situations will become for the foreseeable future more supportive of efforts to improve social and human services.

Nonetheless, a large number of problematic situations face our society and have implications for us all. (1) The United States has entered a "war against terrorism," a war that requires increased public expenditures to counter the terrorist threats, to conduct the war, and to repair the damage inflicted in several ways on our society. (2) These public expenditures will erode the Social Security trust fund and perhaps deplete the predicted surpluses even more than had been done with the massive tax cuts enacted in 2001. (3) It is expected that funds for public investment in social and human services will have to compete even more strenuously against these other necessary expenditures for defense, fostering a sense of security and physical safety for citizens, and ensuring the economy is maintained into the future.

(4) The economic fallout from terrorism accompanied an economic slowdown and the safety net has holes in it. TANF (the "public assistance") program set five years as the limit for most recipients of public assistance. The five year limit for many people arrived in 2002. Welfare-to-work makes sense when the economy is strong and work plentiful. It is unclear, however, what will become of those who have no chance of work when employment becomes scarcer. Unemployment compensation has become more and more difficult to get. Job training and low-income housing have been shrunk by budget cuts. State budgets are experiencing lower tax receipts because of the slowing economy. Social services broadly defined are usually not at the head of the priority list. (5) We have a large and expanding number of aging persons and attending to their problems such as Social Security and Medicare will require changes and/or more dollars. How will our society pay for the rapidly increasing life expectancies of citizens, especially if a weakened economy reduces the financial wealth of many aging persons?

It is not clear how all these problems can be dealt with simultaneously. Our society may have to return as during the Viet Nam War to choosing between "guns and butter." Or, contrariwise, our nation can seek to maintain morale, social cohesion, and a feeling that "we are all in this together" by enhancing social welfare provision. No one can accurately predict the future but decisions about social welfare will be made within the complex context suggested above.

We have attempted in this book to achieve two sometimes mutually exclusive objectives. First, we have written a book with a point of view—one that examines social welfare issues critically, focuses on concepts, and invites challenge and alternative interpretations. Second, we have tried to produce a usable textbook, covering detail and fact in an organized manner, useful for all those concerned with social welfare and human services in our society.

The success of our work can only be judged by individual readers, whom we hope will be challenged to reach their own conclusions about the issues discussed. We will have succeeded if readers attain knowledge and understanding to aid them in decision making both as professionals and as informed and participating citizens.

We are grateful to a number of persons whose reactions and advice have helped us to improve the book: Ana Alvarez, Aaron Dolgoff, Eliana Dolgoff, William Jackson Jr., Heejung Koh, Richard Larson, Margie Simon, Dr. Raju Varghese, Dr. Donna Harrington, Dr. Howard Altstein, and Rex Rempel (who asks good questions). We also want to express our appreciation to Bernetta Hux and Tammy Derry for their assistance and to the librarians, as well as to the Health and Human Services Library of the University of Maryland, Baltimore and the Milton S. Eisenhower Library of the Johns Hopkins University.

This revised edition reflects change in the social welfare system through the publishing process. In addition to a complete updating, we have tried to anticipate the issues and proposed solutions to various social problems. We have maintained the main theme and focus on the impact of societal structure and change on the nature of peoples' needs and problems. In this edition we have added or augmented material on the following:

- Trends data and discussions are all up-to-date, including programs, income, poverty and wealth.
- Bush administration philosophy, goals, agenda, and early actions have been included as well as identifying its "waiting list" of desirable legislation.
- Expanded traditional residual, institutional, and developmental models by adding a new category and extensive description of Socio-Economic Asset Development.
- Expanded discussion on national policy for church and state and social welfare.
- Expanded section on services for children.
- New section on Mental Health Services for Children and youth.
- Early Hispanic experiences in the Southwest expanded and decimation of Southeastern indigenous peoples given more emphasis.
- Policy issues and discussion related to gay men and lesbians expanded and up-dated.
- New expanded section included on Corporate and Taxpayer Welfare.

To communicate with the authors, contact Ralph Dolgoff at rdolgoff@ssw.umaryland.edu. We will respond to your comments as soon as possible.

We are appreciative of the support our families have provided. Special thanks is due to Sylvia Dolgoff, who at various stages has contributed in many ways.

Finally, we want to express our deep appreciation to our students, whom we have taught and from whom we have learned.

Many people have contributed to the development of this book, including our reviewers: Dr. George T. Patterson, New York University; Barbara Chandler, New Mexico State University; and Marion Wagner, Indiana University. Nonetheless, the book is ours and we are responsible for its limitations. On each re-reading we, as do all authors, become aware of things we should have written or written better. But we hope we have come close to the expression of the aims with which we started and that our readers find this book stimulating and helpful.

About the Authors

Dr. Ralph Dolgoff
is a professor at the School of Social Work at the University of Maryland, Baltimore, where he also served as Dean. Previously, he served as acting Dean and associate Dean at the Adelphi University School of Social Work, and as senior program specialist at the Council on Social Work Education. Dr. Dolgoff is coauthor (with Frank Loewenberg and Donna Harrington) of *Ethical Decisions for Social Work Practice* (6th Edition). He has published widely on social and welfare services, ethics, social policy, and social work education.

Dr. Donald Feldstein, Associate Executive Vice-President, Council of Jewish Federations (Retired)
has had a distinguished career in Jewish Communal Service and in Social Work Education. He is the author of numerous monographs and articles in the previously mentioned fields.

Understanding Social Welfare

1

Socio-Economic Structure, Human Needs, and Mutual Responsibility

Competition…is a law of nature…. if we try to amend it, there is only one way in which we can do it. We can take from the better and give to the worse. We can deflect the penalties of those who have done ill and throw them on those who have done better. We can take the rewards from those who have done better and give them to those who have done worse. We shall thus lessen the inequalities. We shall favor the survival of the unfittest, and we shall accomplish this by destroying liberty. Let it be understood that we cannot go outside of this alternative: liberty, inequality, survival of the fittest, not-liberty, equality, survival of the unfittest.

—William Graham Sumner[1]

Overview

Embedded in Sumner's statement is a deep American belief: Those who have done well materially are better than those who have done not so well. Those who have prospered have done so because of their own individual talents and efforts. The corollary is that those who have not done well have done so because of some personal defect. They are immoral, lazy, unmotivated, or not so bright. Poor people, for example, are individually responsible for their poverty. According to this perspective, each person is responsible for whatever situation in which he or she finds him- or herself. The most important values are self-reliance and the avoidance of dependence. One should not be a burden to family, others, or—especially—society. Essentially, those who are disadvantaged, victimized, poor, or disabled somehow

1

are responsible for their condition; if they were better or more adequate people, they would not be in a dependent position.

We begin this book by noting this perspective because it has had a profound and continuing impact on the nature of social welfare in the United States and re-emerged as a widespread force during the 1980s and 1990s. However, this emphasis on individual responsibility is not the only driving force in U.S. social welfare, which is influenced by a mixture of motives rather than one unified, impelling force. Altruism, a refusal to ignore the suffering of others, a sense of fairness, and a concern for mutual aid are also viable American values. Social welfare also functions to meet the maintenance needs of society by preventing instability and providing for social continuity. In part, one's views of the functions of social welfare depend on one's personal perspective, but in reality the U.S. social welfare scene is marked by ambivalent motivations rather than one pure and straightforward intention.

The values of a society, even implicit values, can influence the nature of its social welfare system. What are the roots and several manifestations of social welfare in U.S. society? What are the components of American tendencies to focus on individual responsibility as a major influence on social welfare? How are these and other values expressed in social welfare? And what are the biases of the authors that will inform this volume?

The Impact of Social and Economic Structures

Many Americans and most students and practitioners in the helping professions have been socialized to think in a certain way—primarily to understand case situations in individual, family, and group terms, often minimizing the effects of the multiple factors and levels of the social environment on human behaviors and lives.

In this book, in addition to individual responsibility and effort, we want to consider the impact of social and economic structures on us all. Although this approach is not completely explanatory, it does provide a contrasting view and offers other ways of understanding what happens to people.

One way of understanding the difference between individual and structural causes is provided by C. Wright Mills, who defined "private troubles" and "public issues":

> *Troubles* occur within the character of the individual and within the range of his immediate relations with others; they have to do with his self and with those limited areas of social life of which he is directly and personally aware.

Whereas troubles refer to one's immediate milieu and, to some extent, to one's willful activity, they are essentially private matters. On the other hand, *issues*

> have to do with matters that transcend these local environments of the individual and the range of his inner life. They have to do with the organization of many milieux into the institutions of an historical society as a whole, with the ways in

which various milieux overlap and interpenetrate to form the larger structure of social and historical life.

A public issue is a communal matter, an economic and political crisis in institutional arrangements. If a few people are unemployed because they resent authority and have difficulty with supervisors, it is a private matter. However, if thousands or millions are unemployed because of the nature of the structure of employment opportunities, their difficulties have origins far beyond their personal, individual control, despite their strenuous efforts.[2]

The following studies illustrate that many social problems are associated with, influenced by, even caused by social and economic structural factors. From 1970 to 1996, the social indicators (measures of socially important conditions in a society) for some social problems improved, others worsened, and still others shifted in their performance. Among those problems which *improved* were infant mortality, the high school drop out rate, the poverty rate for those over 65, and life expectancy at age 65. Among those that *worsened* were child abuse, child poverty, youth suicide, health care coverage, wages, inequality, and violent crime. Those whose performance *shifted* included teenage drug use, teenage births, affordable housing, and unemployment.[3]

Despite exceptional, strong, and sustained economic performance during the 1990s, nevertheless, the following reports illustrate that many social problems are associated with, influenced by, even caused by social and economic structural factors:

1. Poverty is the best predictor of poor health outcomes for children, including mortality, activity limitations, and utilization of health care.[4]
2. People who experienced financial difficulties in childhood are at greater risk of both low educational attainment and poor health at age 23 and in adult life.[5]
3. Poor children are more likely to have physical and mental health problems, to suffer from stunted growth or lead poisoning, to score lower on reading, math, and vocabulary tests, and to drop out from school compared to non-poor children.[6]
4. Studies have found large percentages of child-abusing fathers and stepfathers were unemployed during the year and/or at the time they were abusers. Reports show that both the number and severity of child-abuse cases increase during recessions, with the greatest number of abuse problems found in counties with the highest unemployment rates. Family service agencies found that family violence increased during a recession, and case studies document an upsurge in the use of child welfare services following the closing of industrial plants. Recessions are stressful for those maintaining continuous employment *and* for those who lose their jobs.[7]

Unemployment and poverty are inextricably tied to the structure of the economy. Among these structural factors are a shift from a goods-producing, manufacturing economy to service-producing industries; the polarization of the labor market into low-wage and high-wage sectors; increasing technology; and the dispersal of manufacturing and other jobs to suburban and overseas locations. Although these structural factors—such as the nature of the job market, the job preparation of potential workers, geographic factors, and racial and other discriminations—affect everyone in our society, they impact differentially on different groups, as we shall see in more detail in chapter 8.[8] For example, the structure of jobs and wages has changed. Many industries require more able and highly skilled workers. Such workers are generally in short supply, bidding up their wages and increasing the gap between their incomes and those of workers with lower educational levels and skills.

Poverty in the United States has become more urban, spatially concentrated, and clustered with other indicators of disadvantage. The residents of neighborhoods of concentrated poverty who experience multiple forms of social and economic disadvantage are disproportionately members of minority groups. Changes in the wage structure over the past two decades have impacted negatively upon non-college educated minorities living in inner cities. Declining real wages overall, rising inequality in wage and income distribution, growing numbers of low wage jobs have been accompanied by an increase in joblessness, especially among black minority youth in cities.[9]

Opportunities for job advancement by low-skilled workers have decreased. Nonetheless, there is a paradox. Unemployment overall has decreased, and many workers hold more than one job. Those who face the most difficulty are those poorly educated, school dropouts, and minorities.

Finally, there is a concern that inflation be kept under control. However, doing so has accompanying costs. Productive output is lost, jobs are lost, business opportunities are bypassed, and tax receipts are lost. Incomes end up lower than they would have been without these efforts to forestall or ameliorate inflationary threats in the economy.

We will return to these issues and concepts in later chapters. For now we need to recognize the impact of structural factors such as business cycles; the shifts in the number, types, and degrees of skilled labor required by various industries; international trade and competition; and technological change. Additional significant factors are discrimination, immigration, changes in the age and educational composition of the work force, and unionization and the lack of it, as well as changes in the political climate.[10]

Defining Social Welfare and Social Work

Social welfare is referred to throughout this book. What is social welfare, and what do we mean by this term? The definition is not simple and is discussed at some length at the beginning of chapter 6. But the reader is entitled to a brief definition early on. For reasons explained in chapter 6, we define *social welfare* as follows: *all social interventions intended to enhance or maintain the social functioning of human beings.* We limit our consideration, however, to those parts of the broadest social welfare system that are not clearly the domain or territory of other fields or disciplines such as education, police, and fire services.

Social work is discussed in chapters 12 and 13, where the emergence of the profession, its current functions, the context within which it operates, and other selected issues are examined. At this point, however, it is important that the reader understand that *social work* is a *professional occupation that delivers social welfare services.*[11] Although social work serves preponderantly in the social welfare societal institution, social workers also deliver services in a large number of societal institutions that are not the social welfare institution per se, including business and industry, military defense, and criminal justice, as well as educational, health, and religious institutions, among others. The reader should keep this distinction in mind, differentiating the societal institution of social welfare from the profession of social work.

Our aim in this book is to examine U.S. social welfare and social work. We are mindful of the interconnections and interdependence of U.S. society, in all its aspects, with other parts of the world. The United States in contemporary times is affected by developments in many nations and regions far from our shores. Although the world is a series of societal and ecological interconnections, and these systemic relationships impact on the U.S. economy and general culture—including social welfare, both directly and indirectly—our priority focus will be social welfare and social work within the U.S. context.

The American Myth of the Hero

For more than five centuries people have come to America: the secular Zion, the golden nation, the land of possibilities. Leaving behind families, traditions, and the familiar, people set out for America. Although we note these migrations to a land of dangers and dreams, there was—of course—a major exception. In the case of African Americans, they were forcibly taken to this land.

From the Puritans seeking religious freedom in Massachusetts, to the debtors escaping imprisonment in Georgia, the earliest American settlers were a mixture of indentured persons, craft workers, paupers, businesspeople, sailors, artisans, and adventurers. They were seeking to escape, and they were searching for new horizons beyond the ocean and beyond the constraints of more developed societies.

The pioneers were seen as rugged individualists, self-reliant and independent. The reality was quite different from the myth. A communitarian spirit was needed in frontier territories and pioneering times. Settlements developed, and people became interdependent. In *The Americans*, Daniel Boorstin described the reality this way:

> But, of all the American myths, none is stronger than that of the loner moving West across the land. Without having thought much about why, we have taken for granted that, on landing, the colonial traveler no longer needed his community. The pioneering spirit, we are often told, is a synonym for "individualism." The courage to move to new places and to try new things is supposed to be the same as

the courage to go it alone, to focus exclusively and intensively and enterprisingly on oneself.... There was, of course, the occasional lone traveler and individual explorer.... In history, even the great explorer has been the man who drew others to a common purpose, in the face of unpredictable hardships.... To cross the wild continent safely, one had to travel with a group...When American ways were taking shape, many, perhaps most, of the people who were the first to settle at a distance from the protected boundaries of the Atlantic seaboard, traveled in groups.[12]

Even the early U.S. government aided the individual with mechanisms similar to those used today. Puritan communities paid a salaried town doctor in a sort of community-supported medicine. New Englanders attempted to regulate wages, prices, and interest rates. Laws were passed to ensure the quality of workmanship and goods. Public officials scrutinized the regulation of weights and measures, as well as ferries, mills, and inns.[13] In fact, the government during early U.S. history played an affirmative role in the economy in regard to credit, a national bank, currency and coinage, public lands, and other matters. During Jefferson's first administration, the Cumberland National Road linked the eastern seaboard with the Ohio Valley. The government also owned stock in the Chesapeake and Delaware Canal Co., as well as in the Dismal Swamp Co. of Virginia and the Chesapeake and Ohio Canal Co. These governmental interventions had many purposes, chief among them the encouragement of travel and trade.[14]

The complexity and specialization of modern society makes interdependence greater and more necessary than ever. Each of us can perform only a small fraction of the functions necessary to help ourselves and society to survive. The astronauts are heroic figures even while they are excellent symbols of the necessary interdependence of "heroes." They need each other's skills; they are dependent on teams of scientists and technicians. Even so, we are left with Americans still idealizing images of self-sufficient persons.

The American idealized myth includes the following:

1. The best people are rugged individualists who are physically strong, psychologically independent, and able to flourish without help.
2. "Making it" is what counts and is to be respected and admired.
3. Everything is possible. Those who try hard enough, no matter how humble their beginnings, can "make it."
4. Humans strive for material gain. If it were not for the carrot of material gain or the stick of hunger and deprivation, motivation for work might disappear. Other motives are shadowy, unreal, or idealistic.
5. The corollary of all the above is that those who fail to "make it" are at least incompetent, and perhaps even lazy and immoral (synonyms).

Although the entire mythology has created some of the strains in American life, it is this final corollary that places personal responsibility and independence at the heart of American values. Somehow, if things do not go well or if one fails, then one is to blame. Other cultures have extolled ambition and progress. It is the combination of this striving philosophy with the corollary that people determine both their successes and failures that makes American society particularly unusual. Not all Americans accept the mythology. At different periods it is stronger or weaker. For example, during the Great Depression of the 1930s people felt simultaneously that they were inadequate and that the social system had failed them.[15] As Americans experience a tension between individualistic and communitarian values, there are trends away from and toward this American mythology. These trends are discussed in chapter 14, because these views continue to have profound effects on life in the United States, particularly regarding social welfare.

This mythology needed nurturing to grow and develop, and the United States supplied it. The United States has been a land of opportunity to a degree unmatched by other societies. There was and continues to be more physical and social mobility in the United States than elsewhere. One price of that mobility has been the assumption that the nonmobile are inadequate.

According to the historian Frederick Jackson Turner, the idea of a constant frontier is central to the American spirit, and it was only in the last decade of the nineteenth century that the frontier was officially declared closed. Illustrative of this idea was the young and vigorous Kennedy national administration that in 1960 named its program "The New Frontier." The idea of a constant frontier stays before the United States in several forms: the reach to fulfill the American dream, to fulfill the potential of the nation and all its citizens, to explore space, to develop the contributions of science and technology for human betterment, and to create throughout our urban centers, suburbs, and rural areas "user-friendly" habitats for all citizens. However, even where agreement exists as to the goals, as we shall see later, there is much and intense disagreement about how to achieve these goals.

Intellectual, scientific, and religious currents all fed the mythology. In chapter 2 we discuss the relationship between the views of human nature in any society and its welfare approach and programs, but it should be noted here that the ideology of industrialism, the development of the Protestant ethic (particularly the Calvinist strain), and social Darwinism each contributed to our placing priority on individual responsibility.

Industrialism drove people from their traditional homes and pursuits to cities and encouraged mobility, material gain, and competition. Industrialism resulted in the amassing of capital, something frowned on in more traditional Christian theology. Industrialism demanded a large pool of low-paid working people. Religion and science generated a rationale and justification for these developments. The element of Calvinist philosophy that concerns us here is that the successful and wealthy are seen as God's elect, whom God has chosen to reward. We need not, therefore, overly pity the poor for receiving their just desserts at the hand of God, nor should we hate the rich, who are God's elect.

Additional support came from economics and evolutionary theory. The theories of laissez-faire capitalism suggested that society functions best and that the common good is furthered most when there is constrained governmental interference in the affairs of the market. The market is a grand anonymous stage in which each commodity finds its own value. If labor is underpaid, this reflects its market value. Any attempt to interfere by regulation lessens the ultimate good to society.[16] Social scientists went further. They took the ideas of natural selection developed by Charles Darwin and created a social equivalent. The theory of natural selection, most simply stated, is that in nature the most fit survive and the least fit die. Similarly, according to this view, in society, in the free market (nature), there is a natural tendency for the best (most fit) to succeed, and any attempt to interfere with this "natural selection" only perpetuates and gives favor to those who can contribute least.

According to these views, social welfare measures, which help the weak, only weaken society. The kindest approach, in the long run, is to let the weak fall. Laissez-faire philosophers acknowledged the value of charity, but more to foster uplifting the soul of the philanthropist than for aiding the victim. President Herbert Hoover claimed that enterprise builds society while charity builds character.

All of these ideas and forces had their impact in shaping the American myth. They were particularly functional to a young, vigorous, and expanding country in which there were many casualties of that expansion, from the indigenous Native Americans to the enslaved African Americans, the working poor, small shopkeepers, and the waves of immigrants in each generation.

It is not our intent here to try to counter the arguments of these philosophies. They are discussed further in chapters 2 and 3. Many Americans reject them on face value, but many others believe them. It is suggested that we live in a welfare society, and "they" are expected to be able to do something about our social problems. Most Americans believe the destitute should be helped. But so deep and pervasive in the American psyche is the philosophy of individual responsibility and competition[17] that we still find ourselves, in many overt and subtle ways, repeating the patterns that belong to ideologies many have long since rejected. Many others believe these ideologies are true and best for each of us and for the nation. We will discuss important ways in which this American myth is still active and particularly how it affects social welfare in the United States.

Balancing Individual and Societal Responsibilities

An overemphasis on individual causation (personal troubles are mainly a result of personal failures) can be harmful; similarly refusing to recognize "public issues" that must be dealt with can be equally destructive. Nonetheless, an emphasis on individual responsibility for one's situation regardless of the context and structural factors in society is very much alive and very much with us. In fact, this deeply ingrained value judgment and perception is rather ubiquitous and is found often where one might least expect it. For example, Peggy Say, the sister of Terry A. Anderson, who had been snatched off the streets of Beirut and held captive in Lebanon for many years, reported, "I won't tell him of the accusation that 'he shouldn't have been there in the first place....'"[18] Every important social problem—crime, mental illness, civil disorder, unemployment, child abuse, health care, slum housing—has been analyzed within the framework of the responsibility of the individual. Those who experience the problem are poorly motivated, lack information, have the wrong characteristics, have poor judgment, or are not acculturated.

What are some of the reasons we shift responsibility from community and society entirely to the individual? To do so serves certain purposes. It makes us feel superior; it allows us to express our hostilities toward relatively safe objects. It also separates and distances us from those in need and allows us subtly to defend the status quo in regard to the poor.

When we consider Mills's differentiation between "private troubles" and "public issues," we can see, in the latter case, that the solution does not lie within the range of opportunities available to a few people. Even divorce, commonly viewed as a personal matter, becomes a "public issue" or structural issue involving the institutions of marriage, the family, and other societal institutions. As we saw earlier, public issues such as unemployment and wages may result in "personal problems" of various types, in which people "carry" the public issue.

To define all personal problems as private troubles is to suggest that individuals can control their fates. However, to understand and accept the point of view implied by "structural" explanations of public issues suggests that something should be done to alter the structure that affects us all, a structure that affects some more positively and others more negatively.

To understand the personal milieu and "private troubles" of people, we often have to look beyond the immediate to the societal context. The sector of the economy, the degree of unionization, the geographic part of the country one resides in—all these and other factors, as we shall see in greater detail in chapter 8, impact on one's well-being. Events in distant locations can have enormous implications for persons and families, events over which, in this interdependent world, we often have little, if any, control.

The Authors' Perspective

The reader deserves to know something more about the biases of the authors. We move from multiple perspectives:

1. Many problems of people in our society are largely caused by the institutional structure of society and not by their own inadequacies or actions.
2. Although societal structures impact on individuals, people ultimately are responsible for their actions and behavior, if not for their fates. There is free will within the boundaries of the opportunities available, boundaries that are defined by both objective and subjective realities.
3. Social policies and programs can have a profoundly positive influence on society.
4. Private troubles and public issues are interrelated. Private troubles are embedded in public issues, and public issues are embedded in private troubles.

All of these perspectives are important. People may be oppressed and be irresponsible or even criminal. That may be society's fault, and it may be society's responsibility to restructure itself so that such people will be less likely to make such destructive choices. Nonetheless, there are those persons who choose to harm others. Because of the circumstances in which people are born and raised, there are different obstacles and opportunities confronting each individual. There are unequal capacities among people, and there are oppressive social forces. We do not deny these factors as part of the reality that confronts each individual in relation to his or her own responsibility. Moreover, people are sometimes so incapacitated that their impairment makes it impossible for them to control their own actions; therefore, they do not have a full measure of responsibility. These exceptions and external forces create dilemmas for human beings, but, it seems to us, we must hold people responsible for their actions precisely because such a claim upon them maintains their very humanity and dignity. The question is this: To what extent are people really human without assuming responsibility for their actions?

Persons who kill other persons must ultimately be considered responsible, or we deprive them of their very humanity. The public official who engages in corruption because he goes along with the others, the Nazi who obeyed orders, and the mugger who must support a heroin habit—all are finally responsible for the acts they commit. There is a song in the musical *West Side Story* in which the juvenile delinquents are addressing their tormentor, Officer Krupke. After several humorous verses in which they mock society's shuttling them from judge to psychiatrist to social worker, the delinquents insist that it is not environment or upbringing that caused their plight but, "Deep down inside us, we're no good."

To make this claim is their way of insisting that they be recognized as individuals in their own right, that there is a certain kind of sociological jargon that is dehumanizing. If one is human, one is deserving of faith in ultimate worth, in capacity to grow. But being human implies being responsible for one's acts in spite of adversity. There is a patronizing element in portraying vandals as social revolutionaries, and there is racism in suggesting that any group cannot be expected to live up to standards for responsible behavior.

At the same time, we believe that poverty and other social problems derive largely from the institutional arrangements of the society in which we live. These arrangements result from an interplay between philosophical beliefs, such as those that have been reviewed here, and the demands of our society. These factors are structural in the society and not simply the by-play of individuals with equal opportunity making their demands felt in a free-market economy. From the tax structure, which is much less progressive than it was in recent decades, to the availability of social services and supports, to the punishments meted out by the penal system, we observe vast inequalities in how people are treated by society. There is a kind of "welfare" for the wealthy and for large industries not available to the poor. It is our point of view, therefore, that solutions to social problems must be sought mainly in institutional and structural arrangements rather than in the rehabilitation of vast numbers of sick, disturbed, or uncultured people. Although we believe that individuals may need and deserve individual services, the greatest help will come to the most people through institutional change such as jobs, improved housing, and health services.

Recent rhetoric from the highest levels of the U.S. government portrays government as the enemy of social progress, ignoring the impact of societal structure. That rhetoric suggests that government programs can only make problems worse; only the voluntary efforts of people in local communities can really make a difference. There have been poor government programs and exciting local voluntary programs, but this basic proposition is essentially false. Major and massive social problems have, throughout our history, been amenable to amelioration only through major government efforts, including the application of fiscal resources. From the Social Security system to Medicare to any number of other significant programs, changes and improvements in the social system have come about only through such major public efforts, most often national—not local.

We live in a highly complex postindustrial society in which we are all very interdependent. We are not the mythological self-reliant, autonomous, and independent beings we are led to believe are the highest order; we are, in fact, integrally dependent on others. We cannot all assemble automobiles, build roads, grow corn, and teach ourselves, and we are deeply dependent on others who are, in turn, dependent on our own specialized skills and knowledge.

We also believe there is an alternative reading of the information on evolution, which leads us to cooperation and survival. In nature there is competition, but there is also cooperation. There is selfishness, but there is also mutual aid and self sacrifice. Ashley Montagu, the noted anthropologist, suggested:

> Clearly, the degree of sociality, of co-operativeness, prevailing in any group will constitute an important factor in influencing its fertility rate as well as its survival rate. It cannot be too often repeated that all animals are members of social groups, and that there is no such thing as a solitary animal, even though some groups are much less integrated than others. Social life is, among other things, a means of ensuring reproduction. To the extent, therefore, that any group is less social, less fully integrated, than another, it is likely to be differentially less fertile. All other factors being equal, with the exception of the degree of social integration, it should be obvious that the group in which its members are closely integrated, are often together, is the group that is likely to leave a greater surviving progeny than the group whose members are less integratedly social.[19]

Contrary to the argument put forth by the social Darwinists with which we began this chapter:

> animals...are strikingly unselfish, particularly with their own species—giving warning of predators, sharing food, grooming others to remove parasites, adopting orphans, fighting without killing or even injuring their adversaries. They work dutifully for their communities instead of being hard-bitten, self-seeking individualists.[20]

However, the fact that altruism is natural does not mean it is inevitable. Altruism is in keen competition with other values, is fragile, and has not been socially nurtured in recent U.S. history. Altruistic behavior depends on social structures within which we live. It is neither essential nor a universal characteristic of human nature, and the structural choices our society makes either support or undermine altrusitic behaviors.[21]

We see the poor as the outcome of imperfect systems. We believe this is not the only choice in society and that other options are available. Finally, we suggest that the middle class is also injured by structural factors. Although economically less disadvantaged, the middle class, too, is caught in a snare of individualism run rampant, in which blame for one's situation and mishaps is self-directed. Members of the middle class, often ineligible for public welfare programs and unable to pay for private ones, frequently believe that their problems, too, are the result of individual failure: "If we were really equal to the task, all things would be possible. Whatever our difficulties, they are the result of our failures." The overreaction to this belief system, the other side of the coin, is the tendency among some contemporary groups to deny their own humanity, to disclaim responsibility for their behavior, to despair of achieving progress when "they" don't respond immediately to a political campaign, or to retreat to utopias and inactivity. This is a kind of self-victimization.

It is clear U.S. society has several predominant values in regard to social welfare, sometimes conflicting and always interdependent. An emphasis on self-reliance, individual responsibility, and social Darwinism are strong currents in American thought. However, U.S. society is also influenced by the value of mutual aid, the ideal of equal opportunity, and the "second chance" philosophy. Our social welfare system, as we will see, has been profoundly affected by the English Poor Laws. Even so, when the pain is distributed broadly enough in our society, Americans begin to think more in terms of improving society than of "we" and "them."

There are several strong themes in social welfare. For example, Americans suspend their judgmental values about persons with problems on the basis of human tragedies, especially widespread disasters that affect persons across the board and also in regard to special categories of persons, such as war veterans. We do suggest, however, that an emphasis on individual responsibility is a crucial perspective that is unduly influential in U.S. society. A major thesis of this book is that values inform social welfare, and this theme will be explored as we proceed.

Even though we believe that all persons in the United States are entitled to the inalienable rights provided by the Constitution, they are entitled not on the basis of their problematic situations, but simply because they are human. We do not believe individuals should have to demonstrate how beaten down they are before government intervention helps them out. Similarly, we do not believe that groups should have to contest with each other over how persecuted they have been in order to qualify for necessary benefits and resources. The basic question is: How can U.S. society ensure equal rights and equal opportunities for all? Thus, we see societal values as having profoundly affected the social structure in the United States, particularly in social welfare. We see humans, however imperfectly, as being capable of adopting more humane values and of structuring a more humane society.

Summary

In chapter 1, we introduced the ideas of self-reliance and individual responsibility as driving forces in U.S. social welfare and suggested the importance of societal structures as they impact on our lives. We briefly defined social welfare and social work; explored the American myth of the hero; and introduced intellectual, scientific, religious, and socioeconomic factors contributing to the state of U.S. social welfare. Finally, we introduced the authors' perspectives. Students and readers are entitled to know our perspectives because of the importance we assign to values as determinants of each person's and our society's views regarding social welfare. We hope readers will be encouraged to consider how values play a part in determining how our society deals with social welfare.

We turn now to chapter 2, in which we review the relationship of perspectives on human nature in any society and the approach the society takes to welfare. Early history and examples of social welfare practices over time will be explored.

Electronic information sources are growing in importance. In appendix A, you will find sources of information that you can use to enrich your learning.

Questions for Consideration

1. Can you identify problems and issues that seem to be caused more by societal structures than by individual responsibility?

2. Can you identify in your community and perhaps in your own life experience a "blaming the victim" psychology?

3. Before you have read further in this book, what do you believe social welfare is?

4. What are your reactions to the values expressed in the authors' perspective?

Notes

1. William G. Sumner, "The Challenge of Facts," in *The Challenge of Facts & Other Essays*, Albert G. Keller, ed., New Haven, CT: Yale University Press, 1914, p. 25.

2. C. Wright Mills, *The Sociological Imagination*, New York: Oxford University Press, 1959, pp. 8–9.

3. Marc Miringoff and Marque Luisa Miringoff, *The Social Health of the Nation: How America Is Really Doing*, New York: Oxford University Press, 1999.

4. Edward L. Schor and Elizabeth G. Menaghan, "Family Pathways to Child Health," in *Society and Health*, eds. Benjamin C. Amick III, Sol Levine, Alvin R. Tarlov, and Diana Chapman Walsh. New York: Oxford University Press, 1995, pp. 18–45.

5. Michaela Benzeval, Andrew Dilnot, Ken Judge, and Jayne Taylor, "Income & Health Over the Lifecourse," in *Understanding Health Inequalities*, ed.

Hilary Graham, Philadelphia: Open University, 2000, pp. 96–112.

6. Children's Defense Fund, *The State of America's Children Yearbook*, Boston: Beacon Press, 1999.

7. Loring Jones, "Unemployment and Child Abuse," *Families in Society: The Journal of Contemporary Human Services*, Vol. 71, No. 10, December 1990, pp. 579–588.

8. William J. Wilson, *The Truly Disadvantaged: The Inner City, the Underclass, and Public Policy*, Chicago: University of Chicago Press, 1987, p. 39.

9. William J. Wilson, *When Work Disappears: The World of the New Urban Poor*, New York: Alfred A. Knopf, 1996, pp. 25–26.

Martha A. Gephart, "Neighborhoods and Communities as Contexts for Development," in *Neighborhood Poverty: Consequences for Children*, Vol. 1,

Eds. Jeanne Brooks-Gunn, Greg J. Duncan, and J. Lawrence Aber, New York: Russell Sage Foundation, 1997, 1–43.

10. Norman S. Fieleke, "Is Global Competition Making the Poor Even Poorer?" *New England Economic Review,* November/December 1994, pp. 3–16.

11. The purpose of social work is to promote or restore a mutually beneficial interaction between individuals and society in order to improve the quality of life for everyone. To achieve these aims, contemporary social work practice focuses on the transactions among individuals, families, groups, organizations, and communities and their respective social environments, as well as the problems and opportunities that grow out of these interactions. This perspective seeks helping strategies predicated on such an interactional view; by broadening the bases for comprehending a problematic situation, social work tends to avoid focusing exclusively on either individuals or their environments.

12. Daniel J. Boorstin, *The Americans,* New York: Vintage, 1967, pp. 51–52.

13. William B. Scott, *In Pursuit of Happiness: American Conceptions of Property from the Seventeenth to the Twentieth Century,* Bloomington, Ind.: Indiana University Press, 1977, p. 11.

14. Frank Bourgin, *The Great Challenge: The Myth of Laissez-Faire in the Early Republic,* New York: George Braziller, 1989, pp. 24–25, 142, 171; Walter I. Trattner, "The Federal Government and Social Welfare in Early Nineteenth-Century America," *Social Service Review,* Vol. 50, No. 2, June 1976, pp. 243–255.

15. "Everybody...blamed himself....There was an acceptance that it was your own fault, your own indolence, your lack of ability.... We all had an understanding that it wasn't our fault. It was something that happened to the machinery." These contradictory excerpts are from an oral history of the Great Depression. Studs Terkel, *Hard Times,* New York: Pantheon, 1970, pp. 52, 90.

16. Adam Smith's free-market ideas have been invoked by conservatives to support laissez-faire philosophy to an extreme. However, Smith supported labor unions, believed in public works, was suspicious of businessmen, and was not opposed to redistribution of income to the poor. Sylvia Nasar, "Adam Smith Was No Gordon Gekko," *New York Times* (January 23, 1994), p. E6.

17. An educational psychologist, when asked about cooperative learning (a movement to reduce student rivalry and encourage students to help each other), said it is "doomed to failure" because "it goes against the American grain, the individualism that creates the entrepreneurship we as a people have historically espoused. In a Utopia it would be wonderful. But education should prepare kids for life in a particular culture. In reality the name of the game is dog eat dog. Kids have to learn that you get something through your own smarts." William J. Warren, "New Movement Seeks to Replace Rivalry in Class with Team Spirit," *New York Times* (January 4, 1989), p. B11.

18. Peggy Say, "Free At Last," *New York Times* (December 5, 1991), p. A33.

19. Ashley Montagu, *Darwin, Competition, and Conflict,* New York: Henry Schuman, 1952, pp. 102–103.

20. Helena Cronin, *The Ant and the Peacock: Altruism and Sexual Selection from Darwin to Today,* Cambridge: Cambridge University Press, 1992, p. 254.

21. Jerome C. Wakefield, "Is Altruism Part of Human Nature? Toward a Theoretical Foundation for the Helping Professions," *Social Service Review,* Vol. 67, No. 3, September 1993, p. 454.

2

Social Values and Social Welfare

Economic life is deeply embedded in social life, and it cannot be understood apart from the customs, morals, and habits of the society in which it occurs. In short, it cannot be divorced from culture.

—Francis Fukuyama[1]

How selfish soever man may be supposed, there are evidently some principles in his nature, which interest him in the fortune of others, and render their happiness necessary to him, though he derives nothing from it except the pleasure of seeing it.

—Adam Smith[2]

Overview

In the first chapter we described several ways of understanding the situation of the poor. There will be critical differences in the social welfare institutions of a society, depending on where, and to what degree, it places responsibility for poverty. If poor people are responsible for their plights, then, at worst, society will set up rather punitive, or very limited, social welfare services. At best, social welfare services will be directed to improving the poor person. On the other hand, if society assumes that its own deficient institutions are responsible for poverty, then the efforts of the social welfare system may be directed toward correcting and improving those institutions. The social welfare systems a society constructs and operates are direct outcomes of its inherent social values. Often these values are implicit. They are understood as such obvious and commonsense truths that they may not even be stated. And yet they inform the entire approach to social welfare.

15

In this chapter and the next, we examine how various societies base their social welfare systems on predominant views of human nature. Although this chapter cannot be inclusive, covering all social welfare history, we explore the legacy of the past, taking special cognizance of those social institutions and values that continue to be influential in the U.S. social welfare structure. Primarily, we hope to draw out the relationship between societal values and the organization of social welfare, so that in examining the latter the student will always look to the former for greater understanding.

Modern Views of Humanity

Some people believe humans are inherently good, and others believe humans are inherently evil. A classic statement about the evil nature of humans was made by the seventeenth-century philosopher Thomas Hobbes, who pictured human nature so "that during the time men live without a common power to keep them all in awe, they are in that condition which is called war; and such a war, as is of every man, against every man...continual fear, and danger of violent death, and the life of man, solitary, poor, nasty, brutish, and short."[3] No person is to be trusted, and one should anticipate the evil acts of humans rather than expect their cooperation and goodness.

More recently, exponents of the fundamental, biological nature of human aggression and self-seeking behavior have suggested that "the aggression drive is a true, primarily species-preserving instinct [that] enables us to recognize its full danger; it is the spontaneity of the instinct that makes it so dangerous."[4]

Thus, on both philosophical and scientific grounds, some claim that humans are untrustworthy, evil, aggressive, and dangerous. Counter to this view of human nature is the view expounded, for example, by Jean-Jacques Rousseau, an eighteenth-century philosopher. He suggested that people are naturally good and that evil does not originate in human nature but has its source in the external world. (We have contrasted "evil" and "good" for simplicity. People who believe in the capacity of the environment to influence behavior include those who would substitute "neutral" for "good," with the ability to be influenced either way.) Rousseau suggested that we "lay down as an incontrovertible maxim that nature's first movements are always right; there is no original perversity in the human heart: there is not a single vice in it, of which I cannot say how and where it came in."[5] Arguing that humans are born good and that evil derives from institutional arrangements, Rousseau, unlike the novelist Joseph Conrad, looked into the heart of humankind and saw not darkness but light.

In regard to social welfare, if society believes humans are fundamentally evil, then it must guard against evil, which can be defined to include all unacceptable behavior. Thus poverty, mental illness, out-of-wedlock pregnancies, and hyperactive children are attributed not to external forces but to the evil nature of people. Because one cannot trust statements of need or portrayals of plight, barriers are placed in front of people, and those in need are demeaned.

✓ Rousseau's view of people as basically good fosters the idea that the societal arrangements that create evil and human problems should be altered to allow for the well-being of people. For instance, people should escape from the evil influences of cities and live in the natural countryside environment.

In summary, if people are considered evil, societies can explain away their needs and problems as having been created by evil individuals. Societies may use that argument as a rationale to avoid altering the status quo, except to force the evil to do good, to protect the good against those who would do harm, and to punish those who are judged evil as a result of acts of commission (crimes of action) and acts of omission (laziness and being unproductive). On the other hand, if people are considered good, then one can approach social welfare as a means—in Jane Addams's memorable phrase, "to raising life to its highest value." People's lives can be improved and arrangements in society can be altered to reach higher goals for all citizens.

Self-Actualization versus Irritation Response Theories

Just as human nature can be categorized as good or evil, theories about the motivations of humans can be classified into two categories: *self-actualization* and *response to irritation*. The belief that people are inherently self-actualizing or that they only respond to irritation and goading has significant consequences on how we think. Abraham Maslow, for example, was a major proponent of the view that humans are self-actualizing and not driven solely by instincts. In his view each person has a hierarchy of needs, including basic physiological needs and the needs for safety, belongingness, love, self-esteem, and self-actualization. Each person tries to satisfy these needs in ascending order so that the basic needs are cared for first, leaving the person free to work on the next "higher-level" need. Fundamental to this point of view is the idea that there is a universal set of basic impulses found in each person to satisfy ascending sets of needs.[6]

Needs also can be seen as arising from the values of a particular culture, much as in American culture we pass on, through values, the need for individualism and achievement. In other cultures, values determine other ways of living and viewing the world. The Arapesh, for instance, "plant their trees in someone else's hamlet, they rear pigs owned by someone else, they eat yams planted by someone else."[7] This example suggests that human behavior and needs themselves are defined by basic societal values. Given this point of view, society could just as easily be arranged in such a manner that people will work without being forced. If one believes in an inherent drive for self-actualization, one can then trust that those in need do not require irritation and goading so much as the opportunities and social structures to enable them to achieve their aims.

Karl Polanyi made a similar point about the importance of basic social values as determinants of social arrangements. He stressed the relationship of noneconomic motives to the economic system, suggesting that the outstanding discovery of recent historical and anthropological research is that the economy, as a rule, is submerged in social relationships. One does not act so as to safeguard his or her individual interest in the possession of material goods; one acts so as to safeguard one's social standing, social claims, and social assets. Material goods have value insofar as they serve this end. The economic system is run on noneconomic motives.[8] The essential point of Polanyi's argument is that the economic motivation of people and society is subsumed in the social texture of life. Economic factors are real, but the suggestion is also made that humans and societies can be motivated by other, equally real motivations.

The irritation philosophy, on the other hand, demands that poor people live uncomfortable lives based on the perspective that this will motivate them to stronger efforts to succeed. John Romanyshyn suggested that to regard people as evil and naturally lazy, driven to useful work only through hunger and fear of starvation, is to suggest that societies characterized by scarcity require an image of people that will justify social discipline. This discipline is required to get necessary but distasteful toil accomplished. Affluent societies can afford wider freedom of choice and can facilitate the development of new views of people more consistent, perhaps, with their true nature.[9]

So it may not be inherent in people that they need goading and irritation to be productive; it may be that such a "reading" of people derives from scarcity in societies or from societies that do not choose to share sufficiently with those in poverty. Or it may be that such views derive from the need in a particular society to accomplish something in the future. Punitive, irritant behavior has been typical in our society when dealing with those in poverty. Payments beneath the acknowledged level of subsistence, disrespectful behavior toward the poor, and various forms of harassment are all ostensibly aimed at restoring the poor to productive lives.

Economics and Human Motivation

The irritation response theme implicitly runs from Adam Smith to Milton Friedman and from Karl Marx to Mao Tse-tung: A human is an economic being who works for economic gain and whose behavior is economically determined. In this respect, capitalism, communism, and socialism are triplets, in that they all view people in economic terms.[10] To accept as fact the view that a human being works only for economic gain supports a punitive approach to poverty. This view makes "less eligibility" inevitable (no one on welfare can be paid as much as the lowest paid employed person in the community). Although we know in practice there are specific exceptional cases, our societal theory views less eligibility as a necessity. Persons in poverty, it is thought, can be encouraged to rise from their impoverished state only through the discomforts of a life without enough to live on. Thus, if one believes in the economic human being, then less eligibility seems to be almost inevitable, because people would otherwise not work.

Closely related to the view of humans as economic beings is the belief that a market mentality is the central and inevitable reality. This theme suggests that reality is based on economic human beings. The organization of society and the motivations of people are dictated by the market mentality, and other motives are relatively insignificant.

As Polanyi suggests, and as history and the world make abundantly clear, economic relationships are subsumed in social relations. Societies have the ability to create any kind of mechanism to motivate human activity. Economic activity is certainly necessary for the survival of society, but it can be pursued from a multitude of motives, including social ones. Polanyi is critical of the split reflected in the market mentality that humans have two selves: the economic or market self and the other self, which is ideal and spiritual. With such a human-created dichotomy, economic determinism holds sway and inhibits other ways of viewing people and society. Those societies trapped in economic theories of motivation alone make it less probable that fundamental changes in the way we view those in poverty can be attained.[11]

From Polanyi's multimotivational point of view, social motives serve as the engine for society and individuals, not just economic motives. Thus, assistance to poor people could just as well be based on our social responsibility to them. In addition, the motivation of the poor can be stronger as a result of the realization that society holds them as valued citizens and will not let them starve or be punished. Subliminal messages in this case would resound through society: Poor people are to be trusted, cared for, and helped because of our higher social goals.

In our post-industrialized society strong relationships have been established between technology and an emphasis on monetary motivation. Focusing economic effort on production for profit has repercussions on all other aspects of life. Among the results are technological unemployment and the business cycle. This makes it difficult for some people to obtain the fundamental necessities of life. In all nonliterate societies, resources may be meager, and subsistence difficult to obtain, but where there is not enough to go around all go hungry, as all participate when seasons of plenty provide abundance. "No one ever went hungry [among the Baganda of East Africa,] because everyone was welcome to go and sit down and share a meal with his equals," is an expression of the tradition, universal among nonliterate folk, that none must be allowed to want in the face of plenty.[12]

An Overview of History

Altruism and Mutual Aid

Recent discoveries have led to the conclusion that Neanderthals who resembled modern humans in body movement, use of hands, and language lived with elevated levels of risk and yet had a respect for the living. Life was frequently dangerous; nevertheless, injured individuals were apparently cared for by other members of their social groups. There is extensive evidence of the healing of injuries. Some injured persons lived for many years with considerably disabling conditions that would have prevented their actively contributing to the subsistence of the local group. Some skeletons with evidence of trauma, age-related health deterioration, or disability suggest that persons otherwise normal were cared for by the group, as well as children who lost their parents, most of whom did not live beyond 35 years of age. The skeleton of a young male dwarf whose physical impairments would handicap his participation in a nomadic hunting and gathering society is evidence of the tolerance of and care for a severely deformed individual during the Paleolithic era. Even more recently, the body of a four-year-old with a disability and believed to be dead for 800 years was found in Alaska. Her body was located in a secure area and adorned with protective covers, indicating a great deal of care had been taken. Because of her disabilities, she had to have required extra attention throughout her life.[13]

Peter Kropotkin described mutual-aid mechanisms in all types of societies throughout history, including medieval city life and today's unions and business, political, and remarkably diverse voluntary associations. Kropotkin argues that "the practice of mutual aid and its successive developments have created the very conditions of society life in which man was enabled to develop his arts, knowledge, and intelligence; and that the periods when institutions based on the mutual-aid tendency took their greatest development were also the periods of the greatest progress in arts, industry, and science."[14]

Despite the fact that industrial societies clearly require mutual aid and cooperation, the common perception is that the motivations of people are dictated by the market (supply and demand) and the necessity of competition. In the following section we examine briefly nonliterate societies, other past cultures, and nations, focusing on elements of particular interest to our understanding of human nature, on alternative societal arrangements, and on precedents that influence current social welfare theory. As we will see, modern themes have very ancient parallels.

Robert Trivers reports that reciprocal altruism (mutual aid) exists in all known cultures. People help each other in times of danger, sharing food and helping the sick, the wounded, the very young, and the old. They also share implements and knowledge. Although hunter-gatherer groups make adaptations to regulate group size near optimum, there is no evidence that altruistic gestures are curtailed when groups are above what they consider optimum size.[15]

Our complex and specialized society requires even more, not less, complicated mutual aid and cooperation because we don't do many things ourselves and are dependent on many others during every ordinary day. Nevertheless, we foster the myth of individual responsibility and independence, and the "survival of the fittest" is more or less an accepted societal value.

Altruism grows out of a sociocultural reality, as does an overvaluation of individual responsibility. Every culture develops altruistic components required for the survival of the group. The essential factor to recognize is that the degree of cooperation and altruism, or the emphasis placed on individual responsibility, and the role of social welfare are determined by predominant views of human motivation in any society. The point has been made that "the frequency of behavior that we might regard as altruistic is likely to depend more on the social structures within which people live than on any essential and universal characteristics of human nature…All the features of society that make egoism ring true are human creations—creations that could be different, that indeed are different in different cultures, and may have once been different in our own."[16]

As another aid to our sense of perspective, here is a quotation from a pre-colonial letter written by Amerigo Vespucci describing his experience with Native Americans: "They are so liberal in giving that it is the exception when they deny you anything; and, on the other hand, they are free in begging, when they show themselves to be your friends."[17]

In 1493, Columbus in a letter to King Ferdinand and Queen Isabella described the Native Americans he encountered this way: "After they have shaken off their fear of us, they display a frankness and liberality in their behavior which no one would believe without witnessing it. No request of anything from them was ever refused, but they rather invite acceptance of what ever they possess, and manifest such generosity that they would give away their own hearts."[18] Their society functioned effectively and with a complex social system, using mutual aid and without an all- encompassing market mentality.

In the following brief review of ancient cultures, we focus on elements of particular interest to our understanding of certain influences on social welfare today.

Ancient Cultures

Egypt

Peasants in Egypt during the fourth through sixth dynasties (2700–2200 B.C.) planted and reaped their masters' crops. Before the first autumn crops were gathered, it was likely that peasants were close to starvation. Their lives were described as similar to the lives of animals. They were the property of the lords, beasts of burden themselves, and completely dependent on the yield of the land and the whims of the landowner.[19]

The yield of the land was erratic. One result was that as early as the twenty-eighth century B.C. the tradition of seven lean years was known. The prosperity of Egypt depends on the satisfactory flow of the Nile, and Egyptian texts make frequent references to hunger ("years of misery," "a year of low Nile").

> When the entire Upper Egypt was dying because of hunger, with every man eating his (own) children, I never allowed death to occur from hunger in this nome. I gave a loan of grain to Upper Egypt.[20]

Because of the importance of the grain harvest, the state through the king's commissioners paid special attention to planning, production, and distribution. Grain was stored for two seasons and had to be sufficient for those who were building public works, including canal and dike workers, stonemasons, and the builders of pyramids, tombs, and temples. Thus, centralized planning and coordination are not inventions of the modern age, and specifically, careful provision of food supplies was a fundamental social welfare effort directly tied to national intentions and needs.

However, problems arose when there was a breakdown of the economy. For example, an uprising took place in the twelfth century B.C. in which a group in the state labor corps complained: "We have been hungry for 18 days in this month. We have come here by reason of hunger and thirst, we have no clothes, we have no ointment, we have no fish, we have no vegetables. Send word to Pharoah, our good lord, and write to the vizir, our superior, in order that the means of living be provided for us."[21]

Thus we can see workers were accustomed to receiving various supplies, centrally controlled. But in times of trouble, apparently, local self-interest quickly came into play when supplies became limited, and this self-interest became the sole means of defense in the struggle for existence. One lord was quoted as saying, "When Upper Egypt was in a bad state...I closed the frontiers."[22] The frontiers were closed so the available harvest and supplies would suffice for the local population, an early version of residency laws and the forerunner of clashes between national and local political necessities.

At a later time (seventh–sixth century B.C.), Egyptian culture expressed some obligations even toward strangers who were in need. The Egyptians believed God was a protector of the poor against the rich. Around this time, the following instruction was set forth:

> Do not find a widow if thou catchest
> her in the fields (i.e., gleaning the fields).
> Nor fail to be indulgent to her reply.
> Do not neglect a stranger (with) thy oil-jar,
> That it be doubled before thy brethren.
> God desires respect for the poor
> More than the honoring of the exalted.[23]

Egypt was in an anomalous situation when the economy produced an agricultural bounty and also often had the ability to command the resources of its neighbors. Nevertheless, it is important to note that the bottom rungs of society consisted of slaves and serfs whose lives were completely controlled by other people. Most Egyptians worked every day with few exceptions and no day of rest. Social welfare served the needs of the State for survival and development through central planning for social control, to support projects, and to maintain a workforce.[24]

Sumer and Babylonia

As early as the second millennium (2000 B.C.), the Sumerians, an ancient culture that settled in the Euphrates river valley, placed a positive value on the protection of widows, orphans, and the poor. Nanshe, a goddess mentioned in Sumerian mythology, cared for the defenseless:

> Who knows the orphan, who knows the widow,
> Knows the oppression of man over man, is the orphan's mother,

Nanshe, who cares for the widow

> Who seeks out justice for the poorest.
> The queen brings the refugee to her lap,
> Finds shelter for the weak.[25]

Nanshe was also referred to as Truth, Justice, and Mercy.

In the early development of Babylonia, peasants worked the land for the temples. Later they held land either as private property or as rentals. When they assumed the relatively freer state, they then had to brave the onslaught of catastrophes—floods, droughts, blights, and sickness—on their own. Before this the temple had been the owner of everything, including both land and people. Formerly when difficulties had arisen, rations were distributed from the temple granaries to sustain the community through times of trouble.

When peasants were freer they were forced to borrow from the temple at interest, a fact that led to many peasants becoming seriously indebted. This resulted in friction, and there are indications some kings enacted moratoriums on debts, remission of debts, and fixed wages and prices.

During the first millennium (1000 B.C.), several types of persons were dedicated to the temples, in fact entrusted to the care of the temples. Among these were prisoners of war, slaves donated or bequeathed, and persons of free birth including children of poor families handed over in times of famine to save their lives.[26]

There are several noteworthy points to be made about this ancient culture. it set forth *ideals* for social welfare; temples were important economic forces; governments acted to relieve economic burdens in certain circumstances, probably to avoid serious conflicts; and temples served as "social welfare" agencies, anticipating major religious institutional functions to follow in later centuries.

Hebrew and Judaic Societies

Judaic culture developed out of a desert existence in which each person had a responsibility not only to him- or herself but also to the group and the community. This tension between self-interest and group interest was neatly summed up by Rabbi Hillel: "If I am not for myself, who will be? If I am only for myself, what am I? If not now, when?"[27] Judaism established within its own sociocultural reality a God-ordered altruism. When Abraham greets and serves three strangers who approach his tent in the desert, he establishes the principles of hospitality and caring for the stranger.

The Hebrew Bible makes clear provision for the poor based on the agrarian society at the time. Through a series of commandments Judaism established a system of individual responsibility for providing assistance. Several illustrations demonstrate what is in essence a developed system of social welfare, both as an ideal and in fact. For example, Leviticus 19:9–10 states: "And when ye reap the harvest of your land, thou shalt not wholly reap the corner of thy field, neither shalt thou gather the gleaning of thy harvest. And thou shalt not glean thy vineyard, neither shalt thou gather the fallen fruit of thy vineyard; thou shalt leave them for the poor and for the stranger: I am the Lord your God." Gleanings, forgotten produce, and the corners of the field were available for poor people who were free to take food for their own use. Strangers, aliens in the land, were also free to take produce, and apparently there was no such thing as a special amount of time one had to live in the land in order to receive charity. Starvation also was prevented by another commandment:

> When thou comest into thy neighbour's vineyard, then thou mayest eat grapes until thou have enough at thine own pleasure; but thou shalt not put any in thy vessel. When thou comest into thy neighbour's standing corn, then thou mayest pluck ears with thy hand; but thou shalt not move a sickle unto thy neighbor's standing corn. [Deut. 23:25–26]

Public opinion, apparently, enforced this commandment, and there is no record of actual starvation in peaceful times.[28]

These commandments are essentially a tax on producers for the benefit of the poor: the stranger, the fatherless, and the widow (see Deuteronomy 24:19–22). Many centuries later the English poor laws utilized a poor rate as a public tax for the care of the poor.

A tithe was required to be given to the poor. Further, all financial debts still owing by the sabbatical year were canceled. The emphasis on charity of many kinds in the Hebrew Bible did not in itself produce a redistribution of wealth or correct economic inequalities.

Among the Judaic commandments, one series of laws introduced a radical and revolutionary concept: the Jubilee year. Every fiftieth year, slaves were emancipated, and property—with the exception of house property in a walled city—was to be restored to its original owners. This series of laws created a counterbalance to the possible gradual accumulation by a few of most of the property and goods. According to the Talmud and other sources, the observance of the Jubilee was a reality for centuries.

Finally, Deuteronomy introduced the legal requirement for neighborly love. For instance, in Deuteronomy 25:35 the law states: "And if thy brother be waxen poor, and his means fail with thee; then thou shalt uphold him: as a stranger and a settler shall he live with thee." The manner in which charity was given added to its value so that *gemilut hasadim* (acts of loving kindness) is considered one of the three pillars upon which the continued existence of the world depends (*Ethics of the Fathers*, 1:2).

The prophets later stressed the importance of charity and taking care of those in need. Isaiah (58:5–7), in a statement read every year on Yom Kippur, excoriates Jews because fasting and the wearing of a sackcloth and ashes are in themselves not an acceptable offering to the Lord. According to the prophet, an acceptable offering would be giving bread to the hungry, housing the poor, and clothing the naked.

Throughout later rabbinic and other Jewish literature, the performance of charitable deeds is stressed both in spirit and in the giving of things for those who need them. All human possessions belong to God (*Ethics of the Fathers,* 3:8). One interesting device in early times was a community charity box, designed so others would not know whether people were depositing or removing money.

An early social welfare stance of the Jewish community is reflected in an enumeration of some post-biblical communal institutions. These functions are not far removed from some basic social welfare functions: clothing the naked, educating the poor, providing poor girls with a dowry, providing food for Passover, caring for orphans, visiting the sick, caring for the aged, ransoming captives, and providing burials.

Judaism bases its requirements for altruism on essentially two concepts: Tzedakah, a mixture of charity and justice, and Chesed, loving kindness. In the Jewish community, historically, the giver and the recipient both needed each other. Every person has inherent dignity and should strive to live a life in the image of God. Even the poor must perform charitable acts. In regard to its basic view of humans, Judaism postulates both a force for good and a force for evil in every person. Because of these simultaneous drives, humans need the restriction, direction, and support of the commandments that enable people to choose life and avoid death, to be supportive of humanity and justice, and not to become numb either to one's own needs or those of all other humans.

From our perspective today, several important themes appear in the Hebrew and Judaic culture. Social welfare became institutionalized in two important respects: in regard to expected behavior and in provision for the poor in essentially nonstigmatizing ways. Attempts were made to redistribute wealth to offset long-term poverty through diminishing inherited wealth. There appears early to have been provision for the poor as a right or entitlement from individuals and later in an organized fashion. Perhaps these achievements were possible because of the small size of the society. Essentially, a culture developed that valued enterprise but without categorizing the poor as evil or idle. On the contrary, the society and individuals in it would be judged on the degree to which they provided for the poor without demeaning them.

Greece and Rome

In Greece, the beggars scorned by Plato could expect to be sent away from cities. They were viewed by the Greeks as being lazy and not willing to work rather than as lacking opportunity. One Spartan was quoted by Plutarch as saying: "But if I gave to you, you would proceed to beg all the more; it was the man who gave to you in the first place who made you idle and so is responsible for your disgraceful state." Similarly, Plautus made clear the Grecian attitude: "To give to a beggar is to do him an ill service."

Aristotle, in his theoretical State, thought he could avoid the need for charity by making part of the land completely public, thus defraying the costs of providing common meals. Several options were available for the poor and landless. They could move to new colonies, could become mercenaries, could use contraception or abortion, or (with a high incidence of poverty) could resort to infanticide.[29]

Although according to some sources the Grecian poor could only hope for better conditions by starting anew somewhere else, there is also evidence that throughout Greece there were inns or resting places for strangers. Located near or at temples, these places were centers for medical relief and for the poor. Associations for the support of those in need reportedly also existed.[30]

The rejection of beggars illustrates a strong theme in Western culture—actually, it is more a concern with pauperism than with poverty. A *pauper* is a person without means of support, especially someone who depends on aid from tax-based public welfare funds. In modern terms, the issue is how to keep people from getting paid from tax funds when they are not working rather than how to alleviate poverty. This attitude pervades U.S. society and is fundamental, as we see later, to the concept of less eligibility. Harassment of those on welfare continues for reasons probably close to those that motivated the exile of beggars from Greek cities. It is not the desire to alleviate poverty that encourages harassment of the poor; instead, demeaning treatment is used against pauperism and to reduce the extent to which public funds are used to support those in need. The focus on pauperism is one that returns at a later stage as an important ingredient in Western treatment of the poor. The emphasis on preventing funds from being given to those who are not working is a common American aim, a crucial factor in society in general and in social welfare in particular.

Whereas the Egyptians and Hebrews gave the poor special consideration, in Greece hospitality for the stranger was a relationship between nobles or merchants, and the Romans were obliged to give hospitality "only in the case of foreigners of the same standing as the host and [this] was seen as a means of obtaining good relations with them."[31] Nonetheless, by the third century A.D., 175,000 Romans were receiving free food distributions. This was in addition to the system of patrons, in which everyone felt bound to someone more powerful and superior. Patrons distributed both food and money to those who were connected to them in the patronage system. During the second century, there are estimates that almost one half of Rome's population lived on public charity. Of 1.2 million people, all but 150,000 heads of families needed to draw on public resources.[32]

The vast majority of people were always poor and had little to eat. Sheer physical survival was difficult through droughts, famines, harvest failures, and epidemics. Starvation was close at hand.[33] Most labor was unfree. Slaves were owned and the legal property of other persons; serfs were tenants and bound to live and labor without the ability to change their status while forbidden to move from place to place; and there were those in debt bondage.[34]

Over time, grants of land given as rewards for military or other services formed the basis for large landholdings. Fortified manors offered security and refuge to ruined freeholders, poor urban workers, uprooted persons from outlying regions, vagabonds, army deserters, and escaping slaves. All of these became tenants of the large landowners and, in exchange for protection, would pay part of their crops. This system was more easily established in Grecian lands, where hereditary service had been an institution. This relieved landowners of labor worries. This system, tying people to the land in exchange for support from the landowners, as a process led to the medieval system of distribution of wealth and power known as feudalism that later influenced our attitudes and welfare philosophy.

Early Christianity

The development of Christianity introduced an important new variable on the scene, with profound implications for social welfare. Two themes were introduced that influenced social welfare for more than 1,500 years and remain with us even today. Charity and the near sanctification of the poor assumed great importance in societies influenced by Christian thought. A second theme derived from Christian thought was the denigration of conspicuous consumption. Until the Protestant revolution, these themes were fundamental to Western social welfare practices.

Jesus, who had been a wandering preacher in Galilee, was a healer of body and soul who cured the sick and cast out demons. He taught that service to people was service to God. So it became the responsibility of Christians to take care of the poor, widows, and orphans. "Therefore love is the fulfilling of the law" (Romans 13:10).

According to Christianity, there are three abiding gifts: faith, hope, and love, but of these love is the greatest (I Corinthians 13:13). Jesus made it clear that the outcasts of society, such as prostitutes, were worthy of special care. The Christian themes of (1) charity and a sanctification of the poor and (2) a denigration of conspicuous consumption brought with them several significant social welfare themes. Very early Christians in Jerusalem pooled their possessions for relief of the poor. "They sold their possessions and their means of livelihood, so as to distribute to all as each had need" (Acts 2:44, 4:34).[35] In Jerusalem there was a daily distribution of food to widows and perhaps to others.[36] The concept of hospitality also became institutionalized when early Christians met in the homes of church members—the house church—and traveling Christians assumed they would receive hospitality, a concrete expression of Christian love.[37]

Early Christians held an ethic of poverty based on scriptural statements such as, "It is easier for a camel to go through the eye of a needle than for a rich man to enter the kingdom of God" (Mark 10:25) and "Blessed are you poor for yours is the kingdom of God" (Luke 6:20). Early believers came primarily from poor groups and were rewarded with a promise that poverty, not wealth, held the key to the kingdom.[38]

Both love of Jesus and love of people were necessary for the Christian life. Judgment was to be on the basis of how one treated those who were hungry, thirsty, strangers, unclothed, sick, or in prison because Jesus was considered present in all such people. By the late first and early second centuries, Christians placed an increased emphasis on giving alms: "Almsgiving is as good as repentance from sin; fasting is better than prayer; almsgiving is better than either." By the middle of the second century, Christian charity had become organized. Voluntary offerings were collected once a week and deposited with the "president" or bishop, whose responsibility it was to protect orphans, widows, those in distress, prisoners, and strangers—all who were in need.[39]

Although charity and relief of the poor were Christian requisites, early Christians also held strong beliefs about the necessity of work. Three motives for work were held: (1) Christians should not be a burden to others; (2) one should obtain resources with which to help the needy; and (3) non-Christians should be favorably impressed so as to commend the faith to them. By contrast, Greeks thought work a servile activity, and Romans felt work was beneath the dignity of a citizen.[40]

By the fourth century, Christians (encouraged to engage in good works) had built hospitals for the sick and established systematic charitable efforts. State, church, and voluntary social welfare functions overlapped, particularly in regard to the Roman grain dole for Roman citizens, such a widespread practice that a "steward over the grain" was appointed. Privately endowed foundations, especially in Italy, invested capital in real estate mortgages. Interest was paid to towns or to state administrators for charitable uses. By the third century, oil was added to the ration of grain and eligibility for the dole was extended to noncitizens. Bread was substituted for grain by the early fourth century.

Byzantium: Christianity in the East

In the East during the third century A.D., 80,000 people received free food at Constantinople. Requisitions and taxes supported large parts of the population. Constantine thought the poor should be maintained by the wealth of the churches and that the rich should support the needs of this world.[41]

By the fourth century A.D., the period often referred to as the Dark Ages began with the advancing disintegration of Roman imperial government in the West. From the fourth century, when official state protection made possible the open accumulation of ecclesiastical wealth, church leaders developed lists of people in need whom the Christian community assisted. There is evidence that widows, young women, as well as men were fed daily, along with prisoners, the ill in hospitals, the mutilated, and the shipwrecked. People traveling through also were dependent upon church resources.

Christian charity was also administered through institutions that assisted the very old, the very young, the poor, and the blind. Many hostels provided shelter for travelers, pilgrims, the diseased, and suffering aging persons. Also formed were leprosariums, old people's homes, and hospitals. These organizations were typically attached to a church or monastery that was supported by donations and ecclesiastical revenues such as income from properties. In part these institutions were intended to redistribute resources of the wealthy to the needy poor.

In the fifth-century eastern monasteries, the underemployed of the towns were hired for service in the Christian church. However, imperial (state) assistance dominated in the development of Byzantine charity. The imperial treasury and public funds frequently ensured the survival of religious-sponsored institutions for the poor. Funding often included a combination of private, imperial, and ecclesiastical funding.[42]

In Alexandria in the early seventh century, a Byzantine welfare state was developed. There were maternity hospitals, medical facilities, and food rationing, all of which were provided from the revenues of the patriarch.[43]

These developments reflect the ubiquitous creation of social welfare institutions, regardless of time, culture, or society. But developments were not always as completely charitable as one might imagine. As early as the first century A.D., the Christian principle of assisting all those in need was modified in practice by a reluctance to support strangers. Apparently, there were abuses of hospitality by visitors extending their stays more than two nights. True Christians were expected not to stay longer. There are examples of putting travelers to work after a week's stay.[44]

It is important to note that Constantine in the East eased the position of women, children, debt-ridden farmers (a theme that arises frequently), prisoners, and slaves. While the western Roman Empire collapsed, the eastern Byzantine Empire survived, and until the thirteenth century Constantinople was the most prosperous place in Europe.[45] A mixed system of voluntary, religious, and state-supported social welfare was implemented. State funds were administered by a private voluntary group for the benefit of both public and private spheres, thus anticipating a modern funding and administrative device.

Holy Poverty and Expectations of the Wealthy

Later saints, such as Saint Francis of Assisi, and ordinary Christians in some cases renounced material goods and family ties and led lives of poverty, an expression of being one with the wretched of the Earth and a desire to be of help to them. Such acts were viewed as imitations of the life of Jesus. Christianity expected its adherents to emulate the life of Jesus and to help those who were in need:

> For I was hungry, and you fed me,
> I was thirsty and you gave me drink,
> I was a stranger and you welcomed me,
> I was without clothes and you clothed me,
> I was in prison and you visited me.
> [Matt. 25:31–46]

Beyond helping those who were needy, early Christianity demanded that those who had excess worldly goods should share these with the underprivileged. The gift of one's property, received from God through God's beneficence, was a sign that one was imitating the life of Jesus. Church officials and Christians could distinguish between holy poverty, which was chosen by the person, and involuntary poverty. To an extent during early Christianity it was important for Christians of means to divest themselves of property to support those in need in order to show signs of one's religious commitment. As we will see when we examine the early Middle Ages, these Christian values influenced social welfare in important ways and had long-term effects on western European antecedents of U.S. social welfare.

Eastern Cultures

Although not directly linked to early U.S. social welfare, several additional social welfare histories have in recent years begun to affect the U.S. scene and may play more prominent roles in the future.

China

As early as the eighth century B.C., China developed a political system of monarchy with various subordinate groupings organized into fiefdoms. Peasants worked the land to support their superiors, were attached to the land, and were bestowed along with the land. It is probable that peasants were assigned a piece of land to cultivate for their particular superiors and another for the use of their own families. One contemporary saying was that "dukes live on tribute, ministers on their estates, shih (a group between the power group and the ruled) on the land, and peasants on their own toil." Peasants working for their lords were the source of labor and food for the self-sufficient manorial communities but had few rights, opportunities, or pleasures. A passage in Mencius suggests the state of affairs: "If a common man is called on to perform any service, he goes and performs it."[46]

Later, during the sixth century B.C., taxes were instituted based on the amount of land one possessed. Slowly the former responsibility of the lords to feed, house, and clothe their subordinates fell on the peasants themselves. Emancipation from the status of manorial dependent upgraded the peasants' status and afforded them greater freedom; it also relieved the lord from many of his former responsibilities. The peasants then had only themselves to look after for livelihood. Poverty or prosperity became their own responsibility.[47]

By the fourth century B.C., Mencius expressed the Confucian ideal of the humane and righteous king and suggested that the ruler must pay attention to the people's welfare. People need the necessities of life before they can be expected to concentrate on being good. Mencius, like Maslow, hypothesized a hierarchy of needs that must be met in ascending order so higher-level needs can be met. He advised the king to avoid extravagance at court and to open parks and other state lands so people could gather wood and herbs. He also urged that public funds be used for the care of the aged, the poor, and orphans and for public assistance when natural disasters struck.

By the first century B.C., in times of natural disasters such as floods or famines, the government took several steps. Government granaries were opened. Grain was distributed free to those who were unable to pay for it and sold to those who could afford to pay. The rich were called on to give or lend grain from their personal supplies. Gifts from the imperial treasury were sent to establish relief work for the poor. Court commissioners were sent out to encourage the planting of grain for a new harvest. Finally, if necessary, the poor were taken from the ravaged areas and resettled on new lands.[48]

The Sung Dynasty (960–1279 A.D.) reportedly exceeded the benevolence of earlier dynasties. Emergency relief was provided in times of catastrophe such as floods, drought, fire, and warfare when displaced persons lacked food and shelter. Local authorities with permission of the government distributed grain from granaries and cash. The amount distributed depended on the seriousness of the emergency and stopped when the emergency was over. Normal relief was also provided for the general mass of poor people who were unable to sustain themselves, including the aged, widowers, widows, orphans, and the childless old. There were definite periods of operation of normal relief, special administrative officials, and regulating laws. The ancient guiding principle suggested that it is the responsibility of the government to see to it that the living are given sustenance; the sick, medical care; and the dead, burial.

Charity homes were established all over the empire. Cases were checked for veracity and lodging was provided in the homes of those who died without heirs. If such lodging was unavailable, the indigent were lodged in government buildings. Expenses with no time limit were paid out of the property of the heirless.

Medical relief institutions were established, as were public cemeteries for those who could not pay for their own burials or died while traveling away from home. Other welfare measures included distribution of grain in times of bad harvests. The wealthy were asked to contribute money or grain in return for official posts or ranks. If this was insufficient, the palace storehouses would contribute. When winter weather became too severe or commodity prices rose too high, the government would pour its stocks of rice or fuel into the market and sell at low prices. In addition, maternity clinics were instituted for needy women, children abandoned during a flood were cared for, and famine victims were employed to work on dikes so workers profited from wages and the area gained from the irrigation.[49]

Several themes should be noted from these examples from ancient China. With the breakup of a feudal pattern, the peasant was freed from semi-bondage on the manor but was forced to rely on his or her own resources. One can see a tradeoff was made between security on the one hand and mobility and greater freedom on the other. Furthermore, government provided help when people could not care for themselves, particularly in the case of a natural disaster. Moving from place to place to find sustenance must have been done at the expense of the government— an early governmental resettlement program. Perhaps there were additional motives, but specifically the move was made possible through governmental resources when those of the people failed. But Mencius's views reflect a government that had a responsibility for the people's welfare in order to promote the "good" at all times and not just in times of disaster.

India

Aspects of social welfare have been identified in India at least as far back as Buddha (sixth century B.C.). During very early times (fourth and third centuries B.C.), construction projects provided work for the public good. Villagers jointly provided for the care of boys and old or diseased men where they had no guardians or protectors.[50] It was the duty of the village elders to look after the property of minors who lacked a natural guardian until they reached the age of majority, when their property would be returned to them with any accumulated profits.

There also was collective charity. A family would give alms, the residents of a street would give voluntary offerings, or all the inhabitants of a town would do so. Charity (food, clothing, money) was collected especially during times of famine. Gifts supportive of education were highly meritorious. Reportedly, even the poorest person gave something to hungry students. Temples sheltered the homeless. In villages, extended families cared for their aged members, those with physical and other disabilities, and the chronically ill. Caste organizations, guilds, and the *panchayat* (village government in later times) took care of the poor, the aged, the ill, and the disabled and provided housing and food for travelers.

From ancient times all Indian religions have emphasized charity. The responsibility for those needing assistance was shared by the rulers, by the rich, and also by individual members of the general community. Temples and monasteries served as centers for extensive social services and were left endowments for their maintenance; for construction of residences for monks; and as support for the supply of food, cloth, and oil for religious individuals and institutions.[51]

From the medieval period on (thirteenth century A.D.), Indian Muslims provided help to less fortunate persons through payment of the *zakat*, a poor tax, by every Muslim. They also provided endowments for religious and educational institutions, constructed temples and mosques, and established rest houses and *dharamshalas*, a public place of provision for those in need, including travelers, who were given free food and lodging.

Islam

Among the fundamental tenets or requirements of Islam, accepted by all branches, is the obligation to give charity. The Koran contains numerous references to almsgiving to the poor and needy and to those who work for them:

> O ye believers, give in alms of the good things
> that ye have earned, and of what we have brought forth
> for you out of the earth.
> Ye cannot attain to righteousness until ye expend
> in alms of what ye love. But what ye expend in alms,
> that God knoweth.

One was expected to give at least 2.5 percent of what one possessed.[52]

One form of charity is *zakah*, the giving of alms on an obligatory basis. This type of charity requires that one give up a portion of one's wealth in excess of what is personally needed in order to "purify" what one retains. This charity can be paid directly to the poor, to travelers, or to the state. Among others to be assisted were Muslims in debt through pressing circumstances, enslaved persons to buy themselves out of bondage, and for benevolent works. *Sadaqah*, righteousness, was another form of charity that included distribution of a quantity of grain to the poor or its monetary equivalent for every member of a household at the end of Ramadan. A *waqf* is another form of charity in which property is given by will or as a gift in perpetuity to the Islamic state for pious works or for the public good, such as payment for the upkeep of charities and mosques. Those who collected any charity tax were allowed to take their own livelihood from the funds collected.[53]

Summary: Evolving Values and Social Welfare

This brief excursion enables us to draw several conclusions. Most people in most societies were faced constantly with subsistence crises and inequalities existed throughout the ancient world. Many societies proclaimed calls for justice, more often promulgated than honored. "In every city the rich and the poor were two enemies living by the side of each other, the one coveting wealth, and the other seeing their wealth coveted...They regarded each other with the eyes of hate."[54] Nevertheless, from earliest times, all societies in varying forms, created social welfare systems for the poor and needy. Mutual aid and reciprocal altruism conferred benefits on individuals and societies. The ability to work together in groups constituted a competitive advantage for early humans "so those qualities that sustained group cooperation spread."[55] Mutual aid and cooperation have a long human history and "friendship, affection, trust, these are the things that, long before people signed contracts, long before they wrote down laws, held human societies together."[56] Conscience, sympathy, love, and altruism grounded in societal and individual self-interest make social welfare possible and also support the survival of nations.

Motives differ from society to society and situation to situation. Social welfare systems have been based on social, religious, political, economic, and other motives. It is clear that sometimes social welfare and mutual aid were altruistically and benevolently motivated; at other times, social welfare was used as a social control. Mutual aid mechanisms are human inventions that can serve a number of functions; there does not seem to be any historical era or place without them. The availability of a workforce with sufficient energy, aid for victims of disasters, the preservation of life, group morale, the doing of God's will, social justice, the avoidance of violence against the established order—all are reasons for social welfare.

We turn now in chapter 3 to developments during the Middle Ages in western Europe, particularly in England, that have influenced most profoundly U.S. social welfare.

Questions for Consideration

1. Can you identify some ways in which values in your community affect social welfare services or the lack of social welfare services?

2. Are there mutual aid organizations in your community? How many and of what kinds can you identify?

3. Do you see any ways in which the ancient social welfare ideas you read about in this chapter are reflected in today's United States?

4. Religion has always had a major impact on social welfare. Do you think it still does? If so, in what ways?

Notes _____

1. Francis Fukuyama, *Trust: The Social Virtues and the Creation of Prosperity*, New York: Free Press, 1995, p. 13.

2. Adam Smith, *The Theory of Moral Sentiments: Of the Sense of Propriety*, eds. D. D. Raphael and A. L. Macfie, Indianapolis: Liberty Classics, 1982, p. 1.

3. Thomas Hobbes, *Leviathan*, Michael Oakeshott, ed., Oxford: Basil Blackwell, 1946, p. 82.

4. Konrad Lorenz, *On Aggression*, London: Methuen, 1967, p. 40; Richard Wrangham and Dale Peterson, *Demonic Males: Apes and the Origins of Human Violence*, New York: Houghton Mifflin Co., 1996; and Richard Dawkins, *The Selfish Gene*, New York: Oxford University Press, 1976.

5. Arthur M. Melzer, *The Natural Goodness of Man: On the System of Rousseau's Thought*, Chicago: University of Chicago Press, 1990, p. 17.

6. Abraham H. Maslow, *Motivation and Personality*, New York: Harper & Row, 1970, pp. 35–58.

7. Dorothy Lee, "Are Basic Needs Ultimate?" in *Personality in Nature, Society, and Culture*, Clyde Kluckhohn and Henry A. Murray, eds., New York: Knopf, 1956, p. 340.

8. Karl Polanyi, *The Great Transformation*, Boston: Beacon Press, 1957, p. 46.

9. John Romanyshyn, *Social Welfare: Charity to Justice*, New York: Random House, 1971, p. 309.

10. Karl Marx, "Capital," *The Communist Manifesto and Other Writings*, Max Eastman, ed., New York: Modern Library, 1932; Milton Friedman, *Capitalism and Freedom*, Chicago: University of Chicago Press, 1962.

11. Polanyi, pp. 163–164.

12. Melville J. Herskovits, *Man and His Works*, New York: Knopf, 1960, p. 267.

13. Erik Trinkhaus, *The Shanidar Neanderthals*, New York: Academic Press, 1983, pp. 422–423. Also see David W. Fryer, William A. Horton, Robert Macchiarelli, and Margharita Mussi, "Dwarfism in an Adolescent from the Italian Late Upper Paleolithic," *Nature*, Vol. 330, No. 6143, November 5–11, 1987, pp. 60–62; Christopher Stringer and Clive Gamble, *In Search of the Neanderthals: Solving the Puzzle of Human Origins*, New York: Thames and Hudson, 1993, pp. 94–95. "Girl of 8, Going on 800," *The Baltimore Sun*, February 8, 1995, p. 2A.

14. Peter Kropotkin, *Mutual Aid*, Boston: Extending Horizons Books, 1914, p. 296.

15. Robert L. Trivers, "The Evolution of Reciprocal Altruism," *Quarterly Review of Biology*, Vol. 46, No. 1, March 1971, pp. 45–47.

16. Barry Schwartz, "Why Altruism Is Impossible ...and Ubiquitous," *Social Service Review*, Vol. 67, No. 3, pp. 314–343.

17. Wilcomb E. Washburn, *The Indian and the White Man*, Garden City, N.J.: Anchor Books, 1964, p. 8.

18. Jennings C. Wise, *The Red Man in the New World Drama*, Vine Deloria Jr., ed., New York: Macmillan, 1971, p. 27.

19. John A. Wilson, *The Culture of Ancient Egypt*, Chicago: University of Chicago Press, 1951, p. 74.

20. James B. Pritchard, ed., *The Ancient Near East*, trans. John A. Wilson, Vol. 1, Princeton, N.J.: Princeton University Press, 1973, p. 24.

21. Herman Kees, *Ancient Egypt*, Chicago: University of Chicago Press, 1961, p. 277.

22. Ibid., p. 58.

23. James B. Pritchard, ed., "The Instruction of Amen-em-opet," chap. 28 in *Ancient Near Eastern Texts*, trans. John A. Wilson, Princeton, N.J.: Princeton University Press, 1969, p. 424.

24. Bob Brier and Hoyt Hobbs, *Daily Life of Ancient Egyptians*, Westport, Conn. Greenwood Press, 1999, p. 6 and p. 99.

25. Samuel N. Kramer, *History Begins at Sumer*, Philadelphia: University of Pennsylvania Press, 1981, p. 102.

26. H. W. F. Saggs, *The Greatness That Was Babylon*, London: Sidgewick and Jackson, 1966, pp. 171–172, 198.

27. Phillip Blackman, ed., *Ethics of the Fathers*, New York: Judaica Press, 1964, p. 44.

28. Salo W. Baron, *A Social and Religious History of the Jews*, Vol. 1, *To the Beginning of the Christian Era*, New York: Columbia University Press, 1962, p. 86.

29. A. R. Hands, *Charities and Social Aid in Greece and Rome*, London: Thames and Hudson, 1968, pp. 65–69.

30. "Philanthropy," *Encyclopedia Britannica*, Vol. 17, 1970, p. 823.

31. Noel T. Timms, *Social Work*, London: Routledge and Kegan Paul, 1973, pp. 17–18.

32. Jerome Carcopino, *Daily Life in Ancient Rome*, New Haven, Conn.: Yale University Press, 1963, pp. 16, 65.

33. Michael Grant, *Greeks and Romans*, London: Weidenfeld and Nicolson, 1992.

34. G. E. M. de Ste. Croix, *The Class Struggle in the Ancient Greek and Roman World*, London: Duckworth & Co., 1981.

35. Jean Danielou and Henri Marrou, *The First Six Hundred Years*, New York: McGraw-Hill, 1964, pp. 14–15.

36. Robert M. Grant, *Early Christianity and Society*, San Francisco: Harper & Row, 1977, p. 127.

37. Abraham J. Malherbe, *Social Aspects of Early Christianity*, Baton Rouge, La.: Louisiana State University Press, 1977, pp. 67–68.

38. John G. Gager, *Kingdom and Community: The Social World of Early Christianity*, Englewood Cliffs, N.J.: Prentice Hall, 1975, p. 24.

39. Michael Grant, *The Climax of Rome*, London: Weidenfeld and Nicolson, 1968, pp. 126, 128, 131.

40. John G. Davies, *The Early Christian Church*, New York: Holt, Rinehart and Winston, 1965, p. 66.

41. Grant, p. 60.

42. Judith Herrin, "Ideals of Charity, Realities of Welfare: The Philanthropic Activity of the Byzantine Church," *Church and People in Byzantium*, Rosemary Morris, ed., Birmingham, Eng.: University of Birmingham, 1990, pp. 153–158.

43. Peter Brown, *The World of Late Antiquity*, London: Thames and Hudson, 1971, p. 185.

44. Herrin, p. 159.

45. Grant, pp. 83, 99.

46. Cho-yun Hsu, *Ancient China in Transition*, Palo Alto, Calif.: Stanford University Press, 1965, p. 11.

47. Ibid., pp. 109–110.

48. Nancy Lee Swan, trans., *Food and Money in Ancient China*, Princeton, N.J.: Princeton University Press, 1950, pp. 60–61.

49. I-T'Ang Hsu, "Social Relief During the Sung Dynasty," *Chinese Social History*, E-Tu Zen Sun and John De Francis, eds., New York: Octagon Books, 1972, pp. 207, 208, 214.

50. It is unclear how girls were cared for. In Indian languages there are words that are inclusive of both genders, and inattention may be a function of translation lapses. Or the omission in the sources may reflect a historical attitude toward younger women. Because some castes followed matriarchal systems and others were patriarchal, some ambiguity exists on this point.

51. Gurumukh Ram Madan, *Indian Social Problems*, Bombay: Allied Publishers, 1967, p. 15; R. C. Majumdar, "Social Work in Ancient and Medieval India," *History and Philosophy of Social Work in India*, A. R. Wadia, ed., New York: Allied Publishers, 1968, pp. 16–19.

52. Robert Roberts, *The Social Laws of the Qoran*, Atlantic Highlands, N.J.: Humanities Press, 1990, pp. 71–72.

53. Cyril Glasse, *The Concise Encyclopedia of Islam*, New York: Harper & Row, 1989, pp. 132, 341, 417, 430.

54. Numa Denis Fustel De Goulanges, *The Ancient City*, Garden City, N.Y.: Doubleday & Co., 1956, p. 340.

55. Francis Fukuyama, *The Great Disruption*, New York: The Free Press, 1999, p. 174.

56. Robert Wright, *The Moral Animal, The New Science of Evolutionary Psychology*, New York: Pantheon Books, 1994, p. 198.

3

Social Values and Social Welfare

England from the Middle Ages Onward

For the poor shall never cease out of the land; therefore I command thee, saying: "Thou shalt surely open thy hand unto thy poor and needy brother in thy land."

—Deuteronomy 15:11

Overview

In this chapter we examine the chief trends and major social welfare events, primarily in England, from the Middle Ages to the development of the Poor Laws, Speenhamland, the workhouses, and the Poor Law of 1834. We undertake this review to demonstrate that events following the Middle Ages represented a significant departure from the earlier ways in which poor people were perceived. We also do this because U.S. social welfare has been influenced in so many ways by historical developments in England and English perspectives on the poor.

The Early Middle Ages

The Middle Ages have been divided into three separate phases. The first stage was the feudalization of western European society, roughly from the sixth to the tenth centuries, when "barbarian" successor states replaced a collapsed Roman Empire. From the king down, a hierarchy was created in which each person knew his or her place and responsibilities. The manorial system of vassalage (vassals were granted feudal land in return for homage and military service) was a system for control of society and included the lord, his vassals, and serfs (peasants bound to the land). The serf owed work and portions of agricultural produce to the lord, and the lord ostensibly owed protection and support to the serfs who worked his land.

The 1066 Norman conquest of Anglo-Saxon England by William the Conqueror established political feudalism on the basis that all the land belonged to this king, who then granted portions of it to barons (the tenants-in-chief) in return for certain services, generally for military purposes such as guard, escort, and provisioning of troops. The barons granted lands to knights, who became their vassals, and, in turn, the knights could grant lands to others. The land grants included the tenants with their obligations to the lords of the manors. Still relatively few people controlled most of England's land.

Peasants were tied to the manor and owed work and taxes. They had to mill their grain at the lord's mill; bake their bread in the lord's oven; pay a fine at the marriage of a daughter; give the lord their best beast at their death; and answer in the lord's court for failure to perform any required services.[1]

The serf's life was hard. Housing was poor, food was short, and starvation loomed during famines. The lord owned the land; he controlled the meadow and the woods. The serfs owed rents, gave labor service and gifts, and also paid fines to the lords. Each household was expected to give tithes to the church and charity to the local poor. The lord's rulings were final and the serf's status was servile. The lords, on their side, gave protection. Welfare benefits did exist for the serfs tied to the manors on which they were born. They could be released from the year-round work for up to 30 days, if sick. If they died, their wives did not have to serve for the following 30 days. Even so, boon work (additional work at ploughing time and harvest) had to be done or a substitute found and paid.[2]

This agrarian economy produced very little surplus; production for market was low. Rents were paid in labor or in-kind because there was little money in circulation. Upper-class incomes were measured in produce rather than cash. There was little effective demand for luxuries. Town populations were small, with the lords and peasants constituting the overwhelming majority of the population.[3] Life was hard for both landlords and tenants, and famines were common. Between the tenth and fifteenth centuries, there were—excluding local outbreaks—49 general famines.[4]

But it was not just famine and wars that threatened stability. Orders prevented people from withdrawing or avoiding services such as threshing and other manual work.[5] Periodically the demands upon the peasantry would become increasingly burdensome. There might be a demand for higher farm rents, restrictions on the freedom of the tenants on lords' estates, or labor obligations added to the rent. Naturally this increased existing tensions among landholders, serfs, and tenants.[6]

The poor were not without certain protections. Canon law demanded that each parish, the ecclesiastic subdivision on the local level, provide for the poor. Poverty was not a crime. Brian Tierney contrasted the attitude of the English in the early Middle Ages with their views during the early twentieth century, when as late as 1909 an English royal commission assumed that every poor person was poor because of a "defect in the citizen character."[7]

In thirteenth-century society, an individual whose wealth exceeded his needs consistent with his status was obligated to assist the poor. The following canonical directives confirm this: "Feed the poor. If you do not feed them, you kill them." "Our superfluities belong to the poor." "Whatever you have beyond what suffices for your needs belongs to others." "A man who keeps for himself more than he needs is guilty of theft."[8]

It was the responsibility of the clergy of each parish to provide "hospitality" for travelers and other guests, and to take care of the poor. Even St. Francis of Assisi made a distinction between holy poverty and other kinds of poverty. He wrote in his last testament: "I have worked with my hands and I choose to work, and I firmly wish that all my brothers should work at some honorable trade. And if they do not know how, let them learn."[9]

The only grounds for refusing to provide charity was the belief that it would encourage idleness. The "willfully idle" should not be assisted. Every able-bodied person was expected to earn his keep after a few days. Several centuries later, distinguishing between the *deserving* and *undeserving* poor became crucial in determining aid. In the early Middle Ages, however, such distinctions apparently were not clearly defined.

As prescribed by canon law parishes and monasteries practiced charitable acts and provided relief. These efforts may have been somewhat haphazard and were clearly insufficient, but they must be viewed within the broader context of scarcity and want. Consider, for example, the general plight of many peasants:

> They all lived in unsanitary conditions; they had no doctors, and at times pestilence swept away whole communities. Few families could store grain; a year of flood or drought created terrible famines. The peasants could not defend themselves against heavy-armed feudal cavalry, and if their lord became involved in a war they were almost sure to see their fields ravaged and their houses burned. It is not surprising that the span of life was short, that a man of forty was considered old.[10]

The Middle Middle Ages

The second phase of the Middle Ages—from the eleventh to the early fourteenth centuries—brought a growth of the population, an expansion of cultivated areas, some technical progress, and market-oriented production. A surplus appeared owing to three factors: (1) increased technical efficiency; (2) improved administration; and (3) increased pressure to transfer more of the surplus from producers to lords.

The quickened pace of economic activity generally benefitted the urban areas, which became a focus for the efforts of artisans, retail traders, industrial entrepreneurs, unskilled laborers, servants, and other poor people. The movement into the towns also was the consequence of rural overpopulation, which became acute by the end of the thirteenth century. Despite these positive signs, persistent demands for rents, tithes, and taxes by landowners, the church, and the state continued to produce social upheavals and uncertainty.

For example, a village revolt in 1261 at Mears Ashby, Northhamptonshire, was followed by another in 1278 in Harmondsworth, Middlesex. Sometimes these conflicts related to rent collections; at other times they were connected with the collective refusal to provide services for the landlords.[11] Serfdom was degrading, and people were forced into hierarchical relationships. There was confusion regarding individual rights and restraints. But the line between liberty and servitude could never be forgotten. Serfdom meant subordination and arbitrariness, which people feared and resented. At the same time they lacked mobility and freedom.[12]

Still, in the context of U.S. social welfare and our ideas about the poor, one must consider Tierney's view about how the poor were treated in the Middle Ages. He concluded that "in this particular matter, I am inclined to think that, taken all in all, the poor were better looked after in England in the thirteenth century than in any subsequent century until the present one. The only reservation we need make is that perhaps that is not saying much."[13]

Whatever Tierney's judgment as to the treatment of the poor, one has to keep in mind that

> the lord's household could be both a terror and a benefit to the villagers. When a peasant defaulted on payments or revolted, it was the lord's household that would be the ultimate source of discipline.
>
> Members of the household could enter a tenant's house, take his goods, and imprison him with impunity. On the other hand, if the lord wished to look after the interests of his peasants, he would use his household to punish their enemies.[14]

Thus, the relationships of the lords and the peasantry were complicated, reflecting both their need for each other and the tensions relating to their conflicting needs and status differences.

The Late Middle Ages to Elizabethan Poor Laws

In the late Middle Ages, new towns arose, colonization of new lands began, and the growth of international trade spurred the formation of money economies. The feudal system gave way to wage-based relationships, and the serf and the lord severed their allegiances and responsibilities. There was a loss of what economic security existed. By the thirteenth century, many English peasants had become small landholders. Poverty persisted but there also were indications of prosperity: cathedral building and the production of metal, cloth, gold, and other substances. With the rise of wage labor, serfdom declined and those on the land experienced new freedom and independence. The retreat of feudal society was also accompanied by the appearance of vagrants, transients, and migrants. A rooted society was giving way to one in which mobility was becoming more the norm. From a life defined by *status*—the relationship of lord and serf—a new relationship was evolving determined by *contracts* between parties. Power had become a negotiable commodity.

Those needing a steady and dependable labor supply did not appreciate a state of affairs in which people could escape from the traditional roles and places. Nor were they prepared to deal with marauders. *Begging* became widespread and gained a degree of acceptance, especially because the act of giving charity to care for the poor was a religious obligation and both begging and giving had long been practiced with the blessings of the Church.[15]

In addition to individual acts of charity, more than 8,000 *parishes* did charitable work in medieval England. Religious *monastic orders* served both the local poor and strangers passing through.[16] It is of interest, however, that during the Middle Ages, the percentage of monastic income actually devoted to charity varied widely. Estimates ranged from 1 percent to more than 22 percent; however, the national average did not reach 2.5 percent.[17] Strangers were to be helped without discrimination, as well as infidels and excommunicants. Thus, in the thirteenth century, there was little if any discrimination based on eligibility categories or residence.

Other institutions served important roles for the poor. The *guilds*, which were voluntary commercial and social associations of merchants and artisans, functioned as mutual aid societies and charitable organizations for their own members. They built and maintained hospitals,[18] fed the needy on feast days, distributed corn and barley annually, provided free lodgings for poor travelers, and gave other incidental help.[19]

In addition, the guilds provided disaster insurance, specifying assistance for poverty, sickness, old age, blindness, loss of limb, loss of cattle, fall of a house, false imprisonment, and temporary financial problems, as well as losses by fire, flood, robbery, or shipwreck. There were eligibility limitations, and a member could be helped only three times in a lifetime and then only when the crisis was not of his doing.

Another pillar of social welfare was the *private foundation*, created by the bequests and gifts of individual philanthropists. At the time of the Reformation there were in England at least 460 charitable foundations. As much a part of medieval life as they are today, foundations established almshouses, hospitals, and other institutions; provided money for funerals; and disbursed funds on the anniversaries of the benefactor.[20]

Hospitals of various types were established during the Middle Ages, including leper houses, orphanages, maternity homes, and institutions for the aged and the infirm. In fact, in mid–fourteenth-century England there were 600 hospitals.[21] But for the most part, peasants would not have had access to hospitals or monasteries for retirement and terminal illness. They formed voluntary organizations on their own that provided some benefits to the aged and the helpless. Of 507 guilds that returned descriptions of their charters in 1389, about one third (154) provided their members with benefits during disaster or old age.[22]

It is estimated that there were some 500 to 700 hospitals in late medieval England, but only a few specialized in caring for the aged, poor women in childbirth, maimed soldiers, and the "deserving poor." Mostly, they provided temporary shelter, taking persons in for only one night. Furthermore, most were small, serving perhaps a dozen persons. A comment by Henry VII in 1509 suggests concern over this situation:

> There be fewe or non such commune Hospitalls within our Reame, and that for lack of them, infinite nombre of pouer nedie people miserably dailly die, no man putting hand of help or remedie.[23]

Tithing was a feature of life in the Middle Ages, and in England church funds secured from parishioners were divided: one third for the maintenance of the church, one third for the poor, and one third for the priests.[24] Individuals at every level of society were expected to give to the poor. During the thirteenth century, King John—in debt himself—continued to give alms to the poor from his revenues.[25]

Several important factors combined to force upon the English of the late Middle Ages a very different attitude toward the poor. The movement from rural to urban settings was stimulated by the introduction of woolen manufacturing. Within a relatively short period of time the manufacture of woolen goods became in England so extensive that an export trade was established.

With the growth of cities, trade, money economies, and international relations, the expiring feudal system forced large numbers of people into social chaos. Wars created a pool of wanderers who were not eager to stay in one place and who were skilled thieves. People were also displaced from their former positions, physically and psychologically. The old truths were no longer valid. With the necessity for sheep grazing in order to grow wool for the textile industry, land was "enclosed," and peasants were forced from the land, dislocated, unattached, and without means of support.

The fourteenth and fifteenth centuries have been characterized as the third or last phase of the Middle Ages. Prior to the first part of the fourteenth century, the population of England had grown. Severe cold weather throughout Europe from 1200 to 1400 A.D. contributed to erratic eras of drought and flood, abundance and famine. Commencing with flood and famine from 1315 to 1317, the population began to decline. About the middle of the fourteenth century, ensuing events intensified a rapid diminution of the population.

Much starvation and disease followed the first wave of the Black Death (bubonic plague) in 1348. The plague continued through the fifteenth century, which saw the demise of serfdom. The plague revisited England in 1361, 1368, and 1375 and was not completely eliminated until the seventeenth century. Not only was there population loss in England, but also a series of plagues decimated the European population during this time. Although there is a dispute as to the exact dimensions of the population loss, the estimates range from 20 to 50 percent of the population.[26]

Even before the middle of the fourteenth century there were difficulties finding tenants for numerous landholdings. A poor climate for agriculture, famines, continuous wars in northern Europe, as well as plagues decimated many parts of Europe, including England. It was the Plague of 1348, however, that initiated a scarcity of labor of great proportions, and a new value was awarded to the available labor because of this scarcity.

Other changes resulted from these devastating events. In England, per capita bequests were much higher in the 1350s than they had been earlier in the fourteenth century. Prior to the onset of the plague in London, only about 5 percent of all persons registering their wills in the Hustings Court provided funds for hospitals. Between 1350 and 1360, this figure tripled and the amount of the average bequest rose by almost 40 percent. Charity funded institutions helped plague victims and promoted the good works that counted toward salvation.[27]

The loss of population undermined the manorial system by the close of the sixteenth century, and migration to towns created a pronounced shortage of agricultural workers. In England, more than 1,300 villages were deserted between 1350 and 1500, almost all in marginal farming lands. The emancipation of the serfs ground to a halt, and landlords tried desperately to retain the traditional services of their tenants. Free laborers, of course, used the shortage of labor as leverage to demand higher wages.[28]

There was a general breakdown of law and order as the economic and military power of the landholders, as well as their social prestige, declined. Local landholders operated the police and the courts because law enforcement was a local prerogative. This breakdown is reflected by the increased incidence of homicide, which from 1349 to 1369 was about double that of the period from 1320 to 1340.[29]

Because of the shift in power from landholders to workers, the late Middle Ages has been referred to as the "Golden Age of Laborers," and it is believed that real wages were higher in the fifteenth century than at any time in history until the twentieth century. From the beginning of the thirteenth century to the beginning of the fifteenth century, agricultural prices fell by 10 percent, real wages multiplied 2.5 times, and cash wages nearly doubled.[30]

Because of their scarcity, laborers were in a position to seek higher wages and to make demands where historically demands had all come from lords and landholders. Illustrative of this trend is the pay scale for ploughmen:

> A ploughman who was paid 2 shillings a week in 1347 received 7 shillings in 1349 and 10 shillings 6 pence by 1350.... Day laborers not only received higher wages, but asked for and got lunches of meat pies and golden ale.[31]

To deal with the new freedom of the serfs and a scarcity of labor, and to assure a supply of agricultural workers, a series of laws was enacted. In 1349, the *Statute of Labourers* was passed to force those who were able-bodied and without other means of support to work for an employer in their own parish *at rates prevailing before the plague.* This statute is the first of poor law legislation that evolved over the next four centuries.

A national system of enforcement was established that made it illegal to demand or offer higher wages than had been the standard in 1346. Laborers were expected to contract to stay with an employer for a year or another appropriate period, and there was to be no daily hiring. Laborers had to swear an oath that they would obey the provisions of the statute or be placed in the stocks. Those with sufficient land to keep them occupied were exempt from the obligation to work for wages. In some areas, during the first ten years following the statute's enforcement, laborers paid, through fines, as much as one third or one half of the tax burden that the wealthier formerly had paid. But, ultimately, such measures were not successful and ended in a sense of grievance as all efforts to control the workers failed. The landlords discovered the only way to retain laborers was to pay the going rate.[32]

The effects of the bubonic plague not only were problematic in the countryside but affected urban centers and commercial activity as well. The wealthy of the cities also tried to retain what they had, and restrictive guild regulations and city ordinances were enacted. In the twelfth century, any industrious young apprentice might become a master after completion of the appropriate training.[33] By the latter part of the fourteenth century, eligibility for becoming apprenticed in many guilds was limited to the sons of masters or to those who married their daughters. A large group of urban laborers lived at the beck and call of their masters and were forbidden to organize to foster their own interests. Not surprisingly, there was much resentment among these laborers and frequent riots among the peasants, including the French Jacquerie (1358), the English Peasant's Rebellion (1381), and the town revolts by artisans in Bruges (1302), Ghent (1381), and Rouen (1382)—all of which were quickly crushed. One exception occurred in Florence (1378), where workers held control of the city for three years.[34]

The Statute of Labourers denounced not only those who sought higher wages but also, more emphatically, those who chose to beg rather than earn their bread. In an effort to maintain the traditional system, the statute provided that all *able-bodied* persons under 60 years without means of subsistence must work, that alms could not be given to able-bodied beggars, and that runaway serfs could be made to work for anyone who claimed them. In medieval society, work was expected of all; idleness was a crime.

In 1352, in England, workers demanded, and some employers paid, wages two and three times the pay rate before the plague. During the 1350s and 1360s, fugitive laborers were declared outlaws; if caught they were branded on the forehead with an "F," for "fugitive" or "falsity"; stocks were set up for punishment; and imprisonment was often used as a penalty. Those who were wandering and unemployed outside their own parishes were whipped, branded, sent to toil in the royal galleys, or set into stocks for three days.[35]

Begging was permissible for the *impotent* poor, that is, those who could not possibly work. By the last years of the fifteenth century, pregnant women and extremely sick men and women were considered among the impotent. Shortly after, those poor over the age of 60 years were added to the list of the impotent. The categorization of those in need was established, and the beginnings of differentiation between the "*deserving*" and the "*undeserving*" poor were initiated. Thus continued a series of punitive laws that culminated in the Elizabethan Poor Laws in the latter part of the sixteenth century.

Work and Religion

Martin Luther in 1517 presaged still other changes with his momentous posting of the 95 Theses on the door of Castle Church in Wittenberg, the initiator and focal point of a religious revolution. As a result, the foundations of Roman Catholicism were challenged, especially the notion of papal authority, and the Protestant Reformation followed. With this one act a theological conflagration was lit and a political revolution began that weakened the Holy Roman Empire and fostered the development of the modern nation-state.

Luther defined *vocation* as a calling to do God's work in all things; a vocation was an

> exaltation of the common occupations as the appropriate spheres in which to serve God acceptably. The term vocation was transferred by Luther from the cloister to the workshop.... [T]he farmer, the doctor, the school teacher, the minister, the magistrate, the house-mother, the maidservant and the manservant were all of them religious callings, vocations in which one was bound to render no lip service but to work diligently at serving not merely an earthly but also a heavenly master.[36]

Luther's teachings improved the morale of laborers, giving them a sense of duty in doing an honest day's toil; his beliefs also resulted in an elevation of the family, and of individuals as well, in the sense that all callings were important.

During the sixteenth century, Calvinism also began to make its mark. The distinction between the cloister and the marketplace was broken down even more; one could serve God as well in the marketplace as in any other place. Work was a divine vocation and thus a religious activity. Idleness and the temptations of the world distract us from the pursuit of righteous living; work was for the glory of God. Max Weber describes Calvinism in this way: It was "not leisure and enjoyment, but only activity [which] serves to increase the glory of God.... Waste of time is thus the first and in principle the deadliest of sins." Loss of time through sociability, idle talk, luxury, even more sleep than is necessary for health (six to at most eight hours) is worthy of absolute moral condemnation. Work could be viewed as a chief end for life and, as St. Paul suggested, "He who will not work shall not eat."[37]

Paradoxically, the "elevation" of the individual enhanced by the "calling" of an occupation was a double-edged sword. According to Calvinist doctrine, a calling reduced uncertainty—the reality of life—by limiting mobility. For the sake of order, each person had an obligation to remain within his or her calling:

> The best way, therefore, to maintain a peaceful life is when each one is intent on the duties of his own calling, carries out the commands that the Lord has given, and devotes himself to these tasks; when the farmer is busy with the work in cultivation, the workman carries on his trade, and in this way each keeps within his proper limits. As soon as men turn aside from this, everything is thrown into confusion and disorder.[38]

The values of Calvinism very much affected our ideas on social welfare through the centuries. The Calvinism of England in particular stressed personal responsibility and discipline and an intense individualism in social affairs. Pauperism was viewed as a question of character. Calvin himself condemned indiscriminant almsgiving and urged ecclesiastical authorities to visit families regularly to see if they were idle, drunken, or otherwise undesirable. Idleness was a sin against God and a social evil; not to work meant to refuse to listen to God's word. For the glory of God, society must be served. Those who were dependent were somehow "marred."[39] The impulse to work was sacred. Upright character, integrity, and work were the products of faith. If one's economic state was improved as a result of industry, sobriety, honesty, and frugality, this was only a by-product of doing God's work.[40] Conspicuous consumption was still frowned on, so wealth tended to be reinvested, to become capital.

A new system was being created, both economic and social; people were being separated from the land and moving to the cities. Towns and cities were being enlarged for manufacture and commerce, including international commerce. Poor people were not just the victims of famines and war; new forces came into play that victimized them in new ways. Employment became variable, with cycles influenced not only by local events but also by unseen international occurrences.

Serfdom provided some insurance against sickness and old age; now poverty of a new kind developed. During the Middle Ages people were poor, but those who had the greatest difficulty surviving were those we would now refer to as *case poverty* (widows, orphans, the old, the blind, the mutilated, and those infirm from long illnesses) in the sense that they resulted from *individual* tragedies. But from the fourteenth century, English poverty was also of the *structural* type and developed from the changed *economic structure* of society. When living on feudal manors, a person disabled by injury could be assisted at the local level. However, when entire industries located in cities were affected by their international markets and people were thrown out of work, the resources available for those affected were far more limited. People could not fall back on the farmland. Previously famine could cause widespread danger, but now industry and commerce could cruelly cause poverty and do so in complex ways beyond the control of individuals.

Laborers gathered into the crowded towns and cities. The extent of exemptions from taxation on the grounds of poverty suggest at least one-third of the population lived marginally in most cities, and in some cities the percentage was more than one half. Those who migrated into towns were mainly unskilled and found only intermittent work.[41]

The expansion of markets and the creation of new technologies in combination with many other factors gave impetus to the Industrial Revolution. According to one interpreter, many factors contributed to that revolution, including the rise of "factory towns, the emergence of slums, the long working hours of children, the low wages of certain categories of workers, the rise in the rate of population increase …[and] the concentration of industries." All these in the view of Polanyi "were merely incidental to one basic change, the establishment of market economy." But the rise of a market economy demanded certain costs. Polanyi continues, "Machine production in a commercial society involves, in effect, no less a transformation than that of the natural and human substance of society into commodities."[42]

When people are needed to strive in the "satanic mills," to produce for markets within industrializing and urbanizing societies, they become essential parts, as labor, of the grinding wheels. When this role is viewed within the context that productivity is a sign of the elect standing in the world, the burden of poverty falls squarely on the shoulders of individuals, regardless of the more complicated causation that actually creates their impoverished conditions. The message communicated was that individuals demonstrate their spiritual condition through the signs that God has provided. Poverty, then, means unworthiness, and in fact, poor people can be viewed as undeserving.

In 1531 in an attempt to deal with the phenomenon of beggars and vagabonds, the government of England introduced for the first time *the principle of governmental responsibility* and provision. Evolving out of great concern about the numbers of persons who were idle, or committing thefts and murders, this initial act first provided for those in genuine need such as aged and disabled poor persons. Local authorities were authorized to certify these people by letter indicating they were eligible to beg, the first legal assumption by government of responsibility for care of the poor.

The able-bodied poor, however, were treated much differently. Fines were imposed on those who would give "any harboring, money, or lodging to any beggars being strong and able in their bodies to work." An idle man was whipped and after the punishment was forced to return to the place of his birth or last dwelling place and there to "put himself to labour like as a true man oweth to do."[43]

In 1536, Henry VIII, under the Dissolution of the Monasteries Act, expropriated all monasteries with an annual income of less than 200 English pounds. The property and wealth of the monasteries were given to the King's followers. By 1540 all monasteries and their wealth were taken with few exceptions. These actions effectively did away with one of the pillars of social welfare and also minimized the ascetic ideal. The people most adversely affected were those monks who had to rely on rather meager pensions; nuns who had still smaller pensions, who remained unmarried, and were not otherwise employed; domestic servants who found it difficult to obtain alternative employment; and an unknown number of poor persons who relied on the monasteries for charity. Those less wealthy persons who donated livestock or other in-kind resources to the monasteries in exchange for permanent food and shelter were protected by the Dissolution Act and paid in cash rather than in-kind.[44]

Also in 1536, a statute was passed creating a comprehensive English system of relief. The statute provided that those returned after punishment to their former places of residence were entitled to food and lodging every ten miles for one night from the parish constable. Further loitering would be punished by whipping, cutting off the right ear, or even death. Children aged 5 to 14 could be apprenticed out. Church collections were to be used to care for "the poor, impotent, lame, feeble, sick, and diseased people, being not able to work." Where parishes had a surplus it was to be used to provide support for the poorer parishes. The collectors were to be paid "good and reasonable" wages and thus became the first paid public welfare personnel. In addition to registration of need, licensed begging was replaced by funds derived from contributions stimulated through the force of the state and the clergy. Those who were "strong enough to labor" were given employment. Although this responsibility for providing jobs was not spelled out, the important principle of public responsibility to provide work when work could not be found was laid down for the first time in England. Thus work relief was born in the welfare system.[45]

Idlers were detested in English society and by 1547 a V could be marked on their breasts with a hot iron and they could be enslaved for two years. If idlers ran away when captured a letter S could be burned on their foreheads or cheeks and they could be enslaved forever. If there was a repetition of this behavior, the sentence was death. These laws proved to be too severe and were repealed in 1550. Concurrently, licensed begging was revived.

When the nation-state developed as a full-blown institution in society, there was a simultaneous reevaluation of the role of the monolithic church. Where there had been parallel bodies of binding law, the state began to take on many of the responsibilities that previously rested more fully with the church.

As early as 1526 in Spain, Juan Luis Vives set forth a plan for communal care of the poor in his *De Subventione Pauperum* (*On the Supervision of the Poor*). According to his plan, two senators with a secretary were to visit each institution where paupers were housed and investigate the living conditions, meanwhile counting and listing names. Those living in private homes were to be similarly registered. Those who were of a certain age and without a trade were to be taught one. Irksome tasks were to be assigned to those who dissipated their "fortunes in riotous living." Those unable to find work, including the blind, were to be assigned such work. This plan included a communal duty to care for the poor, local-level inquiry into the situations of the poor so as to prioritize them, and the registration and development of different categories of the poor, particularly based on moral grounds. Similar plans were developed in Germany in the early 1520s, in the southern Netherlands in 1524–1525, in Venice in 1528–1529, in France in the 1530s, and in Spain after 1540.

It is instructive to review the Venetian plan for the sake of comparison and to acknowledge the international nature of the problems of poverty and the similar approaches to dealing with those problems. Venice established machinery for discriminating between the worthy and the unworthy poor, developed a system of priorities for giving relief so as to eliminate "social parasites," and distinguished among paupers who were physically handicapped, able-bodied but not employed, and physically whole but ill equipped by upbringing to do manual labor. The Venetians encouraged the greatest number of applicants to be self-supporting: They gave the able-bodied opportunities to work, and they forced those able-bodied who did not want to work to do so through corporal punishment or threat of expulsion from Venice. Beggar children were educated so as to enable them to work and be absorbed into the economic system. The impotent poor, the aged, the crippled, and others were helped through accommodation in hospitals and through distribution of charity to their homes. As a last resort, they were given licenses to beg, which signified their worthiness to be given charity. Paupers were the responsibility of their native communities. Native paupers had priority over strangers, and there was a municipal organization to supervise and administer poor relief.[46]

The Poor Laws

During the sixteenth century, a series of laws called the *Poor Laws* were enacted in England. The result of centuries of periodic social unrest—famines, epidemics, wars, enclosures, urbanization, unemployment and labor supply problems, rising prices, and increases in the number of persons seeking poor relief—the laws consisted of experiments with methods of alleviating distress, preventing vagrancy, and maintaining social stability.

In 1572 the aged, poor, disabled, and other persons born within each county or those who had resided there for three years or more were to be "sought out, registered and assigned for their habitations and abidings." Justices of the peace were to determine weekly charges to maintain them; to tax and assess all inhabitants of every city, town, and village; and to use the proceeds for the relief of the poor. Collectors were appointed as well as overseers of the poor and work relief. Thus was started the first legislation for taxes for poor relief and the institution of overseers of the poor who were to put the able-bodied to work. Those who refused to work were sent to the Houses of Correction. Severe punishments were to be taken against "idlers, beggars, rogues, and vagabonds." These latter types were to receive funds only after the worthy poor had their needs met, and the able-bodied were to be helped only in return for their labor.[47]

The Poor Law Compilation of 1601

Following a period of near famine from 1594 on, there were unusual destitution and periodic disturbances, including small rebellions and an increase in vagrancy. Legislation was enacted in 1597 (39 Eliz. c3) and in 1601 (43 Eliz. c2; see Chart 3.1) that systematized earlier laws and became the basis for the English Poor Law system.

These laws provided for the implementation of a national system. This plan placed greater emphasis on civil power, which now made it compulsory for every parish to provide for the poor by levying a tax on all occupiers of property within its bounds. Relief was to be locally financed and locally administered for local residents. An unpaid parish officer—the overseer of the poor—was appointed whose duties were to collect the tax and see that it was spent on relief, to apprentice the children of paupers to a trade, and to assign work to the able-bodied poor. Piecework was to be arranged for persons in their own homes to repay the charity of the local community. It was the responsibility of the overseers and of the church wardens to take care of the various categories of poor people: able-bodied, disabled, children, aged, blind, or those who for other reasons were impoverished. Direct grants were available for the unemployable and a work policy existed for

CHART 3.1 *The Chief Provisions of the 1601 Poor Laws*

1. A central administration was formed to ensure implementation of the laws throughout England.
2. Each parish was responsible to provide for the poor by levying a tax on occupiers of property.
3. Unpaid officers—overseers of the poor and church wardens—were appointed to collect taxes, spend the funds on poor relief, assign work to the able-bodied, and apprentice the children of paupers.
4. Parents were responsible for their children and grandchildren, as were the grandchildren and children for the grandparents.
5. Justices of the peace were to send to jail those who did not pay their poor taxes or refused to work.
6. Parishes could call upon other parishes when they were unable to provide relief for their poor.

those who were able-bodied. Parents with means were liable for their children and grandchildren. Children with means were responsible for parents and grandparents who were unable to work for their own sustenance.

Justices of the peace could send to jail those who refused to work or send to prison those who did not pay their poor tax. If a parish was unable to support its own poor, it could levy other parishes for additional funds. Beyond this, a central administration was formed to ensure the execution of the laws in all parts of England. Locally financed and locally administered poor relief was for local residents. Although repression did not work, government reluctantly assumed a responsibility to help people who could not provide for themselves.[48]

One emphatic and important alteration in the basic poor laws was the *Act of Settlement of 1662*. This statute "empowered the justices to return to his former residence any person, coming to occupy a property renting for less than ten pounds a year, who in the opinion of the overseers might at some future time become in need."[49] It was expected by the various parishes that they would be protected from the poor who belonged elsewhere—at least back in their own parishes.

The Act of Settlement was passed, in part, to remedy a problem created by masses of disbanded soldiers seeking work. Reportedly, this law was never rigidly enforced because a high degree of labor mobility was needed in an economically expanded society. However, such legislation strengthened the local basis of the poor law, and a strong trend toward residency requirements was united with local responsibility, a theme that has continued to our day. It was only three centuries later, in *Shapiro v. Thompson* (U.S. Supreme Court, April 1969), that residency laws as a factor determining eligibility for public assistance were held to be unconstitutional in the United States. This decision finally recognized the reality that local events, at least in regard to employment, poverty, and rights to freedom of movement, were truly reflective of structural problems on a national scale.

During the eighteenth century, there was a growing tendency to deal stringently with able-bodied poor persons, including granting them relief only within an institution (*indoor relief*) in which they would be required to work. After this strategy failed, *Gilbert's Act* (1782) required that work be found outside the workhouse for the able-bodied (and subsidized out of the poor tax). The poorhouse became an institution for the aged and infirm.

The poor relief system was a ready means for disciplining potentially disorderly persons and the laboring poor. In the closing decades of the seventeenth century and throughout the eighteenth, it is estimated that one third of the population, despite work and good health, were unlikely to be able to support themselves on a regular basis without assistance. This led to people trying by whatever means possible to support themselves and their families. The Poor Laws were seen as a more agreeable means of controlling the poor than dealing with frequent criminal charges and frequent executions.[50]

Problems of poverty on a national scale were thus met in particular ways through governmental legislation. The statute enacted in 1601 is a summary codification of what has come to be called the Elizabethan Poor Laws, incorporating the attitudes and provisions discussed in the preceding pages.

The responsibility for poor relief had been shifted from voluntary charities sponsored by the church, monasteries, foundations, guilds, and private citizens to local governments, which provided orphanages, hospitals, and almshouses for the old. These legal responsibilities were defined by national legislation with accompanying punishments for noncompliance. The control the Poor Laws exerted on individuals was related to productivity and the scarcity of manufactured goods.

> To make them available, it was necessary to have not only land and capital but also human labor. If every human being in society could somehow be converted into an operating unit and induced to work, more manufactured goods would become available. It thus became important to emphasize the virtues of work and the evils of idleness.[51]

What began in the fourteenth century as a means of dealing with a shortage of labor for agricultural work developed by the sixteenth and seventeenth centuries into an entire philosophy that demanded that the undeserving poor (the able-bodied) be controlled and dealt with punitively while deserving poor were treated differently. This change was a result of alterations in the economic, religious, social, and governmental aspects of society. The Poor Laws then stood for almost 300 years as the basis for English and U.S. social welfare.

Speenhamland

The issue of subsidies to individuals and families has often focused upon the Speenhamland experiment. The specific context in which the justices at Speenhamland decided to create a subsidy is significant. In 1794 and 1795 (including the severe winter of 1794–1795), there had been short harvests. Imports were sparse because the Baltic Sea was frozen well into spring, thus delaying food shipments from Poland and southern Prussia. England also was at war with France, which was seizing English vessels, and the armed forces needed grain. These factors led to a steep rise in the price of bread, a staple food, and there were increases in destitution, starvation, discontent, and bread riots.

In 1795, meeting at the Pelican Inn at Speenhamland, Berkshire, England, the justices of the peace decided to pay subsidies to currently employed individuals and families when the cost of bread rose to 1 shilling. The justices chose to provide the subsidy rather than regulate wages. They urged farmers and others to raise laborers' wages, recommended that a few areas be set aside for the poor to grow potatoes for their own use and sale, and suggested that fuel be collected in the summer for cheap sale in the winter. The subsidy, called the "bread scale," received much publicity. The pension list previously consisted of women, many widows, children, invalids, and old men. Suddenly, with the enactment of the Speenhamland system, the majority of new names were of men.

The supplementation of low and inadequate wages was not a new development at Speenhamland. _Outdoor relief_ (relief in one's own home) was widespread from 1760 to 1795, preceding Speenhamland's subsidy. Parishes adopted outdoor relief policies as a response to two major changes in the southern and eastern parts of England: There was a decline in allotments of land for agricultural laborers and a decline in cottage industries. Parishes responded to these forces and the losses of incomes by guaranteeing seasonally unemployed laborers a minimum weekly poor relief income. These subsidies were not intended to cover maintenance needs but were supplementary to low and inadequate wages. There are definite instances where allowances were provided for men with families too large to be supported by their wages. This practice was well established at the close of the seventeenth century.[52] Farmers were thus subsidized by other parish taxpayers because rural areas were dominated by labor-hiring farmers.

There were other results of the subsidy. According to one view, the subsidy led to ambiguity in the distinction between pauperism and independence. The fear was that the Speenhamland subsidy system was undermining the independence of agricultural laborers. Such fears strengthened the idea that no outdoor relief should be given to the able-bodied poor and suggested they should be maintained in a workhouse. Further, their lives should be regulated and made less comfortable than those outside and fending for themselves, that is, they should be "*less eligible.*"

A confusion was institutionalized among wage supplements, providing cash to employed workers to supplement their earnings, and providing family allowances directly to families to assist them. Able-bodied persons became regular recipients of relief, and employers took advantage of the system to maintain wages at a low level.[53]

A prior history and tradition existed for supplementing inadequate wages in the parishes. The poor were put to work on the land where they were needed in a process called "going the rounds" and were given relief at what was considered an appropriate level. Such a system was open to abuse by employers and acted to depress wages.

The *roundsman* system provided for the pauper-laborer to go from house to house seeking work. If work was provided, then he received food for the day and a small wage, while the parish paid a supplemental sum. In some places the Poor Law administrator contracted with employers who would pay a fixed sum for a certain number of poor laborers; the workers' wages were supplemented by relief funds. Another method used was the labor rate. A parish tax was levied to cover the support of the able-bodied unemployed, and a price was set for their services. Taxpayers could employ a number of paupers at the appropriate wage or pay the tax. In all cases allowances were used to restore order by enforcing work at very low wage levels.[54]

Following the implementation of the Speenhamland system in many parts of England, criticism was voiced that has a familiar ring. It was surmised allowances would undermine individual responsibility, lead people to produce children recklessly, and deplete productivity. Furthermore, such allowances, it was thought, would alter fundamentally the basic psychology of "necessary" goading and encourage freedom of choice in regard to work. Moreover, it would cost too much. Essentially this argument derives from the belief that people must be forced to produce. From another point of view, at times subsidies are needed even by the working poor, to prevent starvation and to provide a healthier family life in order to best support productivity and society in general.

After the beginning of the nineteenth century the birthrate did not rise dramatically, and historians differ as to whether productivity actually fell or rose under the Speenhamland system.[55] One of the lessons of Speenhamland is that such subsidies do not necessarily result in less productive workers or increased birthrates.

Debates on wage supplementation continue in our age, following the basic arguments established when Speenhamland was in operation. This is an issue today. So long as we operate on the theory of the economic being, wage supplementation may demean the labor market, in the sense that employers may lower wages by taking the supplementation into account. The basic problem is that of *less eligibility*: the belief that no person on relief should be paid as much as the lowest wage earner in the community for fear such a wage will impair the labor market. For those who accept the economic view of human beings, such wages will prove counterproductive by diminishing the motivations of those at the poverty level and those just above it.

The Workhouse

By 1662, urban poverty was an increasing problem. As we saw earlier, destitute individuals were the responsibility of their parish of birth. When sent to their parish of origin, they often took dependent children with them. These children were strangers to the parish, a factor that was even more problematic for those orphaned or abandoned children who were completely unfamiliar to the parish residents. Children whose parents died or disappeared seemed to have no real connection to the parish to which they were removed. This led to great resentment. Sometimes they were apprenticed at the rate (tax) payers expense and sometimes placed in a workhouse.

In 1723 the English Parliament authorized any parish to establish a workhouse. The poor were to produce goods that would earn money for the state. Typically, notice would be given to the poor that their weekly pensions were to be discontinued. Those who were unable to support themselves could apply for admission to the workhouse.

According to one contemporary quotation, "A workhouse is a name that carries along with it an idea of correction and punishment and many of our poor have taken such an aversion to living in it, as all the reason and argument in the world can never overcome."[56] All categories of the poor were housed under one roof, including "fallen" women, the insane, the old, children, paupers, the sick, the disabled, and vagrants. The problems of the workhouses were so bad that in 1762 the Act for Keeping Poor Children Alive was passed. This law required parishes to maintain records of all children admitted to the workhouses so death rates for institutions and their caretakers could be ascertained.

Infant death in the workhouses took place within a particular historical context. With the rise of the propertyless as a proportion of the population, abandonment and infanticide were stimulated. During the eighteenth century, many abandoned infants were sent to parish workhouses, where they died from starvation, beatings, and disease. Overseers of the poor sometimes received lump sum payments from the father or putative father if the infant was born out of wedlock. These children were sometimes murdered by their caretakers and a profit was made from the lump sum payment upon the early death of a child. At London's Foundling Hospital during its first four years of existence (1741–1745), of the 15,000 children placed there, approximately 10,000 died. In Dublin from 1790 to 1796, of 12,600 children placed in a hospital, almost 10,000 died. Some abandoned children were born out of wedlock. Others, a majority, were from couples unable to support them. There are estimates that in eighteenth-century Europe anywhere from 10 percent to 40 percent of urban children were abandoned.[57]

By the nineteenth century, 3,800 workhouses existed in England with approximately 83,500 residents. Despite the widespread use of the workhouse, relief of the poor in their own homes (*outdoor relief*) was the predominant mode of subsidy, utilizing both in-kind and monetary payments.[58]

Workhouses fell short of their goals. The major aim of the workhouses was the profitable employment of the poor; however, they failed. Workhouse labor had to be inefficient: The laborers were either incapable or unwilling. Workhouses were not capable of providing work in spinning and weaving, precisely those tasks more and more performed by machines. The training some children received proved to be obsolete. In other cases, the use of the workhouse as a punitive deterrent, as a house of correction, was contradictory to the aim of production. Thus, the principles of deterrence and of profitable employment conflicted.

The evidence suggests that workhouses gave only temporary relief to the tax rates. The harshness of the workhouses encountered growing criticism, while many institutions became "unsupervised asylums for a mixed population of the impotent and the vicious, and (unfortunately) children."[59]

The Poor Law of 1834

At the beginning of the nineteenth century, the tax to be paid for the poor rose rapidly, as did per capita expenditures for the poor in the latter part of the eighteenth century. Following the defeat of Napoleon, unemployment increased, food prices fell, many small farmers faced bankruptcy, and starvation forced people to apply for relief. Parishes drove paupers out of their territories, and the enactment of the Corn Law of 1815 increased the price of bread while wages remained low.

In 1832, a royal commission was established to review the Poor Laws. The commission was biased against the poor from the start and was supported by several ideological strands: Adam Smith, Thomas Malthus, and Jeremy Bentham. Adam Smith, a theoretician of laissez-faire capitalism, believed that the private interests of individuals in the market were led by an "invisible hand" toward the interest of the whole society. Government should passively police the market and has only three duties: (1) protect society from invasion and violence by other societies; (2) protect, as far as possible, members of society from injustice and oppression of every other member of it; and (3) develop and maintain public works and institutions that can never be the interest of any individual or small group to create and maintain. He believed in the liberty of the individual and free trade among nations.

Thomas Malthus suggested that the human species would breed itself into starvation and ruin. The geometric increase in population would be greater than the ability of people to produce the subsistence needed because food would be harvested only arithmetically. As a result, Malthus concluded pessimistically that misery and vice would spread. Further, the increase in population would decrease demand for labor and result in lowered wages, which would lead to suffering. The poor could only achieve prosperity by abstaining from reproduction (an impossible task). The resources given to undeserving and unproductive paupers can only be given at the expense of deserving laborers because to do so raises the price of food and reduces real wages. Relief leads to increased poverty. The more severe the attitude toward the poor, the greater the true benevolence.[60]

Jeremy Bentham was an exponent of utilitarianism. The "good" equals adding to the sum total of pleasures or diminishing the sum total of pain for a community. In social and economic matters, government should have a hands-off policy. Yet in certain cases, the pursuit of self-interest by individuals, he believed, might not work to the best interest of all individuals. If the pains endured by the many exceeded the pleasures enjoyed by the few, then the state should step in and do something about it.

In 1834, the Reform Poor Law (the New Poor Law) was enacted. Outdoor relief would be available for the sick and the aged, but not for the able-bodied. No relief would be given to able-bodied persons unless they were residents of the workhouse, a highly stigmatized institution. There would be a three-member central Poor Law commission with the power to group parishes into unions for Poor Law administration and to supervise the work of local authorities. Poor Law guardians elected by local taxpayers would be in charge of the disbursement of local relief. The principle of less eligibility and punitive stigmatization of relief recipients were basic principles of the new law.

The 1834 law was a compromise enactment in that strict Malthusians, laissez-faire economists, and others wanted a law that completely put an end to Poor Law relief. In reality, one of the motivations for the revised law was to reduce poor taxes. This did in fact occur following the enactment of the 1834 law. Good harvests and the building of railways undoubtedly had some effect on this drop. However, the trend reversed itself and taxes began to climb once again, although more modestly than in the past. It is likely that voluntary charity played some part in minimizing the need for more rapidly expanding public assistance. But the intent of the 1834 law was primarily to do away with outdoor relief. Some 15 years after the enactment of the New Law of 1834, five times as many people were relieved outside the workhouses as were being given relief inside them.[61]

Still more complex motivations impelled the attempt to abolish outdoor relief. Farming communities were actually in favor of retaining subsidies such as Speenhamland's. However, Parliament was dominated by large landowners who were convinced that outdoor relief was a threat to their rental incomes. On the other hand, grain farmers developed such subsidies as an inexpensive means to provide income for seasonally unemployed workers. So the original abolishment of subsidies was not because it had disastrous effects on the rural economy. Instead it was because landowners who controlled Parliament feared such future consequences.[62]

Principles of the Poor Laws

As we have seen, the principles by which treatment of the poor was determined changed dramatically after the thirteenth century. The Poor Laws evolved as a result of changing features of society, including the dissolution of the feudal system, the alteration of the churches, the emphasis on individual responsibility, and the growth of international money and trade economies. All these factors combined to ensure a market in which labor was simply another resource to be maintained. The series of Poor Laws was created to maintain a motivated workforce available for productive employment as well as to minimize the number of shiftless vagrants who might commit violent acts and the number of those dependent upon the community.

The Poor Laws themselves were based on and slowly evolved several principles for dealing with the poor. These principles have remained with us, sometimes in disguised form and often explicitly. Secularism was established as the basic direction of social welfare, despite the existence of a religious social welfare subsystem. Whereas during the Middle Ages there existed both a governmental and an ecclesiastic system, along with other voluntary systems, gradually social welfare became a public responsibility—that is, a secular task for the entire body politic. This development is part of the rise of nation-states, with their need to care for their citizens in order to maintain morale and build the nation. It is also a result of the secularization trend that has evolved over centuries, by which certain church functions and controls have been shifted to the public and governmental bodies. The powers of the ecclesiastical system and the demands it could make on people diminished, while the demands of the nation-state on its citizens increased. Although recent U.S. history has seen a shift away from federal responsibility and toward state, local, and voluntary welfare efforts, overall the provision of social welfare for the masses remains the responsibility of the taxing authority: the secular state. (This topic will be explored in greater detail in chapters 5, 9, 10, and 11.)

The concept of risk or categories also developed as a principle. For example, not only were the poor divided into categories—aged, children, lame, ill, and so forth—but also these categories were further defined in moral terms: *the worthy and the unworthy poor.* Such definitions led to *means-testing,* or establishing need on the basis of one's income (which has to be below the level required to purchase necessary goods or services). These definitions were congenial to the view that the poor had caused their own poverty, were morally at fault, and could by sufficient motivation and willpower alter their life circumstances. As we saw in chapter 1, such views of the poor remain with us, accompanied by the idea that poverty should be punished, a remnant of philosophies centuries old. Whereas in the Middle Ages all poor were given assistance without consideration of the "category" they were in, now one differentiates between those who are worthy or unworthy of receiving assistance.

Another principle was the establishment of the distinction between *indoor* and *outdoor* relief. Work was demanded from the poor (a demand present in the early monasteries as well); that is, some poor would have to take shelter in a public house or hospital (indoor), whereas others "more deserving" would be supported in their own homes (outdoor). The outdoor/indoor controversy, of which the workhouse is the prime example, continues today in terms of community care for those with chronic mental illness, persons with developmental disabilities, juvenile delinquents, and others.

Although it almost always costs more to have indoor relief, countermoves are typically resisted with vigor, such as the debate on whether to establish foster homes for persons with disabilities or to place the poor in middle-class neighborhoods. Beneath such resistance can be found fear of differences and also the idea that the unworthy should be shunned and out of sight.

Residency laws, as a principle, required that laborers be tied to their lords and employers and then to their home parishes or place of birth. Binding people to places (a throwback to serfdom) served to minimize their bargaining power through restrictions on their freedom to move and thus set limits on what employers had to pay as wages. Thus, residency laws served important economic purposes and had the intention of maintaining a pool of available labor for production accompanied by control over wages.

The principles of *less eligibility* and *wage supplementation* are hotly debated even today. The question of *less eligibility* (the poor must not be supported at a level as high as that of the lowest employed person in the community) is one of the most intractable problems facing social welfare. With the establishment of less eligibility, a problem of great difficulty was identified and a solution was suggested that assumed that humans are economic beings.

The solution, however, has proved problematic. Although the original intent for less eligibility assumed that the poor could be motivated only in this way, the results of following such a principle are open to question. As we saw in the case of Speenhamland, the "payoff" was really not for the employees, but actually was a use of public means to subsidize the employers: The main effect of the allowance system was to depress wages below the subsistence level. Methods need to be found to deal with this problem, especially ways that recognize the structural nature of high unemployment and poverty in a multinational, technological economy.

Finally, the fact that the social problems of the needy were approached by and large on a *case-by-case* basis has supported the assumption that the problem rests with the individual or family. Such views are still subtly expressed in current social work when insufficient attention is paid to the structural determinants of social need and too much emphasis is placed on the responsibility of individuals and families. Such views have far-reaching implications for social welfare.

Summary

In this chapter, we have surveyed the major trends and social welfare events from the Middle Ages to the early nineteenth century in England. We have also examined some of the moral, religious, philosophical, and economic theories and principles behind the practices, institutions, and laws developed to deal with the poor. We will turn in chapter 4 to the U.S. experience, which is based primarily upon the preceding English history and carries over the values of the Poor Laws. We will examine major themes and significant social welfare exemplars from colonial times to today, keeping in mind the relationship of underlying values to the social welfare choices made historically by U.S. society.

Questions for Consideration

1. What were the benefits and limitations for individuals and families in a *status* relationship and what are they in a *contract* relationship?

2. What relationships can you identify between the Poor Laws and people's ideas about social welfare today?

3. Have any states or the Congress recently attempted to make residency laws regarding

social welfare? Does anything stand in their way? For some groups? For all groups?

4. Did Speenhamland provide a family allowance, a wage supplementation, or a subsidy for employers? Do any of these exist in the United States today?

Notes

1. Clayton Roberts and David Roberts, *A History of England: Prehistory to 1714*, 2nd ed., Vol. 1, Englewood Cliffs, N.J.: Prentice Hall, 1985, pp. 75–81.

2. L. C. B. Seaman, *A New History of England, 410–1975*, Totowa, N.J.: Barnes and Noble, 1982, pp. 114–120.

3. Rodney Hilton, *Bond Men Made Free: Medieval Peasant Movements and the English Rising of 1381*, New York: Viking, 1973, pp. 14–15.

4. Fernand Braudel, *The Structures of Everyday Life*, New York: Harper & Row, 1979, p. 74.

5. Hilton, p. 65.

6. Ibid., p. 86.

7. Brian Tierney, *Medieval Poor Law*, Berkeley: University of California Press, 1959, p. 12.

8. Ibid., p. 37.

9. Ibid., p. 11.

10. Joseph R. Strayer and Dana C. Munro, *The Middle Ages, 395–1500*, New York: Appleton-Century-Crofts, 1970, p. 130.

11. Hilton, pp. 15–16, 86, 88.

12. Richard W. Southern, *The Making of the Middle Ages*, New Haven, Conn.: Yale University Press, 1970, pp. 106–107.

13. Tierney, p. 109.

14. Barbara A. Hanawalt, *Crime and Conflict in English Communities, 1300–1348*, Cambridge, Mass.: Harvard University Press, 1979, p. 31.

15. David Nicholas, *The Evolution of the Medieval World: Government and Thought in Europe, 312–1500*, New York: Longman, 1992, p. 410.

16. Tierney, p. 61.

17. J. Gilchrist, *The Church and Economic Activity in the Middle Ages*, New York: Macmillan, 1969, p. 79. According to Gilchrist, the income expended on charity never exceeded 5 percent. However, Pound suggests the percentage of monastic income devoted to charity ranged from less than 1 percent to more than 22 percent. But even Pound finds that the generosity of some houses was insufficient to raise the national average to 2.5 percent. See John Pound, *Poverty and Vagrancy in Tudor England*, London: Longman, 1975, pp. 21–22.

18. Roland Bainton, *The Penguin History of Christianity*, Vol. 2, Harmondsworth, Eng.: Penguin, 1967, p. 9.

19. de Schweinitz, p. 15.

20. W. K. Jordan, *Philanthropy in England: 1480–1660*. London: George Allen & Unwin Ltd., 1959, p. 41.

21. Gilchrist, p. 79.

22. Hanawalt, p. 235.

23. Ibid., p. 253.

24. de Schweinitz, p. 17.

25. Gilchrist, p. 79.

26. Recent research hypothesizes that the Black Death was not solely the result of Bubonic Plague but probably also caused by anthrax or some similar disease spread by cattle. See Norman F. Cantor, "Studying the Black Death," *The Chronicle of Higher Education*, April 27, 2001, B7–B10.

27. Robert S. Gottfried, *The Black Death: Natural and Human Disaster in Medieval Europe*, New York: Free Press, 1983, pp. xii, xvi, 86.

28. Ibid., p. 135.

29. Ibid., pp. 97–98.

30. Ibid., p. 98.

31. Ibid., p. 94.

32. Hilton, p. 155.

33. Barbara W. Tuchman, *A Distant Mirror: The Calamitous 14th Century*, New York: Knopf, 1978, p. 124. One historian suggests about this period that "if it was a golden age, it was the golden age of bacteria." Sylvia L. Thrupp, "The Problem of Replacement-Rates in Medieval English Population," *Society and History*, Raymond Grew and Nicholas H. Steneck, eds., Ann Arbor, Mich.: University of Michigan Press, 1977, p. 186.

34. Brian Tierney and Sidney Painter, *Western Europe in the Middle Ages, 300–1475*, New York: Knopf, 1978, pp. 511–512.

35. Tuchman, pp. 125–126.

36. Roland Bainton, *The Reformation of the Sixteenth Century*, Boston: Beacon Press, 1964, p. 246.

37. Max Weber, *The Protestant Ethic and the Spirit of Capitalism*, Los Angles, CA: Roxbury Publishing Co., 1998.

38. William J. Bouwsma, *John Calvin: A Sixteenth-Century Portrait*, New York: Oxford University Press, 1988, p. 74.

39. See Bainton; Georgia Harkness, *John Calvin: The Man and the Ethics*, New York: Abingdon Press, 1958; R. H. Tawney, *Religion and the Rise of Capitalism*, New York: Mentor Books, 1950.

40. The distinction must be made between the original writings of Calvin and Calvinism as it developed. Weber and Tawney suggest that Calvinism equates amassing wealth with a sign of individual grace and election. Their view is that Calvinism thus contributed to the development of capitalism. Calvin himself, however, did not regard prosperity in this life as associated with election. See John T. McNeill, ed., *Calvin: Institutes of the Christian Religion*, Philadelphia: Westminster Press, 1960, in particular p. 438.

41. David Nicholas, *The Evolution of the Medieval World: Society, Government and Thought in Europe, 312–1500,* New York: Longman, 1992, p. 410.

42. Karl Polanyi, *The Great Transformation,* Boston: Beacon Press, 1960, pp. 40, 42.

43. de Schweinitz, pp. 20–22.

44. Pound, pp. 16–24 and David Loades, *Revolution in Religion: The English Reformation, 1530–1570,* Cardiff: University of Wales, 1992, p. 90.

45. de Schweinitz, pp. 22–23.

46. Brian Pullan, *Rich and Poor in Renaissance Venice,* Cambridge, Mass.: Harvard University Press, 1971, pp. 239–240.

47. Sidney and Beatrice Webb, *English Poor Law History,* Part 1, *The Old Poor Law,* London: Frank Case, 1963, pp. 52–66.

48. Ibid., pp. 52–66.

49. John R. Poynter, *Society and Pauperism,* London: Routledge & Kegan Paul, 1969, p. 50.

50. J. A. Sharpe, *Crime in Early Modern England,* London: Longman, 1984, pp. 91, 184.

51. Robert Boguslaw, *The New Utopians,* Englewood Cliffs, N.J.: Prentice Hall, 1965, pp. 132, 134.

52. George R. Boyer, *An Economic History of the English Poor Law 1750–1850,* New York: Cambridge University Press, 1990, pp. 265–267; Dorothy Marshall, "The Old Poor Law, 1662–1795," *Essays in Economic History,* Eleanora Mary Carus-Wilson, ed., London: Edward Arnold Publishers, 1954, p. 304.

53. Geoffrey W. Oxley, *Poor Relief in England and Wales, 1601–1834,* London: David and Charles, 1974, p. 113; Michael Rose, *The Relief of Poverty, 1834–1914,* London: Macmillan Press, 1981, p. 8.

54. Catherina Lis and Hugo Soly, *Poverty and Capitalism in Pre-Industrial Europe,* Atlantic Highlands, N.J.: Humanities Press, 1979, p. 199.

55. According to Marcus, a fall in production accompanied a rise in the poor rates (taxes) (Steven Marcus, "Their Brothers' Keepers: An Episode from English History," *Doing Good,* W. Gaylin, Ira Glasser, Steven Marcus, and David J. Rothman, eds., New York: Pantheon, 1978, p. 49). According to Blaug, however, the allowances did not encourage people to "breed recklessly" and did not devitalize the working class; furthermore, after the turn of the century, there was an increase in production. Blaug suggests that the allowance systems were almost entirely a rural problem in particular parts of the country. The device was chosen to deal with surplus labor in a lagging sector of an expanding but underdeveloped economy; it was a method for dealing with problems of structural unemployment and substandard wages. According to this view, the allowance system contributed to economic expansion (Mark Blaug, "The Myth of the Old Poor Law and the Making of the New," *Journal of Economic History,* Vol. 23, No. 2, June 1963, pp. 151–184, and "The Poor Law Report Reexamined," *Journal of Economic History,* Vol. 24, No. 2, June 1964, pp. 229–245).

56. Frank Crompton, *Workhouse Children,* Phoenix Mill, England: Sutton Publishing Limited, 1997, p. 3. Norman Longmate, *The Workhouse,* London: Temple Smith, 1974, p. 24.

57. See Lawrence Stone, *The Family, Sex and Marriage in England 1500–1800,* New York: Harper & Row, 1977, pp. 473–478; John Boswell, *The Kindness of Strangers: The Abandonment of Children in Western Europe from Late Antiquity to the Renaissance,* New York: Pantheon, 1988, p. 10.

58. John R. Poynter, *Society and Pauperism,* London: Routledge & Kegan Paul, 1969, p. 189.

59. John R. Poynter, *Society and Pauperism,* London: Routledge and Kegan Paul, 1969, pp. 14–17.

60. Robert Pinker, *Social Theory and Social Policy,* London: Heinemann Educational Books, 1973, pp. 55–61.

61. Robert H. Bremner, "The Rediscovery of Pauperism," *Current Issues in Social Work Seen in Historical Perspective,* New York: Council on Social Work Education, 1962, p. 16.

62. George R. Boyer, *An Economic History of the English Poor Law 1750–1850,* New York: Cambridge University Press, 1990, p. 267.

4

Social Values and Social Welfare

The American Experience I

The welfare or happiness of mankind consists entirely in the freedom to exercise the natural faculties.... The problem therefore manifestly is how to secure to the members of society the maximum power of exercising their natural faculties.... Abundant nourishment for the body is therefore the first condition of liberty.

—Lester F. Ward[1]

Overview

In the preceding chapter, we described the evolution of the English Poor Law system. In this chapter, we turn to consider factors that influenced social welfare developments in the United States, ranging from the impact of the English system on U.S. social welfare choices; the differential experiences of African Americans, Hispanics, and American Indians; the importance of voluntary mutual aid among all groups; and the impact of the frontier myth. In addition, we review the federal role in social welfare, including the Freedmen's Bureau, the suspension of the ethic for veterans and their families, as well as the important impact of social Darwinism on American values, and the initiation of social insurances in Germany and Great Britain.

American Poor Law Mentality

Eight years after the compilation of the Elizabethan Poor Laws, settlements began to be established by colonists along the eastern seaboard of what was later to become the United States of America. During the early stages of settlement, clashes between ideologies took place. When Jamestown was settled, the Virginia Company required all employees to contribute "the fruits of their labor" to a common storehouse. The food was then distributed to each person according to their needs. This plan was later abandoned and the owners turned to settlers to support themselves with individual gardens.[2]

The first years of the Plymouth colony were based on a common sharing of all property. An emphasis on mutual aid and communal organization reflective of early Christian social organization clashed with the Protestant work ethic reflected in the Poor Laws. For the pious, ownership could never be simply a means for personal fulfillment or gain. It must also contribute to communal well-being, and one was a steward of God's property, which was to be used to serve God and society.[3]

Given the need for work and workers, the Protestant ethic in the form of the Poor Laws was used by the early settlers because that was the natural thing for them to do, in the sense that the laws reflected the traditions of the English founding settlers. The English Poor Laws and their underlying attitudes were implanted early in the Atlantic coast colonies: secularism, the concept of risks and categories, indoor and outdoor relief, residency laws, less eligibility, and approaching the poor on a case-by-case basis. But, also, in these ways, American ambivalence toward the poor began; there is community caring but also an inheritance of the Poor Law mentality.

Settlements, Labor, and Imported "Poor Laws"

European events pushed some to America; others were attracted by opportunities; and some were forced to the colonies. For example, the English made efforts to divert to the colonies some part of a mobile labor force during the seventeenth century. The only way poor persons could practically get to the colonies in the seventeenth century was through some form of *indentured service* (a contract to work for someone for a designated period of time). Of the 155,000 English emigrants during that century, the majority fit into this category. The principal labor supply for early settlements was indentured servants until this supply was superseded by enslaved Africans, when, beginning in the 1680s, the mainland colonies underwent a massive shift from indentured to enslaved labor. Adults were indentured and children were apprenticed. But indentured service for some (those at the margin) turned into multiple terms of indenture. Thus, England's need to deal with its labor force and the colonies' need to recruit emigrants for labor combined to foster indentured service and found both emigrants and those who preceded them in the mainland colonies acutely aware of the Poor Laws and their provisions.[4]

Many immigrants came as indentured servants, apprentices, tenants, "all agreeing to the status of a person who, lacking the means, accepts free transportation as the price of four to seven years of unrelenting servitude to an unknown master."[5] This is how indenture worked. Shippers took whatever money individuals or families could pay to transport them to the colonies. Emigrants were then given fourteen days to come up with the balance of the cost due the shipper. If the required amount could not be produced, they were "sold" into indentured servitude for an amount sufficient to repay their debt. This legal contract tied immigrants to their local place of settlement in exchange for transportation to the colony, food, drink, clothing, and shelter during the term of service, which depended upon the amount of the debt owed.[6]

By 1633, the following provision was made for one of the colonists:

> Thomas Higgins having lived an extravagant life, was placed with John Jenny for eight years, to serve him as an apprentice, during which time the said John competently to provide for him; and at the end thereof to give him double apell [apple], 12 bushels of corn and 20 acres of land.[7]

In Massachusetts, as in other parts of America, poor relief was a local responsibility. The smallest unit of government became the instrument for implementing the readily imported English Poor Law system. By 1642, Plymouth had enacted the following law:

> ...that every township shall make competent provision for the maintenance of their poor according as they shall find most convenient and suitable for themselves by an order and general agreement in a public town meeting. And notwithstanding the promise that all such persons as are now resident and inhabitant and within the said town shall be maintained and provided for by them.[8]

Selectmen administered aid to the poor. Almshouse care was not common until approximately the late eighteenth century. Cases were dealt with individually and were presented to the town at a public town meeting. Settlement laws were also enacted to keep strangers out if there was an incompatibility of religious belief or likelihood of early public dependency.

According to town records in Fairfield, Connecticut, during the seventeenth century, the deserving poor were maintained by the town. However, vagrant and idle persons were warned to leave town, and they and persons who harbored them were subject to prosecution. Thus two categories were again established, the worthy and unworthy poor, with the unworthy poor being made to leave town.[9]

Children were viewed as economic assets rather than liabilities, much as in other agricultural societies. In social welfare terms, however, children were placed with various parties by indenture; parents were forced into service to avoid public expense. If parents with children were aided by the town, they were required to set the children out to work. The poor also were boarded in private homes. Outdoor relief was given as well. Sometimes there were local work-relief programs, especially on projects needed by the community.

Settlement laws also played a part in colonial social welfare, as can be seen in the following example:

> December 11, 1634. One Abigail Gifford, widow, being kept at the charge of the parish of Wilsden in Middlesex, near London, was sent by Mr. Ball's ship into this country, and being found to be somewhat distracted, and a very burdensome woman, the governor and assistants returned her back by warrant, 18, to the same parish, in the ship Rebecca.[10]

In the early scattered American communities (primarily rural with subsistence farming), the local community could indeed handle the few cases that were its responsibility. It was familiar with the people involved and made what it considered appropriate provision.

As early as the seventeenth century, when America was newly settled by European colonists and was primarily an agricultural society, private and voluntary philanthropy and mutual aid developed, on both an individual and cooperative basis. This aid was founded on religious and civic principles and traditions brought from Europe, on the views of the proper role of government, and on the limitations of resources available to governmental jurisdictions. For example, several private benefactors left bequests to Boston that, when combined, enabled the town to build an almshouse. As Pumphrey and Pumphrey pointed out, this "pattern of making individual gifts or bequests to the town, rather than setting up isolated foundations, was regarded as natural. Private benevolence thus provided the capital, but the public was expected to maintain the donated facility."[11]

It was natural that early colonial social welfare should fashion itself on the model set in seventeenth-century Europe. This era was a great period of European philanthropy, one characterized by missionary enterprises, interest in charitable works, tax-supported poor relief, as well as philanthropic associations. There were efforts at colonization and motivation for converting the natives to Christianity, for poor men to be provided with work and land, and for a wilderness to be supplied with institutions of civilization.[12]

Cotton Mather proposed in 1710 that men and women should engage as individuals or as members of voluntary associations in "a perpetual endeavor to do good in the world." Good works were viewed as an obligation owed to God and a reward in themselves. To help the unfortunate was deemed an honor, and sound policy called for effective social control through pious example, moral leadership, voluntary effort, and private charity. These were the means by which competing and conflicting interests could be brought into harmony.[13]

During the colonial period, the line between public and private responsibility was not sharply drawn. A cooperative approach existed. Overseers of the poor called on the churches for special collections. As noted earlier, the bequeathing of property to public authorities during the colonial period was a popular form of philanthropy. In many instances, national, occupational, and religious groups relieved the public sector of the necessity for charitable support.[14]

In American port towns during the 1690s, life compared favorably with the conditions in English, Irish, and Scottish towns. Although lower-level workers labored long hours in unpleasant and unhealthy conditions and, at the ends of their lives, had little to show for their strenuous labors, they did not starve or go unclothed or unhoused. Meanwhile, in English towns, there was much unemployment and acute poverty. In the colonial cities, workhouses had a dual purpose: to deal with the jobless poor and if possible to reduce tax rates through their labor. The incidence of poverty was confined mainly to the widowed, disabled, and the orphaned, who were viewed as wards of the community. There was little stigma attached to being poor, as this was viewed as being generally due to circumstances beyond one's control. Persons in need remained in their homes or in the homes of others and were given outdoor relief such as clothes, firewood, bread, and a small weekly cash payment.

Boston in the 1730s illustrates what happens when poor relief rises. The selectmen and overseers of the poor sought new solutions to a rise in pauperism. They wished to care for the poor while also caring for their constituents' resources. In 1735, Boston enacted a new Poor Law under which the selectmen could eject strangers without first appealing to the county court for a warrant. The law also authorized the erection of a separate workhouse on Boston Common where able-bodied poor would be put to work. This workhouse was specifically for those who were unable to find work. The almshouse was where the aged, ill, and disabled could receive care.

Those in the workhouse were expected to support themselves by picking oakum, weaving cloth, and making shoes. By 1741, 55 persons were living in the workhouse. The expenses exceeded the income. Nevertheless, an inspection committee judged the experiment to be a success since support of this number of persons on outdoor relief would have been far costlier.[15]

The Early Spanish Influence, the Mexicans, and Other Hispanics

Social welfare was not only being developed in the English colonies. It is important to remember that Juan Ponce de Leon explored Florida in 1513 and that Hernando Cortes, the Spanish conquistador, invaded Mexico and conquered the Aztecs in 1519, prior to developed settlements on the eastern seaboard. During the sixteenth and seventeenth centuries, Florida was an outpost of the Spanish empire consisting of a fortified garrison at St. Augustine and a string of missions along the Atlantic coast and across the peninsula, mainly used to convert and control the American Indians. The province was strategically important but was never self-supporting and experienced a series of disasters.

In what is now the southwestern United States, the Spanish established in 1609 Santa Fe de San Francisco and colonized what is now New Mexico and parts of Arizona, Colorado, Texas, Nebraska, and Oklahoma. In the sixteenth century the transplanted Catholic church built missions, convents, monasteries, churches, hospitals, and schools. By the seventeenth century, there were 3,000 missionaries in New Spain, converting nonbelievers but also providing some social welfare services, such as caring for the sick and the poor in almshouses, serving and burying the poor, as well as payment of tithes by non-Native persons and encouraging the giving of charity, especially on feast days.[16]

Spanish rule had two goals: the enrichment of the conquerors and the Christian salvation of the Indians' souls. By the 18th century there were 21 missions in the territories and *encomiendas* (grants of land and control over American Indian lands, labor, and produce) were distributed among the conquerors. The *encomendero*—the holder of the grant—expected to profit from the work on farms, at crafts, in mines, and in households through entitlement to the perpetual service of the natives. In return, they were expected to maintain a church and a priest for American Indians and to keep arms as a kind of militia. The *encomenderos* were supposed to obey certain rules: not to uproot American Indians from their homes, not to send them to work in mines, or on war expeditions except when the crown's representatives called for them to help for defense. They were also not to be made to labor to exhaustion or to the detriment of their own plots of land. But there were flagrant abuses and unethical officials helped to exploit the American Indians.[17]

Members of the clergy objected strongly to the encomiendas, and there were American Indian revolts in 1541 and 1680. American Indians were sometimes hired labor and traders but sometimes forced to labor without pay. Although enslavement of pueblo American Indians was rare, this usually was punishment for certain crimes. Sometimes written permission was given to soldiers to seize American Indian orphans as house servants with the assumption the soldier would be the guardian of the seized orphans, teach and indoctrinate them, and in return for protection the master had a claim on the orphan's services. It is unclear how general this practice was. However, captured Apache boys and girls were commonly used as house servants. Later a substitute method of exploitation was instituted— *repartimiento*. American Indians were forced to accept cash advances or goods were priced high, against the expected harvests. Then they would "sell" the harvested crops at a lower-than market price set by the Spaniards. Thus, they became involuntarily indebted. Sometimes they were forced to buy enough goods from the Spaniard to deliver the amount owed, but to do so without the means to repay the debt. Many families were in perpetual debt.[18]

Catholic friars had use of both cultivatable and range lands. They defended their use of these lands on three grounds: (1) all their food had to be raised on the spot and they had a right to a certain amount of land; (2) in case of famine they frequently fed large numbers of American Indians and Spaniards from their food and livestock reserves; and (3) they had to export cattle and other livestock to obtain funds needed for church purposes not supplied by the Crown.[19]

Hispanics are among both the oldest and newest immigrants to the United States. As we have seen, Spaniards arrived even before colonizers arrived on the east coast and Latinos have come from many different places. Mexico because of its proximity has had a shared complex history with the United States. Mexican lands were fought over and the annexation of Texas in 1845 began a war that ended officially in 1848 with the signing of the Treaty of Guadalupe Hidalgo. This treaty left Mexicans who chose to stay in the United States with cultural autonomy but in marginal and discriminated situations. Many lost their lands and as a result became agricultural laborers. Discriminatory rules affected voting rights, economic opportunities, education, and the use of the Spanish language. Texans, many of whom originated in the American South, transferred their attitudes to Mexican-Americans who, nevertheless, were citizens, albeit treated—for the most part—poorly.

The Mexican Revolution displaced millions of peasants after 1910 and American railroads recruited many of those who came to the United States into track gangs and dispersed them to where they built urban *barrios*.[20] The Spanish influence was intensified by the Spanish-American War, which entangled the United States further into Hispanic affairs in Cuba and the Phillipines. After World War I, Mexicans immigrated to the United States legally because the restrictive legislation of the 1920s did not apply to western hemisphere nations. During the Great Depression of the 1930s, as many as half a million Mexican persons were deported or "encouraged" to return. In 1942, during World War II and from 1948 to 1965, federal legislation encouraged the importation of *braceros* (temporary farm workers) to help with wartime shortages. Others came illegally, slipping across the Rio Grande border. Workers were poorly housed, underpaid, and discriminated against.

During the 1960s as part of the general civil rights era, the Chicano movement began in the southwest, demanding better schools, easier access to higher education, and fostering cultural pride. One group, Alianza, led by Reies Lopez Tijerna, failed in its effort to secede from New Mexico. Probably the persons with the widest influence were Cesar Chavez and Delores Huerta, who organized farm workers into unions and founded the United Farm Workers Organizing Committee. His leadership of a grape pickers strike became a nationwide effort as he enlisted the support of church leaders, organized sit ins, marched on the California State capitol, and initiated a nationwide consumer boycott of grapes. These union organizing efforts and demands for equal treatment did not lead to separatism but, instead, opted for economic and political inclusion.

Puerto Rican migrations mainly took place post–World War II and during the 1950s. Later migrations came following the Cuban revolution 1959 and as a result of civil wars in Nicaragua, Guatemala, El Salvador, and other political upheavals. In chapter 8, the economic situation of Hispanics will be introduced, and in chapter 14 we will discuss the impact of Hispanic groups on the current U.S. political situation.

In summary, Latinos settled early on in what became the United States and provided a social welfare system, mainly through the Catholic Church and its missions, and have enriched American society, the economy, and culture for many centuries, despite loss of lands, cultural clashes, and persistent discrimination.

Voluntary Mutual Aid Efforts

Other voluntary mutual aid efforts were also being organized. The Scots' Charitable Society, first among many such nationality-based groups, was formed in 1657 as a mutual aid society for those of Scottish origin.[21]

Voluntary organizations were formed to aid special groups, for example, the Philadelphia Society for Alleviating the Miseries of Public Prisoners (1787), the Massachusetts Charitable Fire Society (1794), and the New York Society for the Relief of Poor Widows with Small Children (1798). Church charities, another form of voluntary social welfare, were financed by collections and gave relief to members of particular congregations. For example, in 1729 the Ursuline Sisters in New Orleans established a private home for mothers and children left homeless by the Native American massacres.

Mutual Aid among African Americans

Mutual aid among African Americans was based on their cultural heritage from western African society and expressed the positive functions of "Africanity," the heritage of the African ethos: the importance of family, survival of the tribe, the oneness of all being, unity, cooperative effort, and mutual responsibility and aid. In Africa, most black people lived within the context of "tribal socialism," in which patterns of mutual concern and sharing even in times of abundance were highly developed. The entire tribe is an interdependent entity. Existence, including the provision of food, shelter, clothing, protection, and a sense of belonging depends on every member of the tribe, living, dead, and yet to be.[22] W. E. B. DuBois observed that "of charity as such there was no need among Africans, since all shared the common fund of land and food."[23]

Blyden, a nineteenth-century Africanist, described African life and culture in this way: "We, and not I, is the law of African life." African social philosophy could be summarized in a folk saying: "I am, because we are; and since we are, therefore I am." Furthermore, no matter how much wealth or power a man attained, he could not place his individual interests above those of the group. This rule applied as well to chiefs, priests, and others of high authority who could not hoard while others were unsheltered or hungry.[24]

In the United States, even during slavery, enslaved persons created mutual aid and burial societies, although usually not openly. In every city of any size in Virginia, organizations operated surreptitiously to care for the sick and to bury the dead. As soon as enslaved persons were emancipated, these mutual aid societies began to be openly formed as fraternal, mutual aid societies and churches.[25] One of the earliest of these organizations was the African Methodist Church (1787). Groups such as the African Union Society, the Free African Society, the Black Masons, and the Negro Oddfellows supplied medical, educational, and burial services, in addition to helping to resolve disputes. In Boston a Masonic Lodge was formed by free African Americans in 1784,[26] and in 1787 they formed the Philadelphia Free African Society. The latter society was formed, according to its mission statement, without regard to religious tenets. Persons should live "an orderly and sober life, in order to support one another in sickness, and for the benefit of their widows and fatherless children." The members of the society made insurance payments, and benefits were paid provided this necessity was "not brought on by their own imprudence." If a member became sick, he or she was exempt from payments and eligible for benefits. In addition, there were benefits for widows and children's benefits, including schooling and apprenticeship.[27] Soon after the Philadelphia Society was formed, similar associations were formed in Newport, Boston, New York, and Charleston.[28] The intention of these mutual aid societies often was to lessen the need for benefits from public funds.

There were almost 500,000 free African Americans in the United States at the outbreak of the Civil War, approximately half in the South and many "well to do." The free African-American community created churches, literary debating societies, fraternal organizations, and other mutual aid groups.[29] But even in slavery there was a system of social obligation among enslaved people for other enslaved persons, and there are many examples of extravagant giving in relation to available resources. Among formerly enslaved people, the indigent or helpless were supported by relatives, parents, friends, and relief associations.[30] In fact, it has been suggested that similar altruistic behavior by freed people over the entire South is an important reason why over the full lifetime of the Freedmen's Bureau it materially assisted only 0.5 percent of the 4 million freed people.[31] Obligations to kin were transformed into larger social and communal obligations such as setting aside a piece of land for a community purpose or supporting free schooling for poor children. The following comments of an African American regarding a school in South Carolina illustrates the mutual aid values of the freed African-American community: "…they were all poor, and each could do but little, but this was a work for many.… Should each man regard only his own children, and forget all the others? Should they leave that poor neighbor widow with her whole gang of children, and give them no chance for a free schooling?"[32] In addition to the development of cemeteries and educational facilities, in the latter part of the nineteenth century, hospitals, homes, and orphanages were organized, out of which later developed cooperative businesses and insurance societies.

Constitutional conventions following 1865 in the southern states were dominated by old Confederate leaders at a time when 4 million African-American enslaved people were freed and insufficient industry existed in which they could be employed. It was at this time that southern state legislatures passed the *Black Codes*, which relegated African Americans to a status somewhere between slave and free. These codes were intended to restore forced labor conditions on plantations, that is, controlled labor for agricultural production.

The Black Codes fixed a legal place for formerly enslaved persons in the postwar South, restricted African Americans' occupations and property ownership, slowed mobility, reduced bargaining power, and limited access to the judicial system, making appeals difficult. Any freed person who refused to work at the prevailing wage could be defined as a "vagrant" or "loiterer," or, lacking employment, could be forced to labor. Such forced labor could also be imposed on children whose parents were unable to support them. Employers could control wages in collusive arrangements, and every African American had to show a license from the police or a written labor contract to prove employment. Any African American quitting a job could be arrested. There is some evidence that these Black Codes successfully oppressed African Americans until their repeal by the constitutional conventions of 1868 and the new Reconstruction legislatures.[33]

Harsh vagrancy laws and the Black Codes, particularly where nonagricultural employment was restricted, were attempts to stem the tide of freed persons to the cities and to maintain them as landless laborers for agriculture. The purpose of these laws was to keep these persons working as laborers for white employers—not as an enslaved person and yet not as a completely free person either. Although there are no exact parallels, the Black Codes share certain characteristics and purposes with the vagrancy acts of the Poor Laws of the fourteenth through sixteenth centuries in Europe. Essentially, both sets of acts attempted to control a labor supply for the benefit of the employing class and set harsh measures to maintain legal restrictions on mobility, work conditions, and the relationships among communities, employers, and those recently freed.[34]

The vagrancy laws, as Leon Litwack points out, were more harshly enforced in regard to African Americans than to whites:

> Enforcement of the vagrancy laws revealed an all too familiar double standard. If a white man was out of work, as many were in 1865, that was simply unemployment, but if a black man had no job, that was vagrancy. If a planter refused to till the fields himself, that was understandable, but if a former slave declined to work for him, that was idleness if not insolence.[35]

In the decades following the Civil War, none suffered more than freed, formerly enslaved African Americans, but white subsistence farmers who fought in the Confederate army and their families also suffered. In a period of disorganization, their land, buildings, and tools were not cared for properly. Also, there were famines, food could not be transported to remote areas, and there was general economic desolation. Many subsistence farmers borrowed in order to grow cotton, amassed debts, and had their farms foreclosed. Many were forced into sharecropping. Others became migrants, moving from the Old South to Texas and further west.

Voluntary and Public Responsibilities

Consistently throughout American history there were voluntary, private social welfare efforts. In New York City, prior to the Civil War, the New York Association for Improving the Condition of the Poor and the Society for the Prevention of Pauperism in the City of New York were organized. Both perceived poverty and antisocial behavior as results of alcoholism and idleness. There also were numerous groups concerned with social issues and problems, including political reform, women's rights, economic and land reform, abolition of slavery, and temperance.

Following the Civil War, state boards of charities were formed in Massachusetts, Connecticut, New York, Wisconsin, Rhode Island, Pennsylvania, Michigan, Kansas, and Illinois. Representatives from the first four states met in New York in 1874 and formed the Conference of Boards and Public Charities, an important beginning for the development of a communication network among social agencies, both public and private. It was only eleven years earlier that the first state board was created in Massachusetts to supervise charitable, medical, and penal institutions.

The development of both public and private agencies was a result of societal forces. Six percent of the American population lived in cities in 1800; by 1870 this number had risen to 25 percent. The problems of rapidly industrializing cities and the hordes of people moving into them for employment had to be handled in new ways. Social agencies developed on the local and state level to meet the needs of a changing society.

The long-term trend toward public assumption of major responsibility for social welfare in England and the United States always was joined by a continuous involvement of private, religious, and other organizations in the social welfare arena. According to one major early study of social welfare, by the early part of the twentieth century, in the United States private and public social welfare seemed to be assigned different functions:

> The advantages of private charities over public ones are that they afford on the average a somewhat larger share of personal sympathy, that their benefits cannot logically be claimed as a right (although they often are), that they do not oppress the poor by increasing taxation, and that they are supposed to bring a somewhat smaller degree of degradation to the recipient of relief.
>
> The probable lines of demarcation between the field of public and private charity seem to lie between those dependents requiring some degree of control, and those that may be allowed their freedom; between measures for chronic dependents and those looking to prevention; between institutional care on a large scale and private aid to the needy in their homes. Generally speaking, private charity is best fitted to conditions where much personal, individual sympathy is required; public charity, to problems requiring large funds, equipment and control. Finally, private charity, under the stimulus of some individual enthusiast, will mark out new paths which when proven may be adopted by the State.[36]

As we shall see later, the Great Depression of the 1930s confronted the United States with problems on a scale that could only be dealt with by public action at the federal level. But as we can see from the preceding paragraphs, some relief functions shifted to the public sphere long before the cataclysmic social upheaval of the 1930s.

From rural, colonial, agrarian America to the modern, industrial, and urbanized United States, private voluntary welfare, formal and informal, played an important part in meeting human needs. Informal, natural helping systems always played a significant role in social welfare. Extended families, friendship circles, churches, and neighborhood, ethnic, and religious groups have all contributed to individual and family welfare. Although the long-term trend in American society has been toward formalization of social welfare functions, one should not forget that informal, spontaneous helping outside formal channels has been and remains a significant portion of American social welfare.

The American Frontier: The Myth and Values

America existed as a physical frontier and also as a psychological frontier. It was a place where a new life was possible, where dreams of freedom or sustenance or success could be fulfilled.

The fact that America was a frontier land in which the horizons always beckoned influenced how people viewed themselves and how they viewed others. The frontier myth declared all things possible; the land was open for the benefit of those who were hardy and brave enough to venture forward. Beyond the next hill, beyond the next river, or beyond the next mountain range, life would be better. One part of this frontier philosophy was the belief that riches belonged to those who dared to seek them and who were strong enough to earn their way. The other side of this frontier myth and the frontier people was that those who did not or could not venture forth or "make it" financially were suspect.

Into the frontier land of America came waves of immigrants. At first, during the colonial period, immigrants to America were English, German, and Scottish, with small numbers of French Huguenots, as well as indentured servants and enslaved people exploited for the development of a new country. Later Irish, Swiss, Swedish, Danish, Italian, Portuguese, Spanish, and West Indian immigrants came to America, to be followed by yet other groups.

Immigrants to the colonies came for political, religious, and social reasons. Later immigrants came to the United States primarily for economic reasons in order to make a living. As the various immigrant waves reached America, the earlier settlers would accuse the later settlers of depressing wages and of causing various social problems. Cultural conflicts abounded between the various groups and within ethnic groups. Religious differences caused some conflicts. Within some groups there were conflicts over whether the culture and language of the "home country" should be preserved. And there were differences of race. In addition, many immigrants came from rural homes and had to deal with urban problems in America. The experiences of the waves of immigrants coming to America created a strong "we–they" feeling and attitude. For example, Chinese immigrants who came to the western United States during pioneer days and during the gold rush were viewed as economic competitors; by 1882 Chinese laborers had been excluded from immigration on the basis of race alone.

Of course, immigrant groups found ways to help each other and carried into American society their own unique mutual aid efforts. Chinese were among the servants of Spaniards, sailing between the Philippines and Mexico after 1565. From Mexico, Chinese moved north to Los Angeles and Monterey. The first documented arrival of a Chinese person on the east coast occurred in 1785. From 1850 to 1882, when the Chinese Exclusion Act went into effect, more than 322,000 Chinese entered the United States and worked as merchants, artisans, and mainly as unskilled laborers in railroad construction and mining.

Chinese immigrant organizations derived their structure from loyalty to clan, dialect, or region and were called the "company." They banded together for social and charitable purposes during the nineteenth century to greet new immigrants, help find places to live and eat, borrow and lend money, find work, patronize stores owned by persons from their native locality, provide protection, care for the sick, adjudicate disputes, and help return the dead to China for burial. Subsidiary organizations maintained the cemetery. As early as the 1850s, guilds modeled on organizations for artisans and merchants in China served mutual aid functions.[37]

The Mexicans, or Chicanos, were the first large ethnic group incorporated by annexation following the separation of Texas from Mexico. Between 1845 and

1854, the United States acquired about half the territory belonging to the Republic of Mexico, including all or part of Arizona, California, Colorado, Nevada, New Mexico, Texas, Utah, and Wyoming. Most *sociedades mutualistas* (mutual aid societies) were formed in the late nineteenth or early twentieth century as local organizations or as chapters of regional or national Chicano organizations. These organizations were the focus of social life and provided assistance to families in need, emergency loans, legal services, mediation of disputes, as well as medical, life, and burial insurance.[38]

Italians, too, had their mutual benefit societies, which provided insurance and helped newly arrived immigrants to deal with sickness, loneliness, and death. The hat was passed for members in trouble, guaranteeing help at minimal expense for all concerned. These organizations also provided for attendance at funerals, proper burials, and stipends in the event of sickness or disability. Later such organizations added recreational and social functions.[39]

A similar mutual aid ethic assisted immigrants whether they came to the United States from the South, East, or West; whether over land or over the Atlantic or Pacific oceans or over the Caribbean; whether enslaved, indentured, or free. Norwegians had their *bydelag* societies; Jews, *landsmanschaften*; Japanese, *kenjinkai*; Greeks, *topikas*; Koreans, *kei*; Ukranians, Hungarians, Finns, Czechs and Slovaks, West Indians, and all other groups banded together for social and mutual aid purposes.

The existence of a "we–they" attitude was strengthened by economic competition. However, the attitude that one person was better than another on the basis of some ethnic difference also played a part in how Americans viewed those who were different from themselves, including those who were in need of help, financial or otherwise: They somehow did not fit in. In addition, as the different waves of immigrants came to America, it was always "they" who needed help. Mutual aid may have been retarded and racism and rugged individualism advanced by the notion that it was always some other ethnic group, not one's brothers and sisters, who needed help in America.

As we noted in chapter 1, the myth of individualism, particularly "rugged individualism" as a part of the American frontier tradition, needs to be modified in our understanding of American culture by the influences of mutual aid and social control, even in the evolving West. Ray Allen Billington casts a different light on the idea of American "rugged individualism":

> Actually, the legend of frontier individualism rested on what people thought should be true, rather than on what was true. The West was in truth an area where cooperation was just as essential as in the more thickly settled East. The danger of Indian attack, the joint efforts to clear the forests or break the prairie sod, the community of labor required for the variety of enterprises necessary in establishing a settlement, all decreed that new communities be occupied by groups, and never by solitary individuals.[40]

Billington points out that common perils served as a cohesive force among those who were homesteading the Great Plains "no less than among earlier pioneers, for these grass fires, grasshopper invasions, and cattle wars banded the people together to combat mutual enemies."[41] Communities and individuals benefited from cooperative enterprises that built churches and schools. Laws were also adopted to regulate economic behavior, including the regulation of trade—the price of bread was sometimes fixed, fees were regulated, weights and measures were checked for accuracy.[42]

For one group immigration was not voluntary. In 1619, one year prior to the arrival of the Mayflower, twenty Africans who had been captured by a Dutch vessel from a Spanish vessel en route to the West Indies were traded for food into indentured servitude at Jamestown, Virginia. For forty years or more the first African-American settlers accumulated land, voted, were able to testify in court, mingled on an equal basis with whites, and owned other black servants, some of whom they imported and paid for.[43] From such a relatively small event at Jamestown, however, a tangled web of black–white relationships and problems developed that has confronted American society continually throughout its history.

Some colonial communities made the indenture of African-American paupers harsher than that of whites. Special rules were sometimes established making slavery the punishment for African Americans who became paupers.[44] In 1641, Massachusetts became the first colony to legally recognize slavery, thus institutionalizing different treatment for African Americans and whites. After the middle of the seventeenth century, all African Americans—and only African Americans—came as enslaved persons.[45] In the 1680s, there was a massive shift from indentured to enslaved labor. Until the onset of the Civil War and the promulgation of the Emancipation Proclamation (1862) most African Americans were enslaved by whites, with their only security being the best interests of the slaveholders as the slaveholders saw them. This reality and the fact that the United States was settled at the expense of nonwhite Native Americans has produced a backdrop of racism and oppression of minorities of color throughout U.S. history.

American Indians and U.S. History

One ethnic group preceded European immigration, and its fate at the hands of the immigrant majority was particularly cruel. The early generosity of American Indians stands in marked contrast to the values of the early American colonists. It is a trait remarked on by the earliest colonists both in the East and the area that has become the southwestern part of the United States. The American Indians have been described as people who "at times...even gave their possessions away for nothing to those who asked for them."[46] The kind and caring quality of American Indians was noted by Christopher Columbus in a letter to the king and queen of Spain: "So tractable, so peaceful are these people that I swear to your majesties, there is not in the world a better nation. They love their neighbors as themselves and their discourse is ever sweet and gentle, and accompanied with a smile; and though it is true that they are naked, yet their manners are decorous and praiseworthy."[47]

Later, the American Indians almost universally greeted the British settlers with friendship and assistance. Interestingly, this overt friendliness was viewed by the colonists with suspicion. A contemporary observer reported:

> All accounts agree that for some reason the Indians did daily relieve them for some weeks with corn and flesh. The supplies brought from England had been nearly exhausted, the colonists had been too sick to attend to their gardens properly, and this act of the Indians was regarded as a divine providence at the time.... What was the real motive for the kindly acts of the Indians may not be certainly known, but it probably boded the little colony a future harm.[48]

Early American legal commitments to American Indians were respectful. A much-violated document, the Northwest Ordinance (1787) states:

> The utmost good faith shall always be observed towards the Indians; their lands and property shall never be taken from them without their consent; and, in their property, rights, and liberty, they shall never be invaded or disturbed, unless in just and lawful wars authorized by Congress; but laws founded in justice and humanity shall from time to time be made for preventing wrongs being done to them, and for preserving peace and friendship with them.[49]

Following the Revolutionary War, through a series of treaties the United States acquired lands and assumed legal responsibilities for American Indians. Tribes ceded their lands and the federal government made commitments in return. From 1830 to 1850, American Indian land east of the Mississippi was "exchanged" for land west of the boundary. Almost the entire American Indian population in the southeastern United States was coerced and removed—in a trek described by the Cherokees as a "trail of tears"—to the west, where they were placed on reservations and promised material and political assistance.

The European colonists and later Americans took American Indian lands by theft, fraud, deceit, purchase, and military force, pushing the American Indians before them, removing them from the land, decimating them as they moved westward. By the end of the nineteenth century, a policy of assimilation developed in which American Indians were forced by the Bureau of Indian Affairs to forsake their religious, social, and cultural practices through control of everything from hairstyles to language. Children were separated from their American Indian environments and forced to adopt white ways. Treated as wards of the state, they were not allowed to make decisions about their own lives and were forced into the "melting pot," dependent on rations and assistance.

Although the United States' public policy was creating a dependent group—the American Indians—it was also creating many social problems among them as immigrant Americans destroyed the fabric of American Indian life. By contrast, there is evidence, for example, that in the 1820s, left to their own social welfare devices, "there were no paupers in New Mexico at that time, nor could there be any."[50] This observation, made by a Mexican lawyer in 1827, only confirmed earlier evidence. In the southwestern culture a poor person would go to a rich livestock and land owner and offer to assist him by herding sheep. The shepherd would give of the future increase, and wool would be contracted at the current market price. Materials from the sheep would be used to construct housing; milk and meat were used as food; and the wool was marketed as blankets, stockings, and the like. Thus the necessities of life were supplied.

Illustrative of the suffering of American Indians is the "trail of tears" episode, the forcible uprooting in 1831 of the "Five Civilized Tribes" (Cherokees, Choctaws, Chicasaws, Creeks, and Seminoles) from their homelands in the East to present-day Oklahoma. They were removed during winter over snow-covered trails. Shelter was inadequate and food was scarce as hundreds died, including entire families and in some cases entire communities. The Cherokees suffered most. Many opposed their removal and the Georgia militia invaded the Cherokee nation, destroying crops, burning homes, and scattering families. The tribe members were herded into "concentration camps" by Federal troops in order to control the situation. Eventually, one fourth of the tribe perished. The Seminoles also fought a war when federal authorities insisted they honor a fraudulent and deceptive treaty. As a result, the U.S. army removed the Seminoles and forced them westward.[51]

With passage of the General Allotment Act (1887), known as the Dawes Act, the United States intervened to break up tribal communal landholdings and distribute them into individual 40-, 80-, and 160-acre shares for agricultural and grazing purposes. (A blood code that assigns one's racial or other status on the basis of familial descent patterns was used to legally define who was an American Indian.) The American Indian would become a voting citizen if his residence was maintained separate from the tribe and if he became a farmer. This was contrary to the tribal and communal property traditions and values of the American Indians. The result was that many lost their land. From 1887 to 1934 American Indian landholdings were cut down from 138 million acres to 47 million acres, a two-thirds' loss. Entire tribes became landless. Today, American Indian tribes retain only about 5 percent of their original land.[52]

By 1934, the Indian Reorganization Act permitted tribes to reorganize their own institutions and to handle many of their own concerns. Nevertheless, the Bureau of Indian Affairs sustained for itself a veto power over most tribal decisions. In the 1950s the U.S. government terminated control over certain tribes over which it was thought federal responsibility was unnecessary, and jurisdiction was shifted to state governments. Americans Indians were also physically relocated from reservations to urban areas.

In the 1960s, as part of a general claiming of ethnic identities and as part of the Civil Rights movement, American Indians expressed vigorously their rights to their cultures and civil rights within American society. Although it was quite late and much damage had been done, groups of American Indians set out to lay claim to their languages, general culture, and a rectification of the history of broken white promises and treaties. As a result, a series of court cases was instituted holding the United States liable for lands belonging to the tribes.

Treaties recognized American Indian tribes as sovereign nations since the eighteenth century, when the government pledged to provide public services such as education and health to the American Indian nations in exchange for land, other resources, and peace. Despite the independent status of the tribes, the U.S. federal government maintained tight management of these public services until 1974.

A movement began to expand and make permanent a restoration of independence to American Indian nations. In 1974, the federal government made a fundamental change in its policy regarding American Indians when it passed the Self-Determination and Education Assistance Act (amended 1988). The act granted 554 tribes greater autonomy and authority over federal programs designed for their benefit and affirmed their right to be self-governing.

During the 1980s, American Indian programs, like other federal programs, were cut or eliminated despite the trust and treaty relationship. The total privatization of reservation economic development and the application of market forces to American Indian policy was fostered, except where states wished to retain control, such as tribal gaming. There also have been complaints that the federal government has stalled in carrying out the self-determination act.[53]

From 1980 to 1999, the Native American population increased 54 percent in the American Indian population, a result of Americans with American Indian heritages increasingly identifying with the group and an improved count by the Census Bureau. Over 2 million Americans say their race is American Indian and there are estimates that as many as one in every thirty-five persons claim some American Indian ancestry.

The number of American Indian–owned businesses increased 64 percent between 1982 and 1987, as tribes attempted to create sustainable, self-reliant economies, in part to provide jobs and offset unemployment and the problems that accompany it. There are both legal and political efforts to reduce the sovereignty of American Indian tribes at the same time the number of American Indian lawyers increased substantially. Among these efforts are those challenging the tax status of the tribes and efforts to prevent tribes from taxing businesses on their territories. There are proposals in Congress to limit the expansion of American Indian sovereignty, holdings, and jurisdictions. Gambling casinos and tourism, which have enriched some tribes, have also attracted criticism from those who maintain that businesses within a state should be taxed and regulated by the states. The law that legalized the opening of gambling casinos by American Indians on reservations allowed this as long as the states agreed in a contract (called a compact) that is renegotiable. These businesses, especially the casinos, increase revenues, which in turn create new political power. Critics include those who want more tax revenue for the states, those businesses that compete with the casinos, and those who oppose the extra-territoriality of the tribal territories where a complex set of legal arrangements exist with states, localities, and the federal government. Still others challenge the success of the tribes on other grounds. An example of the intensity of these conflicts is the decision in Utah by the Skull Valley Band of Goshutes (with barely 100 members) to lease part of their reservation as the temporary storage ground for high-level civilian nuclear waste. The governor and the congressional delegation tried to block this lease arrangement. Tensions about these matters have become intense and the challenges of many kinds have created stronger cooperative arrangements by the tribes in defense of their rights. Important factors that affect these conflicts and challenges include (1) the Supreme Court's shrinking of the concept of American Indian country and giving states more power to limit Native American gambling and (2) the trend in Congress to move power and decision making from the Federal to the state level.[54]

The Federal Role in Social Welfare

As in the English Poor Law tradition, the U.S. system provided social welfare services at the local level with certain limited supports provided at the state level. Federal governmental intervention in economic matters began during the early years of the republic and included tariff legislation; disposition of the public domain; creation of a banking system; and canal, road, and railroad construction. The active role of the federal government in social welfare has been traced to two early forms of assistance—cash and other types of assistance to victims of floods, fires, earthquakes, and other disasters, and aid provided to two charitable institutions: the Connecticut Asylum for the Deaf and Dumb (a private institution, in 1819) and the Kentucky Deaf and Dumb Asylum (a public institution, in 1826). But these were isolated events and set no pattern of federal intervention in the social welfare domain.[55]

In 1854, Dorothea Dix, who worked strenuously for better treatment of the indigent insane, managed to get the Indigent Insane Bill passed by Congress to provide funds to improve the care of such people. The bill would have granted 10 million acres of public lands to the states, in proportion to their congressional representation. The states could then sell the land and use the proceeds for the perpetual care of the indigent insane. The bill was a popular one because it provided "payoffs" for both land speculators and philanthropists. However, President Franklin Pierce vetoed the bill, and his veto was sustained by Congress, thus halting a landmark advance in U.S. governmental philosophy concerning social welfare.

Pierce used several arguments, including one that President James Madison earlier presented in an 1811 veto: that the federal government could not give legal sanction to charitable governmental acts. Furthermore, if help was to be given to the indigent insane, he suggested that all the needy would have to be helped eventually. Pierce also used President Andrew Jackson's argument that lands given to the states must be used for the common good. In addition, financial expediency played a part: Pierce claimed the lands were security for the Mexican War debt.

However, Pierce intimated he would approve land grants to railroads. The purpose of granting lands to the railroads, as Pierce viewed it, was to enhance the value of the whole nation. The crucial assumption, however, is that property owners need help through governmental assistance while people do not. Interestingly, Pierce previously gave land to soldiers and to railroads but would not do so for the benefit of disabled and ill persons. One editorial interpretation at the time suggested the veto halted an erosion of states' rights. Another argument used by Pierce was based on a strict construction of the U.S. Constitution: If the Founding

Fathers had wanted such programs, they would have made it explicit in the Constitution. Essentially, Pierce refused to make "the Federal government the great almoner of public charity throughout the United States."[56] And yet the federal government, so reluctant to assume a welfare role, did so in several instances.

The Freedmen's Bureau

Following the Civil War and during the period of Reconstruction, the Freedmen's Bureau (Bureau of Refugees, Freedmen, and Abandoned lands) was created as part of the War Department. The Freedmen's Bureau was an experiment in social policy. Among its responsibilities was the introduction of a workable system of free labor in the South, finding employment for formerly enslaved people, supervising labor contracts affecting freedmen, establishing freedmen on homestead lands, fixing wages and terms of employment, providing transportation to new-found homes, and forming settlements of African Americans.

The Freedmen's Bureau had other daunting responsibilities. There was an expectation the bureau would adjudicate disputes among African Americans and between the races, attempt to secure equal justice from state and local governments, and provide aid for the destitute, aged, ill, and insane. One of its important functions was the arrangement of family reunions. As part of that effort, prior marriages of enslaved persons were formally, religiously recognized and made official, and the children of the deceased were adopted by relatives and friends. By 1870, a large majority of African Americans lived in two-parent family households.

The bureau had a role in health care as well and assumed the operation of hospitals that had been established by the army in larger cities during the war. It also established dispensaries in other less-populated areas. Although the bureau was hampered by limited resources (most of its budget was spent on relief and hospitals) and did not itself establish schools, it did coordinate the activities of northern societies and groups involved in establishing schools. By 1869, there were almost 3,000 schools, which served more than 150,000 African-American pupils in the South. In addition, there were evening, Sunday, and private schools run by missionary groups and by African Americans themselves in which adults, children, and sometimes whole families learned. These schools were influential in establishing a foundation for public education in the South.[57]

True to American experience and values, the administrator of the bureau, Commissioner General Oliver Otis Howard (for whom Howard University is named) stated proudly that the bureau had not been "a pauperizing agency."[58] By the end of 1868, the Freedmen's Bureau ceased most of its activities and was officially abolished in 1872.[59]

Important legacies were established by Reconstruction and the Freedmen's Bureau. But when Reconstruction ended, most energies were directed toward separate public institutions for African Americans and whites with the inferior services designated for African Americans. This pattern culminated in the "separate but equal" Supreme Court ruling in 1896 (*Plessy v. Ferguson*), which gave legal sanction to segregated facilities. Nevertheless, the suggestion has been made that a number of positive accomplishments rose out of public welfare efforts in the South during the period 1865–1880: Universal public education was established, attention was paid to children, agencies were created to improve health conditions, and poor relief was implemented at the local level more than at the state level.[60]

The importance of the Freedmen's Bureau for our discussion lies in its example of governmental intervention during a time of stress to assist people with their problems rather than to leave them entirely at the mercy of events. Thus there was a commitment by the federal government to meet the fundamental welfare needs of people, despite the earlier Pierce veto. Furthermore, governmental programs of a diverse nature provided a comprehensive series of services to deal constructively with serious social upheaval and foreshadowed across-the-board, comprehensive programs like those of the Great Depression and the War on Poverty in the 1960s.[61]

Veterans and a Suspension of the Ethic

The federal government, when motivated by political and pragmatic reasons, established and administered social welfare programs. Welfare services for one group are based on the suspension of the Protestant ethic. Considering the veteran's sacrifice (and our collective guilt?), the veteran is viewed as entitled to help even if he or she is personally unworthy. Following the Revolutionary War, veterans were recipients of generous grants to western lands.[62] An anonymous quote from the period following the War of 1812 makes a straightforward argument: "Who but the Soldier and his family should eat the bread from the Soil his own blood has enriched?"[63]

Although most social welfare efforts during the late eighteenth century were local, beginning in 1776 there was a series of pension acts that generally provided assistance to disabled veterans. But other types of aid were also given. In 1818, the Revolutionary War Pension Act was passed. This federal poor law

> assumed, prima facie, that every Continental soldier was worthy of aid, so the only question to be asked was whether he needed it. Once judged in need of aid, the claimant was not granted relief rated to his need but rather awarded a lifetime pension at a rate higher for officers than for ordinary soldiers. By passing the War Department's means test, the veteran was transformed from an alms seeker into an honored pensioner with a guaranteed annual income for life.[64]

Most social welfare during the nineteenth century was provided by state and local governments, but there was a federally funded pension system for Civil War veterans who fought in the Union army. The costs of these pensions for disabled soldiers and the widows and dependents of deceased soldiers became the largest single item of federal expenditure, except for debt service, in every year from 1885 to 1897, and reached 34 percent of the federal budget in 1890. Following 1890, veterans no longer had to claim a relationship between their disabilities and Civil

War military activities, a liberalization that affected three-quarters of a million former soldiers, their widows, and dependents.[65]

Other federal social welfare supports emerged during the nineteenth century. The Homestead Act (1862) made it possible for any American citizen to obtain 160 acres of unoccupied government land if he or she lived on it for five years. By 1870, special privileges were given to soldiers who fought in the Union army. Such soldiers could count their time of military service toward the five-year prerequisite homesteading period. Widows could count the full term of their husband's enlistment.[66] Following every war, various techniques were found to provide resources for veterans and their families.

Although in many cases benefits were specifically meant for those who have been disabled, at other times these benefits were more universally available for all veterans. Following World War II, 10 million veterans had to be reintegrated into civilian life. The Servicemen's Readjustment Act (1944, the "GI Bill") guaranteed loans to buy a home, farm, or business, and provided 52 weeks of unemployment insurance at $20 per week to any unemployed veteran. Among the benefits were job placement services and up to four years of federal aid for learning or training at any level, including tuition and monthly allowances. These benefits were available to each veteran whether or not the veteran had been disabled and, more importantly, whether or not the veteran had actually been engaged in battle. The GI Bills were extended to veterans of the Korean and Vietnam conflicts. These benefits are examples of a type of universal program, which is more the exception than the rule.[67]

The federal government enacted such legislation out of complex motivations. In addition to rewarding veterans, one important factor was the idea that giving benefits to veterans and their families would have a long-term beneficial effect on the total society, raise the average educational and skill level, provide needed technical and other training to be used by society, and enhance social and governmental future income from the improved earnings of the veterans and their families. The GI Bill after World War II is also credited with helping to avoid a postwar depression. Historically, investments in veterans have been viewed as exceptions to the Protestant ethic. Therefore, the eligibility rules do not in general call for rigorous "means testing" (a financial test of one's level of income).

For our purposes, treatment of veterans may be seen as an example of what might be possible were we able to free ourselves from the values of Calvinism, dependency, and our terror of idleness. The veterans who received GI benefits included the majority who used the time to prepare for or to seek work. Some might have used this "dole" to postpone entry into the workforce. Still, the net effect of these programs was (1) to avoid a major economic depression as millions of soldiers were rapidly demobilized and thrown into a civilian economy, and (2) to upgrade the quality and earning power of the American work force for a generation.

In the case of the GI Bills, by forgetting about who was worthy and unworthy, about means tests and the like, a dignified welfare program benefited the whole economy. In fact, if one takes the cost of the GI program following World War II and balances it against the tax revenues gained from a better-educated workforce, the treasury has come out ahead. The avoidance of depression, crime, and the like also must be considered. Thus a shift in values makes possible a shift in types of welfare programs. What might result if all U.S. citizens were deemed as worthy as veterans?

Social Darwinism

In 1859, Charles Darwin published *The Origin of Species,* a book that had a remarkable impact on the world. Essentially a biological study, it postulated the concepts of natural selection and evolution. To this scientific interpretation of biological phenomena, social Darwinism added social, philosophical, and theological elements. From the point of view of a social Darwinist, those who become wealthy in the struggle for existence do so because they are superior people.

Admittedly, the nineteenth-century capitalist economy was the scene of struggle and competition in which morality as such had limits. Almost anything and any action was permitted by some in the capitalist struggle. Beyond this, however, social Darwinism viewed the struggle and competition as justifiable and glorifying the natural order and even God's will.

These ideas were justification for those who had enriched themselves through ruthless competition. In this way, predatory competition in business and industry was provided a philosophical rationale. Herbert Spencer (1820–1903), an English philosopher, sociologist, and coiner of the phrase "survival of the fittest," defended the moral aspects of individualism and laissez-faire economics. He asserted the poor "were unfit...and should be eliminated. The whole effort of nature is to get rid of such, to clear the world of them, and make room for better."[68]

Given these perspectives, some people were "elected" to survive and prosper. Logically then, the poor, ill, and disadvantaged were responsible for their limitations and their poverty, perhaps through lack of God's grace but surely through their being unfit. This tangle of interrelated concepts led directly to the assignment of responsibility for one's personal situation. The impoverished were all responsible in some way for their own plights. The way of the world was just as it should be. The status quo reflected not only human achievements and limitations but also God's will. Furthermore, social welfare efforts, however well meant, interfered with the process of natural selection and, in the long run, injured society.

The Coming of Social Insurance

Just as the early American social welfare system was influenced by the English Poor Laws, later American developments were influenced by the coming of social insurance in Europe, a forerunner of the U.S. Social Security Act of 1935.

In a Germany recently united during the 1870s, Social Democrats were urging the workers of a rapidly industrializing nation to demand a republican form of government, a bill of rights, and support for the international socialist movement. In the political and industrial ferment of middle Europe, the socialists were gaining strength. As a result, in 1879 antisocialist laws were enacted that forbade parties aimed at "overthrowing the established state or social order."[69] Otto von Bismarck (chancellor of the German empire) shifted from laissez-faire economics and free trade to protectionism, as indicated by the institution of tariffs in 1879.[70]

Since the antisocialist laws created enemies among the workers, Bismarck decided something needed to be done that would assure more contented workers in a period of great industrialization. In 1881, all workers in mines and factories whose earnings did not exceed 2,000 marks per year were insured against accidents. There followed in 1883 the enactment of a Sickness Insurance Law; in 1884 an Accident Insurance Law; and in 1887 an Old Age and Invalidity Law.

Bismarck presented a remarkable argument in his 1881 speech to the Reichstag in which he proposed social insurance: "I am not of the opinion that laissez faire, laissez aller, 'pure Manchester policy,' 'everybody takes care of himself,' 'the weakest must go to the wall,'...can be practiced in a monarchically, patriarchically governed state."[71] As his arguments were presented in favor of social insurance and of governmental intervention, Bismarck amalgamated several themes into one: The state has a responsibility to intervene when it assumes that industry cannot handle the problem. These themes are noted in Bismarck's comment that

> an appropriate title for our enterprise would be "Practical Christianity," but we do not want to feed poor people with figures of speech, but with something solid. Death costs nothing; but unless you will put your hands in your pockets and into the state Exchequer, you will not do much good. To saddle our industry with the whole affair—well, I don't know that it could bear the burden. All manufacturers are having hard times.[72]

By 1889, the method of financing these social insurances included contributions from employers, employees, and the government. Social legislation did not halt the rise of the Social Democratic party because German workers did not trust the government's motivation and workers really wanted improved working conditions and higher wages.

Bismarck, who, however contradictory it might appear, had taken a liberal stance in regard to the creation of social insurances, stubbornly refused legislation on working hours, woman and child labor, factory inspection, or changes in government policy regarding labor unions, which were carefully controlled. He emphasized that the social insurances were intended to bind workers to the state, not only through loyalty but also through self-interest. For the state was all-important, and Bismarck had given all his energies to the creation of Germany under Prussian leadership. Social welfare was a tool directed toward turning the sense of loyalty away from the locality toward the nation. When it suited his purposes, he reverted to Manchester laissez-faire arguments. But the historic principle of contributory social insurance was institutionalized in a modern nation-state for the first time. The reverberations of this event have been felt in every modern society, and the principle of various forms of "social security" continue to be developed and refined.

For a sense of perspective, one can note that social insurance instituted in Germany was soon followed by the United Kingdom and a number of European

and South American nations, as well as Australia, Canada, and New Zealand decades earlier than the United States. In the United Kingdom, the Old Age Pensions
Act (1908) took a step away from the traditional Poor Law but used a means test:
Only deserving persons and those with annual incomes below a certain point were
entitled to the benefit. According to the act, the undeserving were those who had
habitually failed to work according to their ability and personal need, those who
had not saved money regularly over a period of years, and those who had been
convicted of habitual drunkenness. Interestingly those dependent on the head of
household were also perceived as undeserving. In 1911 the National Insurance Act
(Part 1, Health Insurance; Part 2, Unemployment Insurance) was instituted. Precedents existed in cooperative friendly societies and trade unions and the program
was based on contributions by employers, employees, and the state.[73]

Society, Social Values, and Modern Views of Human Nature

In preindustrial societies those who were dependent often were deemed worthy of
assistance. In times of catastrophe, as we have seen, the larger community had the
duty of providing the essentials for survival. Assistance was provided in many ways.

Problems developed in the fourteenth century when "able-bodied" poor, the
"sturdy beggars," became visible. As a result of their increased numbers and
threat, there began the regulation and differential treatment of beggars.

In general, with the development of industrial society, it was hoped the able-
bodied would gain employment through economic expansion. For the rest, self-
help, mutual aid, charity, and ad hoc emergency measures would be used. Public
assistance would be only for those least able to cope and for those caught up in
catastrophes.

In the latter part of the nineteenth century, it became clear that the "invisible
hand" (Adam Smith's idea that each individual promoting his or her own self-interest in the marketplace is led by an invisible hand frequently to promote society's best interest more effectively than when the person consciously intends to
promote it) of the self-regulating capitalist economy just might not be an invisible
hand. The capitalist economy might not be self-regulating. Furthermore, it left
many by the wayside, a seemingly natural concomitant of the "self-regulating"
mechanisms.

The growing influence of the working classes, of the nearly poor and the
poor, resulted in the evolution of economies in which (as in Germany in the 1880s)
it became important to create welfare for the vast majority of persons for the sake
of productivity and for the cohesion of the society. Dealing with pauperism
became a part of the problem of minimum standards for all citizens.

In the early stages of industrialization, it could be argued that punitive welfare laws were necessary to maintain a pool of motivated workers. In this sense,
the Poor Laws were functional in that they supported the industrialization of society and thus the creation of more wealth. As welfare systems evolved, especially

after the creation of social insurances, support systems for more and more people were indeed built into Western societies.

The historic disjunction that occurred in the late Middle Ages and created 500 years of punitive social welfare legislation was undoubtedly connected with the many trends, ideas, and technical developments we have reviewed. But if changes of such tremendous importance could take place, there is a suggestion that the future also could be different. On the basis of prudence, societies could decide to treat those in need humanely, to avoid clashes, make human relations more peaceful, and assure that all citizens are treated with respect and are sustained.

Summary

In this chapter we reviewed the major developments and themes in U.S. social welfare including the impact of the imported Poor Law mentality, differential experiences of African Americans, Hispanics, and American Indians, mutual aid, federal roles and American ambivalence about them, social Darwinism, and the creation of social insurances. In chapter 5, we turn to periods in U.S. history when poverty was highlighted as a social problem, an exploration of the two divergent social policies and programs resulting from different philosophies and values, a brief history of later American events, a look at the Poor Laws today, modern views of human nature, and human nature and the American dream.

Questions for Consideration

1. What support can you find for either the American myth of the individual hero or the role of mutual aid and cooperation in American life?

2. Do you believe President Pierce was correct in his interpretation of the U.S. Constitution? If yes, what are your arguments? If not, what are your arguments?

3. What did Bismarck mean by "death costs nothing"?

4. Is social Darwinism alive and well in the United States today?

Notes

1. Lester F. Ward, *Applied Sociology,* New York: Ginn & Co., 1906, pp. 25, 327.

2. William B. Scott, *In Pursuit of Happiness: American Conceptions of Property from the Seventeenth to the Twentieth Century,* Bloomington: Indiana University Press, 1977, p. 6.

3. Ibid., pp. 8, 10.

4. Bernard Bailyn, *The Peopling of British North America,* New York: Knopf, 1986, p. 60, and Peter Kolchin, *American Slavery 1619–1877,* New York: Hill and Wang, 1993, pp. 10–11.

5. John Van der Zee, *Bound Over: Indentured Servitude and American Conscience,* New York: Simon & Schuster, 1985, p. 11.

6. Abbott E. Smith, *Colonists in Bondage: White Servitude and Convict Labor in America 1607–1776,* Chapel Hill, N.C.: University of North Carolina Press, 1947, pp. 20–21.

7. Robert W. Kelso, *The History of Public Poor Relief in Massachusetts, 1620–1920,* Montclair, N.J.: Patterson Smith, 1969, p. 95.

8. Ibid., p. 92.

9. Ralph E. Pumphrey and Muriel W. Pumphrey, *The Heritage of American Social Work,* New York: Columbia University Press, 1961, p. 24. Colonial society stigmatized unmarried females. In addition, from one third to one half of a town's paupers were likely to be female. See Mimi Abramovitz, "The Family Ethic: The Female Pauper and Public Aid, Pre-1900," *Social Service Review,* Vol. 59, No. 1, March 1985, p. 124.

10. Pumphrey and Pumphrey, p. 20.

11. Ibid., p. 27.

12. Robert H. Bremner, "Private Philanthropy and Public Needs: Historical Perspective," *Research Papers: The Commission on Private Philanthropy and Public Needs,* Vol. 1, *History, Trends, and Current Magnitudes,* Washington, D.C.: Department of the Treasury, 1977, p. 90.

13. Ibid., pp. 91–92.

14. Ibid., p. 103.

15. Gary B. Nash, *The Urban Crucible: Social Change, Political Consciousness, and the Origins of the American Revolution,* Cambridge, Mass.: Harvard University Press, 1979, pp. 21, 125–126.

16. Bernard L. Fontana, *Entrada: The Legacy of Spain and Mexico in the United States,* Albuquerque, N.M.: University of New Mexico Press, 1994, p. 37; Elizabeth A. Foster, ed., *The Motolinia's History of the Indians of New Spain,* The Cortes Society; University of New Mexico, 1950, pp. 143, 154–155; Bonnie G. McEwan, ed., *The Spanish Missions of Florida,* Gainesville, Fla.: University Press of Florida, 1993, pp. 89, 91; Albert Prago, *Strangers in Their Own Land,* New York: Four Winds Press, 1973, p. 33; Engel Sluiter, *The Florida Situado: Quantifying the First Eighty Years, 1571–1651,* Gainesville, Fla.: University of Florida Libraries, 1985, p. 1.

17. Alice B. Kehoe, *North American Indians,* 2nd Edition, Englewood Cliffs, N.J.: Prentice Hall, 1992, p. 83.

18. Alice B. Kehoe, *North American Indians,* 2nd Edition. Englewood Cliffs, N.J.: Prentice Hall, 1992, p. 88

19. Himilce Novas, *Everything You Need to Know about Latino History,* New York: Penguin Books, Inc., 1994, pp. xiii, 38, 56, 58; France V. Scholes, "Civil Government and Society in New Mexico in the Seventeenth Century," in Vol. 1, *Historical Themes and Identity,* Antoinette Sedello Lopez, ed., New York: Garland Publishing, Inc., 1995, pp. 27–67.

20. Roberto Suro, *Strangers among Us,* New York: Alfred A. Knopf, 1998, p. 20.

21. Pumphrey and Pumphrey, p. 30.

22. Wade Nobles, "Africanity: Its Role in Black Families," *The Black Scholar,* Vol. 5, No. 9, June 1974, pp. 11–17.

23. Andrew Billingsley and Jeanne M. Giovannoni, *Children of the Storm,* New York: Harcourt Brace Jovanovich, 1972, p. 46. James O. Horton and Lois E. Horton, *In Hope of Liberty,* New York: Oxford University Press, 1997.

24. Joanne M. Martin and Elmer P. Martin, *The Helping Tradition in the Black Family and Community,* Silver Spring, Md.: National Association of Social Workers, 1985, pp. 12–13.

25. W. E. B. DuBois, *Economic Cooperation among Negro Americans,* Atlanta, Ga.: Atlanta University Press, 1907, pp. 20–21.

26. E. Franklin Frazier, *The Free Negro Family,* Nashville, Tenn.: Fisk University Press, 1932, p. 16.

27. Herbert Aptheker, ed., *A Documentary History of the Negro People in the United States,* New York: The Citadel Press, 1951, pp. 17–18; James S. Olson, *The Ethnic Dimension in American History,* New York: St. Martin's Press, 1979, p. 152.

28. E. Horace Fitchett, "The Tradition of the Free Negro in Charleston, South Carolina," *The Making of Black America,* August Meier and Elliott Rudwick, eds., New York: Atheneum, 1969, pp. 206–215.

29. Frazier, p. 16.

30. Herbert G. Gutman, *The Black Family in Slavery and Freedom, 1750–1925,* New York: Pantheon, 1976, pp. 224–225.

31. Ibid., pp. 224–229.

32. Ibid., p. 229.

33. James S. Allen, *Reconstruction, 1865–1876,* New York: International Publishers, 1966, pp. 57–59; Peter Kolchin, *American Slavery 1619–1877,* New York: Hill and Wang, 1993, pp. 209–210.

34. Leon F. Litwack, *Been in the Storm So Long: The Aftermath of Slavery,* New York: Knopf, 1979, pp. 366–371 and passim.

35. Ibid., p. 321.

36. Amos G. Warner, *American Charities,* New York: Thomas Y. Crowell, 1908, pp. 393, 395.

37. H. M. Lai, "Chinese," *Harvard Encyclopedia of American Ethnic Groups,* Stephan Thernstrom, ed., Cambridge, Mass.: Harvard University Press, 1980, pp. 218–219, 221, 222.

38. Carlos E. Cortes, "Mexicans," *Harvard Encyclopedia of American Ethnic Groups,* Stephan Thernstrom, ed., Cambridge, Mass.: Harvard University Press, 1980, pp. 698–699, 709.

39. Humbert S. Nelli, "Italians," *Harvard Encyclopedia of American Ethnic Groups,* Stephan Thernstrom, ed., Cambridge, Mass.: Harvard University Press, 1980, p. 552.

40. Ray Allen Billington, *America's Frontier Heritage,* New York: Holt, Rinehart and Winston, 1966, p. 143. Also see Mody C. Boatright, "The Myth of Frontier Individualism," *Turner and the Sociology of the Frontier,* Richard Hofstadter and Seymour M. Lipset, eds., New York: Basic Books, 1968, pp. 43–64.

41. Billington, p. 145.

42. Ibid., pp. 145–147.

43. Lerone Bennett Jr., *Before the Mayflower: A History of Black America,* New York: Penguin, 1984, pp. 29, 35. Also see Madeleine Burnside, *Spirits of the Passage: The TransAtlantic Slave Trade in the Seventeenth Century,* New York: Simon & Schuster Edition, 1997.

44. Billingsley and Giovannoni, p. 26.

45. Thomas R. Frazier, ed., *Afro-American History: Primary Sources,* New York: Harcourt Brace Jovanovich, 1970, p. 29. An African-American pilgrim, Abraham Pearce, settled in the Plymouth Colony in 1623. Pearce owned land, voted, and had equal standing with others in the community. "Plymouth Historian Says a Black Settled at Pilgrims' Colony," *New York Times,* August 20, 1981, p. A28. Peter Kolchin, *American Slavery: 1619–1877,* New York: Hill and Wang, 1993, pp. 10–11.

46. Lewis Hanke, *The First Social Experiments in America,* Cambridge, Mass.: Harvard University Press, 1935, p. 30.

47. Quoted in Dee Brown, *Bury My Heart at Wounded Knee,* New York: Holt, Rinehart and Winston, 1974, p. xiii.

48. Fremont J. Lyden and Lyman H. Legters, eds., *Native Americans and Public Policy,* Pittsburgh, Penn.: University of Pittsburgh Press, 1992, pp. 14–15.

49. Ibid., p. 15.

50. David J. Weber, ed., *Foreigners in Their Native Land,* Albuquerque: University of New Mexico Press, 1973, p. 38.

51. E. Hoxie Fredrick, ed. *Encyclopedia of North American Indians,* New York: Houghton Mifflin Co., 1996, pp. 639–640.

52. Ward Churchill and Glenn T. Morris, "Key Indian Laws and Cases," *The State of Native America: Genocide, Colonization, and Resistance,* M. Annette Jaimes, ed., Boston: South End Press, 1992, p. 14; Peter Nabokov, ed., *Native American Testimony: A Chronicle of Indian-White Relations from Prophecy to the Present, 1492–1992,* New York: Viking Publishers, 1991, p. 306; Fremont J. Lyden and Lyman H.

Legters, eds., *Native Americans and Public Policy,* Pittsburgh, Penn.: University of Pittsburgh Press, 1992, pp. 18–24, 69.

53. Paul Nyhan, "Senate Clears Bill Giving Tribes More Authority Over Programs," *Congressional Quarterly Weekly Review,* Vol. 52, No. 40, p. 2961.

54. Timothy Egan, "Mending a Trail of Broken Treaties," *New York Times,* June 25, 2000, *Week In Review,* p. 3. Some Native Americans suggest the casinos have a destructive impact on Native American culture and lead to internal conflict.

55. Walter I. Trattner, "The Federal Government and Social Welfare in Early Nineteenth-Century America," *Social Service Review,* Vol. 50, June 1976, pp. 243–255.

56. Carlton Jackson, *Presidential Vetoes: 1792–1945,* Athens, Ga.: University of Georgia, 1967, pp. 100–102.

57. Eric Foner, *Reconstruction: America's Unfinished Revolution: 1863–1877,* New York: Harper & Row, 1988, pp. 142–151; Peter Kolchin, *American Slavery: 1619–1877,* New York: Hill and Wang, 1993, pp. 208–210, 221–222.

58. Foner, p. 152.

59. Ibid., pp. 84, 142–144, 151. Also see Victoria Olds, *The Freedmen's Bureau as a Social Agency,* unpublished doctoral dissertation, New York: Columbia University, 1966.

60. Howard N. Rabinowitz, "From Exclusion to Segregation: Health and Welfare Services for Southern Blacks, 1865–1890," *Social Service Review,* Vol. 48, No. 3, September 1974, pp. 327–354.

61. Victoria Olds, "The Freedmen's Bureau: A Nineteenth-Century Federal Welfare Agency," *Social Casework,* Vol. 44, No. 5, May 1963, pp. 247–254.

62. Cortez A. M. Ewing, *American National Government,* Norman, Okla.: University of Oklahoma, 1958, p. 583.

63. Marcus Cunliffe, *Soldiers and Civilians,* New York: Free Press, 1973, p. 81.

64. John P. Resch, "Federal Welfare for Revolutionary War Veterans," *Social Service Review,* Vol. 56, No. 2, June 1982, p. 191.

65. Theda Skocpol and John Ikenberry, "The Political Formation of the American Welfare State in Historical and Comparative Perspective," *Comparative Social Research,* Vol. 6, 1983, pp. 95–97.

66. John D. Hicks, George E. Mowery, and Robert E. Burke, *The American Nation,* Boston: Houghton Mifflin, 1963, p. 96.

67. *Those Who Served: Report of the Twentieth Century Fund Task Force on Policies toward Veterans,* New York: The Twentieth Century Fund, 1974.

68. Richard Hofstadter, *Social Darwinism in American Thought,* Boston: Beacon Press, 1967, p. 41.

69. Louis L. Snyder, *Documents of German History,* New Brunswick, N.J.: Rutgers University Press, 1958, p. 234.

70. Ibid., p. 234.

71. Ibid., p. 245.

72. Hajo Halborn, *A History of Modern Germany,* New York: Knopf, 1969, p. 292; Daniel Levine, *Poverty and Society: The Growth of the American Welfare State in International Comparison,* New Brunswick, N.J.: Rutgers University Press, 1988, pp. 51, 52, 55.

73. M. Penelope Hall, *The Social Services of Modern England,* London: Routledge and Kegan Paul, 1959.

5

America, Poverty, Two Paths

The American Experience II

Every modern industrial society is a welfare society. None permits natural or social contingencies fully to determine the life chances of its members. All have programs whose explicit purpose is to protect adults and children from the degradation and insecurity of ignorance, illness, disability, unemployment and poverty.

—Gutmann[1]

Three Discoveries of Poverty

In part the programs that exist today in the United States result from three "discoveries of poverty" and the ways in which American society focuses on poverty. The divergent social welfare paths for dealing with the issue result from different societal values and views of human nature.

Social Darwinism did not go unchallenged during the latter part of the nineteenth century. Among those groups that countered the arguments of the social Darwinists were the Grangers, Single Taxers, trade unionists, populists, and socialists who challenged the existing pattern of free enterprise, demanded reforms by state action, or insisted upon a thorough remodeling of the social order.[2] As early as a century earlier, Thomas Paine argued that the United States had the potential for abolishing poverty and that security could be provided for the aged through the use of inheritance taxes and ground rents.[3]

Social Darwinism was a fatalist, status quo philosophy, useful for those who controlled industry and business. Paradoxically, this conservative philosophy took hold when—because of science and technology—it was thought that human beings could achieve whatever they chose, including modifying society.

Lester Ward, a sociology pioneer, argued against social Darwinism and suggested that restraining power is needed to regulate the conduct of individuals toward one another and to prevent the wholesale exploitation of the weak by the strong. Without constraints, liberty and happiness would be impossible. The highest aim of true individualism is to maximize individual liberty; accomplishing this requires some governmental restraints. From this perspective, the doctrine of laissez faire *at the extreme* is incoherent and futile.[4]

Prior to the 1890s, the predominant attitude in the United States was that society and the community had no real obligation to the poor. Until the last decades of the nineteenth century, reform movements in the United States did not focus on the problem of poverty or on its elimination. During these decades one response of churches to slums and poverty was to preach the *Social Gospel*. Walter Rauschenbusch was a prime proponent of the Social Gospel, which was "the application of the teaching of Jesus and the total message of the Christian salvation to society, the economic life, and social institutions...as well as its individuals." Socially conscious ministers suggested that Jesus came to establish a new environment and that all Christians should work to change the world by acting to reform wages, housing, and working conditions. Some defended the demands of labor unions and preached against the economic doctrine based on social Darwinism. Although these ministers argued there are Christian solutions for all social problems, their influence did not reach the mass of churchgoers.[5]

Furthermore, the laissez faire philosophy that prevailed during the intense rush to industrialize America was modified. In 1887, the federal Interstate Commerce Commission was formed, although limited in power, and helped to uncover business and political corruption. This action affirmed the right of the federal government to regulate interstate business, a key ingredient for effective regulation yet to be built. There was a growing interest in improving the living conditions of the poor, illustrated by numerous exposés of dangerous and unhealthy work and home environments. Another force leading to reform were the "muckrakers," journalists who were active in exposing social ills, including corruption in business, city governments, child labor, food packing, and other spheres of life.

First Discovery

The progressive era that spanned the first decade and a half of the twentieth century marked the *first discovery* of poverty in America: Progressives, during this period, had an intense belief in the possibility of social progress and a deep concern for reform in politics and business. They were committed as utopian thinkers to the idea that progress toward social justice was possible and necessary, and they viewed poverty as a result of the structure of society. It was agreed that the community had to take some responsibility for alleviating poverty, criminality, prostitution, poor housing, and intemperance. The expectation was that remedial work should be focused on the capacity of the individual for self-improvement but that society also could be altered. So, this first discovery of poverty also reflects a "can-do" attitude, the idea that government and the people can fix problems, even poverty.

It also was during these years that various insurance laws were enacted. These were mostly related to unemployment and disability protection, and their initiation was partly stimulated by the earlier German experience. During 1900–1914 (the Progressive Era), the federal government intervened for the first time since the Freedmen's Bureau, and much social legislation was passed, including antitrust laws, civil service reform, creation of the Children's Bureau, child labor laws, health and safety laws, the income tax, direct election of senators, and other laws with major social consequences but requiring limited federal expenditures.

The Fading of the First Discovery

With the onset of World War I, the progressive era of legislation faded and with it the focus on poverty. In the United States, disillusionment with and fear of left-wing philosophies, including socialism and anarchism, dampened the interest in initiating social legislation.

During the 1920s, there was a return to the philosophy of governmental non-intervention and the hope that the country could return to the "good old days." Thus the first discovery of poverty passed, leaving a wave of social welfare legislation in the states and on the federal level.

The one exception to the return to the laissez faire philosophy was the enactment of the Sheppard-Towner Act in 1921 (following the enfranchisement of women in 1920). This was the first federal program to provide grants to states to develop preventive health services for mothers and children. Despite common knowledge about high maternal and infant death rates, those opposing the act suggested the act threatened the basic values of the nation. Among those who opposed the bill were anti-suffragists, anti-feminists, and anti-communists. It was also opposed by states who feared a loss of power and by the American Medical Association, which feared state-sponsored medicine. By supporting federal intervention for a national social problem, the Sheppard-Towner Act was a conceptual link between the earlier progressive period and the New Deal to follow; despite the fact that it was proven effective, the act was eliminated just before the Great Depression.[6]

Second Discovery

A *second discovery* of the problem of poverty occurred during the Great Depression of the 1930s. So many people were unemployed and poor during the 1930s that the federal government was forced to act. It was no longer "they" who were poor; it was "us." President Herbert Hoover initially thought a return of confidence would correct the failing economy. He was also deeply committed to a conservative, free-enterprise philosophy based on a belief in individual and family responsibility. He was opposed to efforts to expand the federal role—for example, the provision of federal grants to states for direct relief, federally funded public works projects, or any federal-state employment role. Federal assistance was viewed negatively. At first, Hoover limited himself to confidence-instilling statements, which failed to deter the continued deterioration of the economy. He attempted to expedite private relief efforts, to no advantage. Finally, the Reconstruction Finance Corporation was created to lend money to banks, railroads, and other institutions, and Hoover supported federal loans to states for their relief efforts.

The New Deal era initiated by President Franklin D. Roosevelt involved a very different strategy to counteract the Great Depression and was marked by an enormous variety of legislation designed to deal with the many human problems. Among these actions were federal protection for bank depositors and stock market investors, federal credit to ease the debt burdens of farmers and home-owners, programs such as the Civilian Conservation Corps and the National Youth Administration to put unemployed youth to work, fair labor standards, emergency relief and work-relief programs, public works programs such as the Tennessee Valley Authority, lending programs for middle-class homeowners to repair old houses or build new ones, and building low-income housing. Other in-terventions included rural electrification, legislation to support farm prices, a na-tionwide unemployment exchange system, and monetary, food subsidy, and banking laws.

Although there had been efforts to introduce various types of social security in the states and on the federal level, until the Great Depression, Congress had failed to enact social insurance. Then, in 1935, as part of a wave of New Deal legis-lation, the Social Security Act was passed. Based on contributions by employer and employee, the plan was federally administered and included unemployment compensation, public assistance, and services.

This second discovery of poverty faded during World War II, probably be-cause of the focus on the war effort and the full employment it engendered. The decade of the 1950s was not unlike the decade of the 1920s in that social legislation in general played a low-key role in regard to social welfare.

Third Discovery

The first American discovery of poverty in the early twentieth century came at a time when poverty was viewed as a personal and moral fault of the poor. However, so many persons were poor during the second discovery period in the 1930s that the systematic and structural nature of poverty was clear, and invidious moralizing necessarily was limited. However, the *third discovery* of poverty began in an afflu-ent period—the 1960s. Then, as we shall see, the key to poverty was thought to be a lack of "opportunity."

In the late 1950s, the general belief, exemplified by Kenneth Galbraith's *The Af-fluent Society*, was that poverty as a social problem in the United States was past. There was still residual poverty, in Appalachia and other isolated pockets, and case poverty among those with low level skills or with emotional problems. It was be-lieved the personal characteristics of poor persons contributed greatly to their being poor. Therefore, it was believed that such poverty could be reduced by having more trained social workers in welfare departments rehabilitating the poor.

This latter perspective was the thrust of amendments to the Social Security Act in 1962, which sought more trained social workers in public welfare in order to rehabilitate those on "welfare." Although for the short run this was good for social workers, it involved ignoring the societal and structural aspects of poverty.

Into this atmosphere came Edgar May's book *The Wasted Americans* and Michael Harrington's *The Other America*. These books pointed out that, if in the depression of 1933 one of every three Americans was poor, in 1960 one in four was still poor. Furthermore, this 25 percent was essentially constant and had not decreased since World War II. Dwight MacDonald popularized these ideas, and the idea of a poverty "line" below which people should be considered poor, in a series of articles in *The New Yorker* magazine. These articles and books caught the attention of advisors to President Kennedy who were seeking programs to stimulate the economy. After the Kennedy assassination, these advisors brought their preliminary thinking to President Johnson. Johnson supported them, and thus was born the Economic Opportunity Act of 1964—the so-called "War on Poverty."

The strategies chosen to deal with poverty did not include transfers of money directly to the poor. Instead, like the 1962 amendments to the Social Security Act, the strategy focused on services and offered opportunities for self-advancement. This focus on services was—although subtly—victim-blaming. Implicit in the emphasis on services was the suggestion that one was poor because of personal shortcomings or because of a lack of equal opportunity, a structural approach. The problem of inadequate income was viewed as inseparable from these personal limitations and structural limitations, which in turn limited opportunities.

The nature of the poverty war was related to the values and philosophies of the period. The antipoverty agencies developed on the basis of strategies demonstrated earlier. The Ford Foundation in the 1950s and 1960s addressed itself to urban issues. Gradually its priorities shifted from study and research to direct action grants, particularly the "grey areas" programs that focused energy on deteriorating central city areas with the aim of transforming political and social life through community organization. Congress enacted the Juvenile Delinquency and Youth Offenses Control Act (1961) to provide multifaceted antidelinquency projects by providing a package of federal services to communities. Federal efforts were often implemented in tandem with efforts supported by the Ford Foundation.

At one time, delinquency was seen as related to certain genetic or physical characteristics of the delinquent. A more "modern" approach was to view the juvenile delinquent as psychologically disturbed. Sociologists then claimed that delinquent behavior represented normal participation in a separate delinquent subculture. But the theory current in the late 1950s was "opportunity theory" as developed by Lloyd Ohlin and Richard Cloward.[7] The delinquent gang did not operate in a separate culture with different values and aspirations. Instead, delinquents shared the same desires for a car and a house with a picket fence and the like. It was the gap between these aspirations and available opportunities that caused delinquent behavior. Opportunity needed to be opened. Therefore, it is no surprise that the War on Poverty was the Economic *Opportunity* Act and that its programs stressed access, opportunity, and participation for the poor. Out of these participatory efforts grew the later demand for income transfer itself.

The 1960s focused the most attention on the problems of poverty since the 1930s. The president, Congress, and the society at large agreed to attack poverty through the enactment of legislation. There was a federal, state, and local approach to the problem, one which brought some but not all resources to the task.

How did the third discovery of poverty develop? Two different points of view hold special interest because they reflect the realities of the 1960s and identify the development of a relatively new feature in society. Furthermore, they may be instructive in pointing out the directions from which future reforms will come.

The first view was suggested by Senator Daniel P. Moynihan, then assistant secretary of labor, that a new phenomenon had occurred: the professionalization of reform. The question of poverty was now being dealt with, planned for, and coped with by administrators, professional organizations, doctors, teachers, social workers, and others, and special initiatives were being taken by government-employed professionals and foundations. The Ford Foundation and others designed methods to help people move out of poverty and selected cities for funded experiments. It is noteworthy that North Carolina during Governor Terry Sanford's administration sought to apply techniques that formerly focused on urban centers to an entire state, including rural sections, and received funding from the Ford Foundation and the Babcock and Reynolds Foundations, matched by local funds and grants from Federal agencies. Within a year following the inception of the North Carolina program, Congress appropriated funds for a national war on poverty, unleashing experiments in every state.[8] Moynihan's argument was that the Office of Economic Opportunity (OEO) programs were the result of this "professionalization" of reform.[9] Based on social statistics, newly available for use, and expanded social science research, OEO included high-level planning by professionals and "maximum feasible participation" by the poor in the development of programs. Furthermore, Moynihan argued, these programs had the effect of re-creating ethnic politico-social organizations in the big cities. According to Moynihan, for the first time in history professionals took the lead in the search for reform. They had access to information, they had expertise, and they knew where the entry points to the gates of power were located. Thus, in a way, the search for reform had taken a new turn. Professionals, with whatever motives, took on the mission of reforming society as a part of their own job definitions and responsibilities. The War on Poverty had not resulted from marches, demonstrations, or popular demand but rather from ideas emanating from intellectual and professional circles.

Richard Cloward and Frances Fox Piven, on the other hand, claimed that the War on Poverty was a response to the Civil Rights movement, the beginnings of unrest in the cities, and political payoffs to poor urban constituencies to whom the Democratic party owed a debt.[10] According to this view, OEO was the continuation of a political process. The Cloward and Piven perspective contrasted with the Moynihan point of view that no one was specifically "banging on the door" for a War on Poverty. Where the two points of view apparently intersect is in the fact that maximum feasible participation, as a principle, was invented by the professional planners but was also inherent in political realities among the poor. Enhanced participation by the poor is found in their demand for greater recognition and involvement in the political process. Both theories are correct but incomplete.

There would have been no War on Poverty without the unrest Cloward and Piven describe; yet it might not have developed when and in the way it did without the process described by Moynihan.

The War on Poverty

During the ten-year period from the mid-1960s to the mid-1970s, the average annual growth rate in spending on social programs (social insurances, public assistance, health and medical programs, veterans' programs, education, and housing) expanded nationally from 11.5 percent (1965) of the gross national product to 19.5 percent (1976).[11] A major factor contributing to the rise was an administrative action by President Johnson that counted all trust funds officially in the budget beginning in fiscal year 1969. The surplus in Social Security in the "unified budget" in a sense obscured the budget deficit that reflected increased costs of the war in Vietnam.

President Johnson achieved an impressive series of legislative successes in his "Great Society" program. In 1965 alone, the following laws and programs emerged: Medicare, Medicaid, general federal aid to local public schools, federal scholarships and loans for college students, the Voting Rights Act, the National Foundations for the Arts and Humanities, rent supplements for poor persons, highway beautification, grants, loans, training programs for physicians and other health professionals, and developmental assistance for Appalachia.

The Economic Opportunity Act (1964) was only one element in the call by President Johnson for the nation to conduct a War on Poverty, mainly a set of services. When we think of a War on Poverty, we think of a massive effort. However, the budget of the Office of Economic Opportunity, between 1965 and 1974, ranged from a low of $328.5 million to a high of $1.896 billion.[12] Although these may seem like large sums, in a nation such as ours they are quite modest.

The War on Poverty and its leaders in Community Action Programs around the country adopted many of the tactics and slogans of a radical tide in the United States at the time. There were confrontations, sit-ins, and demonstrations. However, if by "radical" we mean a fundamental restructuring of the social order and by "conservative" we mean staying with the status quo, then the War on Poverty was an essentially conservative program. It mandated no fundamental new income maintenance program. Our social welfare structure remains based on the Social Security Act rather than on the new developments of the 1960s. In fact, one may argue that, by focusing on local issues, the War on Poverty deflected true radical reform. It must be noted that in reality the major impact on poverty came from income transfer programs and health insurance, not from War on Poverty programs themselves. The biggest change in the social welfare system in the 1960s came through the adoption of Medicare and Medicaid, which were not a part of the War on Poverty.

Expectation and Delivery

If there is one criticism of the War on Poverty on which most analysts agree, it is that the expectations engendered by the promises were far beyond anything the program had the capacity to deliver. Success often was called "failure" when newer and higher goals implicitly replaced original program goals. Elimination of poverty was not enough. Expenditures for goods or services going to the poor must be effective, efficiently managed, and equitable. Participation of the poor in managing an antipoverty budget was replaced by assuring their participation in all matters that affect them. Some escalation of goals is evidence not of failure but of problems of success, perhaps intensified by failing to make goals more specific and limited.[13]

Some people see this as not all bad, because it created a sense of entitlement. Others criticize the War on Poverty precisely because it encouraged this sense of entitlement. There are those who believe that the gap between expectation and delivery may have been in part responsible, along with the Vietnam War, for some of the violence characteristic of U.S. society in the late 1960s. Perhaps Aaron Wildavsky put it best:

> A recipe for violence: promise a lot; deliver a little. Lead people to believe they will be much better off but let there be no dramatic improvement. Try a variety of small programs, each interesting but marginal in impact and severely under financed. Avoid any attempt at solution remotely comparable in size to the dimensions of the problem you are trying to solve.... Get some poor people involved in local decision making only to discover that there is not enough at stake to be worth bothering about.[14]

There were at least seven developments that resulted from the War on Poverty and governmental intervention:

1. The poverty rate was reduced from 22 percent in 1960 to 11.2 percent in 1974.

2. The community became involved in decision making. "Maximum feasible participation" was a phrase little understood by Congress when it voted for the Economic Opportunity Act, the basis for the War on Poverty, but it is a dramatic illustration of the power of guideline writers and bureaucrats. They were able to give meaning to this phrase by demanding the participation of the poor in the governance of Community Action programs. Out of this came a concept of community involvement that is so much a part of social welfare today that the younger student will find it hard to imagine the degree of change. Before the mid-1960s, it simply would not have occurred to social welfare planners to ask residents or local leaders if a new hospital or center should be placed in their community. Most people agree today that there should be community input and involvement. This general acceptance grew directly from the activities of the War on Poverty and its successor programs.

A latent consequence of the involvement of local people in community affairs during the War on Poverty was the training and emergence of indigenous leadership that moved beyond the local scenes. There are governmental leaders in Washington, D.C., and elsewhere whose training began on the local level during the Civil Rights movement and the War on Poverty of the 1960s.

3. Similarly, the client's right to know and to gain access to information grew dramatically with the War on Poverty. Before the War on Poverty, welfare rights organizations would have to have pages of welfare manuals surreptitiously photocopied

so that clients could learn about regulations and processes. Today the right of access to information is legally supported (although sometimes not honored). In addition, client brokerage and advocacy are viewed as legitimate social service functions.

4. Evaluation of the Head Start program found that graduates as young adults performed better in school, were more interested in going to college, and were less likely to get into criminal difficulty than persons with similar backgrounds who were not in Head Start. Whatever the limitations of the Head Start program, it made the following contributions:

   a. It strengthened the legitimacy of early intervention;
   b. It supported the value of day care; and
   c. It improved nutrition and health care for young children and enhanced parental involvement in education.

5. There was a major change in the concept of legal services that grew out of one of the programs of the War on Poverty. Not only criminal but civil legal service for the poor is now an accepted fact. This has occurred even though legal services have been poorly funded and there have been executive and legislative efforts to limit or eliminate the role of such programs.

6. Through the Job Corps and other job-creation programs, the War on Poverty helped to develop a consciousness and, at that time, an acceptance of the potential role of public service employment. Later events placed much greater emphasis on private-sector employment. It remains to be seen whether the special employment and training needs of a number of groups can be accommodated within the private sector alone.

7. Through the Vista Corps, which followed up on the successful Peace Corps launched during the Kennedy administration, the War on Poverty established that there is a human reservoir of idealism and a willingness for voluntary action that can be mobilized on behalf of social issues. The "thousand points of light" concept promulgated by President Bush in some ways is an extension of this principle.

8. The New Careers movement encouraged the use of indigenous members of the community as paraprofessional workers in the human services. Career ladders in education, often through community colleges, were established.

The "Skirmish" against Poverty

Although there was certainly no acknowledged war on poverty in the 1970s, there was a scarcely noticed confluence of legislation that might best be viewed as a "skirmish" against poverty. Though seldom recognized, this series of legislative actions made important contributions to the antipoverty effort:

   1. The Supplemental Security Income program (1972) replaced the former state-run old-age assistance, aid to the blind, and aid to the permanently disabled programs.

2. Title XX of the Social Security Act (1975) was enacted to give more flexibility to the states in designing their social service programs.
3. The Earned Income Tax Credit (1975), a form of negative income tax, provided cash supplements for working parents with relatively low incomes.
4. The Comprehensive Employment and Training Act (1974) and the Special Supplemental Food Program (Women, Infants and Children [WIC]) (1972) provided food assistance and nutritional screening to low-income pregnant and postpartum women and their infants, as well as to low-income children up to five years of age.

Although not precisely aimed at poverty, during these few years there was a flurry of other legislation with implications for social welfare: The Drug Abuse Office and Treatment Act (1972); the National Health Services Corps (1972); the Child Abuse Prevention and Treatment Act (1974); The Child Nutrition Act (1974); the Rehabilitation Act (1973); the Housing and Community Development Act (1974); the Developmentally Disabled Assistance and Bill of Rights Act (1975); the Education of All Handicapped Children Act (1975); the Revenue Sharing Act (1972); the School-Age Mother and Child Health Act (1975); and the Legal Services Corporation Act (1974). Among other creations were the Environmental Protection Agency (1970), the Occupational Safety and Health Administration (1970), and the Juvenile Justice and Delinquency Prevention Act (1974).

President Carter's administration, although not averse to governmental intervention, was not particularly active in regard to social welfare matters. Following the Carter administration, there occurred a reversal when President Reagan set out "to get government off the backs of people" to clear the way for the private sector to solve society's problems. Tax cuts initiated during President Reagan's first term, when combined with a large federal deficit, served as a major obstacle to attention to poverty and to antipoverty spending. Instead of closing the gap between the rich and the poor, there in fact developed greater income inequality. Fiscal and tax policies were implemented that redistributed income upward rather than down the economic ladder; those who had less channeled money to those who had more. Those who favored supply-side economics argued that investment by the wealthy would "sprinkle" dollars downward and thus help those who were not well off. Others argued that what really was needed was a "bubble up" strategy in which many people had more expendable income and their purchases would restimulate the total economy.

Comprehensive antipoverty programs require funding, an accepting political climate, and political leadership at the presidential and Congressional levels. As the first decade of the 21st century unfolds none of these politically necessary ingredients were present, nor were they visible on the near horizon.

Families, Children, and Poverty

Earlier we saw how societal values influence the types and delivery of social welfare. U.S. society produces programs influenced by underlying values. This underlying structure of values results in opposing eligibility categories—the deserving and undeserving, the worthy and unworthy, those employed and unemployed. It is instructive to trace the evolution of two programs as exemplars of this two-track value system—Aid to Families with Dependent Children (AFDC), which is now entitled Temporary Assistance to Needy Families (TANF), and Old Age and Survivors Insurance (Social Security). Because so many values swirl about them, they are the nexus for major concerns in social welfare and in U.S. society. Observing how they have changed over time can highlight how they exemplify and reflect major values and trends in social welfare provision.

Aid to Families with Dependent Children ("Welfare")

Given impetus by the 1909 White House Conference called by President Theodore Roosevelt on the Care of Dependent Children, mothers' pensions to enable widows and deserted women to care for their children were first introduced statewide in 1911 by Illinois. Only two years later, these "pensions" had spread to 19 states.

By 1920, 40 states had enacted mothers' pensions. These provisions, although inadequately financed, provided numerous children more support than they would have had under earlier poor laws or private charity. But, the laws were not mandatory, and many counties did not follow them. Nevertheless, mothers' pensions did prevent many children from being placed in orphanages, poor farms, or institutions for delinquent children. In 1931, more than 80 percent of the recipients were widows; smaller percentages were deserted mothers or divorced. In that same year, only 55 beneficiaries in the entire United States were unmarried mothers.[15]

Although these programs multiplied rapidly, unanimity in regard to government-provided mothers' pensions was absent. Opposition came from business and economically conservative forces, as well as most charitable groups, including national associations such as the National Conference of Charities and Corrections. Most private charities defended their own voluntary measures for assisting widows and children and were critical of relief for the poor outside of institutions.[16]

The Report of the Committee on Economic Security (January 1935), which led to the Social Security Act, described mothers' pensions in this way:

> These are not primarily aids to mothers but defense measures for children. They are designed to release from the wage-earning role the person whose natural function is to give her children the physical and affectionate guardianship necessary not alone to keep them from falling into social misfortune, but more affirmatively to rear them into citizens capable of contributing to society.[17]

As one can observe, the intentions at that time were to maintain the family together, to keep mothers at home to raise their children out of institutions, and to prevent their children's inadequate supervision and potential delinquency. In 1935 *Aid to Dependent Children* (ADC), a federal-state cash grant program, became a part of the Social Security legislation to enable states to aid needy children without fathers. With the 1939 amendments to the Social Security Act, surviving wives and dependent children became eligible under certain criteria in 1940 for social security payments. It was thought at that time that ADC would fade away when the family survivorship benefits started. Viewed as a transitional program, ADC was considered necessary and helpful for deserving women and children. Between 1940 and 1955, the average number of families on ADC decreased.

At the end of the 1950s, the Social Security insurance program had grown but ADC also had increased numbers of recipients and costs, becoming the chief public assistance program of the United States for society's most vulnerable families. Divorce rates rose, and many persons migrated from rural farming communities to urban centers often unprepared for the demands of city life. Despite sustained economic growth and greater employment freedom for women, the ADC program kept expanding and became a worrisome social policy issue. Instead of aging widows, dependent children, and orphans, ADC began to serve unmarried, divorced, and deserted women. The name of the ADC program was changed in 1962 to *Aid to Families with Dependent Children* (AFDC), recognizing societal changes.

In the interim, there were various attempts to deal with the "welfare mess." In 1961, ADC was changed so that families with an unemployed parent could become eligible for assistance. However, coverage for families in which the primary wage earner was unemployed was not required of states, and half the states chose not to offer this provision. The 1962 amendments to this program mainly focused on rehabilitation and services to help people become economically self-sufficient. But social services proved to be unequal to the societal forces expanding the AFDC rolls.

AFDC, which began as a program to keep mothers at home to raise their children, now shifted its focus to encourage employment and work. The Work Incentive Program (WIN, 1967) was developed to provide opportunities for able-bodied adults to acquire vocational skills and work experience. However, prior to 1967, there was no "earnings disregard." If an AFDC parent earned $100 from working, she lost an equal amount from AFDC. After 1967, if working, she could retain a portion of the total earned. As a result, she would receive more than if she were not working.

The amendments of 1971 required all able-bodied AFDC recipients without children under 6 years of age to register for WIN services and states to provide training and work experiences. The promotion of opportunity was the theme of these changes, but their impact never met expectations and criticism continued.

During the early stages of the Richard Nixon presidency, the *family assistance plan* (FAP, 1969) was considered. This reorganization of the welfare system was designed to encourage AFDC recipients to work. The proposal called for a minimum cash payment for a family. If an AFDC recipient worked, the recipient could retain half of earnings above the minimum guaranteed annual income. The program also intended to shift the emphasis from services and rehabilitation to money and to make it possible for two-parent families to obtain AFDC. Food Stamps, a cash equivalent for AFDC families, were included in the package.

This plan was a radical departure from the traditional approach and was criticized by both conservatives and liberals. Some objected to a program that implied welfare assistance was a right. Others were concerned about the potential costs. Still others were concerned about the relationship of FAP to other benefits and work disincentives. Objections also were expressed about women being forced to go to work for low wages. One outcome of the debate was the 1972 creation of the Supplemental Security Income (SSI) program, which federalized benefits for the universally recognized deserving poor, aging, disabled, and blind.

In 1977, President Carter proposed the *Program for Better Jobs and Income*. The deserving poor would receive a guaranteed annual income. Those who were expected to work would be granted a lower sum and the possibility of raising their incomes through public-sector or government-subsidized private-sector employment. The proposal failed to win congressional approval because it required the creation of a huge number of jobs.

The thrust throughout the Reagan administration was toward tightened eligibility requirements and reduced benefits. The poor were viewed as responsible for their poverty, able to extricate themselves if they tried sufficiently, and better off with less governmental assistance.

In 1988, Congress passed the *Family Support Act*, which essentially defined AFDC until radical change was introduced in 1996. AFDC operated in all 50 states, the District of Columbia, the Virgin islands, Guam, and Puerto Rico. The program assisted children in families in which need was brought on by the incapacity, death, continued absence, or unemployment of a parent. The program benefits (55 percent on average) and administration (50 percent) were financed by uncapped federal funds and state matching funds based on formulas, generally in inverse relationship to the per capita wealth of the State. The total cost of benefits depended on the number of eligible persons receiving benefits. Such entitlement is usually associated with the individual applicant; but, in reality, it was the states that were entitled to reimbursement from the federal government for all those to whom they paid benefits.

There existed from mid-century general frustration and discontent with the nature, size, and cost of the AFDC rolls. In 1988, Congress passed the Family Support Act, which essentially defined AFDC until radical change was introduced in 1996. The Act stressed the mutual obligation of government and the welfare recipient to promote the self-sufficiency of AFDC families. During the early 1990s, more than 40 states received waivers allowing them to test their own ideas, including special behavioral rules, rewards, penalties, and welfare to work strategies. By 1994 enrollment had soared to an all-time high (5 million families and one in every twelve U.S. children). More than half of AFDC children were born out of wedlock and three-quarters had an able-bodied parent who lived away from home. Almost half the families had received benefits for more than five years, when counting repeat spells. Benefit costs also peaked in 1994.

A growing number of policymakers advocated that Congress put a cap on AFDC funds to control costs. Others argued that offering permanent help for needy children in single-parent families encouraged family breakup, promoted unmarried births, and fostered long-term dependency. Efforts to reduce welfare use and promote self-sufficiency generally had been less successful than hoped for. Rehabilitative services, work requirements, work rewards, education and training, support services such as child care, child support enforcement, and provisions to establish paternity on out of wedlock children all failed to stem the growth of welfare use.

An Old-New Path

President Clinton promised during the 1992 election campaign to "end welfare as we know it." Following the Republicans' gaining control of Congress in 1994, they too promised as part of their "Contract with America" to reform public welfare. Thus, both the President and Congress were committed to changing public welfare.

Following intense debates and two prior vetos, in August 1996, Congress passed and President Clinton signed the radical Personal Responsibility and Work Opportunity Reconciliation Act (PRA) abolishing the AFDC program, thus reversing a federal guarantee of support for these families enacted in 1935 as part of the original Social Security Act.

The PRA resulted in momentous shifts in social policy. The new legislation gave states vast power to run their own welfare and work programs. In signing this legislation, President Clinton fulfilled his promise, and the Republicans also laid claim to having fulfilled their promise.

During the long debate, opposing ideologies played an important role, minimized somewhat by general agreement that public welfare needed to be reformed. Many forces coalesced to support changes. Among these factors were the following:

1. Many had distinct views of the proper distribution of governmental power, particularly Article X of the U.S. Constitution (the powers not delegated to the United States by the Constitution, nor prohibited by it to the states, are reserved to the states respectively, or to the people). Political devolution to the states was an important factor, a process whose efforts began with President Nixon's revenue-sharing program and accelerated during the Reagan administration. The claim was made that states, being closer to the people, could administer public welfare programs more efficiently, more flexibly, and with greater knowledge of what is needed. Forgotten was the fact that the program became federalized because states were not doing the job.

2. The legislation assumes the poor can best be motivated to compete successfully in a job market by being forced into it. This view dominated despite the existence of a job market that does not have a sufficient number of jobs reasonably available at a living wage for unskilled and semi-skilled persons.

3. Despite many positive achievements, genuine concern was expressed by all sides in the debate about the dysfunctions of the public assistance system, including multi-generational receipt of benefits, administrative complexity, and undermining self-reliance.

4. Both parties used reform efforts as a political strategy to gain votes during the upcoming presidential and congressional elections. The President's original intention was to create new and expanded training programs, expanded child care, universal health care, and—if necessary—government-supplied jobs as employer of last resort for those who would exhaust his proposed two-year time limit. However, his early welfare plan would have added $10 billion more to the budget for spending on the poor, a proposal that was not acceptable politically.

5. The original public welfare system served widows and deserted mothers with children, not those who were divorced or never married, in the midst of the Great Depression. Those who favored radical change compared the nature of the poverty population today with those originally served and thought change was needed.

6. Policymakers expected that projected savings (approximately $55 billion over six years) would reduce substantially the federal deficit and/or make possible federal tax cuts or maintenance of middle-class entitlements.

Few people defended the system that many believed undermined values such as work, family, personal initiative, and independence. Although the new legislation was a revolutionary departure from the past, supporters of the legislation suggested that a new system could hardly do worse than the system then in place, viewed it as a magnificent new experiment, claimed it would free millions of people from dependence, restore them to self-reliance, and save billions of dollars. Opponents foresaw a grim future for approximately one million children who would be pushed further into poverty. Critics suggested the legislation was a retreat from a 61-year commitment that Republicans and Democrats, U.S. presidents, and Congresses of both major parties made on behalf of poor children. Still others thought this change was a precursor and the first step to dismantling the social contract that was in place since the mid-1930s, including Social Security and other social insurances.

A third group rejected radical change. This group pointed out that as a result of waivers approved by the Clinton administration, 45 states were engaged in public welfare experimentation at the time the new legislation was passed. Their suggestion was that the most prudent course was to examine the results of these experiments and choose among the most positive plans on the basis of real experience rather than a leap of faith. Proponents countered this view by suggesting the possibility of change deserves a leap of faith. Thus, AFDC had changed in many parts of the country and a quiet revolution was proceeding.[18] The Personal Responsibility and Work Opportunity Reconciliation Act (PRA)—the program that supersedes AFDC—will be described in Chapter 9.

Social Security

The historical path of Social Security has been quite different from that of AFDC. Instituted during the Great Depression as an old-age retirement program, Social Security was an omnibus legislative act that included a social insurance ("Social Security old age benefits") designed to provide monthly benefits to retired workers aged 65 years and over and a lump-sum death benefit to the worker's estate.

The Act also contained provisions for old age assistance, unemployment compensation, aid to dependent children, and maternal and child welfare. Gradually the old age and survivor's program was broadened to include benefits for dependents and survivors (1939), followed by coverage for the permanently disabled and their dependents (1956) and health insurance for the aging (1965). However, when people refer to Social Security, by and large, they are referring to Old Age and Survivors' Insurance.

Social Security amendments provided that monthly cash benefits would be increased through automatic cost-of-living adjustments, which keep pace with inflation. One can observe that the Social Security program continued to expand the number of beneficiaries and the benefits. However, even this program, which is designed for "worthy" workers, was not received with open arms during the Great Depression. Resistance, for example, came from the U.S. Chamber of Commerce and the National Association of Manufacturers, among others. Some argued the program was a threat to the American way of life and would deprive citizens of their personal liberty. The compulsory nature of the payroll tax was objectionable to many who suggested the program should be voluntary.

Others argued the act did not go far enough. Initially, Social Security deliberately omitted inclusion of health insurance to avoid attacks by the medical lobby. A full-employment policy was dropped because it was too expensive and tainted by the temporary public works programs of the depression. Another inhibiting force was the fear that unless states and local governments significantly controlled eligibility, the expansion of federal activities would be found unconstitutional by the then-conservative Supreme Court.

Contrasting Values and Aims

In contrasting Social Security and Aid to Families with Dependent Children (replaced by TANF), we find they embody different American values. Despite some initial resistance, as described previously, Social Security has always received broad-based political support. Note the relative frequency of proposed and actual changes to the AFDC program compared with the relative infrequency of major changes to the Social Security program since its inception. This widespread consensus is derived from several features: Social Security is a national insurance program, one pays into the program prior to receipt of benefits when eligible, the benefits are standardized, and they are related to one's personal *employment*. One has earned the benefits. People of every social and economic class in all parts of the nation are served by the program. Today there are millions of recipients, many of whom have highly developed political skills.

Aid to Families with Dependent Children, on the other hand, has been a focus of controversy. The purpose of AFDC shifted over time. The original purpose was to encourage the care of needy children in their own homes, followed by strengthening family life and promoting family self-support (1956). There is no national consensus or standard rules and benefits supporting it. The program differs from state to state. There is no cost-of-living adjustment to offset inflation. The recipients are not viewed in terms of their work histories but are seen as dependent and unproductive beneficiaries of the general revenue taxes paid by those who are currently employed. They are perceived as unworthy, and the prevailing attitude is that benefits provided should be as short and as sparse as possible. Myths abound as to the race, age, duration of benefit receipt, and other characteristics of the beneficiary group.

The Poor Laws Today

Despite the passage of time and the many changes that have taken place in our society, the Poor Law mentality discussed in chapter 3 remains with us and recently has been reemphasized in TANF "welfare." The welfare system, broadly defined, is the nexus for conflicting values: humane and punitive.

The major trend toward secularism continues. Related to this is a blurring of the private and public sectors. In many respects, the private sector, including sectarian-sponsored social agencies, has become simply another vehicle for the delivery of services based upon the aims of government. This issue of private and public sectors will be examined in greater detail in chapter 11.

Risks and categories also remain with us. Poor persons are classified as either worthy or unworthy, disabled or able-bodied. During the 1980s and 1990s, both physically and mentally disabled persons were excluded from certain benefits. In fact, the Reagan administration enforced severe eligibility requirements, forcing many disabled persons off the rolls during the early and mid-1980s. These actions—later overruled by court decisions—suggested that poor persons, including even the disabled, were viewed as unworthy.

Public welfare categories have traditionally favored the aging, the blind, the disabled, and female-headed families. It was only the aged, blind, and disabled who were included in the national SSI program. General assistance designed for single adults and married persons without children continues to receive far fewer resources, to the point of not existing in some states. So categories remain, and it appears unlikely that in the foreseeable future the United States will design a welfare system that abolishes categories and deals with people strictly on the basis of need. It has become possible that entire programs will be curtailed. Those people formerly served may have few places to turn, in which case, categories themselves become irrelevant.

There are few claims that indoor relief is cheaper or more productive than outdoor relief, although the desirability of indoor relief has been proposed again by conservatives. In general, we have learned that institutionalization is more expensive than outdoor relief (except where costly technology and other intensive service are required), for both the short and long term. A respect for independent functioning also serves to support outdoor relief. However, deinstitutionalization, especially of the mentally ill, has not worked out successfully in all areas. The funds required by the system to implement the outdoor community services needed have not been forthcoming. At the same time that there are significant problems with deinstitutionalization, there has also developed a clearer recognition that institutional care is absolutely necessary for some persons, and the dream that most—if not all—institutionalized persons could be served successfully in their communities cannot be fulfilled.

Residency laws are being eroded as the United States moves in certain respects toward a national society. Greater mobility has been brought about by new modes of transportation and the need for workers in various parts of the nation. The connections between what occurs in Mississippi, for example, and what happens in major metropolitan areas of the northern or western states have increasingly become clearer as the various regions become much more aware of their interconnections. The erosion of residency laws also has been supported by court cases. Attempts by States to reinstitute certain residency requirements did not survive several recent challenges.

Nevertheless, the local responsibility/local control argument is strong. In the revolutionary TANF program (1996), to be discussed in chapter 9, the state rather than the federal level is viewed as the most desirable arbiter of social welfare policy and program priorities. Localities, it is argued, know better what their needs are.

The issue of less eligibility remains, even today, one of the most difficult and intractable problems in social welfare. Benefits for social welfare payments are typically computed on the basis of a percentage of the minimum level subsistence. Thus, those who receive "welfare" assistance are helped only at a subsistence level.

The treatment of poverty on a case-by-case basis has been changed primarily in the sense that our understanding has been broadened to appreciate structural components that contribute to poverty in individual cases. We understand better the relationship between public issues and private troubles. Even so, psychological counseling and moralizing are the treatments of choice for many of those with private troubles, as though the "fault lies in ourselves." Further, policy attention focuses on individual and family responsibility and avoids confronting how the structure affects lives.

Stigma remains a part of welfare today, and there is much victim-blaming. As the Poor Laws utilized stigma to control people's lives, creating a climate in which people would be punished for not working, it is reasonable to assume that today's remaining harsh attitudes also serve such purposes.

Human Nature and the American Dream

In every society people express their values about human nature and the image of the good society. We have seen that throughout history each society acts on its ideas through its social welfare system. In a sense, all modern societies are at the lead of long marches across time. Slowly, continuous historical processes have brought each society forward.

In the United States, according to the Constitution, we are to seek the "general welfare," but how should we seek it (with what means) and what is it? As in the beginning of our discussion in chapter 1, we arrive at values. Views differ as to the relative responsibilities of individuals and society to achieve the general welfare. Certainly in the United States both mutual aid and individual responsibility are valued, some persons placing major emphasis on the former and others on the latter.

Besides our values, however, we have seen that other constraints enter the picture. Social welfare is intricately related to the view of humanity held by citizens, especially decision makers, but it also reflects our view of ourselves and the society we wish to create. Even on pragmatic grounds, it appears there is much to be said for an openhanded social welfare policy, because what is sown now will be reaped in a few years.

But American values are mixed. Along with the Protestant ethic and social Darwinism, there is an impetus toward egalitarianism, democracy, and a belief in mutual aid. The American dream also calls for equal opportunity. Although it does not make claims for all persons being equal, it does demand that American society strive to give all persons equal opportunity; which is to say that all persons, including those who need help from the society, have a right to equal opportunity to health, education, and the basic necessities of life. They, too, are building America.

The ideal of equal opportunity is as yet unfulfilled. The degree to which the dream remains unfulfilled is dependent not only on the will of our society to fulfill it, but also on the inherent difficulties in achieving the dream. The fulfillment of the dream of equal opportunity for one individual may diminish that opportunity for other individuals; the enhancement of one group's, neighborhood's, or region's opportunity may have adverse effects on others. The complete resolution of such dilemmas about the American dream remains before us.

Finally, the American dream includes pluralism—many groups, many lifestyles, and many ethics—and this pluralism and differentiation must be respected by the law. Social welfare, as an important institution in our society, has to deal evenhandedly with all who need help, regardless of their values or their differences. The American dream is enacted in "minute particulars," in the way each person is dealt with under the law and by the professional social worker who makes decisions about a person's future.

Summary

Turning now from values and the historical precursors and development of American social welfare, in chapter 6 we will introduce the major philosophical and sociopolitical assumptions and perspectives that influence the choices our society makes regarding the nature of the social welfare programs it chooses and does not choose to implement, along with a brief description of our federal and pluralist decision-making system. In addition, we will introduce economic concepts that can help one's understanding regarding the forces affecting social welfare.

Questions for Consideration

1. Do you believe Lester Ward's ideas make sense today? In what ways?

2. What are the positives and negatives of laissez faire philosophies for modern American life?

3. Is there any way around the idea of less eligibility?

4. If someone asked you to state *your* vision of the American dream, what would you say?

Notes

1. Amy Gutmann, ed., *Democracy and the Welfare State*, Princeton, N.J.: Princeton University Press, 1988, p. 3.

2. Richard Hofstadter, *The Age of Reform*, New York: Vintage, 1955, p. 165.

3. Merle Curti, *The Growth of American Thought*, New York: Harper & Row, 1964, p. 165.

4. Henry Steele Commager, *Lester Ward and the Welfare State*, New York: Bobbs-Merrill, 1967, pp. xxxi, 223.

5. Ronald C. White and C. Howard Hopkins, *The Social Gospel. Religion and Reform in Changing America*, Philadelphia: Temple University Press, 1976, p. xi.

6. J. Stanley Lemons, "The Sheppard-Towner Act: Progressivism in the 1920s," *Journal of American History*, Vol. 55, December/March 1968, pp. 776–786; Kristine Siefert, "An Exemplar of Primary Prevention in Social Work: The Sheppard-Towner Act of 1921," *Social Work in Health Care*, Vol. 9, No. 1, Fall 1983, pp. 87–103.

7. Richard C. Cloward and Lloyd E. Ohlin, *Delinquency and Opportunity: A Theory of Delinquent Gangs*, Glencoe, Ill.: Free Press, 1960.

8. Terry Sanford, *Storm over the States*, New York: McGraw-Hill Book Company, 1967, pp. 174–175.

9. Daniel Patrick Moynihan, "The Professionalization of Reform," *The Public Interest*, Fall 1965, pp. 6–16.

10. Frances F. Piven and Richard A. Cloward, *Regulating the Poor*, New York: Vintage, 1993, pp. 256–263.

11. Ann K. Bixby, "Public Social Welfare Expenditures, Fiscal Years 1965–1987," *Social Security Bulletin*, Vol. 53, No. 2, February 1990, pp. 12–13.

12. Robert D. Plotnick and Felicity Skidmore, *Progress Against Poverty: A Review of the 1964–1974 Decade*, New York: Academic Press, 1975, pp. 8–9.

13. Aaron Wildavsky, "What Does It Do for the Poor?—A New Test for National Policy," *The Public Interest*, Vol. 34, Winter 1974, pp. 66–82.

14. Aaron Wildavsky, quoted in Daniel P. Moynihan, *Maximum Feasible Misunderstanding*, New York: Free Press, 1969, inside cover page.

15. Theda Skocpol, *Protecting Soldiers and Mothers: The Political Origins of Social Policy in the United States*, Cambridge, Mass.: Harvard University Press, 1992, pp. 424–426, 467.

16. Ibid., pp. 424–426.

17. *The Report of the Committee on Economic Security of 1935, 50th Anniversary Edition*, Washington, D.C.: National Conference on Social Welfare, 1985, p. 36.

18. Center for Law and Social Policy, *The CLASP Guide to Welfare Waivers: 1992–1995*, Washington, D.C., 1995.

6

Concepts for Social Welfare

The definition of politics is this: In politics, there are no right answers, only a continuing flow of compromises between groups, resulting in a changing, cloudy and ambiguous series of public decisions, where appetite and ambition compete openly with knowledge and wisdom.

—Senator Alan K. Simpson[1]

There is a liberal myth that poverty is bad for kids.

—Robert Rector at privatization conference[2]

Politics is mostly about which part of the electorate gets the money. Saying so is usually said to be cynical, but this is one of those periodic times in American history when the question of who gets the money is too blatantly in the open to be ignored.

—Russell Baker[3]

Overview

In the previous chapters, we discussed the history of social welfare and the impact of social values on social welfare. In this chapter we will examine closely the concept "social welfare" and define important terms, including social policy, social services, and social work. We will discuss information about ideology, political decision making, and economics useful for understanding the context that influences social welfare policy.

What Is Social Welfare?

One can attempt to define social welfare in narrow or broad terms. In its narrowest sense, social welfare includes those nonprofit functions of society, public or voluntary, that are clearly aimed at alleviating distress and poverty. Just about everyone would include the Temporary Assistance to Needy Families program as part of the U.S. social welfare system. Similarly the Food Stamp program, hospital social service programs, social service departments in homes for the aged, and the like would be seen as part of the social welfare system. Perhaps a broader definition such as the following can be more helpful:

> ...a nation's system of programs, benefits, and services that help people meet those social, economic, educational, and health needs that are fundamental to the maintenance of society.[4]

Such a broadened perspective that is not limited to the nonprofit sectors includes activities by voluntary (nonprofit), for-profit, and governmental programs, utilizing a wide variety of professional personnel such as social workers, physicians, nurses, lawyers, educators, ministers, and others, including family members.

This wider perspective reflects more nearly the contemporary reality in that no modern industrial state "permits natural or social contingencies fully to determine the life chances of its members. All have programs whose explicit purpose is to protect adults and children from the degradation and insecurity of ignorance, illness, disability, unemployment, and poverty."[5]

Some activities—collective goods—of society are primarily directed at the requisites of the society itself, such as national defense or flood control, and only indirectly and ultimately toward the fate of the individual. Other activities of society are those that provide direct services to meet immediate needs of individuals and families, such as subsidized housing, counseling, and medical and hospital services. It is in this last group that what we call social welfare tends to fall.

Neither the narrow nor the broad definition is perfect. Narrow definitions tend to exclude the most important and effective social welfare programs of society. They define social welfare in what will be defined later on as *residual* terms. Social welfare is seen as the activities directed toward helping people for whom the market failed. What links these definitions is the breadth of the activities included. Certainly, social welfare has a priority concern about those who are disadvantaged—the poor, ill, distressed, and vulnerable. But social welfare also has a broader aim. As President Franklin Roosevelt stated, "If, as our Constitution tells us, our Federal Government was established, among other things, 'to promote the general welfare,' then it is our plain duty to provide for that security upon which welfare depends."[6]

Programs of prevention or insurance—such as the Social Security system, which covers almost everyone today, social programs for the retired to meet a broad need for leisure and recreation, and Workers' Compensation for rich and poor alike—all evolved from the broad definition. Temporary Assistance for

Needy Families, Food Stamps, and Medicaid, which focus on the needy, derive from the narrow definition.

Even the broad definitions of welfare are not fully inclusive, and at the same time, they suffer from being somewhat too inclusive. On the one hand, by distinguishing between the profit sector and the welfare sector, they appear to exclude the growing delivery of social services for profit in the context of the private sector. Private hospitals, nursing homes, day-care centers, and private practice by social workers and other helping professionals all deliver services that are definable as social services and are part of the social welfare system, and yet they are not divorced from the private sector. As we will see further on, the division between private and public has become increasingly blurred in the United States.

Stated simply, even the broadest definitions may not cover everything that will come to be recognized as social welfare. Furthermore, the broad definitions tend to focus on formal as opposed to informal social welfare institutions. But policymakers are becoming increasingly aware that social welfare as an institution in the United States needs to be cognizant of and more connected with the informal, natural helping systems that people use. For example, the neighbors in the garden apartment complex who provide cooperative child care or who refer a person for counseling, the parish priest, the police who intervene in family disputes, the bartender who encourages a customer to go for help—all are, in a sense, part of the helping system and need to be taken into account as part of a full appreciation of the scope of social welfare.

On the other hand, the broad definitions of social welfare are too all-encompassing when they claim to cover all collective interventions to meet needs. Such broad definitions intrude on territory that has come to be defined institutionally as belonging elsewhere. The non-market portion of society also covers police and fire services, education, medical care, and the like, and we do not subsume all of these under our definition of social welfare.

What then are we to do? Should we throw up our hands and admit defeat in an attempt to define social welfare? To an extent, we must. The sophisticated student must realize that social welfare is an ambiguous, changing, and blurred concept. Still, we generally know what we are talking about when we discuss social welfare, and it is possible to suggest a definition that will serve for working purposes. Our guiding definitional principles will be the following:

1. Social interventions that are intended to enhance or maintain social functioning of human beings may be defined as social welfare in the largest and broadest sense. Titmuss even goes so far as to try to break down all these interventions into three basic categories of welfare: fiscal, occupational, and social.[7]

2. As social welfare programs enter the mainstream of society and become more universally used and widely accepted, they tend to lose their identity as social welfare services. This blurring will confuse the picture, but we need to understand it. The best social welfare programs are those so accepted that they cease to be commonly defined as social welfare. The kindergarten movement started as a social welfare program in settlement houses. As it became accepted as an important part of the U.S. educational system, it moved into the public school system, and now is seen as part of the domain of education. There is no need for us to claim kindergarten or to study it in a text on social welfare, although students should be aware that, in the largest sense, kindergarten and the entire public school system is a welfare program. Social Security, universally used and accepted, has become less identified as social welfare than it once was. Recipients of Social Security do not think of themselves as "welfare" cases in the same way that recipients of means-tested programs do. Nonetheless, it is essential to study Social Security as part of the social welfare system of the United States. It is not part of any other domain.

3. Our definition will tend toward the broad rather than the narrow approach to what social welfare is. We will include interventions for the enhancement of social functioning, even where they are in the profit-making sector or where they are part of an informal, less clearly institutional structure. For the sake of practicality, however, we limit our consideration to those parts of the broad social welfare system that are not clearly the domain or territory of other fields or disciplines, such as education, medicine, and police and fire services. This, too, will pose problems, because the domains are not always clear. Health insurance and care can be said to be part of the domain of social welfare, whereas medical practice clearly is not. Similarly, there are social welfare programs and concerns related to corrections and public justice even though police science is not social welfare.

Our definitional guidelines are complex, but a student needs to understand this as the necessary concomitant of a society that is mixed in its functions between market and nonmarket activities and that is specialized and multidisciplinary in its provision of services. There is no easy answer or way out. But we think that the boundaries we have suggested will give us relative clarity in seeing what is part of our social welfare system and what is not. Briefly, everything for the enhancement of social functioning is encompassed, except those activities and functions clearly part of another domain or territory.

Social Policy, Social Services, and Social Work

Before proceeding, there are a few other terms that frequently come up in social welfare and need to be defined.

Social Policy

Social policy refers both to the social decision-making process by which a course of action is selected, defined, and promoted (policy making) and to the product or outcome of that process (the resulting policy). Although social policy may be made in both the public and private sectors, the preponderance of social policy is determined by what governments choose to do or not to do. They regulate certain behaviors, organize bureaucracies and programs, distribute benefits, and collect taxes. Our concern is with social policy and its relationship to social welfare.

Social Services

It is probably simplest to think of *social services* as those activities conducted by social welfare institutions. Occasionally, such services will be delivered by institutions that are not recognizable as social welfare institutions, and therefore, it is helpful to think in terms of services delivered rather than simply of social welfare institutions. To the extent that an institution delivers a social service, one could argue that it is, by definition, a social welfare institution. But the distinction is helpful, because often a largely nonwelfare institution will deliver a social service; for example, social services are provided by the Department of Defense, Corrections, and Industry but neither defense, corrections, nor industry as institutions can be considered social welfare institutions themselves.

Social services include both *personal services* (services to individuals based on relationships) and more *institutional services* (income programs, housing projects, and the like). Social services do not merely replace or seek to correct the family or earlier social forms; they are also new responses to new social situations. Alfred Kahn defines social services in terms of the functions they serve:

1. To strengthen and repair family and individual functioning with reference to ongoing roles.
2. To provide new institutional outlets for socialization, development, and assistance, roles that once were but are no longer discharged by the nuclear or extended family, neighbors, or the kin network.
3. To develop institutional forms for new activities essential to individuals, families, and groups in the complex urban society even though they are unknown in a simple society.[8]

Social Work

It is important that *social work* not be confused with social welfare or social services. Social work is a *professionalized occupation*. It operates largely in the delivery of social services and in social welfare institutions. Social welfare is the primary arena in which it operates. Social services are what it provides. Social work is the major professional provider in the social welfare arena. If an analogy might help, think of medical doctors as the professional group in the arena of health services. However, not everyone who provides social services is a social worker, just as not everyone providing medical services is a medical doctor.

The distinction can become very important. Headlines around the country, on occasion, proclaim that a "social worker" had failed to save a child from brutal abuse by a parent. Most times this person was not a professional social worker, but there is a tendency to use the term for anyone working in the social services.

Ideology, Social Policy, and Government Intervention

Decisions regarding government action or inaction and regarding program design are predicated on particular views of the society and its functions. These basic beliefs reflect values strongly held by diverse groups, which have different assumptions about the nature of society, the role of government, and the path to attain the general welfare.

During the early 1960s, Daniel Bell and others introduced the idea that ideology had become tangential, a thing of the past, or only of value in developing nations.[9] According to the "end of ideology" thinkers, developed nations such as the United States, those of western Europe, and even the former Soviet Union were confronted not by conflicts of values or ideology but instead by issues of strategy, bureaucracy, and expertise. From this perspective, all developed nations, regardless of economic system, faced one central issue: how to make the system work. The trend that Bell described in the 1960s seems to be confirmed by recent events in the former Soviet bloc. In addition to moves to democratize their societies, the former Soviet Union splintered into separate nations, and other eastern European states are moving from centrally planned economies and toward more or less free enterprise—driven economies. The outcomes of these efforts remain to be seen because there are also countervailing forces in eastern Europe and elsewhere.

However, Francis Fukuyama of the U.S. State Department's policy planning staff—stressing the power of ideas—concluded that the era of "post-history" had arrived. Liberal democracy had triumphed. Fukuyama suggested what we may be witnessing is not just the end of the Cold War, or the passing of a particular period of postwar history, but the end of history as such—that is, the endpoint of mankind's ideological evolution and the universalization of Western liberal democracy as the final form of human government.

According to this view, there is no viable alternative ideology; liberal democracy—politics and culture—will have the field to itself. Others thought the future would remain, as always, contingent, changing, unforeseeable, and replete with unanticipated events. But there has not been a universal acceptance of market-based, capitalist democracies. Economic crises in Asia, Russia, South America, and Mexico, all had to be handled by governmental and international organization interventions as the shortcomings of markets and global capitalism became problematic.[10]

Samuel Mencher, in a prescient 1967 work, "Ideology and the Welfare Society," challenged the idea that social policy is chiefly determined by technical problems. In his view, ideological conflict is endemic to issues of expertise, governmental involvement in welfare, the balance of social and individual interests, and the goals of state policy. Ideology drives policy decisions critical to social welfare and social work. Ideology and values help to determine policies related to such questions as this: To what extent should the distribution of income resulting from the private economic market be permitted to be the final determinant of the distribution of income among the members of the society? And to what extent should the use of national income be dominated by private or public choices?[11]

The answers to these questions are based not only on ideological assumptions but also appear to be determined by the context in which they are asked. The Wall Street panic of October 1929 led to the Great Depression, and by early 1933 one in every four persons in the labor force was unemployed. Very few, if any families, were unaffected by a world that seemed to be crumbling. Within that context, President Franklin D. Roosevelt shifted ideological gears and instituted a New Deal, calling upon new governmental methods of intervention to meet unprecedented conditions. Pragmatically moving on many fronts, the New Deal attempted to shore up the economy, bring order and hope into a society experiencing conflict and pain, and restore as quickly as possible humane living conditions for as many people as possible. The failure of the unlimited free market required counterbalances, so the New Deal created and utilized Social Security, unemployment insurance, home mortgage guarantees, rural electrification, farm price supports, bank deposit insurance, and other social programs to improve the general welfare.

When President Ronald Reagan stated in his first inaugural address that "government is not the solution to our problem; government is the problem," he sought to enhance a laissez faire attitude, reflective of a conservative philosophy. In general, the Reagan ideology promoted reduced taxes; deregulation of industry; return of powers to the state and local levels; less government, particularly at the federal level; "getting government off the backs of the people"; and encouragement of the business community while reducing the social welfare efforts of U.S. government—all intended to spur individual initiative. Minimal government with a spartan welfare state was the ideal Reagan sought.

Many persons saw these directions as an effort to return to social Darwinism. During the Reagan era, the focus on individualism and materialism were enhanced, while the thrust for public purposes, governmental responsibility, and mutual aid were blunted.

Social policy literature during this period supported this philosophy. Jude Wanniski, in *The Way the World Works: How Economics Fail—and Succeed*, wrote of the world that will ultimately reject all systems that do not revolve around the individual.[12] George Gilder championed an unbridled supply-side economics and capitalism of "high adventure and redemptive morality."[13] Charles Murray went a step further to claim in *Losing Ground* that social programs, including income transfers, were "disastrous for poor people of all races, but for poor blacks especially, and most emphatically for poor blacks in all-black communities." According to this view, "it is indeed possible that steps to relieve misery can create misery."[14] The theme of the destructiveness of social welfare continues, and Marvin Olasky's highly influential *The Tragedy of American Compassion* indicted all governmental social welfare, affecting the Personal Responsibility and Work Opportunity Reconciliation Act (1996). According to him, the War on Poverty was a disaster; an emphasis on entitlements displaced a focus on need; and the United States should return social services to compassionate private and religious institutions.[15] For some, these books were clarion calls for individualism and laissez faire.

Others saw a return to social Darwinism as the Reagan administration challenged social welfare programs, shifted expenditures from domestic and social concerns—especially those to help poor people—to defense, and called into question social welfare supports that had been won and accepted over many years. To some, the retrenchment of aid to the poor and vulnerable was understood as a social Darwinistic "blaming the victim" in the sense that spending for the poor was somehow responsible for the nation's problems and that—according to this view—the poor, regardless of general economic conditions, should be able to fend for themselves.

These examples reflect the expression of two major U.S. political ideologies, which can be roughly categorized as liberalism and conservatism. Liberals place an emphasis on equality before the law, equal treatment by the state, the protection of individual rights and freedoms, and government as a necessary protector of individuals from abuse by the market and other societal forces. The belief in the use of government as a corrective to foster justice and equality of opportunity is combined with a desire to preserve the rights of individuals and the right to own private property, including the means of production. Liberals support government intervention in the economy to offset the failures of capitalism and the market economy. On a more philosophical level, liberals generally believe in the possibility of improvement of the human condition and the possibility of progress. Things can be made to work; the future will bring improvements; barriers can be overcome. Liberals believe that the nature of modern society — technology, industrialization, internationalization—requires to one degree or another governmental programs to remedy the loss of liberties by those who are less well-to-do. The combination of affirmative governmental action with a politics of compassion is stressed in order to foster the development and well-being of each individual.[16] Further, liberals can be expected to disfavor legal enforcement of private morality; to favor greater sexual, political, and economic equality while attempting to reduce stark economic inequality through economic and welfare programs; and to favor neutralism—the government should take no side on moral issues and treat all citizens as equals. Finally, liberals do not insist on equality of result, only equality of access and opportunity.[17]

Conservatism emphasizes a defense of the status quo and resistance to major proposals for change in the economy and in the political sphere. Change should be moderated and the role of government limited, especially in regard to regulation of the economy, thus placing greater emphasis on economic free enterprise. Conservatives encourage individual achievement and favor the expansion of the private sector wherever possible, demonizing governmental action, idealizing the voluntary sector, and promoting entrepreneurialism, all as countervailing forces against government control. Major tenets of conservatism focus on private property rights and a belief in free enterprise. Conservatives believe that the private sector is capable of handling many societal problems and resist turning to the federal government for solutions to societal problems such as the amelioration of poverty, much preferring to turn to state and municipal action before federal action. Stability is a priority for conservatives in regard to the dollar, economics, politics, and international affairs. This emphasis on stability is also found among conservatives who believe that the traditional values of hard work, ambition, and self-reliance will lead to individual and family well-being. From a societal point of view, conservatives believe that individual effort, tax reductions, and a free economy will best achieve economic and social welfare. Their goal is equity. That is, if everyone is provided with an equal opportunity to compete, conservatives want to minimize policies that are designed to shape the final result.[18]

These descriptions of the traditional beliefs of conservatives provide an incomplete picture. Conservatives have both a social and an economic agenda. Although they may favor individual rights in regard to gun possession and property rights, or less regulation for businesses, they may concurrently argue against certain personal liberties such as abortion, family planning, sex out of marriage, homosexuality, and pornography. At the same time conservatives wish to conserve certain parts of the economy and society, they are more change oriented regarding deregulation, tariffs, immigration, and tax relief for the wealthy and reversing some values they find repugnant. They do, however, believe with some consistency that social injustice and inequality are best overcome through personal initiative and effort. Almost everyone, they believe, can improve his or her situation within an unregulated free-enterprise system.

The liberal-conservative conceptualization introduced here is generalized and is often encountered in discussions as social welfare decisions are contemplated. However, it is important to understand that these are ambiguous definitions and that each of the major camps include opposing perspectives. In addition, when it suits both the left and the right they can move from ostensibly ideologically pure positions. There are libertarian conservatives who defend individual private freedoms, want a sharply limited state and government, and advocate no governmental interference regarding private sexual activity. Libertarians emphasize both personal and economic liberty and believe that free markets in all aspects of life lead to free minds. Other conservatives favor governmental interference regarding such issues as abortion, "Baby Doe" cases, pornography, prayers in public schools, and private sexual behavior. Liberalism is also not monolithic. Some liberals may uphold the absolute right of free speech and assembly while others support censorship of movies, musical recordings, access to pornography, and seek limitations on harmful, "too free" speech.

From a political point of view, the United States has been relatively inhospitable to radical groups of either the left or right; democratic socialists and Marxists on the one hand and fascists or radical conservatives on the other have failed historically to win mass support. Although radicalism can emerge from either extreme, extreme radicalism never took hold as the dominant ideology. In general, radicalism has arisen from the right. One of the reasons that the United States has been inhospitable to radical groups has been its relative success in providing for the needs of most people, more so than most other societies. While there are many individual exceptions and ambiguities, and although it is very difficult, if not impossible, to describe definitively the two main political streams in American life, we view liberalism and conservatism as general trends and descriptions that are incomplete shortcuts to understanding—but nevertheless convey political stances and directions.

As a further aid toward understanding the basic assumptions that influence our thinking about social policy and program choices, we examine briefly several major sociopolitical theories. The predominant perspectives are *structural-functional* theory (sometimes called "integrator theories") and *conflict* theory. The major assumptions of structural-functional theory include the following:

- *Stability.* Institutions serve positive purposes, contributing to the maintenance of society and the realization of its main goals;
- *Harmony.* The various parts of society cooperate for the good of the whole; and
- *Evolution.* Change occurs through adaptation to meet new needs and demands.

All of this occurs in general through consensus. From the perspective of structural-functional theory, an observer wants to know the nature of the social structure and what the consequences are of that structure. This theory supports a more static, conservative analysis of social systems which implies a preservation of the status quo.

Conflict theory views the world as continual conflict and change. Society is replete with competititon and conflict, and there are always winners and losers. There is an emphasis on stress and conflict and the ways in which they contribute to social change. The major assumptions of *conflict theory* include the following. *Competition for scarce resources is at the heart of all relationships, and competition rather than consensus is characteristic of human relationships. There is structured inequality* so that those who have power and get the rewards strive to maintain them. From the perspective of conflict theory, observers want to know who benefits from the social structures and how those who benefit maintain their advantage. Paradoxically, conflict theorists want to know how the society is functional for whom.[19] Despite the contradictory assumptions of the structural-functional and conflict theories, a synthesis of the two models involves perceiving society as having "two faces of equal reality   one of stability, harmony, and consensus, and one of change, conflict, and constraint." This combination of opposites suggests that a more realistic model has to combine both the order and and the conflict perspectives. A more complex understanding of society views both perspectives as concurrent and complementary.[20]

As we noted earlier, social policy is both the decision-making process and its outcomes concerned with social welfare, social services, and closely related spheres. Social policy thus refers both to the decision making by which a course of action is determined and to the resulting policy—which is a statement about the aims and planned activities in regard to a particular social problem. From our point of view, social policy can be positive governmental statements or can set direction through omission. To have no stance, or a "hands-off" policy, about a particular problem— that is, to relate to a problem in a laissez-faire manner—is also a policy position.

Four Routes to Social Policy.   Social policies are determined in four basic ways, as indicated in the following paragraphs.

Legislation.   When a legislative body enacts laws that establish the directions the society will take in regard to a particular social problem or issue, it establishes a formal social policy that expresses the aims and expected activities of the society. For example, in 1965 the Congress explicitly set forth several aims of the nation in regard to a growing aging population. The Older Americans Act created the Administration on Aging, and the Social Security Act provided for Medicare, a national system of health insurance for the aged. In 1972, the Supplemental Security Income program shifted aid for the aged, blind, and disabled to a national level from state administrative responsibility.

Governmental Guidelines for the Implementation of Legislation.   Governmental bureaucracies influence social policy in many ways. The guidelines drawn up by the agency charged with implementing certain legislation may be vague or alter the original purposes of the legislative enactment; the staff may not be trained to fulfill the necessary tasks; or governmental agencies can skew the policy through reduced activity. As was noted earlier, the interpretation of the phrase "maximum feasible participation of the poor" made dramatic changes in the War on Poverty, beyond the intent of the original legislation. Passage of a law does not guarantee its implementation consistent with the intentions of the legislators. Writing regulations is a quasi-legislative function, in large part hidden from public view.[21]

Judicial Decisions.   Decisions by courts at various governmental levels can also enunciate social policy and give direction to governmental and societal action. In *Shapiro v. Thompson* (1969) the courts struck down laws requiring a period of in-state residence as a condition of eligibility for public assistance. The Supreme Court decision in *Roe v. Wade* (1973) set forth the constitutional guarantee of the right to privacy and its application to a woman's decision to terminate her pregnancy. *Wyatt v. Stickney* (1972) established for the mentally ill confined in hospitals the right to adequate and effective treatment, a humane physical and psychological environment, adequate numbers of properly trained staff to provide treatment, and individual treatment plans. Similarly, *Youngberg v. Romeo* (1982) established a constitutional right to proper treatment for persons with mental retardation in state facilities.

Following the enactment of the Personal Responsibility and Work Opportunity Reconciliation Act (PRA, 1996), States began to challenge former court rulings related to public assistance such as *Shapiro v. Thompson*. At least eighteen states and the District of Columbia adopted some sort of restrictions on benefits to new residents in their Temporary Assistance for Needy Families programs. These changes were made despite evidence suggesting people do not move to gain public assistance benefits. Various tactics were used: pay new residents the benefit available in their former states for a period of six months or a year; a 30 percent reduction in benefits to all new residents for one year regardless of the state from which they came; denial of benefits for periods of time. These variations were challenged and the California statute that limited the maximum welfare benefits available to newly arrived residents was found unconstitutional by the U.S. Supreme Court in Saenz v. Roe (Supreme Court 1518, 1999). In essence the ruling found that citizens have a right to travel interstate and Congress has no right to authorize the States to violate the Fourteenth Amendment.

Informal Processes.   There is a fourth means for determining social policy; however, it is a matter of *informal* processes rather than formal. Public decision making and choices of societal direction also can be accomplished through a spontaneous understanding of a large-scale public will. Because of this, certain laws stop being enforced or are reversed, such as prohibition or speed limits on highways.

The Federal and Pluralist System

Legislation is a major determinant of social policy and is the result of a political process that involves political parties, special interest groups (for example, agriculture, business, organized labor, professional, religious, environmental, consumer groups), and the media (television, books, films, radio, magazines, and so on, which influence public opinion). In addition, the executive, legislative, and bureaucratic parts of the government also play parts in the process.

The United States is a federal governmental system in which power does not rest solely with the central government nor with the 50 states but, instead, depends upon a sharing of power between a strong central government and strong states. Further, the states share certain powers with local governmental units, which also play important roles, so that power is dispersed among the federal, state, and local governments.

Decision making and implementation in a federal system may involve actions at the federal, state, and local levels by executive, legislative, judicial, bureaucratic, and nongovernmental individuals and organizations within the context of the Constitution. Nongovernmental groups include both the proponents and opponents of particular policies or programs. Added to the complex of potential participants, there also exist regional *quasi-governmental bodies*. For example, in many metropolitan areas, there is significant decision making on issues such as metropolitan transportation, airport, water supply, ports, and solid and hazardous waste authorities formed by the adjoining governmental jurisdictions. Neither the directors nor their staffs are elected. They are responsible to governors or other elected officials but not accountable directly to the electorate. This type of quasi-governmental organization exists in a number of metropolitan and regional areas and exerts enormous influence on people's lives. It can determine the cost of bridge and tunnel tolls, transportation patterns, location of jobs, and so on. As a result, regional semi-governmental organizations are another important player in what is already a highly complex political configuration.

Federalism divides political power among political authorities in the United States. Three and sometimes four governmental jurisdictions (nation, state, county, city) have a set of relationships in which there is no one source for leadership, which tends to result in compromise and piecemeal action. Through public and special interest opinion, certain problems come to the forefront. Many of the groups mentioned previously play a role in the formulation of policy alternatives. Several conflicting proposals are discussed. The potential policy is debated (for example, to change or not change the eligibility rules for a program), and ultimately, a policy is adopted. Successful implementation of the policy depends on the availability of sufficient knowledge for effective implementation, positive attitudes of the implementers, and adequate additional resources (people, dollars).

The Economic Sphere

Social policies are decided and implemented in the context of diverse values and ideologies and political and economic factors. The context and these policies affect every citizen's life and the life of the nation. At this point, we introduce selected *economic* concepts that can assist us in understanding the economic factors that affect social welfare decisions.

Economics is the study of income, production, and distribution of goods and services and is the study of social systems used to allocate scarce resources for different uses. In general, there are two major concerns of policymakers: growth and equality. *Growth* is the increase in total output; *equality* is concerned with how that output is divided among the population.

The economy of the United States is capitalist, by which we mean that the basic raw materials, means of production, and the goods produced are primarily privately owned. However, even in the United States state ownership can be found in electric power utilities, housing, transportation systems, public forests, and parks. In socialist societies, the productive assets are predominantly state owned. In regard to state and private ownership, nations can be found along a continuum. Over time, ownership patterns have in general been shifting toward the private sector, but most nations have a mixed pattern.

The United States utilizes a market system in which decisions are decentralized and made through the interaction of individuals, businesses, and other organizations. People are free to work where they wish but must compete for jobs. One is free to buy or sell whatever one possesses or has sufficient resources to purchase. It is often assumed that in capitalism free markets most effectively allocate goods and services to their best use. The way in which that allocation takes place in market systems is through prices. Prices act as signals to people to make their economic decisions and reflect their preferences, desires, and costs.

Conversely, other systems utilize centralized decision makers who decide what is to be done and issue directives to achieve certain desired ends. Individual choice is constrained by the expectations and regulations of the centralized system. In the decade following the collapse of the Soviet Union and following the problems of the debt crises that strained the governmental budgets in developing countries, there has been a shift more toward market systems and away from planned economies.

The federal government (and state and local governments) exists within our capitalist society and may use fiscal and monetary policies for various purposes, deliberately or not: to increase employment and reduce unemployment or vice versa, achieve price stability, enhance productivity, and redistribute wealth or income.

Fiscal Policy

Fiscal policy is the use of *government spending* and *tax policies.* Government expenditures directly and government taxation indirectly through disposable income affect the demand for goods and services. The timing, size, and combination of these actions are important factors. When the federal budget is balanced, tax revenues and expenditures are exactly equal. If revenues are more than expenditures, the budget is in surplus. The reverse means the budget is in deficit. Deficits require an increase in borrowing by the government, obtained from the private sector or the central bank by selling treasury bills and bonds, a promise to repay a stated amount sometime in the future (both short term and long term). A government bond is to be paid in the more distant future.

The government can purchase goods and services or make infrastructure investments. In addition, the government transfers payments through social insurance programs, public assistance, and subsidies to agricultural, business, and industrial components of the nation.

Tax policy, the pattern by which individuals, families, and businesses are taxed, influences the amount of income/wealth available to individuals and businesses. There are three types of taxes. A tax is *progressive* if the average tax rate is higher for those with higher incomes: Those who are wealthier pay a higher percentage of their income. The tax rate percentage is larger as income rises. For example, a person whose income is $20,000 might not pay a tax or pay at a low percentage rate, while those who earn $300,000 pay at a 35 percent rate. A graduated income tax is an example of this type. *Regressive* taxes are those that take a larger percentage of income in taxes from poorer persons than from wealthier persons. Examples are sales taxes, the social security payroll tax, cigarette, gasoline, alcohol and beer, and airplane taxes. Thus, there is a larger relative burden on low-income persons than on those with higher incomes. A *proportional* tax is one in which all taxpayers pay exactly the same proportion of income, a constant percentage of their incomes. An example of this is the Medicare tax as part of the overall Social Security tax. The crucial differences are whether the tax takes from higher-income people the same fraction of income as from those with lower incomes (proportional), a larger fraction of income from wealthier people (progressive), or a smaller fraction of income from wealthier persons than it takes from lower income people (regressive). In Table 6.1 one can observe the differences/similarities of these three types of taxes.

A new form of taxation was introduced as a major issue during the 1996 presidential campaign—the *flat tax.* Although first introduced during the 1992 campaign by Edmund G. ("Jerry") Brown Jr., a former governor of California, it did not make headway but became a prominent issue. The flat tax would simplify an elaborate and complex tax system by eliminating a sliding scale of tax rates and make all taxpayers pay the same percentage of their income. Almost all deductions would be

TABLE 6.1 *Three Types of Taxes*

Income	Regressive Tax Paid/Income%		Progressive Tax Paid/Income%		Proportional Tax Paid/Income%	
$10,000	$1,000,	10%	$1,500,	15%	$150,	.015%
$50,000	$1,000,	2%	$12,500,	25%	$750,	.015%
$100,000	$1,000,	1%	$40,000,	40%	$1500,	.015%

removed so that wealthier persons could not use deductions available only to them. Some persons argued that the elimination of "loopholes" would be fairer and reduce the size and cost of the internal revenue system.

Charitable deductions, income from interest and stocks, mortgage interest payments, and other deductions would be eliminated. The claim was made by proponents that people would support charities sufficiently without the ability to claim that deduction. Also it was suggested that people would not object to very wealthy persons avoiding taxes on interest and dividends because they would believe this income would already have been taxed at the corporation level.

Democrats and many Republicans argued against this type of tax, claiming it would have to be set at a level higher than claimed by proponents in order to gain sufficient tax income to balance the budget and reduce the federal debt, and the tax would favor the rich. Bankers and insurance and real estate companies were early opponents of the idea.

Another proposal is to tax consumption by instituting a national retail sales tax. A simple, single-rate sales tax would be paid on all new goods and services. Included would be a tax refund system so families would not pay taxes on the purchase of necessities. Called the Fair Tax, critics claimed the math supporting the plan was faulty and a third of the estimate of revenue was based on taxes the government would pay to itself. Furthermore, one fourth of the anticipated sales taxes would be paid on things like church services, free care at veteran's hospitals, and free checking accounts and other difficult-to-tax financial services.[22]

Monetary Policy

In the United States the central bank, the Federal Reserve Board, controls the banking system. It is through this mechanism that the government's monetary policy is executed. The Federal Reserve System ("the Fed") began operation in 1914 after passage of the Federal Reserve Act (1913). There is a board of governors appointed by the president. The seven members serve 14-year, staggered, nonrenewable terms of office, which overlap presidential administrations. The chairperson is appointed to a 4-year renewable term. (All appointments are confirmed by the Senate.) There are 12 Federal Reserve regional banks that serve various regions of the nation. The Federal Open Market Committee (FOMC) is composed of representatives of the board of governors and the regional Federal Reserve banks. The

Federal Reserve Bank of New York (FRBNY) is the most important regional bank, executing much of monetary policy and acting in the international economy, in addition to other responsibilities. The board of governors is now relatively independent of both executive and congressional controls, but in the past from time to time has been more easily pressured by the administration or Congress.

One of the most important functions of the Federal Reserve is control of the supply of money. The Federal Reserve, through *"open-market operations,"* can purchase or sell government securities on the open market, which contracts or expands the money supply. When the Federal Reserve buys a bond or bill from a household or firm, it pays money into the person's or firm's bank account, increasing the supply of money both for the individual or firm and for the bank. Conversely, when the Fed sells securities, it "soaks up" the money available for spending or loans. Dollars held by the Fed are not counted as part of the money supply. Dollars held by banks, individuals, and firms are counted as part of the money supply.

The Federal Reserve can also control the supply of available money by raising or lowering banks' deposit requirements—that is, the *required reserves of banks.* A bank's reserve is the amount of money it must set aside as an assurance toward its ability to pay out money owed to depositors. Money kept in reserve is unavailable for being lent out. It is the bank's money-lending ability that gives it its special role in the creation of money. The higher the required bank deposit reserve, the less money is available for banks to lend; the lower the requirement, the more money available for lending.

There are still other ways in which the Federal Reserve controls the supply of money. Banks may borrow from the Federal Reserve and from other banks. In the first case, the Fed sets a *discount rate* (the rate at which the Fed will lend money to banks). By increasing or decreasing the discount rate at which banks can borrow from it, the Fed influences the rate that banks can charge potential customers. Banks pass on the higher interest rates to their customers. The higher the rate, the lower the number of consumers who will borrow. The lower the rate, the easier it is to borrow. In the second case, the Fed sets the *federal funds rate*, which is the rate banks pay for interbank borrowing of money overnight.

Money supply and money demand interact to determine the price level and interest rates. Interest rates are important because they provide an incentive for firms or individuals to make real decisions regarding investment, consumption, borrowing, and lending. The importance of money and hence monetary policy comes from the three roles money plays: (1) as a store of value—inflation eats away at this stored value; (2) as facilitator of transactions—unstable prices make economic transactions complex and difficult; and (3) as a unit of account—businesses and households need an accurate measurement of what they are worth.

The Importance of Fiscal and Monetary Policy

The importance of fiscal and monetary policy for social welfare is that the state of the economy—for example, how many and the types of jobs available, inflation (too many dollars chasing too few goods) and deflation (too many goods chasing too few dollars), and where jobs are located—is determined in part by these policy decisions. Fiscal policy is an important factor in managing the economy through alterations in government spending, borrowing, and tax rates.

One governmental role reflects the economic theories of John Maynard Keynes, a British economist. Keynes viewed economic depressions as a result of individuals and businesses decreasing substantially or stopping spending altogether and investing because interest rate changes or price changes were insufficient inducements to spend. These spending reductions cause a drop in output, usually with both job losses and wage decreases. Increased governmental spending or tax reductions can increase *the demand side of the economy,* which in turn leads to higher output and employment. High inflation, on the other hand, can be countered by raising tax rates or cutting government spending, unlikely events, to reduce demand. It is obvious how governmental expenditures or taxes (along with private decisions) influence the well-being of the citizenry. Monetarily, an increase in the money supply can offset a sluggish economy when unemployment is high. There is a belief that there is a "natural" rate of unemployment below which inflation will be accelerated, referred to as *NAIRU,* the nonaccelerating inflation rate of unemployment. The goal is to have inflation and unemployment in equilibrium, inflation neither rising nor falling. Recent evidence about this phenomenon has raised questions about the assumed rule.[23]

During the 1980s, the Reagan administration stressed quite a different economic theory known as *supply-side* theory (yet it was still "Keynesian" to the extent that output could be influenced by government tax and spending policies). This theory emphasized *tax cuts,* thought to *encourage saving, increase investment,* and thus *improve productivity.* To make the tax cuts more acceptable, some economists argued that with sustained growth in the economy, tax revenues would increase even with the tax break, offsetting any revenue lost through the initial tax cuts. However, the actual experience was that government deficits increased dramatically, and the substantial federal debt (the total of all previous deficits) created problems for the nation: high interest rates; overvalued dollars, which leads to increased imports and decreased exports; and future tax liabilities.

During the Reagan administration, in addition to a massive tax cut during his first term, spending in total dollars was increased. (In percentage terms, social spending for entitlements grew quickest.) The result of these actions was an increase in federal budget deficits and a tripling of the federal debt. An important factor that determines the ability of the nation to repay the debt is the *gross national product* (GNP), which includes all U.S.-owned production within the United States or at any other location and excludes production in the United States owned by foreigners. Another statistical summary is the *gross domestic product* (GDP), which counts all the production within the nation's borders regardless of whether the firm is owned by U.S. citizens.

Huge federal debts carry several problems. They may strain the ability of the nation to repay them in a timely manner. These debts shift tax burdens to future generations for the actions of current governmental services. The interest on an overlarge national debt is in itself a great burden on the budget and moves dollars away from private-sector productive investment by individuals and households ("crowding out"). To reduce deficits and the debt, the government has to either raise taxes, cut governmental spending, or use inflation to erode the value of the debt. These are not popular governmental actions.

There are several other economic concepts that students should become familiar with in order to think about social welfare within the socio-politico-economic context. The economy continually fluctuates in regard to the pace of economic activity. The economy is cyclical with "booms" as well as "busts." Eras of expansion and prosperity are followed by recessions (increased unemployment and lowered demand for goods and services with unused industrial productive capacity) or depressions (deep unemployment, loss of confidence in the future, few new investments). During the 1970s, the United States experienced "stagflation," which was inflation concurrent with unemployment. In the 1990s, during an economic boom some economic "truths" did not hold up. The Phillips Curve suggests that there can be low inflation or low unemployment but not at the same time. In the 1990s, this was not the case because unemployment (officially lowest since 1970, but many unemployed persons are not counted) and inflation both were low. Growth was strong in the 1990s despite fiscal constraints and a reduced federal deficit. The money supply increased rapidly but this did not result in inflation. In the early years of the 21st century, the assumed relationship between productivity, unemployment, and inflation did not hold up.[24]

Cycles are caused by fluctuations in "demand shocks," that is, shifts in consumption, and "supply shocks," for example, the oil crisis. The cyclical pattern derives from leaps and lags in the economy. Investment decisions typically are not made instantaneously; decision makers take time to react to "signals" in the economy, such as interest rates and prices, and the implementation of decisions also takes time. Factors that influence these decisions are changes in consumer preferences and expectations, interest rates, taxes, transfer payments, government expenditures, and technology changes. Another influence on economic fluctuations is change in investment expenditures. These expenditures are related to interest rates and include inventories, residential housing construction, plants and equipment, and infrastructure.

Spending has a *multiplier effect;* that is, the recipients of the payments engage in further spending of their own. New employment and incomes are created and—in turn—create further demand for goods and services. When the economy is in recession, certain social welfare programs (for example, unemployment insurance) provide *counter-cyclical* investments. They provide income to recipients that is spent, thereby offsetting the strength of the recession. During business cycle peaks, more social insurance taxes are paid. The effect of these counter-cyclical actions is to modify the sharpness of the business cycle.

An International Economy

Goods and services flow constantly among nations—food, raw materials, machinery, microchips, financial consultation, engineering, and so on. In almost every sphere of life, we can see the impact of imports and exports as international trade has expanded. Our nation exports goods such as Chevrolets, Coca Cola, teachers, banking and finance, construction, and movies, and imports goods and services such as Toyotas, Gucci, Absolut, Guinness, Volkswagen, software design, and Nestlé, Shell, and Heineken. In addition, U.S. firms own and produce goods in overseas locations, while other nations do the same in the United States. When U.S. industries as multinational corporations operate overseas subsidiaries, there are limits to the extent they can be controlled by the United States. A number of U.S. corporations depend to a significant extent on the profits of these overseas operations.

Production, marketing, and finance have become internationalized so that the decisions of boards of directors meeting in Germany can affect the economy of South Carolina and decisions made in Japan can affect the types of jobs in California and Ohio. Similarly, decisions made in Detroit or Dallas have an impact in many parts of the world.

The international economy is extremely complex but has importance for social welfare in several ways: (1) International trading influences the overall well-being of our society. Trade patterns and exchange rates influence the pattern and types of jobs in the economy. (2) The productivity and competitive ability of U.S. industries is forced to compete in this complex arena. (3) In general, the interdependent world economy has its greatest impacts in two ways: (a) capital mobility affects investment, inflation, interest rates, and the effectiveness of government policies across countries and (b) individual decisions affect micro-level consequences—where jobs are, what they pay, and what is traded. Our citizens, as well as the citizens of other nations, have to live with these decisions. (4) Decisions in one country—for example, the United States, Canada, or Mexico—can cause harm to other nations through "exporting" inflation, transferring capital, labor, or other resources, by the creation of pollution, acid rain, over-fishing, and other factors. (5) Groups of countries can join together to raise or lower the price of commodities through creating monopolies or otherwise controlling the market. Finally, (6) the ways other nations deal with their social welfare systems in relation to their contextual factors—unemployment, budget difficulties—give signals and form a climate of opinion about what is proper and permissible.

A Second Welfare System—Corporate Welfare

As we examine specific programs commonly identified as social welfare in chapters 9 and 10, one should keep in mind there is another welfare system, one that benefits individuals and corporations through tax breaks and subsidies.

Tax expenditures are revenue losses attributable to provisions of the federal tax laws that allow special exclusions, exemptions, or deductions from gross income or that provide special credits, preferential tax rates, or deferral of tax liabilities. They are, therefore, any reductions in individual and corporate tax liabilities that result from special tax provisions or regulations that provide tax benefits to particular taxpapers. These tax provisions are referred to as tax expenditures because they are analogous to direct spending programs, both of which may have similar budget policy objectives. Tax expenditures are most similar to direct spending programs that have no spending limits and are available as entitlements to those who meet the established statutory criteria.

To gain a sense of the dimensions of tax expenditures, estimates for the fiscal years 2002–2006 prepared by the Office of Management and Budget would result in an anticipated total of $3.85 trillion dollars over the five years. Among the larger expenditures are mortgage interest deductions by home owners, enhanced oil recovery credit, capital gains, depreciation of machinery and equipment, and exclusion of employer contributions for medical insurance premiums and medical care.[25]

Individual and corporate welfare costs taxpayers as much or more than means-tested assistance programs such as Temporary Assistance to Needy Families, Food Stamps, housing assistance, and child nutrition. Many expenditures are to encourage business, trade, development of natural resources, and other economic developments. One way in which government supports corporations is through research grants and subsidies. Even where no business will reap large profits, it may be necessary for the federal government to fund basic research in areas that have potential for enriching society. One never knows the potential of basic research or the possibilities of programs such as NASA, materials science, biotechnology, or other investigations. So one can assume there ought to be a federal role in which industry is subsidized, but questions can be raised about the aims, dimensions, and efficacy of such subsidies. Some subsidies provide housing or health care but others may be little more than political payoffs to constituents or business expense expenditures that businesses might be expected to pay themselves. It is interesting to note that the calls during the 1990s for reform and cutting of social programs were forceful and intense, but the call to reduce individual and corporate welfare through the tax system was muted.

A Changed World—New/Old Ideology, New Politics, New Economic Forces, New Social Policy, and New Social Services

Global issues that concern many nations and the broad spectrum of society have arisen and hold special importance for social welfare. The world has entered an age of intense international competition related to economic growth, employment, productivity, budget deficits, taxation, motivation, as well as ideologies deemed to be supportive of successful economic competition.

A backlash arose against social welfare provision in widely separated places, including western Europe, Canada, New Zealand, central and eastern Europe, and in the United States. In a number of South American and Caribbean nations social security pensions have been devalued and health services have deteriorated. Chile moved to privatize its social welfare system.

In the United States there has been a return to traditional anti-federalism, a focus on individual and family responsibility as social welfare strategies that do not cost tax dollars, and these along with voluntary efforts have once again become ascendent values. Many citizens and legislators turn away from governmental action and social welfare programs on the basis of political ideology. In their view, governmental action and social welfare programs are incompetent, untrustworthy, and cost-inefficient; undermine self-reliance by encouraging dependence; are tilted against freedom and autonomy; and undermine economic productivity. Such attitudes tap into deeply held beliefs by Americans. Only 34 percent of Americans basically trust the government, and there is a sense that politicians are corrupt. Nevertheless, two-thirds of Americans have positive views of federal workers and particular federal agencies, a view that contrasts with their negative view of Government as a whole.[26]

Among the factors that support these new directions are reevaluations of welfare financing, aging populations, technological innovations, and widespread aversion to taxes. Various groups have used the current situation to begin "rolling back" welfare programs. Major congressional figures have argued that people are not entitled to anything but opportunity. Calls for cost-containment and efficiency affect social welfare programs at every level and, undoubtedly, will continue to affect social welfare's future.

Until recent times, the creation of the modern world has brought with it the welfare state. However, as we entered the 21st century, the thrust of social welfare in the United States since the Great Depression was challenged by Republican and conservative forces, often joined by members of the Democratic party and by other former supporters of governmental action and services for people. This major challenge took place in a context that included a large federal debt, popular resistance to taxes, general discontent with government, shifts in federal funding expectations of the states, and a desire by conservatives to cut taxes and return federal functions to the state level. Critics charged that social welfare was too expensive, undermined the traditional family, encouraged the increase of single-parent families and children born out of wedlock, failed to reduce the number of poor persons, and fostered dependence.

Social welfare in U.S. society developed in a piecemeal and incremental fashion; it attacked one problem, relatively without regard to other problems that might contribute to the creation of the problem or that influence its dimensions. Although experience might teach that comprehensive and coordinated approaches could offer better solutions to problems and reduce the inadequacies of one program overburdening other programs, comprehensive approaches to social welfare have been impracticable in U.S. society.

Social workers and others may see the needs of people and the positive and negative effects of social welfare programs. But the individual observations of social workers are not made within a vacuum. On the contrary, they take place within the context of a national society at a particular time and state of development. Social welfare is in fact the collective supply of resources, a sharing of the burden or the risk. Two questions have to be asked: (1) What needs should be supplied by the collective action of the society and which left to individual effort? (2) What can the society afford?

What should and can be done to eliminate poverty or to deal with other social problems depends on the ideologies and values of those who make legislative decisions. A "backlash" has grown against social welfare provision in Western Europe. In the United States, a seismic shift is occurring in which individual responsibility is the ascendent philosophy. Many citizens and legislators turn away from governmental action and the programs designed to assist the poor.

Some attribute the successes of pro-market and anti-welfare governments to the fact that many welfare supports were in place minimizing the shock and burden of unemployment. Certainly, to a significant extent, such social welfare benefits minimized the shock and burdens of unemployment in the United States.

But various events have caused nations with highly developed social welfare systems to reevaluate their efforts. High unemployment rates in France, Italy, Spain, and Germany and other industrialized nations during the mid-1990s reached the highest levels those nations experienced since the recovery from World War II. The prospect of chronic joblessness led to examining assumptions about salaries, benefits, and tax policies. There was agreement that one important reason their economies are unable to create sufficient numbers of jobs is the high cost of occupational and social benefits. This led to revisions in the social welfare benefits provided. In addition to unemployment, other pressures reinforcing a need for this reexamination included aging populations, global economic competition, and widespread aversion to taxes.

A Changed Context

Is the modern welfare state self-limiting? To what extent can a viable economy tolerate a welfare state? On the other hand, to what extent can a modern industrial or post-industrial state do without social welfare programs and services? Mass production demands mass purchasing power. Social welfare programs, particularly income maintenance programs, serve the society as *economic stabilizers*. Nevertheless, they must be funded, and these funds are made available through taxation of current or future generations. The complexity of modern society becomes focused on the issue of whether social welfare will expand. The decision is not simply one of social justice or morality but is part and parcel of an economic scene in which taxation grows and is resented. Comprehensive tax legislation based on decade long future forecasts was passed by Congress during Spring, 2001. Doubts were raised because the surplus was committed; there was uncertainty about whether the anticipated surpluses would occur; and concern about what spending priorities would be, chief among them effects on the futures of Social Security and Medicare. Much will depend upon the effects of the War on Terrorism and the anticipated cyclical economic recessions.

At the same time that tax policy alters the nature of social services because of the demands of various parts of the population for fiscal relief, another trend affects social welfare. The entire premise of progressive, liberal thought has become suspect, and questions of a serious nature are being asked about the limits of "doing good." The two-edged nature of social welfare has been recognized, that is, How does a greater emphasis on market exchange (exchanges between buyers and sellers that depend on their relative powers) affect social welfare? This focus on individuals and family responsibility defines the social good as the sum of individual desires and detracts from ideas of communal and societal responsibility. Efficiency is the overriding goal of social policy and results in market-based social policies.

Before we turn in the next chapter to the structural components, alternative characteristics, and evaluation of social welfare programs, we want to introduce here the major contextual factors that affect social welfare ideas, policy, planning, and program decisions in the United States. As one proceeds through the following chapters, be mindful of these background factors:

1. The United States is relatively secure from the threat of war and has no major rival around the world. However, potential global threats include recession/ depression, poverty, pollution, disease, hunger, political disenfranchisement, terrorism, drug trafficking, cultural conflicts, and shortages of fresh water and arable land.
2. There has been a shift in power from governments to markets.
3. The national budget is balanced. Unemployment is down. But looming in the background is a significant federal debt that impedes attention being paid to social programs. At the same time, a budget surplus was achieved for the first time in 30 years. Furthermore, it is unclear how surpluses, if any, can and will be used following massive tax cuts, mainly aimed at the wealthy.
4. The chasm between the rich and the poor continues to increase.
5. There are strong forces that believe that government is ineffective and want to reduce further governmental action and service.
6. The shift from government to the market and voluntary efforts results in the following:

    A. *The privatization of public services.* There has been a shift from governmental provision of social services to provision by corporations. This often results in lower wages, fewer benefits such as health care, and more part-time employment.
    B. *There has been a shift to user charges rather than taxes to finance public services.* It is unclear whether this improves efficiency of services, but the substitution for taxes results in greater monetary burdens for the poor.
    C. *Universal services are replaced by services for those willing and able to pay.* Deregulation ends the requirement to serve low volume places or to price goods so as to ensure universal service.
    D. *Capital mobility has an impact on jobs, people, and communities.* Constraints on plant closings are loosened and jobs are transferred to lower tax or pay scale communities.
    E. *Welfare reform.* The terms of the social welfare debate are shifted from the level of benefits (Can a family live on this benefit?) to a focus on dependency and self-sufficiency. Attention is shifted from societal responsibility and the political and economic systems to individual and family behavior.
    F. *The New Federalism.* Society needs more market discipline, including federal, state, and local governments.[27]

7. Medicare has serious funding problems. Social Security has less serious problems that need to be addressed. There is a growing dominance of managed care plans.

As our society deals with these problems and makes decisions that limit and/or reduce social welfare, there will be positive outcomes but also negative consequences. The balance between positive and negative remains to be weighed. However,

> we can degrade people by caring for them; and we can degrade them by not caring for them.... All interventions have consequences, and one of the things we should learn to keep in the forefront of our consciousness is that the most important consequences of any intervention almost always turn out to be those consequences that were not intended or planned upon or could not have been calculated beforehand.[28]

Summary

In this chapter, we have looked closely at the concept of social welfare and defined and distinguished some essential terms such as social policy, social services, and social work. We have also given an overview of the ideological, political, and economic forces influencing how social policy is determined, social services delivered, and social work practiced. In the economic sphere, we've given a brief overview of monetary and fiscal policy and the types of taxes supporting social welfare. Also introduced are the major contextual factors that will influence for the foreseeable future the potential policy, funding, planning, and program decisions affecting social welfare in our society.

Questions for Consideration

1. We have presented a broad definition of social welfare. Do you agree? How would you change it?

2. Suggest some ways in which ideology impacts on social welfare in your community.

3. Do you know the legislative process in your state regarding social welfare policy and legislation? What advocacy groups play parts in the process? Is it always the same groups?

4. (a) What kinds of taxes support social welfare in your state? Are they fair? (b) Has your state and social welfare been affected by the international economy? In what ways?

5. Does your state provide individual and corporate tax expenditures? To whom?

Notes

1. Adam Clymer, "Simpson Joins Ranks of Pragmatists Leaving Senate," *New York Times,* December 4, 1995, p. B5.

2. Ruth Conniff, "Welfare Profiteers," *The Progressive,* Vol. 61, No. 5, May 1997, p. 33.

3. Russell Baker, "Used to Talk, Now Shrieks," *New York Times,* June 29, 1996, p. 19.

4. Robert L. Barker, *The Social Work Dictionary,* 3rd Edition, Washington, D.C.: NASW, 1995, p. 357.

5. Amy Gutmann, *Democracy and the Welfare State,* Princeton, N.J.: Princeton University Press, 1988, p. 3.

6. Gutmann, p. 3.

7. Richard Titmuss, *Essays on the Welfare State,* "The Social Division of Welfare," Boston: Beacon Press, 1963, pp. 34–35.

8. Alfred J. Kahn, *Social Policy and Social Services,* New York: Random House, 1979, p. 16.

9. Daniel Bell, *The End of Ideology,* New York: Free Press, 1960.

10. Francis Fukuyama, *The End of History and the Last Man,* New York: Free Press, 1992. Charles Wolf, Jr. "Rely on markets to be unreliable," *Baltimore Sun,* January 17, 1999, p. 6c.

11. Samuel Mencher, "Ideology and the Welfare Society," *Social Work,* Vol. 12, July 1967, pp. 3–11.

12. Jude Wanniski, *The Way the World Works: How Economics Fail—and Succeed,* New York: Basic Books, 1978.

13. George Gilder, *Wealth and Poverty,* New York: Basic Books, 1981, p. x.

14. Charles Murray, *Losing Ground: American Social Policy, 1950–1980,* New York: Basic Books, 1984, pp. 9, 223.

15. Marvin Olasky, *The Tragedy of American Compassion,* Washington, D.C.: Regnery Publishing, 1995.

16. James MacGregor Burns, J. W. Peltason, and Thomas E. Cronin, *Government by the People,* Englewood Cliffs, N.J.: Prentice Hall, 1987, pp. 435–436.

17. Ronald Dworkin, "Why Liberals Should Believe in Equality," *New York Review of Books,* Vol. XXX, No. 1, February 3, 1983, pp. 32–34.

18. J. M. Burns, J. W. Peltason, and T. E. Cronin, p. 437.

19. David B. Brinkerhoff, Lynn K. White, and Suzanne T. Ortega, *Essentials of Sociology,* 2d Edition, New York: West Publishing Co., 1992, pp. 10, 12–13; Neil J. Smelser, *Sociology,* Cambridge, MA.: Blackwell Publishers, 1994, pp. 26–27.

20. D. Stanley Eitzen, *In Conflict and Order: Understanding Society,* Boston: Allyn and Bacon, 1985, p. 45.

21. See John W. Kingdon, *Agendas, Alternatives, and Public Policies,* Boston: Little, Brown, 1984.

22. Robert S. McIntyre, "Kooky, the 23 Percent Solution," *New York Times,* January 23, 1998, p. A25.

23. Louis Uchitelle, "Epitaph For a Rule That Just Won't Die," *New York Times,* Business, July 30, 2000, p. 4; Michael M. Weinstein, "Unemployment's natural rate may have a mind of its own," *New York Times,* April 22, 1999, p. C2.

24. Sylvia Nasar, "Unlearning the Lessons of Econ 101," *New York Times Week in Review,* May 3, 1998, p. A26.

25. The White House, Office of Management and Budget, Table 22-4. *Tax Expenditures by Function, www.whitehouse.gov/omb/budget/fy2002/bud22_4.html,* June 11, 2001, 1–11.

26. Katharine Q. Seelye, "Americans Take a Dim View of the Government, Survey Finds," *New York Times,* March 10, 1998, p. A15.

27. Peter S. Fisher, "The Economic Context of Community-Centered Practice: Markets, Communities, and Social Policy," in *Reinventing Human Services,* Paul Adams and Kristine Nelson, eds., New York: Aldine DeGruyter, 1995, pp. 41–58.

28. Steven Marcus, "Their Brothers' Keepers: An Episode from English History," in *Doing Good: The Limits of Benevolence,* Willard Gaylin, ed., New York: Pantheon, 1978, pp. 65–66.

7

Examining a Social Welfare Program

Structural Components, Alternative Program Characteristics, and Evaluation

It is a hard thing to be a poor man in any culture, but hardest to be a poor man in a rich culture.

—Max Lerner[1]

Overview

What tools does a student need in order to develop a coherent understanding of a social welfare program, some intelligent analysis of its characteristics, and some informed opinion as to its desirability? First, a student needs to know what basic components there are in any social welfare program. Second, he or she needs to know what some of the basic issues are about various ways of organizing social welfare programs and various characteristics that they may possess. Third, a student should have some beginning background in the political, social, and economic context that affects human need and social welfare decisions to meet those needs. Finally, the student needs to know what criteria he or she must apply to any social welfare program in order to evaluate it.

This chapter presents a rigorous schema for understanding and analyzing a given social welfare program. Prepared with this schema for examining the structure of a welfare program, a student can then apply it to a variety of social welfare programs in the United States, both economic security programs and programs that are generally termed the "personal social services." The schema for examining a social welfare program is summarized in Chart 7.1.[2]

Structural Components

What Are the Needs and Goals to Be Met?

Social welfare programs, like all other governmental and private programs, are intended to meet certain needs, deal with specific problems, or enhance life. They are implemented to achieve particular goals in relation to needs such as economic security, child care, and health care; to ameliorate such problems as teen pregnancy, homelessness, and substance abuse; to enhance life through such means as education, socialization, and recreation. These goals may be stated or unstated in the legislation, but nevertheless, they are real and influential in determining the nature of the legislation and of the program. The Food Stamp Program, for example, has a stated objective to alleviate hunger and malnutrition by enabling low-income households to purchase a nutritionally adequate diet. It also seeks to expand the market for domestically produced food by supplementing the food-

---

CHART 7.1   *A Schema for Examining Social Welfare Programs*

  I. Structural components
     A. What are the needs and goals to be met?
     B. What is the form of benefit that the program produces?
     C. Who is eligible for the program?
     D. How is the program financed?
     E. What is the level of administration?
 II. Alternative program characteristics
     A. Residual, institutional, developmental, or socio-economic asset development
     B. Selective or universal
     C. Benefits in money, service, or utilities
     D. Public or private
     E. Central or local
     F. Lay or professional
III. Evaluating the program
     A. Adequacy
        1. Horizontal
        2. Vertical
     B. Financing
        1. Equitable
        2. Priority use of funds
        3. Efficient: cost and benefit
        4. Cost-benefit analysis
     C. Coherence
     D. Latent consequences

---

purchasing power of eligible low-income households. Similarly, the School Lunch Program is intended to safeguard the health and well-being of the nation's children and to encourage the consumption of domestic commodities.

Thus, these two programs have the stated goals of alleviating hunger and malnutrition but also of expanding the market for, and consumption of, domestically produced foods. But Food Stamps may not be used for the purchase of alcoholic beverages and tobacco, pet food, and cleaning and paper products, including toilet paper. Implicit in a portion of these restrictions is a moral objective to control the behavior of the recipients.

The stated or unstated goals for particular programs may differ from group to group: Farmers, warehouse workers, teamsters, wholesalers, retailers, salespersons, and those who do business with them all have their own sense of investment in the goals of the program and benefit in different ways as their own individual goals are met by the program.

What Is the Form of Benefit That the Program Produces?

This is simply another way of asking: What does the program produce? For instance, unemployment insurance produces a certain amount of cash income for a certain number of weeks. A family agency might "produce" individual or group counseling, or help in negotiating other social systems. A housing project might "produce" apartments at low cost. The concept is simple enough. Among the first things anyone who examines a social welfare program will want to know is what the benefits are and what form they take. It is important, to begin with, to get a good fix on precisely what the benefits of a given program are so that the program can be understood and evaluated on its own terms. We will see that the form the benefits take is a major issue. Should they be in the form of money such as rent, personal services such as tenant counseling, or the provision of a new social utility such as a housing development? The question of the level of benefit in programs is crucial. Is the level of cash benefit in an economic security program adequate? Is the kind of counseling available in a personal service agency adequate or underadequate or overadequate for the task?

Who Is Eligible for the Program?

Another way of saying this is: What risks of human existence are covered by the program? The concept of covering certain risks of living, or categorical programs, is basic to the Western social welfare system. At least since the English Poor Laws, and probably of necessity in any modern society, there are few agencies that simply provide "help." Even most generalized multiservice centers can offer services, provide information, and make referrals to others only for people within a given geographical area or a certain age range.

Criteria for eligibility are critical. In order to receive food stamps, for example, a person needs to meet federal poverty guidelines. To be eligible for service in a community mental health center, a person must live within a certain district; if not, the person is referred to another community mental health center. To be eligible for Medicare, a person must be above a certain age level, be disabled for a period of time, or have end-stage renal disease. Workers who have worked long enough in covered employment, their dependents, or survivors are eligible to receive Social Security benefits. To be eligible for day care, a person must be below a certain age. So along with the question of what the benefits or output of a program are, one must ask the companion question: For whom are the benefits? How is eligibility determined? The choices in determining eligibility raise major issues in the characteristics of social welfare programs, as we will see. But if the student knows the answer to the questions of what the benefits are, and who is eligible for the benefits (what class or classes of people are eligible), he or she can get a good beginning understanding of the nature of the program.

Later in this chapter, the issue of *financial equity* will be introduced. Financial (economic) equity means that all individuals who have paid the same amount of money for some good (insurance, mortgage, or some other form of property) are entitled to receive the same amount of benefits. This is the principle of "you get what you pay for."

But equity also has a different meaning in social welfare. In social welfare, *equity* refers to similar cases being treated similarly. The use of criteria of similarity limits the discretion of those in authority and results in like decisions being made in like cases. Equity then in social welfare means that all individuals that are in the same circumstances (income, size of family, age, and so on) are entitled to receive the same social assistance irrespective of what they have contributed to the program or to society financially through taxes. In this case, you receive what you need—a form of social equity.[3]

How Is the Program Financed?

Financing is a crucial component of any social welfare program, and one that can be overlooked by those who are concerned only with the benefits of the program. The availability of the resources, where they come from, and in what proportion they are used are all crucial to what is produced. A social welfare program may be financed by any one or by a combination of sources including the following.

1. *General revenues.* At each level of government—local, state, and national—there are general tax funds collected from income taxes, sales taxes, and the like that go into a general purse. Out of this general purse the legislature allocates monies for various social functions—defense, highways, safety services, and social services. Some social welfare programs are financed completely or partially from such general revenue monies. In discussing financial equity as part of the evaluation of a social welfare program, we will see that whether monies come from general revenues or other sources can make a tremendous difference. The private or voluntary sector often has a rough equivalent of general revenues. In most communities there is a United Way branch that raises money for the social service needs of a whole variety of local agencies such as scouts and family service agencies. These funds become a kind of general revenue source for making allocations to the various member agencies for their own general operations.

2. *Earmarked taxes.* Sometimes the local, state, or national government will develop a special tax or revenue-collecting program, the money from which is earmarked in advance for a special purpose. A federal gasoline tax is an interesting example. Proceeds from this tax are kept in a special trust fund for purposes of transportation. A state lottery may designate its proceeds for education or the aged. It sometimes makes taxes more palatable if the general public understands that the proceeds from a given tax are going to some agreed-on important purpose. This approach, however, provides for limited flexibility. For instance, there was much argument and litigation about using a transportation trust fund for public transportation as well as for the building of highways. Again, the umbrella funding agencies in the voluntary sector have a mechanism roughly equivalent to the earmarked tax when, in addition to the general fund-raising drive, they may have a special drive for a new building or for a specific local agency. Also, the option is offered to United Way donors to earmark their contributions for specific agencies.

3. *Employer/employee taxes.* A number of social programs are financed by taxes on employees or employers or both. Such programs tend to be for the social insurances. They connote, in some ways, an insurance concept: that a person pays for insurance out of his or her earnings and is thus getting back what was put in when a claim is filed. We will see in our discussion of Social Security that these are not really insurances in that the person who is contributing is not buying benefits with this contribution. But they do have the advantage of creating a sense of personal possession of the right to the benefit on the part of the payee. On the other hand, as we will discuss further under financial equity, these kinds of taxes to finance social programs tend to be regressive. We will be using the terms *progressive, regressive,* and *proportional* in describing taxes as introduced in chapter 6.

4. *Payment by the recipient of service.* Many social welfare programs derive at least a portion of their income from payments by the recipients of the services or "user fees." Payment is often on a sliding scale based on ability to pay; those who can do so, pay more. Those with lower incomes pay progressively less. Some services in social welfare are available only to those who can pay an additional fee for those services, such as Part B of Medicare, the supplementary medical insurance program.

5. *Third-party payments* and *purchase of services.* A growing phenomenon on the U.S. social welfare scene has been the financing of services through the purchase of services and third-party payments. This can mean different things. In its simplest form, a governmental unit is mandated or decides to provide a certain social welfare service. It may decide that, rather than create a new social service on its own, it may be more economical to purchase service from an existing institution or social agency or a new one created for that purpose. Thus the state agency that wishes to provide homemaker services may develop a homemaker division of its own or may purchase homemaker services for eligible clients from some voluntary or private for-profit organization. A public agency may pay the cost for placing children in day care or residential treatment rather than create a network of such centers of its own. This is what is generally meant by purchase of service. Although one can see where this might be economical, it is also easy to see where it could be wasteful. It can lead to a lack of accountability (or very expensive policing procedures so that there will be accountability) and opportunities for "sweetheart deals" between private contractors and the government.

Third-party payments usually refer to a more generalized form of this phenomenon. Here there is no plan, intent, or possibility of the social welfare program providing the service directly. The social welfare program itself consists entirely of payment to a "vendor," an external deliverer of services. Medicaid is an example of such a program. A Medicaid recipient goes to a medical facility, and payment may be made directly to the facility by the Medicaid program. There is a problem with such a system, particularly with regard to cost containment. This is because there is little motivation to keep prices down, and costs keep escalating. This escalation of health service system costs in the United States is one of the problems that accompanied the growth of third-party payments as a form of financing health and social welfare programs.

6. *Combinations.* Increasingly, social welfare programs are financed through a combination of some of the previously mentioned methods. A social welfare program or agency may be required to raise some of its own funds through fees. A voluntary agency may be receiving some money from insurance payments, the government, private foundations, the United Way, and individual contributions as well as other sources, some for general purposes and others earmarked. The complexity of financing may affect the efficiency of an agency operation. The time allotted to satisfying the accountability requirements of different grantors may be excessive. In the extreme and not uncommon case, an agency may recast its services, not in terms of the needs of its community, but in terms of the purposes for which funds are available.

To study a social welfare program, it is crucial to know just what the sources of funds are. We will see in examining specific social welfare programs that these questions affect the outcome.

What Is the Level of Administration?

Some programs such as Social Security or Medicare are completely federal or national programs. That is, although there may be offices in each locality, the program is a single one for the entire nation, consistent in its administration and its benefits. Local employees are employees of the national government, and policies are made in Washington, D.C. Other programs are under state, regional, or county auspices.

As with financing, there is a growing trend toward combinations of levels of administration and, particularly, greater emphasis on administration by states. There is a peculiar U.S. institution known as the grant-in-aid, which contributes to this complexity. In a grant-in-aid, one unit makes funds (a grant) available to another level of government or to a voluntary or private agency and allows that unit to administer the program itself, so long as it is in keeping with some general guidelines that are set by the granting agency. Some examples may help to clarify the grant-in-aid concept: The federal government provided 50 percent or more of the cost of public assistance to each state with a public assistance program. In order to receive that money, the state complied with certain regulations that are set down by the federal government when it gives its 50 percent. For example, it had to provide the opportunity for fair hearings or appeals by clients who are found ineligible. The public assistance program is administered on the state and local level, but to the extent that the administration must meet certain guidelines from the federal government, even administration could be viewed as also being federal. Temporary Assistance to Needy Families (TANF) provides states with block grants (one sum for benefits and administration) and reduces federal controls without ceding all decisions to the states.

And so in developing a basic understanding of a social welfare program, the student of such a program will want to know the following:

1. What are the needs or problems being addressed, and what are the goals of the program?
2. What are the benefits of the program?
3. What are the eligibility requirements for the program?
4. How is the program financed, at what level, or from what combination of sources?
5. How is the program administered, by whom, and at what level of government, or in what combination?

Alternative Program Characteristics

No matter what the basic structure of the social welfare program under study may be, the program may choose among alternative program characteristics. There are different ways in which the program may be organized and different philosophies that it may embody. We will examine some of the alternative program characteristics of social welfare programs.

Residual, Institutional, Developmental, or Socio-Economic Asset Development

Over time social welfare programs tended in their approach to be more or less residual, institutional, or developmental. In recent years, another approach has been introduced and has gained recognition: socio-economic asset development. The *residual* or minimalist concept of social welfare is based on the premise that an individual's needs should be met through the market economy and through the family. Occasionally, however, individuals are unable to utilize the market system or the family; for example, there is some sort of disruption that hits the market system, such as a recession, or a family faces a crisis. In these cases, the social welfare system comes into play. It is seen as a kind of necessary evil, a backup system for the market and the family. Theoretically, the social welfare system is supposed to withdraw when these institutions of society—the family and the market—can once again function. We see this in the perspective that argues that if society were only properly organized, there would be no need for social work or that the goal of the public assistance system is to do away with itself—get everyone off welfare and into the job market. Few people seriously believe that this is a real possibility, and yet the whole public assistance program is structured as though it were only a necessary evil. Its success is evaluated on the basis of how many people leave the welfare rolls and its failure by how many come on. The residual concept in social welfare leads to the kind of programs in which eligibility is based on proving a need, that is, proving the breakdown of the other normative systems that should be working.

The *institutional* view of programs implies no such breakdown. From this perspective, it is accepted that we live in a complex, difficult environment and social welfare is a legitimate function of modern society. It is assumed, for instance, that when people become elderly they will cease working and may be faced with the problem of a lack of income. Therefore, an institutional structure such as Social Security meets a normal need. Similarly, it is assumed that there will be some industrial accidents. Therefore, Workers' Compensation is set up to meet the risks of working, so that people who are injured can get medical care and some income protection during the period of their absence from employment. The institutional point of view sees social welfare as regularized, permanent, necessary, and a desirable part of the social structure.[4]

What we are calling the *developmental* conception of social welfare moves one step beyond the institutional concept to focus on human development. The institutional view assumes some social problems that a social welfare institution is set up to prevent or correct. The developmental view, however, assumes that all citizens in a modern, complex society may need "a variety of socially provided goods and services to develop their capacity to participate in society and to achieve and maintain a desirable standard of living."[5] It is possible for society to set up a social welfare institution simply to make living better, to improve the quality of life, and to fulfill human development, not necessarily to solve a problem or to aid those in distress.

As an example, in social welfare if day-care services are instituted because certain parents are not yet properly trained or are incapable of taking care of their children as should be the norm, this is a residual concept of day care. If it is assumed that many parents in industrial society will need to work and will need the help of day-care services, this would be the institutional concept. If, on the other hand, a society simply said it would be better for the quality of life if parents in every neighborhood could have a nursery to drop their children off for an hour or two while they were shopping or taking courses or simply for a respite, and the society instituted a network of drop-in nurseries in neighborhoods, this would be a developmental approach to social welfare.

The *socio-economic asset development* perspective evolved through attempts to harmonize social welfare with efforts directed at economic development that focus on ways in which social welfare can contribute efficiently and effectively to economic development through social investment.

The socio-economic assest development approach suggests that social welfare to one degree or another manages social problems, meets needs, and should provide opportunities for advancement to individuals, families, groups, communities, and even whole societies. Based on the work of the past half-century in developing nations, social development seeks ways that create human and social capital and foster peoples' welfare by simultaneous productive economic activities. Social welfare is thus linked to economic development and policies.[6]

The distinctions made here among the categories are not always that clear; there is no single on or off switch that can differentiate between residual and institutional programs, or institutional, developmental, or socio-economic developmental. It is more a question of the attitude toward the program, the way it was conceived, and what it is intended to do. Nonetheless, this is a rather fundamental issue in social welfare and affects the question of whether people are treated humanely or whether they are stigmatized, and whether a program is starved or encouraged.

There are alternative program characteristics in social welfare programs that are similar to the residual, institutional, and developmental ideas. The view of a social welfare program as a *right* versus a *charity* is one such alternative. The charity concept is very much like the residual concept. Because it is not a basic and permanent part of the system, it is something that society does for people, in a sense, out of the goodness of its heart. To the extent that social welfare is institutional or developmental, it is more like a basic social right of citizens in a given community. In the 1960s, we saw the development of welfare rights organizations, which tried to build on the assumption that entitlement to social welfare programs was as much a right of eligible citizens as the right to vote or to be treated without discrimination. On the other hand, the stigma and other concerns associated with many welfare programs, particularly the residual ones, continue to support the notion that social welfare is a charity.

Several decades ago, a number of Supreme Court decisions underscored public assistance as a right. *Shapiro v. Thompson* (1969) eliminated length-of-time residence requirements from public assistance programs. *Smith v. King* (1969) eliminated the man-in-the home rule and held that the presence of a man not their father living in their residence may not be considered a factor of children's eligibility for assistance because he has no legal responsibility for their support. The Court ruled in *Goldberg v. Kelly* (1969) and *Wheeler v. Montgomery* (1969) that aid cannot be discontinued prior to a hearing on a decision at issue until an evidentiary hearing is held. These Supreme Court rulings clarified the principle that citizens could not be deprived of welfare benefits without due process, at that time a revolutionary concept. Nevertheless, there is a sense of ambivalence around the issue of public assistance and rights.[7]

The history of seeing social welfare programs as a charity has led to evaluation of who is the worthy versus the unworthy poor—that is, who is deserving of the benefits of these special programs. When programs become more institutionalized or developmental, it is difficult to enforce this concept, and the very notion begins to change. For example, recipients of Social Security benefits feel that this is their right.

Another closely related conceptual design is the degree to which a social welfare program is seen as *minimal* or *optimal*. That is, does it seek to provide a basic floor below which no citizen should be expected to fall, or does it try to create an institutional structure that goes beyond the basics and adds to the quality of life? For instance, most income maintenance plans (public assistance or other kinds) attempt to be minimal at best. They establish a floor below which it is impossible to maintain any sort of living standard, and they may bring people up to that level. Beyond that level, it is expected that market mechanisms should take over and should provide for the other amenities of life. On the other hand, certain institutions, such as public libraries, are more institutional or developmental in concept and therefore more optimal than minimal in design. It is simply decided that the social system rather than the profit-making market system should be given responsibility for providing libraries to optimize the quality of life. It certainly goes beyond the minimal. It is also, in a sense, striving for equity in certain areas of life.

In income maintenance, it is not considered necessary or even desirable that everyone should have equal incomes. What is usually seen as desirable is that each person should have a certain minimum income in order to survive. To the extent, though, that tax laws are made more progressive, there is an attempt to provide more equity in society between rich and poor and not simply to provide minimum standards. To the extent that the same fire services are made available to everyone in society despite his or her contribution, such social welfare programs are organized to provide equity rather than minimum. Any social welfare program may be designed essentially to provide a floor or minimum, or to provide more equity, or to optimize the quality of life in a given area. This, too, can be seen as another expression of the residual, institutional, and developmental concepts.

In examining or designing social welfare programs, residual, institutional, developmental and socioeconomic asset developmental concepts need to be considered. They will affect how the program is structured, who is made eligible for it, the nature of the benefits, how it is financed, and so on.

Selective or Universal

A crucial question in any social welfare program is the degree to which that program is selective or universal. Here the definitions are a little more precise. A *selective* program is one in which eligibility is based on a determination of need and the individual financial means of the potential client. A *universal* program is one that is open as a right to anyone who meets certain class, category, or regional criteria. The benefit is provided to all who meet the criteria no matter how high the total cost to the public treasury. If a person has to prove eligibility based on individual financial status, that program is selective no matter how generous the provisions or how broad the coverage. For example, if anyone who is under 3 years of age or over 65 years of age, is a resident of Chicago, is a veteran, or has been laid off is eligible for a program without a test of individual financial means, that program is, by our definition, universal. The difference between the two concepts is crucial.

Public assistance, Medicaid, and Food Stamps are all selective programs. Unemployment insurance, Workers' Compensation, Medicare, and Social Security are all universal programs. Somewhere between might be those programs, such as family services and some day-care services, that are open to everyone but on a sliding scale, based on an examination of individual ability to pay.

Universal programs normally provide benefits that are legally due one as a right. They are not based on a means test of one's income or assets. Programs that are residual in their concept, such as Temporary Assistance for Needy Families, will tend to be selective. Programs that are institutional or developmental, such as Social Security, are in concept more likely to be universal. If the program is more institutionally conceived—such as the Social Security system: all persons with specific needs who meet the criteria are treated equally as a right based on prior contributions. Although there is no "up front" means test for benefit eligibility, in Chapter 9 we will see there is a "backdoor" means test for receipt of benefits.

The student should be aware that residual concepts and selectivity go together and institutional concepts and universality go together, although not in perfect step. For instance, in disasters, floods, or earthquakes, programs may be set up that are residual in nature—that is, temporary and necessary because of the breakdown of a system that ordinarily meets people's needs—but may be operated universally—that is, anyone who needs help may avail him or herself of disaster relief without proving eligibility based on financial need. Student loans and scholarships may be universally available but selective and provided on the basis of financial means tests.

Why should a program be selective or universal? What are the advantages and disadvantages of each? The most obvious advantage of the selective program is limitation on cost. Few programs or societies have all the resources or all the funds to do everything that might be desirable. Therefore, there is a natural tendency to try to limit a program to a specific target population—the one that is most in need. The simplest answer appears to be for a program to be limited to people who meet certain criteria of financial eligibility on an individual basis. This is the heart of the argument for selectivity.

It is also ideological in the feeling that society "should not" pay for services that can be afforded privately. Sometimes no real money difference is involved. For example, if I pay $5 in taxes to help support my poor neighbor for medical services and I pay $5 to my own doctor for my medical services, medical care is costing me $10. If I pay $10 in taxes for medical care that will cover both me and my neighbor, I am paying the same $10. The question becomes, Should only those who are unable to afford private services be subsidized by a state system and should others pay privately, or would it be better for society, for a variety of other reasons, to have one medical care system for all with my $10?

There are other reasons besides the basic financial one for preferring selective programs. For one, there is a fear on the part of some social planners that universal programs are "creamed" by the rich and middle class. That is, when a program is available to all, it is the wealthier and the more sophisticated who have better access to it, who hear about it, and who take advantage of it the best, leaving less for the poor. The public library that is kept quite busy by the middle class may not develop the kind of accessible services to provide reading opportunities for those without means of transportation. It is this fear of "creaming" that causes some people to favor services specifically targeted.

Why, then, might one prefer universal services over selective ones, if they do tend to cost more and if there is the danger of creaming, of not having the services go to the most needy population? There are several reasons many favor universal programs.

First, universal programs limit the sense of being demeaned that goes with an examination of one's income. The idea of being a welfare client still carries a stigma in society. A universal program eliminates this stigma. Anyone in a given category is eligible. There is no scrutinizing of one's individual savings or income.

Second, many have despaired of finding any fair formula by which one can administer a selective program. For instance, let us assume that you and I each earned $30,000 a year for 10 years. At the end of those 10 years, both of us found ourselves without employment or other insurance and turned to welfare. You had saved $1,500 a year of your salary and now had $15,000 in the bank. I had spent all my salary and had nothing but debts, including car loans, credit card debt, and a home. Should I be eligible for welfare and you ineligible because you had saved? Should you be penalized for your thrift? If you say no, what if you had $30,000 or $40,000 or $50,000 in the bank? How does one develop a fair system without trying to legislate public morals? The whole selective system lends itself to a continuation of judgments being made by others of who is the worthy and who is the unworthy poor, a distinction deeply embedded in the English Poor Law tradition.

Third, some persons argue that universal programs help poor persons without stressing that as their major aim. A universal program such as Social Security attracts major support, yet is able to target and assist those who have been lower earners during their lives.

Just as creaming may limit the availability of universal programs to the poor, there are other factors that limit the ability of selective programs to serve the poor. Selective programs have a limited constituency of those financially in need. Because these programs lack broad support from a large constituency, they also tend to lack the legislative power to improve programs and often find their budgets constrained or reduced. Yet universal programs, despite costs, tend to be improved and expanded. They are more difficult to change, and it is quite difficult to reduce their benefits. There are those who believe that programs for the poor tend to become poor programs.

Because of concerns about possible cheating, investigations and roadblocks are set up for recipients of selective programs. For example, recipients of public assistance are frequently recertified. This may lead many of the needy people who would be eligible to not apply. Because selective programs are not easily accessible, many of the poor never find their way onto their rolls. Under the former AFDC program it was estimated that there were as many people eligible for welfare who were not receiving welfare as those who were on the welfare rolls.[8]

Whenever the system is attacked, there are allegations of misuse of funds by ineligible recipients. However, there is also a certain amount of financial waste in selective programs. Although money is not "wasted" on the rich in these programs, there is a great deal of waste that is called *cost inefficiency*, the proportionate cost of a program used in its administration. Selective programs demand much more administrative budget than do universal programs because there need to be procedures for determining eligibility, investigators, checks, and double-checks. The vast universal Social Security retirement system is operated from a single computerized facility and serves its clientele with only a small percentage of the total funds used for administrative purposes (less than 1 percent). State TANF programs, by contrast, use nationally a significant amount of funds (10 percent) to administer their own operations.

The waste in using the money allocated for a program in large measure on administration is called cost inefficiency. The so-called waste in having large amounts of the money go to people who are not needy or not the original targets of having such a program is called *benefit inefficiency.*

Even to the extent that universal programs generally serve those who are not poor, the benefits may go to those who are near poverty. Many social planners would not consider this wasted or benefit inefficient at all. People just above the poverty line may be in need as well as those below the line. This is another reason many planners favor a universal approach to social services.

Universal programs tend to be cohesive factors in U.S. society. Selective programs tend to pit recipients against nonrecipients. So long as I am getting some benefit from a program, I am willing to pay for it, even if you are getting a little bit more benefit from that same program. I am willing to see that program expand and improve. But as long as I am paying for a program for which I am ineligible, I will tend to be unenthusiastic and perhaps resentful of its recipients. Because of this, low- and middle-income persons often are hostile to the poor. Selectivity tends to perpetuate what is only a partial myth: that to get services in the United States one needs to be very rich or very poor.

It has been argued that with new technology the stigma associated with selective programs can be avoided. Each American would have a health credit card. A person would go to a health facility for care and have the card punched on the way out. The poor would get the service without cost and the rich would be billed for the same service. Thus you could have a selective program without the stigma normally attached to selectivity.

This argument does not eliminate the problems of how one determines in a fair way who is eligible and who is ineligible; neither does it deal with the complexity that has grown up in the U.S. welfare system as programs have been added. The more selectivity, the more problems associated with what has been called the *"notch" effect*: As people's incomes rise, they become ineligible for other kinds of selective programs so that their net positions may be worse than before. This is one of the disincentives to work that has been built into the current welfare system. For instance, if a person starts earning more than she had earned before, she might suddenly find herself ineligible for other benefits. Universal programs eliminate this notch disincentive.

Finally, even in terms of cost, if one keeps in mind that there is an input and an output side to the social welfare program equation, the problems of the cost of universal programs can be solved. Tax policies and tax rates can be designed to recover through *"clawbacks"* whatever portion is deemed desirable for a welfare program for which the rich are eligible. To the extent Social Security income is considered taxable income, those who are wealthy and have other income from stocks and dividends will return a portion of this so-called wasted money to the tax treasuries. Other income tax policies can be formed so that universal programs can be less benefit inefficient.

Theda Skocpol and others, mindful of the political forces that impose limitations on U.S. selective programs aimed specifically at the poverty population, have suggested an expanded use of universal programs to deliver services for the poor. Skocpol points out that from the beginning the Social Security system gave proportionately higher—although never absolutely higher—retirement benefits to formerly lower-income workers. Her argument is that universal policies support the development of coalitions that, in turn, support extension of benefits. Thus, in her view, some universal, cross-class programs may be viewed as having selective features and have the best chance of sustained assistance for the poor while helping families from all social classes. Others have argued that there are political problems with such programs because of their large costs and because the political power of universal programs can be overstated. Further, the political strength of the elderly—a potent group—does not apply to other groups who are not elderly, severely disabled, or do not work or work very little. There is an important distinction made between those who earned their benefits and those who are recipients of "welfare."[9]

There is probably no program characteristic more crucial to social welfare in our society than the question of selectivity and universality. The bias of the authors is toward a universal approach to social welfare. However, readers should be aware of the arguments for and against both types and utilize these concepts as they approach social welfare programs.

Benefits in Money, Services, or Utilities

Under the question of structural components, we have indicated that the nature of benefits is a crucial concern. The nature of a benefit, beside the question of amount, may take several forms. Benefits may come in the form of *money*—cash income or vouchers with which to purchase goods or services. Benefits also may come in the form of *services*—as a concrete service (such as an apartment or a medical exam) or as counseling. Services may take the form of *public social utilities* parallel to public utilities such as transportation, water supply, and postal systems. These can be universal programs, serving people facing ordinary circumstances, not limited to those who pass a means test, although they may charge fees that differ according to a user's income. Public social utilities can include day care, public health, a public library, museums, and parks.

From time to time, there is a strong push away from the provision of services in favor of what has been called an income strategy. Services sometimes can be simply a sophisticated form of victim-blaming or of deciding who is the worthy or unworthy poor. Providing cash in place of services is a rather attractive philosophy in many respects. Social services do have a tradition of being judgmental. This has an appeal consonant with the free-enterprise and marketplace perspective. There is a straightforwardness to the idea of giving eligible people money and then letting them go out into the market and do what they wish with it. In fact, there was an interesting similarity of views on this question between conservatives who believe in a total free-enterprise society and liberals who believe in welfare rights. The former, since they had to accept some welfare program in a society that would not allow its casualties to starve, preferred to put that program in the form of cash (so that the recipients could function in the market) rather than to create governmental services and bureaucracies.

The poor themselves preferred the neatness of an income strategy. Earlier, a potential client for public assistance would meet a worker in the social service system who would become his or her worker, and that worker would determine eligibility, provide the monthly checks, offer counseling, and give whatever other help was supposedly needed to help that client do better budgeting and find a way to more independent living. The objections of the poor were that poverty did not imply any inability in social functioning and that a person should be able to establish eligibility independent of whether he or she needed other forms of assistance. There should, for example, be no presumption that being in poverty is the equivalent of a need for counseling. If they were eligible, they would get financial assistance. Applicants might separately request or be offered other public services, such as family planning and counseling, but one would have nothing to do with the other.

It is not necessarily true that whenever a choice is possible, an income or money strategy is better than a service strategy. It has been suggested that instead of public housing there should be vouchers (cash equivalent) that may be used for housing. Instead of aid to education, the poor should be given vouchers with which to help buy education. In some cases, vouchers may be desirable. In other cases, society as a whole may do a better job of creating a social institution rather than giving people money and sending them into the market.

One can give people money to buy medical services, or one may create a medical clinic. In some cases one may be desirable, in some cases the other, but we would be very cautious about abandoning the concept that social services, counseling or concrete, may be the best form for some social welfare programs. This is particularly true when the social services take the form of a utility or amenity to human life such as child and adult protective services, assistance for crime victims, disaster aid, and services for older persons. The same may be said of fire, park services, and other social services that are not strictly identified as social welfare. The same consideration should be applied to all social welfare services before we decide that an income strategy is the answer to all problems. Even people with adequate incomes may and often do need services.

Public or Private

The *private sector* can be divided into two parts: (1) the *private nonprofit sector* (often called voluntary), such as a philanthropic organization operating with a community board of directors (community members and leaders, philanthropists, and others in a cross-section of responsible people who are not members of its staff), which bears corporate responsibility for the enterprise, rather than by an arm of the government. These are the agencies that provide direct services, advocacy, fund-raising, and planning and coordination services in various communities; and (2) the *private proprietary* organization that is in the business of making a profit but in a social welfare-related area, for example, nursing homes or child care agencies. If the staff delivering services or their relatives serve as officers, it is most likely a proprietary agency. A proprietary agency may show no corporate profit; instead it may pay salaries and benefits to its staff and officers, who also are its owners. The difference between the two types of private agencies is usually in the form of accountability. Both the private nonprofit and the private proprietary sectors are important features of the U.S. social welfare scene. We have introduced this topic briefly here. In chapter 11 we will examine the private sector and its many issues in greater detail.

Central or Local

Another program characteristic is the degree to which any social welfare program is operated or administered on a local as opposed to a state or national level. What is the appropriate level of administration and control for various kinds of programs? Again the United States, because it is a federal society with a background of states' rights, has a peculiar history. In most countries of the world, policies are made much more centrally, even though local offices may exist to administer policy and may even have some discretion in administering policy. However, in the United States, one has a Social Security or Medicare or Veterans Affairs program, which is on a strictly national basis, and public assistance and Medicaid programs, which combine state and local benefits with national support and guidelines, and, for example, a correctional system, which can be local, state, or federal. In general there exists a crazy-quilt pattern for the administration of social welfare services. What are the trends and what is the appropriate level of control for each program?

From the early 1970s, concern grew in many quarters that the New Deal programs of the Great Depression and the Great Society programs of the 1960s shifted too much power to the federal level and away from the states and localities. The federal government was viewed as too intrusive and too large and that decision making and administration should devolve to the state level.

Paradoxically, both conservatives and liberals argued that power centralized in Washington is too removed from the "people" and politicians and bureaucrats do not know what is needed at the state and local levels. According to this view, the more layers of intervention between the people and the decision makers, the more decisions become confused, diluted, or sabotaged. Turning control over to states and localities and away from the federal government remains a high-priority goal for many persons.

What is being overlooked, in fact, is that state governments are not without their own traditions of corruption, ineptitude, discrimination, and the fact they are even more accessible to special interest groups. Furthermore, some of the best social welfare programs in the United States in terms of service to people and efficiency are administered federally, such as the Social Security system. It is even possible that direct federal programs need not have many layers between them and the people they serve. The issue may not be efficiency or even effectiveness but where the power lies.

It is hard to see how giving states a blank check increases the responsibility or power of the people over their own decisions. Social workers need to understand community input and community control as vital elements of good social programs, whatever their source. But this is not the same as suggesting that state or local administration is better necessarily than federal administration of any given program, neither is the reverse true.

As a result of the struggles of the 1960s, the principle that the recipients or a local community needed to be consulted on a social welfare program envisioned for that community found its way into legislation in all areas related to social welfare. This is a principle that all social workers need to accept. But community input is not community control. For example, community control has at times meant states' rights, white supremacy, and the ability of some groups to dictate what books would be permitted in local libraries and what a school's curriculum will be. Only federal constitutional amendments abolishing slavery and establishing equal protection principles could overcome local attitudes. The problem is how to maintain community participation and neighborhood vitality and activity without sacrificing the rights of minorities. The decision that is made on the local level cannot begin to take the entire public need into account.

Therefore, I elect legislators who represent me and who are supposed to be able to consider the larger picture in making decisions. I may recall or not reelect them if I am unhappy with their decisions. Similarly, in social welfare it is necessary to have a body that can make the overarching decisions about public policy, although, one hopes, without ignoring the input of local communities. How much local input and control are necessary in which kinds of programs are hard decisions that have to be made, issue by issue. Which social welfare program is best administered by the state or federal government or by the local community will also vary based on the nature of the community and program, but there are no pat answers.

In the 21st century debates continue as efforts are made to shift responsibility for social welfare from the federal to state levels and to place ever more responsibility upon individuals and their families and away from government. There are critical problems with this. First, poverty, recession, and social problems cut across state boundaries. The federal programs of the New Deal (Great Depression) were necessary to provide answers to problems that could not be solved at the level of the states. Second, there are great disparities between states in their fiscal and administrative capacities, in their costs of living, and in their benefits. For example, some states expend several times as much per capita on welfare benefits as do others. The major social problems in the United States of economic security, housing, employment, crime and corrections, and others are not going to be solved by states alone. What is needed are major legislative changes and adjustments in priorities and funding on the national level, in addition to the efforts of states and localities.

Perhaps the greatest genius of the late Martin Luther King Jr. was his ability to merge local and national concerns. He operated on issues of community control and local significance such as voting in Selma, Alabama, and segregated seating on buses in Montgomery. Each of these issues was legitimate on the local level and in its own right, met people's needs, developed local leadership, and had all the assets of community control. But each of them was an orchestrated step toward changing national policies on segregation and voting, which was always kept in mind as the goal and target. It is that broad vision that all of us in social welfare need to maintain even while we work on the state and local level.

Lay or Professional

There are two major senses in which a social welfare program may have more of a lay or professional orientation. On the simplest level, there is the question of who delivers the services. There does not exist the general public acceptance of a body of hard skills that only the professional may apply, as there does with engineering or medical practice, for instance. In fact, social workers themselves believe that there are important roles for citizens to play in human services. Therefore, there is some confusion and often conflict over the appropriate division of labor between lay and professional involvement in social service programs. What kinds of tasks demand professional work skills, what kinds of tasks demand the skills of other allied disciplines, and what kinds of tasks can be performed by community leaders, volunteers, and untrained workers? How these questions are answered will affect the quality, cost, and legitimacy of a given program. There are times when for a specific purpose, such as maintaining contact with an indigenous community for a particular social service program, there may be more reliance placed on lay people, whereas in other situations more emphasis may be placed on professional skills.

In another sense, the question of lay versus professional is the question of control, policy, and decision making. What are the decisions that are legitimately the "people's" decisions in social welfare? What are the decisions that absolutely require professional judgment? For instance, no community board should tell a medical doctor what medicine to prescribe for a certain illness. However, medical doctors ought not make unilaterally the decisions about what kind of national health insurance plan the nation should have. Similarly in social welfare, there are professional judgments that social workers should make and other policy decisions that should be made by community advisory groups or boards of directors. How well a program confronts these issues will often determine its success or failure.

Evaluating the Program

Let us now assume that you have the basic tools for understanding any social welfare program. You understand the nature of the program in terms of the five basic structural components discussed previously. You also understand the program characteristics, whether it tends to be more residual and selective or more universal and institutional, the degree to which its services are seen as a right or as a charity, and all the other characteristics that have been discussed thus far. You have also formulated an opinion as to which characteristics would be most appropriate for a specific program in question. Finally, how will you evaluate whether the program is effective? On the basis of an understanding of the preceding discussion, the following are some of the questions that need to be asked about any program in its evaluation.

Adequacy

Is the program adequate to meet the problem for which it was set up? Adequacy has to be judged on two axes, which we will call horizontal and vertical. On the *horizontal* axis we want to know whether the program reaches the target population. Let us assume that we are setting up a teenage pregnancy prevention program for a city of 300,000 people. The services that the program offers may be exemplary in their quality, may even change people's lives dramatically. But if it is only geared to serving 10,000 people, if information about its availability does not reach the rest of the population, or if long waiting lists develop, then the program is horizontally inadequate. It cannot meet the problem for which it was set up. So one basic question we must ask of any program is whether it has the coverage, capacity, will, resources, and means of access to cover its target population. The allocations for many programs are based on the assumption that a major percentage of those who might be eligible will not hear of it, apply for it, or actually participate.

One needs to ask how *vertically* adequate the program is. Is each recipient sufficiently covered? For example, an AIDS prevention program may "reach" in a sense an entire city of 300,000, but its services may consist only of TV ads. In this case the coverage for each person served is not adequate and is not of sufficient depth and substance to effect major changes in people's lives. The program is horizontally adequate but vertically inadequate. Each program needs to be weighed in terms of its adequacy, horizontal and vertical, to see whether it is doing the job it was set up to do. How many are served? How well is each served?

Financing

There are a number of questions about financing that need to be addressed in the evaluation of every program.

1. *Is the program equitably financed?* The Social Security system may be a relatively excellent program in terms of the benefits it provides to people, the needs and risks it covers, and the universality and neatness of its operation. But if it continues to be financed by a regressive tax that draws more heavily on the poor than on the wealthy, this is a serious shortcoming in the program. One needs to look not only at the output side but at the input side in order to evaluate a program. There is little point in redistributing income to the poor on the output side of the program if this is done by taking money from the poor on the input side of the program. And so the student needs to evaluate how a program is financed and how this needs to be changed to be made more fair, if necessary.

2. *Does this program represent a priority use of funds?* If resources were infinite, this question would not need to be asked. But because resources are finite, every time a dollar is spent on one program there is an *opportunity cost:* the loss of the opportunity to spend that dollar on some other program. Does the particular social welfare program have a high priority in terms of the needs of the community or nation? This is the kind of question about financing that the student needs to ask.

One can observe in Table 7.1 the sources of federal revenues and how they shifted between 1965 and 2000 so that revenues are derived from the same sources with different weightings.

3. *How cost or benefit efficient is the program?* In our earlier discussion we pointed out that all programs lose some resources one way or another. Administrative costs of operating a program will take away some portion of every dollar spent for the program. Money spent on service to those other than the target population can also be seen as a kind of waste or benefit inefficiency. If a program is

TABLE 7.1   *Federal Revenues by Source for 1965 and 2000 as a Percentage of Total Revenues and Gross Domestic Product 1965–2000*

Percent of Revenues			Percent of GDP		
	1965	*2000*		*1965*	*2000*
Individual income	41.8	49.6	Individual income	7.1	10.2
Corporate income	21.8	10.2	Corporate income	3.7	2.1
Social insurance	19.0	32.2	Social insurance	3.2	6.6
Excise	12.5	3.3	Excise	2.1	.7
Estate and gift	2.3	1.1	Estate and gift	.4	.3
Other	2.6	3.3	Other	.4	.6
			Total	16.9	20.5

Note: An excise tax is an indirect tax collected by the federal government on a specific good—gasoline, alcohol, tobacco, and so on.

Source: Congressional Budget Office, *The Budget and Economic Outlook: Fiscal Years 2002–2011,* January 31, 2001. Appendix F. Historical Data. Table 6 Revenues by Major Source, Fiscal Years 1962–2000 (In billions of dollars). Table 7 Revenues by Major Source, Fiscal Years 1962–2000 (As a percentage of GDP). www.cbo.gov/showdoc, June 21, 2001.

set up to distribute funds, for example, but uses 30 percent of the funds for the staff needed to distribute them, this is severely cost inefficient. If a program is set up to do family counseling, but 30 percent of its funds goes for rental of facilities, this is cost inefficient. On the other hand, if a program is set up to serve a particular need of a particular group, and members of other groups use up 30 percent of the service, this is benefit inefficient.

Every program needs to be evaluated in terms of whether its dollar is being spent as well as possible in the delivery of the services to the target population for which the program was set up. It is almost impossible for any program to be 100 percent efficient, but the degree of inefficiency that can be tolerated needs to be part of the evaluation. Universal programs, as has been mentioned, tend to be much more cost efficient because they do not get involved in investigatory bureaucracy. Selective programs may be more benefit efficient in that they limit their eligible beneficiaries more stringently.

4. *Cost-benefit analysis.* A generally accepted mechanism for making evaluations of social programs is referred to as *cost-benefit analysis,* which differs from the cost and benefit efficiency discussed previously. Cost-benefit analysis is a frame of reference for relating costs to program results and attempts to identify the program effects produced by a particular program and the direct and indirect costs. These are then translated into monetary terms—dollars. The ratio of benefits to costs is then supposed to indicate the return society receives from its investment in the program.

Some examples of the kinds of questions one must deal with when considering costs and benefits are the following:

- What are the costs and benefits of inpatient therapy and community-based therapy for adults and children with emotional problems?
- If training or health care is provided for welfare recipients, what benefits and costs result from various approaches? What programs are most cost beneficial in regard to reducing poverty or improving health?
- What are the costs and benefits of returning people to communities from general or mental hospitals prematurely?
- What are the costs and benefits of different methods for dealing with child abuse or ensuring adequate childhood nutrition?

It is possible to overestimate the validity of cost-benefit analysis because many people are somewhat awed by its "economic" and "scientific" aura.[10] It is important to realize that such analyses have their limitations. Among the cautions one must be aware of is the fact that the method involves insisting that dollar costs and benefits must be assigned. However, some benefits are not easily translated into dollar terms. What monetary value should be assigned to enhanced self-esteem? Or, to participation in civic life when one formerly did not? Not everything can be converted into dollars. Both short- and long-term program achievements that depend on forecasting the future must be converted into present-time values. Future forecasting is always prey to uncertainties. Furthermore, it is very difficult to account for all costs or benefits; many can only be approximated.

Despite these limitations, in 1993 Congress enacted the Government Performance and Results Act (GPRA) that requires as of March 31, 2000 all agencies to set performance objectives expressed in *objective, quantifiable, and measurable* form for their programs and to compare and evaluate actual program results with the performance goals.

Coherence

In evaluating a program, a student needs to ask the question: Is this program coherent, that is compatible with other social policies and programs? Very often certain social policies may operate at cross purposes and undermine other social policies and programs. For example, when the government through fiscal or monetary policy slows the economy to avoid inflation, this encourages job layoffs which—in turn—can create many problems for families. Medicare focuses more on treatment and less on prevention. Is this a coherent approach to enhance health and minimize costs? Or, the use of tobacco or alcohol is dealt with as a health risk by one governmental department while they are subsidized through other governmental actions.

Latent Consequences

Programs never exist in a vacuum. As a result of one program, other things happen. Sometimes effects are anticipated and intended; sometimes they are unintentional and actually undermine the program itself, creating new problems.[11] We will see examples of this as we discuss the various social welfare programs. For instance, a jobs-creation program is often seen as a way of stimulating more jobs. As a certain number of people are put back on payrolls and earn incomes, they purchase more, creating the opportunity for still more jobs and a rising economic cycle. This is called a *multiplier effect;* a way in which a small investment in a social program can have consequences that will multiply its effects in the direction desired.

On the other hand, sometimes a latent consequence of a program undermines its very purpose. For example, in the unemployment insurance program, which will be discussed in chapter 9, an incentive was given to employers not to lay off workers. If they fired fewer workers, the insurance rates they paid for unemployment insurance would go down, thus saving them money. It was intended that this would keep employment higher. However, one of the latent consequences was that some employers were reluctant to hire new workers when they were not sure that these people could be kept on. Rather than take the chance of having to fire them later and have their insurance rates go up, the employers did not hire them in the first place. Thus the latent consequence of the program had the precise opposite effect to what was intended. Sometimes latent consequences are neither multipliers nor saboteurs of the program's intent but create new and different problems.

It is important to recognize that programs have both *anticipated* (expected and intended) and *unanticipated* (unpredicted and unintended) consequences. Both anticipated and unanticipated consequences may prove to have either positive or negative impacts. It is important that social programs have "feedback" mechanisms that provide information on their consequences. When dysfunctional (negative) consequences are identified, policy and program planners then have the option of corrective actions.[11]

These are just some of the points to be considered in evaluating any social welfare program. Prepared with this schema of analysis for understanding and evaluation, it should be possible to examine a number of social welfare programs, to understand them much more clearly, and to identify their strengths and limitations.

In the next chapter, we will look at the question of who is a client of social welfare, examine several definitions of poverty, present a profile of those in poverty and the factors associated with poverty, as well as examine income and wealth disparities.

Summary

This chapter has laid out a thoroughgoing schema for analyzing and understanding any social welfare program. It provides the student, or any citizen, with the tools to comprehend the structure and characteristics of the program, as well as to evaluate its effectiveness in delivering the services it claims to offer, in wisely using the funds that support the program, and in its coherence and latent consequences. Later, in chapters 9 and 10, we will apply this schema to a wide variety of social welfare programs currently in place in order to more fully understand their development, contexts, operation, and effectiveness.

Questions for Consideration

1. Take one social welfare program and identify its five major structural characteristics.

2. Ideally would you make all social welfare programs institutional, developmental, selective, or residual?

3. Since cost-benefit analysis translates the "bottom line" into dollars, do you think that is an acceptable way to evaluate all social welfare programs?

4. Can you identify some conflicting social policies and social programs in the United States?

Notes

1. Max Lerner, *America as a Civilization*, New York: Simon & Schuster, 1957, p. 339.

2. The authors assume responsibility for the model that follows. It should be noted that it is, however, drawn from the schema developed by Eveline Burns in her writings and teaching.

3. John Rawls, *A Theory of Justice*, Cambridge, Mass.: Harvard University Press, 1971, pp. 237–238.

4. Harold L. Wilensky and Charles Lebeaux, *Industrial Society and Social Welfare*, New York: Russell Sage Foundation, 1958, pp. 139–140.

5. Alfred J. Kahn, "Therapy, Prevention and Developmental Provision: A Social Work Strategy," *Public Health Concepts in Social Work Education*, New York: CSWE in cooperation with the Public Health Service, Department of Health, Education, and Welfare, 1962, pp. 132–148.

6. James Midgley, *Social Development: The Developmental Perspective in Social Welfare*, Thousand Oaks: Sage Publications, 1995; James Midgley, "Toward a Developmental Model of Social Policy: Relevance of the Third World Experience," *Journal of*

Sociology and Social Welfare 23, No. 1, 1996, pp. 59–74; Michael Sherraden, "Administrative Lessons from the Civilian Conservation Corps (1933–1942)," *Administration in Social Work,* 9 (2), 1985, pp. 85–97; Michael Sherraden, *Assets and the Poor,* Armonk, N.Y.: Sharpe, Inc., 1991.

7. Social workers and other citizens should know that professional social workers refused to make surprise "raids" on clients' homes, visits usually intended to see if a man was living in the home of a welfare mother. With the help of the profession, a social worker, Benny Parrish, was upheld by the courts in his right to refuse this unprofessional duty. *Benny Max Parrish v. The Civil Service Commission of the County of Alameda,* State of California, District Court of Appeal, 1 Civil No. 22556, San Francisco: Pernau-Walsh Printing Co., 1965.

8. See Committee on Ways and Means, U.S. House of Representatives, *Overview of Entitlement Programs, 1994 Green Book, Background Material and Data on Programs within the Jurisdiction of the Committee on Ways and Means,* Washington, D.C.: U.S. Government Printing Office, 1994, p. 399.

9. Theda Skocpol, "Targeting within Universalism," Christopher Jencks and Paul E. Peterson, eds., *The Urban Underclass,* Washington, D.C.: Brookings Institution, 1991, pp. 411–436.

10. Peter H. Rossi and Howard E. Freeman, *Evaluation: A Systematic Approach,* Newbury Park, Calif.: Sage Publications, 1993; Evert Vedung, *Public Policy and Program Evaluation,* New Brunswick: Transaction Publishers, 1997.

11. Nathan Glazer, "The Limits of Social Policy," *The Limits of Social Policy,* Cambridge, Mass.: Harvard University Press, 1988, pp. 51–58.

8

The Welfare Society
and Its Clients

It's no shame to be poor, but it's no great honor either.
—Fiddler on the Roof

Wealth is well known to be a great comforter.
—Plato, *The Republic*

Overview

In this chapter, we will answer the question as to who is a client of social welfare, present various definitions of poverty, and then give primary attention to a profile of those in poverty and the factors associated with poverty. We also examine income and wealth inequality in the United States and suggest the major means for dealing with the problem of poverty. Finally, we will present the current dominant philosophy regarding social welfare as reflected in the United States during the first years of the twenty-first century.

In chapters 9 and 10, we turn to an examination of the specifics of major programs, reflecting the relationship of values, ideology, political decision making, and social policy.

Who Is a Client of Social Welfare?

As discussed earlier, definitions of social welfare differ. Given a very narrow definition, one could conclude that only those who are public assistance recipients are on "welfare." Given broader definitions of social welfare and looking at the many nonmarket functions that serve most citizens, we see that we are all clients of the welfare society.

For example, a U.S. senator offered the following scenario about one family illustrating the omnipresence of social welfare programs in people's lives. A veteran returning from service went to college on the GI Bill; bought his house with a Federal Housing Administration loan; saw his children born in a Veterans Administration hospital; started a business with a Small Business Administration loan; got electricity from the Tennessee Valley Authority; and, later, water from an Environmental Protection Agency project. His parents retired to a farm on Social Security; got electricity from the Rural Electrification Administration; and used soil testing from the U.S. Department of Agriculture. When the father became ill, the family was saved from financial ruin by Medicare and a life was saved with a drug developed through the National Institutes for Health. His children participated in the school lunch program, learned physics from teachers trained in the National Science Foundation program, and went through college with guaranteed student loans. He drove to work on the interstate and moored his boat in a channel dredged by army engineers. When floods hit, he took Amtrak to Washington to apply for disaster relief and then spent some time in the Smithsonian museums.[1]

Social welfare is pervasive throughout the breadth of the "welfare" society. According to Richard Titmuss, all collective interventions to meet certain needs of the individual and/or to serve the wider interests of society can be broadly grouped into three major categories of welfare: *social welfare, fiscal welfare,* and *occupational welfare.*[2] Welfare then may be found in diverse locations, including tax deductions or credits, employer-subsidized health programs, as well as Social Security and unemployment insurance.

The income tax system serves as one major *fiscal welfare* vehicle through which the government develops social welfare programs. Whether the government gives a person money (for example, the Temporary Assistance to Needy Families program [TANF]) or permits a particular tax deduction, the effect is the same: a transfer of funds to people for some socially determined good. Contributions to voluntary social agencies, for instance, are tax deductible. Such support is really another method for the government to support social welfare programs and voluntarism. But there are other ways in which the tax system functions as a welfare system. When a corporation or individual deducts given sums from taxes owed, these sums—because they are not to be paid and are retained by the taxpayer or corporation—are in reality "tax expenditures." That is, the retained monies are really payments to the persons or corporations.

Some observers have suggested that in the United States we have capitalism for the poor and socialism for the rich.[3] Just as social welfare guards against certain risks, there are those who believe that society has been more ready to share risks for large businesses than for individuals. The larger the business, the greater the protection afforded. Big businesses may be able to write off losses or be bailed out through government guarantees. Direct and indirect subsidies have helped large business. In this way, U.S. society has demonstrated greater generosity to the business enterprises than to salaried employees, who ultimately depend in many cases on their social insurances and public assistance.

Occupational welfare is generally associated with having employment. For example, if you are employed, you and your family may be the recipients of insurance benefits that cover health and hospital care, disability, retirement, dental work, and perhaps legal bills. In this way, to varying degrees, employment and occupations also serve as means for distributing welfare benefits, but only to those who are employed or their dependents.

We can see that social, fiscal, and occupational welfare systems are widespread throughout our society. Most people, if not all, are served by these different but functionally similar systems. All of the social welfare services described in this book, both economic security programs and personal social services, are forms of welfare. Many of these services (from social security to mental health programs) serve Americans of all classes. We are all "welfare clients" in one way or another. The issues are simply who benefits and to what degree from each program.

Still our concern here is primarily with the poor and the disadvantaged, and so we want to focus in large measure on the programs for alleviation of poverty in the United States, even while we recognize the universal nature of welfare in its several guises.

What Is Poverty?

There are different perspectives, complexities, and problems associated with the concept and definition of poverty. However, for our purposes, poverty is economic deprivation, a lack of economic resources by which to obtain the goods and services necessary for a minimally adequate standard of living. There are several ways in which poverty is defined. Basically, they fit into these three categories: (1) Poverty means a person or family has less than an objectively defined minimum; (2) They have less than others in society; or (3) They feel they do not have enough to get along.[4] Decisions about the choice of definition to be used are made on pragmatic grounds (What data is available?), political grounds (Which groups favor one definition or another?), and historical grounds (What has been our experience with particular definitions?).

Absolute Poverty

One way of defining poverty is to draw a clear poverty line, a dollar figure, and suggest that this absolute level represents an "objective" minimum. Below the established minimum, one is poor; above it, one is not poor. The poverty threshold is established for income and size of family. In 2002, the poverty line for a four-person family was $18,100 (except for Alaska and Hawaii). Such a line indicates that every four-person family below the line is in poverty, and every family of the same size whose income is greater is above the poverty level. For example, in

2000, using absolute thresholds, there were 31.1 million poor persons, representing 11.3 percent of the U.S. population.

The poverty standard most used is the index originated at the Social Security Administration by Mollie Orshansky, a Labor Department economist, in 1964. Now calculated by the Census Bureau, it became the official federal definition of poverty thresholds for statistical use. This index was based on earlier data that found that American families of three or more persons spent approximately one-third of their income on food and another survey that outlined the cost of a minimal subsistence budget (the economy food plan). The index used an estimate of the least costly economy food plan—a temporary, low-budget, nutritionally adequate diet—and multiplied the cost by three. A slightly different ratio was used for two-person families and for individuals. Originally, the thresholds were computed for households of different sizes, sex of the family head, ages of individuals, and whether the family lived on a farm. Adjustments for the sex of the family head and farm or nonfarm residence were abolished in 1981. Because it only involves considering money income, the index does not reflect noncash benefits such as Food Stamps, Medicaid, and public housing. It does include cash benefits such as Social Security and unemployment insurance. The threshold is adjusted for inflation every year in relation to the Consumer Price Index (CPI). In addition to the Census Bureau's threshold, a simplified version is derived by the Department of Health and Human Services and used for administrative purposes—for example, as an eligibility criterion for federal programs.

In addition to the impact these statistics have in regard to social welfare benefits directly, they affect many financial decisions, from monetary policy and the federal budget to buying a new house and expanding a business, from Social Security payments to union wage increases and individual tax brackets. The quality and accuracy of these critical governmental statistics have been criticized, just as government in general has been. A panel of economists appointed by the Senate reported that inflation as reflected in the CPI may be overstated by more than 1 percent. Much is at stake in defining the CPI, and a debate continues among legislators, administration officials, economists, and the Bureau of Labor Statistics to seek a consensus for action. Many experts counseled caution in considering revisions because of the value, technological, and political ramifications of decisions in this area. Projected changes annually could save many billions of dollars without forcing a single vote on spending or tax hikes. Among the options are: legislation altering the computation of the CPI, leaving it unchanged, or subtracting a particular percentage from each published index figure and then using the lower figure for indexation purposes.[5]

The efficiency of such standards lies in their ability to make possible comparisons over time. If we state that 22.4 percent of the population was in poverty in 1959 and 11.3 percent was in poverty in 2000, we have a basis for comparison over time. Even if we argue that the poverty line, as defined, is inadequate, there is a certain neatness in the concept of defining poverty as being anything below x dollars of income per year.

There are several limitations to this poverty line concept. The identification of progress in combating poverty can be deceptive. When there is dramatic change such as the reduction of the poverty population from 22 percent in 1959 to 12 percent in 1969, we know there has been progress. Such changes can make clearer whether there has been progress or retrogression. But even here, our estimate of the extent of poverty may be faulty. One has to place poverty into a context.

The poverty line excludes the near-poor and may give a deceptive picture of the population. Another limitation is that definitions do not include wealth or assets. There is a vast difference between two elderly people, each receiving $400 per month in Social Security benefits, if one owns a home free and clear while the other does not. Further, personal needs may differ according to such factors as disabilities, illnesses, and special dietary needs.

A further limitation of such an income-only–based poverty level, as noted before, is that it counts only cash received (including governmental cash benefits) but does not include in-kind assistance such as food or medical assistance. Government spending on noncash benefits has increased more rapidly than spending on means-tested cash benefits over the years. The poverty measure does not take into account that changes in the cost of basic goods (food and housing) have changed relative to other goods since the early 1960s when the poverty measure was developed. Costs do not reflect geographic location nor do they make allowances for increased expenses and economies of scale associated with increasing family size. These omissions are serious, and as a result, questions are raised as to the validity of the definition being used.

In considering definitions of poverty, one must ask questions such as: What are the new consumption patterns and what is "necessary" for people today? What goods and services are available today that were not available when the index was created? What proportions of income are needed for life's necessities? It is clear that in recent years, Americans have needed to spend much larger percentages of their income on housing and child care than on food.[6] Which is the fairest measurement of the number of poor persons? What should be included in the contemporary "market-basket"? What impact should a generally improving standard of living have on defining poverty? An accurate and fair count matters because our society needs to know realistically how many poor persons there are, who they are, and where they live. These facts tell us much about how our economy is performing and the nature of our society. Knowledge of the dimensions of poverty is one of the bases upon which arguments can be made either for or against governmental intervention.

In 1995, a panel of experts formed by the National Academy of Sciences at the behest of Congress recommended that the poverty threshold represent a budget based on disposable income (that is, the amount left after a family pays taxes and essential expenses such as for food, clothing, shelter, transportation to work, child care, and health care). The budget also includes a small additional amount to allow for other expenses such as household and personal care and transportation unrelated to work. According to the proposal, the family's cash income would be counted as well as noncash government benefits like Food Stamps, housing assistance, school lunches, and home energy assistance. Inclusion of these items would increase family income.

The panel recommended that the poverty threshold be based on actual consumer expenditures over the three previous years. Also, the poverty level would be adjusted to reflect the needs of different types of families and to reflect regional differences in living costs. Family resources, according to this proposal, would be the sum of money income from all sources together with the value of money equivalents, such as Food Stamps, that can be used to buy goods and services, minus expenses. These latter expenses include income and payroll taxes, child care and other work-related expenses, child-support payments to another household, and out-of-pocket medical care costs, including health insurance premiums. This new poverty threshold would be updated every year and would assume children need fewer resources than adults. The suggested new index would include families (including cohabiting couples) and unrelated individuals sharing a household.[7]

The Census Bureau is conducting research to refine some of the panel of expert's measurement methods and to examine how the recommendations will affect the number of the poor and the poverty rates. Four experimental technical measures are being tested. These include: (1) A close implementation of the panel's recommendations; (2) Estimates of child care expenses; (3) Adjustments for changes in expenses as family size increases; and (4) Study without adjustments for geographic location. Of course, different definitions yield different poverty rates.

Actually changing the measure of poverty is extremely complex and difficult. The poverty index is integral to both federal and state governmental activities (and in certain cases those of the private sector). In addition to the potential impact on various governmental agencies, there is uncertainty about the public reaction if it were found there are many more or many fewer poor persons. Further, resources distributed to states are often based on the number of poor people in the various states, individuals and families are deemed eligible or not for benefits based on how they are classified, and various societal groups will be affected differentially. All of this suggests the political difficulty of altering the poverty definition.

Some advocates for the poor postulate that the only problem of those in poverty is lack of money. They suggest that no theories or experts are needed, just an adequate annual income. But no matter what is established in any society as the income floor, there will still be relative inequality. The new floor becomes, in effect, the poverty line. Still, defining poverty as some amount under x dollars per year gives us a handle on poverty and suggests ways of combating it.

Relative Comparison Poverty

Relative Threshold.   Some people have suggested the utilization of other thresholds that better indicate the standing of poor people in our society. In 2000, the poverty level for a family of four was $17,050. Would a better indicator of poverty be to define four-person families as poor if they had less than 50 percent of the median U.S. family income? In 2000, the median family household income was $51,751, 50 percent of which is $25,875. This figure is $8,825 more than the 2000 poverty level.

There are those who argue that such a relative threshold, by being tied to some average income level, would be a better indicator of who is poor in our society. Others suggest the costs of implementing such a threshold would prove too great. The value of a relative indicator is that it places the poor in relation to other members of our society and is more suggestive of where poor persons stand at a particular time in a certain context.

Relative Deprivation.   Peter Townsend proposed a "deprivation" index and argues that money is an inadequate measure of poverty and does not demonstrate what people need. Those who are poor lack certain commodities that are common in the society in which one lives. This definition is based on the concept of *relative deprivation*. His suggestion is that it is necessary to raise the poverty level to a point that allows people to live a basic civilized existence. Disabled people need more, as do families with children. This argument raises questions such as: Should poor children be able to have birthday parties? Should a poor family be able to afford a car or VCR? Should a poor parent be able to have a vacation? According to this view, the relationship of poor persons to their families and neighbors and the common experiences in their communities, and not money alone, are crucial. There is a point at which, without access to these basic existence activities, one is in a state of deprivation.[8]

Subjective Poverty.   There is another way of defining poverty, which uses a subjective strategy. This measure does not provide a cutoff line prepared on the basis of the statistical data per se. Instead, the subjective measure uses the assessments of household members as to the "just sufficient" dollar amounts of income needed, in their estimation, by people like themselves to get along. If they have less than their estimate, they are said to be poor.

Capability Deprivation.   Another approach is to compare "capabilities," that is, to compare the extent to which for one reason or another a person is able or not able to do the various things they value doing, leading the life they value living or being the kind of person they desire to be. These states can range from adequate nourishment to being able to participate in the community. Poverty then is *capability deprivation* because the people are unable to do many of the things they value doing. These approaches suggest that instead of experts determining the needs of community members, the people affected should offer their views of what they consider to be impoverishment.[9]

A Description of the Poor

When you are poor in the United States, you are poor in one of the wealthiest nations on earth. Poverty in the United States is often hidden from the eyes of the middle and upper classes. But wealth and luxury are not hidden from the eyes of the poor, who see in movies and on television how the "good life" is lived. Moreover, no matter the odds, the societal expectation is that adequate people should be able to find adequate income. The following discussion uses the U.S. Bureau of the Census poverty threshold, an absolute measure, which is increased each year by the same percentage as the CPI.

As Table 8.1 illustrates, in 2000, there were 31.1 million poor persons in the United States. This represents 11.3 percent of all Americans, or almost one out of every eight persons. The poverty threshold for a four person household in 2000 was $17,050 or 40 percent of the median income $42,148. Thus, the median household

TABLE 8.1   *Selected Median Household Income, By Type, Race and Hispanic Origin, Earnings of Full-Time, Year-Round Workers, and Per Capita Income (2000)*

31.1 million poor persons; 11.3 percent of the population	
Poverty threshold, family of four	$17,050
Households	
U.S. median household income	$42,148
Married couple families	$59,346
Male householder, no wife present	$42,129
Female householder, no husband present	$28,116
65 years and older	$23,048
Race and Hispanic Origin of Householder	
White households	$44,226
White, non-Hispanic	$45,904
African American households	$30,439
Hispanic households	$33,447
Asian and Pacific Islander	$55,521
Native Americans and Alaska Natives (1997–99 average)	$30,784
Region	
Northeast	$45,106
Midwest	$44,646
South	$38,410
West	$44,744
Earnings of Full-Time, Year Round Workers	
Male	$37,339
Female	$27,355
Per Capita Income	
White, non-Hispanic	$25,278
African American	$15,197
Hispanic	$12,306
Asian and Pacific Islander	$22,352
Native Americans and Alaska Natives (1990)	$8,284

Source: Carmen DeNavas-Walt, Robert W. Cleveland, and Marc I. Roemer, U.S. Census Bureau, Current Population Reports, p 60–213, *Money Income in the United States: 2000,* U.S. Government Printing Office, Washington, D.C., 2001, p. 2 and U.S. Census Bureau, Table 44 "Social and Economic Characteristics of the American Indian Population: 1990," *Statistical Abstract of the United States: 2000* (120th edition), Washington, D.C., 2000,

income in the United States in the United States that same year was almost 2½ times the poverty level for a four-person household.

In Table 8.2 we observe the numbers of poor people in various groupings. Of the 31.1 million poor in 2000, three fourths of the poor lived in metropolitan areas, including almost 13 million residing in central cities. We can observe that there were 11.6 million poor children under 18 years of age, including almost 4 million under 6 years living in poor families, many of whom lived in families headed by the 3.1 million female householders with no spouses present.

We can focus directly on the well-being of people with lowest incomes by examining the poverty rate. Throughout the 1960s and the early 1970s, the poverty rate fell dramatically, from more than 22 percent to just over 11 percent in 1973. Remaining low through the 1970s, the poverty rate fluctuated little during that decade. In the 1980s, the poverty rate rose dramatically, then decreased in the second half of the decade to reach 12.8 percent in 1989, then rose again until 1993 when it began to decrease once again until it reached 12.7 percent in 1998.

In Table 8.3, we observe that groups experience poverty at different rates. We can note that all poor persons constituted 11.8 percent (1 in 8 persons) of the total population. But the differential rates among groups form a pattern. For example, married couple families—white and African American—have relatively low poverty rates, but the rate increases rapidly for children, central city residents, minority persons, and female householders without husbands present. African American female householders with no husband present experience poverty rates *8 times* the rate for married couples. One can observe other such relationships.

TABLE 8.2   *The Number of Poor Persons, Families, and Unrelated Individuals (2000)*

Population Group	U.S. Population (in millions)	Population Group	U.S. Population (in millions)
All persons	31.1	Midwest	5.9
In metropolitan areas	24.2	Northeast	5.4
White	21.2	Children under 6 years in families	3.9
Inside central cities	12.9		
South	12.2	Persons 65 and over	3.1
Children under 18 years	11.6	Female householder, no spouse present	3.3
African American	7.9		
West	7.5	Married-couple families	2.6
Hispanic	7.1	Asian and Pacific Islander persons	1.2
Outside metropolitan areas	6.8		
All families	6.2	Native American persons	.7

Source: Joseph Dalaker, U.S. Census Bureau, Current Population Reports, Series p. 60-214, *Poverty in the United States: 2000,* U.S. Government Printing Office, Washington, D.C., 2001.

TABLE 8.3 *Poverty Rates for Selected Groups (2000)*

Population Group	Poverty Rate (%)
African American female householder, no husband present	34.6
Hispanic female householder, no husband present	34.2
African American related children under 18	30.7
Hispanic related children under 18	27.3
Female householder, no husband present	24.7
Native American/Alaska Native (1997–99 average)	25.9
African American	22.1
Hispanic	21.2
White female householder, no husband present	20.0
Asian and Pacific Islander female, no husband present	19.9
African American families	19.1
Hispanic families	18.5
Related children under 6 in families	16.9
Inside central cities	16.1
Related children under 18 in families	15.7
Married couple, Hispanic	14.1
Outside metropolitan areas	13.4
South	12.5
All persons	11.3
Asian and Pacific Islander	10.8
65 years and older	10.2
White	9.4
Asian and Pacific Islander families	8.8
In families	8.6
White families	6.9
Married couple, African American	6.1
Married couple family	4.7
Married couple family white, not Hispanic	3.3

Source: Joseph Dalaker, U.S. Census Bureau, Current Population Reports, Series p. 60-214, *Poverty in the United States: 2000*, U.S. Government Printing Office, Washington, D.C., 2000.

Tables 8.2 and 8.3 indicate various factors associated with poverty. One's chances of being poor are compounded by the interplay and effects of multiple risk factors.. When several factors are considered in combination, the risk of poverty soars. Consider that in 1999, 11.8 percent of all persons were poor, over 20 percent of Hispanic families and almost 22 percent of African American families but almost 40 percent of African American female householders and Hispanic female householders without spouses were poor.

One can see in Tables 8.2 and 8.3 some of the important variables associated with poverty, and comparisons among groupings can be made. Taking the white poverty rate of 8.6 percent as the basis for comparison, one can see that almost 21 percent of all persons under 18 years of age were poor (one in five children). There are 14.5 million poor persons under 18 years, 4.2 million poor female householders without spouses, and 3.4 million poor persons 65 and older—just over 22 million poor persons. Thus, 60 percent of the poor can be found in those three categories. Until 1974, the poverty rate for the elderly exceeded that for children. However, since then, the poverty rate for children has been higher than for any other age group, particularly so for those younger than six. These configurations reflect how vulnerable women of any age and children are to poverty. There are strong suggestions that insecure employment and low earnings for fathers are important determinants of childhood poverty because of their direct effect on family income and because of their indirect effect through the rise of mother-only families. Mothers' employment, in turn, contributes to the poverty of children through the income mothers bring into the home and indirectly through facilitation of separation and divorce.[10] But this vulnerability is not limited to those children raised in single-parent families.

Most Americans experience significant fluctuations in their economic well-being on a regular basis. About three-fourths of the population experience their economic well-being go up or down by at least 5 percent from one year to the next. These fluctuations result from changes in living arrangements, program participation, work status, or other circumstances.[11]

Thus, your chances of being poor differ by personal characteristics (minority status, age, sex), family composition (married, female householder, single person), place of residence (central cities or rural areas, region in the United States), education (less than high school education completed), as well as employment and types of employment, among other factors. Some major groups overrepresented among the poor are persons in families with a female head of household, children under 18 years of age (and especially very young children), African Americans, and Latinos. Trends confirm earlier predictions that by the year 2000 the poverty population will be composed primarily of women and their children.

One serious misconception about the poor is the belief they do not work. In fact, the poor work more than is generally believed. Employment plays an important part in determining whether or not one is living at the poverty level, but employment does not explain everything. Having a job, even a full-time job, does not guarantee an escape from poverty. In 2000 44.5 percent of the poor had one full-time worker in the family. The implication of these figures is that many jobs pay less than is needed to lift families out of poverty.[12]

For those who lack education and skills, employment opportunities are difficult to find. Manufacturing jobs have grown scarcer. Technology is used in place of people where possible. Where potential jobs exist in the service area, they are usually lower-paying and without benefits such as health insurance and pensions. Furthermore, technology has begun to affect the service sector as well. Another phenomenon affects employment opportunities: A "contingent workforce" has developed. These persons have no direct ties to a corporation. They are part-timers, temporary full-timers, and contract workers.

But poverty is not simply a matter of unemployment or underemployment. In 2000, the median earnings for year-round, full-time employed males was $37,339 whereas the median earnings for year-round, full-time employed females was $27,355.[13] Thus, the average woman working full-time and year-round earned less than three-fourths of that of a man working in the same pattern. This ratio, while up from 60 percent since 1980, indicates there is still a significant gap between the earnings of men and women. Following the all-time high achieved in 1996, the drop in the earnings ratio is mainly attributed to the larger growth in the earnings of men. Another consideration is the fact that in 1997 8.5 million workers held two or more jobs and 30 percent of them said they did so in order to meet regular household expenses[14]

Even if an individual or family has a high income, they can still be financially vulnerable. Wealth (net worth) rather than income is a better indicator of the long run security or lack of it.[15] We turn now to how income and wealth are distributed in the United States. This will help us better understand the context in which one is poor in this nation.

Income and Wealth Inequality

Poverty also can be approached from another perspective. Statisticians use two common methods to measure the degree of inequality. The *Gini coefficient* or *ratio* is expressed as a scale running from 0 to 1 on which 0 signifies perfect equality (everyone has the same income) and 1 indicates extreme inequality (one person or group has all income). In 1999, the Gini index was 0.457, essentially unchanged since 1993. The other method looks at the share of total income earned by various percentiles. In this case, one examines the total income of the nation to see how much of it went to the poorest 10 or 20 percent of the population and how much went to the richest 10 or 20 percent. Either method can indicate over time whether there is progress in sharing the wealth more equitably. We will look at the respective shares of income and wealth for groups.

Not income alone, but wealth is an important factor. In general, the term *income* refers to the amount of money received in any one year before taxes. *Wealth* usually means property and assets that have market value and can be exchanged for money or goods. Complex definitional issues abound about these two terms, depending on the purposes of the definitions. As many as fifteen alternative measures of income are being tested by the Bureau of the Census. Alternative measures of income are being tested to account for noncash governmental benefits, capital gains, federal and state income taxes, the value of Medicare and Medicaid, the earned income credit, as well as the estimated equity return on one's own home. In regard to income, should in-kind income or services be included? Should a definition of income include money spent on taxes, home production of food or clothing, employee fringe benefits, or expenses required to earn income? Wealth may be in the form of assets of many kinds such as stocks, bonds, annuities, businesses and industries, housing, insurance, trust funds, personal or corporate properties, and so on. Should personal skills or personal contacts be considered forms of wealth? Licenses and credentials?

Income inequality has gown in the United States and the gap between rich and poor households has reached the widest point recorded since the 1930s. One can observe in Table 8.4 that in 1972, the poorest one-fifth of U.S. households received 4.1 percent of national income; the top one-fifth received 43.9 percent. By 1999, the income received by the lowest fifth decreased to 3.6 percent (*14 percent decrease*) and the richest one-fifth received 49.4 percent of the country's total net income (13 percent *increase*). The top 5 percent received 17 percent in 1972 and 21.5 percent in 1999 (a 26 percent *increase*). Almost three fourths of all income went to the top 40% of all households.

A study by the Congressional Budget Office showed that the average after-tax income of the richest one percent of Americans grew by $414,000 between 1979 and 1997, after adjusting for inflation, while average after-tax income fell $100 for the poorest 20 percent of Americans. The average after-tax income of the middle quintile grew by $3,400. The gap between income received by rich and poor and between the rich and the middle class widened in both the 1980s and the 1990s, reaching their widest point in 1997, the latest data available.[16]

Income and its distribution are intricately tied to structural factors and cannot be separated from social and economic trends, including those on the international level. Possible sources of income disparities are changes taking place in the nation's

TABLE 8.4 *Share of Aggregate Income Received by Each Fifth and Top 5 Percent of Households, by Race and Hispanic Origin of Householder (1972 and 1999)*

	Lowest Fifth	Second Fifth	Third Fifth	Fourth Fifth	Highest Fifth	Top 5%
All Races						
1972	4.1	10.5	17.1	24.5	43.9	17.0
1999	3.6	8.9	14.9	23.2	49.4	21.5
Whites						
1972	4.3	10.8	17.2	24.3	43.4	16.8
1999	3.9	9.1	15.0	23.1	49.0	21.5
African Americans						
1972	3.9	9.2	15.8	24.9	46.2	16.9
1999	3.1	8.3	14.7	24.0	50.0	20.0
Hispanics						
1972	5.3	11.2	17.2	24.0	42.3	16.2
1999	4.1	9.5	15.2	23.4	47.9	19.9

Source: U.S. Census Bureau, Current Population Reports, p. 60–209, *Money Income in the United States: 1999,* Table B3, U.S. Government Printing Office, Washington, D.C., 2000, pp. B6–B7.

labor market, a shift from goods production to service production, widespread low-wage, nonunionized jobs, a shift of power away from workers and toward managers and shareholders, deregulation, globalization, relocation of manufacturing industries out of central cities and overseas, and technology. These factors have reduced the typical employee's bargaining power and no institution has arisen to exert counter forces.[17] Although higher wages have been available for highly skilled workers, wages for less-skilled workers have not kept pace, and there have been fewer job opportunities for the unskilled in manufacturing. Other potential contributing factors are the curtailment of public services and benefits, the number of persons divorcing, and the number of single-parent, female-headed households.

Although these variables affect everyone, it is important to note that there are differential impacts by diverse and significant factors such as the nature of the job market, the nature of the job preparation people have received, and geographic factors (living in center-city or rural areas). Discrimination on racial, ethnic, gender, and other grounds, as we saw earlier, contributes to these differential effects.

Wealth in the United States has become extraordinarily concentrated. In 1992 (latest data available) the share of wealth held by the top 1 percent was 37.2 percent. In 1992 the top 20 percent held 84 percent of the total wealth, that is the bottom 80 percent held only 16.3 percent of the total wealth. The assets held primarily by the wealthy were stocks, bonds, trusts, business equity, and non-home real estate. In contrast, almost two-thirds of the wealth of the bottom ninety percent of households was invested in their own homes.

Here too there are differences by race and minority status. In 1992 only 48.9 percent of Hispanics, African Americans, American Indians, and Asians as a group owned homes compared to 69 percent of non-Hispanic Whites. During that same year, the median financial wealth of the latter group was $62,000 while that of the former group was $12,200, 5 times less. While the non-Hispanic Whites had an average net worth of $265,000, the combined group's average net worth was $83,500, more than 3 times less. Similarly 13 percent of non-Hispanic White households had zero or negative net worth while almost 31 percent of the combined group had zero or negative net worth.[18]

The social structure of the society determines the options available to people and affects almost every sphere of our lives, from where one lives to how one spends leisure time. When the United States was compared with other nations, it was consistently found to have a relatively high rate of upward mobility over time. Some of the findings of mobility studies follow: (1) There is a great deal of occupational inheritance; (2) Mobility rates among black men are substantially lower than those among white men; (3) There are regional differences in the rates of mobility; and (4) Geographic mobility is related to vertical mobility. Those who don't move have a higher rate of downward mobility. Some of the factors that influence mobility are industrialization, class differences in fertility rates, immigration rates, and institutionalized ethnic and gender discrimination.

Despite a long history of such upward mobility, *today the data is conflicting.* A study of intergenerational mobility (the income status of fathers and sons) based on national longitudinal data found our society is less mobile than described in earlier research. Another study found that 60 percent of those children in the poorest 20 percent in the early 1970s were still in the bottom group ten years later. Almost 90 percent in the bottom group remained in the bottom two income groups ten years later. There was no change in these figures for the 1980s. Others report there is widespread mobility, generally upward, and "overwhelmingly, across generations, most Americans are movers, not stayers in the occupational hierarchy." This latter group suggests intergenerational mobility patterns have been influenced by the large-scale shift away from farming and blue-collar occupations and the corresponding increase in white-collar, middle class occupations.[19]

The Effect of Some Government Programs

One may ask: What part do governmental programs play in alleviating poverty, especially those programs aimed at economic security? What is the antipoverty effectiveness of governmental cash and noncash transfers (including federal income and payroll taxes)? Table 8.5 addresses these questions. The number of poor elderly persons and children in the United States in 1998 who were counted as poor prior to the receipt of any governmental transfer was 15.6 million elderly persons and 15.4 children. One can observe the effectiveness of and contribution of social insurances (Social Security, Unemployment Compensation, and Workers' Compensation), means- tested cash benefits (Temporary Assistance to Needy Families, Supplemental Security Income, and General Assistance), means-tested noncash benefits (food stamps, housing benefits, and school lunch), and federal payroll and income taxes and the Earned Income Credit (EIC) to the reduction of poverty.

The table presents alternative measures of poverty to the official standard. Included are the number of elderly persons and children below the poverty line before any government benefits are taken into account, after each type of benefit is added to income, and after the government cash and noncash benefits and Federal taxes and the EIC are added to or subtracted from income. Prior to transfers, almost one half of the elderly were poor. After considering the impact of these governmental programs, the poverty rate for elderly persons (8.8 percent) was among the lowest on record. Similarly, the poverty rate among children before transfers was 21.5 percent in 1998 and after considering the programs their rate was 14.3 percent, the lowest level since 1979 and almost five percentage points lower than in 1993. Special note should be taken regarding the powerful contribution of social insurances to the reduction of the number of the poor, particularly of the elderly.

There are numerous complex and perplexing problems associated with counting as income the value of in-kind benefits, not the least of which is the initial problem of what value one will place on a particular benefit. If one adds such benefits from one program to the "income" of poor persons, does that mean they will become ineligible for other programs? There are other quandaries in such valuations. If Medicaid benefits are to be treated as income for the poor, shall Medicare and employer-provided health care be counted as income for those who are not poor? There are political and other pressures to include in-kind benefits in

TABLE 8.5 *The Impact of Market Income and Safety Net Programs on Poverty: 1998: The Elderly and Children*

Elderly Individuals and Children (In 1,000s)			
Total Elderly Population	32.4	*Total Child Population*	71.3
Cash income before transfers	15.6		15.3
Plus social insurance (Unemployment Insurance, Workers' Compensation, Social Security)	3.8		14.1
Plus means-tested cash benefits	3.4		13.4
Plus means-tested non-cash benefits	2.8		11.7
Less federal taxes (Including Earned Income Credit)	2.9		10.2
Number (in thousands) removed from poverty due to:			
Social Insurance	11,836		1,234
Means-tested cash benefits	382		664
Means-tested non-cash benefits	525		1,718
Federal taxes (including EIC)	–4		1,519
	Total: 12,739		Total: 5,135
Percent removed from poverty due to:			
Social insurance	75.9		8.0
Means-tested cash benefits	2.4		4.3
Means tested non-cash benefits	3.4		11.2
Federal taxes (including EIC)	–0.0		9.9
	Total: 81.6		Total: 33.4

Before transfers and taxes, 48.2 percent of the elderly and 21.5 percent of children were poor.

Source: Committee on Ways and Means, U.S. House of Representatives, *2000 Green Book, Background and Material and Data on Programs within the Jurisdiction of the Committee on Ways and Means,* Washington, D.C.: U.S. Government Printing Office, 2000, pp. 1320–1323.

poverty line calculations. The search for fair and objective measurements that include cash and noncash benefits as well as taxes has spurred the type of calculations reported in Table 8.5.

There are three ways of assigning values to in-kind benefits that have been used for measuring poverty: (1) market value, (2) recipient or cash-equivalent value, and (3) poverty budget-share value. The market value is equal to the purchase price in the private market of the goods received by the recipient. The recipient or cash-equivalent value is the amount of cash that would make the recipient just as well off as would the in-kind transfer. This reflects the value that would be set on the benefit by the recipient and is usually less but never more than the market value. This measure is difficult to estimate, particularly for medical care. The poverty budget-share value is tied to the current poverty definition and limits values assigned to food, housing, or medical transfers to the percentages spent on these items by persons at or near the poverty line in particular years. Valuations of in-kind benefits currently in use are those based on a market value technique that attempts to measure the private market cost of benefits provided in-kind.

Transfer programs are powerful forces that can bring people out of poverty. However, as we have indicated previously, the working poor account for large numbers of those in poverty (one in six of the heads of poor families work full-time year-round). The interrelation of poverty, employment, wage levels, and income security programs is clear, and the reduction of poverty cannot be accomplished by income-transfer devices alone; obviously other interventions will be required.

The Near-Poor and Expectations

The "near-poor" struggle with incomes that are only somewhat above the official poverty line. They too are in need of services, but overall, the near-poor are ineligible for many of the benefits for which those below the poverty line may be eligible. Some near-poor may, in certain instances, be eligible for means-tested programs because, implicitly, the government recognizes that the poverty line is too low. But they too have to pass a means test, which is considered demeaning, stigmatizing, and a situation many persons prefer to avoid. It is from this group, but not from it alone, that much of the backlash against selective programs arises.

The poverty line itself, as discussed previously, is an arbitrary division. Although it has been adjusted to account for inflation since the mid-1960s, it does not take into account the rising expectations or the norm of American living. Therefore, the gap between the official poverty line and comfortable living may be growing greater, and a large army of near-poor and nominally lower-middle-class people are really poor and feel discriminated against: women, children, racial minorities, and the working poor.

The poverty problems of women, children, the aging, and racial and ethnic minorities are clearly disproportionate, but it is important to note that the problem of poverty is endemic to our society and endured by many groups. The problem is widespread, and every group has a share in the burden, although some carry inordinate loads. But the problem of poverty cannot be understood or approached without also considering the groups whose income is slightly more than those in poverty.

At different times, different groups have been most discriminated against. Usually the latest wave of immigrants took the brunt of the oppression. For whites, the major force of such oppression may end, but for African Americans, Latinos, and Native Americans, there has been a continuity to the discrimination aimed at them, and their poverty has persisted even in the best of economic times. Although some Asian-American groups have made more rapid progress even while identified as "minorities of color," one in ten of them are poor.

Those who are in poverty are besieged by their difficulties. It is natural that one group or another should claim that the discrimination aimed at them is the most difficult, the most trying. Although programs aimed *selectively* at particular groups hold a certain fascination and promise easier success, they often have accompanying costs.

Counter to programs aimed only at particular groups is the need for *universal* services that offer equal access to opportunity for all groups. Universal coverage in a welfare society would meet basic needs and provide for the development of individuals, families, and communities. It is a truism that universal services are generally higher quality services and must meet overall community standards, not just those for the poor. However, universal services aimed at improving the conditions of all in society do not reduce the distance between those at the top and those at the bottom. This, too, can be questioned. More people are transferred out of poverty by the universalistic Social Security system than by selective public assistance programs.

Other Views of Poverty

In spite of all the programs and progress, widespread poverty and near-poverty persist. If poverty is to be combated successfully, it must be understood and there must be a will to do so. But there are very different ideas about what poverty is. A common way of understanding poverty is as the result of individual failure, the traditional victim-blaming theory of causation. But if one adopts the idea that structural causes have the greatest impact on the incidence of poverty in our society, then more investigation and different interventions to deal with the problem are required.

The only convincing explanation of lagging health, education, and income associated with particular groups is that discrimination is structured into our society. But we are all losers in many ways because of such institutionalized discrimination.

We look next at the major definitions of poverty itself. This may seem overly simple at first. We all "know" what *poor* means. And yet there are significantly different explanations of what constitutes poverty, and the differences have profound implications for what should be done to minimize it. Technology, the need for higher level skills and knowledge, an international economy, discrimination, and other institutional factors need to be examined in order to understand poverty.

In the United States, for most purposes, *poverty* is defined as simply having income below an established dollar figure, a measurable cutoff minimum, and so we focused earlier primarily on the distribution of income and wealth. But there are other ways of understanding poverty, and we turn now to several of these perspectives.

Relative Inequality

According to some persons, the problem is basically one of rising expectations, which are in infinite acceleration. The standard of living has gone up, and so have expectations over time. An automobile was an unusual thing to own in the 1930s. As we entered the 21st century, it is practically impossible in many parts of the

United States to work or live without one. Television, which was unusual in the early 1950s, is accepted as a typical, if not necessary, part of the home, as are VCRs. Similarly, the gap between the poverty line and median family income today is greater. Relative inequality is thus greater. It is this perception of relative inequality that is one of the most difficult problems of poverty, because relative poverty is an inescapable concomitant of poverty. An absolute poverty line suggests there is a definable minimal income needed to exist in our society. But defining such a line does not remedy the fact there will always be richer and poorer persons regardless of what the standard for poverty might become.

In addition, definitions of the expected services of a society alter over time. At one time in the United States, there was an expectation generally held that people might complete the eighth grade. Today it is widely accepted that almost everyone will complete high school and many will proceed to college. Health care was a privilege, and today it is coming to be judged as a right. Thus evolving rights also serve to alter the perception by those in poverty of what their situation means to them and change the definition of poverty.

Poverty may be defined as a standard of living less than the expectation of a society or as an unfair gap between one's resources and that of others. On one level this definition could become ludicrous. Is the ultimate goal the elimination of all difference, of all inequality? Obviously not. It is not necessary to be trapped into such absurd arguments. The answer to how much equality is wanted can be the same as American labor leader (1850–1924) Samuel Gompers's answer to the question of what the U.S. labor movement wanted: "more." The rich have the infinite capacity to invent new luxuries as yesterday's luxuries become today's necessities for many. Absolute equality is not achievable or even desirable. But the feeling that people live in a society that fairly allocates the necessities of life is one key definition of nonpoverty. Titmuss pointed out that in wartime, when rich and poor lined up for rationed food, no one felt poor. It is the lack of something that others have and to which one feels entitled that defines poverty. Inequality is a less-exact definition of poverty than an absolute definition, but it may be more realistic. Accepting an equitable distribution of life's necessities as a solution to poverty suggests transfers of resources, through both income redistribution and amenities (utilities) equally available to all.

Lack of Power, Access, and Inclusion

Titmuss also suggested that "command over resources" is a measure of wealth and thus, by implication, poverty is the lack of command over resources. Paradoxically, as certain benefits become available to different categories of people, the "command" that controls access by some creates relative inequality for those who do not have such access.

Credentials and entitlements are a major form of wealth in our society. These entitlements vary. They include seniority and tenure, licenses and franchises, academic degrees and union membership, and many others. Each has a certain value translatable into tangible wealth, and some may be transferred or even inherited.

The value of many credentials and entitlements is compounded to the degree that they serve as a form of capital rather than simply as a form of consumable wealth. An acre of land has an immediate market value or may produce a certain amount of grain. The same acre of land can also be used as collateral for additional purchases or can serve as the base for a high-rise apartment building. Similarly, a credential or an entitlement can be a building block for the development of additional wealth. A college graduate has the option not only of working and earning money as a result of having a degree, but of "investing" that degree in an advanced degree to bring still better returns in the future.

In the past, certain groups have been denied a fair share of, and access to, traditional forms of wealth. Now demands for greater equity are worldwide, and each society to some degree redistributes and transfers income. But as this "new property"—credentials or entitlements—grows more important, it becomes the focus of attempts to achieve greater equality. Without greater access to this form of wealth, the poor are doomed to continuing poverty or dependence. Not only do the economically deprived have less access to credentials, but there exist fewer safeguards for the protection of those credentials. In the long struggle for more economic opportunity and equality, certain gains have been made. If a person works for wages and does not receive them, he or she has access to the courts. But the credential system still exists largely in self-regulating and self-determining programs less subject to the legal safeguards that have developed around the marketplace. Diplomas and licenses are often awarded or withheld with broad discretionary powers. Individuals and governments are not allowed to walk into homes and steal a person's tangible property, but the state may strip a person of benefits or some other entitlement. Not all hearings of government regulatory agencies are subject to the same safeguards and restraints as are present in the legal tradition.

Privilege and aspects of an industrial and technological society combine so that the poor have less power and less access to resources. In large part, the poverty of many people is the result of the opportunity structure of our society.

To what extent is it possible for our society to create sufficient jobs for all potential workers on the basis of an unregulated labor market? Given a willingness to create jobs, to what extent can these jobs be productively targeted at those who are the least able and least trained and who are ill-equipped to do tasks that require high levels of skill? To what extent is the job market open to upward mobility for those who enter at very low levels of employment?

Racism, age discrimination, and sexism are all forms of denial of access. If a person is denied access to jobs, to entitlements, to respect, and to knowledge about where to go for service, that person may be defined as poor. Although few would argue that lack of power to affect the political system or discrimination is a complete definition of poverty, it can hardly be ignored as a factor. A whole variety of inclusionary strategies is needed if one sees this as a key factor in poverty.

The Underclass/Culture of Poverty Thesis

Poverty consists of economic inequality and also of noneconomic features. In a nation in which social honor, prestige, and self-respect as well as quality of life are important, poor persons are viewed as lacking in such honor and prestige and derive their self-image from society's view of them. To a degree, their sense of aspiration is battered and the gap between early aspirations and real opportunities grows large, resulting in behavior that assumes "making it" is impossible.

According to one point of view identified as the "culture of poverty" thesis, structural factors gave rise to poor persons who have particular behavioral characteristics, and these characteristics are transmitted from one generation to another because of their effects on children who cannot take full advantage of their opportunities.[20] Among the attributes suggested are inability to defer gratification, a present orientation with less emphasis on the future, lack of aspiration for upward mobility, female-centered families, alienation, a freer sexual code, and less investment in child rearing.

In recent years, the culture of poverty thesis has been replaced by the term *underclass*. The issue for both terms is the existence and persistence of poverty. There are two basic ways in which they explain poverty: the result of cultural or structural forces. According to the *cultural* view, poor persons have certain psychological and behavioral characteristics listed previously. These include motivational, cultural group, and lifestyle factors. The *structural* perspective emphasizes major economic and political systems which place various groups at risk. The importance one places on each of the perspectives differentiates explanations.

Exclusion from participation in paid employment and the general cash marketplace can lead to apathy, alienation, and family and community disruptions and disorganization. Cultural elements and discrimination do contribute to the extent of poverty (among other factors), but empirical evidence is lacking for the culture of poverty claim of intergenerational transmission. Family, social networks, and community provide buffers from some economic shocks and can serve as sources of strength.[21] Studies have found that the poor are not as distinctive in their values, attitudes, and aspirations as the culture of poverty thesis suggests.[22]

It would be foolish to ignore the fact that poverty influences behavior. What is crucial is that if the poverty is removed, the behavior tends to change, and social and economic mobility are frequent occurrences. For those who are tempted to believe that contemporary poverty groups are truly different in culture, the following excerpt written around the turn of the century may be instructive:

> The...race stock is inferior and degraded;...it will not assimilate naturally or readily with the prevailing "Anglo-Saxon" race stock of this country; that intermixture, will be detrimental; that servility, filthy habits of life, and hopelessly degraded standards of needs and ambitions have been ingrained...by centuries of oppression and abject poverty;...they are incapable of any adequate appreciation of our free institutions and the privileges and duties of citizenship; the greater part are illiterate and likely to remain so.[23]

The author was talking about immigrant Italians and assumes some intrinsic cultural failure among Italians similar to things said about other groups today. But generations later, Italians are generally believed to be among America's most achieving ethnic groups.

Strategies for Fighting Poverty

At least six major strategies for dealing with poverty have been identified: *social utilities, investment in human capital, transfers, rehabilitation, participation,* and *aggregative* and *selective economic measures.*[24] Each of these approaches has to be considered within the context of rationality, political feasibility, and value preferences. Each approach rests on particular assumptions about the definition or cause of poverty. Each has both positive and negative or functional and dysfunctional aspects. In short, social programs directed against poverty are usually mixed in the sense that they require trade-offs of certain gains against other losses.

Social Utilities

Social utilities are services that contribute to strengthening and enriching the quality of life. Access to birth control methods, family planning, or health services is in effect a transfer of money to the poor. Where our society makes available $1,000 worth of medical care for a poor family, we are providing, inside (health benefits as part of a job, including tax protected health spending accounts) or outside the market (means-tested health care), an equivalent of income for that family. Other examples are parks, free education, public libraries, police and fire services, employment information, and subsidized housing. Some persons oppose social utilities and amenities because they require government planning and bureaucracy. One variation is to provide poor persons with vouchers worth a certain amount of money that they then can spend on food, education, or housing. In this latter case, vouchers support the free market and may or may not give the poor person more options, depending on the terms of the voucher and the realities of the marketplace. The great advantage of amenities or social utilities is availability. Typically, social utilities are nonstigmatized services because the community recognizes the necessity for particular services in a complex and changing society, and they are available to all.

Vouchers run the danger of enriching purveyors of services without equalizing services. Universal social utilities are a form of income transfer and a form of reducing inequality by offering opportunities. Those who see lack of access as a key to poverty also may favor the development of utilities as a strategy.

Investment in Human Capital

This approach to poverty attempts to improve the capabilities of the poor by investing in them through education, health, job training, and the like. Just as investment in capital goods such as machinery and new plants increases productivity, so does investment in the quality of the work force.

One of the important contributors to U.S. growth has been its world leadership in universal, free public education, a form of investment in human capital. For example, literate farmers in the United States have read pamphlets and journals and utilized new methods; while farmers in some other countries, often illiterate, have farmed traditionally, producing less. Public school education in the United States had this effect on farmers and consequently on the agricultural production of the United States. Essentially, this strategy is an indirect service strategy through education, enhancement of workers' knowledge, health, and skills, social services, and other services.

Perhaps the best example of investment in human capital occurred in the period that followed World War II. During the war, unemployment was almost entirely erased. But economists feared a return of massive unemployment after the rapid demobilization of millions of service persons. Two factors prevented this: First, people had savings and money in their pockets as a result of the war effort, enjoyed high employment, and experienced a shortage of consumer goods. There was a backlog of demand that created jobs. Second, millions of discharged veterans took advantage of the educational opportunities made possible through the GI Bill, deferring entry into the job market and eventually improving the quality of the labor force. One payoff for the United States has been higher tax revenues from those who took advantage of the opportunity. Several million people paying taxes through their lifetimes on incomes generated by a college education (rather than on income generated by a high school education) have more than repaid the society for its investment in education. Other payoffs have been less crime, higher morale, new inventions, social stability, and a more productive society. Consider the alternative if 11 million returning veterans had not been either absorbed into the labor market or given other options.

Investment in human capital—training programs, low tuition community colleges and the like—is one way of bringing poor and disadvantaged groups into the system and therefore a way of combating poverty for specific target groups. These programs work best in an expanding economy where opportunities for moving up are more available. This type of investment is another approach to fighting poverty.

Income Transfers

Income transfer systems take money from one population group and redirect it to another. Such transfers can be made from middle-aged persons to the elderly, from the employed to the unemployed, and from the rich to the poor (or in some cases from those with less to those with more). There are two ways in which such redistributions can be made: Either money is redistributed vertically in the sense that those who have more channel their money through a tax system to those who have less; or redistribution can be made horizontally in that those who have, say, fewer dependents (including children) contribute through the tax system to those who have more dependents. The essential assumption of income transfers is that poverty is equivalent to a deficit of income. Although this is a main factor in poverty, as we saw earlier, it is not the complete definition of poverty.

However, a very strong taboo in American culture stands in the way of making such a commitment. There is something abhorrent in the American value system about giving money directly to both the "worthy" and the "unworthy" or able-bodied poor. Such an abhorrence seems ingrained in some Americans. Although programs such as public assistance, social insurance, family allowances, and earned income tax credits (negative income taxes) all have their potential uses in an attempt to minimize poverty, the essential issue is not one of technology (that is, the techniques by which poverty could be overcome most effectively or efficiently), but instead one of values. Specifically, to what extent do Americans want to redistribute income to do away with poverty? Who would support whom? What are the benefits in such a move? And what are the losses, such as higher tax rates, that supposedly would minimize investment in capital goods? However, such questions do not ask whether it could be done. They are all questions about aims and the trade-offs that would have to be made and the identification of who would pay at what price. None of these arguments denies that problems in social engineering exist in devising appropriate income transfer programs. But additional transfer in some form will need to be an essential part of any strategy to eliminate or minimize poverty.

Rehabilitation

Rehabilitation is aimed at changing people through psychological and sociopsychological methods to restore and enhance social functioning. The underlying assumption of some approaches to guidance, social casework, and psychotherapy is that the fault lies within the person or the family and not in the societal context. The assumption is made that people who are poor have problems for which they need help—that is, problems other than lack of money. Such programs are aimed at helping persons manage their emotional and interpersonal problems to a sufficient extent for them to be successfully employed. Such programs tend to be limited in scope and in their capacity to affect poverty.

However, this path has been a traditional major approach to the issue of poverty. The Social Security Act amendments of 1962 actually suggested that more trained labor power—social workers and others—would result in lower welfare rolls. If sufficient numbers of trained social workers, it was thought, were prepared, they could be expected to rehabilitate so many welfare recipients that this would serve as a means of eliminating poverty. However, the basic fallacy in such an approach is that it substitutes personal and familial causation for structural causation. The economic cycles of the nation are greater determinants of the rate of growth or decline of poverty than is the pool of trained social workers. This is illustrated by the fall in the numbers of persons on public assistance during periods of economic and employment expansion.

Nevertheless, rehabilitation has legitimacy because there are people who will have emotional and other problems and need support even in the best of worlds. Some people have special needs as situational crises occur, and they will be driven into poverty or be unable to drag themselves out of poverty without rehabilitation. Rehabilitation cannot be used as an effective, and certainly not as an efficient, means of eliminating poverty, but it is one of the legitimate ways of coping with some poor people as it is with helping some people of every class.

Aggregative and Selective Economic Measures

Aggregative economic measures are those that purport to help the poor at the bottom of the economic scale through economic growth that results from tax reductions, low interest rates, and incentives meant to increase hiring and production. A growth economy is required if we want to minimize poverty. An economy that is healthy and growing with high employment makes the greatest contribution to defeating poverty. A healthy economy in which labor is in demand and productivity and consumption are high may do more than specific programs to lessen the brunt of poverty.

The U.S. Congress in 1946 passed the Employment Act creating the Council of Economic Advisors. A commitment to stimulate high employment was reaffirmed in the passage of the Humphrey-Hawkins Full Employment and Balanced Growth Act in 1978. But a commitment to a full employment policy in which government provides jobs as the employer of last resort has never been seriously implemented. As a result, the coincidental phases of U.S. economic cycles have done more to create poverty or to do away with it than the employment policies of the government.

Selective economic measures are designed to create jobs, raise wages (the minimum wage, the "living wage"), and provide other opportunities to reduce poverty for those poor who could benefit. Although these strategies seem attractive, almost all those persons receiving public assistance are women and children. The redesign of jobs and the creation of jobs will not in themselves move all women and children off public assistance. However, where there is economic uncertainty because of unemployment, underemployment, or even the threat of unemployment, family instability often follows.

For this reason, job creation is of great importance for economic, psychological, and social reasons. The well-being of individuals and families, as well as the society, is tied to work and gainful full-time employment at a living wage. In general, recent efforts to create jobs focused increasingly upon the private sector and minimized the role of government. Governmental efforts—which primarily utilize the private sector to deal with this problem, which is connected to other significant problems in our society—will be described in chapter 10.

There are dangers to a targeting approach. These selective programs present several difficulties because, accompanied by high expectations, they are typically aimed at groups with complicated problems. These problems are not those of particular individuals but are related to societal and structural factors such as the shift from manufacturing and goods-producing to service employment; changes in the geographic location of industries, including what jobs are located where; and to international economic trends. Because of the complexities and difficulties presented by such factors, these programs do not seem to work sufficiently well and fall short of overly optimistic expectations, inviting criticism and political "backlash" directed at the program. Further, there is always the possibility of such selective programs contributing to the divisiveness that they can create in society as one group or another feels left out.

An intense debate focuses on the question as to whether a higher minimum wage reduces poverty. Some argue that raising the minimum wage leads to higher unemployment and more poverty because it reduces the number of jobs available for persons who are semi-skilled or without skill or work experience, while pushing other levels of wages higher. One study found that a higher minimum wage would significantly reduce poverty among working families. Evidence shows that low-income working people do in fact receive most of the wage gains and that almost ten percent of those with jobs benefit from the increase.[25] Another study found, contrary to expectations, that increases in the minimum wage resulted in an *increase* in wages accompanied by an increase in employment. It also was found that creation of businesses continued in the industries studied. Furthermore, it was found that workers earning the minimum wage were disproportionately drawn from families with lower earnings and the minimum wage had a modest effect on the standard of living of those families.[26] According to Robert M. Solow, a Nobel laureate in economics, the evidence of job loss due to raising the minimum wage is weak. This does not still the voices of opponents, some of whom resist any increase in the minimum wage and others who want to repeal the law. The consistent conclusion of a series of minimum wage studies found that no large disemployment effects would result from modest increases (10 percent) in the minimum wage.[27]

Growth in the *gross domestic product* (GDP)—that is, the total value of all goods and services produced—is a key ingredient in any program to reduce poverty. Growth is needed. As discussed, during World War II, there was practically no unemployment, and poverty was reduced through employment associated with the war effort. A bigger pie means potentially more for everyone, including those poor who may be recipients of redistributive efforts made possible by rising tax revenues, which result from an expanding economy. However, growth per se does not guarantee a reduction in poverty. Most people who seek to eliminate poverty are not satisfied that enough benefits will automatically trickle down to the poor. Other strategies are needed. But economic growth is a precondition for other efforts to succeed, or often, even to be tried.

Participation and Organization

Participation and organization programs are intended to promote *social inclusion* and *influence* and to reduce problems among the poor by providing them with a stake in society. Whether there are behavioral problems or problems of access or lack of power, or whether the key is discrimination, one strategy is to bring people into the mainstream through organizing efforts. Such programs are meant to raise the self-esteem of poor persons and to raise their honor and prestige in society by enhancing their political power. Such programs involve antidiscrimination laws, special programs for non–English-speaking children, zoning rules, access to municipal contracts and jobs, educational advancement programs for climbing the job ladder, access to the political process, voting, and direct engagement in political decision making. All these programs are devoted to the theory and policy of inclusion.

Ideology Revisited

In earlier chapters, we introduced the importance of values and ideology as key factors contributing to decisions about social welfare. The congressional elections of 1994 resulted in Republican majorities seizing control of both the House of Representatives and the Senate for the first time in 40 years. The essence of the Republican program was to return the society to one more reflective of laissez faire philosophy, to devolve programs from the federal level where possible to the control of states, to reduce taxes in the belief that tax reduction is needed to encourage greater risk-taking and expansion of the economy, to reduce the size of the federal government and the number of governmental employees at all levels, and to reduce governmental regulations for business and industry and in regard to the environment. Joined with tax reduction, they wanted to balance the budget while reducing federal deficits and overall debt. The ideological aim was to limit governmental responsibility. Concurrent with limiting governmental responsibility, individuals and families would be expected to be independent and governmental assistance for individuals and families would be reduced. On the basis of all these actions, it was expected productivity would increase and the GDP would rise sufficiently to generate higher living standards for the society.

When President Clinton assumed the presidency, the financial situation of the federal government appeared bleak with mounting deficits and a very large debt. During his administration, the Democratic party was nudged toward the Center during an unbroken series of years of high economic growth. President Clinton led the nation during the initial post-Cold War years but did so in the face of a nation grown skeptical of government action. It was commonly said that President Clinton found a "third way" between the left and the right. His early attempt through the efforts of Mrs. Clinton in 1994 to make comprehensive change in the nation's health system failed. The federal budget was brought into balance for the first time in a generation, deficits were avoided, a major restructuring of the welfare system was achieved, and enormous future budget surpluses were projected. It was a period throughout which there were tense, conflicting, and often acrimonious efforts by both Democrats and Republicans.[28]

Although there were debates as to who and what were responsible for the nation's economic bounty, some persons suggested the administration's work on reducing the federal deficit and management of the economy were crucial, others that technological advances and productivity were responsible for generating a flow of unanticipated tax revenues. Whatever the reasons, the nation experienced an unprecedented period of growth that led to revenue surpluses. The unemployment rate fell, incomes rose, poverty fell, interest rates were low, prices were stable, and jobs were plentiful, although many were in service industries where workers received few benefits and were low paid. Critics claimed that President Clinton rode a wave that began in the 1980s, was interrupted by the Persian Gulf War of the early 1990s, but resumed forward motion during his terms.

In fighting poverty, President Clinton joined with Republicans to emphasize programs that reward work such as the Earned Income Credit for the working poor and turned away from "welfare." The Personal Responsibility and Work Opportunity Act expressed these values through programs that encouraged work and individual and family responsibility. Welfare rolls did decline as had been anticipated. From this point of view—widely shared in the nation—levels of dependency had been drastically reduced.

The Bush Administration

During the last months of the Clinton administration, the economy remained fundamentally solid with low unemployment, stable inflation, rising wages, and benefits from continued advances in technology but it also began to slow its pace, threatening a recession, perhaps part of a typical economic cycle—"boom" followed by "bust". As President George W. Bush assumed the presidency, despite the prediction of massive federal budget surpluses, lurking beneath the surface were potentially serious problems including: low savings rates, an expanding aging population, huge and growing trade deficits, and education and skills level of the work force insufficient to meet the needs of many employers.[29]

Although the Bush administration used the theme of "compassionate conservatism" to identify its values, its priorities were familiar: laissez faire philosophy, devolution of programs to the states and away from the federal level where possible, reduce taxes, reduce the size of the federal government, reduce regulations for business and industry, and enhance the ability of faith-based social services, that is, encourage religious organizations to provide "welfare" services broadly defined.

In the initial months of the Bush administration, a $1.3 trillion tax cut was approved by the Congress weighted heavily toward the wealthiest one percent of the population. As soon as it was approved, critics began to raise issues, many of which were identified but either not debated or overridden during the votes.[29] In the first budget submitted there was provision for discretionary spending for the military, medical research, and education but little else. The Congress was on record supporting the tax cut before even seeing the spending cuts that would be necessary. The effect of these actions was to "freeze" government, create scarce room for maneuver, and produce many problems and issues concerning programs and where the money would come from. The massive tax cut made it extremely problematic to deal with serious problems and set up a political struggle. Congress will want more money for elementary and secondary education, defense, a Medicare prescription drug benefit as a part of Medicare, a reform of the flawed farm support program, the President's energy plan and assistance to those without health insurance. Many persons suggested the cost of the tax cuts will force dipping into the Social Security and Medicare surpluses to pay for the income tax cuts scheduled for 2004 and 2006, the marriage-penalty relief to start in 2005 and the elimination of the estate tax in 2010.

The social welfare priority initiatives of the Bush administration included: *Promotion of safe and stable families* (assist states to keep children with their biological families, if safe and appropriate, or place children with adoptive families, education and training vouchers for youth "aging out" of foster care to develop skills needed to lead independent and productive lives); *Creating after school certificates* (grants to states to assist parents in obtaining after-school child care with a high-quality education focus); *Promoting responsible fatherhood* (strengthen the role of fathers in the lives of families, utilize faith-based and community organizations to help unemployed or low-income fathers and their families to avoid or leave cash welfare and to provide programs that promote successful parenting and strengthen marriage); *Supporting maternity group homes* (community-based, adult-supervised group homes or apartment clusters for teenage mothers and their children who cannot live with their own families because of abuse, neglect, or other extenuating circumstances); and *Encouraging compassion and charitable giving* (start-up capital and operating funds to qualified charitable organizations that want to expand or emulate model programs, support and promote research on "best practices" among charitable organizations, and encouragement of states to create tax credits for contributions to designated charities, as well as allow states to use federal Temporary Assistance to Needy Families funds to offset revenue losses.

The initiatives cited above are policy changes and programs are important but "at the margin." The Bush administration on principle challenges the federal government's role and fosters the roles of the private market, individual and family responsibility, and the states. Thus, their agenda included major challenges to Medicare, the delivery of health services to the elderly, to be accomplished by restructuring the program to enhance the private sector's role; and advocating privatization of at least a part of the Social Security program. Furthermore, although unknown at the time this is written, actions were awaited that will impact Medicaid, administration of cash assistance programs, and food stamps. In these areas as well it is unclear how the private enterprise goals will affect for-profit and non-profit organizations as they become further involved in the delivery of services.

Finally, the last several decades have fostered a pro-market, pro-competition ideology. This approach was supported by the major economic expansion of the 1990s. But the United States entered a period of economic uncertainty and anticipated a long-delayed recession accompanied by increasing unemployment during the early years of the Bush administration, an administration that won an extremely close and contested election, that stimulated a major tax cut, followed by declining tax revenues, and had yet to fund many programs it proposed, not to mention such matters as prescription drugs becoming part of the Medicare program.

As this is being written, the nation began a "War on Terrorism" and entered a recession. The United States was beset by many difficult domestic and international issues, including defense issues, continuing terrorism threats, Anthrax cases purposely caused by persons unknown, economically, socially, and in terms of human welfare. The freedom of action (debt reduction, huge tax cuts and/or new services) that years of anticipated huge budget surpluses could provide were now viewed as tenuous as money was taken to deal with a series of new threats. Because of the all-consuming attention to countering the many threats facing the nation, there were suggestions that social welfare and other agenda proposals by the Republican administration and the Democrat party would be put "on hold". Perhaps some parts of their agendas will be enacted and some will be more or less permanently tabled.

Among the social welfare issues that were to be considered were the following. (1) Is there a real or manageable crisis for the Social Security program? In either case, what will be done? (2) Will a Patient's Bill of Rights be enacted and what will be its nature? (3) What solutions will be enacted for dealing with the problems of Medicare? (4) Can a drug plan for senior adults be enacted and what will it provide for whom? (5) The "charitable choice" initiative emphasized by the Bush administration appeared to be dormant. Will it regain momentum? (6) Can the recessionary economy being confronted by the Bush administration like good Keynesian economists (demand side spending) be contained and recovery be encouraged? (6) What will be done about the many low-income persons and others who will be hurt by the economic setbacks, especially how will the 5-year limit on TANF be dealt with in the middle of not "good times" but "bad"? Furthermore, what effects will the long-standing income and wealth gaps mean for societal stability, motivation, and productivity? Thus, the United States early in the 21st century entered a challenging and stressful time with implications for social welfare, broadly defined.

Ideology Once Again

What should be the contract between an individual and society? Is society's purpose the "general welfare"? If so, how it it to be achieved? What are the responsibilities of individuals and families for themselves and for society? Interestingly, the debates about "welfare" and "responsibility" omit consideration of the economic and structural features of the nation and the kind of governments that developed in the United States. To what degree can people be held responsible when economic forces produce "social issues" beyond the power of individuals and families?

Should society set a minimum standard and ensure that the oppressed and needy are raised to that level? Or, is society to ignore a minimum standard as individuals and families pursue their own well-being? What is and should be government's role? This question can be asked in almost every sphere of life. Further, what should be the respective roles of the federal, state, and local governments? What responsibilities should be maintained at what levels? To what degree will cutting the costs of programs undermine purchasing power and the countercyclical effects of social spending? Is there some point at which reductions in the total budget, if made too quickly or too broadly, will lead to recessions and even major depression? These have not been considerations to date in the debates as two ideologies have faced off in regard to discrete programs without weighing the total impact of multitudes of program reductions and eliminations.

Summary

In this chapter, we have seen how broadly based the beneficiaries of social welfare programs are, discussed several definitions of poverty, introduced a profile of the poor, examined the distribution of income and wealth, described the chief strategies for ameliorating poverty, introduced the importance of ideology, and reviewed the major trends of the Clinton administration and the philosophy and early relevant actions of the second Bush administration. A number of structural factors contribute to the extent of poverty in the United States. Among these factors are the nature and performance of the economy, particularly in regard to productivity and the economic growth rate; the federal fiscal deficit or surplus and their implications for potential governmental interventions; trends in regard to marriage, divorce, and the increase in the number of female-headed families with children; the nature and location of employment opportunities; salaries and the fringe benefits associated or not associated with those jobs; discrimination; the employment of young people, especially minority young adults; and the pattern of taxation at the federal, state, and local levels as they affect the poor and the working poor.

Some outcomes of the ideological conflict and context described previously will be reflected in our discussion in this and the next two chapters. We will examine the major social welfare programs in the United States using the concepts and schema introduced in chapter 6. These programs were created in particular contexts and have evolved influenced by complex political, social, and economic values and factors. As you read about the programs, you might begin to formulate what you think would be the best set of programs both to deal with the problem of poverty in the United States and to deal more effectively with the general welfare of all citizens. At the end of chapter 15, we will suggest an approach to dealing with the problems of poverty and human need.

Questions for Consideration

1. We presented a broad characterization of social welfare clients. Do you think it is accurate? If you agree or disagree with the definition, why?

2. If the United States were to use a relative measure of poverty, what do you suggest it be?

3. When you review the tables in this chapter, what stands out?

4. In what ways have ideologies affected recent social welfare legislation in your state? in the nation?

Notes

1. Senator Ernest Hollings of South Carolina, quoted in "The South Carolina Hybrid," George F. Will, *Newsweek,* December 20, 1982, p. 92.

2. Richard M. Titmuss, *Essays on the Welfare State,* Boston: Beacon Press, 1969, p. 42.

3. This is a theme in Michael Harrington's *Toward a Democratic Left,* Baltimore: Penguin, 1969.

4. Aldi Hagenaars and Klaas de Vos, "The Definition and Measurement of Poverty," *The Journal of Human Resources,* Vol. XXIII, No. 2, Spring 1988, pp. 211–221.

5. Dean Baker, ed. *Getting Prices Right: The Debate over the Consumer Price Index,* Armonk, N.Y.M.E. Sharpe, 1998.

6. Patricia Ruggles, *Drawing the Line: Alternative Poverty Measures and Their Implications for Public Policy,* Washington, D.C.: The Urban Institute Press, 1990, pp. 20–23.

7. Constance F. Citro and Robert T. Michael, *Measuring Poverty: A New Approach,* Panel on Poverty and Family Assistance, National Research Council, Washington, D.C.: Academy Press, 1995.

8. Peter Townsend, *Poverty in the United Kingdom: A Survey of Household Resources and Standards of Living*, Berkeley: University of California Press, 1979.

9. Amartya Sen, *On Economic Inequality*, New York: Oxford University Press, 1997.

10. Matthew McKeever and Nicholas H. Wolfinger, "Reexamining the Economic Costs of Marital Disruption for Women," *Social Science Quarterly*, 82 (1), 2000, pp. 202–217 and Patricia A. McManus and Thomas A. DiPrete, "Losers and Winners: The Financial Consequences of Separation and Divorce for Men," *American Sociological Review*, 66 (2), 2001, pp. 246–268.

11. U.S. Department of Commerce, Census Bureau, *Current Population Reports*, P70-56, "Dynamics of Economic Well-Being: Income, 1992 to 1993, Moving Up and Down the Income Ladder," June, 1996.

12. U.S. Census Bureau, *Poverty in the United States: 2000*, Current Population Reports, P60-214, September 2001, p. xi.

13. U.S. Census Bureau, *Poverty in the United States: 2000*, p. xiii.

14. U.S. Department of Labor, Bureau of Labor Statistics, "When One Job Is Not Enough," Issues in Labor Statistics, Summary 00-15-01, August 2000, www.bls.gov, November 2, 2001

15. Edward N. Wolff, *Top Heavy: The Increasing Inequality of Wealth in America and What Can Be Done About It*, New York: The New Press, 1996 and U.S. Census Bureau, "Asset Ownership of Households: 1995: Highlights, www.census.gov/hhes/www/wealth/1995/wlth1995-4.html, July 2, 2001 and www.census.gov/hhes/www/wealth/1995/wlth/1995-4, July 2, 2001.

16. Center on Budget and Policy Priorities, Pathbreaking CBO Study Shows Dramatic Increases in Both 1980s and 1990s in Income Gaps Between the Very Wealthy and Other Americans, www.cbpp.org/5-31-01tax-pr.htm, July 9,2001.

17. Frank Levy, *The New Dollars and Dreams: American Income and Economic Change*, New York: Russell Sage Foundation, 1998.

18. Wolff, op.cit.

19. Wolff, *op.cit.*; Paul W. Kingston, *The Classless Society*, Stanford, CA.: Stanford University Press, 2000, p. 85 and Michael M. Weinstein, "America's Rags-to-Riches Myth," *New York Times*, Editorial Observer, February 18, 2000, p. A30.

20. Oscar Lewis, *La Vida*, New York: Random House, 1966, p. xiv.

21. Rural Sociological Society, Task Force on Persistent Rural Poverty, *Persistent Poverty in Rural America*, San Francisco: Westview, 1993, p. 8.

22. Michael Morris, "Culture, Structure, and the Underclass," in *Myths about the Powerless*, ed. M. Brinton Lykes, et al., Philadelphia: Temple University Press, 1996, pp. 34–49.

23. Joe R. Feagin, *Racial and Ethnic Relations*, Englewood Cliffs, N.J.: Prentice Hall, 1989, p. 112, quoting Eliot Lord, et al., *The Italian Americans*, San Francisco: R and E Associates, 1970.

24. Martin Rein and S. M. Miller, "Poverty, Policy, and Purpose: The Dilemmas of Choice," *Economic Progress and Social Welfare*, Leonard Goodman, ed., New York: Columbia University Press, 1966, pp. 20–64.

25. Robert Pollin and Stephanie Luce, *The Living Wage*, New York: New Press, 2000, pp. 12, 30.

26. David Card and Alan B. Kreuger, *Myth and Measurement: The New Economics of the Minimum Wage*, Princeton, N.J.: Princeton University Press, 1995, pp. 387, 391; Linda R. Martin and Demetrios Giannaros, "Would a Higher Minimum Wage Help Poor Families Headed by Women?" *Monthly Labor Review*, Vol. 113, No. 8, August 1990, p. 36.

27. Louis Uchitelle, "Minimum Wage and Jobs," *New York Times*, January 12, 1995, pp. D1, D19; "New Minimum Wage Research: A Symposium," *Industrial and Labor Relations Review*, Vol. 46, No. 1, October 1992, pp. 1–88.

28. Todd S. Purdom, "Striking Strengths, Glaring Failures," *New York Times*, December 24, 2000, pp. 1, 12 and Richard W. Stevenson, "The Wisdom to Let the Good Times Roll," *New York Times*, December 25, 2000, pp. 1, 12.

29. Richard Stevenson, "Troubles that Lurk beneath Prosperity's Surface," *New York Times*, December 18, 2000, p. C3 and Robert D. Reischauer "Don't Count on that Tax Cut," *New York Times*, June 7, 2001, p. A31.

9

Current Social Welfare Programs—Economic Security

Security was attained in the earlier days through the interdependence of members of families upon each other, and the families within a small community upon each other. The complexities of great communities and of organized industry make less real these simple means of security. Therefore we are compelled to employ the active interest of the nation as a whole, through government, in order to encourage a greater security for each individual who composes it.

—Franklin D. Roosevelt[1]

Overview

As you read this and the next chapter, it will be obvious that there is no comprehensive and unified social welfare system in the United States. The U.S. "system" has developed incrementally in a crazy-quilt pattern. In reality, the U.S. social welfare institution is a series of systems, although they are sometimes more or less interrelated.

The scope of social welfare programs and services in the United States is so broad and complex that it is not possible to review all the social welfare programs in depth here. Each program is complicated, and the reader should be aware there are many details and intricacies that are not included in this discussion. In our discussion, we will introduce programs in general outline and try to indicate the nature of changes enacted or being considered.

Because these programs affect all our lives, it is important for social workers and all citizens to know about the various social welfare programs, their aims, for whom they are intended, benefits, funding, and administration. As we saw in chapter 1, emotional problems and family disturbances, stress, and income insecurity are intricately interwoven. Recessions, job loss, unemployment, and low incomes are all related to personal and family stress.

In this chapter, we review programs that provide for the income security—to varying degrees—of the citizenry, and in chapter 10 we will discuss programs designed to improve the quality of life by providing supports for health care, housing, nutrition, child welfare, mental health, and other human needs.

In chapters 6 and 7, we presented concepts and a paradigm for the description and analysis of social welfare programs. This chapter is an exercise in the use of the analytical tools presented earlier. We will use the paradigm and analytical tools here and in chapter 15 when we consider alternative social welfare programs for several important areas of social concern.

As you read this chapter, it will be helpful to analyze in turn each of the programs as they are described so you can compare your own conclusions with the analysis provided. At the end of chapter 15, we will propose a program to minimize poverty.

Social Insurance Programs

Universal social insurance programs provide benefits to which recipients are entitled without reference to income or assets. Eligibility is a function of an individual's relationship to employment. The major income support insurance programs are Social Security, Unemployment Compensation, and Workers' Compensation.

Social Security (OASDI)

The Social Security Act of 1935 was a watershed piece of legislation establishing several assistance and insurance programs, but when people refer to Social Security, they usually mean Old-Age, Survivors, and Disability Insurance (OASDI). This program was originally enacted as old-age insurance designed to replace some income that is lost when a worker retires because of old age. The program as we know it today emerged through a series of legislated amendments. In 1939, even before the original program was fully operational, benefits were extended to workers' dependents and survivors and, in 1956, the disability insurance component was added. Over time, more categories of workers were added so that approximately 96 percent of jobs are now covered, in contrast to the 55 percent covered when the program was initiated. The full program is now referred to as OASDHI; the "H" is for hospital (that is, Medicare, which is discussed in chapter 10).

Details of the OASDI program regarding eligibility, benefits, and financing undergo numerous changes and continue to face changes. Therefore, it is necessary here to focus on the skeletal structure of OASDI rather than on specifics, which may be obsolete by the time they are read.

Who Is Eligible for the Program?   Coverage is generally compulsory but some of the 96 percent of the paid workforce is covered voluntarily. However, more than 6.8 million workers in 1999 were not covered by Social Security, the majority of whom were state and local government employees. As of 1983, state government entities may not terminate Social Security coverage, and all federal employees hired after 1983 are covered for OASDI. Beginning in 1984, all employees of nonprofit organizations became covered, and in 1991 state and local employees who were not members of a public retirement system were mandatorily covered under Social Security.

To be eligible for retirement benefits a worker must be 62 years old or over with the required number of quarters of covered employment (worked a requisite number of years). If one retires before age 65 years, reduced payments are received. For disability coverage, a worker must be assessed as unable to engage in substantial gainful activity by reason of a physical or mental impairment that is expected to last not less than 12 months or to result in death, be under age 65 years, and be fully insured under Social Security. There are special eligibility rules for workers age 55 and over whose disability is based on blindness. From 2003 through 2008 the retirement age will gradually rise to 66 from 65 years, then from 2021 through 2027, it will gradually rise to 67. In 1999, the average age at retirement was 63.7 years.[2] Dependents' benefits are payable to the spouse of a retired or disabled worker if a currently married spouse is at least 62 years of age or is caring for one or more of the worker's entitled children who are disabled or are under 16; or a divorced spouse aged 62 years or older, not married, and the marriage to the worker lasted at least ten years before divorce became final. A divorced spouse may be entitled independently of the worker's retirement if both the worker and the divorced spouse are age 62, and the divorce has been final for at least two years.

Survivors must be dependents of deceased workers who were fully insured at the time of death. A monthly survivor benefit is paid to a widow(er) (aged 60 years or 50–59 years if disabled, with a waiting period) if he or she is unmarried or remarriage occurred after the widow(er)'s first eligibility for benefits. Dependent, unmarried, biological or adopted children, stepchildren, and grandchildren of a retired, disabled, or deceased worker receive a monthly benefit if under age 18 years, a full-time elementary or secondary student under age 19, or a disabled person age 18 or over whose disability began before age 22 years.

A monthly survivor benefit is payable to a mother (father) or surviving divorced mother (father) if the deceased was fully insured, if the beneficiary is not married and has one or more entitled children of the worker in his or her care. In the case of divorced persons, the child must be a natural or legally adopted child under the age of 16 years of age or disabled. A monthly survivor benefit is payable to the parent of a deceased fully insured worker who is 62 years of age or over, and has not married since the worker's death and was receiving at least one-half of her support from the worker at the time of the worker's death. Proof of support must be filed within two years after the worker's death or the month in which the worker filed for disability. Eligibility for benefits is universal and not related to wealth, assets, or unearned income.

What Is the Form of Benefit?   Benefits are in the form of a monthly check or funds transfer to a bank account. The amount ranges from a minimum to a maximum, depending mostly on the worker's covered earnings. The formula changes from time to time but has remained generally related to contributions. Beginning in July 1975, monthly payments were increased whenever the consumer price index (CPI) increased by 3 percent or more. In 1986, this cost-of-living benefit increase (COLA) was made contingent on any upward movement of the CPI in the past 12 months. The automatic benefit increase granted to all recipients is equal to the actual rise in the CPI.

The benefit amount may change if the beneficiary continues to work. The most recent legislative change in 2000 eliminated the earnings limit for those who have attained the full retirement age (65). Those below the full retirement age (incrementally increasing until 67) could earn up to $11,280 in 2002 through self or other employment. This limit rises each year at the same rate as average wages in the economy or as set by law. For those non-disabled beneficiaries under the increasing full retirement age who exceed the earnings test, $1 was lost for every $2 of earnings, except during the year in which they reach full retirement age. *The earnings test does not apply to those who have reached the full retirement age.* Disabled persons are subject to separate limits on earnings known as substantial gainful employment.

Other recent changes created equity between husbands and wives if either spouse retires or dies and granted higher bonuses for delayed retirement. The amount of the bonus rises to 8 percent for those retiring workers attaining 65 years of age after 2007, and the retirement age rises gradually. Persons who opt for retirement from 62 to 67 years of age will do so with a penalty when their benefits are computed.

How Is the Program Financed?   The OASDI program is financed by an earmarked tax (Federal Employees Contribution Act [FICA]) by covered employees, by employers, and by the self-employed. This tax is a fixed percentage of the wage, up to a certain maximum. In 2002, the tax rate was 7.65 percent; the first $84,500 of earnings was taxable at this rate for OASDI. There was no limit on the maximum taxable payroll earnings for Medicare. Of the 7.65 percent tax, 6.2 percent is allocated for Social Security and Social Security Disability; 1.45 percent for Medicare. The self-employed paid 15.3 percent and were able to deduct for income tax purposes half of the tax to allow for the fact that employees do not pay income tax on the employer's portion of the FICA tax.

Benefits are taxed at either 50 percent or 85 percent, depending on whether one files income taxes as an individual or a joint return and how much income one receives. This helps to finance the system more progressively, but also serves as a "backdoor" means test. Proceeds from those taxed 50 percent are credited to the OASDI Trust Funds and from those taxed 85 percent credited to the Medicare Hospital Insurance (HI) Trust fund.

What Is the Level of Administration?   The OASDI program is administered by the Social Security Administration with offices located in various parts of the United States. Because it has no up-front means test and is centrally administered, the Social Security system is among our most cost-efficient programs; costs typically constitute less than 1 percent of annual benefit payments.[3] Claims are reviewed in regional centers. The Treasury Department collects taxes, prepares checks, and maintains trust funds. Disability determinations are made by state agencies and reviewed by the Social Security Administration. The taxation or recoupment of benefits where incomes rise above particular levels is handled through the income tax system.

Discussion. The OASDI program is a national, universal, and institutional social welfare program. There is no means test, and everyone in the category is eligible for assistance. It is seen as a necessary and desirable element in society to provide some support for people who have retired or who have become totally disabled or for the dependent families of breadwinners who have retired or died. It is viewed as a right by those who receive it and does not bear the stigma attached to public assistance and some other social welfare programs. Central to this psychology of acceptance of Social Security has been its connection to employment and contributory nature—that is, those who ultimately are to receive benefits are those who have, to some degree, made contributions to the system. Thus it has a spirit very much akin to private insurance, and beneficiaries feel that they are entitled to receive the benefits—that they are in a sense being repaid their own money. All of this has contributed to making Social Security our largest income transfer program and the bedrock of social insurance in the United States.

When created Social Security included "insurance" in the title to indicate a social welfare program designed to ensure against a certain risk. However, Social Security is like insurance in that (1) in order to receive benefits one must contribute to the program and (2) people who pay very little get less in benefits than those who pay the maximum, and benefits are graduated along the scale from a very small minimum amount to the maximum contribution.

However, in at least three other ways Social Security is not like private insurance and should not be confused therewith:

1. Benefits are not exactly related to contributions. Although benefits will increase for those who contribute more, it is not in a direct relationship. Social Security benefits are skewed toward the bottom end; that is, the lowest earners receive replacement of approximately 52.8 percent of their preretirement income; average earners, 39.2 percent; and maximum earners, approximately 23.7 percent.[4] Thus, while benefits increase with contributions, they do not increase in a way that would be "fair" in private insurance. Social Security serves as a supplementary pension plan for those who contribute most, but also as a "welfare" program for those most in need.

2. Social Security is unlike private insurance in that the benefits are not due by contract at the time of entering the program. The benefits are based on whatever the current legislation is and not on any insurance "right." This can work to both the detriment and the benefit of the recipient. Thus one's benefits under Social Security are dependent on current legislation rather than on contributed funds. In order to make this possible, it is necessary for there to be the third and most important difference between Social Security and private insurance.

3. Benefits are paid essentially from current funds received rather than from reserves. In a private insurance system, the company may set aside a reserve fund to get started, but eventually the funds collected from contributors must be calculated to be sufficient to pay benefits as they are claimed by beneficiaries. Not so with Social Security. Funds contributed in the past by those now collecting Social Security would be insufficient to meet the current benefit levels. Although there is a reserve fund that helps to meet sudden emergencies and fluctuations, the benefits that are being paid to current recipients are for the most part the receipts from those who are now paying Social Security taxes. When those now paying Social Security taxes are eligible for Social Security, they will depend for their benefits on legislation that will be forcing those then working to contribute to the system. Thus, Social Security is an intergenerational transfer program. Even with a massive insurance reserve some people become concerned when they think of Social Security in terms of private insurance. The backing of the Social Security system, however, is not weak; it is the legislative power of the U.S. Congress—the power to tax—whether that tax is euphemistically called a contribution to an insurance system or one that goes to the general revenues.

When the problems confronting Social Security are considered, highlighted is its relationship to the "baby boom" generation, a large group of Americans born after World War II. Following this boom, there ensued a declining birth rate, producing fewer workers to support the huge baby boom generation retirees and those who follow. This ratio by itself, however, does not determine Social Security's future. Some experts argue that productivity matters more than the ratio of workers to beneficiaries: The total income that workers generate in relation to the costs of benefits is more important than the mere number of workers in relation to the number of retirees. Two other factors also play a part: the lengthening of the average life span and periods of less than full employment when receipts diminish.

A continuing argument about Social Security has to do with the concept of minimal versus optimal levels. Social Security was never intended as a full-retirement system; it was seen as a way of supplementing people's savings, private insurance, and pension plans. Increasingly, current retirees do have other assets to draw on, but there remain many elderly who have no other insurance program, and the minimum level of Social Security benefits is too low to maintain adequate living standards for most people. To improve the minimum benefits to the point of adequacy would seem burdensome to taxpayers who resist having massive amounts of money spent for universal programs, because some of this would go to the rich who have other forms of income and do not need this higher minimum. However, not to improve it condemns many elderly to unrelieved poverty. The compromise has been to supplement Social Security minimums where there is no other income by using a means-tested program, formerly called Old-Age Assistance and since the 1970s known as Supplemental Security Income (SSI), which is discussed subsequently. Thus the problem of vertical adequacy, at least at the minimum level, is somewhat covered. With the improvements in Social Security coverage since its inception, horizontal adequacy is good, and almost all workers are covered today. It is the size and power of its constituency and broad inclusion that give the program its political strength, because it touches almost every family in the nation. This inclusivity also encourages societal cohesion rather than divisiveness, a mark of means-tested, selected programs. Beyond the immediate assistance Social Security provides recipients, there are indirect benefits for middle-aged families who have their parents cared for, thereby not forcing them to choose between supporting their parents and their own children.

The most serious argument in recent years has been over Social Security's form of financing. Social Security, as we have pointed out, is not really an insurance program. The contributory form has been very valuable in affording beneficiaries dignity and giving people a sense of right of entitlement to benefits. It also has meant that the Social Security system is in reality a social welfare program financed by a most regressive tax somewhat offset for low-income workers by the Earned Income Tax Credit. Essentially, the policy choices are the following: lower benefits for future generations, add revenue to the system, have workers work longer, and invest some of the income in the stock market, performed either by individuals or as a part of the trust funds.

To recapitulate, the OASDI program is financed by a fixed-percentage tax on the wages of employees, employers, and the self-employed equal to the combined tax paid by employer and employees. All of this is up to a fixed maximum, which has been raised from time to time over the years. However, these two components—a fixed-percentage tax and a tax only up to a maximum—have added up to regressive taxation: So long as the person earning $25,000 a year and the person earning $85,000 a year are both paying, let us say, a 6 percent tax for Social Security contributions, this is regressive, because 6 percent of the poorer person's tax is much harder to afford than 6 percent of the higher-income worker's tax.

A progressive tax, as explained in chapter 6, is one in which the percentage of contribution goes up with income. However, the second feature of Social Security makes the tax even more regressive. If the maximum taxed income is, let us say, $85,000 per year, then someone earning $300,000 or more per year is paying the same total tax to Social Security as the person earning $85,000. This compounds the regressivity of the Social Security system. So long as the system is contributory and so long as benefits are related to contributions, some regressivity seems inevitable. To raise the level of contribution to an unlimited amount would make it necessary also to raise benefits exceedingly, beyond the intent of the Social Security system for the higher-income person. Numerous ways around this problem have been suggested, from raising the maximum base of amount taxed for the employer share only, so that benefits for the workers do not have to be raised, to infusing the Social Security system with some partial relief from general revenues that would make it more progressive, even while keeping the contributory system as a base. A partial solution legislated in 1983 was to tax benefits of those Social Security recipients who have other significant income, but the basic question of the equitable financing of the Social Security system is likely to continue to be an issue.

Another problem with the Social Security system is its coherence with other social policies. If we are entering an age of automation, then we might want to push for earlier retirement benefits. On the other hand, if we need all the labor power we can get, then the availability of retirement at age 62 and at full funding even at age 67 years might be incompatible with this policy. Social Security policy has been related to our approach to employment. When laws are passed regarding the legality of mandatory retirement ages, this has an impact on the Social Security system.

The question of gender equity has confronted Social Security policymakers for many years. Legislative changes have eliminated distinctions based on gender. In 1950, husbands and widowers who were financially dependent on their wives became eligible for spousal benefits. In 1961, men were permitted to retire at age 62; women had been given this prerogative in 1956. In 1983, amendments to the Social Security Act further reduced inequities for men.

Notable gaps regarding women remain. Women who do not work outside their homes receive no benefits for work performed there. Women who divorce within ten years of marriage are not entitled to any benefits based on their former spouse's earnings. Older women who are divorced after a longer-term marriage and have never entered the workforce receive a generally inadequate benefit based on a percentage of their former spouses' primary insurance amount. Divorced older women receive an often deficient spousal benefit when their ex-husband retires.

Working married women are entitled to their benefit or one based on their husband's earnings, but not both. Because of the way benefits are currently determined, inequities may arise. The survivor of a two-earner couple, for example, often receives a lower benefit than the survivor of a one-earner family with the same total average indexed monthly earnings. Some of these issues are related to the fact that, as noted earlier, Social Security benefits are not directly linked to contributions. Others require consideration because of the high rate of divorce and the large numbers of women in the workforce, both factors not present when Social Security was designed in the 1930s.

Suggestions for enhancing benefit adequacy and equity in the Social Security system have been proposed. In the earnings sharing plan, the yearly income of both husband and wife are combined and divided evenly. In the double-decker system, each individual who is 65 years of age or disabled receives a guaranteed minimum monthly income. In addition, each can receive additional monthly monies related to prior earning. At this second level, the combined covered earnings of husbands and wives would be the basis for a married couple's benefits. Homemaker credits, in which homemakers earn Social Security credits for caregiving years out of the paid work force, also have been recommended. In view of current demographic trends, these problem-solving approaches may very well receive further attention in the next decade.[5] Another question regarding equity is raised by younger people who support the system but feel they will receive fewer benefits than the current retirees. While the Social Security tax burden generally falls on the employed, middle-aged population, careful computations would have to be done in order to compute exactly where the costs to society may rest. For example, the cost of retirement benefits may be offset by reduced benefits for smaller average-size families and increased numbers of women in the workforce.

Another unresolved issue regarding Social Security is the expanding monies in the OASDI trust funds. There have been several suggestions, from leaving it to collect interest to giving some back to using it for social welfare programs, to giving it all back and letting people provide for their retirement as they wish. This latter suggestion plays a part in proposals for altering Social Security as we shall see in later discussion. In any case, when the economy is expanding Social Security taxes increase and stave off future problems.

Reducing the regressive tax has been viewed by some persons as one way to increase the spendable income of low-paid workers. A related concern is that the surplus that by law can only be invested in government securities is included in the budget, thereby reducing—at least on paper—the size of the federal budget deficit and its rate of growth.

Social Security is one of those social welfare programs that have counter-cyclical consequences. That is, in times of high employment fewer people will be retiring so that less benefits will be pumped into the economy and more Social Security taxes will be taken out of the economy from working people. When unemployment is high more people will retire, and therefore, more benefits will be paid out while less money comes in. This is described further in discussing unemployment compensation, a classic counter-cyclical program.

The advent of Social Security also brought tremendous consequences for the development of leisure time activities: the culture of retirement. The fact that the benefits are national rather than local led to the possibility of retirement communities. If the benefits are mine wherever I go, then I can move to warmer states or to places where living costs are lower. This mobility is a consequence of the Social Security system. In fact, the availability of benefits no matter where the beneficiary goes has led a number of people to emigrate after retirement to countries where the cost of living is lower. Social Security has contributed to helping older people form perhaps the most powerful lobby in the nation and to establish a political system in which Social Security is almost sacrosanct in terms of the level of benefits. This is the most dramatic example we have of the degree to which universal social welfare systems tend to be improved even while selective ones may be cut.

Social Security is not the only federal retirement program. The United States Civil Service Commission, Bureau of Retirement, administers a federal civil service retirement system. This is funded by employer and employee contributions, and cash benefits are paid to retirees because of age or disability and to survivors under certain conditions. In 1934, the federal government mandated a similar system based on the Railroad Retirement Act for railroad employees. This program provides retirement, disability, and survivor annuities to workers whose employment was connected with the railroad industry for at least ten years. In 1974, some integration of this program with the Social Security program was developed by Congress, and Social Security credits earned during workers' employment careers are included in the benefit computation. Benefits are financed through a combination of employee, employer payroll taxes, income from a Social Security financial interchange, income from investments, federal general revenues, and a tax levied on railroad carriers. In 1999, there were 748,500 beneficiaries of the Railroad Retirement System at a cost of approximately $8.2 billion.[6] The Department of Defense administers a retirement program, as do many local and state public employee systems.

The Future of Social Security.   Retirement income rests on a four-tier system of arrangements: Social Security, employer-sponsored pensions, individual savings, and Supplemental Security Income (SSI). As it happens, the longer range picture for Social Security has become somewhat problematic. Problems include the long-term balance of funds, the ratio of contributions and benefits, and public confidence. Changes made in 1983 prevented insolvency of the program but expenditures are expected to exceed income by 2041 and to remain high thereafter. Long range projections are complex and based on assumptions, any of which can prove false. The Board of Trustees of the Social Security System and the Congressional Budget Office both make projections about the health of the program, the former for 75 years and the latter for a 10-year period. Their 2000 projections reported that for the next 10 years a large babyboom generation at peak earning years combined with the retirement of a "slim" generation born during the Great Depression years will ensure large trust fund reserves.

For the long-run, however, the projections are somewhat troubling. The Trustee's projection for the next 75 years shows that on-average Social Security annually would pay out more than its income. The trust fund would peak in 2024 and be drawn down as the Baby Boom generation retires. They expect that by 2041 the OASI trust fund would not be able to pay all benefits when they are due; this date, however, was delayed by 12 years since estimates made in 1997. Furthermore, if the trust fund is depleted, the system (*without alteration*) would be able to pay approximately 75 percent of promised benefits out of payroll revenues.[7]

These projections are based on assumptions about the pace of the growth of the gross domestic product (adjusted for inflation), the rate at which wages will rise, the increase in the cost of living, the degree of unemployment, and the ages at which persons will retire. However, during the next decades the baby boom generation is working and the Depression era group is retired. Together these projections make for a stable ratio of workers to recipients. When the Baby Boomers begin to retire in 2010, the ratio will erode, and by 2025 there will be a fast increasing number of retirees, with a declining ratio of workers to recipients. To restore long-run solvency, income must be raised or expenditures cut. Much depends on the assumptions that are used and what actually occurs. When the principal in the trust funds begins to be drawn down, the government would then have three options: raise taxes, curtail other spending, or borrow money from financial markets. There is nothing in the law that determines what actually will happen or be done but using more optimistic economic and technical assumptions can suggest the program will remain sound for 75 years.

Debates about changing Social Security are ideological, political, and technical. Early in the Bush administration, a proposal was made to overhaul Social Security by including personal investment accounts in the program. President Bush appointed a Commission co-chaired by former Senator Patrick Moynihan and Richard Parsons of AOL Time Warner and including economists, business executives, and former government officials.[8] While the Commission included Republicans and Democrats, early on it became clear the Commission favored the creation of private accounts. Before the Commission was able to report officially its proposals, the attack on the Twin Towers took place and the projected federal budgets, the economy, the focus of priority attention and decisions about changing the system were unclear. Furthermore, the stock market lost significant amounts of money and 401K personal retirement accounts invested in the stock market were diminished.[9] The approaches to the problems of Social Security and the proposed solutions reflect diverse and many ideological stances.

Possible solutions that have been proposed include the following: (1) Create individual investment accounts, that is privatize a part of the Social Security funds. On the one hand, doing so provides an opportunity for nearly all workers to build wealth by investing in stocks and bonds. This option depends on the expectation that such investments would gain a greater return than is available currently. According to this scheme, each person would be guaranteed a benefit payment but lower than currently received. Those who oppose this option state that individuals would face the risks of financial markets, an example of which occurred in the first six months of the Bush term. Benefits would be unequal and depend on the investing skill or luck of the person. The costs of administering a private system of accounts are expected to be significant. Also it was expected that the creation of such accounts would require deep cuts in the guaranteed amounts or large tax increases.

(2) Another approach would establish a government investment board much as states, cities, and counties currently handle their retirement systems. To do so proponents expect lower administrative costs, market investments would be spread across income levels and generations, and the returns would close a substantial part of the anticipated gap. Those who argue against more government investment in the market do not want government becoming more involved in private enterprise and believe that politicians would subject decisions to political influence.

(3) Increasing the retirement age would reflect increased life expectancies, keep constant the proportion of one's life spent in retirement, and could eliminate some of the long-term problems. Those who object to increasing the retirement age note the age is rising gradually over the next two decades; persons who do physical work cannot be expected to continue doing so; and older persons who lose their jobs would be penalized. (4) Some persons favor raising the amount of income taxed and would put more of a burden on those who can most afford it. Those who are against raising the cap argue this would be a substantial tax increase and since upper income persons feel that Social Security is not a "good deal" for them raising the tax would further harm them. (5) There is agreement among many economists that the consumer price index *overstates* inflation and thus provides cost of living increases which are not truly reflective of the rate of inflation. Another group suggests the consumer price index *understates* the real cost of living for the elderly. (6) Yet another group favors altering the benefits for those who are wealthy. According to this group, those who can most afford it can contribute more either through tax increases or benefit reductions. Given these

changes being made at certain levels many of the long-term system problems can be eliminated. However, taxing those who get high levels of benefits might hurt those who have sparse additional income.

The Commission charged with modernizing and restoring fiscal soundness to Social Security used six guiding principles: Modernization must not change Social Security benefits for retirees or those near retirement; the entire Social Security surplus must be dedicated only to Social Security; Social Security taxes must not be increased; modernization must preserve Social Security's disability and survivors insurance programs; and modernization must include individually controlled, voluntary personal retirement accounts, which will augment Social Security.

Unexpectedly, the Commission presented a variety of approaches rather than one comprehensive plan as anticipated. They found that it is possible to create personal investment accounts and improve Social Security's long-term financial situation but at an extremely high cost. Also, they found that it would take $2 to $3 trillion in new revenue to shore up the system for 75 years. This money could only come from increased borrowing, higher taxes or spending cuts in other programs. The best answer the Commission could produce required a combination of reductions in currently scheduled guaranteed benefits and increased large funding from general government revenue. None of these suggestions were politically palatable to legislators.[10]

A key element in the debate is the issue of privatization, the creation of personal accounts. Those who favor their creation suggest the personal invested accounts will receive greater returns and benefits. Americans are entitled to their private property by owning their own Social Security retirement accounts and having the choice of using their funds at retirement or leaving them to family members. According to this position, those enrolled would become shareholders in the United States economy and accumulate wealth. Because people would control their own retirement security, they would be empowered and see results related to their hard work.

Those who question private accounts suggest that the financial "problem" does not justify a major overhaul but could be handled through modest tax increases, slight increases in retirement age, a decision to raise benefits at a rate less than inflation or to adjust the cost of living index by a slight amount. This group suggests the drive to privatize is an excuse for Conservatives to begin incrementally dismantling the program. They do not want to risk the successful record of poverty reduction for the elderly that Social Security has achieved. Markets go up and markets go down and there have been prolonged periods when stocks were poor investments, often following periods of extraordinary returns. There is also the suggestion that the government would have to guarantee an income for those who experienced stock markets that do very poorly. While many people are entranced by the idea, there are many workers who are fearful of tinkering with a program that has a proven track record. This group also believes the attempt to privatize is impelled by the financial industry that wants to reap payment for administering and being paid for millions of individual accounts. These administrative expenses can only come from the profits, if any, available to the beneficiary.

Perhaps the most important criticism of the privatization proposal becomes obvious when we remember that Social Security is a transfer system from those employed to those who are retired. Any plan to convert Social Security to private personal accounts would require placing aside those funds to pay for personal retirements. However, there would remain a massive need to finance payments for those already retired or soon to do so. There are estimates that a diversion of two percentage points of payroll tax would approximate $1 trillion over the next decade. But, by not using that money to reduce the federal debt, the government would have to increase borrowing and increase the interest it has to pay. Thus, about $1.3 trillion dollars would be needed to finance the private accounts plan.

Other criticisms have been identified related to women and privatization. Women earn on average less than men, so less money would go into their accounts. Women are viewed as typically more conservative investors, thus being protected when the market does poorly but falling behind when the market would do well. Women who amass as much as men would have to draw out less than men because they must anticipate living longer on average. None of the proposed plans provides monthly payments to a divorced spouse. When a worker dies today, a spouse can get the entire benefit. With private savings plans, the worker can take money as needed, so spouses get no income guarantees.[12]

Social Security has been a highly successful program. In chapter 8 we observed the important role it plays in raising people out of poverty. Benefits are currently kept up-to-date with wages before retirement and with prices following retirement. As one's standard of living rises, the Social Security benefit automatically rises with it. Thus, beneficiaries are guaranteed inflation proof. This inflation protection is particularly important for aging people as it offsets their personal savings' depletion over time. Other advantages include the opportunities created for younger workers when older workers make room for them and the multiplier effects of the economic activity generated by the recipients' expenditures. Finally, Social Security provides not just for retirement but also for family protection and disabilities, even relieving the burden of caring for aged parents by those who are raising families themselves.

Unemployment Compensation

Goals.   Unemployment compensation (UC) is a federal-state program designed (1) to provide temporary and partial wage replacement to involuntarily unemployed workers who were recently employed and (2) to help stabilize the economy during recessions. The first governmental unemployment compensation program was created in Wisconsin in 1932 and was the forerunner of the unemployment compensation program included in the Social Security Act of 1935. By 1937, all states, the then-territories of Alaska and Hawaii, and the District of Columbia enacted programs. Puerto Rico joined in the 1950s.

Who Is Eligible for the Program?   States developed diverse and complex methods for determining eligibility under federal and state laws. In 1999, 97 percent of all wage and salaried workers were covered by UC but only 38 percent of unemployed persons actually received UC benefits. To receive benefits, persons must have worked recently for a covered employer for a specified period of time and earned a certain amount of wages. States are not required to cover nonprofit organizations, State-local governments, certain agricultural labor, and certain domestic service. Special legislation provided coverage for federal civilian employees, ex-military personnel, and railroad workers. Among those excluded from federal coverage are self-employed workers, those employed by their families, members of the judiciary, elected officials, legislators, and those employed by a nonprofit agency that has fewer than four employees. States have the option of covering groups not included in federal legislation, and many do so. However, in general, states do not cover students, individuals unemployed because of family responsibilities, professional athletes between sport seasons, school personnel between academic years, and illegal aliens.

To be eligible, an individual worker must meet a state's specifications regarding the amount of wages earned and/or length of time worked during a "base period." The worker must be able to work, be available for work, and be registered for work at the state unemployment office. Some evidence of an active job-search effort is required by most states, and the person cannot refuse an offer of, or referral to, "suitable work" without good cause. In addition, the worker cannot be viewed as responsible for his or her unemployed status. Such circumstances as being fired because of misconduct, leaving a job without good cause, refusal of suitable work, and involvement in a labor dispute may lead to disqualification for all or part of the benefit year.

There is no assets test, and income from rents, dividends, or earnings of other family members is not used to determine eligibility. This is an insurance benefit available to anyone who qualifies, regardless of wealth; if you are laid off, seeking work, and unable to find it, you are probably eligible for UC. States' UC programs vary in how much proof they demand of unemployed workers regarding their weekly efforts to seek work.

The Balanced Budget Act (1997) provided that age and claim information can be disclosed to the Department of the Treasury, the Social Security Administration, and State Child Support Enforcement agencies. Also, the Taxpayer Relief Act (1997) requires individuals filing new claims for UC to disclose whether they owe uncollected overpayments of Food Stamps. If so, repayment will be made through deductions from the individual's UC benefits based on an agreement by the individual and Food Stamp agency. Administrative hearings are available to applicants who disagree with a denial of benefits or other issue, first appealing before an administrative law judge and later to the Unemployment Insurance Appeal Board. The case may ultimately be presented in the Appellate Division of the State Supreme Court. An employer who disagrees with a claims decision may use the same appeals procedure.

What Is the Form of Benefit?   Cash benefits are provided in varying amounts determined by wages earned during a "base period." States establish minimum and maximum benefits. The national average weekly benefit amount projected for 1999 was $215 for an average of 15 weeks. The Tax Reform Act of 1986 made all unemployment compensation taxable when unemployment benefits plus other earnings exceeded certain levels. The additional revenue was to be used for offsetting the cost of supplementary benefits for persons unemployed for lengthy periods. Such tax plans serve to concentrate unemployment benefits at the lower income levels and away from middle- and upper-income families.

The regular state programs usually provide benefits up to 26 weeks. The federal-state extended benefits program provides up to 13 additional weeks of benefits when a state's unemployment rate is relatively high. An additional 7 weeks is available under an optional trigger, but only eight states have chosen to use this provision. In times of serious economic recession, temporary federal programs augment the permanent program extending the number of weeks covered. If a worker remains unemployed after the benefit period expires, he or she may be eligible for TANF or general assistance.

In 1994 Congress enacted the General Agreement on Tariffs and Trade (GATT), which requires each state to establish a system for withholding federal income tax from UC payments so that withholding can occur at the option of the claimant. This change became effective at the beginning of 1997. The Social Security Independence and Program Improvements Act (1994) gave states the option of excluding from coverage services performed by aliens admitted to the United States under temporary visas.

Several states added a small tax to cover temporary disability that is not work related. This has been one of the "cracks" between social insurances through which some people fall. Additional benefits are made available in the form of free placement and counseling services for use by employers, veterans, and employees. Work training and retraining programs may also be available.

How Is the Program Financed?   The unemployment compensation program is financed by a payroll tax paid by employers on their total payroll. The federal tax is 6.2 percent of the first $7,000 of each worker's covered wages. Employers in states with federally approved programs and with no delinquent federal loans may credit 5.4 percentage points against the 6.2 percent tax rate. This makes the generally applicable rate 0.8 percent. The federal share of the tax is earmarked for federal and state administrative expenses, the federal share of the federal-state extended unemployment compensation program, and a federal account for state loans. The funds returned to the states are supposed to finance the regular state programs and half of the federal-state extended benefits program. Any payments made to a state's unemployment compensation program are credited toward the federal tax. The actual tax paid depends on the stability of an employer's employment history. In almost all states, stability is measured by the amount of unemployment benefits paid to an employer's former workers. Generally, those who discharge fewer workers are granted lower tax rates on their payrolls. This system of "experience rating" was introduced to discourage layoffs. The tax is collected and deposited in the federal treasury in the U.S. Unemployment Trust Fund and then invested, and each state is credited with its share of the interest. States draw as necessary for payment of benefits.

What Is the Level of Administration?   The UC program is administered through the Employment Security Administration of the United States Department of Labor. The collection of taxes is the responsibility of the United States Department of the Treasury. But states each administer their own benefit programs. Programs vary by states, as do the governmental structures used to administer the program. The Consolidated Appropriations Act (2001) treats Indian tribes similar to state and local governments. Services performed in the employ of tribes will no longer be subject to the Federal Unemployment Tax Act and are required to be covered under state unemployment insurance laws. However, the tribe becomes liable for Federal unemployment taxes if they failed to pay into the states' insurance funds. In these cases, the state may remove tribe services from state coverage. The Victims of Trafficking and Violence Protection Act (2000) called for a national study of state unemployment insurance laws that address separation from employment due to circumstances resulting from domestic violence and receiving or not receiving Unemployment Compensation.[13]

Discussion.   Unemployment compensation is a classic example of the grant-in-aid described in chapter 7. The federal government never formally forced states to adopt UC programs. Instead, the federal government simply legislated a payroll tax on employers throughout the nation. If the state wanted to get the bulk of those taxes back into the state, it had to follow the guidelines for receiving that rebate; namely, setting up a state unemployment compensation system. State programs vary in maximum benefits, number of weeks covered, and so on, but all must meet certain basic guidelines of the federal legislation. This is the grant-in-aid principle: Money and guidelines come from a higher level, and the administration and some local initiative remain at the lower level. The incentive was so great to get the grant-in-aid and not lose the money for the state that within two years of the establishment of the Social Security Act all states enacted programs.

Unemployment compensation is a universal and institutional program to meet the reality that in our society there will be temporary dislocations that result from shifting market needs, new job locations, and changes in the industrial system. Thus in the best of all economies, some businesses should close, change, and move locations, and some workers will be dislocated. Unemployment compensation is to give these workers breathing space so that the labor market is not degraded and they are not forced to take the first available job at a lower level of skill. It protects the worker, allowing time to seek employment at his or her level.

The UC reserves tend to build up in periods of high employment when there is little call on them by unemployed workers. This situation suggests that the benefits should be raised because the reserves are building up unnecessarily. However, during periods of a rise in unemployment or a recession, unemployment funds are drained, and the UC system is used as a quasi-public assistance system.

The public assistance program is so degrading and stigmatized with its means test that there is great pressure on Congress to extend the benefits of UC for longer periods of time when many people need this kind of help. But the UC system was never set up to meet this massive need. All UC benefits are taxable, suggesting its being viewed as a public assistance program.

Not only is the UC program an income stabilizer, it is an economic stabilizer as well. The UC system is a classic example of a counter-cyclical program. Usually, in a capitalist or "free-enterprise" economy, the normal business cycle moves up and down like a wave every few years, through periods of high economic activity (high employment and the danger of inflation) to periods of low economic activity (high unemployment and the danger of recession). Government has viewed its role as trying to flatten these waves, to take steps that will counter the expected business cycle, deflating the economy in times of boom and pumping up the economy in times of recession. Programs that automatically have this effect are called counter-cyclical. Unemployment compensation is one such program. Some other social welfare programs also have the same effect. During a time of high employment, when there is an economic boom, little money is paid out of the UC system because there is less unemployment; more money is squirreled away in reserve funds because more people are working and there are more payroll taxes to be collected. This taking of money out of the economy is a deflating move, flattening out a tendency for economic boom. On the other hand, when unemployment is high in times of recession, the unemployment compensation system is collecting less funds because fewer people are employed and is pumping more funds back into the economy in the form of benefits because more people are collecting. This money added to the economy serves to generate more economic activity and is, thus, counter-cyclical.

Two principles are illustrated by the concept of experience rating, described previously. Experience rating is a way of rewarding the "good" employer who does not lay off workers. This is supposed to serve as an incentive to keep employees on the job. However, it shows the strains in every insurance program between the insurance principle and the incentive principle. The whole concept of insurance is to pool or share a risk. For example, if there are 40 people in a class and the odds are that one person will break a leg during the year, each of the 40 contributes something so that whoever breaks a leg will have adequate compensation. However, if an analysis is made of the likelihood of each person's breaking a leg and the amount each person contributes is based on that, we no longer have a true insurance system but a system in which each person is paying for his or her own care. Thus in health insurance, in auto insurance, and in the social insurances, experience ratings of specialized groups by age, sex, geographic location, prior experience, and the like, tend to break down the whole concept of pooled risk. On the other hand, some people feel that if one were not to reward safe drivers and good employers, for example, with financial benefits, one would take away the incentives. There is no "right" answer to this balance. The trade-offs are constantly argued by economists and social welfare experts.

But experience rating is also an example of how latent or unanticipated consequences may undo the purpose of a program. As explained, an experience rating was initiated to keep employers from laying off workers in order to maintain their lower insurance rates. However, it may also work in reverse. The concerned employer may not take on new employees or may lay them off before they have worked long enough to become eligible for unemployment compensation just to protect an experience rating. Thus the experience rating may produce just the opposite effect from that originally intended.

Some persons think that unemployed persons remain unemployed longer than they would if benefits were lower and that some unemployed persons end up with more money than some full-time, tax-paying workers. Those who take this point of view contend that benefits discourage aggressive searches for employment. Others suggest that unemployed persons do not obtain jobs because jobs are unavailable, especially during times of recession. The initiation of taxation of such benefits is viewed by some as a significant step toward the taxation of other governmental benefits paid by the federal government.

Despite the fact the program is a universal one, in actuality it has not been operating in that way. In 1999 only 38 percent of those covered and unemployed received benefits when unemployed. This low percentage was attributed to several factors. The relative importance and order of their estimated contributions to the downward trend follow: Changes in state program characteristics (increase in base period earning requirements, increase in income denials, and tightening up other non-monetary eligibility requirements); decline in the proportion of the unemployed from manufacturing industries; geographic shifts in the composition of the unemployed among regions of the country; implementation of partial taxation of benefits; and changes in the measurement of unemployment.[13]

The amount and duration of benefits differs from state to state. But, the weekly benefit amounts generally replace between 50 and 70 percent of an individual's average weekly pre-tax wage up to some state determined maximum. The wage replacement rates tend, as does Social Security, to vary inversely with the claimant's average pre-tax wage and the bias of the benefits is toward low-earners. Nevertheless, the average weekly benefit amount as a percent of the average weekly covered wage was only 35 percent in 1999.

The relationship of UC to public assistance may become an issue. As welfare recipients are moved into employment, one can expect they will be at special risk of unemployment even in the best of times because of their limited education, work skills, and work experience. There are expectations that former welfare recipients are expected to have jobless rates twice the national average, but it is unlikely changes will be made to enhance or change benefits to deal with this group.[14]

Trade Adjustment Assistance.   Trade Adjustment Assistance for Workers (TAA; Trade Act, 1974) consists of trade adjustment allowances, employment services, training and allowances while in training, and job search and relocation allowances for qualified workers. Administered by the Employment and Training Administration of the Department of Labor through State agencies, the state agencies act as federal agents to provide program information, process applications, determine individual worker eligibility, issue payments, and provide reemployment services and training opportunities. Criteria are used for eligibility related to layoffs, decreased sales, and imports resulting from federal policies to reduce import restrictions that contributed to the layoffs and declining production.

The North American Free Trade Agreement (NAFTA, 1993) established transitional adjustment assistance as a new part of the Trade Act of 1974. The benefits provided are similar to those of the TAA program, but the imports must be from Canada or Mexico. These programs are funded from federal general revenues. Eligibility depends on the "impact" date and whether the worker was employed for at least 26 weeks in the preceding year at wages of $30 or more per week; was entitled to unemployment compensation; had exhausted all rights to any UC entitlement, including any extended benefits; and was enrolled in or had completed an approved training program.

Workers' Compensation

Goals.   Workers' compensation (WC) is designed to provide cash and medical benefits to persons with job-related disabilities and survivors' benefits to dependents of those whose death resulted from work related accidents or illnesses. This program protects workers from two of the problems of the industrial era. In a wage economy, workers are dependent on wages. "Out of work" means "out of wages." It is this risk that WC seeks to insure people against.

Workers' compensation was the first widespread form of social insurance in the United States. In 1902, Maryland enacted the first state compensation law in which benefits were paid without proof of fault, but the United States Supreme Court declared the law unconstitutional. In 1908, the federal government initiated a similar program for federal workers employed in hazardous work. By 1920, all states but six had WC laws; and by 1948, all states had such programs, but they differ greatly in extent of coverage, level of benefits, and insurance underwriting methods used. In addition, the federal government operates WC programs for government employees and for coal miners afflicted with pneumoconiosis ("black lung" disease). There are, therefore, not one, but many WC programs. In our discussion we will focus on their common features.

Prior to the enactment of these programs, the common law principle was well established that a worker had a right to recover damages only if it were proven that the employee's injury or death resulted from the employer's negligence. In such a system, workers were at a disadvantage because of the expense and other resources needed to challenge the employer.

It is easy to see why workers' compensation was the first system of social insurance not only in the United States, but also in England and Bismarck's

Germany. Preceding it was an anarchic system in which the worker was never sure of compensation for work-related injury. Even if he or she did receive benefits, they only would come after long litigation. Thus the worker was not covered during the crisis period, and a good deal of the cost of the system went to pay attorneys. Even the employer had to live with uncertainty because eventually there could be a very large liability settlement that could be injurious to it as well. Therefore, both parties could see benefit in a no-fault insurance system, which is what WC is.

Who Is Eligible for the Program?   In 1996, 114.6 million workers (90 percent of wage and salary workers) were covered. Coverage is compulsory for most private employers except in Wyoming and Texas. If employers reject coverage in those states, they lose the use of common-law defenses against suits by employees. Many state programs exempt employees of nonprofit, charitable, or religious institutions, as well as very small employers, domestic and agricultural employment, and casual labor. Coverage for state and local public employees differs from state to state.

Although a worker is generally eligible regardless of fault or blame, most states do not cover injuries resulting from an employee's gross negligence, willful misconduct, or intoxication. Although claims for occupational disease account for small percentages of WC claims, amendments to and interpretation of state laws covering illnesses with long latency periods is expected to increase this percentage. In addition, medical advances have identified different types of disorders such as traumas caused by constant repetitive motion, pressure, or vibration. This type of disorder accounts for approximately half of all occupational illnesses.

Disputes regarding WC claims can be heard by a Workers' Compensation Law judge. The judge's decision in turn can be reviewed by the Workers' Compensation Board. Ultimately, participants in disputed claims can be heard by the Appellate Division of the State Supreme Court.

What Is the Form of Benefit?   Most WC benefits are paid by insurance companies through policies purchased by private employers and are tied to the requirements of state and federal workers' compensation laws covering the employers. Cash benefit levels are established by state formulas and are usually calculated as a percentage of weekly earnings at the time of the injury or death (typically two thirds) and are periodically paid during the time of disability. Each state (and the federal government for federal workers) sets a maximum benefit level, which they periodically adjust. Medical care and hospitalization costs are covered. In the case of death, payments, including burial expenses, are made to survivors.

A brief waiting period for eligibility is often used to eliminate short duration cases and serves to decrease the cost of the program. When the disability lasts longer than the period specified in law, payment of benefits is made retroactive to the date of injury. It is assumed that sick leave or savings can cover the average worker through time-limited crises.

Cash benefits are limited either by duration or amount. There are differences between benefits for permanent and temporary disabilities. Many states pay temporary total disability for as long as the worker is disabled. Some states have a maximum number of weeks for benefits for temporary disabilities. Some have maximum total payments. For permanent total disability, payments are made for life in a high proportion of the states. In other states, payments are limited to maximum amounts for a maximum number of weeks. Survivors' benefits are provided to spouses until remarriage and until the children reach a particular age. State provisions differ widely in regard to compensation and medical care for injured workers and death benefits and pensions for dependents of workers killed on the job.

Benefit amounts are based on the wage at the time of the accident or at the onset of illness. Temporary total disability, permanent total disability, permanent partial disability, and death of a breadwinner are usually compensated at two-thirds of the wage, up to a limited maximum. For the black lung benefit program, there is an established federal rate, which is reduced if the state's WC program is also covering the disease. If a worker becomes permanently disabled, he or she may be eligible for cash benefits under both WC and the Social Security Disability Insurance program. However, total benefits under both programs cannot exceed the higher of 80 percent of the worker's former earnings or the total family benefit under Social Security.

Medical services, as needed, are also provided. However, some states have limits on such care, which can be extended under certain circumstances. Rehabilitation services are also provided in some states, as are maintenance payments during the rehabilitation period. Most states provide training in new jobs for workers who cannot continue in their old work because of injury. The federal government and almost all states have laws covering compensation for occupational diseases.

How Is the Program Financed?   The funding of workers' compensation is almost entirely borne by employers. In a few states, employees contribute to medical care, and in some states contributions are made from general revenues to the WC fund. Several states have exclusive state WC insurance that employers fund. About a dozen states have state insurance funds and private insurance funds, and employers select their preference. In most states, there is no state fund, and employers are simply mandated to contribute to some private insurance fund. In most states, there is a penalty if an employer does not have insurance. In states where employers have the option, some large firms are self-insured. There is no federal government trust fund, and workers' compensation is dominated by commercial private and self-insurance. Premiums are based on the size of the firm and the nature of the risk involved in the work. Firms are assigned experience ratings on the basis of the use of insurance funds by their employees. This rating is an attempt to introduce a degree of equity into the programs.

The black lung benefit program is funded by general revenues and a federal trust fund supported by a tax on coal.

What Is the Level of Administration?   Workers' compensation is enacted through state laws and is state administered through state departments of labor or independent WC boards, by insurance companies, or by state agencies and insurance companies together. The Office of Workers' Compensation Programs in the Department of Labor administers the federal program. As of 1988, the administrative expenses of private insurance carriers as a percentage of the premiums earned was 22.7 percent; the same feature for state-operated funds was 10.6 percent.

Three major trends are reflected in the most recent legislation enacted by states. One focus is on dealing with fraud; a second is providing premium discounts for employers who maintain drug-free workplaces; and the third is a move in 2000 by a number of states to increase their workers' compensation rates for disability and/or death.[15]

Discussion.   As one can see, the WC system is a universal form of social insurance. There is no means test based on the workers' income, and it is viewed as an insurance and as a right by the injured worker. Workers' compensation represents an institutional kind of social service program, recognizing that some degree of injury is inevitable in an industrial system, and seeks to provide a simple and equitable compensation for that eventuality. There are several principles that are illustrated by the WC system.

First, it is a basic no-fault system. The no-fault concept can be understood in comparison to its alternative: the liability concept. In the liability concept the person or institution that caused the injury or accident has to be determined. If there is fault or liability, then the faulty or liable party must pay damages to the injured party. In addition to paying for all the costs of the injury and making up for the loss, there may also be punitive damages for having been at fault. This is seen as an incentive for safety. In the no-fault system, there is no attempt made to assess liability. The insurance simply covers the injury and its related costs, and there are no punitive damages. The advantages of no-fault insurance are immense: It eliminates a waiting period and uncertainty; it reduces legal fees and litigation; and it avoids massive punitive damages that may destroy a somewhat innocent party who was responsible for the accident.

However, there are civil liberties purists and others who feel that the no-fault system and WC are unfair, that they deprive the citizen of a constitutional right to sue for damages. It is also argued that, since the original enactment of WC, there are now public assistance and other vehicles by which the injured party can get temporary relief while waiting to go through the courts. Finally, some see no-fault as injurious to incentives to maintain safety. However, the majority view seems to be that the current insurance system represents a dignified approach that serves the interests of the U.S. industrial system best, and there is no major movement to change its basic form.

Another principle that is illustrated by WC is that when a system is financed completely by the employer, as is the case in most states, rather than by employer-employee contributions or by general tax funds, the employers tend to have controlling interests in the regulatory boards and state commissions that govern WC. This has acted, according to workers' groups, to prevent the improvement of the

WC system, has caused narrow definitions of what constitutes a work-related versus a non–work-related injury, and so on. It is easy to understand why unions often support employer-employee contributions to systems, even though it costs the worker money: It gives the workers "a piece of the action."

If one may borrow phraseology from community mental health, it is possible to see the evolution of systems for workers' safety in the following ways. The original system of suing for liability is a tertiary kind of care for the injured party, giving rehabilitative relief well after the fact. Workers' compensation represents a secondary level of care that is prompt, universal, and more adequate. The Occupational Safety and Health Administration (OSHA) attempts primary prevention by creating the kinds of conditions in the industrial society where accidents are less likely to occur. The concept of society's working to guarantee safe conditions has been challenged only by free-enterprise purists who believe that the government should stay out of this area completely.

The major criticism directed against the WC system is its still-incomplete horizontal adequacy. This gradually gets corrected as coverage broadens state by state. Whether a worker is declared partially or totally disabled makes a critical difference in the benefit received. The system is also criticized on the level of vertical adequacy. The maximums are seen as too low in some states—hence the calls for maximums up to average weekly wage levels or other such formulas. There is some cost inefficiency in the determination of whether an injury is work related or not. This would be eliminated in a national health insurance plan that covered all medical care regardless of cause. Apart from such a development, it is hard to see how this cost inefficiency can be eliminated. The total coverage of medical care makes it possible for doctors to prescribe whatever is necessary. On the whole, WC is one of the least criticized social insurance systems in American life and one that has found broad acceptance.

Workers' compensation is also a good example of a state welfare system as opposed to a federal one, with all the problems and benefits therein. The problems come from great variations among states, with workers sometimes being unaware of what benefits they actually have, particularly if they move, and the lack of a large federal insurance pool. On the other hand, the fact that there are state variations has allowed progressive states to move faster than the nation might have moved as a whole.

Cost increases for workers' compensation premiums are expected to moderate as the number of lower-risk service jobs grows much more rapidly than those in goods-producing industries. More hazardous employment tends to produce more serious injuries and higher benefit levels. The changing occupational mix in the United States should lead to smaller increases in the total premium amounts per worker paid by employers.

Income Support Programs

To this point, we have examined programs that are "insurances," but there are a number of means-tested economic security programs as well. In this section, we review three public assistance programs—Temporary Assistance for Needy Families, General Assistance (both commonly called "welfare"), and Supplemental Security Income. We also discuss the Earned Income Tax Credit, a negative income tax program that aids low-income working persons.

Temporary Assistance for Needy Families

Temporary Assistance for Needy Families (TANF) is the replacement program for Aid to Families with Dependent Children and is emblematic of a revolution in social welfare policy. Here we will review briefly its major outlines, report on early findings as a result of its implementation, identify various issues to be confronted as part of re-authorization legislation, and discuss the current situation.

Goals. Created by the Personal Responsibility and Work Opportunity Reconciliation Act (1996), TANF has four goals: (1) to provide assistance to needy families so that the children may be cared for in their homes or in the homes of relatives; (2) to end the dependency of needy parents on government benefits by promoting job preparation, work, and marriage; (3) to prevent and reduce the incidence of out-of-wedlock pregnancies and establish annual numerical goals for preventing and reducing the incidences of these pregnancies; and (4) to encourage the formation and maintenance of two-parent families.

What Is the Form of Benefit? The program provides cash assistance based on need, income, resources, and family size. Nearly all recipients must work after two years in unsubsidized or subsidized employment, on-the-job training, work experience, community service, or 12 months of vocational training. Child care is to be provided for individuals participating in work or community service (but there are no guarantees), child support is enforced, and medical coverage is made available. Exceptions are made for six weeks of job search time, parents with a child under 6 years who cannot find child care, and single parents with a child under age 1 year. A year or more of transitional health care is provided for those who leave welfare for work.

Who Is Eligible for the Program? States make an initial assessment of a recipient's need, income, resources and skills and develop personal responsibility plans that identify needed education, training, and job placement services. Families cannot spend more than five cumulative years on TANF. States can specify fewer years and exempt up to 20 percent of the caseload from the time limit. After the time limit is exceeded, States can choose to provide noncash assistance and vouchers to families by using Social Services Block grants to state funds. States are expected to reduce rolls by 50 percent by 2002.

Unmarried minor parents are required to live with a responsible adult or in an adult-supervised setting and participate in educational and training activities in order to receive assistance. States are also undertaking efforts to prevent non-marital teen pregnancy.

State eligibility for block grants depends on operating a child support program, participation in the Federal Case Registry and National Directory of New Hires. Child support can be withheld directly from wages, and paternity establishment is emphasized. Cash assistance will be reduced by at least 25 percent in cases of failure to cooperate with paternity establishment. Uniform interstate child support laws, central registries of child support orders and collections, and toughened enforcement of child support are all implemented.

How Is the Program Financed?   This program is financed by federal general revenues through a fixed basic federal grant of $16.5 billion annually through 2002, plus expanded child care funding. These grants are based on prior federal expenditures for AFDC and a supplemental fund for certain States with low TANF grants relative to poverty and high population growth; a bonus fund for states that reduce out-of-wedlock birth rates without increasing abortion rates; a bonus fund for "high performance" states; a contingency fund for states that experience high unemployment and/or increased Food Stamp caseloads; and welfare-to-work grants. All these grants are capped.

What Is the Level of Administration?   States are largely responsible for administering TANF within certain federal conditions. In addition, the law authorizes states to administer and provide TANF services through contracts with charitable, religious, or private organizations. Beneficiaries who object to the religious nature of organizations must be provided an alternative provider. Federally recognized Native American tribes have the option of designing and operating their own cash welfare programs with funds subtracted from their state's TANF block grant.

The TANF program was passed to drastically reform the welfare system to place a greater emphasis on work and personal responsibility and to provide states with flexibility to create what they consider to be the best approaches to these aims for their particular circumstances. Even before the Personal Responsibility and Work Opportunity legislation was enacted 43 states through federal waivers had altered their welfare programs into work-focused programs. Major emphases were: reduce projected spending, to require work, limit assistance to certain durations, make work pay, improve child support enforcement, encourage parental responsibility, and give more power and authority to states to encourage innovation and creativity in welfare policy.

The Third Annual Report to Congress (2000) by the Department of Health and Human Services (Administration for Children and Families) reported the following. (1) There has been a dramatic increase in employment of current welfare recipients. (2) The percentage of working recipients reached an all-time high in 1999 compared to much lower percentages prior to TANF implementation, mainly in paid employment but also in work experience and community service. (3) Average monthly earnings for those employed increased. (4) Early data suggest employment of long-term recipients earned $700–800 more than they received on public assistance. More recent applicants who were previously and recently employed showed no effect on their earnings. The Urban Institute found average earnings of those who left welfare are above minimum wage—$6.60–$6.80 for hourly wages.

The Report concluded that research on family income, food security and hunger, health insurance status, child outcomes, and other family experiences did not as of the date of the Report provide a definitive picture. Early systematic reports from Minnesota found increased income across a broad range of families. It was found that long-term recipient families experienced a reduction in children's behavior problems, an increase in attachment to and performance in school, a dramatic reduction in domestic violence, increased access to child care and health insurance, and an increase in the percentage of children living in two-parent families. The number of paternities established tripled from 1992 to 1998 and the teenage birth rates fell in all states and the District of Columbia. Child poverty was reduced from 1993 to 1998, the largest five year drop in 30 years. This latter point is undoubtedly due to the vigorous economy during those years.[16]

Other reports were not so "rosy." The House Committee on Ways and Means reported that "millions of American families that have left welfare are worse off economically today because many state governments are not spending the federal funds intended to help them transition into work or take care of their children." The Committee stated: (1) States have failed to use more than $8 billion authorized by Congress for needed child care, transportation, education, and job training; (2) In spite of a booming national economy, the average people living in poverty are poorer today than they were a decade ago; (3) more than half of those who have left welfare for work are unable to pay rent, buy food, afford medical care, or keep their telephone or electric service from being disconnected.

Most research about welfare-to-work focused on young children and how their lives would change under welfare reform, how their daily care would be different. Early studies found positive impacts on young children, but the effect on adolescents were surprisingly negative. In Florida and Minnesota adolescents whose families were enrolled in welfare-to-work were compared to others in welfare programs where the parents were not in such programs. The adolescents with enrolled families did worse in school, were more likely to be suspended from school. In mother-headed families that had been on welfare only a short time when the program began, there was an increased likelihood of arrests, convictions, and other involvement with the police.[17]

TANF serves eligible poor families but most of the eligible poor are not being served, making TANF horizontally inadequate. A report by the Center for Law and Social Policy pointed out that there was almost a 50 percent drop in the public assistance caseload following the PRWO. But the caseload fell more rapidly than child poverty. Most poor children do not receive TANF assistance. In 1994, two thirds of eligible poor children received AFDC while only 47 percent receive TANF.[18]

Discussion. Temporary Assistance for Needy Families, the nation's largest public assistance program, is at the heart of what is commonly referred to as the "welfare problem." Society is often depicted as needing to protect itself against a horde of unwed mothers and other "cheats" striving to live off the public dole.

This image is inevitable given the kind of program that public assistance is and persisting negative perceptions of those in need. Interestingly enough, AFDC started in 1935 as a method of keeping mothers in the home to prevent family breakup and to spare mothers from the necessity of having to work. Today, a major objective of the program is to encourage mothers, except for those with very young children, to go to work outside the home. Thus the same program has been altered to meet changing values and priorities in society.

There is probably no way in which the stigma and the ugliness can be completely removed from a massive means-tested program such as TANF. If there were more social insurances, such as childrens' or family allowances or less unemployment or other means by which the rolls could be reduced dramatically, it might be possible to develop a more responsive system, but this is not an immediate prospect.

The question of whether and at what point welfare destroys the incentive to work has been with us since the Poor Laws introduced the principle of less eligibility—that a person on public assistance should not do as well as or better than the lowest-paid working person. This idea is related to the view that the individual requires motivation to work and if given a choice, would not.

Discussion. Potential issues to be considered when welfare legislation is to be re-considered during 2002 are dependent on the state of the economy and the political context which changed drastically in 2001 as a result of the attacks on the Twin Towers in New York and the Pentagon. The 2002 debates are likely to be extremely important for discussions of national poverty policy and family policy. Among potential issues are the following. Should the purposes of TANF be altered? Major parts of the spending are focused on services and activities other than providing cash assistance. Should there be a greater emphasis on providing supports and assistance to the working poor? The employment rate of single mothers rose steadily from 57 percent in 1992 to almost 71 percent in 1999. Their rate exceeded that of married mothers. At the same time, fewer mothers—even poor ones—are receiving cash welfare. Welfare-to-work programs generally increase employment and often increase average earnings and decrease cash assistance payments. The strong economy over this period had a very positive impact on the employment of single mothers.[19]

Should an even greater emphasis be placed on engaging fathers in family formation, reunification, and maintenance? The number of single mothers increased rapidly between 1989 and 1993 but remained relatively constant from 1993 to 1998. Some people believe this population stopped growing because of changed attitudes and policies but the reasons are unclear. In Minnesota the program found the percentage of family breakup decreased and the rate of marriage among single or cohabiting parents increased.[20]

Overall from 1987 to 1998 income has grown and poverty decreased among mothers raising children alone. These trends are probably due to increased work and less reliance on welfare among these mothers. However, among the very poorest mothers (the lowest 20 percent) income fell because they lost more in cash welfare and food stamps than they gained in earnings and the Earned Income Tax

Credit. Many evaluations found that welfare-to-work programs that succeed in moving persons to jobs often do not raise family income. Increases in earnings did not offset reductions in cash benefits and food stamps. However, a bigger share of income came from earnings and a smaller share from public assistance. Programs that combine mandated employment with generous earnings disregards (recipients can keep more of their welfare benefits) were effective in raising earnings and employment.[21]

Should federal funding and requirements that state maintenance of effort be changed? Since the caseloads declined, some persons will argue that federal funding is too high. Others will argue that the adequacy of the funds cannot be judged until the inevitable recession occurs and the cash demands on the system increase. Or, states could use remaining funds for broader efforts on the part of low-income families. How should state performance be measured? What should be the respective priorities among: caseload decline, reduction of child poverty, or increased attention to out-of-wedlock births and family formation issues? Should there be more federal safeguards? Family sanctions account for part of the caseload decline. How much flexibility should states have to promote employment and reduce caseloads? Some argue that state discretion led to some families leaving welfare without work and deepening poverty for the very poorest female-headed families. How much emphasis should be placed upon addressing literacy barriers, health, substance abuse, mental health or disability-related reasons before imposing full-family sanctions? Should there be greater federal requirements that states assist and work with those/families with the greatest barriers to employment, the hard-to-place group? Among the many other issues are domestic violence, access to education and training, families in which members have disabilities, linkages between the welfare systems and the employment systems.

Welfare reform took place during an unusually extended and positive period for the economy. The inclusion of a five year time limit on welfare benefits (some states have shorter limits) raises some concerns, considering the inevitability of a recession. This limit may cause problems for families. The federal law allows exemptions up to 20 percent of the caseload. However, given the great decline in the caseload, there is concern whether the 20 percent exemption will be sufficient to cover large numbers who play by the rules but still have difficulties. Furthermore, some of those who are left behind are those who have serious barriers to employment such as illiteracy, mental illness and substance abuse, homelessness, learning disabilities, criminal records, health problems, and language barriers.

It is certain the forthcoming debates about the future directions of welfare policy will focus on costs, performance effectiveness, and incentives for government, individuals, and families. The debates will depend on the economic and political context at the time and questions will be considered which cut across many programs, not just TANF. How can government better assist poor, working families? How to assist working families where barriers interfere with their desirable participation? What steps should be taken in regard to marriage, out-of-wedlock births, fathers, and family formation? Finally, what should the balance be between federal responsibility and state discretion?[22]

For how many will TANF improve their lives and for how many make life more unbearable? Will states compete to attract tax paying families and corporations by reducing taxes and expenditures for TANF? What will happen to children whose families lose benefits, even partially? The true testing of TANF will come when the economy moves into more turbulent waters. Then states will be faced with fewer jobs and more children in need, and Congress will have to decide the extent to which it will attempt to bail out states and localities. In any event, TANF benefits are often inadequate both horizontally and vertically, and yet in the states where TANF is very low there is little inclination by society to raise benefits. On the horizontal side, there are large numbers of potentially eligible people who will never reach TANF because of shame, ignorance, or roadblocks put in the way of their applying. It will take some time before the TANF experience will be completely understood, and that requires a period when the program is not undergirded by a prosperous economy.

TANF is the classic example of cost inefficiency because of the massive problems of means testing and the administrative cost and effort that this entails. It is financed as equitably as possible under our tax system and is a highly necessary program, with all its faults. But the consequences of this form of welfare are stigma, cheating, indignities, and wasted money.

That these income support programs are viewed as something more than a product of government largesse is suggested by the fact that they, as the social insurance programs, have procedures for client appeals of agency decisions. All states, in order to receive federal funding for these programs, must administer hearings that incorporate certain due process mechanisms. Among these are the right to timely and adequate prior notice of an agency action, to cross-examine witnesses, to representation, to a prehearing examination of evidence, and to aid continuing until a hearing decision. The 1970 *Goldberg v. Kelly* Supreme Court decision recognized the constitutional bases for procedural due process in welfare hearings.[23]

Supplemental Security Income

Goals. The Supplemental Security Income (SSI) program is a means-tested, federally administered, income assistance program to provide monthly cash payments in accordance with uniform, nationwide eligibility requirements to needy aged, blind, and disabled persons. As originally envisioned, it was hoped the program would assure those eligible they would not have to subsist on below poverty-level incomes.

The SSI program—implemented in 1974—instituted a national assistance program and replaced three state-administered federally reimbursed programs: Old Age Assistance (OAA); Aid to the Permanently and Totally Disabled (APTD); and Aid to the Blind (AB). These had been part of the grant-in-aid public assistance program established by the Social Security Act. SSI is available in all states.

Who Is Eligible for the Program? To qualify a person must meet the program criteria for age, blindness, and disability as well as income and assets criteria.

Recipients must be U.S. citizens or lawfully admitted aliens living in the United States with limited income and resources or a child of a military person or family stationed overseas, or a student temporarily abroad. If not a citizen, the recipient must be a refugee or asylee (a particular type of refugee) who has been in the country for less than seven years or be a "qualified alien" who was receiving SSI as of August 22, 1996 or was living in the United States on that date and later became disabled. Qualified immigrants who entered the United States on or after August 22, 1996 are barred from SSI and Food Stamps. They are subject to a five-year bar on non-emergency Medicaid, the state Child Health Insurance Program (CHIP), and TANF. After the five-year bar, exemptions can be made for up to one year for some battered spouses and children and those at risk of going hungry or becoming homeless. After the five-year bar, states still retain the option to determine immigrant eligibility for TANF, Medicaid, and social services block grants (Title XX). Other ineligible persons include certain active duty armed services personnel, honorably discharged veterans and their spouses and dependent children, and lawful permanent residents who have worked for ten years or more. A recipient must be 65 years of age or over, or legally blind, or unable to engage in any substantial gainful activity by reason of a medically determined physical or mental impairment expected to result in death or that has lasted, or can be expected to last, for a continuous period of at least 12 months. Generally, the person must be unable to do any kind of work that exists in the United States, taking into account age, education, and work experience. If disabled, the person must accept vocational rehabilitation services if they are offered.

Children may qualify for SSI if they are under age 18 years (or under 22 years if a full time student), unmarried, and meet the applicable SSI disability, blindness, income, and resource requirements. The Personal Responsibility and Work Opportunity Reconciliation Act established a new disability definition for children under age 18 years that requires a child to have a medically determinable physical or mental impairment that results in marked and severe functional limitations, and that can be expected to result in death or has lasted or can be expected to last for a continuous period of not less than 12 months. Previous criteria based on a Supreme Court ruling (*Sullivan v. Zebley,* 1990) were generally considered less stringent. Payments may not be made to individuals who are fleeing prosecution for a felony crime or fleeing to avoid custody or confinement after conviction for a crime that is a felony, or violating a condition of probation or parole imposed under either federal or state law.

The SSI law permits six months' benefits to be paid to applicants before a formal decision is made when available information indicates a high probability that the person will be eligible. Among other disabilities, Social Security field offices may find that an individual with HIV or AIDS whose disease manifestations are of listing-level severity is presumed to be disabled. This ruling has been challenged in at least one state on the grounds it discriminates against women because the course of the disease differs for them.

In 1996, Congress passed legislation that ended drug and alcohol addictions as conditions that qualify individuals for SSI benefits. Substance abusers, thus, became ineligible. However, where a person has more than one disability, it is possible for the benefit to be retained.

In 1999, nearly 6.6 million persons received federally administered SSI payments (1.3 million aging; 5.2 million disabled; and 79,000 with blindness). Over 700 thousand of those receiving benefits on the basis of disability or blindness were over the age of 65. Approximately 4 million recipients received only Federal SSI payments and 2.2 million received a combination of Federal and State payments.

If an individual or couple has countable income, there is a dollar for dollar reduction made of the SSI benefit against the maximum payment. Ineligibility occurs when countable income equals the Federal benefit standard plus the amount of state supplementation, if any. Not all income is counted. The major exclusion is the first $20 of monthly income from almost any source (such as Social Security) and the first $65 of monthly earned income plus one-half of the remaining earnings. Work related expenses are disregarded in the case of blind or disabled applicants. Income and resources set aside as part of a plan for achieving self-support (PASS) are also allowed to pay for education, vocational training or starting a business.

There has been a steady decline in the number of persons receiving SSI on the basis of old age; a recent decrease in the number of blind and disabled children under 18; a continuing increase in the number of persons 18–64 receiving benefits on the basis of disability or blindness.

What Is the Form of Benefit?   Cash benefits are paid on a monthly basis. As of January 2000, the maximum SSI payment from the federal government for an individual was $512 and $769 for a couple living in their own household. For those living in another's household, the amounts were respectively $341 and $512. Persons residing in Medicaid institutions (where more than half of the bill is paid by Medicaid) receive $30 per month, and those who live with an eligible person and who are considered necessary to provide essential care and services for the person receive $256, provided they meet criteria related to relationship and history.

Benefits automatically increase whenever there is a Social Security cost-of-living increase. Many states supplement the federal grant. To prevent reduction of income when persons were transferred to the new national program, states were required to supplement the federal payment to bring it up to what the state level had been. Many states have continued to supplement federal SSI payments, but the total grant is combined administratively into one check for the recipient. All but seven states and jurisdictions provide some form of state supplementation.

States provide Medicaid for SSI recipients under three options: (1) A state makes all SSI recipients automatically eligible for Medicaid, (2) the recipient must complete a separate application for Medicaid, or (3) the state may make eligibility criteria more restrictive than SSI criteria, as long as the criteria are no more restrictive than those for the state's Medicaid plan as of a certain date. Except in California, which converted Food Stamp benefits to cash included in the state supplemental payment, SSI recipients may be eligible to receive Food Stamps. Children who lose SSI will continue to receive Medicaid only if they are eligible on other grounds.

Related to an increase in Social Security coverage, there has been a steady decline in the number of persons receiving SSI benefits on the basis of old age. As of 1996, other trends included a slight increase in the number of blind children under 18, a very large increase for children with disabilities, and a sharp increase in the number of adults receiving benefits on the basis of disability.

How Is the Program Financed?   All costs of the benefits and administration of the federal SSI programs are funded through monies from federal general revenues and from states providing supplementation. The administrative costs of federally administered state supplements also are funded in this way.

What Is the Level of Administration?   The Social Security Administration manages the SSI program through regional and district offices located in many parts of the nation. The Social Security Administration may contract for state or local agencies to administer SSI operations. Some states administer the state supplement portion of SSI themselves, but most states that offer this additional benefit have the federal government administer the entire program. There is continuing "outreach" to notify two groups of Social Security beneficiaries: those about to reach age 65 and those disabled persons who have been receiving Social Security for 21 consecutive months and will soon be eligible for Medicare. There are several outreach efforts to better meet the needs of the homeless, especially for individuals who suffer from mental illness or AIDS. Outreach efforts to elderly single females particularly can make a great difference.

Discussion.   Supplemental Security Income is an interesting potential predecessor of what many thought might become a federalized public assistance program. As we saw in chapter 5, in the early 1970s, there was a move toward a national assistance plan, a little bit like a negative income tax. When this proposal failed, Congress was able to take the less controversial parts of public assistance—the categorical sections of aid to the aged, disabled, and blind—and to federalize them. This occurred because there was not at the time the same pejorative picture of these categories as there was of other welfare recipients, nor are those categories so large. With the blind and the aged, society seems to be more willing to accept the fact that continued public support at some level will be necessary. However, this is not true for those who are substance abusers.

In any event, SSI is a good forerunner of what welfare would be like if TANF were federalized as well. The level of aid is higher than it was in the average state, although not as high as the most generous states were paying. SSI's more humane and reasonable approach permits people to have some minimal assets before becoming eligible, but fundamentally it is simply public assistance on a federal level rather than on a state one. This makes little difference to the client and to the benefit of society but relieves states of a major burden and transfers this burden to the federal government.

The point has been made by some that SSI could be removed from public assistance altogether instead of simply being federalized if (1) the money spent on this program was contributed from general revenues to the Social Security system and (2) the Social Security minimum simply became the SSI minimum. The problem with this is that Social Security, being universal, would also give this minimum to people who had other income. However, most of the people on the minimum level of Social Security are people who are generally poor and who do not have other sources of income—the same people who are applying for SSI.

Reports of substance abusers using SSI payments to purchase drugs led to a representative payee for each substance abuser, mandatory treatment and expected progress in addiction treatment, and the limitation of benefits to a three-year period.

A 1999 survey found that few states fully replaced the benefits that immigrants lost as a result of the Personal Responsibility and Work Opportunity Act (PRWO, 1996). In general, states with large numbers of immigrants ordinarily provide a substantial "safety net" for citizens. Those with higher per capita incomes provide broader access to their "safety nets" for immigrants. Nevertheless, a 1999 National Survey of Families found that hardship is greater for children of immigrants than for children of U.S. natives in regard to food, housing, and health care.[24]

General Assistance

Goals.   The goal of general assistance (GA) is to provide benefits to low-income persons ineligible for federal assistance. Based on the concept of local responsibility for the destitute, 41 states (including the District of Columbia) have GA programs. Of these 34 have programs throughout the state and the remainder provide GA only in a portion of the state. These are programs of "last resort."

Who Is Eligible for the Program?   In 1999, of the 41 states with GA programs, approximately 10 provided assistance to all financially needy persons ineligible for federally funded cash programs. The eligible categories differ among states, including disabled, elderly, or otherwise unemployable persons, low-income children or families with children, including pregnant women with their first child, emancipated minors in school and over 18, awaiting Supplemental Security Income determination, and persons who reached the durational limits of TANF. Some states do not provide GA for employable adults. Persons must be financially needy, and asset limits differ by state. Most states limit assistance to citizens and legal aliens. A number of states require drug and alcohol treatment where needed. A number of states require registration with the employment service, and employable adults to enter work or training programs to maintain eligibility. These programs are means tested, and there is no income that is disregarded. In addition to the usual relative-responsibility rules (husbands for wives or vice versa and parents for minors), some states' GA programs also consider adult children responsible for their parents and make siblings, grandparents, and grandchildren responsible for other family members.

What Is the Form of Benefit?   Benefits range from extremely low cash payments, usually insufficient to cover basic necessities, to free groceries and shelter in emergency situations. Most GA recipients are also eligible for Food Stamps and commodities. Medical care may also be provided. Transportation may be offered to return a person to his or her place of residence; burial is provided for deceased indigents.

How Is the Program Financed?   No federal funds support these programs. Using general tax revenues, the GA programs are financed by state funds, combinations of local and state funds, and, in some cases, solely by local funds.

What Is the Level of Administration?   General assistance programs are administered by state public assistance departments on a local level, by local government jurisdictions supervised by the state, or by local governments alone. Most common is administration on a county basis. There are also combinations of state, county, and local administrative organizations.

Discussion.   General assistance to some degree and in some form probably will be necessary in the best of societies. No matter how tightly one tries to develop a social insurance system, there are likely to be emergency situations and people needing assistance who fall between the cracks of the system. The categorical eligibility requirements in the current federal public assistance programs eliminate many financially eligible persons, for example, nondisabled adults without children or the physically and mentally disabled who do not meet SSI's criteria.

General assistance is both horizontally and vertically inadequate, rarely providing enough to cover basic necessities. When several states terminated or limited their GA programs in recent years, relatively few former recipients found employment after their benefits were terminated. When they found jobs, they were usually part-time or temporary. Some supported themselves working at odd jobs; others depended on friends and relatives or panhandled on streets. Many able-bodied GA recipients need assistance to overcome serious barriers to employment, including lack of job skills, poor health, and inadequate transportation. Several studies found that almost half of GA recipients did not have a high school diploma or GED (general education development) certificate. When GA was eliminated in Michigan, a study two years later found that in Detroit the cancellation placed even greater financial burdens on the federal government because of disability payments and on Michigan, which was forced to spend more for emergency shelters.[25]

Among suggestions for reform are facilitating the movement of disabled GA recipients onto SSI; providing a more adequate level of benefit for recipients; providing for those with temporary physical or mental disabilities ineligible for SSI, including persons who are unemployable because they care at home for a disabled relative (This appears to be an increasing category.); supporting the able-bodied person's attainment of job skills and education; and, in addition to providing job search and unpaid work experience, offering educational and training services to those who are employable.[26]

GA is contracting. The federal safety net has shrunk, heightening the need for GA programs. With the poor law mentality persisting in the major public assistance programs' categorical approach to eligibility, a national response in the near future is unlikely, despite the need.[27]

Earned Income Tax Credit

Goals.   The Earned Income Tax Credit (EITC) was added to the Internal Revenue Code in 1975 to give cash income refund supplements to working parents with dependent children and other working adults with low incomes who pay taxes.

Who Is Eligible for the Program?   The basic EITC in 2001 was available to taxpayers who met the following criteria:

1. There is a qualifying child living in the home in the United States for more than six months.
2. The taxpayer has earned money during the year.
3. The earned income and adjusted gross income is less than $31,152 when the family includes more than one qualifying child.
4. The employee, a spouse, and those children included must have assigned Social Security numbers.
5. Eligibility is denied for ten years if a fraudulent claim is submitted; two years if the claim is a result of reckless or intentional disregard of rules.

Those eligible are families with dependent children in which a family member works and the family income is below a specific amount and low-income workers over age 24 to 64 years without qualifying children. The maximum eligible income is indexed to inflation. A person must file an income tax return; couples must file a joint return. Eligibility is restricted for those persons with investment income (interest, dividends, rent, royalties, capital gains) that exceeds $2,400, a threshold which is indexed. Military families, including those posted overseas and those in which a family member is overseas unaccompanied by their families, may also be eligible. In 2000, the projection is that 18.4 million families will receive benefits amounting to $30 billion for an average credit of $1,625 per family.

What Is the Form of Benefit?   More than 87 percent of payments are received as a lump-sum refund following the filing of an income tax return, or the EITC can be used to reduce the amount owed. The benefit also can be given in increments as part of a worker's paycheck after furnishing a certificate of eligibility to the employer. The credit amount rises with earned income as a percentage of annual earnings up to a specific earnings level and then is phased out. In 2001, the maximum credit for families with two or more children who qualify was $4,008. The maximum for taxpayers with no qualifying children was $364. The amount of the benefit is indexed to inflation on an annual basis.

EITC benefits are not counted as income or assets and do not jeopardize a family's eligibility for and benefits from these programs: TANF, Medicaid, SSI, Food Stamps, and low-income housing programs.

How Is the Program Financed?   The program is financed entirely by the federal government out of general revenue.

What Is the Level of Administration?   This is a federal program administered through the Internal Revenue Service. Information is shared between the Treasury Department, State and local governments regarding child support orders and Social Security Administration records may be used to enforce the tax laws, including the EITC.

Discussion.   The EITC traditionally has been supported by persons across ideologies. The program was designed originally to give low-income employed families with children who had been excluded from income transfer programs incentive to stay in the job market and off public assistance. Part of the motivation for the creation of EITC resulted from complaints about the regressivity of the Social Security payroll tax for low-income employed households and the rising cost of living. Although EITC offsets social security taxes for the employee and does provide money and is a supplement to earnings, it also allows employers potentially to pay lower wages when they consider the credit.

EITC is a negative income tax program, a refundable credit as a cash grant, which serves to offset the Social Security payroll tax. Most of the paperwork for this credit is done through the federal income tax system, so there is no public stigma. The amount of money provided is, of course, helpful to a family with dependents.

This program is an example of a residual, means-tested program that has minimized stigma and is aimed precisely at those families needing economic assistance and avoids work disincentives by adding to the wages of low income workers. Attacking poverty, the EITC enables single parents to stay off welfare and underscores the value of work. This program has been supported by legislators and presidents from both major parties because it offsets the Social Security tax, adds to the minimum wage, and makes work more profitable than public assistance.

This program has special importance because it provides incentives for TANF families to work by subsidizing *earned* income. This incentive is enhanced because the program is not stigmatized yet it makes a crucial difference for families. Almost 30 percent of the families receiving EITC had incomes below $10,000 and 60 percent had incomes below $20,000. The EITC in 1999 raised close to 5 million persons above the poverty line, including 2.6 million children, and many low-skilled welfare recipients.[28] Although EITC is valuable for those employed and their children, the extent to which it is used by employers to subsidize wages is unclear.

Some criticize the fact that benefits are increased only up to two children when additional children also cost money to raise. Another issue is that many recipients receive payments as one lump sum, an unhelpful pattern on a day to day basis. Also, many families remain unaware of the program. The earlier criticism that foster children were not covered has been rectified. Some of those who complain about the regressivity of the Social Security tax suggest the exemption of dollars of wage income from that tax, an idea rejected mainly because it would complicate employers' implementation of the payroll tax and perhaps undermine the claim of workers to Social Security benefits. At least fifteen states and the District of Columbia offer tax credits for low and moderate income working families based on the Federal EITC, thus helping families close the poverty gap. If this type of benefit were expanded it would bring a large number of children and their families out of poverty. Since poor families pay regressive sales and other taxes, state EITCs also would lessen the burden of those taxes on poor families. Furthermore, by rewarding work and increasing spendable income such a program is supportive of welfare reform.

When we consider this type of program, however, implicit in our review are several other questions: How can the society be helpful to low-earner families without undermining work incentives? What should be the limits of such help? These families have low earnings but are playing by the rules. What should be the role of universal family support programs such as family or children's allowances? After all, it is only one step to making such a program universal for all parents with children. The same mechanism of the tax system could be used to "claw back" the funds provided for families over particular income levels. In this way, an effective and efficient income support for families becomes possible.

Socioeconomic Asset Development

Wealth inequality has always been more extreme than income poverty. Today wealth inequality is more unbalanced in the United States than in any other industrialized nation.[29] Corporate welfare is mirrored by an individual and family welfare system for the middle class and wealthy in the form of tax expenditures (mortgage interest deductions, retirement accounts, etc.). These are designed for the benefit of those who own homes and who are able to save for retirement security. Although not readily visible, these arrangements are essentially redistribution devices not downward for the poor but upward for those who have more. Our current policy structure supports this redistribution and is a slightly hidden asset-based policy, but one which is heavily subsidized by social policy. Gaining wealth is not just the result of prudent and wise saving but also a result of this redistribution upward.[30]

Traditionally, social welfare and social workers have favored helping poor persons through income support and other programs and paid sparse attention to this other less visible system. During the past several decades, a growing conservatism in American society began to question the choice of income supports and subsidizing consumption as the policies of choice in order to help the poor. This shift in values and attitudes was reflected in the enactment of the Personal Responsibility and Work Opportunity Act (1996) that altered social welfare and public assistance approaches. Instead of subsidies, the new programs expected responsibility and work.

Advocates of socio-economic developmental welfare approaches searched for new anti-poverty strategies and proposed programs that are contrary to traditional social welfare approaches. Their proposals created new approaches to poverty and preceded the enactment of major reform. Midgley, for example, advocates the socio-economic developmental approach as an alternative to both residual and institutional welfare models because social welfare needs to be linked and contribute positively to economic development. Social development can generate returns on investment and contribute to economic growth by assisting in the mobilization of human capital, providing increased opportunities for productive employment and self-employment among low-income and special needs groups, and through investment in education, childhood nutrition, health care, and skills training.[31]

Sherraden argues for investment that increases present and future productivity through asset development among non-income groups. Incentives and resources should be provided that encourage savings and asset development among the poor so they can accumulate the social investments needed to meet their needs and those of their children. Instead of an emphasis on subsistence income and consumption by poor persons, the focus should be on savings, investment, and accumulation in order to help them become "stakeholders" in society. When persons hold assets and have a stake in the system, they overcome their poverty economically, socially, and psychologically. Among these asset builders are Individual Development Accounts (similar to Individual Retirement Accounts) available to everyone in the United States, a universal program, connected to activities that promote individual and national development such as completion of schooling, high school graduation, post-secondary education, housing, self-employment, and retirement, and so on. Subsidized for poor persons and families, the accounts would be tax-favored (tax deferred or tax exempt) and could be used only for specific purposes.

Studies suggest there are positive effects of asset ownership on life satisfaction and self-efficacy and negative effects on depression and alcohol abuse. They also are positively associated with health throughout adulthood and old age. For women, assets are associated with higher levels of social status in the home and community, increased contraceptive use, and improved material conditions for their families. Several studies found a relationship between asset ownership and lower levels of marital violence. Positive relationships have also been found been parental asset ownership and self-esteem among their adolescents, including teenagers staying in school.[32]

Another type of socio-economic development program has evolved across the United States over the past several decades. Micro-enterprises and self-employment projects serve some Temporary Assistance to Needy Family (TANF) clients and others. Programs may offer self-employment training classes, employment readiness and job placement services. An example of this type of program is the preparation of clients to become family day acre providers through classroom training and child care internships before opening their businesses.

Some persons refer to welfare capitalism that includes: (1) wage supplements such as the Earned Income Tax Credit (EITC), the Work Opportunity Tax Credit (Federal income tax credits to encourage private sector employers to hire job seekers most in need of employment opportunities that help them gain on-the job experience.) and direct supplementation of wages; (2) Individual Development Accounts mentioned above and microcredit. (It is difficult if not impossible for poor persons, particularly women, to obtain credit without very high interest rates. Without loans they cannot start income generating projects. Microcredit organizations provide "start up" capital to poor people. The availability of the loan often leads to starting a business and learning basic math and bookkeeping skills.); and (3) community capitalism in which communities develop their own financial institutions such as community development banks and credit unions. One crucial problem associated with many of these programs is that many poor persons do not have bank accounts and commercial banks charge fees, often inversely related to the amount of money in your account.[33]

An additional and innovative way for people who have few resources to gain assets is through *time dollars.* Individuals, community groups, church groups, neighborhood associations, and social agencies whose mission is community building can create neighbor to neighbor time banks. Time Banks are located in the United States, Japan, Great Britain and elsewhere. When tasks are completed (home repairs, house painting, child care, attending to errands for someone who needs assistance) the person has the work and time recorded in a central registry. All time and work provided is equally valued whether by an expert or amateur. A person can "buy" services needed from other persons who belong to the time dollar plan. When a participant needs some service and it is available in the association, they can pay for the service from their time bank account. Participants can save their time, give it to someone else such as a family member, friend, or neighbor or donate it to someone who is in need. Basically, the time dollar plan works on a local level by establishing a system of mutual credit and, concurrently, by building communities. The unemployed, single heads of household, persons with disabilities and others have the possibility in this system of being rewarded for their unpaid labors, many of which they are doing without compensation. Thus, time dollars empowers people to convert their personal time into purchasing power.

Still another socio-economic developmental program is the encouragement of poor persons to continue their education at post-secondary schools. Currently, Federal policy is interpreted variously in different states. Some states allow poor women with children to attend college only up to 12 months. Other states count class and homework time as part of their work participation requirement. In some places supports such as child care and transportation are available, in others they are lacking. The completion of two and four-year degrees is associated with better economic and social returns for women, their children and families, and society at large.[34]

All of these programs can contribute to the betterment of lives and the reduction of poverty but it is unclear as to the extent to which they can separately or together remove people from poverty. As was noted in Chapter 8 many poor people are employed year-round in full-time jobs but their pay and benefits (if any) are insufficient to support their families above the poverty level.

The socio-economic development approach suggests that social welfare to one degree or another manages social problems, meets needs, and should provide opportunities for advancement for individuals, families, groups, and communities, and even whole societies. Based on the work of the past half-century in developing nations, social development seeks ways that create human and social capital and foster peoples' welfare by simultaneous productive economic activities. Social welfare is thus linked to economic development and policies.

Summary

In this chapter, we have reviewed the major income support programs currently available in the United States. These programs are both universal (Social Security, unemployment insurance, WC) and selective (TANF, GA, SSI, EITC). Some were initiated with the New Deal or shortly thereafter; others are the product of more recent efforts to provide income security. Incrementally developed, the programs are flawed by insufficient benefit levels and gaps in populations covered. Other programs, however, help address the issue of adequacy as they attempt to enhance the quality of life for those in need. Some of these programs are examined in chapter 10.

Questions for Consideration

1. Why does Social Security have such a high degree of acceptance in the United States? Interview someone who knows what life was like for people before Social Security was created. On balance, what do you think the benefits of this social insurance are?

2. Would you try to ensure the future of Social Security? Is yes, what approach would you take and why?

3. What is your state's current program designed to assist poor families with children? What income security program would you suggest to bring poor families with dependent children, particularly those headed by females householders, up to some minimum income level?

4. How many people in your state receive benefits from the EITC? Why do you think both liberals and conservatives favor this program?

5. Do you agree with the statement made by President Franklin D. Roosevelt with which this chapter began? If yes, why; if no, why not?

Notes

1. Franklin D. Roosevelt, *Message to Congress,* June 8, 1938, *The Public Papers and Addresses of Franklin D. Roosevelt,* Vol. 3, New York: Random House, 1938, p. 288.

2. Committee on Ways and Means, U.S. House of Representatives, *Overview of Entitlement programs: 2000 Green Book, Background Material and Data on Programs within the Jurisdiction of the Committee on Ways and Means,* Washington, D.C.: U.S. Government Printing Office, 2000, p. 53.

3. *2000 Green Book,* p. 36.

4. *2000 Green Book,* p. 57.

5. Robert Lewis, "Women vs. Social Security," National Retired Teachers Association, Division of American Association of Retired Persons, May 1992, Vol. 33, No. 5, pp. 1, 12.

6. *2000 Green Book,* p. 316.

7. Richard W. Stevenson, "Image and Reality on Social Security," *New York Times,* May 6, 2001, Business, p. 3.

8. Richard W. Stevenson, "President to Name Panel on Social Security Plan," *New York Times,* May 2, 2001, p. A15.

9. Danny Hakim, "401K Accounts Are Losing Money For the First Time," *New York Times,* July 9, 2001, pp. 1, A12.

10. President's Commission to Strengthen Social Security, *Guiding Principles, http://csss.gov/,* October 15, 2001 and Richard W. Stevenson, "A Finale in Three-Part Harmony," *New York Times,* December 12, 2001, p. A21.

11. Cato Institute, "Social Security Privatization," www.socialsecurity.org/faqs.html, October 15, 2001.

12. Jane B. Quinn, "Some Social Security Changes Would Be Costly for Women," *The Baltimore Sun,* February 16, 1998, p. 15C.

13. Robert Kenyon, Jr. and Loryn Lancaster, "Changes in Unemployment Insurance Legislation in 2000," *Monthly Labor Review,* 124 (1), January, 2001, 29–34.

14. Wayne Vroman, "Effects of Welfare Reform on Unemployment Insurance," http://newfederalism.urban.org, October 1, 1998.

15. Glenn Whittington, "Changes in Workers' Compensation Laws During 2000," *Monthly Labor Review,* 124 (1), January 2001, 25–28.

16. Department of Health and Human Services, Administration for Children and families, *Third Annual Report to Congress,* www.acf.dhhs.gov/programs/opre/annual3execsum.htm, September 13, 2001.

17. Tamar Lewin, "Surprising Result in Welfare-to-Work Studies," *New York Times,* July 31, 2001, p. A16.

18. Mark Greenberg, Jodie Levin-Epstein, et al, *Welfare Reauthorization: An Early Guide to the Issues,* July 2000, www.clasp.org/pubs/TANF/packa.htm, September 30, 2001.

19. *2000 Green Book,* p. 1408.

20. *2000 Green Book,* p. 1408.

21. *2000 Green Book,* p. 1409.

22. Mark Greenberg, *op.cit,* p. 32.

23. Goldberg v. Kelly, 397 U.S. 254 (1976)

24. Randy Capps, "Hardship Among Children of Immigrants: Findings from the 1999 National Survey of America's Families," Urban Institute, www.newfederalism.urban.org/html/seriesb/b29.html, October 8, 2001 and Urban Institute, "Patchwork Policies Lead to Partial Benefits for Immigrants," www.urban.org/news, September 30, 2001.

25. Joyce Purnick, "When Welfare Is Gone: A Cautionary Message," *New York Times,* February 27, 1995, p. B3.

26. Marion Nichols and Kathryn Porter, *General Assistance Programs: Gaps in the Safety Net,* Washington, D.C.: Center on Budget and Policy Priorities, 1995.

27. Cori E. Uccello and L. Jerome Gallagher, "General Assistance Programs: The State-Based Part of the Safety Net," Washington, D.C.: The Urban Institute, http://newfederalism.urban.org/html/anf_a4.htm, August, 1998.

28. Making Wages Work: Reducing Dependency and Poverty Through Income Supplements, "Earned Income Tax Credit and Other Tax Benefits," www.makingwageswork.org/earned.htm, October 7, 2001; Internal Revenue Service, Earned Income Tax Credit (EITC), www.irs.gov/ind infor/eitc4.html, October 7, 2001; Nicholas Johnson, "How Much Would A State Earned Income Tax Credit Cost?" Center on Budget and Policy Priorities, www.cbpp.org/11-11-99sfp.htm, October 8, 2001.

29. Thomas M. Shapiro, "The Importance of Assets," in *Assets for the Poor,* eds. Thomas M. Shapiro and Edward N. Wolff, New York: Russell Sage Foundation, 2001, pp. 11–33.

30. Michael Sherraden, "Asset Building Policy and Programs for the Poor," in *Assets for the Poor,* Thomas M. Shapiro and Edward N. Wolff, Eds. New York: Russell Sage Foundation, 2001, pp. 302–323.

31. James Midgley, *Social Development: The Developmental Perspective in Social Welfare,* Thousand Oaks, Sage Publications, 1995; James Midgley, "Toward a Developmental Model of Social Policy: Relevance of the Third World Experience," *Journal of Sociology and Social Welfare,* 23 (1), 1996, 55–74; Michael Sherraden, Asset Building: Integrating Research, Education, and Practice," *Advances in Social Work,*1 (1), Spring 2000, 61–77.

32. Deborah Page-Adams and Michael Sherraden, "Asset Building as a Community revitalization Strategy," *Social Work,* 42 (5), 1997, 423–434.

33. David Stoesz and David Saunders, "Welfare Capitalism: A New Approach to Poverty Policy," *Social Service Review,* 73 (3), 1999, 380–400.

34. Shanta Pandey, Min Zhan, Susan Neely-Barnes, and Natasha Menon, "The Higher Education Option for Poor Women with Children, " *Journal of Sociology and Social Welfare,* 27 (4), 2000, 109–170.

10

Social Welfare Programs

Sustaining the Quality of Life

We the people of the United States in order to…establish justice…promote the general Welfare, and secure the Blessings of Liberty to ourselves and our Posterity.…

—The Constitution of the United States

Overview

In the previous chapter, we reviewed the major social insurance and public assistance programs as well as socio-economic asset development. These focused on income for the aged, disabled, unemployed, and parents or guardians with dependent children. In this chapter, we will study an array of programs whose purpose is to sustain the quality of life, either by providing in-kind benefits to meet a person's basic needs for food, housing, and medical care or by improving the physical and psychological well-being of the individual. We also discuss two social welfare programs designed for targeted groups—veterans' benefits and corrections.

Over the past two decades the programs reviewed in this chapter were the focus of intense political maneuvering as budget considerations and ideologies clashed. A major factor influencing health and mental health care with implications for social welfare and social work is managed care, which created a new environment for the delivery of services. In order to understand more completely the environment in which health and mental health services—as well as other services—operate, we present information about managed care and follow it with a discussion of the various programs.

Managed Care: A Radical Change

Traditionally, most people who had health insurance were covered for most health expenses through indemnity or fee-for-service plans but had to find their own practitioners and arrange for their own care. In these cases, the insurance company paid for all or part of the bill for any doctor, hospital, or other health care provider a person chose. *Managed care* was propelled by rapidly rising health care costs well beyond the rate of inflation resulting from a number of factors: a growing aged population, technology and costly new treatments, the frequent ability to keep people alive at a cost, an emphasis on acute care rather than preventive services, varying standards of treatment according to geographic locations, among others.

There is no standard, all inclusive definition of *managed care*. Suffice it to say that managed care attempts to lower costs by providing care at predetermined or discounted fees by specifying which health care providers and hospitals a person can use and overseeing treatments and referrals. Managed care evolved through at least three generations: (1) Placing some limits on benefits through deductibles, cost sharing, utilization review, second opinions, and other means; (2) different types of benefits in and out of the system; and (3) advanced provider selection, patient care monitoring, and the utilization of quality measures.

Managed care organizations try to balance access, quality, flexibility, control, and accountability while remaining fiscally viable. An enrollee or subscriber receives health care from a group of approved health professionals and hospitals. Typically, the provider network assigns a primary care doctor who provides routine health care and decides if the enrollee needs to see a specialist. Managed care contracts directly with health care providers to set payment for services and restrict the use of costly services. Providers discount their standard fees. Out-of-pocket costs are lower for those enrollees who use providers in the network. If at the end of the year, money paid by employers and employees is left over, the HMO keeps it. If there is a loss, the HMO is responsible.

Major Organizational Types

Managed care is implemented through a variety of mechanisms. The major types are described in the following sections.

Health Maintenance Organizations.   Health maintenance organizations provide a wide range of health services to covered members for a fee or premium paid by an employer, a government, or a person or family. A member chooses a "gatekeeper" physician who provides care and makes treatment recommendations and referrals to specialists. Premiums are usually lower than traditional plans, and there are no deductibles or co-insurance payments; however, there are low co-payments. Members are limited to using the HMO's personnel and hospitals and must get approval for treatment and referrals.

Point-of-Service Plans.   With the point-of-service (POS) plan, members make a decision about the care they need at the point of service when the service is required. These plans allow members to go to health care providers outside of their HMOs for care, provided the member pays the extra cost.

Preferred Provider Organizations.   A preferred provider organization (PPO) is a network of independent health care professionals that contract to provide care at discounted rates. Providers must agree to utilization management and fixed reimbursement rates. A member may use health services *in* or *outside* of the network but must pay a higher co-payment for going outside the network of providers.

Physician Sponsored Networks.   With the physician sponsored network (PSN), large groups of health professionals join together and accept the financial risks of covering their patients' health care needs. This arrangement substitutes for the traditional role played by insurers and maintains health provider autonomy while reducing administrative and other costs.

Managed care contains conflicting purposes. Health services are delivered but benefits are reviewed, controlled, and managed. Reviews can focus on whether services can be provided, what the type and scope of the benefits will be, access to providers, and control of costs. Patients may be preauthorized to receive particular treatment or denied access; the treatment can be reviewed and continued or terminated. The treatment of choice can be determined by the managed care organization rather than the practitioner.

Impact on Services and Practitioners

Managed care is an industrialization of the delivery of health care. There are those who believe the emphasis is more on controlling costs and increasing profits than on access or quality of care. In fact, there can be adversarial priorities. Altruistic professionals are trained to be helpers, but they must operate within a context of cost-consciousness and profit seeking. These conflicting purposes have a heavy impact on social workers and others involved with health and mental health care.

These radical changes in social services, health, and mental health have strongly affected mental health systems and practitioner roles. The traditional mental health care system has been largely dismantled. In-patient psychiatric care has been reduced; there are limits on long stays. Health care practitioners are forced to find places on mental health panels (from which practitioners are assigned cases) to which they may or may not be accepted. The practitioner must agree to a case manager determining who and how to treat persons referred. There are protocols for the length and nature of care on the basis of diagnostic related groups (DRGs). Further, there is an emphasis on biological and cognitive-behavioral treatments.

Proponents

The proponents of managed care claim that the short-term consequences will be uncomfortable but the escalating costs of health care must be controlled, especially since the baby boom generation is approaching retirement age. According to these proponents, more people will be provided with cost-effective health care. Treatment decisions will be based on what is considered "best practice," which in turn rests on outcome research.

Criticisms

Approximately 43 million Americans are without health insurance and perhaps 15 million others, many of whom are chronically ill and unable to buy insurance through an employer, even high cost insurance with bare-bones coverage. Although much attention is paid to denial of care, health experts suggest the greater problems are related to quality of care. A committee of the Institute of Medicine concluded that too little of what physicians do is backed up by scientific evidence. There are estimates that 20 to 30 percent of medical procedures are wrongly prescribed. A 1999 report showed that hospitals lack basic systems to catch mistakes before they kill or maim patients, leading to as many as 100,000 deaths annually from preventable errors.[1]

Professionals have been disempowered as their professional judgments may be overruled by case managers whose training may be less than that of the practitioner, and costs continue to rise. One fallout from these activities is the demise of high quality traditional agencies that contributed for long periods to communities. Collateral interventions are not allowed (school visits, family members, legal representatives, public assistance, landlords, employers) or not reimbursed, and the emphasis is on face-to-face contacts. All these factors result in rationing services for all but the wealthy.

Few federal standards apply to private or employer-provided managed care, and this is viewed critically by many persons. States apply and enforce standards in different ways while people are mobile. What happens if one becomes ill while away from home? Do people receive the services they contracted and paid for? Are good practice standards enforced universally? Such standards will require a combination of state and federal legislation and means for enforcement.

There also are implications of managed care that shift social work practice far from its historic two-track methods—casework (clinical) and macro (organizations, neighborhoods, and communities)—and diminish attempts to achieve goals in the external environment. Managed care focuses almost entirely on the presenting problems of individuals, and there is little if any reimbursement for collateral interventions. This fact can serve to isolate the individual client and restrain practitioners from attempting to influence larger systems.

Research on Quality of Care

One study compared the performance of HMOs with that of fee-for-service plans by analyzing 37 peer-reviewed studies of managed care plans. The study found there were an equal number of significantly better or worse results for HMOs. In several instances, Medicare HMO enrollees with chronic conditions showed worse quality of care. Fears that HMOs uniformly would lead to worse quality of care were not supported by the evidence.

The author identified three factors that make for unfavorable results: payment incentives, disincentives, and inadequate information. In many cases, financial payments do little to reward quality on the part of plans and providers. There are disincentives to care for the sickest and most expensive patients. Consumers and purchasers (employers, the government, and individuals) lack sufficient information on access to care and quality of care. Further, improved quality of care requires new processes, but practitioners change clinical processes only slowly.[2]

Strategies to Achieve Profits

Schamess identified the strategies by which HMOs generate their profits from standard business practices applied to problems that are not amenable to business solutions:

- Denying coverage to people with preexisting conditions or those who seem likely to use services extensively;
- Limiting and/or denying treatment to people whose difficulties do not respond to standardized treatment protocols;
- Replacing professional judgment with multiple levels of organizational decision making;
- Increasing requirements for record keeping and report writing;
- Removing case managers responsible for utilization review from direct contact with both patients/clients and practitioners and providing them access only through overloaded telephone lines;
- Requiring clinicians to comply with insurer policies and protocols or risk their employment;
- Instituting difficult appeal procedures;
- Using economic power to drive down payment rates to treatment institutions and practitioners; and
- Promoting managed care as the most efficient, if not the only approach to cost containment.[3]

Public Criticism and Legislation

Public anger over managed care elevated citizen concerns to a major national issue and legislation was introduced in Congress to define and protect the rights of patients and to regulate managed care companies. In 1998 The Patient Protection Act and the Patient's Bill of Rights Act both failed to move forward because of lobbying by the insurance industry and the personal difficulties confronting President Clinton. These defeats underlined again the difficulty of passing health care legislation affecting physicians, patients, lawyers, insurers, and employers of all sizes. A focus of the debates is whether or not health insurance companies should be treated just like any other person or institution in the health profession, that is be held responsible for actions that harm patients. Previously, in 1997 Congress set similar standards for health plans serving people under Medicare.

During 2001, the first year of the Bush administration, Patient Rights legislation was passed by both the House of Representatives and the Senate following five years of struggle. President Bush favored patient rights legislation during his campaign for the presidency. In fact the State of Texas when he served as Governor was a laboratory for the expense of litigation where such suits are allowed: Although estimates of the increase in health plan premiums nationwide if patients were free to sue insurers for denial of care were 1.2 percent, the actual costs in Texas were a .1 percent increase in total spending per member per month of full-service HMOs.

The major issues confronting legislators were: Should patients be allowed to sue in federal or state court, or both? Should the federal government impose limits on punitive or other damages? Should patients be required to exhaust their rights to administrative appeals before going to court? Should employers have any liability if they participate in decisions denying claims for benefits?

Both the House and Senate bills shared some features. They provide patients with prompt access to emergency care and specialists, such as pediatricians and gynecologists, without a referral from a primary care physician. This benefit was provided by many H.M.O.s on their own or by state law. The crucial differences between the two measures involved the enforcement of benefits. The Senate bill would allow HMOs to be held accountable in state courts, as are doctors, for their medical decisions. The House Bill as this is written allows suits in state courts but only under restrictive federal rules that would make it difficult for patients to prevail against their health plans. Insurance companies would have an important voice in the selection of outside review panels. The House bill has a lower limit on damages and forces patients to prove the H.M.O.'s negligence was the sole cause of harm. President Bush favored the House bill.

Forty states already give patients an independent medical review of any plan's denial of care and ten states allow patients the right to sue in state court under traditional medical malpractice law. Under the House version, those patient protections would be lost.

Congress was to consider reconciling the differences in a conference committee of the House and Senate. The context in which compromise legislation would be considered found President Bush vowing to veto any bill that did not limit suits to federal court where damages are often lower than in state courts, thus leaning in the direction of the insurance industry. Strong advocates for legislation included health insurance lobbyists and the major national business groups. On the other side were patient and consumer coalitions. Many state officials expressed serious doubts about federal legislation on patients' rights, especially the House bill because it would override state laws that provide greater protection to millions of consumers. When this was being written, it was unclear whether an agreement can be reached or that President Bush will sign.

Social workers provide services in inpatient, outpatient, medical, rehabilitation, psychiatric, private practice and other health care settings, all of which are affected by managed care. Although there are fewer opportunities for autonomous decision making by practitioners, social workers must deal with case managers and help clients to avoid the loss of options, including type, duration, and place of service. When clients lose their service options, professionals lose autonomy about such decisions as well.

Munson and Shapiro identified several negative impacts of managed care on social work practitioners. There are effects of "speeding up" practice when it is clear more time and sessions are needed for clients to be helped sufficiently. As one can imagine, the relationships between clients and practitioners also are being altered by the managed care policies described previously. There are administrative costs to managed care, particularly as necessary to control costs. A lack of privacy for clients and patients is enhanced by the number of organizations and people who have access to personal files and case information. Little is known about the effects of the discontinuation of services. Clients (as well as practitioners) must constantly be concerned with whether their request for benefits will be honored. Managed care establishes an environment in which clients cannot be certain they should place trust in the relationship because the treatment can be discontinued by decision makers outside their relationship with the practitioner, decision makers whose goals may not be quality treatment but cost savings.[4]

In practice, social workers advocate for their clients or patients with case managers and managed care organizations, work to improve the delivery of services, and participate in efforts to change health and social service policy for the better. A growing number of social workers are involved in managed care organizations directly in many roles, from owners to case managers. The degree to which social workers will be advocates for clients and families from within these organizations remains to be seen. Social workers also have roles in trying to influence managed care systems so they provide quality services for beneficiaries.

Managed care is not limited to physical and mental health services. In attempts to balance the cost of services with quality and access issues, for example, managed care is utilized in child welfare services (foster care, adoptions, residential treatment, etc.), aging, corrections, developmental disabilities, child care, and for the collection of child support payments.

Health Care Programs

In the mid-1960s, two health programs were introduced under the Social Security Act: Medicare and Medicaid. Medicare is insurance based, whereas Medicaid is a means-tested program.

Medicare

Goals. The Medicare program is a national insurance program (HI) to provide health care for the aged and certain disabled persons. Hospital insurance (HI) is provided through Part A and supplementary medical insurance (SMI) through Part B.

Who Is Eligible for the Program? Most Americans 65 years of age or older are automatically entitled to protection under Part A (the hospital insurance program) by either themselves or their spouses having paid the Hospital Insurance (HI) tax on earnings covered by Social Security or the Railroad Retirement Systems. Part A also provides coverage after a 24-month waiting period for persons under 65 years of age who are receiving Social Security disability cash benefits but their dependents do not. Most persons, regardless of age, who need a kidney transplant or renal dialysis may also be covered. Persons aged 65 years or older who are not automatically entitled to Part A may obtain coverage by paying the full actuarial cost, which was $301 in 2000 or $166 for persons who had at least 30 quarters of covered employment. In fiscal year 1999 Part A covered an estimated 38.8 million aged and disabled persons, including those with end-stage renal disease.

Part B is voluntary. All persons 65 years of age or older (even those not entitled to Part A) and all persons enrolled in Part A may enroll in Part B by paying a monthly premium ($45.50 in 1998). In fiscal year 1999, Part B covered an estimated 36.9 million aged and disabled persons. Voluntary enrollees in Part A must enroll in Part B.

What Is the Form of the Benefit?   Part A provides coverage for inpatient hospital services, up to 100 days of post-hospital skilled nursing facility care, home health services, and hospice care. The first 60 days of *inpatient hospital services* in a benefit period are subject to a deductible ($776 in 2000). A benefit period commences upon entry and ends when the person has not been in a hospital or skilled nursing facility for 60 days. For days 61–90 in a benefit period, a coinsurance amount ($194 in 2000) is imposed. If more than 90 days are needed in a benefit period, a patient can choose to draw upon a 60-day lifetime reserve. There is a coinsurance charge for each reserve day ($388 in 2000).

Skilled nursing facility care is provided up to 100 days following hospitalization for those who need continued daily skilled nursing care and/or rehabilitation services. After the first 20 days, there is a daily coinsurance charge ($97.00 in 2000).

Certain *home health care* services are provided. *Hospice care* is provided to terminally ill beneficiaries with a life expectancy of 6 months or less for two 90-day periods, followed by an unlimited number of 60-day periods. Ill persons must be recertified as terminally ill at the beginning of 60-day periods.

Part B generally pays 80 percent of the approved amount (fee schedule, reasonable charge, or reasonable cost) for covered services in excess of an annual deductible ($100). Coverage includes *physician's services* (surgery, consultation, and home, office, and institutional visits; limitations apply to services provided by dentists, podiatrists, chiropractors, and treatment of mental illness); *other medical and health services* (laboratory and other diagnostic tests, x-ray and other radiation therapy, outpatient hospital services, rural health clinic services, durable medical equipment, home dialysis supplies and equipment, artificial devices other than dental, physical and speech therapy, and ambulance services as required); *specified preventive services*, mammography screening annually for all women over 40 years of age, a screening pap smear and pelvic exam once every three years, except for women who are at high risk of developing cervical cancer, and specified colorectal screening, diabetes self-management training services, bone mass measurements for high-risk persons and prostate cancer screenings.

Medicare in general does not provide for outpatient *prescription drugs or biologicals*. Part B pays for immunosuppressive drugs for 36 months following an organ transplant, drugs for treatment of anemia for persons with chronic kidney failure, and certain specified oral cancer drugs. The program does cover flu shots, pneumococcal pneumonia vaccines, and hepatitis B vaccines for those at risk. *Home health services* include an unlimited number of medically necessary home health visits for persons covered under Part A. The 20 percent coinsurance and $100 deductible do not apply to such benefits. There is no income or assets test for Medicare eligibility.

Medicare beneficiaries have the option of enrollling in a private health plan, typically an HMO. As discussed under managed care, such a program receives a predetermined per capita payment from Medicare for each enrolled beneficiary. Most services are provided by *Medicare-Choice*. This program was designed to expand the availability of health plans in markets where access to managed care plans was limited or non-existent and to offer new types of plans in all areas. However, the program has not been as successful as anticipated. As a result, only about 16 percent of the Medicare population has enrolled. Under the Balanced Budget Act (1997) every individual entitled to Medicare Part A and enrolled in Part B will be able to elect the existing Medicare benefits through either Medicare fee-for-service (traditional Medicare) or a Medicare-Choice plan.

Those beneficiaries who choose traditional Medicare have to pay out-of-pocket for deductibles and coinsurance, as well as all services not covered by Medicare. Beneficiaries who want to fill the gaps in Medicare purchase Medigap or Medicare Select policies from private insurance companies. These companies are allowed to sell 10 standardized Medigap policies or a policy that limits your choice to the plan's network of providers. Each plan differs in respect to benefits and costs.

In order to increase enrollment in Medicare managed care and to allow beneficiaries options similar to those in the non-Medicare market, Medicare-Choice provides several plans such as HMOs (a managed care plan primarily owned and operated by an insurer that also provides services to the enrollees), provider sponsored organizations (typically groups of physicians and hospitals), preferred provider organizations, medical savings accounts, on a demonstration basis, private fee for service, and a combination of a medical savings account (MSA) and contributions to a Medicare-Choice MSA.

The MSA demonstration plans reimburse Medicare-covered services after a specified high deductible is met. The difference between the premium for the high-deductible plan and the applicable Medicare-Choice per capita payment is placed in an account for the beneficiary to use to meet medical expenses below the deductible. Funds from an MSA used for other than medical expenses are included in one's gross income and are subject to an additional tax. This program was limited to 750,000 taxpayer participants. After 2000, no new contributions may be made to the program except by or on behalf of those who previously made contributions. As of 2000, no Medicare beneficiary was enrolled in an MSA and there were no contracts for preferred provider organizations.

In 1988, the Catastrophic Coverage Act was passed by Congress. The bill was designed to assist with a very expensive, lengthy illness and to prevent severe depletion of resources. Its provisions included unlimited inpatient hospital care with only one annual deductible, 150 days of skilled nursing care without a preadmission hospitalization, respite care for caretakers of the elderly or disabled, a limit on doctor's bills, and payment for prescription drugs. However, in a very unusual action, Congress repealed this act one year later largely because of lobbying efforts by seniors, who opposed the bill because it was funded through a tax levied only on them.

How Is the Program Financed? Medicare Part A is Hospital Insurance (HI) financed by an earmarked payroll tax paid by the employer, employee, and those who are self-employed. Additional sources of income include transfers from the Railroad Retirement account, reimbursements from general revenues for certain persons, premiums from voluntary enrollees, payments for military wage credits, taxes on Social Security benefits, and interest. Employers and employees each pay a tax of 1.45 percent on all earnings. Self-employed persons pay 2.9 percent, and there is no limit on earnings subject to this tax. Medicare Part B supplementary Medical Insurance (SMI) is financed by monthly premiums paid by the aged, disabled, and chronic renal disease enrollees (25 percent of costs) adjusted yearly and by federal general revenues (75 percent). In 2000 the premium was $45.50. These premiums and federal contributions are kept in the federal Supplementary Medical Insurance Trust Fund (SMI). The monthly premium is deducted from the enrollee's Social Security, Railroad Retirement, or federal Civil Service Retirement annuity. All states must pay Part A and B premiums and other expenses for certain aged and disabled Medicaid beneficiaries eligible for Medicare.

Part B is financed from premiums paid by the aged, disabled, and chronic renal disease enrollees and from general revenues. The premium rate is computed annually based on the projected costs of the program for the coming year.

In 1983 a system of DRGs was established by the federal government. Under DRG, Medicare's reimbursement rates to hospitals are set according to illness category. If a patient remains in the hospital beyond Medicare's predetermined discharge date, Medicare ceases payment. The DRG system, despite an appeal process and mandated discharge planning, is said to cause premature discharge and other difficulties for some Medicare recipients.

What Is the Level of Administration? The Centers for Medicare and Medicaid Services (CMS) of the Department of Health and Human Services has the overall responsibility for the administration of Medicare. The daily work of reviewing claims and making payments is done by intermediaries for Part A and carriers for Part B. These are usually commercial insurers or Blue Cross/ Blue Shield plans.

Discussion. Medicare disbursements began to exceed income in 1995, and it is projected that Part A (the HI program) will be insolvent in 2030.[5] It is noteworthy that in 1997 projections concluded that the Trust Fund would be depleted in 2001. By 2002, the depletion was projected to be delayed until 2030, due to many factors but crucially related to the earlier "booming" economy. The future size and shape of this extremely popular health care program has to be decided in the near future. The program faces the increased numbers of the baby boom generation, the shift in the ratio of covered workers supporting each HI beneficiary, costs rising faster than income, and the increasing size of the program relative to other parts of the economy.

Costs, consumer choice, the range of available services, the roles of prevention and cure, greater efficiency and effectiveness, and ideological issues focusing on the role of government and the roles of the marketplace all are important considerations. Medicare has been horizontally adequate, efficiently reaching all persons 65 years of age or older (most of the recipients). Questions have been raised about its vertical adequacy in relation to preventive services, prescription coverage, and long-term health care costs, but recent changes have implemented some new preventive services. Virtually all of its funds are used for services; but guarding against waste, fraud, and abuse is very important.

Some people believe that Medicare is benefit inefficient because many persons who could afford to pay for their health care receive services. Others think that a major strength of the program is its universality. All proposals for change shift costs to the elderly, either directly or indirectly, which raises questions about fairness, especially for those with low incomes.

Some proposals for change include increasing monthly premiums, raising deductibles for Part B, increasing the eligibility age to 67, setting annual limits on the growth of Medicare spending, relaxing antitrust laws so that doctors and hospitals could more easily form health networks to serve Medicare beneficiaries (doctors would be able to set their prices in consultation with other doctors), and setting limits for noneconomic legal damages such as pain and suffering. Finally, included in suggested revisions are means testing for participants so that subsidies for Part B (out of general revenues) would be phased out at a set income level, thus ending the universal nature of the program and shifting it incrementally toward selectivity.

Critics also suggest that budget cuts result in too few dollars to deliver quality health care because they do not keep up with health care costs. Limits on the annual growth of per capita payments to HMOs in some parts of the country have proven to be insufficient to attract HMOs. Furthermore, because there would be no limit on the growth of private health care premiums, low-income persons might have to choose low-cost plans while higher income persons could purchase more extensive services, creating a more inequitable system. Concern is also expressed that retirees could choose the tax-free accounts when they are well and choose the traditional Medicare program when they become ill. Other critics suggest that cuts in Medicare and Medicaid could be used to balance the budget and pay for tax cuts for the middle class and wealthy.

Aside from the financial and ideological issues, there are several underlying issues which are seldom discussed but are implied in the debates: What is basic health care? Should health care be provided only in the marketplace? Are those who have not cared for their health (e.g., by smoking or substance abuse) entitled to the same treatment as those who have?

Medicaid

Goals.   Medicaid, authorized under the Social Security Act in 1965, is a federal-state matching entitlement program to provide means-tested medical and health-related services to low-income individuals and families.

Who Is Eligible for the Program?   In 1999 27.6 million persons were covered by Medicaid, some of whom—for example, elderly persons—may have had other coverage such as persons who have Medicare. The requirements of Federal law joined with the decisions of the individual states regarding Medicaid determine who is eligible in particular states. Adding to the complexity of the program are the states' decisions about the limits of allowable income and resources. Thus, one can be eligible in one state and ineligible in others with the same income and resources.

Before the enactment of the Personal Responsibility and Work Opportunity Act (1996) there were two paths to Medicaid for low income families and children. Receiving cash assistance through Aid to Families with Dependent Children or Supplemental Security Income made one automatically eligible for Medicaid. The second route was for low-income pregnant women and children unrelated to the public assistance system. The creation of TANF in 1996 severed the automatic connection between cash assistance provided for low income families with children and Medicaid.

At the time this is written, over 50 distinct population groups may be eligible for Medicaid, some are mandatory groups that all states must cover; others are optionally eligible. Currently, the following categories of people are among the groups eligible for Medicaid. (1) TANF eligibility does not automatically confer Medicaid eligibility. Nevertheless, those persons who meet the requirements for the former AFDC programs that were in effect in their states on July 16, 1996 remain eligible even if they are currently ineligible for TANF. (2) States are required to cover pregnant women and children under age 6 with family incomes below 133 percent of the Federal poverty income guidelines. Since 1991, States have been required to cover all children under age 19 who were born after September 30, 1983 and whose family income is below the federal poverty level. States may cover pregnant women and infants under 1 year of age whose income is between 133 and 185 percent of the federal poverty level. (3) Transitional medical assistance is provided to avoid the loss of Medicaid for those who successfully obtain employment. (4) A number of eligible groups are tied to former AFDC rules and eligibility.

(5) States must continue Medicaid for recipients of adoption assistance and foster care. The Foster Care Independence Act (1999) allows states to extend Medicaid coverage for former foster care youth under age 21. (6) The State Children's Health Insurance program (S/CHIP), although separate from Medicaid, allows states to receive funds to cover targeted low-income children through group health or other insurance that meets specific standards. (7) Other individuals may be covered by extending coverage to those who otherwise might not be entitled. This is by state option when higher income and resource levels are permitted.

Most states that choose this option do so only for low income children and families or to enroll recipients in managed care plans.

(8) States are required—with one exception—to provide Medicaid coverage to SSI (aged, blind, and disabled) recipients. The one exception is that states may elect the option of using income and resource standards no more restrictive than those in effect in 1972 before the implementation of SSI. (9) Certain low-income individuals are entitled to assistance in paying their Medicare part B premiums and other Medicare cost sharing through Medicaid. (10) States may provide Medicaid to certain otherwise ineligible persons because their income is too high to qualify for SSI or state supplemental payments but who are in nursing facilities or other institutions. (11) Legal immigrants arriving in the United States after August 22, 1996 are ineligible for Medicaid benefits for 5 years. Coverage after the five years is a state option. Legal immigrants residing in the United States who were receiving Medicaid benefits as of August 22, 1996 and later became disabled are eligible; refugees for the first seven years after entry into the United States; asylees for the first seven years after being granted asylum; individuals whose deportation is being withheld by the Immigration and Naturalization Service for the first seven years following grant to withhold deportation; lawful permanent aliens after being credited with 40 quarters of Social Security coverage; honorably discharged military veterans, active duty military personnel and their spouses and unmarried dependent children. Eligible for emergency Medicaid services are qualified aliens and nonqualified aliens who meet financial and categorical eligibility requirements.

(12) Finally, a large number of states and other jurisdictions provide Medicaid to some groups of "medically needy" persons. These are persons who meet the non-financial standards for inclusion but who do not meet the applicable income and resource requirements for eligibility. The state may establish higher income or resource standards of the persons may "spend down" to the medically needy standard by incurring medical expenses.

In addition, states may provide Medicaid to certain otherwise ineligible persons who are in nursing facilities or other institutions or who would require institutional care if they were not receiving alternative services at home or in the community. Home and community-based services may be provided to individuals who otherwise would require institutional care. Services may also be provided for persons who would be eligible if they were in an institution. These include children being cared for at home, persons of any age who are ventilator dependent, and persons receiving hospice benefits in place of institutional services.

What Is the Form of Benefit?   The benefits are in-kind medical care services. There are no cash benefits for beneficiaries; payments are made directly to the providers of services. Although Medicaid recipients receive a wide range of health services, the largest number of recipients obtained prescribed drugs, used physician services, and/or utilized out-patient hospital services. Each state within Federal guidelines designs and administers its own program. This results in substantial variation among the states in coverage, types, and scope of benefits offered and the amount of payment for specific services. The State of Oregon uses a prioritized list of health services for its Medicaid program, listing services from most important to least important for their comparative benefit to the population served. Health services for recipients are thus rationed based on the funds available, a phenomenon which may be a harbinger of health care's future.

How Is the Program Financed?   There is no preset limit (cap) on the total federal expenditures for Medicaid. The federal government assists states with the cost of Medicaid services through a variable matching formula, which is adjusted annually. The federal matching rate is inversely related to a state's per capita income, ranging from 50 to 83 percent, although in 2000 the highest rate was 76.8 percent. The federal share of administrative costs is 50 percent for all states, except for certain items for which the match is higher. All funds are obtained from general revenues both on the state and federal levels. Total U.S. expenditures in 2000 were $203 billion.

What Is the Level of Administration?   Medicaid is a state-administered program. At the federal level, Centers for Medicare and Medicaid Services (CMS) of the Department of Health and Human Services is responsible for overseeing state operations. There must be one state agency that administers Medicaid, and it is typically the state Department of Social Services, the state health agency, or an umbrella human resources agency. The one responsible agency may contract with other state organizations to conduct some program functions. States may process claims for reimbursement themselves or contract with other organizations or health insuring agencies to process claims. An increasing number of states are requiring Medicaid recipients to receive their services from HMOs.

Discussion.   Table 10.1 illustrates the differences between Medicare and Medicaid. The problems with Medicare and Medicaid regarding their adequacy are the classic problems of selective and universal programs. Medicare, which is universal, has excellent horizontal adequacy for the aged, at least in the automatic hospital insurance portion, but its benefits are limited and often run out for the elderly, forcing them to use up their limited assets until they become eligible for Medicaid. Medicaid serves as the long-term care safety net. Many Americans quickly deplete their savings and qualify for Medicaid. Cuts and restrictions in Medicaid spending for nursing home care mean greater burdens can be expected to fall on informal caregivers, and given such restrictions by states, there would be little recourse for those in need. One option is to reduce the number of people served, many of whom are severely ill. Another option is to cut reimbursement. This latter choice leaves decisions to cut up to the nursing homes themselves. Further, there is little optimism about states raising taxes to provide broader coverage. There is an additional issue related to potential reductions in Medicaid funding for nursing home care: The families of nursing home residents—spouses, adult children—could find themselves responsible for the burden by either the state or their own sense of

TABLE 10.1   *Differences between Medicare and Medicaid*

	Medicare	*Medicaid*
Who is eligible	All aged recipients of Social Security for hospital insurance; all aged recipients of Social Security who contributed for medical insurance; people disabled after 2 years; and those with end-stage renal disease	All needy, as per means test
Form of benefit	Partial hospital and medical service	All medical services
Funding	Payroll tax on employers, employees, and self-employed for hospital coverage; general revenues match voluntary insurance	General revenues from the federal government with a share of the contribution for medical cost from the general revenues of the states
Administration	National, using various insurers to process claims	Grant-in-aid; federal guidelines, state variations, and administration

obligation. If Medicaid were not available for them, adult children could be forced to choose between their parent's need for nursing home care and providing their own children an education.

Medicaid is vertically more adequate, at least technically, because just about all kinds of medical care and services are covered, but it is not as adequate horizontally because it is means tested. Even the vertical adequacy of Medicaid is affected by the degree to which all programs for the indigent become "poor programs" and in the degree to which the poor are provided "mass-produced" medical care. Moreover, because Medicaid is not an insurance program and because states can expand or contract covered services, Medicaid cannot be said to provide a national health system for the poor.

The unprecedented congressional repeal of the Catastrophic Care Bill one year after its passage raised some crucial questions. Why, in contrast to Social Security and the rest of Medicare, was catastrophic care to be funded only by beneficiaries? Why would Congress not alter the controversial financing format instead of abolishing the program? How will the growing aging population pay for lengthy, costly, serious illnesses? What will happen to the millions of elderly persons who are ineligible for Medicaid but cannot afford private insurance (Medigap) to cover costs not currently assumed by Medicare?

Coverage for catastrophic illness is not the only problem in the current health care system. Perhaps the most critical issue is the estimated over 40 million Americans totally without health insurance. Many of these persons are ineligible for Medicare and Medicaid but cannot afford private insurance. In addition, persons with disabilities must wait two years before being eligible for Medicare. Many children are among the more than 40 million people without insurance. The

Balanced Budget Act (1997) gave states the option to provide Medicaid coverage for about half those children regardless of whether they continue to meet income eligibility tests and to presume eligibility for low-income children while that eligibility is being determined.

The latent consequences of this system are many and were not all anticipated. The emphasis in Medicare on hospitalization tends to encourage physicians to treat those who are ill according to the way they are insured, thus causing a run on the most expensive services of all and increasing health costs. Another latent consequence that led to the escalation of health costs is the third-party payment system described in chapter 7. For all of these reasons, Medicare and Medicaid are critical stopgaps in meeting health needs, but they are inadequate for a comprehensive rational system of health insurance for the nation. To contain escalating health care costs and improve access to Medicaid, states have increased their use of managed care, discussed earlier in this chapter.

Because states have to fund the program, Medicaid competes for general revenue funds with other state budget items such as education and transportation. State governors have complained about the costs of Medicaid, many of which have been mandated by congressional action; the paperwork required to comply with federal regulations; and bureaucratic rules that limit state flexibility.

Nutrition Programs

Nutrition programs help low-income persons meet their nutritional needs. The Food Stamp Program is a means-tested entitlement program, and the Supplemental Food Program for Women, Infants, and Children has a budget cap, and is not only means tested but targets a very specific category of recipient.

The Food Stamp Program

Goals. The Food Stamp Program is designed primarily to increase the food purchasing power of eligible low-income households so they can buy a nutritionally adequate low-cost diet.

Who Is Eligible for the Program? Eligibility is based on financial, employment/training, and categorical tests. A means test requires that those eligible have monthly income and assets below limits set by law. Certain household members must register for work, accept suitable job offers, and fulfill work or training requirements such as looking or training for a job. The law limits Food Stamp eligibility for able-bodied adults without dependents to 3–6 months in any 36-month period unless they are working half time or in a work or training activity. Eligibility rules make some persons automatically eligible (many TANF, SSI, and general assistance recipients) or others ineligible (strikers and most noncitizens, postsecondary students, and people living in an institutional setting). Applications cannot be denied because of the length of time the household lived in the welfare agency's jurisdiction or because the household has no fixed mailing address or does not reside in a permanent dwelling. Many non-citizens are barred from eligibility for Food Stamps, except for children, the elderly, and the disabled who were legally resident before August 22,1996, refugees and asylees for a limited period of time, veterans, those with a substantial history of work under Social Security, and certain limited groups of aliens.

There were almost twenty million recipients in 1998, with the exception of two years, the lowest number since 1980. A number of theories are proposed for the drop: improved economy, more restrictive food stamp eligibility rules, changing administrative practices in public assistance offices, and being discouraged or not understanding that being dropped from public assistance does not mean automatic ineligibility for food stamps. One example of a barrier to eligibility is the fair market value set on cars. A real value of $4,500 in 1977 (when it was set) is now equal to close to $13,000. This federal policy no longer meets the transportation needs of low-income, working families. In 2001, states were given new authority to set vehicle asset policy.[6]

What Is the Form of the Benefit?   Low-income persons receive Food Stamp booklets of coupons of specified amounts. They then can use the coupons like cash to purchase most foods for consumption from participating stores. Most states use electronic benefit transfer (EBT) systems, which replace coupons with an automatic teller machine–like card and with which purchases are deducted at the point of sale from the recipient's account. Food Stamp allotments are not taxable, and Food Stamp purchases may not be charged sales taxes. Receipt of Food Stamps does not affect eligibility for benefits provided by other assistance programs, although it may influence the level of a benefit. Purchases are made in approved grocery stores and include food for home preparation and consumption (not alcohol, tobacco products, or hot foods intended for immediate consumption); seeds and plants for gardens to produce food for personal consumption; for the elderly and SSI recipients and their spouses, meals prepared and served through approved communal dining programs; and meals prepared and served to residents of drug addiction and alcoholic treatment programs, small group homes for the disabled, shelters for battered women and children, and shelters serving the homeless. Homebound aged and disabled persons who cannot prepare their meals may use Food Stamps for Meals-on-Wheels. Some other products are not eligible: For example, pet food and cleaning and paper products may not be purchased with food stamps. In 1999, the average monthly benefit per person was $72.30, and the four-person maximum monthly allotment was $419.

How Is the Program Financed?   The entire cost of benefit payments is covered by the federal government from general revenues, except where states pay for issuing Food Stamp benefits to ineligible noncitizens or those made ineligible by the new work rule for able-bodied adults without dependents. The federal government is also responsible for its own administrative costs: overseeing program operations, printing and distribution of coupons to welfare agencies, redeeming stamps through the Federal Reserve, and payments to the Social Security Administration for certain intake services. In most cases, the federal government provides half the cost of state public assistance departments, including their outreach activities. The federal share can be increased 10 percent if the state has a very low rate of erroneous benefit determinations. The federal government shares the cost of employment and training programs as well as support services for food stamp recipients involved in employment and training. States are allowed to retain a portion of improperly issued benefits (other than agency errors) that are recovered, fraud cases, and other circumstances.

What Is the Level of Administration? At the federal level, the Food Stamp program is administered by the U.S. Department of Agriculture's Food and Nutrition Service, which gives direction to welfare agencies through federal regulations that define eligibility requirements, benefit levels, and administrative rules. It is responsible for arranging for printing Food Stamp coupons and distributing them to welfare agencies, overseeing state programs for EBT and approving and overseeing participation by retail food stores and other outlets that accept Food Stamps. Administrative roles of other federal agencies are as follows: the Federal Reserve System redeems stamps and has some jurisdiction over EBT methods; the Social Security Administration is responsible for the social security numbers that recipients must have, providing limited intake services, and verification of recipients' income; the Internal Revenue Service provides assistance in verifying recipients' income and assets; the Immigration and Naturalization service helps welfare offices confirm alien applicants' status; and the Secret Service and the Agriculture Department's Inspector General are responsible regarding counterfeiting and trafficking investigations.

States and other jurisdictions implement administrative responsibilities through their local welfare offices, determining eligibility, calculating benefits, and issuing Food Stamp allotments following federal rules. They also carry out employment and training programs in cooperation with the Employment Service of the U.S. Department of Labor through state employment offices that administer the Food Stamp Program's work registration requirements.

Discussion. The Food Stamp program is a means-tested, selective program whose federal and state expenditures totaled $21.1 billion in 1998, funding which decreased 22 percent from 1994 to 1999. Vertically the program is adequate in that it helps low-income households to obtain a more nutritious diet. A good diet is associated with health, learning, worker productivity, and becoming earners who pay income and other taxes. The program's horizontal adequacy is questionable. While the program is coherent with other public assistance programs, nevertheless, only 4 of 5 TANF recipients also receive food stamps and only 4 in 10 recipients of SSI do so. Many who may be eligible do not apply or additional factors may be operating.

The Food Stamp Program is a good example of a program initially not particularly favored by social welfare experts, but that has come to be viewed as highly valuable. To begin with, almost all social welfare planners would have preferred to use the money involved in financing the Food Stamp Program to increase general welfare benefits. This was seen as more dignified and would have eliminated the administrative expenses involved in setting up a Food Stamp operation. However, as the program grew each year and as more poor people came to depend on it, it became harder for people concerned with the poor to oppose it.

Among the objections to the program was that it forced the recipient to parade a dependency in stores whenever a purchase was made. The program also lent itself to abuses inherent in a selective program. Although the issue of stigma remains, and although some may still advocate replacing Food Stamps with cash benefits, the Food Stamp Program has notable strengths. It helps the poor meet basic nutritional needs, providing federal assistance in all states, including those in which additional state allocations for the poor would be highly unlikely. It is therefore an income supplement program.

Moreover, benefits are entirely federally funded, and there are uniform national benefit levels. Unlike TANF, then, inequities in benefit levels are eliminated. The Food Stamp Program also requires funds outreach to potential recipients, and recent legislation has sought to assist vulnerable populations such as the homeless.

Special Supplemental Nutrition Program for Women, Infants, and Children

Goals. The Special Supplemental Nutrition Program for Women, Infants, and Children (WIC) provides food assistance, nutrition risk screening, and related services such as nutrition education and breast feeding support to low-income pregnant and post-partum women and their infants, as well as to low-income children up to age 5 years.

Who Is Eligible for the Program? Participants in the program must have family income at or below 185 percent of poverty and must be judged to be nutritionally at risk, defined as detectable abnormal nutritional conditions, documented nutritionally related medical conditions, health-impairing dietary deficiencies, or conditions that predispose people to inadequate nutrition or nutritionally related medical problems. State WIC agencies may set lower income standards but seldom do so. Receipt of TANF, Food Stamps, or Medicaid assistance also can satisfy the WIC program's income test.

What Is the Form of the Benefit? Recipients receive supplemental foods monthly in the form of actual food items or, more generally, vouchers for purchases of specific items in retail stores. The law requires that the WIC program provide foods containing protein, iron, calcium, vitamin A, and vitamin C. Among the items that may be included in a food package are milk, cheese, eggs, infant formula, cereals, and fruit or vegetable juices. These food packages are tailored for age level, special dietary needs, and pregnant, nursing, and postpartum women and are prescribed by a WIC health care professional. Recipients must also receive nutritional education. In 1999 the national average federal cost of a WIC food package after rebates from infant formula manufacturers was $32.50 per month, and the average monthly administrative cost for each participant was about $12.

Benefits are received for a specified period of time and sometimes are recertified if there is continuing need. Pregnant women may continue to receive benefits throughout their pregnancy and for up to six months after childbirth without recertification. Nursing mothers are certified at six-month intervals, ending with their child's first birthday.

How Is the Program Financed?   The WIC program is federally funded from general revenues. It is not an entitlement program, and participation is limited by the amount of federal funding appropriated, whatever state supplementary funding is made available, and the extent of manufacturers' infant formula rebates.

What Is the Level of Administration?   Federally funded, the WIC program is administered by state and local health agencies. This program was authorized by the Child Nutrition Act of 1966, In 1999, there were on average 7.3 million recipients, including 1.9 million infants and 3.6 million children. Because of insufficient funding, many of those who are income-eligible and at nutritional risk do not receive WIC.

Discussion.   WIC is a selective, means and diagnostic tested program. In 1996, over 60 percent of WIC enrollees were found to have family income below the Federal poverty guidelines.[7] The program is coherent with TANF, Food Stamps, and Medicaid since receipt of those benefits also satisfies the WIC program's income test. Since the program depends on limited federal appropriations, not all persons who need the services can be accommodated. When this occurs, agencies make waiting lists and then use a priority system to determine who will receive WIC benefits. The program is horizontally inadequate and vertically adequate. Aside from those who simply do not apply, there were estimates that based on anticipated funding for the fiscal year 2002 200,000 to 250,000 eligible women, infants, and children will be turned away.[8] Cost-benefit studies have found that prenatal participation is associated with substantial savings in Medicaid costs. The savings range from $1.77 to $3.13 for every dollar spent for newborns and their birth mothers during the first 60 days following birth.[9]

School Lunch and Breakfast Programs

Goals.   The School Lunch and School Breakfast programs provide federal cash and commodity support for meals served by public and private nonprofit elementary and secondary schools and residential child care institutions that enroll and guarantee to offer free or reduced-price meals to eligible low-income children.

Who Is Eligible for the Program?   Both the Breakfast and Lunch programs have a three-tiered system that allows children from families with incomes below 130 percent of the poverty line to receive free meals; children from families from 130 to 185 percent of the poverty level to receive meals at a reduced price; and provides a small subsidy for children whose family income does not qualify them for free or reduced price meals or whose families do not apply. Children in TANF and Food Stamp households may automatically qualify for free school meals without an income application and the majority actually receive them. During 1999, 27 million children on average participated daily.

What Is the Form of the Benefit?   The programs provide breakfasts and lunches to children.

How Is the Program Financed?   Both programs are funded from federal general revenues through the budget of the Food and Nutrition Service, Department of Agriculture.

What Is the Level of Administration?   These programs are administered on the federal level by the Food and Nutrition Service and administered locally by school districts, individual schools, and certain nonprofit residences. Other federal child nutrition programs include the Child and Adult Care Food Program and the Summer Food Service, which provides subsidies for meals served during the summer months to children participating in recreational and other programs in low-income areas. The National School Lunch Program (NSLP) and the School Breakfast Program (SBP) provide cash and commodity support to participating public and private schools and nonprofit residential institutions that serve meals to children.

Discussion.   The School Breakfast Program serves far fewer students (1.3 billion lunches) than does the School Lunch Program (4.5 billion breakfasts). This means tested and selective program meets federal nutrition standards and thus provides healthful food to many children whose families are unable to do so. It makes more sense to increase the availability of breakfasts without diminishing the availability of lunches as that can enhance student health and learning throughout the day.

Low-Income Home Energy Assistance

Goals.   The Low-Income Home Energy Assistance Program (LIHEAP) is aimed at helping eligible households pay their home heating or cooling bills, providing assistance for low-cost weatherization, and providing assistance during energy-related emergencies.

Who Is Eligible for the Program?   States have considerable discretion to determine eligibility criteria and the types of assistance to be provided. Recipients of SSI, TANF, Food Stamps, or means-tested veterans' benefits may receive benefits. States can also opt to make payments to households with up to 150 percent of federal poverty guidelines or 60 percent of the state's median income, whichever is greater. States cannot establish an income ceiling below 110 percent of the poverty level. Priority for assistance may be given to households that meet criteria based on home energy burden in relation to household income; and households with younger children, frail elderly, or persons with disabilities and those energy needs that arise from a natural disaster or other emergency.

In 1996, LIHEAP served 3.9 million households, a twenty-five percent decrease in one year's time.

What Is the Form of the Benefit? States may provide three types of services: (1) help eligible households pay their home heating or cooling bills; (2) use up to 15 percent of their LIHEAP allotment for low-cost weatherization; and (3) provide assistance to households during energy-related emergencies. States may provide cash or vendor payments, two-party checks, vouchers/coupons, and payments directly to landlords.

How Is the Program Financed? The LIHEAP is a block-grant program funded entirely by the federal government. Funding reached a high of $2.1 billion in 1985 and a low of about $696 million in 1996.

What Is the Level of Administration? At the federal level, the program is administered by the Administration for Children and Families of the Department of Health and Human Services. States, Native American tribes, and territories administer LIHEAP programs through the state welfare agency or at the local level and must provide for hearings for those denied benefits, public participation, and public hearings in the development of the plan.

Discussion. This program illustrates the problems that occur when a needed service is not an entitlement. Because funding for this program is capped, once the available dollars are spent, those who come for heating and cooling assistance are turned away. The program is horizontally inadequate; it is vertically inadequate as well because, especially in severe weather, the available dollars are not equal for many persons in relation to their needs.

Housing

Goals. The primary purpose of housing assistance is to reduce housing costs and improve housing quality for low income households by providing decent and safe rental housing for eligible low-income families, the elderly, and persons with disabilities. Other goals include promoting residential construction, expanding housing opportunities for disadvantaged groups and groups with special needs, promoting neighborhood preservation and revitalization, increasing home ownership, and empowering the poor to become self-sufficient. Approximately 1.3 million households live in public housing units.

Who Is Eligible for the Program?   Public housing is limited to low-income families and individuals based on annual gross income whether as an elderly person, someone with a disability, or as a family.

What Is the Form of Benefit?   Among the benefits of the various housing programs are the following: rental subsidies through reduced rents and certificates for reduced rental rates and vouchers; insured and reduced mortgages, property taxes, and insurance costs; interest subsidies to the mortgage lender on behalf of lower-income families; rent supplement payments equal to the difference between fair market value rental for particular housing and a percentage of the family income. There are also efforts to increase the supply of affordable housing for low-income families through the provision of federal grants to state and local governments to be used for rental assistance or for the acquisition, rehabilitation, or, in limited circumstances, construction of both rental and ownership housing. Counseling and technical assistance are sometimes available. The McKinney Act provides for some support services for the homeless, including grants for emergency shelter, supportive housing, rehabilitation of single room occupancy dwellings and the Shelter Plus program (housing assistance for hard-to-serve homeless persons and their families living in places not intended for habitation or in emergency shelters). These persons have disabilities such as chronic mental illness, alcohol and drug problems, and AIDS and receive other supportive services.

Beginning in 1996 the HOME Investment Partnerships Block Grant program provides grants to State and local governments. These funds are used for tenant-based rental assistance or assistance to new home buyers. They may also be used for acquisition, rehabilitation, or in limited circumstances, construction of both rental and owner-occupied housing. In addition, the Fair Housing Program is administered through this department to eliminate discrimination in housing on the basis of race, color, religion, sex, and national origin.

Section 8 housing provides several forms of benefits. Households may rent an apartment in a Section 8 project or rehabilitated building. Rent will be low and based on the household's income, size, and expenses. Under the voucher-certification program, a family rents a unit of its choice from a private landlord who agrees to participate in the Section 8 program. In most cases, the family pays no more than 30 percent of its adjusted family income for rent, and the government pays the landlord the difference up to an approved rent level. The voucher-certification program is an ongoing benefit. If a recipient household moves out of one apartment, it can use the benefit in another rental unit. If the family has a voucher, it can carry its Section 8 benefit anywhere in the United States. Under the certification program, the family can transfer the benefit only in its local area. In addition to affordable rents, all Section 8 recipients benefit from the fact that rental units must meet established standards, and the Section 8 lease must offer certain protections.

Each year some low and moderate income households are helped to become homeowners by long-term reductions of their mortgage interest either through direct mortgage loans at low interest rates, roughly equivalent to long-term government borrowing rates or through provision of guarantees for private loans that cannot exceed those set by the Department of Veterans Affairs.

Funds are also provided to county and city governments for housing-related activities such as the rehabilitation of properties and the improvement of public facilities. In addition, there is housing assistance for veterans, which is not means tested, and guaranteed mortgage loans, which have made it possible for millions of people to purchase homes.

How Are the Programs Financed?   These housing programs are financed by federal general revenues, state and local monies, special insurance funds, closed-end appropriations, rental excesses over costs deposited to special funds, loans, a revolving rural housing insurance fund, and the like. Because federal legislative commitments run from 1 to 40 years, the appropriations are actually spent gradually over many years, thus expanding the pool of available aid and increasing the number of households served.

What Is the Level of Administration?   The major housing programs are administered by the U.S. Department of Housing and Urban Development (HUD) through area offices and local public housing authorities and the U.S. Department of Agriculture's Farm Service Agency (FSA), which administers housing programs for rural families and domestic farm laborers through state and county governments and with county committees appointed by the secretary of agriculture. The Office of Indian Housing of HUD administers the Indian Housing Program. The Veterans Administration housing program is administered through regional offices of the Department of Veterans Benefits.

Homelessness has continued as a national problem. The major federal response is the Stewart B. McKinney Homeless Assistance Act of 1987, which provides funds for emergency, transitional, and permanent housing for the homeless.

Discussion.   The total number of households receiving housing assistance from HUD more than doubled between 1977 (2.4 million) and fiscal year 2000 (5.1 million). Most rental subsidies for new commitments and for renewal of expiring contracts are funded for one year. During the 1980s, appropriations were dramatically cut, slightly reversed during the early 1990s, and dropped again after 1994. Total HUD expenditures increased steadily over the past quarter of a century, a fact explained by the increase in assisted households and the increase in the average subsidy. Housing assistance has been targeted increasingly toward poorer persons, also requiring larger subsidies.

There are anecdotal suggestions that new recipients of Section 8 certificates and vouchers in some parts of the country have difficulty finding units in which they can use their housing assistance because of very tight housing markets or a lack of landlords willing to participate in the programs. There are expectations that because of the Multifamily Assisted Housing Reform and Affordability Act (1997) rents in certain Section 8 housing with federally ensured mortgages will be reduced to market levels as the contracts expire. On the other hand, it is expected that because of the Preserving Affordable Housing for Senior Citizens and Families into the 21st Century (1999) rents will increase in other Section 8 housing.

There is a continuing debate between those who favor vouchers or other systems to make private housing and the open market available to the poor and those who believe in public housing, housing developments, and similar projects. The former argue that major housing developments have tended to re-create slums and resegregate people and are expensive to maintain. In their opinion, it is a lot simpler to provide cash assistance with enough dollars for the poor to give them the opportunity to live in decent housing in the community. Actually, the record of housing developments in "projects" is mixed. Some have been quite successful, but most publicity goes to the major big-city, high-rise public housing projects that re-create slum conditions. It is important to remember that the major effort in social welfare housing has been to help the middle class move into private housing through mortgage guarantees and loans. The federal government has expended much more on this over the past years than it has on public housing. There are growing efforts to replicate "middle-class-type housing" programs for the poor by helping them move from impoverished areas and center cities to residences in suburban middle-class and mixed-income neighborhoods. These efforts are viewed as incentives for those moved to maintain their new domiciles and as supports for improved education and financial betterment.

Affordable housing is a pressing national problem. Rising housing costs have put home ownership out of the reach of many young families. Rentals have escalated to the point that low- and moderate-income persons are often unable to afford even inadequate housing. Some have joined the swelling ranks of the homeless. Many existing old units were abandoned, demolished, or converted into higher-cost housing. The issue of housing provides a graphic example of how governmental, economic, and social forces can complement each other and contribute to the rapid development of a major social problem. Numbers of homeless persons in every part of the country are evidence of the consequences of such a confluence of forces. Efforts have focused on increasing allocations for and designing new approaches to meeting the nation's housing needs. Among these were the aforementioned home ownership for low-income persons, more funding for the nonprofit sector, and housing and related social services targeted to special needs populations.

Veterans' Benefits

Goals.   Veterans' benefit programs are provided as recognition of service to the nation.

Who Is Eligible for the Program?   Eligibility for most veterans' benefits is based on discharge from active military service under other than dishonorable conditions for a minimum period specified by law; family members or survivors of deceased veterans are also eligible. "Active service" generally means full-time service as a member of the Army, Navy, Air Force, Marines, or Coast Guard or as a commissioned officer of the Public Health Service, the Environmental Services Administration, or the National Oceanic and Atmospheric Administration. Completion of at least six years of honorable service in the Selected Reserves also provides for home-loan benefits for those not otherwise eligible. Certain veteran's benefits require wartime service.

What Is the Form of Benefit?   The Department of Veterans Affairs (VA) programs include veterans' compensation and pensions, readjustment benefits, medical care, and housing and loan guaranty programs. Also provided are life insurance, burial benefits, and special counseling and outreach programs.

"Service-connected" compensation is paid to veterans who have disabilities from injuries or illnesses sustained while in service. The amounts of monthly payments are determined by disability ratings based on presumed average reductions in earning capacity caused by the disabilities, ranging from 10 to 100 percent. Death compensation, or dependency and indemnity compensation, is paid to survivors of veterans who died as a result of service-connected causes. In fiscal year 1999, about 2.3 million disabled veterans and 324,000 survivors received compensation payments.

Veterans' pensions are means-tested cash benefits to war veterans who have become permanently and totally disabled from "non-service-connected" causes, and to survivors of war veterans. Under current law, benefits are based on family size, and the pensions provide a floor of income (In 2000 an eligible veteran living alone received $8,989.) Less generous benefits are available to survivors.

Several VA programs support readjustment, education, and job training for veterans and military personnel who meet certain eligibility criteria. The largest of these programs was the Montgomery GI Bill (MGIB). The MGIB provides educational assistance to persons, who as members of the Armed Forces or Selected Reserves, elect to participate in the program. Active duty personnel contribute monthly for the first year of enlistment. This program provides an entitlement to basic educational assistance and provides educational assistance to help in readjustment to civilian life, to aid in recruitment and retention of qualified personnel in the armed forces, and to develop a more highly educated and productive work force. Benefits are contingent upon length of service: The maximum benefit of three years requires three years of continuous service. Vocational rehabilitation is provided for disabled veterans, and the Department of Labor provides employment counseling and job training for veterans.

The VA provides an array of inpatient and outpatient medical services through medical centers, nursing homes, domiciliaries, ambulatory clinics, and readjustment counseling centers. Free medical care, both inpatient and outpatient, is provided for service-connected conditions and to low-income veterans for non-service-connected conditions. (The latter program is means-tested.) As facilities and resources permit, the VA provides care to veterans with non-service-connected conditions with incomes that exceed the income conditions but co-payments are required. Nursing home care is provided, with priority given to those with service-connected disabilities. The VA can contract with private facilities when it is determined to be in the best interest of the veteran and cost effective for the VA. VA nursing home care is augmented through contracts with community nursing homes and with per diem payments to state-run homes for veterans.

The VA provides programs to improve health care services for veterans, including priority counseling and treatment for sexual trauma for eligible veterans. The trauma may result from a physical assault or battery of a sexual nature or sexual harassment that occurred while on active military duty. Sexual harassment is defined as repeated, unsolicited verbal or physical contact of a sexual nature that is threatening in character. This service was scheduled to continue to the end of 2004.

Former prisoners of war; those suffering from medical problems that may be related to exposure to Agent Orange (a herbicide used extensively during the Vietnam Conflict that is linked to cancer, miscarriages, and birth defects in laboratory animals), or radiation from nuclear testing; those eligible for Medicaid; and those 65 years of age or older are among those who receive free care regardless of their income or assets. Gulf War veterans are being reached out to in order to determine and assist those who can help to identify the causes of Persian Gulf War veterans illnesses.

The VA also provides educational benefits to eligible dependents of certain veterans under the Survivors' and Dependents' Educational Assistance Program. Dependent children and spouses of veterans who died or are permanently and totally disabled as a result of a service disability are eligible, as well as the dependents of veterans who died from any cause while such service-connected disability was in existence; service persons missing in action or captured in line of duty by a hostile force; and service persons forcibly detained or interned in the line of duty by a foreign government or power. These persons may be eligible for up to 45 months of education benefits.

The VA also provides educational benefits under the Post-Vietnam Veterans' Educational Assistance program (VEAP). This program provides educational and training opportunities to eligible persons who contributed to VEAP while on active duty. If veterans (or in some cases, active-duty personnel) meet certain criteria (dates of service, contributions to VEAP, duration of service, release from service other than dishonorable), they may be eligible for up to 36 months of educational benefits. There are also several employment and training programs for veterans, including transition assistance for persons scheduled for separation from active duty and programs for veterans who have been unable to find employment following military service.

How Are the Programs Financed?   The VA is funded from federal general revenue, except where military personnel contribute or copayments are required. In 1999, a total of $44.1 billion was expended.

What Is the Level of Administration?   The VA is a federal program administered nationally by the Department of Veterans Affairs in coordination with other agencies where appropriate to the service to be provided, including—among others—the Department of Labor, the Farm Service Agency of the Department of Agriculture, Department of Housing and Urban Development for mortgage insurance, and the Small Business Administration.

As discussed earlier in this book, after World War II the GI Bill was one of the major factors in upgrading the U.S. workforce and in preventing a disruptive depression when millions of veterans were discharged in 1945 and 1946. In recent years, veterans' benefits have become less adequate compared with the cost of tuition and maintenance, and some have argued for an increase in benefits. Others have said that there is no reason this educational program should be limited to veterans if, as seems to be the case, it has enhanced the U.S. economy so greatly.

Veterans are also eligible for a variety of other benefits. For example, they may receive money from a limited income maintenance program based on need, free burial, prosthetic appliances, and home modifications to accommodate a disability. The astute social worker will always want to know if the client needing help or a member of the family is a veteran because, depending on the period during which the person served, the benefits might be worth looking into and might prove helpful.

Discussion.   It is interesting that, in contrast to the rest of the U.S. health care system, the veterans' medical program is a true form of nationalized medicine. There are no third-party payments or the like. Doctors and other staff are salaried, and all medical care is available for the eligible veteran. Evaluations of this system differ. Although veterans' facilities have been criticized for a variety of defects, on the whole the hospitals are not considered to be less adequate or less well funded than other medical systems in the United States, and the system has been of great benefit to many thousands of people. If the United States ever moves to national health insurance, the question of how veterans' medical care would be integrated in such a plan is a major one.

Services for veterans mingle selective and universal programs. Some programs are means tested and others are not. Veterans who are not eligible for some programs may be eligible for other services. Criticisms have been voiced about changing eligibility rules as well as problems of access. However, these services play very important roles. Poor veterans are the predominant users of VA health care services.[10] The VA reorganized in 1997 when it cut 40 percent of its hospital beds and shifted services to clinics, consolidated services, and trimmed services, thus placing a greater emphasis on out-patient treatment rather than on in-patient care.

From time to time suggestions have been made to "fold" VA health services into universal health care programs, but to date none of these suggestions have been accepted. Services for veterans and their families have been staunchly defended. No group is considered more deserving than veterans disabled while on active duty. In addition to other support, veterans and their families comprise a large number of voters.

Employment Programs

The Workforce Investment Act (WIA, 1998) created a system designed for a "work first" approach that uses the labor market to evaluate the pool of workers seeking employment and training assistance. A second emphasis of the legislation strengthened links between the workforce investment system and the reauthorized adult education, literacy, and vocational rehabilitation programs.

Linkages are established through state workforce boards with authority to guide the development of the system, local area workforce boards, One-Stop systems, unified state plans, and accountability. Eligibility is expanded for core employment services (job search, assessment, information and referral) to all adults, not just disadvantaged or dislocated workers. Core services must be provided through one-stop employment and training centers. Job training providers are to be screened according to their performance on key outcomes. The use of individual vouchers is promoted rather than contracts for obtaining job training and services. The legislation also restricts training to adults who are not employable after receiving core services or who are employed but need training to become self-sufficient.

Among the programs for adults are: training programs to teach job skills and provide job placement services for economically disadvantaged adults, including workers affected by massive layoffs or closures. Others included are those with outdated skills, those who jobs lost because of import competition or shifts in production outside this country, farmers who lost their farms, self-employed persons who are unemployed, and homemakers who have lost their main source of income, American Indian programs to provide training and employment services for economically disadvantaged, unemployed, and underemployed American Indians; training and employment services for migrant and seasonal farmworkers; the United States Employment Service; technical Skills training for domestic workers to fill some occupations currently occupied by temporary workers admitted from other nations; apprenticeship training; a variety of services to help hard-to-employ welfare recipients to get and keep jobs that will lead to self-sufficiency; unemployment insurance information, assistance, and benefits, including extended benefits and trade adjustment allowances; employment and training for workers affected by shutdowns or downsizing; and the senior community service employment program for economically disadvantaged persons aged 55 and older.

Youth programs are also administered by the U.S. Department of Labor and funded in state and local communities. The School to Work program helps students to earn credentials, prepare for first jobs, and increase their opportunities for further education; the Job Corps provides residential education and job training for "at risk" youth 16 to 24 in a public-private partnership; Youth Opportunity provides help for youth seeking to achieve academic and employment careers, to improve their educational and skill competences and connections to employers. Included are mentoring, supportive services, apprenticeships, on the job training and classroom instruction to improve their skills levels for employment.[11]

The National Council on Disability makes recommendations to the President and Congress on disability policy. The 21st century Workforce Commission called for regional leadership to establish partnerships of education, business, and government to address critical shortages of skilled workers in information technology jobs. Unemployment Insurance, Food Stamps, and TANF utilize employment services for recipients.

Among the programs are the JTPA; the Job Corps; the Employment and Training Administration of the Department of Labor; the Senior Community Services Employment Program; Employment and Training Assistance for Dislocated Workers; the Veteran's Employment Program; the Native American Employment and Training Program; the Women's Special Employment Assistance Program; and the Federal Work-Study Program. The President's Committee on Employment of People with Disabilities is designed to enhance the employment of persons with disabilities. Unemployment Insurance, Food Stamps, and TANF utilize employment services for recipients.

In addition, the Carl Perkins Vocational Applied Technology and Education Act of 1990, administered by the U.S. Department of Education, provides much of the funding for displaced homemakers' programs. A little-publicized but important employment-related program, which is operated through the states with federal funding, is vocational rehabilitation. Under this program, people with various disabilities are eligible for support and educational benefits for education and training programs that are calculated to make them more likely to be self-supporting and to develop careers. Vocational rehabilitation is still an important welfare program of which social workers should be aware. All these programs are now subsumed under the WIA (1998).[11]

Personal Social Services

Historically, five major social welfare systems have been identified: education, income maintenance, health, housing, and employment. Comparative international studies led to the identification of a sixth system with a long tradition—the personal social services. These services are intended to meet the normal anticipated social needs that arise in modern industrial nations.[12]

As we now look at the personal social services, the point must be made that some of them are integrated into other systems; that is, counseling or employment programs may be tied to public assistance. We also will discuss mental health, although in another sense it is part of the health system.

The functions of personal social services are the following:

- Contributing to socialization and development;
- Offering daily living and growth supports for average people (not just problem groups);

- Disseminating information about and facilitating access to services and entitlements anywhere in the social sector, inclusive of all six social welfare fields;
- Securing for the frail and aged, the handicapped, those with mental retardation, and the incapacitated a basic level of social care and aid necessary to support functioning in the community or in substitute living arrangements;
- Arranging substitute home or residential care or creating new, permanent family relationships for children whose parents are not able to fulfill their roles;
- Providing help, counseling, and guidance to assist individuals and families facing problems, crises, or sickness to reestablish functional capacities and overcome their difficulties;
- Supporting mutual aid, self-help, and activities aimed at prevention;
- Overcoming problems in community living;
- Advocating changes in policies, programs, and service planning;
- Integrating the variety of appropriate programs or services as they influence individuals and families, to assure coordination for maximum effect; and
- Controlling or supervising deviant individuals who may harm themselves or others, while offering care or opportunity for assistance, guidance, growth, or change.

What Is the Form of the Benefit?   A cursory look at the functions listed above can suggest the variety of benefits associated with this great diversity of aims and functions.

Who Is Eligible for the Program?   Eligibility for these services is based on a determination of need, including an assessment or diagnosis, and the individual financial means of the potential client.

How Is the Program Financed?   In the private sector, services are funded by membership and user fees, grants, bequests, purchases of service, third-party payments, and donations which often are tax deductible.

What Is the Level of Administration?   There is no central coordinating organization that gives direction to the personal social services. Services may be administered locally and relatively autonomously, or by state associations, or in combinations of national, state, regional and local organization as well as through umbrella organizations. Increasingly, states and localities purchase services from voluntary social agencies or private vendors.

The personal social services respond to needs of all citizens, not the poor alone: the aged in need of community support systems, parents choosing day care for their children, people who need help with "normal" life contingencies, the ill/young/old and those with disabilities requiring community protection, and victims of the addictions. In the public sector, many of these services are provided through categorical programs. At one time, public attention shifts to the needs of children; at another time, the aged, those with mental illness, those with mental retardation, the physically disabled, and others. Constant competition occurs among various groups for available public funds.

From a cursory look at the many programs available, one can see that boundary questions exist as there is overlap between programs. Does one ask for child welfare or family welfare, family welfare or mental health care, mental health care or drug and alcohol rehabilitation? Undoubtedly, greater coordination among services is needed. Under what circumstances is it possible to provide integrated personal or social services in the public sector? What should be the relationship between personal social services delivered by the public sector and those offered by nonprofit and for-profit agencies? Furthermore, which personal services should be provided universally as social utilities available on demand? Which should require means or diagnostic testing?

Who Is Eligible for the Programs?   Eligibility for public social services varies by state and, for nonprofit services, by agency. Some persons purchase services in the marketplace. Some personal social services such as child guidance and psychiatric treatment require a diagnostic assessment or other determination of need and eligibility. Fees may be charged to consumers on the basis of income or may be available free to all who have a particular status—for example, use of a public library or an information and referral service by a town's residents.

Title XX

Goals.   The purpose of Title XX (of the Social Security Act) Social Services Block Grant program is to assist states in furnishing services aimed at one or more of these goals: (1) achieve or maintain economic self-support to prevent, reduce, or eliminate dependency; (2) achieve or maintain self-sufficiency, including reduction or prevention of dependency; (3) prevent or remedy neglect, abuse, or exploitation of children and adults unable to protect their own interests, or preserving, rehabilitating or reuniting families; (4) prevent or reduce inappropriate institutional care by providing for community-based or home-based care, or other forms of less intensive care; and (5) securing referral or admission for institutional care when other forms of care are inappropriate, or providing services to individuals in institutions.

Who Is Eligible for the Programs?   States are given wide discretion to determine the services to be provided and the groups that may be eligible for services, usually low-income families and individuals.

What Is the From of the Benefit?   In 1997 at least 35 states used Title XX funds for the following services: daycare for children, foster care services for children, home-based services (homemaker, chore, home health, companionship, and home maintenance), prevention/intervention (assessments, family centered early intervention, home evaluation and supervision, preventive and restorative services), and protective services for children. Title XX also permits a few universal and free services—for example, information and referral and adult and child protective services.

How Is the Program Financed?   This program is a capped entitlement program. Block grants are given to states to help them achieve goals such as preventing child abuse, increasing the availability of child care, and providing community-based care for the elderly and disabled. From 1996 through 2000, the entitlement ceiling for the program was set at $2.38 billion. However, after 1996 the actual appropriations have steadily been reduced.

The Balanced Budget Act (1997) provided that states can transfer up to 10 percent of their TANF allotment to Title XX. This percentage was reduced in fiscal year 2001 to 4.25 percent and the entitlement was capped at $1.7 billion. Previously, they were authorized to transfer funds from Title XX to the Child Care and development Block grant. The welfare reform law stipulated that any TANF funds transferred to Title XX must not be used for families with incomes higher than 200 percent of the federal poverty guidelines, may be used for families ineligible for cash assistance under TANF because of time limits, or for children denied cash assistance because the family was already receiving benefits for another child. Up to 10 percent of the of the annual Title XX grant can be transferred to certain health care grants and the Low-Income Home Energy Assistance program (LIHEAP).

The Omnibus Budget Reconciliation Act (1993) made $1 billion available grants-in-aid funds under Title XX for states to provide social services in qualified empowerment zones and enterprise communities. In 1994 President Clinton selected 105 areas to participate in the program, which requires that criteria in the Internal Revenue Code be met and that a strategic plan be formulated. Social services provided must be directed at three goals of the basic Title XX grant funds. These funds remain available for expenditure for ten years.

The overwhelming majority of social welfare funds, even in personal social services, comes from the public sector. Such transferred funds can only be used for children and families under 200 percent of the poverty level. The implication of these funding cuts is fewer services for low-income families with children and homeless and disabled individuals.

What Is the Level of Administration?   Title XX is administered on the state and local levels.

Discussion.   The consolidation block-grant tactic and reduced allocations forced states to choose among programs and the levels of their funding. For example, should they give less to the aged or more to the disabled? Provide services for children or assist needy adults? Block grants for the social services distributed in this way meant that bargaining for funds had to be accomplished at the state level, a divisive situation in which very difficult decisions had to be made. Questions also have been raised about the competence of the states to deliver necessary services with less money, with fewer resources available, and with conflict in the relationship between states and localities, as well as special interest groups within the states.

Public monies, until recently, increasingly supported private services. Budget cuts and accompanying tightened eligibility requirements have compromised widespread utilization of some personal social services. The United States does not have a coordinated network of personal social services. As with income security programs, the personal social services are diversified, decentralized, and incrementally developed.

We can look somewhat more closely at services provided for families and at those focused on children as exemplars of the personal social services. We want to look particularly at those services in which social work is the profession that provides leadership.

Services to Families

In the best of times, all families need services that enrich their lives and the general nature of community living. As we have grown interdependent as a society, not everyone can be an expert at everything, and it is normal for families to call on experts and services in many ways. Some families will be unable to cope with harsh economic situations, loss of jobs, and financial, interpersonal, and intrafamilial difficulties. Divorce and separation, family and domestic violence, parent–child conflict, strained relationships between husband and wife or domestic partners, as well as the difficulties of combining families all are among the types of family problems for which people seek help.

It is important to keep in mind that not everyone who seeks help is experiencing problems out of the ordinary and that seeking help cannot be equated with mental disturbance. For example, family services are provided for those individuals and families experiencing special stresses such as single-parent families, families with children or parents with disabilities, and families experiencing various traumas. Family services are also provided for prevention and for life-enhancement purposes. Social groups, respite centers for parents and guardians, parent education, family life and sex education, stress management workshops, seminars on improving family communications, preparations for retirement, and household management and budgeting are among the many life-enhancing services available. Greater attention has been paid in recent years to the impact of ethnic, racial, socioeconomic, religious, gay and lesbian, and group-living arrangement factors among others as these patterns have more often replaced traditional domestic relationships.

The impact of home care services, a personal social service, for example, reduces the time some persons are institutionalized or required to be in hospitals, and can in some instances prevent hospitalization, can enable wage earners to continue working when illness or other crises strike, and can assist others to cope with the world when it is beyond their strength to cope alone.

Assistance in family matters also is provided in the public welfare sector. Public welfare personnel provide information and advice; referrals for jobs, housing, employment, and health care; and adult and child protective services to families in need. Intensive social work with families is provided in cities across the nation by nonprofit nonsectarian and sectarian family service agencies affiliated with the national Family Service America, Inc. These local agencies in larger and smaller cities provide psychosocial help and certain concrete services for families, particularly in relation to marital and domestic problems, parent–child difficulties, and problems specific to children and adults. There has also been a movement among these agencies to expand their educational, preventive, and life-enhancement efforts through programs offering family life education and parent education. Many provide a broad range of services to meet contemporary family problems, such as domestic violence, teenage pregnancy, care of the elderly, employee assistance programs, and substance abuse. In addition, these family agencies may offer case advocacy services for individuals and may engage in cause advocacy activities such as coalition-building and legislative lobbying.

Other organizations also provide some family services. The VA, National Travelers Aid, and local mental health agencies provide counseling for individuals and families. In addition, many Americans purchase help for personal, familial, and interpersonal problems in the marketplace by paying fees to social workers, psychiatrists, psychologists, and family therapists.

Services to Children

Child welfare services have two broad emphases: (1) the enhancement of the functioning of all families and all children and (2) services provided for families and children with special needs. All families and children face developmental stresses and problems. The social health of families determines to a large extent the welfare needs of children. There are basic services in our society that are supportive of family life and the lives of children. Income security and employment opportunities are fundamental to the social health of families and their children. Housing; nutritional aid; maternal, child, and family health care; child care programs; education; recreation; mental health; and a host of personal social services assist families to deal with issues and needs that arise as they deal with the various life-cycle developments and socialization (e.g., pregnancy and birth, early years, school entry, major milestones, divorce, separations, death). Counseling and rehabilitation services are helpful where needed. Mutual aid groups have arisen in recent years, and information and referral services enable families and children to find the proper service for particular needs.

Dimensions.   During 1999, almost 3 million reports about child maltreatment were made to Child Protective Services in the United States. Of this large number, approximately 60 percent were investigated or assessed. The other 40 percent were screened and not pursued. Over half the reports were received from professionals. Others came from lay persons, including family and community members. Almost 30 percent of the cases investigated were either substantiated or indicated child maltreatment. In over half the cases, child maltreatment was unsubstantiated.[13]

The Victims.   Nationally, there were an estimated 826,000 victims of maltreatment, at a rate of almost twelve per one thousand children. Almost 60 percent suffered neglect; just over 20 percent were physically abused; and just over 11 percent were sexually abused. Others were victims of different types of maltreatment. The highest rates for victimization were among those children from birth to three years and the rates declined as ages increased. Many types of maltreatment were approximately the same for males and females, but the rate of sexual abuse was higher for female children than for males. Rates did differ by race/ethnicity. Asian/Pacific Islanders were maltreated at the lowest rate and African-American children at the highest rate. Finally, children who had been maltreated prior to 1999 were much more likely to experience a repeated episode during the first six months following their first victimization than those without a prior history.

Perpetrators.   Who maltreats children? Slightly over 60 percent of the perpetrators were female (perhaps because of the over-representation of low income female-headed families in the data), females who maltreated were younger than the males who maltreated children. Almost 90 percent of all victims were maltreated by at least one parent, most commonly by a female parent acting alone. Female parents neglected and physically abused the greater percentage of victims. Male parents were the highest percentage of those who sexually abused a child.

Fatalities.   Child fatality estimates are based on records of Child Protective Services and other agencies. During 1999, there were 1,100 children who died of abuse and neglect. Just over 2 percent of these fatalities occurred while the child was in foster care. Almost half of the dead were younger than a year; those younger than 6 years accounted for 86 percent of those killed. Maltreatment deaths were more often associated with neglect situations. Of those children who died, one in ten of the families had received family preservation services in the five years preceding the deaths while a much smaller number had been returned to the care of their families prior to death.

The Estimated Economic Cost of Maltreatment.   Child abuse and neglect have social costs for the individuals, families, and society. The trauma affects the lives of individuals both short and long-term. The suffering and trauma experienced by these persons and their families are not measurable but many studies have documented the connections between abuse and neglect and medical, emotional, psychological, and behavioral disorders. Abused and neglected children are more likely than others to suffer from depression, alcoholism, drug abuse and severe obesity. They are more likely to require special education in school and to become juvenile delinquents and adult criminals.

Very recently, the first attempt was made to document the national costs that result from abuse and neglect.[14] The costs were in two categories: *direct* (costs associated with the immediate needs of abused or neglected children) and *indirect* (costs of long-term and/or secondary effects of the abuse or neglect). The study attempted to use conservative estimates. Only harmed children were included who were classified as abused or neglected under the more stringent standard of the U.S. Department of Health and Human Services. Nor were all indirect costs included such as provision of public assistance to adults whose condition is a direct result of the abuse and neglect they suffered in their childhoods.

Nevertheless, the study conservatively estimated that child abuse and neglect annually cost $94 billion. The direct costs of $24.4 billion included: hospitalization, chronic health problems, mental health care, the child welfare system, law enforcement, and the judicial system. Indirect costs were included for: special education, mental health and health care, juvenile delinquency, lost productivity to society, and adult criminality, totaling just under $70 billion[15] Of these costs, it was estimated that in 2002, governmental subsidies for child welfare services, promoting safe and stable families, foster care, administration and training, the independent living program, and adoption assistance would cost approximately $7.2 billion.[16]

Child Welfare Services. The goal of child welfare services is to promote the safety and well-being of children and their families and to improve or provide substitutes for functions that parents have difficulty performing. The range of services provided differs from state to state, however, typical services include protection of abused or neglected children, support and preservation of families, care of the homeless and neglected, support for family development, and provision of out-of-home care, including adoptions. Services may help a family cope with problems or protect children while the parents learn parenting skills.

It is commonly agreed that in most circumstances it is better for children to live with their parents and family. In order to accomplish this, preventive and rehabilitative services are provided and there are attempts to limit the duration of foster care placements. If a child must be removed, social workers seek permanent living arrangements for the child. They can return children to their homes as quickly as possible or they can place the child in adoption or other long-term arrangements.

There are many private, voluntary and governmental agencies that provide child welfare services to families in need. However, the primary responsibility for child welfare services is governmental and rests with the states. Each state has its own legal and administrative programs that address the needs of children. The major program service areas are: protective and preventive services, out-of-home care services (foster care), adoption services, child day care, health care services, substance abuse services, housing and homelessness assistance, and youth services, and public assistance (Temporary Assistance for Needy Families).

The Federal and State Governments. Child welfare programs are supported and influenced by national, state, and local laws. The federal government sets policy, promulgates regulations, provides financial assistance to the states, and monitors program operations. States have the major responsibility for development of the programs, administration, and operation of child welfare programs. Child welfare practice and services generally are influenced by legislation and funding. Among the many issues controlled by law are state intervention into the family; prevention of out-of-home placement; foster care reviews; termination of parental rights; adoption of children in foster care; roles of courts and attorneys; interagency collaboration; and the rights of children, birth parents, foster parents, and adoptive parents.[17]

Some of the major legislative acts which give direction to child welfare services include the following: The Child Abuse Prevention and Treatment Act (1974) responded to citizen concerns about child abuse identified during the early 1960s as "the battered child" syndrome. This act provides financial assistance for demonstration programs for the prevention, identification, and treatment of child abuse and neglect, and established a National Center on Child Abuse and Neglect. The law also initiated systematic reporting of known and suspected instances of child abuse and neglect, thus beginning the collection of data about the nature of the problem.

Title XX of the Social Security Act designed to support a broad array of state social services also provides some funds, which are used for child welfare purposes. The states are permitted to select their own pattern of the goals and allocation of services. The Indian Child Welfare Act (1978) created safeguards in matters regarding the custody and placement of Indian children. Tribes have jurisdiction over Indian children, with several state exceptions. The Adoption Assistance and Child Welfare Act (1980) was succeeded by the Adoption and Safe Families Act ([ASFA] 1997). The former act recognized the problems of the child welfare system and promoted empirically validated interventions. The act discouraged state use of custodial foster care, focusing instead on pre-placement preventive services for families in crisis and permanency planning for children to stay with their families. Fiscal incentives were offered to support the use of "best practice" standards in order to provide services to keep families intact. When family preservation is not possible, the act emphasized the provision of continuity of care, time-limited plans, and a range of placements such as guardianship, adoption, or long-term family foster care.

It is estimated that at least one-third of children placed in foster care will never be returned to their birth parents; they need permanent homes. Certain groups wait longer than others to join a new family. Minority children (who make up over 60% of the children in foster care) wait about twice as long as others. African-American children have a lower possibility of adoption than other children. The Multi-Ethnic Placement Act (1994) eliminated laws that favor same-race placements. The law is meant to prevent discrimination in the placement of children in foster care and adoption on the basis of race, color, or national origin, to decrease the time children wait to be adopted, and to ensure agencies recruit a pool of foster and adoptive parents reflecting the ethnic and racial diversity of the children available for adoption.

The Adoption and Safe Families Act (1997) aims at improving the safety of children, promoting adoption and other permanent homes for children who need them, and support for families. This law does the following: Continues and expands the Family Preservation and Support Services program; continues adoption subsidies to children whose adoption was disrupted; provides adoption incentive payments to states; requires states to document efforts to adopt; expands health coverage for eligible adopted children with special health care needs; provides funding for technical assistance to promote adoption; requires states to develop plans that overcome geographical and cross jurisdictional barriers so timely permanent placements can be accomplished; establishes a kinship advisory council; suggests that states should make it possible for parents who are chronically ill or near death to designate a stand-by guardian for the child, without surrendering their own parental rights; and requires states to file a petition to terminate parental rights and concurrently to identify, recruit, and process and approve adoptive homes for any child (regardless of age) who has been in foster care for 15 out of the most recent 22 months.

Poverty and Other Stresses.   We introduced in Chapter 1 the fact that unemployment and poverty contribute to child abuse and neglect and the effects of such poverty will be examined in greater detail in Chapter 15. Suffice it to say that children growing up in many poor families are impacted in a multitude of ways, including that in some families they are abused and neglected and these are exacerbated by the fact that their families are poor. Family problems necessarily impact in subtle and significant ways upon the lives of children. Child welfare services are meant to protect the welfare of children from neglect, abuse, exploitation or delinquency; to prevent unnecessary separations of children from their families and to restore children when possible to their families; to place children in adoptive families when appropriate; and to ensure adequate foster care when children cannot be returned home or be placed for adoption.

There is evidence that poverty and low income are related strongly to child abuse and neglect and to the severity of child maltreatment. Despite the fact that the vast majority of parents with low incomes do not abuse or neglect their children, it is clear that children from low-income families are greatly over-represented in the incidence of child abuse and neglect. Every national survey reports a preponderance of reports involving low income families. These findings, however, have been challenged on the grounds that the studies found correlations between poverty and abuse and neglect and not causation.[18]

Family Preservation Services.   Family preservation services are intended for children and families, including extended and adoptive families that are at risk or in crisis. Services provided include help to reunite children with their biological families—if appropriate—or to place them for adoption or another permanent arrangement; programs to prevent the placement of children in foster care, including intensive family preservation services; follow-up services to families after a child is returned from foster care; respite care to provide temporary relief for parents and other caregivers (including foster parents) and services to improve parenting skills.

Time-limited reunification services aim at facilitating the safe and appropriate reunification of children removed from their homes and placed in foster care. The goal is to do so within 15 months from the date they entered foster care. Some of these services for children and their families are: counseling, substance abuse treatment, mental health services, interventions into domestic violence situations, temporary child are and therapeutic services.

There are differing findings regarding the results of family preservation efforts. According to Ruth McRoy family preservation services have been found to be very effective for many families and can keep children out of the child welfare system. They have been found to improve family functioning, provided service providers emphasize family strengths, provide concrete services, and focus on the developmental needs of each child and family, are culturally competent, and focus on preventing the recurrence of abuse and neglect. Howard Altstein reports, however, that the greater number of researchers examining whether family preservation works in measurable ways set forth by the program designers found no strong association between family preservation and the measurable results. He suggests the efficacy of family preservation, despite the important need for positive interventions and solutions for family dysfunction that affect so many children, is not demonstrated by the evaluation studies conducted.[19]

Family Foster Care.   Family foster care provides planned, time-limited care by families who substitute for the families that cannot care adequately for their children. Social services are also provided for these families to help resolve the problems that led to the placement of the child. The functions of family foster care include emergency protection, crisis intervention, assessment and case planning, reunification, preparation for adoption, and preparation for independent living. Among the types of foster care are: emergency foster care, kinship foster care, foster care by unrelated families, treatment foster care, foster care for children with special medical needs, and small family group home care.

Adoption.   Adoption creates a legal family for a child when the biological family is unable or unwilling serve as parents. Adoption creates new families, expands existing families, and involves new adoptive parents, including relatives' guardianships. Adoption takes many forms. *Independent adoption* of children, most often infants, occurs when children or infants are placed without the prior review of agencies. This sentence seems out of place here. *Agency adoptions* occur when the infant or child is relinquished directly to the agency. The *Adoption Assistance* Program provides help for states to develop adoption assistance agreements with parents who adopt eligible children with special needs. Provided are assistance payments for qualified children who are adopted; administrative expenses for the expenses incurred with placing children in adoption; and training of professional staff and parents involved in adoptions. A special needs child is one who has a specific condition or situation such as age, membership in a minority or sibling group, or a mental, emotional, or physical disability that prevents placement without special assistance. The state must determine the child cannot be returned to the biological family and that reasonable efforts have been made to place the child without providing adoption assistance. States have some discretion in defining special needs eligibility criteria. Some states include religion or not being able to place the child without subsidy to the definition of special needs.

　　Open adoption refers to a continuum of degrees of contact and communication between members of an adopted child's biological family and adoptive family. At one extreme, there are confidential or closed adoptions in which there is no contact and any information shared is general and non-identifying. Intermediate relationships are those in which birth family and adoptive parents communicate using a liaison person, typically a staff member of the adoption agency, but anonymity of both parties is preserved. If there is telephone contact, no names or addresses are revealed. The other extreme is fully disclosed adoptions in which there is direct contact between some birth family members and some adoptive family members.[20]

There are a variety of *residential services* for children and adolescents. Among these services are: group homes for adolescent status offenders; residential treatment for emotionally disturbed children; state schools for adolescent delinquents; shelter care for street children; respite care group homes for developmentally disabled adolescents; group residences for "dependent/neglected" children; and boarding schools for troubled adolescents.

Foster Care Independence Program. The Independent Living Program (the Foster Care Independence Program) was established to assist youths who eventually will be emancipated from the foster care system. This program was initiated when it was discovered that a significant number of homeless shelter residents were recently discharged from foster care. Among the services provided are: counseling; educational services; employment-readiness programs; life skills training; (communication skills, problem solving and decision making, self-management and control, techniques for handling stress, and household and financial skills); mentoring programs that utilize adult volunteers as advocates, teachers, and friends; transitional services from foster care to independence such as supervised apartment living to independent apartment living in the community. Finally, social support networks are provided to ease the transition to independence through association with former foster youth, support groups, and linking the youth to other supportive formal and informal social supports.

Issues. There are recent creative developments designed to provide homes for children who might otherwise not be adoptable such as older children, those from minority backgrounds, those with disabilities, including those with AIDS and babies born addicted to crack cocaine. Social workers in schools, mental health agencies, hospitals, and other settings increasingly recognize the special problems experienced by gay and lesbian young people. Among the new approaches are broadened eligibility rules for adoptive parents. For example, people who are single, older, less wealthy, gay or lesbian are all more readily accepted as adoptive parents today in many locations.

There is research that suggests there are interventions that work in family preservation and family support; in the prevention of child abuse and neglect; in treatment for abused children; in out-of-home care; adoption services; child care; and services for adolescents, including substance-abuse prevention and treatment, and day treatment for delinquent adolescents.[21] But there remain many issues that are debated. Some issues being debated are: Does child abuse result in irreparable harm in adulthood; should foster parents be given first preference in adoption of their foster children; should child welfare workers be graduate social workers; are legal definitions of child abuse too broad; should adoption records be opened; does institutional care do more harm than good?[22]

Mental Health Services

Who Is Eligible for the Program? The intensified need for mental health services during World War II, especially in the military, led to the passage of the National Mental Health Act (1946), which focused attention on the mental health needs of the populace and emphasized treatment and prevention services. This initial step was followed by the establishment of the National Institute of Mental Health in 1959. In 1963, the Mental Retardation Facilities and Community Mental Health Centers and Construction Act provided funds for the construction of community mental health centers, and subsequent amendments funded personnel. Medicaid and Medicare also provide psychiatric services for eligible persons.

Mental health services are designed to promote and maintain mental health, prevent mental illness, and treat and rehabilitate mentally ill persons. Mental health problems involve a range of behaviors—severe impairments requiring hospitalization, behavior that is mildly impairing, as well as the promotion of maximum mental health. Mental health services have not been restricted to treatment of mental illness but also provide supports during life transitions and difficult stresses. However, there has been a shift toward aiming services more toward those with seriously disabling conditions and away from aims such as personal self-fulfillment. This trend has been intensified by managed care and other funding mechanisms. The interrelationship of biological and psychosocial factors has received more emphasis in recent years.

Mental health facilities include both public (state and county) and private psychiatric hospitals. One can either voluntarily commit oneself or be involuntarily committed for treatment on the basis of a court order or following certification by two physicians. When discharged from a hospital, aftercare is often provided for discharged patients in a local community facility. Some psychiatric hospitals also provide ambulatory care. There has been an increase in the number of general hospitals that provide emergency and acute psychiatric services. The VA also provides inpatient, outpatient, and supportive psychiatric services for veterans, as does the federal government for Native Americans.

Community mental health centers provide a variety of services, including emergency services, diagnosis, treatment, referral, and community education and coordination. Community residences and other outpatient services are provided for those who are reentering the community or need less than total hospitalization. Other service providers are self-help groups and nursing homes.

What Is the Form of Benefit? The benefits received in mental health programs are diagnosis, treatment in the hospital or community, long-term or emergency consultation, professional care, case management, and educational services in the community. Recent years have seen the development of community-based services for the chronically mentally ill, with special focus on those who are multiply disabled—for example, mentally ill substance abusers and persons with developmental disabilities who are mentally ill. The homeless who are mentally ill and the minority patient population also have been targets of new initiatives. Community support programs designed to promote functioning in the community and prevent reinstitutionalization have been developed. Under these programs, a case manager coordinates services and advocates for the client. There also has been a growing emphasis on consumer participation. The client gives input into the treatment and medication plan and has access to records.

In addition, there has been increasing interest at the federal level in mental health services for children. To receive federal funding, each state is required to develop a comprehensive service plan for children as well as adults. Mental health services for children and adolescents will be examined in Chapter 15.

How Is the Program Financed?   Using monies from federal block grants, state mental health departments or state health departments operate statewide networks of mental health services. Mental health services are sometimes financed by state departments of education through special education programs. User fees also provide some funds, often on a means-test basis and with sliding scales for clients based on income. Recently, more health insurance plans have become restrictive in their coverage for mental health services, including those provided by social workers. Indigent patients are served by the public mental health system.

What Is the Level of Administration?   The Substance Abuse and Mental Health Services Administration of the U.S. Department of Health and Human Services administers the federal block grant. The National Institute of Mental Health is responsible for the Community Support Program. Other mental health programs are supported by the U.S. Department of Veterans Affairs, the Office of Vocational Rehabilitation, and the Department of Defense. The federal government also provides mental health services to Native Americans. In addition, state and local governments administer mental health systems in every state. A large number of professional associations are involved in mental health services on the national, state, and local levels, as well as organizations such as the National Mental Health Association, a voluntary organization. There is an active consumer movement, including the National Alliance for the Mentally Ill, which supports research and inclusion of family members in treatment planning.

Discussion.   Deinstitutionalization has not lived up to its expectations. Community living is preferable to residence in mental hospitals but persons following discharge require therapeutic and supportive settings and help for using them. Community care has not received the support it needs. This has resulted in many persons being discharged from hospitals still in need of care. In many places this resulted in homeless persons on the street, many of whom are unable to navigate the world and some of whom are dangerous to themselves and others. The mental health system is not well designed to care for the homeless who are mentally ill.

Needed is a well-funded and well organized mental health system with qualified personnel drawn from a wide variety of class and cultural backgrounds, minimization of stigma, more preventive programs (protection of persons at risk), and improving the public acceptance of the need for community programs.[23]

A number of issues confront those concerned with mental health care. What will the future role of state hospitals be? How can additional community resources be found? Will sufficient attention be paid to the need for psychosocial rehabilitation as well as preventive services? What will be the effects of privatization? How can appropriate and sufficient services be provided for minority groups, women, children and adolescents, older adults, the homeless, and those with AIDs? Solutions for these issues depend on financing, civil rights questions, advocacy, as well as planning and coordination.[24]

Corrections

The Massachusetts Bay Colony built a jail in Boston in 1632, adding a correctional alternative to fines, lashing, branding, and mutilation. By 1655, every county in the colony was ordered to erect a correction house for drunkards and petty offenders. Correctional facilities have a long history in the United States.

Who Is Eligible for the Program?   Today youth and adults become "eligible" for correctional services by being convicted of violating federal, state, or city laws, being detained in a correctional facility on a pretrial basis, or being found to be in need of supervision.

What Is the Form of Benefit?   The number of Americans in local jails and state and federal correctional facilities reached 1.2 million in 1997. Many states adopted tougher sentencing laws; some states abolished parole, and other states' parole boards have less discretion than formerly. Also an increasing number of prisoners are incarcerated for parole violations. As one can imagine, a number of additional problems beset prisoners, including those with AIDs and mental illness. There are estimates that more than one in ten people behind bars are suffering from the most severe mental illnesses. Ostensibly, correctional services have as a goal the rehabilitation of the offender. However, in reality, rehabilitation is not the major thrust of the correctional system today so much as are incarceration and punishment. Some say rehabilitation as a goal has proven to be an illusion and should be discarded in favor of crime deterrence. Others claim that rehabilitation has never really been given an adequate trial. Nevertheless, there are correctional services that aim at rehabilitation. Probation departments conduct pretrial investigations of defendants, which enable the court to make a disposition of the case on an informed, individualized basis. Probation is used by the courts as an alternative to incarceration and often includes a mandate for treatment as a condition of release. The offender remains in the community under conditions imposed by the court, under the supervision of a probation officer. Probation officers use the resources of the community to assist the offender to become rehabilitated.

Parole is for offenders who have served some time in a state or federal correctional facility but who are released into the community under supervision and treatment by a parole officer. Jails are city or county custodial institutions in which detainees are held for pretrial determinations and sentences less than a year for a misdemeanor. Prisons are correctional institutions where persons are incarcerated for longer than a year and are state or federal institutions.

Community correctional services include release programs, treatment centers to reintegrate offenders into the community, work-release programs, halfway houses, therapy, counseling, and assistance with training, employment, housing, and other life problems. Probation departments offer diagnostic assessments in order to judge an offender's eligibility for community placement as part of the presentence investigation process. In addition, voluntary community agencies often provide diagnostic and treatment services for pretrial detainees. Both assessment processes are part of a growing movement toward community-based alternatives to incarceration.

Some jails and prisons offer services such as basic adult education, vocational training, alcohol and drug programs, group and individual counseling, job development, and placement services. In recent years, criticisms arose against "coddling" prisoners with recreation, television, and other programs. Most state and federal prisons have mental health programs that offer counseling and psychiatric care.

Certain juvenile delinquency programs sponsored by various subdepartments of the Department of Health and Human Services provide diagnosis, treatment, rehabilitation, and prevention services to delinquent and predelinquent youth, and develop community-based alternatives to imprisonment.

Among new trends in corrections are the expansion of drug treatment programs within the prison system, privately owned and operated prisons, and attention to the needs of special populations—for instance, women caring for young children in prison, the elderly, and persons with AIDS. Shock incarceration programs are a new and expanding alternative approach for young adult offenders. In these programs, offenders spend several months in a highly structured experience similar to military boot camps and then may be supervised in the community. On the other hand, there is also a trend toward more client-oriented, flexible approaches in juvenile detention, including minimum security detention, in which a more positive, supportive environment is developed.

Although some persons have lately despaired of rehabilitation as a goal of corrections, most people agree that jails and prisons tend to reinforce criminal attitudes. Therefore, the tendency is to support the idea of incarceration only for the "hardened" criminal as both a deterrent to crime and as a protection to society, and to use various community-based programs for the "nonhardened" criminal. Therefore, the social welfare system is likely to increase its interaction with corrections in the coming years.

How Is the Program Financed?   The Violent Crime Control and Law Enforcement Act (1994) emphasized the construction of new prisons, boot camps, and other facilities, funding for additional police officers, and prevention programs.

The Bureau of Prisons and Board of Parole, funded by general federal revenues, is part of the U.S. Department of Justice. State and local correctional programs are funded by state and local jurisdictions from general revenues.

The federal role in the criminal justice system has several facets. Within the Department of Justice, the Bureau of Prisons is responsible for federal prisons and community-based facilities. The National Institute of Corrections provides technical assistance and training for state and local correctional agencies throughout the country and provides grants for research, evaluation, and program development. The Community Corrections and Detention Division is responsible for the Bureau's community corrections and detention programs. The Bureau of Justice Statistics is responsible for collecting, analyzing, publishing, and disseminating statistical information on the criminal justice system, crime, its perpetrators and victims, probation, and parole at all levels of government. The National Institute of Justice is the primary research and development agency to provide the knowledge needed to prevent and reduce crime and improve the criminal justice system.

The Office of Juvenile Justice and Delinquency Prevention oversees grants to states, and provides funds to public and private nonprofit agencies and individuals to foster new approaches to delinquency prevention and control and to the improvement of the juvenile justice system. The Research and Program Development Division sponsors research about national trends in juvenile delinquency, drug use, serious juvenile crime, the causes of delinquency, prevention strategies, program evaluation, and improvement of the juvenile justice system. The division also sponsors training for juvenile justice practitioners and technical assistance in planning, funding, establishing, operating, and evaluating juvenile delinquency programs. Data on adults and juveniles are collected by the Federal Bureau of Investigation for its Uniform Crime Reports, including violent crimes, property crimes, and status offenses. Although not precisely part of the correctional system, the Social Security Act through Title XX makes funds available at the discretion of the states for programs for Persons in Need of Supervision (PINS) and Children in Need of Supervision (CHINS). These youths have not broken the law or committed an offense. They are, however, seen as being in need of supervision because of incorrigible behavior. Many of these children are treated through the voluntary child welfare system in either group homes or residential treatment settings often funded by the school districts under their Committees for Special Education.

What Is the Level of Administration?   The offices mentioned previously administer research and program demonstration grants on a federal level and assist state and local authorities in the correctional field. As noted, the Bureau of Prisons, National Institute of Corrections, Community Corrections and Detention Division, the Bureau of Justice Statistics, the National Institute of Justice, and the various units in the Office of Juvenile Justice and Delinquency Prevention all administer various parts of the correctional system. The Department of Defense also administers a correctional facility program. State and local governments operate their own facilities and programs, but there has been an increase in contracting jail services to private corporations. There is no overall coordination of the several levels of correctional programs, and facilities and combinations of state and local correctional programs take many forms.

Summary

In chapters 9 and 10, we examined public programs that provide the major income security and life-sustaining services. In chapter 11, we will describe and examine social welfare in the private sector, including the roles of voluntary, nonprofit organizations and of profit-making enterprises. We will discuss their interrelationships with each other as well as with the predominant public, governmental sector.

Questions for Consideration _____

1. Aside from Medicare's contribution to health care for the elderly, what economic and social roles does it play for the children and other family members of beneficiaries?

2. Can you locate any research findings that relate school lunch and breakfast programs to student learning?

3. What are the arguments for and against the federal and/or state governments' serving as "employers of last resort" for those who cannot obtain employment?

4. Identify and make a list of the personal social services, both public and private, in your community. Can you categorize them in some way?

Notes _____

1. Michael M. Weinstein, "Will Patients' Rights Fix the Wrongs?" *New York Times, Week In Review,* June 24, 2001, pp. 1 and 4.

2. Tracy Miller, "Managed Care Regulation in the Laboratory of the States," *Journal of the American Medical Association,* Vol. 278, No. 13, October 1, 1997, 1102–1109.

3. Gerald Schamess, "Who Profits and Who Benefits from Managed Mental Health Care?" *Smith College Studies in Social Work,* Vol. 66, No. 3, June 1996, 217–218.

4. Carlton E. Munson, "Autonomy and Managed Care in Clinical Social Work Practice," *Smith College Studies in Social Work,* Vol. 66, No. 3, June 1996, 241–260; Joan Shapiro, "The Downside of Managed Mental Health Care," *Clinical Social Work Journal,* Vol. 23, No. 4, Winter 1995, 441–451.

5. *2000 Green Book,* p. 118.

6. Ray Honig and Stacy Dean, "States' Vehicle Asset Policies in the Food Stamp Program," Center

on Budget and Policy Priorities, www.cbpp.org, July 30, 2001; Elizabeth Becker, "Millions Eligible for Food Stamps Aren't Applying," *New York Times,* February 26, 2001, pp. 1, A11.

7. *2000 Green Book,* p. 960.

8. Robert Greenstein, "Latest Data Show Significant Cuts in WIC Program Would Be Necessary in 2002 Under Administration's Budget and House Bill," Center on Budget and Policy Priorities, www.cbpp. org/8-14-01bud.htm, September 28, 2001.

9. U.S. Department of Agriculture, Food and Nutrition Services, Barbara Devaney, Linda Bilheimer, and Jennifer, Schore, *The Savings in Medicaid Costs for Newborns and Their Mothers From Prenatal Participation in the WIC Program,* Vol. 2, www.fns.usda.gov/wic, July 30, 2001.

10. Elliott S. Fisher and H. Gilbert Welch, "The Future of the Department of Veterans' Affairs Health Care System," *Journal of the American Medical Association,* Vol. 273, February 22, 1995, 651–655;

James A. Pittman, "The Future of Veterans' Affairs: Utilization, Costs, Politics, and Presentism," *Journal of the American Medical Association,* Vol. 273, Editorial, February 22, 1995, 667–668.

11. The Workforce Investment Act of 1998, http://www.reg10.doleta.gov/wia_nga.htm, October 11, 1998.

12. Robert Morris and Delwin Anderson, "Personal Care Services: An Identity for Social Work," *Social Service Review,* Vol. 49, No. 2, June 1975, 157–174.

13. The following descriptive statistics are from the National Clearinghouse on Child Abuse and Neglect Information, "Highlights from *Child Maltreatment 1999,*" www.calib.com/ccanch/pubs/factsheets/canstats.cfm, September 21, 2001.

14. 2001 Prevent Child Abuse America, "Total Estimated Cost of Child Abuse and Neglect in the United States: Statistical Evidence," www.preventchildabuse.org, September 21, 2001.

15. Ibid.

16. Committee on Ways and Means, U.S. House of Representatives, *2000 Green Book, Background Material and Data on programs Within the Jurisdiction of the Committee on Ways and Means,* U.S. Government Printing Office, Washington: 2000, p. 648.

17. Peter J. Pecora, James K. Whitaker, Anthony N. Maluccio, and Richard P. Barth, with Robert Plotnick, *The Child Welfare Challenge: Policy, Practice, and Research,* New York: Aldine D Gruyter, 2000, p. 302.

18. Leroy H. Pelton and Joel S. Milner, "Is Poverty a Key Contributor to Child Maltreatment?" in *Controversial Issues in Child Welfare,* Eileen Gambrill and Theodore J. Stein, Eds. Boston: Allyn & Bacon, 1994, pp. 16–28.

19. Howard Altstein and Ruth McRoy, *Does Family Preservation Serve a Child's Best Interests?* Washington, D.C.: Georgetown University Press, 2000.

20. Richard P. Barth, Noelle Gallant, Harold D. Grotevant, and Gina Alexander, "Adoption Services," in *What Works in Child Welfare,* Miriam P. Kluger, Gina Alexander, and Patrick A. Curtis, Eds. Washington, D.C.: Child Welfare League of America, 2000, pp. 215–265.

21. Kluger, Alexander, and Curtis, op. cit.

22. Gambrill and Stein, eds. Op cit.

23. Philip Fellin, *Mental Health and Mental Illness,* Itasca, IL: F. E. Peacock Publishers, Inc., 1996.

24. Bernard J. Gallagher III, *The Sociology of Mental Illness,* 3rd Edition, Englewood Cliffs, NJ: Prentice Hall, 1995.

Nonprofit and Private Social Welfare

As soon as several of the inhabitants of the United States have taken up an opinion or a feeling which they wish to promote in the world, they look out for mutual assistance; and as soon as they have found each other out, they combine.

—Alexis de Tocqueville[1]

Overview

For centuries, the efforts of nonprofit or voluntary social welfare agencies enriched the social welfare offerings and capabilities of U.S. society, unleashed the energies of millions of persons in creative helping efforts, and developed a diversity of mutual aid and nonprofit social welfare organizations. In recent decades, the nonprofit or voluntary sector has been joined by a growing phenomenon: social welfare services provided for profit. In this chapter, we examine the contemporary situation and issues of the nonprofit and private sectors within the context of U.S. society. To do so, we must understand the complexity of the U.S. economy, including the *nonprofit* (voluntary), *private for-profit*, and *governmental* (public) sectors. The nonprofit sector has been identified in several ways, including the charitable, independent, voluntary, tax-exempt and civil society sector.[2] We will refer to profit-seeking organizations as *private*, although historically nonprofits also have been referred to as voluntary private agencies.

Early Patterns

During the colonial period in America, the line between public and nonprofit responsibilities in the area of social welfare was less sharply drawn than in later times. In fact, there was a cooperative approach. The overseers of the poor called on churches for special collections when funds were needed, and the bequeathing of property to public authorities was a favored form of charity.[3]

Both nonprofit and public social welfare tended to be small-scale, local efforts provided for neighbors in relatively small settlements. At later stages, as we saw earlier, nonprofit social welfare became more varied and expansive and, still later in the 1930s, public welfare burgeoned in response to massive human need.

The Nonprofit Sector

There are several types of nonprofit and private social welfare. Because of the changing nature of this social welfare sector, certain characteristics of nonprofit organizations and for-profit businesses have become ambiguous and confusing.

Both *nonprofit* and *private* organizations fulfill ideological roles. Those who favor limited government wish to enhance both the nonprofit and private sectors in order to minimize what is perceived as governmental growth. Others who fear governmental intrusion in personal and communal life also wish to encourage these approaches. There are still others who wish to encourage nonprofit social welfare because to do so promotes a sense of mutual aid and community participation.

Several theories have been suggested for the existence of the modern nonprofit sector:

1. This sector exists to supply goods and services that are needed as a result of market and governmental failures or that are not yet offered through public policy. These goods and services are not desired or needed by society as universal commodities; therefore the nonprofit sector exists to provide services needed by only a segment of the community. As such, they are vehicles for the expression of diverse opinions and new ideas. The more pluralistic and diverse the population, the greater the expected size of the nonprofit sector.

2. Because nonprofit agencies are not in business to make money, it is assumed that their primary motivation is the delivery of services of quality. They can protect those who are most vulnerable, such as the frail elderly or those who are disabled. They may be the most appropriate or best vehicle to provide an advocacy and ombudsperson function for the sake of clients, sometimes in an adversarial position with the government. Such a function will always remain needed in the best of societies, and it is only the nonprofit agency that can devote itself to such causes.

3. Nonprofits are a first-line series of services, not just secondary supports. They can specialize in a problem or a method of intervention. They can advocate on behalf of people with special needs. And they can help organize peer self-help and other consumer-sponsored organizations.

4. Nonprofit agencies are thought by some to have greater potential than governmental agencies to minimize bureaucratization, rigidity, and impersonality. This is because it is difficult to mobilize governmental action in relation to many social problems.

5. The nonprofit, voluntary agency is the only one that appropriately should deliver sectarian services or services for any special ethnic or interest group. Public services are and should be open equally to all citizens and should not be geared toward a specific position or point of view. On the other hand, it is quite legitimate in a plural society for Catholics, for example, to want to instill values of Catholicism among Catholic youth and to do this in the context of recreational or leisure-time activities. It is quite legitimate for African Americans to appreciate their common heritage and seek their empowerment. Ethnicity and cultural pluralism are hallmarks of the United States scene and should be nurtured and continued. And it is only the nonprofit agency that can devote itself to such causes.

6. There is a growing recognition of the importance of self-help groups from Alcoholics Anonymous to postmastectomy groups. These groups harness volunteer energies of citizens, save money, and provide a unique form of help, which is impossible in a more bureaucratized or public system.

Nonprofit organizations create social networks and relationships that connect people to each other and to institutions. As they work together for mutual goals, trust and cooperation—essential for the functioning of society, politics, and the economy—are built.

Nonprofit services also have certain limitations. Among these are the following: (1) They focus on particular problems, groups, or individuals. By focusing in this way, gaps are created, and nonprofit aid may be uneven and constantly changing. (2) Nonprofit resources are often insufficient, (3) The use by government of nonprofits to deliver services can buffer government from criticism, diverting credit or blame but also potentially undermining support for needed governmental programs; (4) Wealthy communities can provide for their own needs but fail to provide taxes for education and health services needed by low income persons.[4]

Types of Nonprofit Agencies

Classic Nonprofit Board-Directed Agency.   Historically in the United States, nonprofit social welfare agencies served myriad social welfare aims. These nonprofit agencies initially were staffed by volunteers and only later turned to employed staff. They were incorporated by the state under specific legislation. They have boards of directors, which are accountable for the policy and implementation of all facets of the organization. Members of the board may come from the population to be served or from other backgrounds useful to the maintenance and advancement of the nonprofit organization.

Federated Local or National Service Agency.   The United Way is an example of a federated local or national service agency. It was founded by and is sponsored by a group of agencies and serves to coordinate, raise funds, do research and planning, and generally support the efforts of other nonprofit agencies. Such a federated organization may be formed at local, state, regional, or national levels. A wide range of national service agencies exist to support the efforts of local and state agencies such as the Girl Scouts, Family Service associations, and Catholic Charities, among others.

Indigenous Self-Help Mutual Aid Group.   Alcoholics Anonymous, Nar-Anon, Recovery Inc., and Parents Anonymous are examples of indigenous self-help mutual aid groups. Many groups of this type begin as informal mutual aid efforts by those who are faced with a problem. Later, as the programs develop, there often evolves a need for paid staff members, as there are service constraints that arise with a totally volunteer-run organization. The Association for Help for Retarded Children is an example of an organization begun by volunteers as a mutual aid effort that developed into a highly complex and broad-based organization designed to serve the needs of persons with developmental disabilities and their families. As these organizations evolve, they become more formal and must meet certain legal requirements; they incorporate, elect a board of directors, and in other ways take on the trappings of a formal social welfare agency.

The Conduit or Vendor Agency.   A conduit or vendor agency can serve as the deliverer of public funds and grants or grants from nonprofit foundations, or as the vendor and provider of public services through a nonprofit or for-profit mechanism. Nonprofit and private agencies may deliver services where the public sector chooses not to do so because of cost, a lack of human or other resources, or a philosophical commitment to the nonprofit or private sector. Public agencies may purchase a service for a group of consumers or may provide grants to particular agencies so that they can deliver the service on behalf of the public agency.

Quasi-Governmental Organization.   One hybrid type of agency is the quasi-governmental organization, which is largely or completely dependent on governmental funds, although its structure is like the classic board-directed agency. The RAND Corporation, the Hudson Institute, as well as some institutes for the study of poverty, welfare, law and other "thinktanks" are examples of the quasi-governmental, quasi-nonprofit type of organization. Other examples of quasi-governmental agencies are regional transportation agencies such as BART, SEPTA, or the Port Authority in the San Francisco Bay area, Philadelphia, and New York, respectively. These agencies and others like them are neither governmental nor nonprofit/private. They are run by boards and administrators who are not elected but have been appointed by elected officials.

The Proprietary Private For-Profit Organization

Traditionally, most students of social welfare did not include profit-making organizations as part of the social welfare system. From our perspective in today's world, there is every reason to consider such organizations to be a part of social welfare. Child care agencies, nursing homes, homemaker services, mental health and substance abuse treatment centers, camps, and many other forms of human services are provided through the for-profit sector. Employee assistance programs provide services to workers and sometimes to their families as part of their overall business effort.

In addition, the boundaries between public and nonprofit/private sectors have become more ambiguous as funding for both nonprofit and for-profit agencies often derives from the public sector. In order to grasp the totality of social welfare, it is necessary to account for those services provided under public auspices, those services that are in the nonprofit sector, and those services that are provided by for-profit organizations in the marketplace at large.

A major source of economic security today is private pensions, supplementing income from Social Security and personal savings. These pensions are a part of fringe benefits provided by industry sometimes with worker contributions and sometimes administered by labor unions. Pensions, also, may be based on individual investments subject to government regulation.

Services of the Nonprofit and Private Sectors

One can find a rich array of social welfare and health agencies and services in major metropolitan areas with more limited services available in rural locations. If we look at these agencies more closely, we find that the nonprofit sector emphasizes personal and rehabilitative services, as well as services specifically for ethnic, racial, religious, lifestyle, sexual orientation, and disability groups. In contrast, the public sector provides the primary services for income security, medical and health services, housing, education, human resource development, corrections, and child welfare. The nonprofits may contribute to each of these latter areas to a degree, but the paramount contributions are made by the public sector. For-profit agencies are often found in health care, nursing homes, counseling services, substance abuse rehabilitation, and services for children and aging persons.

People may make use of a number of services and, depending upon their particular circumstances and needs, may not limit their use to public, for-profit, or nonprofit services. For example, in some communities, one can find a number of services for aging persons, including clubs, centers, nutrition programs, counseling, residential facilities, telephone reassurance and emergency services, as well as vacation facilities. Aging persons may utilize concurrently homemaker services, health services, financial assistance, housing services, a senior citizens center, and public transportation to reach the needed services. But it is often the case that persons with particular personal or family needs are unfamiliar with the available resources that could be of assistance. Information and referral services have developed that can enable persons in need to find their way to the appropriate services.

Many local agencies are participants in national coordinating organizations. Membership of local organizations in national bodies—such as the YMCA;

YWCA; Alliance for Children and Families; Child Welfare League of America; and Jewish Community Centers Association—provides the local organization with services, which range from referral of potential employees to providing consultation and publications. The degree of national control varies; some are organized as loose federations, leaving the ultimate authority to the local agency. Others set standards, priorities, and program policy at the national level.

Getting and Spending

Total spending for social welfare purposes in 1930 consisted of $1.474 billion expended in the nonprofit sector (1.6 percent of the gross national product [GNP]) and $4.085 billions spent in the public sector (4.5 percent of GNP) for a total expenditure of $5.5 billion. By 1995, even with retrenchments in social welfare, *public* (federal, state, and local) social welfare expenditures amounted to $1.5 trillion (20.9 percent of gross domestic product [GDP]) and 67.5 percent of total government outlays. The larger shares of these expenditures were made on social insurances (income security and health), education, and a much smaller share on welfare services.[5]

Private-sector social welfare expenditures (health and medical care, income maintenance, education, and welfare services) almost doubled from 7.7 percent of GDP in 1972 to 13.3 percent in 1994. Included in these private expenditures are health and medical care expenditures, education, income maintenance (group life insurance, supplemental unemployment benefits, sickness and disability benefits, long-term disability, and employment-related pension plans), and welfare services, including individual and family counseling and referral services, adoption services, emergency and disaster services, child day care, senior citizen services, residential care (group foster homes, halfway homes, care and shelters for the homeless, recreation and group work, job training, sheltered workshops, vocational and skill training workshops). In 1994, health care alone accounted for more than 57 percent of total private-sector expenditures and welfare services only 9 percent.[6]

The magnitude of public expenditures far outweighed spending by the private and nonprofit social welfare sectors. Nonetheless, in 1994 expenditures by the private and nonprofit social welfare sectors were sizable. One can observe in Table 11.1 that in 1994 $.9 trillion, including health spending, was expended (13.3 percent of GDP). Although these private expenditures were large, they were much smaller than those made in the public sector. Together the public, private, and nonprofit social welfare sectors are major economic forces.

In 2000, Americans contributed $203.45 billion to nonprofit organizations. Approximately 83 percent of this amount was given by individual donors (including bequests) and the remainder was given by foundations and corporations. These contributions have remained relatively stable at 2 percent of the GDP with some minor fluctuation since 1966.[7] All charitable contributions in 2000 amounted to only 13.5 percent of public social welfare expenditures in 1995, only a miniscule proportion of such expenditures in 2000 and later. It should be clear from these fig-

TABLE 11.1 *Private Social Welfare Spending by Category: 1972–1994 and Percent of Gross Domestic Product (in millions)*

Total	Health	Income Maintenance	Education	Welfare Services	%GDP
1972					
$96.3	$55.8	$17.1	$14.8	$7.57	7.7%
1994					
$921.4	$528.6	$204.7	$101.8	$86.2	13.3%

Source: Wilmer L. Kerns, "Private Social Welfare Expenditures, 1972–94," *Social Security Bulletin*, Vol. 60, No. 1, 1997, p. 55.

ures that calls for the nonprofit and private sectors to replace any major government programs are simply political rhetoric. The nonprofit and private sector and the public sector operate on totally different scales. In fact, in 1995 funding public assistance and Supplemental Security Income (SSI) alone would have cost $53 billion.[8]

Contributions generally are allocated by donors in descending order to religion; education; health; human services; arts and culture; public/society (e.g., United Way, community action agencies, research institutes, community economic development); environment; and international affairs. Historically, the major proportion of all philanthropic funding has gone to religious associations.[9]

In addition to the large size of nonprofit social welfare expenditures, another indicator suggesting the complexity of the nonprofit sector is that of the 22.4 million national nonprofit associations in 2000 there were 1.9 million such organizations devoted to social welfare.[10]

As noted earlier, occupational benefits also account for large social welfare expenditures. The dimensions of the pension and health plan coverage for employees reflect the substantial amount of social welfare services provided by private-enterprise, profit-seeking businesses.

In addition to those services provided by business and industry for their employees, in recent years there has been a push to "privatize" many governmental services—for example, mass transit, garbage disposal, and the operation of prisons. Early in the 21st century, there are ongoing attempts to privatize public assistance, job training, placement, and support; child support enforcement; and management, computerization, and child welfare services such as foster care and adoptions. These privatization efforts have not always been successful in efficiency, goal attainment, cost savings, and profitability.

Privatization efforts are a result of ideological, budgetary, and political forces. Olasky in *The Tragedy of American Compassion* indicted all governmental social welfare and argued that all social welfare efforts should be returned to the private and religious institutions.[11] Various arguments are put forward to make a case for privatization. Among these are that privatization means competition and choice. Prices and profits as motivators will do a better job at helping people. Privatized services will become more efficient and therefore less costly; they will serve as a competitive spur to the public sector; and they will prod the public sector on to greater efficiency. Over the past quarter of a century, privatization of community-based social services developed as a primary method of delivering social services, also stimulating more attention to accountability issues in the non-profit and governmental areas.[12]

In 1998, 1 in 20 federal prison inmates was in a for-profit prison. More than one in every eight hospital beds was in investor-owned hospitals. Some want to privatize as one strategy to roll back governmentally provided services. Others, opposing privatization, point out that it sometimes results in a "creaming" of clients. They argue that the difficult and costly clients are avoided and, in fact, referred or channeled to the public sector, which must then pick up the greater per capita cost. There is also no guarantee that privatized services will not suffer from precisely the shortcomings sometimes identified in public sector programs. As pointed out in chapter 10, there are early stirrings of a backlash against complete market philosophies in profit-minded managed care and hospitals. Where the line should be drawn is an important question as our society seeks a balance between market forces and humane concern. Does the public interest coincide with private interests, and if it doesn't, how can private for-profit companies adequately be regulated?

Recent studies found that the privatization movement of the late 1980s and early 1990s lost some momentum during the 1990s. This may be due to several factors, including the political power of public employees and the improving fiscal situation of local governments. Some local governments turned to contracting out (privatization), while others simply dropped the service, which left residents to seek services from other providers.[13]

Few challenge the right of nonprofit social welfare agencies to receive tax- deductible donations. During the early 1990s, however, several United Way scandals occurred concerning the theft of charity funds, excessive salaries, and misuse of funds by high-level administrators. These incidents led to increased mistrust by potential givers and years of declining fund-raising support. Donations began to rise in 1997.

As a result of the United Way scandal, attention began to focus also on some nonprofit organizations' legal but easily abused use of for-profit subsidiaries. Among the types of abuse discovered have been concurrent pay for employment in the nonprofit and for-profit affiliates, nepotism, concealed employee identities, and shifting revenue to the nonprofit and expenses to the for-profit side for tax purposes. Although most experts agree that most charities and foundations operate within the law, detecting which are legitimate and which abusive is sometimes difficult because of the ability of these organizations to operate with high degrees of privacy. On the state level, states have focused mainly on full compensation disclosure, including transactions between an organization and its board members. The Internal Revenue Service (IRS) steps in where there are large sums to be recovered and/or there is blatant fraud. There is some concern that these events diminish donations.[14]

In 1998, the IRS implemented the Taxpayer Bill of Rights 2 (1996) which requires tax-exempt groups to make available copies of their tax returns (Form 990) to anyone who requests to inspect them in person or by mail. They must be made available during regular business hours at the organization's principal office. Only reasonable fees for reproduction or mailing costs can be charged.[15]

Another major challenge to the operation of nonprofit social agencies concerned forays into for-profit territory. Because of reduced government funding, constrained government services, and inflation, some nonprofit organizations entered the competitive marketplace to sell various items and services, from calendars to health club memberships to insurance. Businesses were threatened by such competition, and complaints were registered that nonprofits in certain cases were taking unfair advantage of their tax-deductible status to compete in areas impinging on the potential of the private for-profit sector. As a result, some tax exempt organizations make payments to local government in lieu of taxes.

There are those who recommend that nonprofit organizations be far more restricted from engaging in unrelated business activities that are outside their tax-exempt activities. Generating revenues and making profit, it was argued, is unfair competition, because nonprofit organizations operate under different rules and regulations than private, profit-seeking firms. They have special advantages such as exemption from taxation.[16] Other critics argued that profit-making actions divert the organization from its primary social aims and place strains on management. The ability to define client needs and to shape services may shift to the marketplace, undermining the authority of the staff and board of directors.

There is another economic dimension to the nonprofit sector, the monetary value of volunteering. There are estimates that in 1998 55 percent of the adult population served as volunteers for an average of 3.5 hours per week. Assigning a value of $14.83 per hour (average hourly wage for non-agricultural workers), the estimated annual value of volunteer time in 2000 was the equivalent of $226 billion and over 9 million full-time employees.[17]

Private and Nonprofit Agencies as Social Welfare Programs

Who Is Eligible for the Programs?

Private and nonprofit social welfare agencies provide services for people who have experienced almost every human risk: job loss, poor mental or physical health, low income, and inadequate housing, and so on. They provide preventive, rehabilitative, and personal- and family-fulfillment services. Agencies are sponsored under both sectarian (religious) and nonsectarian auspices. They offer services based on the needs of the local community and neighborhood services directed at particular groups (such as African Americans, Catholics, Latinos, West Indians, women, and persons with disabilities). Services are dependent on the context and history of the community and the agency itself. Programs in the nonprofit sector often are offered on a fee-for-service basis, on a sliding scale according to income, or on membership or user fees. For-profit programs require payment either by the consumer or by a third party. Some nonprofit services, such as American Red Cross disaster relief, are offered on demand without fee. Increasingly, as nonprofit and private agencies administer public programs, the public regulations for eligibility apply. In business and industrial settings, social welfare services are available for the employees and sometimes for spouses and children.

What Is the Form of Benefit?

Almost the total range of social welfare services is present in private and nonprofit agencies, and a significant number and type of benefits are distributed in relation to the workplace. Pensions of varying types are provided by many business and industrial concerns so that long-term economic security is provided in the work arena as well as in the public sphere. Private and union pensions are a significant economic force, and the federal government has established rules to protect the rights of contributors. In addition, benefits found in workplaces include health, medical, and hospital insurance; food, recreation, library, and other facilities; counseling, referral, and mental health services; drug abuse and alcohol treatment; day care; and physical health services.

Nonprofit agencies emphasize, to a greater extent than public agencies, services for social development such as youth services and recreation. These agencies also serve as "guardians." For example, there are consumer organizations that police and critique the government or help clients understand their rights. However, nonprofit agencies since the Great Depression have been involved to a much lesser degree than public agencies in economic security, being limited generally to short-term emergencies or supplementing public funds in special situations.

Nonprofit agencies directly or as vendors of publicly mandated services provide food (hot lunches), housing (nursing homes and residences for the well elderly), homemaker and home help services, rehabilitation, mental health services, child welfare services, and a host of other benefits such as services for military personnel and their families (Red Cross), rehabilitation (Good Will Industries), skills training (Lighthouse for the Blind), family planning (Planned Parenthood), general services to merchant marines (United Seaman's Service), and emergency aid (Salvation Army).

Community centers and settlement houses provide many services including community development, adult education, socialization, and recreation. Hospitals and ancillary organizations provide a range of medical and health care services. Health and welfare councils coordinate nonprofit agencies and their services in a community. The United Way or similar organizations raise money for distribution to the social agencies in a city or region.

How Are the Programs Financed?

Funding for private and nonprofit agencies is derived in varying patterns from a number of sources: private contributions, fees (membership or users' fees), payment for services by individuals or third parties, donations, governmental purchase of services and contracts, funds from communal fund-raising agencies (such as the United Way or a local Federation of Social Agencies), endowment funds, and payments from governmental sources in the form of subsidies, goods, third-party payments, and governmental and private foundation grants.

Contributions to nonprofit welfare agencies are tax deductible, provided the agency is recognized by the Internal Revenue Service as a qualified organization. This policy supports the voluntary factor in society and diversity of nonprofit agencies and services. Local affiliates of national organizations help through dues or other fees to support their national umbrella organizations such as the YMCA; Boy Scouts; Girl Scouts; Jewish Community Centers; Catholic Charities; Alliance for Children and Families; and the Child Welfare League.

Fund-raising organizations have proliferated in every imaginable direction. In addition to competing with more organizations, communitywide fund-raising such as that of the United Way has been influenced by "designated giving," in which contributors specify the particular agencies or programs to which they want their contributions directed. This results in a multitude of donors deciding where dollars will be spent. One consequence of these factors is that communitywide fund-raising efforts originally formed for reasons of efficiency become less so, and efforts at coordinated planning also may be diminished.

Several concerns have arisen because of the purchase of services strategy used by governments. Nonprofit agencies fear their potential loss of independence. In some cases, agencies sell their services to the government for negotiated payments, typically on a unit-cost basis. If the agency does not receive adequate reimbursement, it must make up the deficit by seeking additional funds. In this case, there are hidden costs to the agency related to uses of staff time to offset the losses. If, on the other hand, it is reimbursed fully, the reimbursement rate may be sufficient to entice competitive profit-making organizations into the situation. Furthermore, if there is no cost advantage, the government may decide to operate the program itself. The chase of single, narrow, time-limited grants may shift an agency into fragmentation and veer it away from its original mission. In addition, the pursuit of governmental grants is conducted in an uncertain and anxiety-producing environment where there are frequent policy, legislative, and guideline shifts, constant uncertainty about budgets, and many resources needed for grant seeking.

Over the past few decades, there has been a rapid growth in privatization through purchase of service contracts. In fact this mode has become a primary method for the delivery of services, accompanied by increasing attention being paid to accountability. With an emphasis on client outcomes, the use of performance contracts has spread as non-governmental agencies and businesses have become involved in case management, substance abuse, job training and job placement, adult mental health services, community care for disabled adults, housing assistance for the homeless, supported living for those with developmental disabilities, nutrition, homemaker services, day care, family preservation, and adoption and foster care services.[18]

Another increasingly popular mechanism used by wealthy entrepreneurs is an enhanced privatization or market strategy for the distribution of funds. Instead of simply awarding money through grants to human service agencies, some philanthropists start or purchase companies that will generate profits for philanthropic uses. This is a fast-growing area of philanthropic efforts. The National Venture Capital Association listed 18 (doubled in one year) such organizations devoted to philanthropic efforts but entirely through privatization and the encouragement of business efforts.

What Are the Levels of Administration?

There is no overall organization that administers or coordinates private and nonprofit social welfare agencies, although the national nonprofit agencies do act in concert to protect their interests. Organizations can be established on the local, state, regional, and national levels. There are various degrees of autonomy for social agencies, ranging from independence (with the exception of responsibility and accountability to the state through incorporation and guidelines) to control by a council or national organization. Private and voluntary social welfare agencies are legally responsible to a governmental body and, therefore, are never entirely free agents. The use of nonprofit and for-profit agencies to deliver and manage services is based on the belief that the private sector will provide better care more efficiently because it is open to market pressures to control costs and prices.

There are mixed findings regarding comparative costs; however, one national study uncovered significant information. Utilizing data from a national survey of the Drug Abuse System, public and private (nonprofit and for-profit) outpatient substance abuse treatment units were studied. For-profit units reported that smaller proportions of their clients leave treatment involuntarily or because they are incarcerated. A higher proportion of clients are reported as meeting their treatment goals at the time of discharge. It was also found that for-profit units charge more for their services and generated proportionately more surplus revenues for the services they provide. Other findings included that for-profit units serve a smaller proportion of clients who are under age 20, are unemployed, are unable to pay for treatment, or who have multiple drug problems. It was found that for-profit units serve a less disabled, less vulnerable, and more resourceful pool of clients. The implication of these findings is that for-profit units occupy and operate within a distinct organizational niche or segment of the market. They specialize, and the niche makes it possible for them to be protected from market forces, ironically, the very forces that privatization was intended to draw upon.[19]

These findings indicate that the for-profit units "creamed" the potential clients. This undermines the capacity of the nonprofits and public programs, which lose potential income from clients able to pay for the services and are left to serve those with the fewest resources.

A Point of View

From our perspective, the choice is not governmental services versus private- and nonprofit-sponsored services. Governmental services are neither a totally "good" organizational and philosophical approach, nor are governmentally sponsored social welfare services an "evil" to be shunned at all costs and minimized. But this is also true of the nonprofit and private sectors as well. Instead, there is need for governmental, private, and nonprofit services. The important question is whether a *particular* service can be better performed under governmental, private, or non-profit auspices. For ourselves, we do not view these different types of approaches as completely trichotomous. Furthermore, it is our belief that governmental, non-profit, and private efforts have the ability to "free up" citizen creativity. They have grown in tandem, although governmental services are much larger in scope and funding. The private and nonprofit sectors cannot replace governmental social welfare in its entirety. The proper balance and most effective use of various aus-pices, consistent with American political and economic ideals and realities, is re-quired for a healthy American social welfare system. Further, although nonprofit and private organizations may compete, there is much to be learned about how they most effectively can collaborate with each other and governmental agencies.

Leadership, Class, and Gender

Nonprofit associations are voluntary, mutual aid efforts to provide services. There is no economic profit to be gained by participants in these organizations other than salaries and the perquisites that accompany some high-level positions. In ad-dition to paid staff, many persons participate as volunteers; that is, they receive no remuneration for their services. Some volunteers provide the direct services of the agency while others serve in policy-making and fund-raising roles as members of boards of directors, trustees, committees, or special task forces.

Certain characteristics have been found among persons who serve as volun-teers in the nonprofit sector. One is more likely to volunteer if one's background includes higher income, educational levels, and occupational and family status; if one owns property; and if one volunteers for multiple organizations. Socioeco-nomic status is also associated with the kinds of organizations for which one vol-unteers. Blue-collar volunteers tend to volunteer for churches, unions, fraternal societies, and recreational centers. Middle- and upper-class persons tend to volun-teer in general interest organizations, business and professional organizations, and service, cultural, educational, and political pressure groups.[20]

The vast majority of board membership today consists of persons from higher socioeconomic groups. These people may be more attractive recruits for many non-profit agencies because of their access to money, community leaders, and other re-sources. Volunteers, through their participation, typically value the mission and goals of the organization and gain feelings of security and usefulness. Volunteering also is a social act through which participants enjoy sharing common experiences as well as social contacts and social prestige.

Service to the community is often cited as a major reason for becoming in-volved. Some persons volunteer for "business" reasons and the visibility that par-ticipation provides for increasing their personal or employer's business. Contacts are made through such social networks, and prominence in nonprofit agencies often serves as a powerful business influence. Others become involved so they can express themselves. Some people find after a time that their work or business does not call upon all their potential skills and abilities. Participation in nonprofit agencies for these persons becomes a mechanism for further skill development and opportunities for self-expression. Others use such participation as a form of career exploration to test themselves and to examine how congruent their personalities and needs are within a particular field or type of activity prior to their making serious commitments to job changes, more education, and so forth. Volunteering also plays an important part for people during periods of transitions. They establish social contacts and develop new interpersonal networks and skills, for example, during the entry phase in a new community, after a separation or divorce, or after the death of a spouse.

Although this discussion has focused on volunteering in the nonprofit sector, it should be noted that similar participation occurs in the public sector but to a lesser extent. For example, volunteers serve on advisory boards for public departments and also may offer their services in public hospitals, nursing homes, daycare programs, and so on. There is no limiting principle restricting where people will volunteer, but traditionally volunteers have been most active in the nonprofit sector.

Two thirds of the employees in the nonprofit sector are female; more than half of the volunteers are women. A traditional view is that women find in the nonprofit arena opportunities for leadership, power, and influence not available to them in business and government. More recently, it has been thought that power in the nonprofit sector is not nearly as influential as in business and government. So even when women gain power in the nonprofit sector, they are leading in a societal arena that—with some exceptions—is not a powerful player in the overall political structure.[21]

Private and Public Spheres

Today the relationships among public, nonprofit, and private spheres are more ambiguous than at any time since colonial days. These relationships raise a number of issues: (1) uses of public funds, (2) tax laws and policy, (3) programmatic links, (4) accountability, and (5) national policy.

Uses of Public Funds and Power

Public funds, from federal, state, and local governments, are provided for both the private and nonprofit sectors through purchase of service contracts and through third-party payments. In the 1960s, the federal government through the Economic Opportunity Act (1964) encouraged the use of nonprofit community agencies to develop services. Later, Title XX of the Social Security Act (1975) authorized grants to states for social services to be directed toward achieving or maintaining economic self-sufficiency and preventing dependence. Welfare reform (Temporary

Assistance to Needy Families, 1996) encouraged states to involve nonprofit and for profit organizations in the delivery of social services. States have wide discretion as to which services will be provided and how they will be organized and delivered.

As a result, over the past generation, a mixed economy has evolved in the field of social welfare, in which the conventional differences between sectors have become blurred as nongovernmental organizations have increasingly been used to implement public policy. In the personal social services, purchase of service contracting has become the primary financing method and method of service delivery, often severing funding (governmental) from administration (nonprofit or private) of the delivery of personal social services. Practically, this blurring of auspices led to greater interdependence among government, private, and nonprofit social welfare efforts. This trend is a result of a historical American ambivalence toward and distrust of government as well as budgetary constraints. Such development enables the creation of desired public services without necessarily resulting in the growth of government. In fact, some view these moves as leading to more limited government, apparently stemming governmental growth and extending services without increasing the number of governmental employees.[22] The drive to use private organizations to deliver public services is intensified when governmental budgets are squeezed. It is then that the "less government is better government" ideology joins with fiscal imperatives to retrench public services in order to slow or halt the expansion of the welfare sector, or to shift services so they are privately delivered, as governments try to maintain stability and services. Even where there are some savings, in many cases privatization may produce savings that are largely the result of private companies paying low wages and providing limited benefits. The net result may be that one arm of government saved money while another arm—public assistance and health facilities—may spend more because of the layoffs of governmental employees.

Public money is provided in order to implement a public purpose. However, public purposes and those of the private sector may not always be entirely compatible. Those who pay the bill cannot be viewed as equals in the relationship, and contractual power tends to move in only one direction—toward the public sphere. Use of public funds can also inhibit the ability of the nonprofit and private sectors to question and advocate. There are those who argue that nonprofit agencies that receive public funds are in reality constrained from participating in social action or advocacy. Others argue that such losses of autonomy are exaggerated and that the critical and advocacy roles of the nonprofit sector remain influential.

According to one point of view, when the public uses private agencies to fulfill its own purposes, those private agencies should be viewed as being in reality governmental entities: Because there is guidance and restrictions on how such payments should be used, these agencies are agents of the government. In essence, state power is given over in part to private and nonprofit providers. Paradoxically, contracting results in unprecedented governmental involvement in the affairs of non-profit organizations. From this point of view, child-care institutions that receive the great preponderance of their funds from governmental sources and are the means by which the government discharges its responsibilities cannot be considered private agencies. Such agencies are essentially other governmental institutions, although it is unclear at what point this happens.

Tax Laws and Policy

Public funds are provided for nonprofit social welfare through the tax system as well as through direct public funding. The federal government encourages charitable donations by individuals and corporations and makes provision in law for these contributions to be used as tax deductions, which reduce individual or corporate taxes. This tax policy appears to be solidly entrenched in American values. Only a limited number of persons challenge the use of such charitable donations as deductions. They typically do so not as a challenge to the principle of nonprofit efforts but on the basis of the separation of church and state, arguing that deductible contributions confer a benefit on religious organizations. Because charitable giving is related to the provisions of the tax code, efforts to create new tax systems stimulated widespread concerns that repeal of the estate tax early in the Bush administration (2001) would inadvertently mean the tax would cease being a catalyst for major donations to non-profit organizations, seriously undermining their incomes.

Programmatic Links

Non-profit organizations interact with government in several ways, ways which differ over time and in different fields of service. (1) The non-profit organizations may serve as supplementary service providers; (2) They may serve as complementary partners with government when government provides the finances and non-profit agencies deliver the services when it is cheaper for government to contract them out rather than perform them; and (3) In some cases, they may serve as advocates or adversaries in regard to policy formulation and implementation.[23]

Accountability

The expenditure of funds calls for accountability. Grant-providing agencies need to have some proof of the proper use of the funds provided, and the demand for accountability causes certain dilemmas. Social welfare services are "soft" services when compared to, let us say, engineering. In engineering, the bridge is either built or not; it supports the predicted weights under particular conditions. In the human services area, outcomes and appropriate measurement instruments may be in short supply. What is the optimum expectation in the case of an abused or mentally ill child in a problematic family? Short-term outcomes may be measured in some way, but they would only supply a limited knowledge of real progress. In such a case, it may be necessary to examine long-term benefits to the individuals, the family, neighborhood, and society to gain a proper perspective on the investment being made. Measurements of outcomes are difficult and can only be made over long periods of time, time that is often unavailable to the granting agency. In the

United States, there are strong governmental forces intensified by the Government Performance and Results Act (1993) and the Service Efforts and Accomplishments of the Federal Accounting Standards Advisory Board exerted on programs to include measurable outcome related goals and objectives. One result of this trend is that in the human services there is an intensifying drive to achieve client outcomes through performance contracting with agencies.[24]

In an attempt to provide data for proof of effectiveness, it is possible that prized organizational values may be compromised. Fair value must be given, but freedom for performance is also needed. Thus, there is a tension between independence, the kinds of help needed by persons with particular human difficulties, and accountability. Central control by governmental agencies is required in order to ensure accountability, but the degree and nature of the control are issues that remain to be worked out over time.

National Policy: Church and State

An important issue in regard to the relationship of the public and private spheres is that of the church–state relationship. Church-sponsored social welfare is a significant portion of all social welfare efforts. Indeed, much of social welfare in the United States developed originally out of a religious motivation, and social welfare sponsored by various religions continues to occupy an important role in the totality of such services. Organizations such as Jewish and Protestant Welfare Federations, Catholic Charities, a myriad of hospitals under religious sponsorship, as well as a host of other social welfare efforts are delivered under religious auspices.

Notable social welfare programs are sponsored by churches, synagogues, mosques, and other religious organizations. As an example, African American churches serve their members but also serve the African American community as a whole as they respond to current issues. Among the sponsored programs are housing, anti-drug efforts, family life centers, child care, health services, AIDS education, community and senior centers, home health care, parenting programs, adult education, tutorials, food and clothing, counseling, community-owned businesses, prison ministries, scouts, and so on.[25]

An early dramatic initiative of the Bush administration was "charitable choice," a faith-based initiative to encourage expanded efforts by private groups, including religious ones, to help the poor and others in place of governmental welfare programs. Charitable choice began in 1996 when federal welfare reform legislation banned discrimination against faith-based programs that seek to administer social welfare programs to federal beneficiaries. In addition to involvement in major programs, charitable choice has been extended to welfare-to-work, community services, and substance abuse programs. Consideration was being given to involve faith-based agencies in juvenile justice and other programs.

The initiative to channel more government financing to religious social service programs provoked a major battle. The initiative included three components: (1) remove regulatory obstacles to the work of charities; (2) encourage donations to poverty-fighting charities; and (3) provide direct federal grants to religious groups.

Reactions varied. Some thought that qualifying small, neighborhood-based religious charities would provide more "neighborly" based welfare programs, improving services for beneficiaries. Many non-profit organizations were in favor because they expected they would receive federal subsidies. Others favored the program if it limited funds to mainstream religious groups who would not proselytize the poor and that would not use religious guidelines in hiring, while others wanted religious organizations that receive federal funds to hire only employees who share their religious faith. The plan called for some groups to be eligible for vouchers (placing choice in the hands of the client) while others could receive direct grants, Some religious leaders and others who initially had been proponents expressed opposition out of various concerns, including that religious groups outside the mainstream would be eligible. Other religious leaders were reluctant to submit their organizations to compliance with rigorous guidelines required to become government contractors, and/or potentially losing their religious independence. Coincidentally, early in the consideration of the initiative a court case was opened against a religious organization that hired and then dismissed a lesbian on religious grounds; the president of a drug treatment program testified that some Jewish persons in his program had become "completed Jews," a term used by evangelical Christians to describe Jews who became Christians but also viewed by many Jews as offensive; and the White House declined a request from a religious sponsored charity to be exempted from discriminating against homosexuals. Various groups used such court cases, testimony, and challenges as evidence the president's initiative will result in government-financed proselytizing. A major criticism was that the proposal pitted religious, non-profit, and public agencies against each other and placed the government in the position of choosing among religions. While there was support, questions were also raised about many issues such as separating religious instruction from services.[26]

The case of *Wilder v. Sugarman* (1974) drew attention to complex constitutional issues concerning fundamental questions in social welfare and foster care regarding the First Amendment establishment clause and the role of the state in rearing children. In 1974, the U.S. District Court upheld the right of New York City's private foster-care institutions (nearly half of them sponsored by Roman Catholic organizations) to get state support despite the constitutional prohibition of state aid to religion.

After a long period of litigation and legal review, a federal appeals court approved in *Wilder v. Bernstein* (1988) a settlement reached by the parties that religious-sponsored agencies should place children in foster care on a first-come, first-served basis, except that a preference for religious matching requested by parents will be honored when it does not give a child greater access to a program appropriate for his or her needs over children who have been waiting longer for the program. It also prohibited the display of "excessive religious symbols" in common areas open to children. Furthermore, family planning services for foster children must be made available in their placement regardless of the agency's religious affiliation.[27]

Questions arise from time to time in regard to public monies being used by religion-sponsored social welfare agencies. On one hand, religion-sponsored agencies often wrestle with the notion of accepting public funds because they are fearful acceptance will constrain in some way their own particular goals. Others fear that religious auspices translate automatically into social welfare services that necessarily must be religiously imbued. The relevant constitutional principle is based on the First Amendment of the U.S. Constitution and states that the government cannot utilize religion as a standard for action or inaction, either to confer a benefit or impose a burden.[28]

Governmental action cannot establish religion or interfere with its free exercise. Governmental aid to religious institutions, tax exemptions for religious organizations, purchase of services from religious organizations, adoption criteria, the ambiance of social agencies and institutions, camps, and other organizations, religious garb, and religious dietary requirements and even who can be hired—all are issues for social welfare within the perspective of the church-state tension.

Marketplace and the Nonmarket Domain

One major dilemma that arises when public agencies use private institutions for public purposes is the specific problem of the profit motive. We have seen in this chapter that proprietary organizations play important roles in the delivery of social welfare services. A major criticism of profit-making social welfare services is that encouraging efficiency and profit-making implies risks to the quality of services.

But just as there are reasons to believe that private, profit-oriented institutions will fail to allocate resources efficiently (or equitably) under specified conditions, so too there are reasons to believe that governmental institutions sometimes fail to accomplish their aims and are inefficient and inequitable. There are limits to what both private and governmental institutions can accomplish.

Those who question the independence of the nonprofit sector sometimes categorize it simply as another part of the social control mechanism in a capitalist society. For these persons, it is assumed that a social and economic elite controls social welfare in the private sector (private and nonprofit). Some persons are opposed in principle to the private sector per se; others simply wish the private and public sectors were more decentralized in their decision making and that greater democratic participation across class and other lines were an accomplished fact.

Historically, social services have been viewed as being provided outside the marketplace in a separate domain. The world of social welfare has grown more complex over time. Today, as we have seen here, the line between nonprofit and public agencies is blurred, and it is clear that in order to understand fully the institution of social welfare and the delivery of social welfare services the private profit-making sector must be included in the domain of social welfare. Others who oppose the inclusion of profit-making services within the domain of social welfare find private, for-profit social services insufficiently humane, discriminatory, and not social. The service recipient is a customer who is to provide income, and priority rests with producing a profit for the investors.

Family and Friends

Although somewhat beneath everyday view of others, help provided by relatives and friends for persons who are no longer able to manage all aspects of their daily life is a very important, albeit informal, part of social welfare. In more than 22 million households in the United States care is provided for one, two, or more persons for major illnesses and other problems such as mobility, transportation, grocery shopping and meal preparation, housework and repairs, managing finances, and arranging/supervising outside services. This caregiving is largely provided by females to female relatives.[29] To support these significant volunteer services, the Older Americans Act (2000) was amended to establish a new program—The National Family Caregiver Support Program.

Along with providing informal assistance to others, families also give gifts and bequests. The predominant pattern is parents or other relatives giving to adult children. When asked if they ever gave large gifts or major financial assistance to their children 48 percent of the respondents reported they did so at some time. These gifts are concentrated within families and flow mainly from older to younger family members.[30] The dollars dedicated to such low-visibility connections between generations are not trivial. In 1990, the aggregate amount attributed to private transfers totalled *$1.6 trillion*, largely between age groups. That same year, government transfer payments amounted to just under $700 billion, less than half the total of the private transfers.[31]

Toward the Future

There is a worldwide increase in the number of nonprofit organizations as people organize to improve their living conditions and to attain their rights.[32] Decisions supportive of this major trend develop out of ideological, political, economic, and social factors. Recent Congresses and presidents emphasized the nonprofit sector as part of a strategy to cut back on governmental social spending and interventions. Some legislators advocate the dismantling of the welfare state and turning over many governmental functions to the nonprofit and private sectors, suggesting that helping the needy requires shifting assistance from bureaucracies to neighborly help. Those familiar with social welfare in the United States point out the discrepancy between the scale of efforts required by all levels of government and those of the nonprofit sector. They suggest the implausibility that the nonprofit sector can compensate sufficiently for governmental cutbacks.

Certainly, it is unthinkable that the United States will nationalize the personal social services. Federal control of these services is not a real choice. The devolution strategy expects that local government will provide some services and the nonprofit sector will fill identified gaps. This strategy is consistent with a control of services at the state and local jurisdictions. An emphasis on the use of the profit-making sector to the greatest extent possible has been in effect for a generation. Reliance on competition in the marketplace is viewed as a good in itself. Also valued is faith in and empowerment of the nonprofit sector along with encouragement and greater utilization of nonprofit associations, religious institutions, neighborhood groups, and the primary social systems. This view perceives the nonprofit sector as one means in an attempt to recover the lost sense of community and of defending against the involvement of the state in the private affairs of citizens. The degree to which this strategy can be successful, however, really depends on funding and the feasibility of the assignments thrust on the nonprofit sector.

Thus, shifting away from federal responsibilities, reducing the overload on government, especially lessening the power of the federal government, and utilizing the private and nonprofit sector to provide decentralized services at reduced costs is a major strategy being pursued. Whether the changes that take place will be radical or more incremental remains to be seen.

Pragmatism is also an American value, and the interdependence of government and the nonprofit and private sectors will continue with increased emphasis on accountability, efficiency, and bottom-line effectiveness where governmental funds are used. This pragmatic view of the future seems most consistent with U.S. society and its emphasis on pluralism, incremental change, and its increasingly strenuous commitment in ideology to the private and nonprofit sectors.

Government is not the enemy some see. Government can provide freedom *to do* as well as freedom *from*. There are limits on the intrusion of government into our lives; our constitutional rights are protected in this society. But the efforts of government to create opportunity through health care, educational benefits, housing, child care, and nutrition, support the freedom of those who could not possibly attain self-fulfillment without the assistance of government. Governmental efforts such as those of the Food and Drug Administration and the GI Bill opened up freedom, options, and creativity for many individuals and for our society. The ultimate questions should not revolve around the issue of whether government should intervene but, instead, should be focused on when, where, and how governmental interventions will be most helpful for the individual and for society.

It is clear that the private and nonprofit sectors simply cannot do all the required tasks of a social welfare system in a complex and interdependent society such as ours. Lester Ward, an early American critic of social Darwinism, strongly suggested that governmental intervention was necessary precisely in order to protect freedom. The predatory behavior of unbridled competition works to destroy freedom. According to Ward, such matters as sanitation, health, unemployment, the rights of employees to organize, and many other matters require governmental intervention to protect the freedom of individuals and the community. The proper balance of the public and the private and nonprofit sectors in regard to the delivery of social welfare services remains to be worked out over a long period of time.[33]

The attainment of access to services, adequacy, accountability, effectiveness, and efficiency in social welfare will require the combined efforts of government and the private and nonprofit sectors. Their respective roles in regard to the scope of interventions, costs, benefits, and the mechanisms for the delivery of services remain to be balanced as our society, its problems, and its resources change.

Summary

In this chapter, we examined the place of private and nonprofit social welfare in the overall picture. We can readily see the important and prominent part this sector plays in the delivery of social welfare services. The complete list of role players in the social welfare institution has to include the state, the market, the nonprofit and private sectors, and the household.

In chapters 12 and 13, we will deal with the emergence and development of social work as a profession, a major but not the only professional group that serves in social welfare. Following that discussion, we will examine the functions of social work as a profession, the context within which it operates, and some issues confronting the profession.

Questions for Consideration

1. What nonprofit and for-profit social welfare organizations are there in your community?

2. Suggestions have been made that the nonprofit sector can handle many of our society's social welfare needs. Do you think that could be done in your community? What's your opinion and what facts do you base it on?

3. Can you identify women in your state who occupy significant social welfare leadership roles?

4. For what social welfare services should families be responsible? Why?

Notes

1. Alexis de Tocqueville, *Democracy in America*, Richard D. Heffner, Ed., New York: Mentor Books, 1956, p. 201.

2. Lester M. Salamon and Helmut K. Anheier, *Defining the Nonprofit Sector*, New York: Manchester University Press, 1997, p. 12; Lester Salamon, *America's Nonprofit Sector*, The Foundation Center, 1999, p. 8. (Note: No place of publication)

3. Robert H. Bremner, "Private Philanthropy and Public Needs: Historical Perspective," *Research Papers: The Commission on Private Philanthropy and Public Needs*, Vol. 1, *History, Trends, and Current Magnitudes*, Washington, D.C.: Department of the Treasury, 1977, p. 103.

4. Lester M. Salamon, "The Non-Profit Sector and Government: The American Experience in Theory and Practice," *The Third Sector: Comparative Studies of Nonprofit Organizations*, Helmut K. Anheier and Wolfgang Seibel, Eds. New York: Walter de Gruyter, pp. 219–240. 1990. Elizabeth T. Boris, "Non-profit Organizations in a Democracy: Varied Roles and Responsibilities," in *Nonprofits and Government: Collaboration and Conflict*, Eds. Elizabeth T. Boris and C. Eugene Steuerle, Washington, D.C.: The Urban Institute Press, 1999, pp. 18, 24.

5. Although the 1930 data and later figures are not absolutely comparable, they do indicate the gross weighting and directions of expenditures. See U.S. Bureau of the Census, *Statistical Abstract of the United States: 2000* (120th edition), Table 598, "Social Welfare Expenditures under Public Programs: 1980 to 1995, p. 378 and Table 599, "Social Welfare Expenditures under Public Programs as Percent of GDP and Total Government Outlays: 1980 to 1995," p. 378. GDP is the economic measure now used most equivalent to the measure (GNP) used in 1930. See Chapter 6 for GDP and GNP definitions.

6. Wilmer L. Kerns, "Private Social Welfare Expenditures, 1972–94," *Social Security Bulletin*, Vol. 60, No. 1, 1997, p. 55.

7. American Association of Fundraising Counsel, "Total Giving Reaches $203.45 Billion," July 11, 2001, www.aafrc.org/press3.html,

8. *Statistical Abstract: 2000,* Table 601, "Public Income-Maintenance Programs—Cash Benefit Payments: 1980 to 1995," p. 380.

9. American Association of Fundraising Counsel, *op.cit.*

10. U.S. Bureau of the Census, *Statistical Abstract of the United States: 2000,* Table 1304, "National Nonprofit Associations-Number by Type: 1980 to 2000," p. 773.

11. Marvin Olasky, *The Tragedy of American Compassion,* Washington, D.C.: Regnery Publishing, 1995.

12. Barbara Peat and Dan I. Costley, "Privatization of Social Services: Correlates to Contract Performance," *Administration in Social Work,* 24 (1), 21–38, 2000.

13. Yolanda K. Kodrzycki, "Fiscal Pressures and the Privatization of Local Services," *New England Economic Review,* January/February 1998, 39–50.

14. Reid Abelson, "Charities Use For-Profit Units to Avoid Disclosing Finances," *New York Times,* January 9, 1998, pp. A1, A12.

15. Department of the Treasury, Internal Revenue Service, *Taxpayer Bill of Rights 2,* www.IRS.gov, July 11, 2001.

16. James T. Bennett and Thomas J. DiLorenzo, *Unfair Competition: The Profits and Nonprofits,* New York: Hamilton Press, 1989, p. 1.

17. U.S. Bureau of the Census, Statistical Abstract of the United States: 2000 (120th edition), Table No.637, "Percent of Adult Population Doing Volunteer Work: 1998," Washington, D.C., p. 396 and Independent Sector, "Newsroom," www.independentsector.org/media/voltimePR.html, July 12, 2001.

18. Barbara Peat and Dan L. Costley, "Privatization of Social Services: Correlates to Contract Performance," *Administration in Social Work,* 24 (1), 21–38, 2000 and Lawrence L. Martin, "Performance Contracting in the Human Services: An Analysis of Selected State Practices," *Administration in Social Work,* 24 (2), 29–44, 2000.

19. Anna C. Burke and Jane A. Rafferty, "Ownership Differences in the Provision of Outpatient Substance Abuse Services," *Administration in Social Work,* Vol. 18, No. 3, 1994, 59–91.

20. Jone L. Pearce, *Volunteers: The Organizational Behavior of Unpaid Workers,* New York: Routledge, 1993, pp. 64, 66, 70, 78.

21. Michael O'Neill, "The Paradox of Women and Power in the Nonprofit Sector," in Teresa Odendahl and Michael O'Neill, Eds. *Women and Power in the Nonprofit Sector,* San Francisco: Jossey-Bass, 1994, p. 2.

22. Steven R. Smith and Michael Lipsky, *Nonprofits for Hire: The Welfare State in the Age of Contracting,* Cambridge, MA: Harvard University Press, 1993, p. 193.

23. Dennis R. Young, "Complementary, Supplementary, or Adversarial? A Theoretical and Historical Examination of Nonprofit—Government relations in the United States," in Boris and Steuerle, *op. cit,* pp. 31–67.

24. James R. Kautz III, *et al,* "The Government Performance and Results Act of 1993: Implications for Social Work Practice, "*Social Work,* 42(4), 364–373 and Lawrence L. Martin, *op. cit.*

25. Andrew Billingsley, *Climbing Jacob's Ladder,* New York: Simon & Schuster, 1992, 349–378.

26. Laurie Goodstein, "Battle Lines Grow on Plan to Assist Religious Groups," *New York Times,* April 12, 2001, p. A22; Laurie Goodstein, "Many Churches Slow to Accept Government Money to Help Poor," *New York Times,* October 17, 2000, p. A1 and p. A25; Kate O'Beirne and Ramesh Ponnuru, "Great Society," *Wall Street Journal,* April 30, 2001; Frank Bruni, "Bush Pushes Role of Private Sector in Aiding the Poor," *New York Times,* May 21, 2001, pp. A1 and A15; and Frank Bruni and Elizabeth Becker, "Charity is Told It Must Abide by Antidiscrimination Laws," *New York Times,* July 11, 2001, p. A15.

27. Martin Guggenheim, "State-Supported Foster Care: The Interplay Between the Prohibition of Establishing Religion and the Free Exercise Rights of Parents and Children: Wilder v. Bernstein," *Brooklyn Law Review,* Brooklyn, NY: Brooklyn Law School, 1990, Vol. 56, No. 2, 603–655.

28. Philip B. Kurland, *Religion and the Law of the Church and State and the Supreme Court,* Chicago: Aldine, 1962; Frank J. Sorauf, *The Wall of Separation: The Constitutional Policies of Church and State,* Princeton, NJ: Princeton University Press, 1976.

29. National Alliance for Caregiving and the American Association of Retired Persons, *Family Caregiving in the U.S.: Findings from a National Survey,* Bethesda, MD, June 1997.

30. Robert A. Harootyan and Robert E. Vorek, "Volunteering, Helping, and Gift Giving in Families and Communities," in *Intergenerational Linkages,* Vern I. Bengston and Robert A. Harootyan, Eds., New York: Springer Publishing Co., 1994, pp. 105, 108.

31. Karl Kronebusch and Mark Schlesinger, "Intergenerational Transfers," in *Intergenerational Linkages,* p. 137.

32. Lester M. Salamon, *The Global Associational Revolution: The Rise in the Third Sector on the World Scene,* Paper No.15, Johns Hopkins University, Baltimore, Md.: Institute for Policy Studies, April 1993, p. 6.

33. Henry Steele Commager, *Lester Ward and the Welfare State,* New York: Bobbs-Merrill, 1967, p. 223.

12

Social Work

The Emergence of a Profession

...the good we secure for ourselves is precarious and uncertain, is floating in mid-air, until it is is secured for all of us and incorporated into our common life.

—Jane Addams[1]

Overview

Depending on who is doing the "name-calling," social workers are referred to as "do-gooders," "bleeding hearts," "radicals," captives of and apologists for "the establishment," organizers of the poor, and servers of the middle class. All these are ways in which people stereotype social workers and the functions they perform in society.

As we have seen, social welfare has evolved through a lengthy process, but social work as a professionalized occupation started its evolution at a much later stage, gaining momentum as a result of the Industrial Revolution.

In this chapter and the next, we explore the profession of social work within the context of social welfare. We review historical antecedents of modern social workers and the creation of the profession, describe the functions of social work and the arenas in which social workers perform their functions, and examine a number of current issues that confront the profession.

Social work is a *professionalized occupation* that delivers social services largely in social welfare institutions. Although social work is the major professional group in social welfare, social workers are by no means limited to delivering services in the social welfare area, nor are all services in social welfare delivered by social workers.

The Workers of "Good Works"

Antecedents of professional social workers are found among people who have helped others through the ages. Services have been provided in many forms by religious institutions and charities, public and voluntary services, and by little-known "good Samaritans." Among these predecessors, it has been suggested that Father Vincent de Paul, a seventeenth-century Roman Catholic clergyman—later canonized—initiated the training of social workers. When he founded the Daughters of Charity in 1633, young peasant women who wanted to devote themselves to charitable work were trained especially for nursing the poor. Others pointed out that a century earlier Juan Luis Vives developed a plan of organized relief (1537) at the request of the mayor of Bruges in Flanders that required that good persons "remember that the burden of their neighbor's calamities must be relieved not only with alms but also with their presence in visiting, comforting, helping, and in executing the deeds of pity." Along these lines, in the American colonies as early as 1626 *siecken troosters* (comforters of the sick), after passing an exam, were appointed to visit ill persons at their homes in New Amsterdam (later New York) to offer counsel in relation to spiritual and other matters.[2]

People have always reached out to help other people. Family, church, and other groups often tried to institutionalize this helping function. It was particularly during the nineteenth century that more definitive forerunners of social work as a profession were established. The coming of industrialization and an accelerated movement from rural to urban locations produced social needs and social problems that were beyond the coping capacities of individual families. Along with modernization, functions that traditionally would have been performed by family members soon became the tasks of specialists. For example, rather than milking one's own cows, one obtained milk provided by dairy farmers, dairies, distributors, truckers, and grocers. And today the child with developmental disabilities, who was once cared for entirely at home, is transported to a child-development center for education and training by specialists.

Specialization developed in many facets of American life, including one dealing with pauperism and poverty. Following the War of 1812, a short harvest occurred in 1816 because of weather conditions. Shortly after, there followed the 1817–1821 postwar depression. John Griscom in New York organized the Society for the Prevention of Pauperism. The society aimed to investigate the circumstances and habits of the poor, to devise means of improving the situation of the poor both morally and physically, to suggest plans by which the poor could help themselves, and to encourage economy and saving. Among the remedies utilized were house-to-house visitation of the poor and the flow of charities into one distribution channel in order to prevent cheating.[3]

Around the same time, Thomas Chalmers, a minister and philosopher, believed that his parishioners (the poor included) could provide for themselves through their own resources, the kindness of relatives, and the sympathy of the wealthier members of the community. Taking over a Glasgow parish, he implemented a new plan from 1819 to 1823. All local parish church collections would be left with the parish rather than transferred to a central fund. These funds could be used at Chalmer's discretion to provide for the people of the parish, but would not be used for new families moving into the area.

The parish of 8,000 people was divided into 25 districts. The office of deacon was responsible for providing for all new applications for public assistance. Deacons were given general instructions and individual supervision and advice. For approximately four years, Chalmers supervised the program for relief in St. John's parish. The parish took over the care of individuals previously under the care of the town hospital, and some money was left for the parish school.

At a time when workhouses were used cruelly and indiscriminately, Chalmers created a system of personal influence and individualization outside the framework of the Poor Laws. Investigation and district assignments were systematic techniques. Although Chalmers believed in an ethic of "noblesse oblige" by the wealthy for the poor, he, nevertheless, created an administrative plan and trained persons to implement it, based on the belief that personal factors cause poverty and that the effort of "helping" people could bring them out of poverty. The investigation of individual situations was a factor in the creation of the concept of *casework,* by which we mean that each person or case is unique. Thus benefits were related to the individual assessment.[4]

Among other social work precursors were the volunteers of the New York Society for the Prevention of Pauperism formed as a result of the 1819 depression. Similarly, the New York Association for Improving the Condition of the Poor (NYAICP) was organized in 1843 to relieve pauperism and aid the worthy poor through the use of volunteers. It, however, was not staffed only by volunteers. Instead, employed staff members, primarily missionaries, were used to do administrative work for districts and to train and supervise the volunteer visitors. Families were investigated by the volunteer visitors who provided health, housing, and child welfare services. The family conditions found by the visitors were reviewed by the paid agents serving as district secretaries. By 1866, the district secretaries were dismissed and the NYAICP returned to an almost entirely volunteer effort. However, in the 1870s, paid visitors were once again employed. These paid district secretaries were forerunners of the later social workers. The AICP structure served as a model for succeeding private agencies and the agency later merged with the New York Charity Organization Society to form the eminent Community Service Society of New York.[5]

Still other predecessors of social workers emerged from the Civil War. Members of the U.S. Sanitary Commission, a federation of voluntary organizations, helped to serve the needs of Union troops during the Civil War by supplying bandages, clothing, and food and by establishing lodging places for soldiers on leave, meals while in transit, and assistance with pay claims.[6] The workers in the Freedmen's Bureau for former enslaved persons, created in March 1865, implemented a comprehensive program including temporary relief, food, clothing, hospitals, schools, orphan asylums, homes for the aged and the infirm, lease of lands, job finding, supervising labor contracts, housing and transportation for job seekers, courts, and legal counsel as to rights.

The Freedmen's Bureau was family centered. Designed to minimize the social upheaval of the war and the stressful emancipation of enslaved persons, the Freedmen's Bureau offered—in contemporary terms—child welfare services, income maintenance, medical care, work projects, government housing, provision for the aged and infirm, employment counseling, family location, marriage counseling, legal aid, assistance with resettlement, protective services, and education.[7]

Philosophies and techniques continued to evolve. Franklin B. Sanborn, a New England intellectual associated with John Brown, after becoming the executive secretary of the Massachusetts State Board of Charities in 1863, encouraged the use of homes for delinquent and nondelinquent children. He initiated the use of foster homes for the emotionally disturbed on the basis of observations made in Scotland, Belgium, and France. He also recruited local volunteers, for the most part women, to serve as visitors. These *"friendly visitors"* were middle- and upper-class women who had time and wanted to do good. They would visit the poor and try to teach them to be better citizens and parents, to budget, and to practice sobriety in all matters. The expectation was that through moral instruction one could learn how not to be poor.[8]

A major economic depression in 1873, one of many during the nineteenth century, created severe unemployment problems. It became clear that agencies, programs, and resources were not equal to the tasks they were called on to perform. As a result, during this period an English invention—the *Charity Organization Society* (COS)—caught the imagination of a number of U.S. communities.

A first attempt to form a citywide Bureau of Charities was initiated in New York in 1873 but was abandoned when several influential institutions refused to cooperate. Boston also instituted a charity organization that year, but it was operative only in the North End. The first operational citywide COS originated in Buffalo, New York, in 1877, and similar societies then developed rapidly in a series of cities, including New Haven, Philadelphia, Boston, Brooklyn, Cincinnati, and New York.[9]

It was hoped that charity organizations could meet the pressing social problems of the cities—unemployment, orphans, beggars, the ill, and others—and clarify the interrelations of private and public relief agencies that had overlapping functions and different policies. These new organizations were to assume two different roles: (1) *direct service* to individuals and families; in this respect they were the immediate forerunners of social casework and of family service agencies, and (2) *planning and coordinating* efforts, which preceded the development of community organization and social planning. Thus, implicit in the creation of these new agencies were two different functions, reflecting the two tracks of cause and function, a theme to be discussed further in chapter 13.

The general principles on which the charity organizations operated were

1. detailed investigation of the applicant,
2. a central system of registration to avoid duplication,
3. cooperation among the various relief agencies, and
4. extensive use of friendly volunteer visitors.

Investigative and administrative responsibilities belonged to the paid staff. The major treatment and helping roles belonged to the friendly visitors who as volunteers had the task of directly helping those in difficulty.

Roy Lubove reports that work was viewed at this time as the solution for all problem families. When persons came for assistance, the Conference of the Boston Associated Charities, for example, "boasted that when the poor first called for assistance, they requested 'clothing, money, etc., etc.,' but were refused anything except work."[10] Thus there is an amazing consistency in attitude and approach to the poor in England and America from the fourteenth century until the latter part of the nineteenth century, and although diminished for a time the same theme of individual responsibility continues to this day, unmindful of the altered economic and societal context.

To further illustrate the incipient social work roles and tasks about the same time, a *Manual for Visitors Among the Poor* was developed by the Philadelphia Society for Organizing Charitable Relief and Repressing Mendicancy. The suggestions for friendly visitors are instructive: sympathy and encouragement are more important than money; women are the best friendly visitors; help, if urgently needed, may be obtained from neighbors; personal assistance should take the form of employment; cultivate the habit of looking below the surface of things; poverty is associated with disease and a consequent lack of vitality; know the sanitary laws; the poor have not learned thrift; and so on. The thrust of these instructions places the responsibility on the person or family involved. The effort to make change is marked by "moral suasion."[11]

At this point in the development of social work, volunteers were primarily motivated to change people as "doers of good works." It was through social investigation and attempts to understand family situations that social work began to gestate as a profession. The time and effort required to deal with many cases led to making comparisons among situations and searches for underlying causation. Although there was a strong sense of moral judgment involved, friendly visitors and charity organizations moved toward understanding and took a major step on the road to professionalization.

To the contemporary mind, these forerunners of casework stand out for their judgmental and patronizing qualities and the tendency to place total responsibility for a person's or family's problems solely on them. Although these attitudes were present, it is important to note that these movements set down one of the basic principles of all contemporary social work practice: that each person is unique and has to be understood in individual terms.

Concurrently, *settlement houses* were being instituted in the United States following the establishment of Toynbee Hall in 1884 in London. A group of people from the middle and upper classes would live in a poor neighborhood so they could experience firsthand the realities of neighborhood life and search simultaneously for ways to improve conditions in cooperation with the residents of the neighborhood. Many of the early U.S. settlement house workers were daughters of ministers. No doubt they tried to do away with any airs of superiority and supplant such feelings with neighborliness. By assisting their neighbors, they hoped their experiences would make them more effective social reformers. By 1910, 400 settlement houses had been formed, three fourths founded by women. The settlement house movement was a creative and influential force in American life. Among its creations were new communal organizations such as the National Association for the Advancement of Colored People, which grew out of the Henry Street Settlement (New York, 1909), and the U.S. Children's Bureau (1912), among many other accomplishments.

It is important to place these developments in the context of the times. These women were part of the first generation of women graduating from college in significant numbers, and their career possibilities were limited, mainly marriage or teaching. Life in the settlements was viewed as moral and unselfish. It was semiprotected, and offered a social life as well. Settlement houses and social work offered public roles of potential influence at a time when women were still unable to vote, thus providing an alternative route to influencing policy.[12]

Women's voluntarism preceded the settlement house movement. Beginning in the 1820s Protestant women formed lay organizations. One such organization created before 1870 was the American Female Moral Reform Society (AFMRS). By 1839 this organization had 500 local chapters in New England and New York. During the depression winter of 1873–1874, another Protestant organization—the Women's Christian Temperance Union (WCTU)—began and supplanted the AFMRS. By 1883 there was a branch of WCTU in almost every American county. Their work was not limited to temperance matters. In Chicago, the site of the WCTU headquarters, the organization maintained two day nurseries, two Sunday schools, an industrial school, a mission that sheltered 4,000 homeless or destitute women in a 12-month period, a free medical dispensary that treated more than 1,600 patients a year, a lodging house for men that had by 1889 provided temporary housing for more than 50,000 men, and a low-cost restaurant. Among the ideas they advocated were prison reform, special facilities for women offenders, the eight-hour working day, model facilities for dependent and neglected children, the kindergarten movement, shelters for the care of children of working mothers, social "rooms" other than saloons for the urban poor, mothers' education, and vocational training for women.[13]

Thorstein Veblen, however, commenting on the roles of leisure class women in charity work and social amelioration efforts, did not accept the "philosophy" of settlement house workers quite as benignly as offered and suggested:

> The solicitude of "settlements," for example, is in part directed to enhance the industrial efficiency of the poor and to teach them the more adequate utilization of the means at hand; but it is also no less consistently directed to the inculcation, by precept and example, of certain punctilios of upper-class propriety in manners and customs.[14]

Settlement houses played important roles in cities, especially in immigrant communities. Their focus was on improving housing, health, and general living conditions; finding jobs; teaching English, occupational skills, and hygiene; and attempting to change the environmental surroundings through cooperative efforts. Social casework started in charity organization work. Social group work, community organization, and social action were developed by settlement houses and workers.

In addition to dealing with local problems by taking local action, settlement houses played important roles in gathering facts, promulgating them, preparing legislation, and collecting forces to influence social policy and legislation. Many of the key legislative enactments of the reform era had their inception in the work of the settlement houses. The settlements learned what the realities of life in slum communities were and included staff members who were nationally influential, not only through their social work efforts but also through personal and familial connections. Settlement houses emphasized reform through environmental changes, but "they continued to struggle to teach the poor the prevailing middle-class values of work, thrift, and abstinence as the keys to success."[15]

Jane Addams of Hull House in Chicago thought that settlement house residents could eventually help slum-dwellers to "express themselves and make articulate their desires."[16] By changing neighborhoods, together they would change communities; and through changing communities, they would alter the nation. Settlement houses expressed the ideas of women who wanted to reform American society and, in fact, were wellsprings of reform both locally and nationally. Those who served in settlement houses had a profound impact on American society as they later headed government and voluntary agencies and worked for legislation that shaped in many ways American social policy for the generations that followed.

According to Mary McDowell, settlements in 1896 worked from within the neighborhood and among the people, sharing the fate of the slum-dwellers, whereas the charity organization's visitors came from without and returned to the outside after the visit. The two approaches differed in methodology but complemented each other's efforts, doing together what neither could do entirely as separate agencies.[17]

By the end of the nineteenth century, two major tracks emerged along which professional social work evolved. Future developments would be dramatically influenced by the different natures of the two tracks and by their confluence within social work.

The Process of Professionalization

Harold Wilensky traced the growth of 18 professions, and all follow the same pattern:

1. A substantial number of people begin doing full-time some activity that needs doing.
2. A training school is established.
3. A professional association is formed.
4. The association engages in political agitation to win the support of law for the protection of the group.
5. A code of ethics is developed.[18]

The developmental pattern and professionalization process for social work follows a typical pattern. When charity organizations or societies received contracts to administer relief funds, they began to hire people as executive secretaries to organize volunteers properly and established procedures to show accountability for the money received from the city. These executive secretaries can be considered among the first paid social workers. They began meeting in conferences, and—reflective of the professionalization process—they established standards and training courses.

In the summer of 1898, the New York Charity Organization Society offered the first course in practical philanthropic work to charity workers. By 1904, a one-year program was offered by the newly formed New York School of Philanthropy, and by the end of World War I, 17 programs were members of the Association of Training Schools for Professional Social Work. The American Association of Social Workers (AASW) was formed as a professional association in 1921 following a vain effort to form an association several years earlier. It was not until 1951 that an official code of ethics was prepared by the AASW, followed by the code developed by the National Association of Social Workers (NASW) in 1960.

Social work is a profession whose development in the modern era has been supported by general professionalization trends and the growth of services resulting from industrialization, urbanization, and specialization. The evolution of many new professions in our society supported the rapid strides social work made as a profession, condensing into several decades evolutionary processes that took centuries for other professions. This trend is reflected in the American experience. Professional occupations are expected to continue these growth trends. By 2006, it is expected that 23 million persons will be employed in professional speciality occupations (over 15 percent of total employment and a seventy percent increase since 1986).[19]

A Brief History of Practice and Methods

Mary Richmond, one of the outstanding founders of social work and active in charity organization efforts, could say in 1890 that "only two things are necessary in order to do good work amongst the poor; one is much good will, and the other is a little tact."[20] However, 12 years later, she was defining *social casework* more precisely as "those processes which develop personality through adjustments consciously effected, individual by individual, between men and their social environment."[21]

Physician Richard C. Cabot introduced medical social work to Massachusetts General Hospital in 1905. Soon social workers were employed in schools, child-guidance clinics, courts, and other settings. Building on the investigatory and friendly visiting functions by charity organization volunteers and paid staff, social casework methodologies continued to develop. Initially based on moral categories, the work of the caseworker was to help through persuasion and example. As knowledge developed based on practical experience and as new knowledge became available from psychology, sociology, and psychiatry, the efforts of social caseworkers led to greater understanding of the interaction of individuals and their environment. A "diagnosis" could be formulated and strengths and limitations identified for use in the helping process. Typically, early efforts to make changes were educational and persuasive.

However, it was recognized that there are limits beyond which the individual is not responsible for his or her situation and that society has a reciprocal responsibility for collective action that influences the lives of individuals. The experience of the settlement house confirmed this view. Addams reported:

> We early found ourselves spending many hours in efforts to secure support for deserted women, insurance for bewildered widows, damages for injured operators, furniture from the clutches of the installment store. The Settlement is valuable as an information and interpretation bureau. It constantly acts between the various institutions of the city and the people for whose benefit these institutions were erected.[22]

Not only were early social workers brokers, but they were also advocates, interested not only in techniques for individual and family change, but also in altering society. This perspective of societal change was cogently stated by Florence Kelley, a consumer advocate, in 1905:

> A government which finds it possible, for instance, to take care of the health of young lobsters on the coast of Maine, would seem to have ingenuity enough at a pinch to enable it to make some sort of provision for the orphan children of skilled and unskilled workmen. It may take a long time. It has taken a long time to learn to take care of the lobsters.[23]

An important event took place in 1915 when Abraham Flexner, a significant critic of medical education, turned his attention to social work in a presentation at the National Conference of Charities and Corrections. Training and creation of a scientific method for social work had been advanced, and yet Flexner raised a question as to whether social work was a profession or not. His answer was equivocal and suggested that "if social work fails to conform to some professional criteria, it very readily satisfies others.... In the long run, the first, main, and indispensable criterion of a profession will be the possession of professional spirit, and that test social work may, if it will, fully satisfy." Flexner was strenuous in his criticism, stating that social work lacked a specific skill for a specific function and, insofar as this was true, could not become a profession.[24]

Despite this criticism of social work, several events followed shortly after that energized the continued professionalization of social work. Training schools were formed, a professional association was created, and a formative book was published. Within two years after Flexner's presentation, Richmond published *Social Diagnosis* (1917), a work that organized a theory and methodology for social work. She formulated a common body of knowledge for casework based on collecting information and understanding the meaning of the information. The book was important for the development of the profession because it expounded an orderly professional process consisting of study, diagnosis, prognosis, and treatment planning. Reflective of Richmond's charity organization background, the focus was on the individual or family—the case—in determining what was wrong, what could be done, and how the worker should intervene.

With the advent of medical social work, psychiatric social work, the mental hygiene movement, and psychoanalytic psychology, social work searched for a defined professional methodology and professional status.[25] From the latter years of the nineteenth century until approximately 1915, casework changed from a movement on a one-by-one basis to a method with nascent scientific underpinnings. The "cause" mission of the profession, which had set out to change the world, was changed to focus more on the functions of the social worker and the skills and knowledge that support those functions.

Social workers were employed in a broad diversity of specialized settings. Each social worker identified to a significant extent with particular settings so that professional roles, identities, and functions experienced a centrifugal expansion as social workers identified themselves with the fields in which they practiced. Beyond the development of social work in psychiatric settings, including child-guidance clinics, much of social work became infused with psychiatric knowledge and was especially influenced by psychoanalytic thought, both Freudian and Rankian. Approximately two years following the publication of *Social Diagnosis,* Mary Jarrett, a psychiatric caseworker, rediagnosed the cases presented by Richmond and concluded that at least 50 percent included psychiatric problems.[26] Addams helps to place this influx of psychoanalytic thought and emphasis on individual psyche, technique, and method in perspective. She pointed out that the veering away from social reform can be viewed within the context of the times:

> Throughout the decade (the Twenties) this fear of change, this tendency to play safe was registered most conspicuously in the field of politics, but it spread over into other fields as well. There is little doubt that social workers exhibited many symptoms of this panic and with a kind of protective instinct carefully avoided any identification with the phraseology of social reform.[27]

During the 1920s, many social workers thought of themselves as therapists, or at least believed that there were therapeutic emphases within their social work practice.[28] Social work continued to proliferate in health, school, family, and psychiatric settings. As the proliferation of practice fields continued, concern increased about the specialized nature of social work in many settings, and a systematic study was undertaken to determine what the generic elements of the profession were. A series of meetings was held from 1923 to 1929 to identify the general knowledge shared by all social workers regardless of setting. This work group became known as *"The Milford Conference."* In 1929, the work group, consisting of executives and board members, reported that generic social casework, that is, casework applicable in all potential settings, was viewed as having these common aspects:

1. Knowledge of typical deviations from accepted standards of social life;
2. The use of norms of human life and human relationships;

3. The significance of social history as the basis of particularizing the human being in need;
4. Established methods of study and treatment of human beings in need;
5. The use of established community resources in social treatment;
6. The adaptation of scientific knowledge and formulations of experience to the requirements of social casework;
7. The consciousness of a philosophy that determines the purpose, ethics, and obligations of social casework; and
8. The blending of the foregoing into social treatment.[29]

The Great Depression began soon after the Milford Conference Report on a generic social casework predicated on individual change. Despite the fact that the depression refocused attention on social change, the social casework stream in the social work profession clung to an individual-centered and personality-focused approach.

Meanwhile the overwhelming nature and scope of human need created by the Great Depression caused social policy shifts, which affected social welfare and social work. Everyone was affected; many were unemployed. It clearly was not the result of personal responsibility: Systemic and structural factors were at work. The society and government searched for new security, and new roles for government were accompanied by new social planning trends. These new trends were supported by the general agreement that government should help people—a new assumption in American life.

A myriad of New Deal programs responded to the need for national governmental entry into comprehensive social welfare provision. Concurrently, there was a call for prepared personnel to expand public social services. Because of new public assistance programs, the number of social workers increased rapidly in the 1930s. Numbering 31,000 in 1930, by the 1940 census there were at least 70,000 social and welfare workers. The American Association of Social Workers, the largest professional organization, doubled its size. Seventeen new schools of social work opened, and established schools increased in size.

There was a shift during the 1930s in the relative importance of the public and private sectors of social welfare, the greater weight by far now moving to the public sector. Many social workers were active in starting new programs, including Social Security, and also were employed in public assistance and child welfare. Others continued to work in voluntary agencies and in public institutions such as hospitals. One significant result of the Depression was the introduction of unions into the field of social work.[30]

A major issue arose during the years of the Great Depression centering on the role of social work in an expanding welfare state. Integral to this issue were questions about theories of causation, both personal and societal, and about the roles of social workers in institutional services for normal but disadvantaged persons.

A second issue was an intense struggle, which over the decades faded: the vying between two schools of thought, diagnostic and functional social work. The two schools share the vocation of social casework but differ on underpinning theories of personality. The *diagnostic school*, also known as the psychosocial (the "person-in-situation") school, was based on Freudian thought and stressed the importance of diagnosis and of the powerful role of a person's past interpersonal and intrapsychic experience in the treatment process. The *functional school,* based on a psychology of growth, stressed the impact of the agency's function on the ability to help in the process of casework and emphasized the relationship between the social worker and the client in the here-and-now helping process.

Paradoxically, a psychologically based casework preoccupied with individuals remained the major trend in social casework while the economy was crumbling. Perhaps there is an explanation for this curious persistence. Psychological casework had become the professional tool, developed over decades, of social workers. A therapeutic emphasis also was supported by the Great Depression itself. Social welfare agencies, especially private social welfare ones, sought new roles as public welfare assumed the responsibility for income maintenance, a task completely beyond the resources of private philanthropy. An emphasis on psychologically oriented casework then was an answer to the quest for a professional knowledge base and helped to define the changing functions of private social welfare agencies.

At the same time, social workers affected social legislation and social planning as they developed as part of the New Deal. Among the social workers playing important parts in the "cause" efforts of the 1930s were Harry Hopkins, Frances Perkins, and Bertha Reynolds. They were active and influential in determining governmental policy and the administration of expanded social welfare.

World War II was a time when social work continued to emphasize the therapeutic aspects of treatment as it dealt with family disruption, problems of relocation, and the needs of military personnel at home and abroad. Following the war, social work continued to be mainly influenced by psychodynamic psychiatry, but the social sciences began to be introduced to a greater extent in schools of social work. There was an emphasis on seeking out the hard to reach, working with delinquent youth and multiproblem families, and initiating private social work practice. The commonalities and differences between social casework and psychotherapy were debated.

In the 1960s, the emphasis on the therapeutic function diminished somewhat as social workers became active in community action and advocacy as part of the civil rights struggle and in regard to housing and racial discrimination, juvenile delinquency control programs, neighborhood organization and multiservice centers, draft resistance and anti-Vietnam War efforts, the National Welfare Rights Organization, the efforts for economic security programs such as a negative income tax and guaranteed annual income, and the flowering of minority group organizations of many kinds.

Since the 1960s, social problems and developments in schools of social work contributed to social workers engaging in a broad variety of practice efforts. Among these efforts were social work with HIV positive persons and those with AIDS; practice in industrial and business settings, with immigrants and refugees, substance abuse, domestic violence, the needs of women, the homeless, managed care, gangs, and teen pregnancy; social work and technology; chronic mental illness; suicide prevention; and private solo and group practice, among many others.

In social work education, both graduate and undergraduate, a diversity of practice models were developed, including a focus on social problems (such as substance abuse, women's issues, severe mental illness, and poverty), methods (clinical social work, policy, planning and community organization, political social work, generalist practice), populations at risk (impoverished communities, age, ethnicity, culture, class, physical or mental ability), and fields of practice (aging, children, families, youth, disabilities, health, mental health, and rural).

Development of the Professional Association

Beginning in 1874, the National Conference of Charities and Correction provided an opportunity for social agency employees to meet together on a national basis. Locally, various clubs and social work organizations were formed. The National Social Workers Exchange began operations in 1917 for job placement in social work positions.

By 1918, there was an attempt to organize a national association of social workers, but the effort failed partly because of lack of agreement on membership qualifications. In 1921, the American Association of Social Workers was formed. In addition, social workers from specialized settings formed national organizations, including the American Association of Medical Social Workers (1918), the National Association of School Social Workers (1919), the AASW (1921), the American Association of Psychiatric Social Workers (1926), the American Association of Group Workers (Study Group, 1936; Association, 1946), the Association for the Study of Community Organization (1946), and the Social Work Research Group (1949). In 1955, those associations then in existence combined to form the NASW—the national professional association that now represents the full range of professional social workers.[31]

The professional association provides a variety of services including insurance benefits, regulation and credentialing, standards for several types of practice and services, publications, a register of clinical social workers, continuing education, and practice sections for aging, alcohol, tobacco and other drugs, private practice, and school social work. There are two affiliate organizations, the National Center for Social Policy and Practice and the NASW Communications Network, as well as four subsidiaries: the Research and Education fund, Insurance Trust, the Legal Defense Service, and PACE (Political Action and Candidate Election), which plays an active political action role. The NASW also advocates for sound public policies in health and mental health, economic equity, civil rights, child welfare, and education.

Several smaller groups have developed—for example, national associations of African American, Latino, Native American, and industrial social workers; social workers with groups, community organization and social administration; oncology and clinical social work; social work managers; hospital social work administrators; Commission on Gay Men/Lesbian Women of the Council on Social Work Education, the North American Association of Christians in Social Work, and others. This burgeoning of splinter groups reflects the pluralism in our society, the multiplicity of functions and fields in social work, the creation of new specializations, the difficulty of having one organization satisfy all segments of the profession, and efforts by particular groups to enhance their legitimate goals. In addition, the American Association of State Social Work Boards was organized in 1979 and oversees national credentialing licensing examinations, which can serve to further develop national standards of social work practice.

The membership of NASW multiplied slightly less than sevenfold from 22,027 in 1957 to 149,000 in 2001.[32] Membership is open to baccalaureate and master's graduates from accredited schools and holders of doctorates in social work or social welfare. By comparison, the memberships of some other professional organizations in 2001 were American Medical Association, 297,000; American Nurses Association, 210,000; American Bar Association, 375,000; and American Psychological Association, 151,000.[33]

Social Work with Groups

Social work with groups developed from several sources different from those of social casework. Settlement houses, influenced by the social reform movements of the early twentieth century, focused in part on group services, including cultural and art groups, recreational groups, education, and physical health. They emphasized social participation and association, mutual aid and cooperative problem solving, democratic processes, learning and growth, the encouragement of interaction among persons of different backgrounds, the impact of the environment on persons, and the potential impact of persons on the environment.

In group service agencies such as community centers, camping, and youth service organizations, there was a belief that the road to democracy was through democratic participation. Group service agencies would foster such participation at every level—from children to adults—and from the group itself to the greater society. Support for the evolving methodology came from sociology and progressive education as expounded by John Dewey.

The first course on group work in a school of social work was taught by Clara Kaiser in 1923 at Western Reserve University in Cleveland. The University of Pittsburgh and the New York School (later to become the Columbia University School of Social Work) instituted programs in the 1930s, with other schools soon also offering group work courses.

By 1936, the American Association for Study of Group Work was formed. Noteworthy was a great increase in the use of groups in psychiatric settings during World War II, in part created by the need for the few available trained persons to work with large numbers of persons affected by the war experience. In 1946, the National Conference of Social Work recognized social group work as a part of the social work profession.[34]

Early social group work had several goals:

1. Democratic experiences,
2. Cooperative problem solving and mutual support,

3. Improvement of society, and
4. Character development.

Although there was hesitancy about the place of social group work in the social work profession as early as the Milford Conference Report in 1929, the fundamental methods of social work were "recognized as social case work, community organization, group work, social research, and since social work is almost invariably carried on through the medium of organizations, we may add the technique of administration."[35] Thus the elite group that prepared the Milford Conference Report concluded that group work was an intrinsic part of social work.

Illustrative of the diversity of group workers current service is their work with people with HIV/AIDS, single-parent families, substance abusers, sexual abuse and incest survivors, violent men, inner-city youth, immigrant groups, bereaved persons, cross-cultural and cross-gender groups, holocaust survivors, multifamily groups, persons with Alzheimer's disease, the homebound, and a host of other populations.

Despite the multitude of perspectives, technologies, contexts, and populations served, a core set of values and concepts has been identified as belonging to the social work method with groups. These unifying concepts include the following:

- A systemic perspective—that is, groups are social systems. This view underscores a dynamic view of group development and operation, stresses the reciprocal nature of relationships, and highlights the relationship of the group to its context.
- Group dynamics, including group climate and processes, influences on members, goals, maintenance, and task functions, decision making, developmental stages, norms, conflict, cohesion, and power structures.
- Concepts of intervention, including planning and analysis, worker's engagement, power of the group as the medium of service, individual, group, and environmental interventions.[36]

In recent years, social work with groups has involved exploring the implications of feminist thought for social group work and efforts have been ongoing to define a feminist group work.[37] Social group work, which began with a focus on work with children and youth in settlement houses and in adult education and social action, now is practiced in a great variety of settings. From groups in administration to treatment groups, from informal education to social action groups, and from consciousness-raising to socialization, social work with groups is used for many purposes in many different settings. Today there appears to be a growing utilization of groups by social workers for various purposes, including treatment, support, education, personal, organizational and community development, administration, advocacy, and social action.

Community Organization and Social Planning

Community organization and social planning have their roots in the reform efforts of the latter part of the nineteenth century. The Charity Organization Society originally sought to develop cooperative planning and coordination among local charities and worked for reforms in housing codes, antituberculosis associations, legislation in support of juvenile courts and probation, programs for the care of dependent children, cooperation with the police in regard to beggars and vagrants, and legislation to require absent fathers to support their children. As time went on, and as we saw earlier, settlement houses played major roles in organizing neighborhoods, studying social problems, making policy and program proposals, forming pressure groups, and conducting campaigns. Their efforts eventuated in changes that affected localities, states, and the nation.

Social workers such as Jane Addams and Lillian Wald were much involved in efforts to improve the quality of life in the United States. Following Addams's election as president of the National Conference of Charities and Corrections in 1909, a committee was appointed to undertake a study of the minimum requirements for well-being in an industrial society. In 1911, Florence Kelley, activist and general secretary of the National Consumers League, chaired the committee, followed, in 1912, by Owen Lovejoy, secretary of the National Child Labor Committee.

One outcome of this study was the minimum platform that was created in "Social Standards for Industry": the eight-hour workday, the six-day work week, abolition of tenement manufacture, improvement of housing conditions, prohibition of child labor under 16 years, regulation of employment for women, and a federal system of accident, old age, and unemployment insurance.[38] Social workers were in the forefront demanding new child labor laws, health and safety legislation, and social insurance, and on many issues were in the vanguard, helping to move the nation toward new social welfare ideas.

From these early beginnings to contemporary times, community organization efforts were conducted in many ways, including voluntary organizing efforts focused on the creation and implementation of health and welfare councils and community chests for communal fund-raising, planning, and coordination of services. Other efforts included grassroots organizing to improve the quality of life in neighborhoods through political power and the redress of problems; self-help and community-change organizations of African Americans, Latinos, and Asian Americans; Native American survival and community and tribal development; rural community organization related to electrification, access to water and other resources, mutual aid and cooperatives among rural residents, and the development of basic services such as schools and fire brigades, as well as unionization. Recent years have seen a growing emphasis on organizing by and for women, gays, and lesbians.

In 1939, the Lane Report emphasized community organization as a social work method and suggested that local welfare councils and other coordinating bodies all shared the purposes of local planning and coordination in order to seek the congruence of community social welfare resources and needs. During World War II, community organization was one part of the massive war effort, especially through the U.S. Office of Civilian Defense and the Office of Defense, Health, and Welfare Services to coordinate health and welfare services, public and private, for defense- affected localities. Following World War II, community organization emphasized integrative efforts, consensus, and process-oriented models to increase the capacity for cooperation within society.[39]

Generally, community organization was a method that for a long time focused on cooperative efforts to organize efficiently the social services in a community. The basic methodology was consensual. Conflict was minimized and the attempt was made—as in intergroup work—to utilize a process that led to understanding and cooperation. The process was intended to be enabling in that rival entities could be helped to identify common goals and through cooperative efforts attain their respective goals and a better society.

By 1947, the Association for the Study of Community Organization published *Community Organization: Its Nature and Setting* to clarify issues, terms, roles, and methods.[40] In 1962, the Council on Social Work Education issued a curriculum policy statement identifying community organization as a major social work method.

During the 1960s, our society underwent great change in an atmosphere of participatory democracy. Community organization was an important contributor to efforts to overcome juvenile delinquency, to attain civil rights, and to develop communities through the War on Poverty and model cities programs. A major emphasis during this decade was on grassroots organizing and community participation and action.

Current community organizing efforts include the following models:

1. Neighborhood and community organizing, designed to develop the capacity of the members to organize and to improve the quality of life in the geographic area;
2. Organizing functional communities of like-minded people in a community, region, nation, or internationally to advocate for a particular issue or population;
3. Community social and economic development for improved income, resources, and social supports;
4. Social planning for citywide or regional proposals for governmental or human services;
5. Program and service development and community liaison for a specific population by improving service effectiveness and/or organizing new services;
6. Political and social action, building political power toward institutional change in order to change policy or policymakers;
7. Coalitions to influence program directions or to gain resources related to a specific issue, social need, or concern; and
8. Social movements, action toward social justice for a particular population group or issue.[41]

Among recent organizing efforts are community organizing for neighborhood and economic development, safe and drug-free schools and communities, anti-hunger, increased housing for persons of modest means, health promotion, violence and homicide, "living wage" campaigns, assuring bank loans in low-income neighborhoods, people with HIV/AIDS, development of small businesses, teen pregnancy, the homeless, and the environment and hazardous wastes in poor neighborhoods. Some groups focus on the creation of low-income housing and elections. Other efforts include ACORN (Association of Community Organizations for Reform Now), which developed out of the 1960s welfare rights movement and now organizes low-income neighborhood residents around housing and other issues with a direct action approach. Citizen Action places an emphasis on health questions and tenant organizing. Other groups organize around particular identities and focus on the civil rights of various groups: Latinos, women, gays and lesbians, disabled persons, and others. Self-help and mutual aid groups also organize related to addictions and other problems—Mothers Against Drunk Driving, Alcoholics Anonymous, and advocates for the homeless. There is a new ethnic politics and organization both within and between groups, some of which formerly were in conflict. Community organization efforts raise political consciousness, are training grounds for democracy, and focus on local issues, but organizing necessarily reaches beyond the local to regional, state, and national interventions.[42]

Toward a Unified Profession

Modern social work with individuals and families are the predominant social work methods and have remained in the practice mainstream of the profession, along with group work and community organization. But practitioners have evolved in all methods a plethora of continually expanding models for and approaches to working with people. Theories range from aboriginal theory to ego psychology, from feminist theory to neurolinguistic programming and transpersonal social work.[43]

The need to define a common core and common methodologies continues unabated in social work. Concern about the effect of forces that move away from a common core in the profession is often expressed as there continue to develop diverse types of social work practice. Graduate social work education prepares students for work in direct practice (individual, family, group), community organization and planning, administration or management, and combinations of direct practice and community organization and planning (or administration or management). The largest numbers of students are being prepared for work in mental and physical health, family services, child welfare, and school social work.[44] The types of concentrations increase, but simultaneously, there is a strong sense of concern that a generic core should be maintained for all social workers.

In the professionalization process, social work has created training programs, a professional association, and a code of ethics; is licensed or certified in all 50 states, the District of Columbia, Puerto Rico, and the Virgin Islands[45]; and has created a knowledge base. Notwithstanding these accomplishments and its rapid development and growth, social work is an insecure profession because of its status. This internally and externally generated status insecurity is in part related to social work's association with poor and problematic groups and to its championing unpopular causes, among other factors.

Social work continues to grow. In 1982, there were 88,000 members of the professional association and more than 384,000 social workers employed in the United States. By 1999, more than 813,000 persons were employed in social work positions, more than doubling since 1982; and, as we have seen, the professional association in 2001 had 149,000 members.[46] The overwhelming majority of social workers are women. In chapter 13, we will examine their numbers and the role and status of women in the profession.

So social work as a profession in most respects seems to have very much completed the professionalization process with one important exception: that it does not control its varied "turf." Although some, even within the profession itself, may disagree with this assessment, society, through regulating sanctions, is moving forward in its recognition of social work as a profession. But there remain limits to the ability of the social work profession to control use of its name; and there are two streams of personnel, one professionally qualified and the other consisting of persons who are employed in social work positions but lacking professional education and credentials. Differentiating these two types of persons who occupy positions with social work titles remains problematic for the profession, and this ambiguity often is misunderstood by those not familiar with the profession.

Summary

In this chapter, we have examined the emergence and evolution of the social work profession. We turn next in chapter 13 to a discussion of the functions of the profession, the contexts in which it operates, and several major issues with which social work must deal.

Questions for Consideration

1. What do you think Jane Addams meant by the quotation with which this chapter opens?

2. How many kinds of social workers can you identify in your community?

3. Which would you choose as the better social work approach—charity organization society or settlement house?

4. What social work professional organizations are there in your community?

Notes

1. Jane Addams, *Twenty Years at Hull House*, New York: Macmillan, 1961, p. 92.

2. Karl de Schweinitz, *England's Road to Social Security*, New York: A. S. Barnes, 1975, pp. 30, 35–36; David M. Schneider, *The History of Public Welfare in New York State: 1609–1866*, Chicago: University of Chicago Press, 1938, p. 10.

3. Robert H. Bremner, "The Rediscovery of Pauperism," *Current Issues in Social Work Seen in Historical Perspective*, New York: Council on Social Work Education, 1962, p. 13.

4. de Schweinitz, pp. 100–113.

5. Dorothy G. Becker, "The Visitor to the New York City Poor, 1843–1920," *Social Service Review*, Vol. 35, No. 4, December 1961, pp. 382–396. Also see Brian Gratton, "The Invention of Social Work: Welfare Reform in the Antebellum City," *The Urban and Social Change Review*, Vol. 18, No. 1, Winter 1985, pp. 3–8.

6. Robert H. Bremner, *From the Depths*, New York: New York University Press, 1967, p. 43.

7. Victoria Olds, "The Freedmen's Bureau: A Nineteenth-Century Federal Welfare Agency," *Social Casework*, Vol. 44, No. 5, May 1963, pp. 247–254.

8. Frank J. Bruno, *Trends in Social Work,* New York: Columbia University Press, 1948, p. 11.

9. Frank D. Watson, *The Charity Organization Movement in the United States,* New York: Macmillan, 1922, pp. 178–179.

10. Roy Lubove, *The Professional Altruist,* New York: Antheneum, 1971, p. 8.

11. Ralph E. Pumphrey and Muriel W. Pumphrey, eds., *The Heritage of American Social Work,* New York: Columbia University Press, 1965, p. 170.

12. Judith A. Trolander, *Professionalism and Social Change: From the Settlement House Movement to Neighborhood Centers 1886 to the Present,* New York: Columbia University Press, 1987, pp. 12–13.

13. Ruth Bordin, *Woman and Temperance: The Quest for Power and Liberty, 1873–1900,* Philadelphia: Temple University Press, pp. 13, 98; Kathryn K. Sklar, "The "Quickened Conscience": Women's Voluntarism and the State, 1890–1920," *Philosophy & Public Policy,* Vol. 18, No. 3, Summer 1998, pp. 27–33.

14. Trolander, pp. 176–181; Thorstein Veblen, *The Theory of the Leisure Class,* New York: Modern Library, 1934 (Original, 1899), pp. 339, 344.

15. Dorothy G. Becker, "Social Welfare Leaders as Spokesmen for the Poor," *Social Casework,* Vol. 49, No. 2, February 1968, p. 85.

16. Clarke A. Chambers, *Seedtime of Reform,* Minneapolis, Minn.: University of Minnesota Press, 1963, p. 15.

17. Nathan Cohen, *Social Work in the American Tradition,* New York: Holt, Rinehart, and Winston, 1958, p. 71.

18. Donald Feldstein, "Do We Need Professions in Our Society? Professionalization Versus Consumerism," *Social Work,* Vol. 16, No. 4, October 1971, pp. 5–11, and Ronald M. Pavalko, *Sociology of Occupations and Professions,* Itasca, Ill.: F. E. Peacock, 1971, p. 277.

19. George T. Silvestri, "Occupational Employment Projections to 2006," *Monthly Labor Review,* Bureau of Labor Statistics, November 1997, Table 1, p. 52.

20. Lubove, p. 46.

21. Ibid., p. 48.

22. Addams, p. 167.

23. *Proceedings of the National Conference of Charities and Corrections,* Press of Fred J. Heer, 1905, p. 577.

24. Abraham Flexner, "Is Social Work a Profession?" in *Proceedings of the National Conference of Charities and Corrections,* 1915, pp. 576–590.

25. Pumphrey and Pumphrey, p. 306. Nathan Cohen suggested the search for method came at a time when the profession was eagerly trying to rebut the criticisms of Flexner and at the same time

that psychoanalytic thought was making inroads into American culture. Cohen, pp. 120–121.

26. Scott Briar, "Social Casework and Social Group Work: Historical Foundations," *Encyclopedia of Social Work,* Vol. 2, New York: National Association of Social Workers, 1971, p. 1239.

27. Jane Addams, *The Second Twenty Years at Hull House,* New York: Macmillan, 1930, p. 155.

28. The rise of psychoanalytically oriented casework parallels a movement away from social reform. The climate of the times militated against such efforts. But psychoanalytic thought helped veer social work's understanding of people in difficulty, moving it away from the idea that people with difficulties simply lacked character to an understanding of psychological stress and disability. See Herman Borenzweig, "Social Work and Psychoanalytic Theory: An Historical Analysis," *Social Work,* Vol. 16, No. 1, January 1971, pp. 7–16. However, Leslie Alexander suggested that Freudian theory was little known to social workers and had an influence limited to the professional elite rather than the major part of the profession. Alexander suggests social workers used a more sociological than psychoanalytical approach during the 1920s and also that social reform debates and demands continued in relation to women's rights, child welfare, unemployment, housing reform, and the need for federal action on public assistance and social insurance. Because of the nature of the times, major social reforms had to await the 1930s. Leslie B. Alexander, "Social Work's Freudian Deluge: Myth or Reality?" *Social Service Review,* Vol. 46, No. 4, December 1972, pp. 517–538.

29. *Social Casework: Generic and Specific,* New York: American Association of Social Workers, 1929, Classic Series, Washington, D.C.: National Association of Social Workers, 1974, p. 15.

30. Jacob Fisher, *The Response of Social Work to the Depression,* Cambridge, Mass.: Schenkman, 1980, pp. 233–241.

31. Donald Brieland, "History and Evolution of Social Work Practice," *Encyclopedia of Social Work,* Vol. I, 18th Edition, Anne Minahan, ed., Silver Spring, Md.: National Association of Social Workers, p. 747.

32. *Encyclopedia of Social Work,* Vol. 2, Washington, D.C.: National Association of Social Workers, 1977, p. 1670, and personal communication from Louisa Lopez, Staff Member, NASW, July, 25, 2001.

33. Patricia T. Ballard, ed., *Encyclopedia of Associations,* 2001, Vol. 1, Parts 1 and 2, Detroit: Gale Research Group, 2001.

34. Scott Briar, "Social Casework and Social Group Work: Historical and Social Science Foundations," *Encyclopedia of Social Work,* Vol. 2, New York:

National Association of Social Workers, 1971, pp. 1237–1245.

35. *Social Case Work: Generic and Specific*, p. 78.

36. Janice H. Schopler and Maeda J. Galinsky "Group Practice Overview," *Encyclopedia of Social Work*, Vol. 2, Washington, D.C.: National Association of Social Workers, 1995, pp. 1129–1142.

37. Charles D. Garvin and Beth Glover Reed, "Sources and Visions for Feminist Group Work," in *Feminist Practice in the 21st Century*, Nan Van Den Bergh, ed., Washington, D.C.: NASW Press, 1995, pp. 41–69.

38. Allen F. Davis, *Spearheads for Reform: The Social Settlements and the Progressive Movement: 1890–1914*, New York: Oxford University Press, 1967, p. 196.

39. Donald S. Howard, ed., *Community Organization: Its Nature and Setting*, New York: American Association of Social Workers, 1947.

40. Ibid.

41. Si Kahn, "Community Organization," *Encyclopedia of Social Work*, Vol. I, Washington, D.C.: National Association of Social Workers, 1995, pp. 569–576;

Marie Overby Weil and Dorothy N. Gamble, "Community Practice Models," *Community Organization: Its Nature and Setting*, Donald S. Howard, ed., New York: American Association of Social Workers, pp. 577–594.

42. Robert Fisher, *Let the People Decide: Neighborhood Organizing in America*, New York: Twayne Publishers, 1994; S. M. Miller, Martin Rein, and Peggy Levitt, "Community Action in the United States," *Community Empowerment*, Gary Craig, ed., Atlantic Highlands, N.J.: Zed Books, 1995, pp. 112–126.

43. Francis J. Turner, *Social Work Treatment*, 4th Edition, New York: The Free Press, 1996.

44. Todd M. Lennon, *Statistics on Social Work Education in the United States: 1999*, Alexandria, Va.: Council on Social Work Education, pp. 35.

45. Association of Social Work Boards, "Licensing Information," www.aswb.org/licensing/index.html, July 26, 2001.

46. U.S. Bureau of the Census, *Statistical Abstract of the United States: 2000*, 120th Edition, "Employed Civilians by Occupation, Sex, Race, and Hispanic Origin: 1983–1999, Washington, D.C., 2000, p. 416.

Social Work

Functions, Context, and Issues

> But it is perfectly alright to say that in Darwin's world individuals always act in their
> own interests and the bald principle holds but it is no longer quite clear what an individ-
> ual is. Groups and societies are individuals too. And I think therefore the growing ties
> among us, that universal brother- and sisterhood to which we aspire, is perfectly good
> biology, and the enlarged notion of individuality is not just outdated liberal hope or
> mushy romanticism.
>
> —Stephen J. Gould[1]

Overview

In this chapter we examine the functions of social work, the context within which
social work is practiced, and issues arising from their interaction. Among the
topics explored are the purposes of social work and the relationship between professionals and the organizations in which they practice, including issues related to
authority and professional autonomy. Private practice as an alternative to organi-
zation-based practice is considered, as well as social work's relationship to its assigned societal functions. The evolution of the *"cause" (social reform)* track and the
"function" (case services) track and the historical tensions between the generic and
specialized thrusts of social work are explored. The profession is also reviewed in
the context of racism, sexism, and a pluralistic society.

The Purposes of Social Work

Social work as a profession is committed to the enhancement of human well-
being, to the alleviation of poverty and oppression, and to "raising life to its high-

est value."[2] The profession receives its sanction from public and private auspices and implements its purposes through a broad variety of interventions in practice. The purposes of social work are as follows:

1. To enhance human well-being and alleviate poverty, oppression, and other forms of social injustice.
2. To enhance the social functioning and interactions of individuals, families, groups, organizations, and communities by involving them in accomplishing goals, developing resources, and preventing and alleviating distress.
3. To formulate and implement social policies, services, and programs that meet basic human needs and support the development of human capacities.
4. To pursue policies, services, and resources through advocacy and social or political actions that promote social and economic justice.
5. To develop and use research, knowledge, and skills that advance social work practice.
6. To develop and apply practice in the context of diverse cultures.[3]

There is practically no institution (e.g., education, defense, health, justice, religion) in our society that is without social workers, because social and human problems affect every institution and, in turn, these same institutions affect individuals, families, groups, and communities. Social workers are employed under public and private auspices on the local, state, regional, national, as well as international level. Some social workers are self employed private practitioners

Social workers assist persons, groups, and communities to cope with a multiplicity of issues, covering most of the social problems people experience. The tasks needed to implement the aims of social work include an array of activities ranging from counseling to research, from organizing to administering, and from planning to legislative advocacy.

Several brief examples can give a sense of social workers in action. Suppose a person encountered a series of social and psychological setbacks, including loss of job, serious illness in the family, depleted funds, and conflicts within the family that seem to derive from stress. A social worker would attempt with the client to select from all the client's problems which to focus on and to work on them in order of priority with the person(s) involved. This could mean assistance in finding work, in dealing with hospital or medical personnel, and in assisting the family with its interpersonal problems through social work counseling.

A social worker employed by a community development agency may discover a large number of young adult men and women in the neighborhood who do not have jobs. Because of much time on their hands, frustration, and resultant anger, they are involved in a series of destructive acts, against both themselves and society. Social workers may work with employers, city or county agencies, and other organizations to create jobs, training programs, reentry into schools, and other needed resources. A social worker also may help to form groups of such young people to help them work on personal and family difficulties and in other ways to help them reach their legitimate goals.

Social workers in a family service agency may organize services for aging persons who live isolated and lonely lives, have difficulty shopping, and eat poorly. They may help by arranging homemaker services, organizing a volunteer group that visits with isolated persons and renders simple assistance, organizing shopping assistance, or establishing a Meals-on-Wheels program for those unable to prepare hot meals for themselves.

The Professional within Complex Organizations

As our society becomes more complex and interdependent, as business and other organizations grow in size, there has been more employment within complex organizations, even by professions that in the past have been noted for their "free" stances. Sociologists studying the professions point out this increased organizational employment by professionals: Physicians are now affiliated in larger numbers with hospitals and health maintenance organizations; attorneys with law firms and, in increasing numbers, with industrial corporations; scientists and engineers with industry, government, large independent research organizations, and a collection of institutes and departments in academic institutions.[4]

Professions and complex organizations are intricately tied, but there are real problems for social workers as professionals as they function within these complicated human networks. Essentially these problems can be categorized into two areas: (1) the relationship between organizational structure and professional culture and (2) the structure of authority.

Complex Organizations and Professional Culture

Alfred Kahn suggested that organizational factors and realities may supersede professional ethics. Overall professional and organizational perspectives affect the ways in which a problem is perceived and structured, the values that are held supreme, the priorities given to components of and the sequences in a solution to a person's or family's difficulties, and the "costs" to be tolerated for given outcomes or benefits.[5]

The effects of professional identity within a complex organization include subtle issues. For example, Robert Vinter makes the point that when professionals are present in large numbers and assume elite positions, the organization's dependence on them brings with it limiting commitment to particular ideologies and strategies of change. Alternative approaches are thus denied the organization except as these are mediated through the profession. The risk is that the approaches defined by one or another profession may not be sufficient for achievement of treatment goals, yet the organization is no longer as free to pursue alternative means.[6]

Complex Organizations and Authority

Professional identity and perspectives cause the selection of particular intervention strategies. Generalized professional knowledge and identity, however, are expressed in the individual case. It is here that individual professions may enter areas of potential conflict with their superiors in the hierarchical arrangements in the bureaucracy. Amitai Etzioni suggested that a basic administrative principle is thus put in jeopardy because knowledge is largely an individual property, not the property of the organization; unlike other organizational resources, it cannot be transferred from one person to another by decree. Creativity is basically individual and can only to a very limited degree be ordered and coordinated by the superior in rank. Even the application of knowledge is basically an individual act, at least in the sense that individual professionals have the ultimate responsibility for their professional decisions. Only if immune from ordinary social pressures and free to innovate, to experiment, to take risks without the usual social repercussions of failure, can a professional carry out his or her work effectively.[7]

But these are requirements that are difficult for a complex organization to accept, not only because of internal accountability but because of accountability to the wider community. Peer support for professional experimentation or decision making is one thing, but administrative responsibility and accountability run counter to such freedoms.

The longer the training and the more intense the professional orientation, the greater the tendency to take as one's reference group the profession rather than the employer.[8] This, too, runs counter to a demand of complex organizations. In social agencies or other organizations one method of standardizing the discretionary component in the work is to make rules. Another method is to reduce the number of written rules by employing personnel who have complex rules *built into them*. We generally call these people "professionals."[9] Thus social agencies, when possible, hire professionals to ensure high standards and the delivery of high-quality service. But, paradoxically, being professional in itself runs counter to organizational demands while it meets the need for narrowing the outer limits of discretion through professional training. Perhaps the critical issue is who controls which aspects of daily professional practice.

The Profession and Professional Autonomy

The problem as posed in the preceding section is to reconcile professional autonomy with bureaucratic demands. Willard Richan pondered this question and placed the dilemma in a different context. The individual worker must be viewed within the context not only of the agency and the profession, but the agency *and* worker must be viewed within the context of the profession within the social welfare or other societal institution. The power of the social work profession depends on the cohesion of the profession. Richan suggests "the issues of professional autonomy and professional cohesion are closely related. To achieve the former, the organized social work profession must demonstrate the latter; that is, its ability to speak for the social work community. And both of these depend, in turn, on effective control over social work practice and the social work education process."[10]

Paradoxically, the attainment of greater autonomy for social workers is tied to greater controls. The regulation of practice, control over who practices and the conditions for practice, and licensing and "enforceable expectations"—that is, greater regulation of social workers—is the means for achieving greater autonomy.

An issue that highlights the question of autonomy is social reform and social work's role in it. Social reform is one part of the social work tradition. However, as Kathleen Woodroofe asserted, the struggle to gain professional acceptance in the community accentuated some of the stresses within social work itself. Some of these stresses spring from attempts to fix rightful boundaries to its domain; others from efforts to define its function to new areas and settings. Some spring from limitations of its knowledge and experience; others arise from the nature of its own activity. But perhaps the most serious source of stress has been the attempt to reconcile the caution of professionalism with social work's traditional commitment to reform.[11]

There are other more pedestrian problems and dysfunctions of complex organizations. For example, the specialization of social workers within an organization means task specialization. Such specialization increases the quality and quantity of work, but it also may lead to discrete responsibilities and areas of service. When this occurs, it is often accompanied by disjunctions among the several services available, and people who need service may fall through the cracks.

Work within organizations is accompanied by frustration, lack of congruence between individual and organizational needs, skewed time perspectives, rivalry, and conflict. To the extent that these attitudinal effects carry over into work with clients, members, and others who come for service, they may be dysfunctional in regard to services.

Alternative Roles and Settings

A growing literature has developed aimed at understanding organizational settings and developing ways of operating successfully within them.[12] The range of options available runs from less active and dramatic roles for the social workers to conscious and planned efforts to alter the agencies in order to improve services. Others suggest the need for organizations that decentralize decision making, practice participative management, and are more adaptable and responsive to their members.

According to some social workers, the trend toward private practice is a key lever to offset the forces of bureaucracy that act on social workers. The private practice of social work and employment in private profit making organizations are, indeed, important components of contemporary professional practice. However, when those directions are selected by many, a question can be raised about the social commitment and philosophy of the profession.

To the extent that social workers become private practitioners, they delimit the communal (societal) sanction they receive through social welfare and other sponsoring organizations. Social sponsorship and commitment have been important factors in the development of social work's professional identity. According to some observers, tendencies away from the social commitment of the profession lead to a deemphasis on social action, acceptance of the role of technician-implementer in contrast to policy changer, and an increase in the congruence between social workers' ideas and those of the dominant groups in society.[13] Thus, complex organizations, although subject to criticism, may be better settings for social workers to engage in social change and social action than some of the alternatives offered.

Society, the Functions of Social Work, and Services for People

Society sets certain demands and limits on the profession. Nevertheless, the parameters of social work have been vigorously debated within the social work community. Essentially, the question is, how many functions of social work should there be: rehabilitation, prevention, provision of resources, enhancing human rights, or social justice? The major functions expected of social work determine how social workers must be prepared to implement them.

From one perspective, all roles performed by social work can be viewed as deriving from two basic societal functions: *social control* and *social change*. Society assigns the functions of social welfare, and therefore of social work, in formal and informal ways. Various sanctioning bodies provide that social welfare agencies and social workers will perform specific functions, and these bodies typically determine how these functions will be implemented. These sanctions derive not only from consumer demand but also from legislation, funding, and other formal and informal sources. Thus, the roles and functions of social workers are dependent on the priorities set by society through various control mechanisms. In addition, social agencies themselves exert control over the work of social workers in several ways, including identifying populations to be served, services to be provided, and methods of service. Thus, not only are social control mechanisms manifested through social agencies that wish to socialize clients to dominant societal values, but more subtle controls are expressed through the choice of methods and technologies to be used.

Finally, both on philosophical and empirical grounds, there are social workers who suggest that any profession that focuses primarily on individual change cannot be truly focused on social change. According to this view, individual change is simply inconsistent with the demands of social change and, in reality, such an approach is more consistent with social control. To this group, the fact that social work maintains its clinical, individual, and family focus suggests not social change but social control as the higher professional value.

The "Bottom Line"

Social workers are not "free agents" who can choose whether they wish to be part of a profession of social control or of social change. Regardless of whether the profession operates within organizational settings or as an entrepreneurial service, it is dependent on the sanctions of society. In addition to whatever limitations exist as to knowledge needed for social change or the choices of interventions, social work can only make choices within certain limits. Societies do not hire "social change" agents; rather they hire persons who can perform important functions that serve the society.

The Two Tracks of Social Work:
Cause and Function

In regard to the roles of social workers, a historical tension exists between two tracks of social work that have survived in an uneasy alliance. These two streams have been described variously as *cause* and *function* and, respectively, as the social reform and case service tracks. Almost from the inception of social work, the two tracks came to be associated with particular persons and institutions. The function or *case service* track, which developed from the work of Thomas Chalmers as translated to the United States, is ordinarily associated with the friendly visitors of charity organization societies. The cause or *social reform* track is associated with the settlement houses and social workers involved in seeking better environmental conditions through legislation and other means. The function track is best represented in the United States by Mary Richmond, who developed early casework theory and techniques, and the cause track by Jane Addams, who, as a settlement house founder and director, was active in social reform.

These two tracks reflect separate and different conceptions, and yet the social work profession remains intact. Why this is the case is an important question. Historically the dichotomy—the two tracks—arises in different forms and under different names. During the 1890s, hostility was expressed toward settlement houses and their workers at the National Conference on Charities and Corrections. Originally formed by volunteers who created neighborhood service centers in the midst of poor neighborhoods, the settlement houses and their leadership focused not only on services to individuals, families, and neighborhoods, but also on changing society and the world in which the poor existed. They were not confident of their acceptance by others in the field of social welfare. In 1897, Addams apologized for being at the national conference because "settlements are accused of doing their charity work very badly."[14]

Through her writings and work, Addams represented the social reform track. On the basis of her experiences, she recognized a multicausation for social ills, a fact that suggested multifocused action was needed to change life conditions. In regard to this multicausation in life she stated:

> The settlements have often been accused of scattering their forces; as institutions they are both philanthropic and educational; in their approach to social problems they call now upon the sociologists, now upon the psychiatrist; they seek the services of artists, economists, gymnasts, case-workers, dramatists, trained nurses.... [in order to deal with] bewildering legal requirements, ill health and conflicting cultures which the settlements find so baffling.[15]

Representative of the case service track in social work, Mary Richmond was employed in charity organization societies in Baltimore and Philadelphia, formulated the first global statements of the principles of social casework, taught at the New York School of Philanthropy, and was the author of *Social Diagnosis* (1917), the first formulation of the theory and method of social casework.[16] From the start, the social workers at charity organizations were investigating each needy person and family in detail, attempting to avoid duplication of benefits of any kind, seeking cooperation among agencies, and fostering the use of friendly visitors.

Very early in its development the case service track had an individual and family focus, based on the character of the individual, the relationship with the people to be helped, and a search for technique. On the other hand, the social reform track, while serving individuals, families, and neighborhoods, also stressed more global change through political action, publicity of social problems, legislation, and a greater emphasis on the surroundings in which people lived. This stream of social workers was doing the preliminary work to attain workers' compensation, health insurances, and mothers' pensions, and generally worked to prepare for the financial and other protection of workers and their families.[17]

Thus, in its early stages, social work contained several different kinds of social workers. They were employed or served as volunteers in a wide variety of situations. They were based in settlement houses and focused on societal changes. They were employed as administrators and friendly visitors in charity organization societies, constructing a method for helping individuals and families. They were crafting and lobbying for the preliminary social insurances and for other social legislation.

Despite the differences in emphasis, spokespersons for the two tracks (social reform and case services) agreed there were commonalities between the two tracks, and each had need for the complementary actions of the other. In *Social Diagnosis,* Richmond concluded that the majority of social workers were in casework: "in work, that is, which has for its immediate aim the betterment of individuals or families, one by one, as distinguished from their betterment in the mass. Mass betterment and individual betterment are interdependent, however, social reform and social case work of necessity progressing together."[18]

Various people struggled with this conundrum. In 1929, Porter R. Lee, director of the New York School of Philanthropy, in his presidential address to the National Conference of Social Work, provided a perspective on the tensions that existed between the social reform and the case service aspects of the profession and suggested that social work was both *cause* and *function*. He defined cause as a "movement directed toward the elimination of an entrenched evil"; a function he viewed as an "organized effort incorporated into the machinery of community life in the discharge of which the acquiescence at least, and ultimately the support, of the entire community is assumed."[19]

Thus, Lee defined these two aspects of social work as overlapping and symbiotic; they also were parts of an historical process through which society and social work both change.

> Social work...is cause as well as function. Much of what we do in social work we do because, on the whole, we prefer a civilization in which such things are done to one in which they are not. Some values are beyond measurement.... Efficient social work everywhere means the constant discovery of new evils, of ancient evils in new forms which are taking their toll of men. Good social work creates the necessity for more social work.[20]

In a catchy phrase, Clarke Chambers offered another way of viewing these two social work tracks: He called them the *"retail"* and the *"wholesale"* services; not only do the two tracks differ in regard to cause or function, but they also differ in regard to the size of the population unit to which they give emphasis and in regard to the roles their professionals play. He suggested that

> the two overlapping phases of social work continue to exist, not always harmoni-ously, but certainly in interdependence—the one focused on the individual and his or her welfare, strongly influenced by the psychological disciplines, introspective, dealing in personalized retail services; the other concerned with reform, with re-construction, informed primarily by the social sciences, extroverted, dealing in group or community or wholesale services.[21]

Chambers went further and suggested the two tracks of social work require two different major roles: *priest* and *prophet*. The priest is a "shepherd, he serves, he counsels, he comforts, he reconciles, he listens, he accepts, he judges not, he plays out a ritualistic role, he bears witness to a transcendent concern." The prophet, on the other hand, "holds up absolute standards against which the sins of man and the shortcomings of the world may be measured and judged; his cry is less for charity and compassion than for justice; he is not content merely to stand and serve; repen-tance and reform or doom is his prophecy."[22]

But the argument as to cause and function, case services or social reform, is dismissed by those who suggest that the different methodologies of social work are all conservative, social control forces, the only differentiation being which level of society is addressed for intervention. Some suggest that casework oper-ates on a sociopsychological view insufficiently related to the societal roots of peo-ple's dilemmas and therefore cannot develop strategies equal to making social change. Furthermore, community organization—even through the more radical of its historical interventions—also serves as a conservative force in that whatever changes it accomplishes do not lead to change in the basic structures of society. Others argue that specialization, elitism, and career structures result in profession-alism, which serves the dominant class of society.

In recent years, feminist practice emerged to challenge the assumptions and roles of social work based on five principles: eliminating false dichotomies and arti-ficial separations, reconceptualizing power, valuing process equally with product, the validity of renaming, and making the personal political.[23] Feminist practice re-quires understanding women's lives and experiences, the nature of inequality be-tween the sexes, and the structuring of gender. This type of practice centers on the connections among gender, privilege, social class, culture, sexuality, and the concept of self, thus close attention must be paid to the effects of the social context on the dif-ficulties of the client. Included in feminist practice is a revaluing of behaviors often performed by women, recognizing differences in male and female experiences, re-balancing perceptions of normality and deviance, an inclusive stance, attention to power dynamics, recognizing the personal is political, and empowerment prac-tice.[24] Such a practice focuses on personal and political transformation because personal problems arise from the failures of society. Feminist social work is concerned not just with the problems of patriarchy but "with *all* institutionalized systems and ideologies of domination/subordination, exploitation, and oppression that are inimical to individual and collective self-actualization."[25]

These arguments call for the politicization of social work as a profession. The early social workers of the progressive era took political stands and affected party platforms and legislation to significant extents. Still later, other social workers influenced decision makers and legislation. Over the years, however, as Daniel Moynihan suggested, there arose the "professionalization of reform."[26] This implies a certain objectivity and attention to professional expertise rather than investment in the movement aspects of the professional aims and their achievement. Ideology can be a resource and lead social workers toward the achievement of social reform or help to veer social work onto new professional paths. It is possible that more radical professional stances, including alliances with particular political parties, could serve to create new roles for social workers as their functions change. This might be one method of combining the cause and function dichotomies into unique, new professional configurations. However, the alliance with particular political parties or ideologies is a two-edged sword, which also can cause losses. Given the existence of a democratic United States in which parties move in and out of power, it appears more likely that on balance social work will not choose to become overly identified with one party or to cut off its links with any party or ideology that has the potential of helping create better services for people.

Some social workers have attempted to create pathways out of the two-track dilemma through new methods and new types of professionalism. Others have attempted to reconcile the differences through redefining traditional methods, so that the connections between the two tracks stand out.

William Schwartz, in attempting to reconcile the two tracks, reminds us that certain human dichotomies seem always with us: mass or individual betterment, process or goals, individual or state, freedom or discipline. The emphasis is always on the choice—either one or the other. But, as he suggests, the choices once made seem incomplete. Schwartz joins private troubles and public issues through the mediating role of the social worker. The mediating process between individuals and society—the engagements of people with their systems—are real struggles in which both can change. The professional role of social workers is to help change the nature of individuals and of the society through these engagements, thus tying societal and individual change (cause and function) together.[27]

Another effort to resolve the dilemma revolves around the issue of generalist practice. In generalist practice, the social worker maintains a focus on the interaction among systems—the person/family, their environment, and their transactions. The situation determines the particular practice approach to be used by the social worker. This requires that social workers have a broad knowledge and skill base from which to serve clients or client systems.[28] Through generalist practice, an eclectic knowledge base, professional values, and a wide range of skills social workers are enabled to target any size system.[29] In this way, generalist practice combines the element of cause with the element of function.

Roy Lubove suggested another possible explanation as to why the disparate elements within the profession hold together. Casework, that is, case services, was a key to "a knowledge base and helping technique more 'scientific' and hence more professional." However, "if social work could claim any distinctive function in an atomized urban society with serious problems of group communication and mass deprivation, it was not individual therapy but liaison between groups and the stimulation of social legislation and institutional change" which offers that unique function. Agreeing with Abraham Flexner that social work's unique feature is its "traffic cop" function, Lubove suggests that the clinical case services offer social work a baseline for practice while reform gives the profession its uniqueness, and the two—cause and function, social reform and case services— together form a team that provides the profession with a territory, the arena of social welfare. The functional specialty is needed to give social work a professional image and base, and the cause element is needed to give it distinction from the other therapeutic or helping professions.[30]

But using what is known about cases to move to causes is not simply a matter of differentiating social work from other professions. Advocacy offers a way for agencies and staffs to bridge the gap between the many cases of individual and family need and grievances against social institutions and the broader-scale actions needed to bring about institutional change. The social worker's intimate knowledge of individual families provides a grassroots basis for social action improving the social environment of families.[31]

Generic-Specific Social Work

Even within the relatively homogeneous case services stream of social work, there were and are questions of generic skills, knowledge, and attitudes applicable to a broad variety of practice settings. Simultaneously there were counterforces demanding specific training for specific agencies and fields of practice.

Social work historically juggled tensions between generic and specific qualities just as it has between cause and function. The price of being able to practice in a wide variety of settings (functional diffusion) and the required generic qualities was the workers' limited sense of identity as social workers and a limited sense of the totality of the profession as social work. The more practice settings there are, the more difficult it is to achieve a common professional identity. Constant, in addition, was the early-identified problem of educating workers equally prepared for work in several fields.

In the 1929 monograph *Social Casework: Generic and Specific*, these issues moved to the fore. A work group (the Milford Conference) struggled with the generic and specific aspects and the issues that underlay the concepts. Their work commenced from

a recognition of the importance of the problems of division of labor among case work agencies. This, again, was not a new question. It furnished material for dis-

cussion for a generation. After a generation's discussion, however, it seemed to the group that dividing lines between the specific fields of social case work were still lacking, as well as the fundamental principles underlying the practical working divisions among the case work agencies of the community.[32]

But it was not simply a question of division of labor. The different philosophies (for example, cause or function) and different methodologies (specialized or generic) raised bothersome but important questions. In 1936, Sophonisba Breckenridge, a professor at the University of Chicago, reported the problem and drew attention to its importance. In an article on professional education for social work, she remarked:

> Another subject on which agreement has been slowly developing is the generalized, as over against the specialized, nature of the desirable curriculum. Some schools, possibly because of the nature of their origin, provided instruction in family welfare, in child welfare, and in group work, organizing the instruction in fields quite distinct from the others. On the other hand, some schools have taken the position from the beginning that their responsibility was the education of persons who should enter a field of social work, thus recognizing the probability of a worker's passing from one area in the field to another.[33]

With a social worker's passage from one field of service to another or entry into new settings, the profession became *functionally diffuse* (social workers function in many settings with many different sets of skills to meet many different kinds of needs). This fact, on the one hand, creates problems for the profession, mainly relating to issues of education and professional identification: What are the commonalities of social workers trained in diverse ways who practice in even more diverse settings?

On the other hand, the fact that the profession is functionally diffuse and of a generalized nature allows for the entry of social workers into many different types of employment and service settings. The functionally generalized nature of the profession also makes it possible for it to bring knowledge and skills when the society alters its major concerns or new problems arise. Social work has been quite successful at entering new fields and making contributions. This flexibility is the positive side of the functionally diffuse nature of the profession.

While some view the diversity of social work as a drawback, it can be viewed as an important strength or, even more, as an unplanned strategy related to the achievement of widespread social services. The fact that the profession plays an important intermediary role among different institutions makes it possible for the profession to help people meet varying needs.

Another positive attribute derives from functional diffusion. It has been suggested that specialized roles in organizations allow professionals to carry out their activities with a greater degree of freedom than would be the case where substructures and roles are more generalized. The autonomy of a professional in an organization is supported by the differentiation of roles and consequent specialization.[34] By analogy, the social work profession also may function in this manner.

Specialization tends to support the autonomy of separate divisions of the profession. However, problems of communication, influence, and cooperation may be created because of a lack of a common language and the resistance of different camps to accept the views of others.

Despite the difficulties of diverse preparation and functional diffusion and despite the problems related to professional identity, it is clear that the development of the profession and services for people have been encouraged by this diffuse/diverse feature of the profession. Although difficulties arise, they seem on balance to be outweighed by the gains for society and for the profession.

Ambiguity, complexity, fluidity, and differing assumptions along with multiple and varying visions of the nature of social work practice lead to a plurality of practice modes and theories. In an attempt to prepare social workers with common knowledge and skills, the Council on Social Work Education has required educational programs to implement a generic foundation. The generic foundation includes a liberal arts base, specific social work knowledge such as social work's purpose, the focus of social work on the person in the environment, professionalism, sanction to practice, values and philosophy, basic communication and helping skills, ethnic and diversity sensitivity, the change process, and understanding of human relationships. These core (generic) elements serve as the base for generalist practice—the ability to assess situations, choose the appropriate means of intervening, and to intervene as a worker who possesses a wide variety of skills and/or for specialty practice organized around fields of service, population groups, problem areas, or practice roles and interventive modes.[35]

Professionals and Volunteers

Social work is organized formally with two academic entry points to the profession: baccalaureate and graduate. As of July, 2002 the Council on Social Work Education implemented new *Educational Policy and Accreditation Standards* for baccalaureate and master's degree programs. The baccalaureate programs prepare for generalist professional practice and the master's degree programs prepare for advanced professional practice in various areas of concentration such as fields of practice (e.g., aging, family services, mental health); problem areas (e.g., poverty, alcohol, drug, or substance abuse); and interventive methods (e.g., direct practice, community organization and planning). All social work practice is expected to take place within a configuration of social work values and ethics. Social workers are responsible for their own ethical conduct based upon the Code of Ethics of the National Association of Social Workers, the quality of their practice, and to seek continuous growth in the knowledge and skills of the profession. Emphasis is placed on human diversity, poverty, individual and collective social and economic justice, populations at risk, and the dynamics and consequences of discrimination, economic deprivation, and oppression.[36]

Despite efforts over several decades to retrench social services and social workers, by 1999, 813,000 persons were employed as social workers, 71.4 percent

of them women, 24.2 percent African American, and 7.4 percent Latino. At least 40 percent of social workers are employed by state, county, and local governments in a host of settings. A small number of social workers are employed by the federal government. Others are employed by voluntary, nonprofit agencies, with a number involved in international service as consultants, administrators, and direct service practitioners. There is a growing number of social workers employed by private for-profit businesses, and an increasing number of social workers who conduct private practices.[37]

In Chapter 11 we discussed the extremely important and diverse positions and contributions of volunteers in the social welfare arena. Among the issues confronting social work is task differentiation among professional social workers (bachelor's through doctorates), paraprofessionals, untrained persons employed in social work positions, and volunteers. This is a relatively undefined but important area of concern in social welfare. The entire issue of who may do what is somewhat ambiguous and unsettled. Even the value of volunteerism itself is subject to objections from those who want to enhance employment opportunities and who view volunteerism in some situations as undermining the goal of paid work. And yet the development of citizen leadership and involvement are also basic goals of social work.

Questions about the areas of competency of professionals and of laypersons confound many professions. Which social policy decisions should be decided by laypersons and which only by professional social workers (or by physicians, engineers, and so on)? Some questions about health insurance or public assistance programs may rest in the broader citizen sphere, whereas questions requiring specialized competency (such as whether or not to operate, or whether to place a child in a foster home) belong in the professional sphere. Yet other social welfare policy questions are ambiguous so that it is difficult to differentiate the dividing line between professional and layperson or citizen decision making.[38]

The Number of Social Workers

As one can see by the discrepancy between the number of members in the professional association (149,000) and the number of persons employed in social work positions (813,000, 1999), many persons employed in social work positions as defined by employers are untrained in social work prior to their employment. The implication is that the profession has not been in a position as yet to control sufficiently the use of the professional title or to prepare sufficient numbers of trained personnel. At the same time, social work by 1995 was licensed or regulated in all 50 states, the District of Columbia, Puerto Rico, and the Virgin Islands.[39]

Racism, Sexism, and a Pluralistic Society

The profession of social work has made efforts to deal constructively with racism and sexism within its professional ranks and in society. Social work as a profession has done well compared with other groups. Nonetheless, problems remain, and the efforts need to be continued.

Almost 80 percent of NASW members are female; similarly, 80 percent of graduate students are female; and over 80 percent of baccalaureate students are women. In 1999 one-third of baccalaureate students were members of minority groups; among master's students, 26 percent were from minority groups (29 percent of the full-time doctoral students) while only 10.4 percent of NASW were minority group members.[40]

Estimates of the proportion of females in administrative positions in general social work practice are far below their percentage of professionally trained social workers. In 1999 53 percent of the deans of graduate programs were females and 55 percent of baccalaureate directors were women.

Leadership positions in social welfare organizations associated with higher pay scales go disproportionately to men. Social service employment, generally, is underpaid for both women and men. Recent studies of social workers' pay found that incomes for male social workers continue to be higher than those of females, and this gap exists at all income levels—perhaps reflecting the income gender gap in society at large, and at direct service, supervisory, and management levels. The predominance of women in performing direct service work (lower paid roles) contrasts with the predominance of males in social welfare administration (higher paid roles) and produces differences in compensation and rewards. These findings generally are supported by salary studies of the members of NASW.[41]

At one level, all people are the same and have "common human needs," but at another level, we are all different. One way we deal with differences in our society is by discrimination. As a result, there is a need for affirmative action programs in social work and social welfare, at least for the foreseeable future. One major reason for affirmative action is the need that all groups have for role models to identify with in terms of gender, race, and ethnicity. But this rationale must not be taken too far; we are not arguing that only African Americans can work with African Americans, or that the blind can only work with those similarly disabled, or those who have been addicted with those who are addicted. Social work is struggling with this problem. It is legitimate that a social service in a Latino neighborhood ask that most workers speak Spanish and be familiar with Latino cultures, but to ask that all workers also be Latinos may be going to an extreme.

Race and ethnicity are factors in American culture, and social work's recognition of this has influenced recruitment, admissions, hiring, and promotion patterns. Similar decisions regarding women are being made relative to promotion to leadership positions. These trends are not just personal, professional career decisions affecting individuals; they have an impact on the delivery of social services, resource allocation, and community conflict and consensus. Race, ethnicity, and gender are important areas for social work and social welfare in which significant strides have been made. Continued efforts are needed to attain equitable methods of dealing with people in a pluralistic society.

For all its limitations and ambiguities, the profession of social work is strong, growing, and a fundamental part of contemporary society. However, both internal and external pressures are exerted on the profession. Emblematic of internal criticism are those who suggest that social work has abandoned its mission to help the poor and oppressed and now devote their energies to psychotherapy and private practice. These critics, harkening back to earlier social work times, believe social work's mission should be to build a "meaning, a purpose, and a sense of obligation, and social support" for all. The external pressures derive from the global context in which social work is practiced. The context has dictated leaner budgets, increased paperwork and documentation, briefer treatment, and greater accountability. These affect the quality of services, reduce interventive choices, reduce follow-up efforts, and can lead to alienation between clients and services unable to meet basic needs. All of which may tend toward the devaluation of social workers.

Summary

In this chapter, we examined the functions of social workers and the organizational contexts in which they practice, as well as issues that arise from their interactions. We also examined the roles of social work as a profession in our society as a cause and/or function and the history and tensions between generic and specific social work practice methods. Also discussed were the social work profession today and the contributions and roles of volunteers. Finally, information regarding racism, sexism, gender and the profession were set forth. In chapter 14, we will discuss major societal trends that affect the needs of people and the social welfare responses of society. We will examine growth, demography, and resources; productivity and the service economy; individual and shared goals; ethnicity and pluralism; gender; gays and lesbians; the new property; technological change; crime; and the economy.

Questions for Consideration

1. What do you see in social work that suggests either a dominant social control or social change role for the profession?

2. If it could, should social work better combine the two streams—cause and function? What suggestions would you make to do so?

3. What does feminist social work suggest are the ways the profession should seek to integrate personal and societal transformation?

4. Can you identify the ways in which volunteers and professionals cooperate in the delivery of social services? In what ways might they have conflicting purposes?

Notes

1. Stephen J. Gould, *The Individual in Darwin's World,* Edinburgh: Edinburgh University Press, 1990, p. 33.

2. Jane Addams, *Jane Addams: A Centennial Reader,* New York: Macmillan, 1960, p. 85.

3. Council on Social Work Education, *Educational Policy and Accreditation Standards,* 2001, www.cswe.org, July 26, 2001.

4. Howard M. Vollmer and Donald M. Mills, *Professionalization,* Englewood Cliffs, N.J.: Prentice Hall, 1966, p. 264.

5. Alfred J. Kahn, "Perspectives on Access to Social Services," *Social Work,* Vol. 15, No. 2, April 1970, pp. 95–101.

6. Robert D. Vinter, "Analysis of Treatment Organizations," *Social Work,* Vol. 8, No. 3, July 1963, p. 9.

7. Amitai Etzioni, *Modern Organizations,* Englewood Cliffs, N.J.: Prentice Hall, 1964, p. 76.

8. Ibid., p. 88.

9. Charles Perrow, *Complex Organizations: A Critical Essay,* 3rd Edition, New York: Random House, 1986, p. 22.

10. Willard C. Richan, "The Social Work Profession and Organized Social Welfare," *Shaping the New Social Work,* Alfred J. Kahn, ed., New York: Columbia University Press, 1973, pp. 147–148.

11. Kathleen Woodroofe, *From Charity to Social Work in England and the United States,* Toronto, Canada: University of Toronto Press, 1974, pp. 224–225.

12. See, for example, George Brager and Stephen Holloway, *Changing Human Service Organizations: Politics and Practice,* New York: Free Press, 1978; Ralph Dolgoff, "Clinicians as Social Policymakers," *Social Casework,* Vol. 62, No. 5, May 1981, pp. 284–292; Marie Weil, "Creating an Alternative Work Culture in a Public Service Setting," *Administration in Social Work,* Vol. 12, No. 2, 1988, pp. 69–82.

13. Herbert Bisno, "How Social Will Social Work Be?" *Social Work,* Vol. 2, No. 2, April 1956, pp. 12–18.

14. Allen F. Davis, *Spearheads for Reform: The Social Settlement and the Progressive Movement 1890–1914,* New York: Oxford University Press, 1967, p. 195.

15. Christopher Lasch, ed., *The Social Thought of Jane Addams,* New York: Bobbs-Merrill, 1965, p. 216.

16. D.G. Becker, "Mary Ellen Richmond," *Encyclopedia of Social Work,* Vol. 2, Robert Morris, ed., New York: National Association of Social Workers, 1971, pp. 1135–1136.

17. Roy Lubove, *The Struggle for Social Security 1900–1935,* Cambridge, Mass.: Harvard University Press, 1968.

18. Mary E. Richmond, *Social Diagnosis,* New York: Russell Sage Foundation, 1917, p. 25.

19. Porter R. Lee, *Social Work as Cause and Function,* New York: Columbia University Press, 1937, pp. 3, 5.

20. Ibid., pp. 19, 21.

21. Clarke A. Chambers, "An Historical Perspective in Political Action vs. Individualized Treatment," *Current Issues in Social Work Seen in Historical Perspective,* New York: Council on Social Work Education, 1962, p. 53.

22. Ibid., p. 63.

23. Nan Van Den Bergh, *Feminist Practice in the 21st Century,* Nan Van Den Bergh, ed., Washington, D.C.: NASW Press, 1995, p. viii.

24. Helen Land, "Feminist Clinical Social Work in the 21st Century," in *Feminist Practice in the 21st Century,* Nan Van Den Bergh, ed., Washington, D.C.: NASW Press, 1995, pp. 5–6.

25. Mary Bricker-Jenkins, "The Propositions and Assumptions of Feminist Social Work Practice," *Feminist Social Work Practice in Clinical Settings,* Mary Bricker-Jenkins, Nancy R. Hooyman, and Naomi Gottlieb, eds., Newbury Park, Calif.: Sage, 1991, pp. 271–303; Jeffrey H. Galper, *The Politics of Social Services,* Englewood Cliffs, N.J.: Prentice Hall, 1975, pp. 11–13; David Wagner, *The Quest for a Radical Profession,* New York: University Press of America, 1990, p. 7.

26. Daniel P. Moynihan, "The Professionalization of Reform," *The Public Interest,* Fall 1965, pp. 6–16.

27. William Schwartz, "Private Troubles and Public Issues: One Social Work Job or Two?" *Perspectives on Social Welfare,* Paul Weinberger, ed., New York: Macmillan, 1974, pp. 346–362.

28. Armando Morales and Bradford W. Sheafor, *Social Work: A Profession of Many Faces,* 6th Edition, Boston: Allyn and Bacon, 1992, p. 19.

29. Karen K. Kirst-Ashman and H.Hull Grafton, Jr., *Generalist Practice with Organizations and Communities,* Chicago: Nelson-Hall Publishers, 1997, pp. 7–8.

30. Roy Lubove, *The Professional Altruist: The Emergence of Social Work as a Career, 1880–1930,* New York: Atheneum, 1969, pp. 210–211.

31. Jack Rothman and Jon S. Sager, "Advocacy," *Case Management: Integrating Individual and Community Practice,* Boston: Allyn and Bacon, 1998, pp. 176–192.

32. *Social Casework: Generic and Specific,* New York: American Association of Social Workers, 1929; Classic Series, Washington, D.C.: National Association of Social Workers, 1974, p. 4.

33. Sophonisba P. Breckenridge, "The New Horizons of Professional Education for Social Work,"

Social Service Review, Vol. 10, No. 3, September 1936, pp. 434–444.

34. Bernard Barber, "Some Problems in the Sociology of the Professions," *Daedelus,* Vol. 92, Fall 1963, pp. 669–688.

35. Mona S. Schatz, Lowell E. Jenkins, and Bradford W. Sheafor, "Milford Redefined: A Model of Generalist and Advanced Generalist Social Work," *Journal of Social Work Education,* Vol. 26, No. 3, Fall 1990, pp. 217–230.

36. Council on Social Work Education, "Educational Policy and Accreditation Standards," www.cswe.org, July 27, 2001.

37. Bureau of Labor Statistics, *Occupational Outlook Handbook, 2000–01 Edition,* "Social Work," www.stats.bls.gov/ocohome.htm, July 27, 2001.

38. Donald Feldstein, "Do We Need Professions in Our Society? Professionalization Versus Consumerism," *Social Work,* Vol. 16, No. 4, October 1971, 5–11.

39. Association of Social Work Boards, "Licensing Information," www.aswb.org/licensing/index.html, July 26, 2001.

40. Todd M. Lennon, *Statistics on Social Work Education in the United States: 1999,* Alexandria, VA.: Council on Social Work Education, pp. 28, 32.

41. Margaret Gibelman and Philip H. Schervish, *Who We Are: A Second Look,* Washington, D.C.: NASW, 1997, pp. 149–150; Ruth Huber and Betty P. Orlando, "Persisting Gender Differences in Social Workers' Incomes: Does the Profession Really Care?" *Social Work,* Vol. 40, No. 5, September 1995, pp. 585–591.

14

Social Trends Affecting Social Welfare

Is it possible to make sense of what is going on in the world, to set oneself for the future?
Of course we cannot predict the sudden storms of history. But history is more than
storms; it is also a great Gulf Stream, carrying us along on its broad currents.

—Robert L. Heilbroner[1]

Overview

In this chapter, we will examine national society, individual and shared goals, growth, trends, an international economy, population growth and resources, the United States: a changing population, productivity and the service economy; ethnicity and pluralism; gender; gay men and lesbians; and the place of welfare in a changing context.

National Society

The United States is a national society, one in which events in one part of the society can have immediate repercussions in every other part. A national economy, transportation system, and media of communication have served to develop an interdependent society. In regard to mass media, people receive more and more information from central sources; information is gotten from national—even international—television, national newsweeklies, and nationally distributed papers.

In some respects, as a nation we are developing a mass culture; we attend the same movies, see the same television shows, and in general are developing a culture of a single society. Yet, as we shall see later there are countertrends away from a single set of values toward a multiplicity of values.

Mobility helped to create this national society. Over 80 percent of Americans do not move in a year's time. However, typically, 15 percent of the population change residence each year (42 million people). Most people move within the same county or between counties in the same state. Relocation peaks in the 20s and then declines with age. Among those 65 and older there is almost no movement. Demographers attribute the mobility pattern to an aging population, the growth of two-income families, the decline in family size; perhaps some stay put because they feel there is no place left to seek a better life.[2]

Individual and Shared Goals

For many years, there has been a tide of rising expectations. A nation involved in mass production also has to ensure mass purchasing power. The way in which expectations are met, at least minimally, is through pooling the risks, so that those who are less able to produce are nevertheless entitled to and provided with certain goods. A major theme of the Reagan administration of the 1980s was the firm belief that Americans could "have it all"—lower taxes, stronger defense, and no sacrifice. However, this claim was accompanied by a diminished sense of interdependence and shared responsibility.

As we entered the 21st century, more and more people rejected the idea of providing for those in need. A great shift occurred, which fostered individual rather than shared aims: The market became the arbiter of decisions. At the same time, there has been a concern about individual and group rights. Freedom is no longer defined as freedom for the individual citizen alone, but also as freedom for diverse groups to have equality of rights. Thus two separate trends are occurring: a national ethos of commonality on one level, and individual and group competitiveness, which seek inclusion as well as a greater share of the "pie."

In "The Cultural Contradictions of Capitalism," Daniel Bell discussed the development of hedonism (the pursuit of pleasure) in our capitalist society. Capitalism was generated by and accompanied by the Protestant ethic (delay gratification, put money in the bank, invest it, make it work for you, don't be profligate, spend little, idleness is the worst sin, be productive, work hard, and if you are successful you are blessed by God, but if not you have not received grace). The contradiction, according to Bell, is that when capitalism works, as it has in the United States, the reverse situation is produced. The hedonistic ethic arises in which self-fulfillment, "do your own thing," becomes the result and the keynote of an economy of abundance.[3]

The emphasis on immediate gratification becomes more the American norm. The idea of delayed gratification, the traditional capitalist ethic, is less the common ideal of the American scene. If it feels good, it is right. Bell suggests this changed ethic is the result of the affluent, post-industrial society, but it is a change that may undo society because the common glue for a society may become weaker. Paradoxically, while individuals become focused on immediate gratification, the society concurrently stresses the demands of a capitalistic free enterprise system.

Trends

We will now seek to look at major social trends both international and national and at some of their implications for social welfare. Among these are:

1. An international economy.
2. Population growth and its impact.
3. Food, water, land, energy, and other resources.
4. Issues of productivity and growth.
5. Immigration.
6. A view that government is "the problem" and that more "market" discipline is preferable wherever possible.
7. Individuals and families are responsible for themselves and there is an increasing emphasis on self-sufficiency and minimizing dependency. Societal responsibility is minimized. Less attention is paid to the impact of political and economic systems and more emphasis is placed on individual and family behavior.
8. The role of the federal government should be constrained and the roles of states and localities, voluntary organizations, and individuals and families should be enhanced. Changing population patterns: A rapidly expanding elderly population; decreasing numbers of young adults; diminishing percentage of families are nuclear (two-parent) families; increasing number of couples living together out of wedlock; more women headed single parent families; growth of the minority proportion of the population; and immigrants.[4]

An International Economy

A freeze in Brazil that will affect the supply of coffee becomes known instantly and is communicated electronically to the United States where financial decisions are made within minutes affecting the price of coffee. Foreign companies purchase and administer industries in the United States and the United States companies act similarly in many nations. Money moves with the click of a "mouse" from one nation to another. Jobs that used to exist in Massachusetts, North Carolina, or Texas are transferred among other places to India, China, Mexico, Poland and Russia.

Globalization is the spread of free-market capitalism—free trade and competition. Globalization is made possible through technologies—computers, satellite communications, the internet, fiber optics, etc. The economies of the world have become more and more integrated just as the "World Wide Web" operates without boundaries. Commerce, travel, communication, competition, and innovations are all affected by this globalization. In fact, a company can have offices or workplaces located in three cities around the globe and operate 24 hours a day with different work groups coming on line in order.[5]

The result of this complex globalization is that capital (money) can freely be moved from nation to nation; banking and industrial problems in Thailand, Indonesia, Korea, Japan, Mexico, Brazil, Russia, and Argentina—for example—can rapidly affect financial and monetary affairs in the United States. The American economy as a whole is related to these global factors and local communities can be affected by distant actions. Plants can be shut down and jobs lost. Studies have shown that suicide increases consistently with adverse changes in the economy. Similarly, mental hospital admissions increase; psychological problems are consistently associated with unemployment; criminal aggression associated with alcohol abuse and mortality rates due to cirrhosis of the liver rise in relation to difficult economic times; heart disease is inversely related to the employment rate; infant mortality increases sharply in response to economic recessions; and the overall mortality increases 2–3 years following the lowest point of an economic cycle. Child abuse and domestic violence also increase.[6]

Population Growth and Resources

Environmental alarms have been sounding about impending worldwide disasters for decades. Within a global context, projections of the future are essentially optimistic or pessimistic. The *neo Malthusians (catastrophists)* are those convinced that continued population growth and economic development will lead to starvation, exhaustion of resources, and the "collapse" of the world system. Even earlier than the gloomy predictions of Paul Ehrlich's *The Population Bomb* (1968) and the Club of Rome's *Limits to Growth* (1972) predictions were made that:

> The famines which are now approaching will not last for years, but perhaps several decades and they are inevitable. In 15 years famines will be catastrophic and social turmoil and economic upheaval will sweep areas of Asia, Africa, and Latin America.[7]

Serious questions were raised—and continue to be raised—as to whether the Earth can continue to sustain life.

There have been warnings about global warming, depletion of the ozone layer, vulnerability to epidemics, and the exhaustion of soils and groundwater, all of which are related to population size. Although predictions were made that the population explosion will come to an end before very long, it was also suggested that the only remaining question is whether it will be halted through the humane method of birth control, or by nature wiping out the surplus.[8] More recently there have been predictions that present levels of production and consumption of resources used in rich countries cannot be sustained. Mineral, timber, energy, and water resources will be exhausted and it is not possible for all people to have rich diets.[9]

Another school of thought is somewhat less pessimistic. There is population growth with rising consumption pushing beyond the planet's natural limits. Water tables are falling, oceanic fisheries at their limits, earth's temperature is rising, and plants and animals are becoming extinct at a rapid rate. According to this perspective there is also encouraging news. Fertility rates (the average number of children born to a woman) have fallen steadily in most countries in recent decades. Population projections have been moderated. In some developing countries the population is growing rapidly while in other nations it is stable or declining. The population of the world is expected to expand from an estimated 6.2 billion persons in 2001 to 9 billion in 2054 and level off at 10 billion in 2200, but these projections are not inevitable, although population increases have proceeded at a diminishing rate and it is thought the population surge may almost be over.[10] As nations modernize, the population size stabilizes.[11] The United Nations International Children's Emergency Fund (UNICEF) found that the death rate among small children and infants is declining in much of the developing world. Based on past experience, this trend suggests that parents will voluntarily begin to limit the size of their families because they will not fear the premature death of many of their young.[12]

Those who are more *optimistic (cornucopians)* point out that Malthus's (19th century economist and mathematician) prediction two centuries ago that world population would outstrip food supply has proven false. Lappe, *et al.* challenged certain myths, including the idea that food producing resources are stretched beyond their limits; there is not enough food to go around; and some people will have to go hungry. According to his view, the world produces enough grain alone to provide every human being on the plant 3,000 calories a day and this does not include vegetables, beans, nuts, root crops, fruits, grass-fed meats, and fish.

Most estimates of the population the Earth can carry range from 10 to 14 billion (One estimate is as high as 44 billion). All future projections have been dropping. Fifty years ago, it was predicted that China could never feed its population. With a population that has doubled in the interim, the population is being fed fairly adequately.[13]

Today, experts suggest that hunger persists because of political and distribution problems. Economist Amartya Sen's work demonstrated that famine is not just a consequence of nature but also a human-made disaster, an avoidable catastrophe. Declines in food production rarely account for mass starvation. Typically, there is—even in the midst of starvation—sufficient food to go around or enough money to import it. In fact, there are cases where food is being exported from an area because of market demands at the same time there is famine and starvation. Sen found that disaster strikes when the poorest people can no longer afford to buy food because of unemployment or increases in the price of food. The strategy of choice is now the creation of public works that create jobs to replace the lost incomes of the poor.[14] This argument is buttressed by the report Global Trends 2015, prepared by the Central Intelligence Agency, that found there will be adequate food production to feed the world's growing population, but poor infrastructure and distribution, political instability, and chronic poverty will lead to malnourishment in parts of sub-Saharan Africa; energy resources remain sufficient to meet demand but that water scarcities and allocation will pose significant challenges in certain parts of the world.[15]

Julian Simon, representative of the optimists, approached these issues from the standpoint of an economist and argued that scarcity will be defeated by inventiveness. According to Simon,

1. the per capita food situation has been improving since World War II and famine has progressively diminished;
2. the amount of agricultural land in general has been increasing and in the United States the amount of land used for forests, recreation, and wildlife has increased;
3. natural resources have become progressively less scarce and less costly;
4. the long-term future of energy supplies is as bright as that for other natural resources; and
5. all population growth estimates are being lowered.

Simon's argument is the following. Consumption increases as population and incomes grow, these in turn heighten scarcity and increase prices. Higher prices present opportunities that steer inventors and entrepreneurs to seek ways to satisfy the shortages. Some fail, others succeed. The final result is that we end up better off than if the original shortage had never arisen. The growth of the population brings with it an increase in useful knowledge. There exists technology to provide food and energy and all other raw materials for vastly larger numbers of people than now exist, indefinitely.[15] Simon's argument was supported by a recent Danish study that examined his claims. It was found that the rate of human population growth is past its peak, agriculture is sustainable, pollution is ebbing, forests are not disappearing, there is no wholesale destruction of plant and animal species, global warming is not as serious as commonly portrayed, the price of oil (adjusted for inflation) is half what it was in the 1980s, and calorie intake has increased by a quarter as a whole and by almost 40 percent in developing nations.[16]

Which is the correct vision? Have we reached beyond our resources and beyond the are absolute limits to sustainable expansion? Or, are people a creative resource rather than a burden? The power of innovation will counter scarcity and creativity will produce enough to sustain the world. There is no necessity of believing either the optimistic or pessimistic projections. It is also possible to think it is difficult to believe either view and to choose between the two future scenarios. Many variables, including the development of technology, elasticity of the concept of quality of life, and the ability to adapt in a complex and dynamic system, all play a part in determining the future.[17] If we do not know with any certainty what will develop as a result of continued population growth, it is certainly wiser to be cautious. Therefore, the future must be prepared for and that has implications for everyone, rich and poor. Only continuous growth can begin to deliver in modest degree, what the coming world will require by way of health, welfare, and human dignity.

The line of reasoning of the neo-Malthusians, those who take the pessimistic approach, is congenial to those who are already prosperous; by the same token, the "have nots" essentially have to opt for the "bigger pie" with more for everyone. If we believe the economy and world growth are to reach a stage of stasis, of steady state, then wealth will be static as well. In this case, redistribution can only be resisted by those who are the "haves." Philosopher John Rawls, in *A Theory of Justice*, argued that equity should be based on a reparations approach.[18] However, reparations (redistribution) depend on taking from the rich and giving to the poor. To the extent the "pie" is bigger and expanding, it is more probable redistribution can be accomplished when the wealthy continue to gain wealth, albeit at a diminished rate. Thus growth versus no growth is the fundamental issue that confronts the world's population, our society, and, in turn, social welfare provisions. Continued economic growth, we hope in non-polluting directions, seems to us a prerequisite to improvements in social welfare.

The United States: A Changing Population

The size of the population and its components have special importance for social welfare and needed services. Unlike physical factors, the variables that affect social changes cannot be predicted with great accuracy, and nations cannot know with assurance what events will impact on their future. The 2000 census counted 281 million Americans, or six to twelve percent less than the 300 to 320 million that had been predicted in the late 1950s. Nevertheless, the issue of growth and shifts in the composition of the U.S. population *are* of immediate concern to social welfare. Each of the population features identified below has implications for social welfare planning, policies, and services.

For many years the "baby boom" generation born following World War II has been a dominant factor in American life. With the imminent entry of this cohort into the 65-plus age group, the elderly population will increase rapidly. Those who followed this bulge from birth to death were able to predict the extent of many of the social welfare needs that had to be met. Beginning with social services related to childhood, the pattern of services needed by this large group of people shifted as they entered different periods of life: school, marriage, forming and raising families, and now as this generation moves into the 65-plus age group and retirement a growing number of aging persons will begin to call upon Social Security, Medicare, and other services needed by aging persons.

Changes in the general environment, including technological changes such as birth control methods, the women's movement, a questioning of traditional family patterns, a need for two incomes in families, and a search for personal fulfillment, have led to changes in the family. (1) The marriage rate is decreasing (22 percent less in 1998 than in 1970) but the size of the group is increasing; (2) Marriages are taking place at a later age; (3) The number of those who never married is increasing; (4) The rate of divorce and annulments is holding steady at 4.2 per thousand persons; (5) The birth rate has leveled off as has the fertility rate per thousand women; (6) Families have become smaller as the average size of family decreased from 3.58 (1970) to 3.18 in 1999, an eleven percent reduction in average size; (7) Nevertheless, the total number of family households is increasing, despite the lower marriage rate; (8) For the first time, less than a quarter of all households in the United States are made up of married couples with children. Non-family households almost tripled in number to 32.3 million between 1970 and 1999; (9) More households are led by one parent, mainly female. In 1970 there were 2.9 million female householders with their own children; by 1999, there were 7.8 million such households. Between 1990 and 2000 the number of single fathers with primary custody of their children doubled to over 2 million; (10) More than 2 million grandparents are raising grandchildren under 18 for whom they are responsible; (11) Many couples are living together out-of-wedlock, often with children. (12) Decreasing numbers of teenagers are giving birth to children, but the total remains sizeable; (13) Both parents are employed in a majority of 2-parent families. Two-parent families increasingly consist of Asian and Hispanic immigrants. Almost 70 percent of wives with children under 18 and with a husband present are working outside the home; remarkably, almost 60 percent of wives with children younger than one year are employed in the labor force; (14) Millions of legal and illegal immigrants have entered the society. One in five Americans does not speak English at home; and (15) American society continues to be a mobile one with 15 percent of the population moving annually, however, this mobility rate is the lowest it has been in over 50 years, probably due to the aging of the population.[19] The major demographic trends facing the United States are related to an expanding population of aging persons and increasing population diversity.

As more women achieve economic independence, as more remain in the labor market, and as the legal line between marriage and cohabitation is blurred, the number of "nontraditional" households has increased. Many Americans now live with extended family, roommates, partners, grandchildren, boarders, healthcare providers, or other group caregivers. Unmarried couples, fewer than half a million in 1960, exceeded 5.2 million in 2000.[20]

First marriages occur about 3.5 years later on average now than they did a generation ago; families are having one less child; more women, married and unmarried, are employed (including women with very young children); and more couples are surviving jointly for longer periods after their children marry. All these appear to be crucial changes that are significantly altering family life patterns. While there is disruption of family life and new household and family configurations, social welfare sees as a special concern those families under stress in our society.

Poverty is the greatest nemesis for children and their chances of growing up poor are increased in female-headed households. The participation of women in the work force is a continuing phenomenon with implications for themselves as individuals and for their families. With divorce and remarriage, the number of blended or reconstituted families has become significant. This development poses new issues for family life and for social welfare services. Sexual activity among teens is no greater in the United States than in a number of Western nations even while pregnancy and abortion are. This poses issues for family planning and must be a factor in debates on abortion and the availability of birth control information. One result is that teenage pregnancy and family dependency are major concerns expressed in the Personal Responsibility and Work Opportunity Act and Temporary Assistance to Needy Families (TANF) program, discussed earlier.

The emergence of and problems of the "sandwich generation" (adults caring for both their children and their aged parents) present very great difficulties and are closely related to Social Security and Medicare issues. Situations now exist in which adult children are forced to choose between supporting their aging parents and sending their children to college. Uncertain Social Security or Medicare benefits can compound these difficulties. Furthermore, it has been estimated that many families spend more years as caregivers for their parents than for their children. This outgrowth of longevity and an aging society will be ever more prominent in the next decades.

The future and existence of the American family does not appear to be in doubt. What does appear to be changing are the dimensions of the family of the future: How shall families adjust to poverty, an increasing number of women working, shifting roles within the family, after the children are gone? What are the social welfare implications for struggling immigrant families?

The glorification of the individual, self-fulfillment, and self-gratification are not values that enhance families; rather family life requires loyalty, self-denial, and sharing. It remains to be seen to what extent personal self-fulfillment will supersede or be made compatible with the importance of family life. What effects on children will the changes in family life bring? Social welfare, through its services to families and individuals, will play a role in helping people sort out their options and make choices as to the dimensions of their lives.

Smaller families have effects on child-rearing patterns; the middle-aged will have to bear the brunt of supporting the society as taxpayers; and mandatory retirement ages may have to be postponed. Whichever way the birthrate moves—continuing downward, leveling off, or increasing—there are social welfare implications: size of tax force, family patterns, proportions of age groups within the overall population, resources available for distribution, and other concerns such as living space and number of retirees. Predictions regarding birth trends remain complex. It is unknown what effects the economy, immigration, the "surfacing" of illegal immigrants, and unforeseeable national and international events will produce. Prediction is difficult, but social welfare decisions need to be made nonetheless. What provisions need to be made for those yet to be born and for the life stages of those already born?

Productivity and the Service Economy

Issues affecting social welfare also derive from the nature of *productivity* in U.S. society. A rise in output per employed person is a rise in productivity, which is a major source of economic growth. Productivity creates the "pie" to be divided among the various demands within society. In 1853, an American writer predicted the day would arrive when "machinery will perform all work, automata will direct them. The only task of the human race will be to make love, study, and be happy."[21] So far, the automation revolution has not yet reached that millennium. Quite the reverse. In 1853, almost 33 percent of the total U.S. population was employed. By 1999, the figure more than doubled to 67.1 percent of the civilian non-institutional population.[22]

To the extent that wealth is created through technological and other advances, the social welfare programs of the nation are potential recipients of the "bigger pie." Nevertheless, social welfare has to compete with other "goods" within the society and such competition has been weakened by a political focus on the federal debt, tax cuts enacted under the Bush administration (2001), the requirements of a large and soon to be retired generation of aging persons, and the costs of the War on Terrorism. Increasing productivity in itself does not mean greater emphasis on social welfare concerns. Recessions raise questions about structural unemployment and the growth of the Gross Domestic Product. During recessions, however, when productivity is at lower levels, society has to be much more concerned about how many workers are unemployed or underemployed.

In response to such questions, issues are raised about *structural unemployment* and how to deal with it. Certain sectors of the economy, because of technological changes and competition from other nations, among other reasons, fail to maintain their shares of the world markets. Which industries will be the wave of the future—microelectronics, basic industries such as steel and automobiles, service industries? If we can identify which industries hold out the most optimism for the nation, what should be the role of government in planning, human resource development, resource allocation, funding supports, and so on? The ultimate issue is whether improved productivity and the necessary industrial emphases can efficiently and effectively be made without radical changes in the political and economic system. If need be, how will we adjust to a society in which a growing number of persons could be unemployed? How shall the governmental and private sectors minimize unemployment and maximize productivity, all the while balancing inflation and employment?

Other issues related to productivity affect social welfare, including the shift from production of goods to the production of services and information. Our society has become post-industrial, in the sense that the majority of workers are no longer engaged in manufacturing or the production of goods. We have reached a high level of productivity so that it takes less than a quarter of the work force to produce all the goods to supply the population. In 1999 in the United States, almost 75 percent of the workforce (excluding agriculture, mining, construction, manufacturing, and transportation) was employed in services.[23] The United States is the pioneer but not alone among nations with developed economies.

There are implications for social welfare in the information revolution. The place of work shifts from office to home, if not entirely then partially. The information age has implications for socialization, work styles, family life, and the kinds of personal problems individuals and families experience. Special problems of privacy and confidentiality arise in such systems. The nature of social services in tomorrow's environment cannot fully be predicted. But just as chronically ill persons who are shut in can participate "by remote" in classes, groups, and projects, the use of electronic devices—email, videophones, and so on—counseling and therapy may also be possible under certain circumstances. These changes have implications for social work practice, the delivery of social services, and the organization, resources, staffing, and methods of social welfare agencies. One down-side of a service and information economy is the problem created for those who lack the skills, education, and health needed for higher paid positions. This group does not have the "living wage" opportunities of the past in manufacturing jobs. There are real limits for them in attaining a living wage and benefits equal to supporting a family.

Technology has raised the output of the average skilled worker relative to that of the unskilled. The demand for skilled workers grows compared with that of the unskilled, thus raising the relative earnings of the skilled. This rise in relative earnings of the skilled occurred in virtually every industry. Technological innovation changes the demand for unskilled labor. While there may be jobs created for the unskilled, they typically are low paid and without sufficient benefits.

Some argue that a service-dominated economy is problematic and associated with a productivity decline. For example, if a factory manufactures 100 shirts per hour, a new invention may make it possible to create 200 shirts an hour, so then any one worker can be more productive. But there are natural limits to how many persons can be served by a social worker during any one day. This is an illustration of *labor-intensive* industry. It is an open question as to how productive human services can become. To what extent can social workers, teachers, or other workers be made more productive? Paraprofessionals and technology can be used to increase the productivity of some professionals. Ultimately, however, we are dealing with labor-intensive industries in which it is difficult to raise production. Surprises, however, do occur and dramatic increases in productivity still develop from time to time. The ultimate upper limit remains unknown.

Social welfare has to compete with other parts of the society for resources; this competition is minimized in an era of expanding productivity and made more difficult in an economy in which taxpayers and legislators become very much concerned with costs and priorities. All of the above suggest that social welfare goals can be met only if (1) productivity continues to be increased in manufacturing, farming, and in service areas where productive possibilities need to be exploited and (2) social welfare services themselves can be delivered more efficiently.

Ethnicity and Pluralism

Ethnicity, a growing and visible phenomenon in U.S. society, is an important ingredient in the formation of identity, both for families and for individuals. It is possible that ethnic group identity can serve as a counterforce against the encroaching national forces that make for a certain degree of homogenization. It is also possible that identification with an ethnic group serves to counterbalance feelings of alienation brought on in a technological and enlarged society. The growing phenomenon of group identity and its emphasis in American culture as a political and social force serves as a means of expression and as a means for achieving meaning in people's lives. But what serves as a primary support of social cooperation and order, simultaneously, also is a major source of conflict and division in our society.

The United States is a nation built on immigration from many lands by many different groups of people. Between 1830 and 1930, almost 40 million Europeans crossed the Atlantic Ocean to try to make lives for themselves in America. African Americans were brought first as indentured workers and then as enslaved persons. Mexicans inhabited the Southwest for centuries. Chinese persons were in California as early as 1815.[24] Native Americans were here already.

Ethnic clashes are a part of U.S. history, sometimes based on ideological conflicts but more often based on economic competition, especially for jobs. One reaction to growing diversity is an effort by some persons to defend the *status quo*. These concerns are expressed in various ways, including support for a more restrictive immigration policy. Another result is California's Proposition 187 that sought (ultimately unsuccessfully) to prohibit state and local governmental agencies from providing publicly funded education, health, public assistance benefits, and social services to non-citizens or persons illegally admitted to the United States. Governmental employees were expected to report those suspected of illegal immigration to the Immigration and Naturalization service.

Notwithstanding a history of intergroup conflict, there was much cooperation as well. Two group philosophies arose to point the way to the future. The *melting pot* theory held that Americans of whatever background would become "Americanized" into a happy amalgam. As late as the end of World War II, there were predictions that "the future of American ethnic groups seems to be limited; it is likely that they will be quickly absorbed."[25] This has not happened—quite the reverse. There has been an acceleration of *cultural pluralism* (sometimes referred to as the "salad" bowl), the concept that group identity should be maintained and that the United States can provide a supportive setting for group continuity and group expression within a diverse but democratic society.

Immigration has contributed in an additional way to the growing diversity of American society. Immigration fueled the growth of American Muslims, Buddhists, Hindus, enlarged the number of Roman Catholics, increased the diversity of local congregations, and led to the expansion of some churches overseas. There are 2,000 distinct religious groups in the United States and—amazingly—Los Angeles is the only place in the world that you can find all forms of Buddhism. Not even Asian countries have all forms of that religion.[26] While there may be a degree of truth to the melting pot theory (there is acculturation to a general American culture), the civil rights revolution of the 1960s, particularly the phenomena of black pride and Hispanic advocacy, joined with increased immigration initiated a re-emergence of cultural pluralism. Groups became more aware of their heritages and more sensitive to what they were losing as they ceded their traditions, language, and cultures to some mythical American ideal type.

It is clear that distinct ethnic identities and cultures exist in our diverse society. Assimilationist and anti-assimilation biases coexist in the modern United States. New responses to ethnicity and new methods of accommodation will be necessary during the next decades. African Americans have been the principal minority group in the United States. This is changing as Hispanics surpassed African Americans as the nation's largest minority group.[27] Greater diversity is expected, which will bring many economic and social issues. The fact is that even in a time of a robust economy, means will have to be found to solve issues of distribution of resources such as jobs, government contracts, political power, and others.

However, pluralism is not limited to ethnicity or racial groups. There are other groups that organize to advocate their rights, including those based on disability, religion, income levels, and sexual orientation. These ethnic and other special interest groups occupy important positions in U.S. society.

We have a national society and we have pluralist groupings. Cultural pluralism, in fact, seems embedded in U.S. society. The libertarian values of the United States support pluralism, and pluralism suggests trade-offs and compromises. Compromises between groups suggest political incrementalism, a strategy that operates to preserve the autonomy of multiple interest groups. Thus one value supports another, pluralism reinforcing political trade-offs which, in turn, support ethnic pluralism.

On a personal level, there are psychological and skill implications of living in a diverse society. A pluralistic society requires the ability to live with differences. One result of not fully comprehending the thinking of people with whom one works or lives near is anxiety. Handling such anxiety requires new skills and even new attitudes. For social workers, the delivery of social services for different cultural groups requires knowledge, skills, and flexibility.

This latter point is not simply one of personal psychology. Social services for ethnic groups is a matter of the distribution of resources. Which neighborhoods and people will be served by what means are issues directly connected to questions of intergroup conflict and accommodation. Questions of poverty and inequality similarly have political implications. Which ethnic groups will control a school district? Which neighborhoods will have greatest access to housing or job-training funds? Given such powerful questions, the answers profoundly influence people's lives. With the perspective that ethnic identity is an important reality in relation to decision making about services and control, U.S. society has so far proven to be remarkable for its ability to manage these intergroup balancing acts.

One example of the way in which this conflict between groups is played out is seen in the issue of quotas, goals, and affirmative action. The preferential treatment of one group can usually be offered only at expense to other groups and their members. As a result, group interests and individual rights clash, for example, over admission to colleges and professional schools and preferential hiring. Such issues remain to be worked out within an accommodation that enables our society to balance two "goods" simultaneously—the protection of individual rights and individual merit in contrast with group rights and justice for groups that have been discriminated against.

Caught within this strain among groups in a pluralist society, the human psyche demands a sense of community. The development of ethnic, women's, gay, and other groups may be indications that either humankind or the nation is too vague an entity with which to identify oneself. A person must invent a community if it does not exist. In this way, people become part of groups with a sense of social responsibility. The future will reveal whether ethnic and other groupings in our society are a result of a search for community, a way in which people can express themselves and gain "their" share in this productive society, or, as is likely, both.

Gender

Over the last century, there has been a rapid evolution of the roles of women, family structures, and sexual mores. More women are employed, even while they have young children. As we saw earlier, more women are single-parent heads of households than ever before. Women are choosing to have children even though unmarried. They enter the professions in growing numbers.

These developments challenge male dominance and alter the definition of female and male roles. Increasingly, women have been elected to political offices, including the House of Representatives and the U.S. Senate, run for the vice presidency, have become cabinet secretaries at the federal level, and Supreme Court justices, as well as governors and other state officers. Among the women who have achieved stature in numerous fields are Madelaine Albright, Maya Angelou, Carol Browner, Elizabeth Dole, Marian Wright Edelman, Gale Norton, Jodie Foster, Betty Friedan, Bernadine Healy, Anita Hill, Mae Jemison, Audre Lorde, Wilma Mankiller, Venus and Serena Williams, Angela Oh, Janet Reno, Donna Shalala, Linda Chavez Thompson, Christine Todd Whitman, and Oprah Winfrey.

While there has been progress, women continue to face restrictions, discrimination, and "glass ceilings." Sexual discrimination and harassment, although less open than they used to be, remain serious problems. Women still earn considerably less on average than men. In addition to "old boys' networks" and role models that favor men, many women have the stress of balancing work, family, and caregiving, which makes life as well as career advancement difficult. A recent study of women's perceptions found women believe they are mostly given low- or mid-level jobs, are held to higher standards than men, are discriminated against in life and business, and that young girls are not encouraged to aim for management positions.[28]

The Equal Rights amendment to the U.S. Constitution was not approved by the number of needed states within the required time. Discrimination continues, including that against poor women, especially those receiving Temporary Assistance for Needy Families, and the prevalence of rape, domestic violence, and sexual harassment, all take a heavy toll on women's lives. In chapter 8 we saw how many women are affected by poverty and in chapter 15, we will examine more closely female-headed households, children, and poverty. In addition, most poor, aging persons are women.

In the past several decades, women have made political gains:

The Equal Pay Act (1963) requires that women be paid the same salary as men for doing substantially the same work.

Title VII of the Civil Rights Act (1964) bans discrimination against women and is the basis for claims of sexual harassment.

Title IX of the Education Amendments Act (1972) prohibits sex discrimination in educational programs that receive federal funds.

The Roe v. Wade (1973) Supreme Court decision ensures women the right to have an abortion within certain time limitations.

The Pregnancy Discrimination Act (1978) states that pregnant women must have the same rights as other workers on the job.

The Family and Medical Leave Act (1993) provides reasonable job leaves for medical reasons or for the care of a child, spouse, or parent.

U.S. v. Virginia re Virginia Military Institute and Faulkner v. Jones re The Citadel gained the right for women to attend the last two state supported schools to prohibit women from admission.

From the perspective of social welfare, there are critical unresolved issues concerning gender in regard to poverty, discrimination, equal pay and comparable worth, equal access to and opportunities for education, health care, mental health care, and other resources, violence, changing roles and needs of single and married women, as well as women in other household relationships, including lesbian, "melded" families, and various group living arrangements. Social work has more and more recognized the effects of sexism. Social work, particularly feminist practice, seeks to empower women and remove discriminatory attitudes and policies.

Gay Men and Lesbians

Homosexuality has always been present in human societies. John Boswell found that, in ancient and medieval Europe, homosexuals were not persecuted and were often accepted, influential, and respected. The importance of Boswell's work is that it illustrates the reality that homophobia (an irrational hatred, fear, or dislike of homosexuals) has not always been the norm in Western history.[29] There is evidence of the acceptance of homosexuality in Asia and ancient China as well.[30]

The emergence of gay and lesbian movements in the international context was traced back to Berlin in 1897.[31] The rise of industrialization created new employment opportunities when persons living in rural areas and dependent upon their families could move to the expanding cities. It was there that personal freedom grew and individuals who felt oppressed in rural areas could find havens and gain a new sense of security. It was possible to live alone and survive, meet people like yourself, and also experience privacy. Few people knew who you were in cities and fewer still cared.

It was in the cities that communities of gays and lesbians developed as they began to find one another. Same-sex relationships were often viewed by the larger community as immoral, sinful, or later as a sign of psychiatric illness.[32] It is probable that these stigmatizing terms and mistreatment helped to build gay and lesbian communities as they had need for mutual support in stressful environments.

For gay Americans, World War II was a turning point as the conscription of millions of persons enabled people to travel and to meet in an ever-wider sphere persons who shared their own interests and concerns. Some persons think that the social disruption of war time encouraged sexual experimentation, brought many gay men in contact with one another, and loosened ties to their original communities. The Chicago-based Society for Human Rights, founded in 1924, was the only gay rights organization in existence prior to World War II.

Some identify the appearance of the first stirrings of movement activity among recently demobilized men—following World War II—in the Veteran's Benevolent Association in New York and among working women in Los Angeles. Both groups formed out of existing friendship networks and made no attempt to gain public recognition. It was not until 1950–51 that the Mattachine Society was formed, where gay men could meet and share with each other in a nonsexual environment. This group, named for the medieval Italian court jester who expressed popular truths from behind a mask, took as its mission to unify, to educate, and to lead. The recruitment of members was slow, however, a first Convention was held in 1953.

Homosexuality became caught up in McCarthyism and political "witch-hunts" during the late 1940s and early 1950s. Issues of loyalty were fought on the federal level but repression extended to state and local governments. Many gay men and lesbians were fearful during this era of losing their jobs. Also the Mattachine Society's leadership focused on the "adjustment" of gay men to society. This low profile, accomodationist stance, however, was not an acceptable perspective for those who did not see themselves as having the problem. The first post-war lesbian organization—the Daughters of Bilitis—was formed in 1955 in San Francisco.

In the 1950s and 1960s, making a life as a gay person took considerable courage and problem solving. Gay men and lesbians faced discrimination and ostracism. Openly choosing a gay life meant in many cases the loss of family, friends, career, and community. Nevertheless, many persons made such choices. The early 1960s witnessed a new militance. For instance, the East Coast Homophile Organizations (ECHO) conducted public demonstrations at the U.S. Civil Service Commission, Department of State, Pentagon, White House, and at Independence Hall in Philadelphia.[33]

Influenced by the civil rights, student and anti-Viet Nam War movements, the event that galvanized the homosexual community to advocate gay liberation were the Stonewall Riots of June 27–28, 1969. Patrons of the Stonewall Inn in Greenwich Village in New York City—angry because of continual police raids, harassment, and surveillance—responded to a raid by throwing beer cans and bottles. The riots lasted two nights and involved 2,000 persons battling 400 police. But this event was not an isolated occurrence as rallies were held in Los Angeles against police harassment and radical student caucuses developed.

Stonewall served as a symbolic end to stigmatization and the resulting fear of exposure, which previously restrained gay mens' and lesbians' behavior. Where gay men had previously acquiesced to police brutality, they now fought back. Following Stonewall, "gay power" graffiti began to appear in Greenwich Village—public statements indicating a new phase. The Gay Liberation Front and the Gay

Activists Alliance were formed, and similar groups were organized across the nation. Groups were now focused on fighting back rather than "fitting in" to society. At the time of Stonewall, there were reportedly only about 50 lesbian and gay groups in the United States. By the end of 1973, there were more than a thousand.[34] Noteworthy was the organization of groups promoting the interests of people of color, including the Latino/a Lesbian and Gay Organization (Llego), Black Lesbian and Gay Leadership Forum, and Trikone (Sanskrit for triangle) for lesbian, gay, and bisexual south Asians.

There are a number of social policy issues affecting gay men and lesbians. At the federal level, Congress failed to enact the Employment Non-Discrimination Act which would have created Federal civil rights protections for homosexuals in the workplace. Tax laws do not provide for "domestic partners" and discrimination exists in the military, despite the "don't say, don't tell" policy. The policy has proven less than successful and a Federal appeals court upheld the military's policy.[35] On the other hand, a California judge ruled against the Defense Department policy and ordered the California National Guard to admit openly gay members.[36]

At the state level, discrimination continues regarding jobs, housing, and public accommodation, domestic partner benefits, and laws regarding sexuality. Discrimination also exists in areas of family law: marriage, custody cases, foster care, adoptions, inheritance rights, and spousal benefits for insurance and pensions. Florida, Mississippi, and Utah ban adoption by same-sex couples. August, 2001, a Federal judge upheld the Florida law banning gay men from adopting children. Discrimination also takes a destructive turn when police or others harass gay men and lesbians, when violence is perpetrated against them, and in HIV/ AIDS-related discrimination.[37]

As of 2001, eleven states and the District of Columbia prohibited job discrimination based on sexual orientation. Those states are: California, Connecticut, Hawaii, Massachusetts, Minnesota, Nevada, New Hampshire, New Jersey, Rhode Island, Vermont, and Wisconsin.[38] In 1998 Maine was the first state to repeal its law barring discrimination against gay men and lesbians in employment, housing, credit, and public accommodations.[39]

Courts at the state level and nationally have a mixed record in regard to decisions affecting gay men and lesbians. In regard to employment discrimination, the U.S. Supreme Court rejected without comment a case being appealed from Georgia. The dispute involved a woman who had been offered a job in the state law department in 1991; however, the offer was withdrawn when officials learned she planned a wedding-like religious ritual with her lesbian companion. The woman stressed in her appeal that she was not claiming a right to be married in a legal sense but sought protection against being punished by the government through denial of a public job solely because of her private relationship with her partner. In a similar case, a lesbian was hired as an art therapist and boy's residence supervisor by Kentucky Baptist Homes for Children and revealed her sexual orientation prior to hiring. A federal judge in 2001 upheld as a matter of law the right of a charity receiving tax dollars to act on its anti-gay beliefs. The

Court also ruled the lawsuit may continue on the issue of whether the firing violated the separation of church and state.[40]

The U.S. Supreme Court upheld the Defense Department's policy of "don't ask, don't tell," and reversed the New Jersey Supreme Court ruling that the Boy Scouts of American could not discriminate against the participation of homosexuals. On the other hand, in Romer v. Evans (U.S. 1996) the same court struck down a proposed amendment to the Colorado state constitution barring the state or local governments from forbidding discrimination on the basis of sexual orientation.

In Hawaii, the State Supreme Court ruled in 1993 that it is unconstitutional to ban same-sex marriages and to do so violated the due process clause in the state constitution, unless the state could prove a compelling public interest in doing so. This led to the State Legislature passing a bill to grant gay couples many rights and benefits and placing on the 1998 ballot a measure that would deny legality to gay marriages. The case was remanded to the trial court for the state to justify itself. The Hawaii legislature in April 1997 passed an amendment to the State constitution reserving marriage for opposite sex couples. This amendment was ratified by the electorate November 1998 and December 1999, the Supreme Court of Hawaii reversed the earlier decision of the circuit court.

The issue of marriage for gays and lesbians became an important and widespread political conflict during 1996, a presidential and congressional election year. Concern that the U.S. Constitution's "full faith and credit" clause will require other states to honor whatever Hawaii chose to do led to the Congress passing the preemptive Defense of Marriage Act. The Act defined a marriage as a legal union of one man and one woman as husband and wife. Although, the act does not specifically forbid same-sex unions it withholds federal tax and other benefits, which would deny gay couples many of the civil advantages of marriage. The legislation would also allow all states to ignore same-sex marriages performed elsewhere. A major argument proffered was that the law confirms the right of each state to determine its own policy. In part because of the Hawaiian developments twenty-five states and Congress passed laws against homosexual marriage. At a later point (April 2000), civil unions became legal in Vermont, providing the same state law protections and responsibilities as are available to spouses in a marriage. Whatever the legal situation, clergypersons conducting same sex union rituals have become more common.

Sometimes events in one arena impact on other issues. This may prove to be the case in regard to same sex unions. The Supreme Court curbed the power of major companies to control corporate whistle-blowers. If a company gets a "gag" order against a whistle-blower in one state that order cannot be used to stop that witness from testifying in other states. Although the decision focused on consumer products, it may affect other disputes and the duties of states to respect the actions of other states, clarifying the "full faith and credit" clause that makes court orders in one state valid in others. If gay couples gain the right to marry in particular states, that clause will be directly at issue in the future as gay couples married in those states will undoubtedly seek recognition of their marriages in other states.[41]

Discrimination against gay men and lesbians persists in many parts of the United States, much depends both on laws and on attitudes. Citizens—homosexual and heterosexual—from many types of groups organize to seek civil rights legislation and protection. Others counterorganize. The Supreme Court, in *Bowers v. Hardwick* (1986), upheld the constitutionality of sodomy laws by a vote of 5–4. The decision held that consensual sex between consenting adults is not protected by the Constitution even in a person's own bedroom. The majority opinion cited proscriptions against homosexuality and referred to religious rationales. The minority opinion held that private, consensual homosexual conduct should not be condemned because it does not interfere with the rights of others.

The agenda of policy issues concerning homosexuals includes workplace and life space security, domestic partners' benefits, same sex marriage, anti-discrimination rules, violence, divorce, custody, adoptions, and foster care issues. Harassment in regard to sexual orientation, hate crimes against lesbians and gay men and lesbian and gay youth, and discrimination against homosexuals and lesbians continue. Social work has important roles to play in direct services for homosexuals and lesbians, educating toward attitudinal change for professionals and laypersons, assuring nondiscriminatory work environments, and working for macro-change, including legislative changes.

The Place of Social Welfare in a Changing Context

Until recent times, the creation of the modern world brought with it expanding welfare states. Recently, however, the entire thrust of social welfare in the United States since the Great Depression has been challenged in major ways. These challenges took place in a context that included a large federal debt, popular resistance to taxes which supported enactment of highly significant tax cuts, general discontent with government, shifts in federal funding expectations of the states, and a desire by conservatives to limit and return federal functions to the state level. Critics charged that social welfare is too expensive, undermines the traditional family, encouraged the increase of single-parent families and children born out of wedlock, failed to reduce the number of poor persons, and fostered dependence. Conservatives rejected anti-poverty efforts supported by governmental interventions, other than employment, personal and familial efforts, combined with opposition to raising the minimum wage; and those in favor of even small degrees of governmental intervention found themselves stymied by the national debt, and diminished resources as a result of failing tax revenues. The initial budget major tax cut engineered by the Bush administration in 2001 when Republicans controlled both Houses of Congress together with the costs of the War on Terrorism imposed spending limits that stymied potential spending in a number of areas, including social welfare concerns.

Another factor influencing social welfare is the incremental nature of American political decision making. Social welfare in U.S. society developed in a piecemeal and incremental fashion; it attacked one problem, relatively without regard to other problems that might contribute to the creation of the problem or that influence its dimensions. While experience might teach that comprehensive and coordinated approaches could offer better solutions to problems and reduce the inadequacies of one program overburdening other programs, comprehensive approaches to social welfare have been impracticable in U.S. society.

Social workers and others come face to face with the needs of people and the positive effects of social welfare programs. However, the kinds of problems many Americans encounter including, for example, poverty, mental illness, and child welfare are not visible to many citizens nor are they high priorities in the media or for action by lawmakers. Individual observations of social workers are not made within a vacuum. On the contrary, they take place within the context of a national society at a particular time and state of development. Social welfare is in fact the collective supply of resources, a sharing of the burden or the risk but there are many forces questioning the responsibility of society, even for collective goods in many areas of life. Two questions have to be asked: (1) What needs should be supplied by the collective action of the society and which left to individual effort? (2) What can the society afford to do and to not do?

> The two edged nature of social welfare has been recognized, that is, in the individual case: We can degrade people by caring for them; and we can degrade them by not caring for them;[42] ...

All interventions have consequences, and one of the things we should learn to keep in the forefront of our consciousness is that the most important consequences of any intervention almost always turn out to be those consequences that were not intended or planned upon or could not have been calculated beforehand.[43]

Further, it is important to keep in mind the idea that "it is illusory to see social policy only as making an *inroad* on a problem; there are dynamic aspects to any policy, such that it also *expands* the problem, *changes* the problem, *generates* further problems."

Summary

In this chapter, we have examined major trends that impact on the needs of people and on the social welfare response of society. Among the factors we looked at were national society; individual and shared goals; major trends; the international economy; population growth and resources; a changing population; productivity and the service economy; ethnicity and pluralism; gender; homosexuals and lesbians; and the place of social welfare in a changing context.

In the next and final chapter, we will discuss alternative programs to meet the needs of female heads of household and their children; immigration; the aging and long-term health care; persons with disabilities; and technology and social action. We will also explore alternatives facing practitioners; where we are; and two scenarios affecting social welfare's future and present our proposal for the amelioration of poverty.

Questions for Consideration

1. In the section above entitled Trends fifteen demographic facts were cited. What implications do you see for social welfare for each of the facts and what services do you think will be needed?

2. Can you locate trend data that suggest future social needs in your community in relation to a specific problem: teenage pregnancy, child abuse, depression among the elderly, etc.?

3. What effects of the "baby boom" generation do you foresee for your community in the coming decades?

4. In what ways do you think technological changes impact on social welfare?

5. What human needs do you believe should be supplied through collective action and which left to individual effort?

Notes

1. Robert L. Heilbroner, "Trying to Make Sense of It," *New York Times,* October 10, 1977, p. 29.

2. U.S. Bureau of the Census, "Mobility Status of the Population by Selected Characteristics: 1980 to 1999," *Statistical Abstract, 2000,* Table 28, p. 30.

3. Daniel Bell, "The Cultural Contradictions of Capitalism," *Capitalism Today,* Daniel Bell and Irving Kristol, eds., New York: New American Library, 1971, pp. 27–57.

4. U.S. Census Bureau, *Statistical Abstract of the United States 2000,* (120th edition), Washington, D.C., 2000. Tables 5, 53, 60, 80, 144, 149, 653, and 654.

5. Thomas L. Friedman, *The Lexus and the Olive Tree,* New York: Farrar, Straus, Giroux, 1999.

6. M. Harvey Brenner, "Political Economy and Health," in *Society & Health,* eds. Benjamin C. Amick, III, Sol Levine, *et al.,* pp. 211–246; Carolyn C. Perrucci, Robert Perrucci, Dena B. Targ, and Harry R. Targ, *Plant Closings: International Context and Social Costs,* New York: Aldine de Gruyter, 1988; Loring Jones, "Unemployment and Child Abuse," Families in Society: The Journal of Contemporary Human Services, Vol. 71 No. 10, December 1990, pp. 579–588.

7. William and Paul Paddock, *Famine—1975!* Boston: Little, Brown and Company, 1967.

8. Ted Trainer, "Our Unsustainable Society," in *The Coming Age of Scarcity,* ed. Michael N. Dobkowski and Isidor Wallimann, Syracuse, N.Y. Syracuse University Press, 1998, pp. 83–100.

9. U.S. Census Bureau, *Statistical Abstract 2000,* Table 1350, "Total World Population: 1980 to 2050," Washington, D.C., 2000, p. 821. Barbara Crossette, "Re-thinking Population at a Global Milestone," *New York Times,* Week in Review, September 1999, pp. 1 and 4.

10. Lester R. Brown, Gary Gardner, Brian Halweil, *Beyond Malthus,* New York: W. W. Norton & Co., 1999.

11. Paul Lewis, "Unicef Sees Death of Infants Ebbing," *New York Times,* December 19, 1990, p. A8.

12. Frances M. Lappe, Joseph Collins, and Peter Rosset, *World Hunger: Twelve Myths,* 2nd edition, New York: Grove Press, 1998.

13. Amartya Sen, *Poverty and Families,* Oxford: Clarendon Press, 1981.

14. Central Intelligence Agency, "Global Trends 2015: A Dialogue About the Future With Nongovernment Experts," www.cia.gov/cia/publications/globaltrends2015/index.html, August 2, 17.

15. Julian L. Simon, *The Ultimate Resource,* Princeton: Princeton University Press, 1996, pp. 56, and 12; *The Ultimate Resource2,* ed. Timur Kuran, Ann Arbor, Michigan, University of Michigan Press, 2000, p. 182;

16. Nicholas Wade, "From an Unlikely Quarter, Eco-Optimism," *New York Times,* Science, August 7, 2001, pp. 1–2.

17. Massimo Livi-Bacci, *A Concise History of World Population,* 2nd Edition, Malden, MA: Blackwell Publishers, Inc., 1997, pp. 218, 223.

18. John Rawls, *A Theory of Justice,* Cambridge, Mass.: Harvard University Press, 1971.

19. U.S. Census Bureau, *Statistical Abstract of the United States: 2000,* (120th edition), Washington, D.C., 2000: Tables 5, 28?, 53, 54, 60, 79, 80, 144, 149, 643, 653, 654, 672, 1350, Eric Schmitt, "For First Time, Nuclear

Families Drop Below 25% of Households," *New York Times*, May 15, 2001, pp. 1 and A18; Eric Nagourney, "Study Finds Families Bypassing Marriage," *New York Times*, February 15, 2000, p. D8; Tamar Lewin, "Now a Majority: Families With 2 Parents Who Work," *New York Times*, October 24, 2000, p. A14; D'Vera Cohn and Dan Keating, "Two-Parent families Increasingly Immigrants," *The Washington Post*, www.washingtonpost.com, May 23, 2001; D'Vera Cohn and Sarah Cohen, "Census Sees Vast Changes in Language, Employment," *The Washington Post*, www.washingtonpost.com, August 6, 2001.

20. U.S. Census Burea, Quick tables, QT-01, "Profile of General demographic Characteristics: 2000," http://factfinder.census.gov/servlet/QT, August 6, 2001.

21. Richard A. Peterson, *The Dynamics of Industrial Society*, New York: Bobbs-Merrill, 1973, p. 48.

22. U.S. Statistical Abstract 2000 (120th edition), No. 643, "Employment Status of the Civilian Population: 1950 to 1999," p. 403

23. U.S. Statistical Abstract 2000 (120th edition), No. 672, "Employment by Industry: 1980 to 1999," p. 420 and Organization for Economic Cooperation and Development, Services: Statistics on Value Added and Employment, 2000 edition. Paris: Organization for Economic Cooperation and Development, 2000, p. 24.

24. H. M. Lai, "Chinese," *Harvard Encyclopedia of American Ethnic Groups*, Stephan Thernstrom, ed., Cambridge, Mass.: Harvard University Press, 1980, p. 21

25. Rudolph J. Vecoli, "Ethnicity: A Neglected Dimension of American History," *Overcoming Middle Class Rage*, Murray Friedman, ed., Philadelphia: Westminster Press, 1971, p. 160; Charles Guzzetta, "White Ethnic Groups," in *Encyclopedia of Social Work*, 19th Edition, Volume 3, ed. Richard L. Edwards, Washington, D.C.: National Association of Social Workers, 1995, pp. 2508–2517.

26. Gustav Niebuhr, "Land of Religious Freedom Has Universe of Spirituality," *New York Times*, March 30, 1997, pp. 1, 16.

27. U.S. Census Bureau, Quick Tables, QT-01, "Profile of General Demographic Characteristics: 2000," http://factfinder.census.gov/servlet/QT, August 6, 2001.

28. Judith H. Dobrzynski, "Women Less Optimistic about Work, Poll Says," *New York Times*, September 12, 1995, p. D5.

29. John Boswell, *Christianity, Social Tolerance, and Homosexuality*, Chicago: University of Chicago Press, 1980.

30. Kevin Jennings, *Becoming Visible*, Boston: Alyson Publications, 1994, pp. 52–63.

31. Barry D. Adam, Willem Duyvendak, and Andre Krouwel, eds. "Introduction," *The Global Emergence of Gay and Lesbian Politics*, Philadelphia: Temple University Press, 1999.

32. Warren Johansson, "Psychiatry," *Encyclopedia of Homosexuality*, Vol. 2, Wayne R. Dynes, ed., New York: Garland Publishing, 1990, pp. 1072–1074.

33. Barry D. Adam, *The Rise of a Gay and Lesbian Movement*, Boston: Twayne Publishers, 1987, pp. 58, 62–63; Cynthia C. Poindexter, "Sociopolitical Antecedents to Stonewall: Analysis of the Origins of the Gay Rights Movement in the United States," *Social Work*, Vol. 42 (6), November 1997, pp. 607–615.

34. Margaret Cruikshank, *The Gay and Lesbian Liberation Movement*, New York: Routledge, 1992, p. 69 and Steven Epstein, "Gay and Lesbian Movements in the United States," in Barry Adam, Willem Duyvendak, and Andre Krouwel, eds. The Global Emergence of Gay and Lesbian Politics, Philadelphia: Temple University press, 1999, pp. 30–90.

35. Andrew Sullivan, "Undone by "Don't Ask, Don't Tell," *New York Times*, April 2, 1998, p. A31; Alan Finder, "Court Backs The Pentagon On Gay Rights," *New York Times*, September 24, 1998, p. A14.

36. "National Guard Is Told To Admit Homosexuals," *New York Times*, July 1, 1998, p. A18.

37. Wallace Swan, ed., *Gay/Lesbian/Transgender Public Policy Issues*, New York: Haworth Press, 1997.

38. Human Rights Campaign, "Bill to Prohibit Job Discrimination is Introduced in Congress," www.hrc.org, August 8, 2001.

39. Carey Goldberg, "Maine Voters Repeal a Law On Gay Rights," *New York Times*, February 12, 1998, p. 1, A33.

40. Lyle Denniston, "Supreme Court Rejects Plea to Hear Ga. Gay-Rights Case," *The Baltimore Sun*, January 13, 1998, p. 4A and Janet L. Boyd, "Judge Rules Charity May Act on Anti-Gay Bias," *Women's E News*, www.womensenews.org/article.cfm/dyn/aid/170, August 6, 2001.

41. Lyle Denniston, "Supreme Court Loosens Muzzles On Corporate Whistle-Blowers," *The Baltimore Sun*, January 14, 1998, p. 3A.

42. Steven Marcus, "Their Brothers' Keepers: An Episode from English History," *Doing Good: The Limits of Benevolence*, Willard Gaylin, ed., New York: Pantheon, 1981, pp. 65–66.

43. Nathan Glazer, "The Limits of Social Policy," *The Limits of Social Policy*, Cambridge, Mass.: Harvard University Press, 1988.

15

Alternative Programs to Meet Social Welfare Needs

No choice is a choice.

—Yiddish Proverb

Life's business being just the terrible choice.

—Robert Browning

Overview

At any given moment, there are debates over alternatives in social welfare programs. Old programs evolve; new programs are introduced. All citizens, and certainly social workers, need to have informed and intelligent opinions on alternatives. In this chapter, we want to help the reader not just to understand what currently exists but to develop opinions and to see which of several directions are preferable. We will accompany the reader through an analysis of several programs, studying alternatives and developing a point of view.

The structures of social welfare programs and not just specific benefit levels or provisions are extremely important; in part because these programs, once in place, with few exceptions have tended to maintain their skeletal structures. Since 1935, the Social Security system has been changed and improved many times. Still, the changes have been incremental, and the Social Security system continues to operate within the general outlines of the 1935 enactments, with the basic inequities that have been pointed out almost since the system's inception.

There are so many social welfare programs that it is impossible here to analyze alternatives suggested for them all. For that reason, we focus on program examples in several areas that exemplify the general issues and choices: (1) female heads of household, children, and poverty; (2) mental health services for children and youth; (3) corporate and taxpayer welfare; (4) persons with disabilities; (5) technology and social action; (6) where we are; (7) two scenarios; and (8) our proposal.

Female Heads of Household, Children, and Poverty

A classic election campaign photo opportunity is one in which a campaigner is seen holding and kissing a baby, indicating the campaigner's concern for children. Americans, including our politicians, exude warmth and caring about our children. We are often told children are our future. But when we look closely at what laws are passed and what budget priorities actually are chosen, we are faced with the differences between our societal rhetoric about the importance of children and the reality of childrens' lives.

In the United States, diversity and inequality among American families have grown for several decades. Over time there has been an increase in marital instability. Divorce rates in the United States are among the highest in the advanced industrialized nations. Remarriage has become a common life event but marriages tend to be briefer than earlier. More people are foregoing marriage completely, far more people are co-habiting before and between marriages.[1] As a result, there has been an increase in the numbers of single-parent families. These changes are taking place in the context of growing racial and ethnic diversity with minority populations increasing in number.

In 2000, there were 12.5 million persons living in female-headed households (17 percent of all families). Of those, 3.1 million female householders with no husband present and their families were poor (24.7 percent). Sixteen percent of white (non-Hispanic) such families were poor; 19.9 percent of Asian and Pacific Islander families; 34.2 percent of Hispanic families; and 34.6 percent of Black families. Female householder families composed the majority of poor families. Over 20 percent of these families had one or more employed workers. Women earned on average only 74 percent of what males earned, comparable to the previously achieved high.[2] Almost three fourths of poor children today live in working families that cannot make enough to escape poverty. Three in every five poor children live in female-headed families. It is important to note that the United States is the only industrialized nation without universal health insurance/health care, paid maternal/paternal leave at childbirth, and a family or children's allowance.[3]

The poverty rate for U.S. children is about twice that of most other industrialized nations, and it has increased in the United States in general from the early 1970s. Several causes are suggested for this poverty rise: (1) economic changes have eliminated many blue-collar jobs that paid well; (2) the percentage of children living in single-parent families has increased; and (3) the real value of governmental benefits has declined because of inflation. In addition, policy changes have reduced the dollar amount of benefits and the number of children eligible for them. In addition, (4) the results for this population of the rigorous reform of public assistance begun in 1997 cannot be predicted at this time. The effects of a recession joined with implementation of sanctions for some families may prove to be harmful for children, the most vulnerable group, whose parents are least prepared to support themselves and family through employment.[4]

As indicated here, growing up in a single-parent household is one of the less secure living arrangements for children. There are many mother-headed families whose financial security is undermined by fathers who do not pay child support. After parents divorce or separate, children have been found to be almost twice as likely to be living in poverty than they were before the breakup. These findings underscore the relationship between family structure and economic well-being. A family breakup can cause poverty, but poverty can also cause families to break up.[5] Whatever the reason for a family's being poor, money can buy good food, a safe and decent shelter, opportunities to learn, and good health care, and can reduce family stress and conflict.

As we saw in chapter 1, there are both social and economic costs to poverty for these women and their children. Low-income children are at higher risk for the following:

- death during infancy
- low birthweight
- being abused or neglected
- being partly or completely blind
- physical or mental disabilities
- overall injuries
- hospitalization
- iron deficiency in preschool years
- asthma
- school days missed due to acute learning disabilities and chronic health conditions
- being below grade in school
- death during childhood
- stunted growth
- being partly or completely deaf
- mild mental retardation
- more days in bed because of injuries
- fair or poor health
- pneumonia
- decayed, missing, or filled teeth
- being a dropout at age 16 to 24[6]

Providing adequate nutrition on a below-poverty-level budget is by definition an extremely difficult or impossible task. Nutritional difficulties can lead to other difficulties, and poor housing can contribute to lead poisoning and risks such as living in fire-prone mobile homes. Poverty reduces the number of opportunities to learn at all educational levels. Money reduces family stress and conflict and can provide the opportunity to live in decent neighborhoods and receive health care. Money buys transportation, communication, and economic opportunities. Thus, to be poor is to suffer the impact of many adverse forces. Furthermore, the many effects of poverty on families and their children all interact and are cumulative. Childhood poverty reduces the lifetime productivity output of workers, reduces employment opportunities, and increases ill health and mortality. These adverse conditions have societal economic costs, ranging into the many billions. They result in reduced worker output measured by lower lifetime earnings, and it is clear that the social and economic costs of children in poverty are substantial not just to them personally but also to the entire society.

Studies show that poor children in the United States are poorer than the children in most other Western industrialized nations. There are proportionately more children in poverty in the United States than in other affluent societies. One contributing factor is the shortage of child care in the United States. When inexpensive, high-quality child care is available, it is easier for mothers to return to the workforce. Because these studies excluded in-kind benefits such as free medical and child care services, some claim that the situation for poor children in the United States would compare even less well to these other industrialized nations. Furthermore, the income gap between poor households with children in the United States and affluent households with children is larger in the United States than in any of the other developed nations. Also, welfare programs in the United States are less generous than in these other countries. Finally, households with children in the United States tend to have lower incomes than the national average, a pattern not shared by many other nations.[7]

Social policy and the resulting programs meant to deal with the problem of poverty among single-parent women and their children have never been sufficient to the task. Programs do not focus on preventing a fall into poverty. They provide benefits and services only after families are unable to meet their own needs.

Limitations of Current Programs.   What are some of the limitations of programs that have been designed to assist these parents and their children?

1. The residual nature of the programs and their accompanying means tests cause many people to be declared ineligible because they do not fall completely within specified guidelines, although their need may be real. The stigma associated with means-tested programs leads many persons not to apply because they do not want to be seen as dependent and failing.

2. Benefits are inadequate to the task. Public assistance, the mainstay of many female-headed families and their children, has never provided in any state—other than Alaska and Hawaii—cash and the value of Food Stamps equal to the official poverty level. Few states provide a maximum grant equal to what they define as 100 percent of the "need standard"—the income the state decides is essential for basic consumption items.

3. Poor children tend to live in school districts in rural and inner-city areas which are inequitably financed through property taxes. These school districts are less able to provide a quality education than those in suburban areas.

4. As noted previously, poor children and their families experience difficulty gaining access to medical and dental care for a variety of reasons. They receive poorer quality care and are hospitalized more frequently than persons with private health insurance.

5. They tend to live in unsafe and unhealthy housing.

6. The several programs designed to serve this group are uncoordinated. They are administered at several levels of government, by different agencies and personnel, and with differing eligibility criteria. It is the task of the recipient to ascertain eligibility criteria, meet deadlines, and negotiate varying requirements expected by agencies unmindful of the requirements of other agencies that affect the family's needs.

Improved Social Policy.   What should U.S. social policy be? The basic question is to what degree should the society support female-headed households and their children? There are those whose position is clear: Support women and families to the greatest extent possible for their individual sakes and the sake of the society now and in the future. Others argue that if you improve the conditions for single parents and their families, you undermine the traditional family. The latter argument expresses traditional values that challenge much of what is going on in modern life. The former argument suggests there is no moral alternative and that it is more practical and a higher value for the society to attempt to assist such families with income, educational opportunity, and health care, among other supports. Various industrialized societies react to these questions in different ways.

Sheila Kamerman identified four clusters of policies and programs that are used as strategies in industrialized nations for mother-headed families:

1. *A targeted focus on poor families.* This approach provides public assistance to all poor families and assumes that mothers, whether in one- or two-parent families, will remain at home to rear their children.

2. *Categorical targeting of lone mothers with modest incomes.* These programs assume that most mothers prefer to stay home with their children if financially possible and that women who parent alone have special needs.

3. *Universal support for young children.* Whether married or single, mothers with very young children are covered by these programs. This type of program assumes that financial support and job-protected leaves for parents with children under 3 years of age would find they want to stay home and that children are better off if parents who prefer this choice can do so.

4. *Combining labor market and family policies.* This policy provides cash benefits, services, and other policy supports for working families with children. The goal is to enable parents to enter and remain in the workforce without undue hardship during the child-rearing years.[8] The United States when it instituted Temporary Assistance to Needy Families (TANF), concerned about encouraging dependency, chose to combine forcing as many single parent women as possible into the work force, sometimes with supports and sometimes without sufficient resources.

A Set of Ideal Services. We suggest a combination of strategies (3) and (4): A universal, economic support program for young children and methods that enable parents to enter and remain in the workforce without undue hardship during the child-rearing years. In place of the current scattered efforts for poor single mothers and their children, the United States should seek the welfare of all families and their children. The philosophy we choose to guide social policy for families and their children, not just single-parent mothers and their children, ought to be institutional and universal. Universal, non–means-tested programs should replace selective and means-tested approaches. A focus on poor families that utilizes residual and selective programs intensifies a sense of stigma for those who need assistance. The means-tested approach also excludes those who fall slightly above what is a relatively arbitrary eligibility level.

Some persons advocate changes in public policy such as more stringent divorce laws, holding parents responsible for their childrens' actions, holding fathers responsible for child support, and finding ways for citizens to return to more traditional family values and structures. Others emphasize the provision of material resources such as money, education, health and child care. The provision of additional resources will certainly require reallocation of resources from other sources—the aging, other governmental programs, and families and individuals without children. Certainly, the implementation of Temporary Assistance for Needy Families (TANF) has made the situation of many women and their families more problematic. One way to achieve such a reallocation is through the requirement that employers provide benefits such as paid leave and subsidized child care. The costs of these benefits could be shared among all workers and among consumers. To choose the employer route will avoid certain public budget conflicts. But that strategy will usually be less efficient and less equitable than direct government programs. An alternative way to approach the problem is through government action such as tax credits, subsidies, and child allowances. Choosing this path requires raising taxes, reducing spending, changing priorities, or all three actions.[9]

Raising a family is a normal, legitimate, and necessary function in our society, and our society benefits from healthy, educated, and productive citizens. The needs of families are not abnormal, nor should they be stigmatized. Families should not have to prove their needs in order to be eligible for programs that make it possible for all children and their parents to have a reasonable quality of life. Programs that make this possible should be universal and open to all families and their children below a certain age limit. Such an approach would provide a basic standard of living for all families and the creation of a healthy, appropriately housed, educated, and productive citizenry. Such an approach is preventive, mitigates the structural antecedents of poverty, and supports the morale enhancing idea that our society cares for all its families and their children.

The United States should provide a basic guaranteed annual income and a family allowance to all families with children younger than 18 years of age. The amount provided should be sufficient for the expense of raising children. The cost of these two income security programs can be recouped from those who are well off through the income tax system, which will avoid stigma and create a cost-efficient program. In addition, the minimum wage, whose value has seriously been eroded, should be raised to a level that would allow a working adult to provide at least for a three- person family at the poverty level. (The average public assistance family is slightly fewer than three persons.) The minimum wage should be indexed to inflation to protect its purchasing power. As part of this income security approach, job opportunities—including public work employment and the government's serving as employer of last resort—should be made available for all those able and wishing to work.

Among the other services and benefits that should accompany these economic aspects, our society should strive to provide high-quality public education for all children; safe, affordable, and uncrowded housing for all families; comprehensive and accessible medical and dental care; public and inexpensive transportation; child care for all on a sliding scale; universal application forms, procedures, and eligibility requirements for all services. In addition, agencies serving families and children should be expected to coordinate their services to assist families applying for and receiving the services they need.

One strategy suggested as a complement to these services is "the women's economic agenda." Women and other disadvantaged groups are affected differentially by low and inequitable wages and lack of access to capital. A single mother in a minimum-wage job has to pay from half to three-quarters of her salary for licensed day care. Over one-half of those women starting new businesses have to pay high interest for credit to begin their businesses. Many women workers are also part-time and temporary and so receive few, if any, benefits.

The Women's Voices for the Economy Commission proposed the following agenda:

- Capital to start and expand businesses;
- Job training, continuing education, and skill development;
- Equitable pay and benefits for contingent, temporary workers;
- Flexible schedules; and
- Adequate care for children and the elderly.

This agenda seeks to encourage public-private partnerships in the development of child care centers; support training programs for women who want to work in nontraditional jobs; establish the government as a broker between contractors and service providers; and encourage businesses to offer incentives for investing in their communities. The agenda features partnerships, incentives, individual contributions, and the leveraging of available resources.[10]

Poor children have lower levels of well-being regarding physical health, cognitive functioning, school achievement, and emotional and behavioral outcomes, and were more likely to experience hunger, as well as child abuse and neglect, violent crimes, and fear of going out in their neighborhoods. For low income children, there are indications that a $10,000 increase in average family income between birth and age 5 is associated with nearly a full-year increase in completed schooling.[11] But, it is not just the poor women and their children who would benefit from a better group of services. Our society would also have both social and economic gains by paying greater attention to the needs of these groups. A dollar invested in good early childhood programs for low income children saves $7. A dollar invested in immunizations against diptheria, tetanus, and whooping cough saves $23; a dollar spent in the Women, Infants and Children program (WIC) saves over $3 during a baby's first year.[12]

Later in this chapter, we will examine a second welfare system, often barely discernible to most Americans. By juxtaposing the needs of these two groups, single-parent women and their families and business corporations and higher-income taxpayers, we emphasize the nature of the social policy trade-offs that play a part in determining how Americans will live. An inescapable dimension of social policy is the necessity for trade-offs. No group can get a hundred percent of what they want. As a greater priority is placed on resources and services for one group, the difficulty grows of finding funds for the reforms and social programs needed for poor women and children. In a later section, we will turn to this second welfare system.

Mental Health Services for Children and Youth

The future strength of the United States depends on, among other factors, the physical and mental health of our young people. Many children have mental health problems that interfere with their development and functioning. Nevertheless, because childhood and adolescence are periods of transition and almost constant reorganization, assessment of children and adolescents has to be carefully done within the context of family, social, and cultural expectations about appropriate thoughts, emotions, and behaviors. While the range of what is considered "normal" is wide, children and adolescents do develop mental disorders beyond the usual ups and downs one experiences in the course of development.

Prevalence.   In the United States, one in ten children and adolescents suffer from mental illness severe enough to cause impairment. There are estimates that in any particular year fewer than one in five of these children actually receives the needed treatment. Internationally the World Health Organization predicts that neuropsychiatric disorders will become one of the five most common causes of morbidity (disease), mortality, and disability among children.[13]

The mental health problems of children and youth include the following: *Depression*. There are reports that 3 percent of children and up to 8 percent of adolescents in the United States experience depression, a serious mental disorder, that adversely affects mood, energy, interest, sleep, appetite, and overall functioning. Treatment is critical to prevent impairment in academic, social, emotional, and behavioral functioning and to enable children to reach their full potential. *Anxiety Disorders*. These include generalized anxiety disorder, obsessive compulsive disorder (OCD), panic disorder, post-traumatic stress disorder, phobias, and separation anxiety. One study found that as many as 13 percent of 9- to 17-year olds experienced an anxiety disorder in a year.

There are estimates that 3–5 percent of school-aged children experience *Attention deficit hyperactivity disorder* (ADHD) making this the most commonly diagnosed psychiatric disorder of childhood. Among other illnesses are *eating disorders, bi-polar* (manic depressive) illness, *autism* and other pervasive developmental disorders, *schizophrenia*, and *Tourette's syndrome*. In addition, mental health concerns are related to abuse, learning disabilities, rape, runaways, substance abuse, suicide, and violence.

Mental health problems appear in all social classes and people from all backgrounds. While no one is completely immune to these disorders and problems, there are young people who are at greatest risk because of factors such as: physical problems; intellectual disabilities (retardation); low birth weight; family history of mental and addictive disorders; multigenerational poverty; and caregiver separation or abuse and neglect.[14]

Economic Costs.   There are a multitude of social, educational, productivity, short and long-term health costs, as well as personal and family suffering, pain, and struggle that accompany children's emotional and mental illnesses. There are also economic costs, although a complete estimate is not attainable for the direct and indirect costs. These costs are not limited to direct mental health services but also must include services provided in critical child and youth serving locations such as education, child welfare, and the juvenile justice system. There are estimates that up to half of the children and youth in the child welfare system need treatment and upwards of four in five in the juvenile system.

In 1998 annual expenditures for child and adolescent mental health services, although incomplete, were estimated at $11.75 billion or $173 per child. The costs of serving adolescents accounted for almost 60 percent of the total and the highest per person expenditures. Only an estimated $39 dollar was expended for children one to five years of age. Outpatient services cost almost 60 percent, followed by inpatient treatment (33%), and psychotropic medications that made up 9 percent of the costs. The sources of payments included almost half (private insurance), Medicaid (one fourth) other public insurance (3%) and the remainder were uninsured. State and local governments provided 21 percent of the costs. The costs of institutional care has been reduced by such factors as reductions in length of stay and the rise in out-patient treatment.

Despite the costs of services provided, only 5–7 percent of the children needing treatment receive some specialized mental health services. Furthermore, the

United States Public Health Service estimates that up to 20 percent of children at one time or another have a diagnosable mental disorder. Thus, many children and youth who should be receiving treatment and mental health services are not provided such care, eventuating in social, economic, and other costs.[15]

Mental Health Services.   The mental health needs of children and adolescents have historically been neglected. At the time mental health services in the United States received their greatest boost, services for those groups were almost completely ignored in the Mental Retardation Facilities and Community Mental Health Centers Construction Act (called the Community Mental Health Centers Act (1963). Today state mental health agencies continue spending most of their funds on mental hospitals that mainly serve adults. The Child and Adolescent Service program identifies seriously emotionally disturbed children as a major target group but this is only one group among many with mental health needs. The Education for All Handicapped Children Act as Amended (1986) recognized the need for early intervention. There are several early intervention programs that target infants and toddlers who are developmentally disabled or at risk of disabilities and that attempt to intervene as early as possible in the developmental process.[16]

In the last several decades, a number of changes have occurred in the way children and adolescents with serious emotional disorders and their families are served. *Community-based* systems of care have been expanded with the belief that services should be delivered in the least restrictive setting appropriate to the particular child and problem, ranging from residential to entirely community-focused treatment services.

Several shifts in philosophy and approaches have supported a general change in the ways services are provided for young people and their families. Traditionally, parents—particularly mothers—have been identified as the "cause" of mental health problems experienced by their children. Today attempts are made to have families participate more in the treatment planning process for their children. Earlier it was believed that mental health services could only be provided by placing children in residential centers away from parents, siblings, and their community, that is, removing them from the sources of their illnesses. Today efforts are made to preserve families and to develop a series of services that are "wrapped around" the patient and the family thereby providing intensive services in more natural and familiar settings.

Recent decades have also seen the intensification of culturally competent service delivery systems that acknowledge cultural differences and the need to formulate services that meet varying needs and backgrounds. Help-seeking involves decision-making wherein a person defines a problem, decides to seek help, and then selects a particular source of help to resolve the problem. Help-seeking varies by racial and/or ethnic groups. For example, Asian Americans rarely endorse emotional interpersonal problems as a central problem. These attitudes lead to underutilization of formal mental health services. One study found Asian Americans were 3 times less likely than their Caucasian counterparts to use available mental health services. African Americans and Latino parents were less likely to contact professionals when seeking advice or help regarding their children's problems.[17]

The development of community-based systems of care offset the prior over-dependence upon residential treatment. Included in community-based systems of mental health care are: mental health, social educational, health, substance abuse, vocational, recreational, and other support services such as case management, family support and self-help groups, advocacy, legal services, transportation, and juvenile justice services.

Among the current mix of services are preventive services, early identification and intervention, assessment, outpatient treatment, home-based services, day treatment, emergency services, therapeutic foster care, therapeutic group care, therapeutic camping services, independent living services, residential treatment, crisis residential services, inpatient hospitalization, and outpatient therapy. In regard to early identification of problems, one study found that self-reports by first-graders of depressed moods and feelings predicted later child academic functioning, the need for and use of mental health services, suicidal ideation, and a diagnosis of major depressive disorder by age 14.[18] On the other hand, clinicians have to be wary of stigmatizing and creating self-fulfilling prophecies.

Day treatment is the most intensive form of non-residential treatment but some patients are hospitalized partially or in hospital-based day treatment. These treatment situations often include special education, counseling, family services such as counseling, parent training, and assistance for families with their tangible needs. Some adolescents are provided with vocational training, crisis intervention, and skill building activities, including interpersonal, problem-solving, and practical skills. Other services may include behavior modification, positive-reinforcement, recreation, and art and music therapy.

Some services are school-based whereby school mental health clinicians and teams help to create a network of community resources for youth with emotional and behavioral disorders. They try to provide a structure of services at home, in school, and in the community "wrapped" around the youth and their families. Other services—dependent upon the situation—are delivered primarily in the home. These services are family-focused and their intensity is based on the needs of the particular family. Efforts are made to link the family with appropriate community agencies and individuals such as therapeutic foster care—a relatively new form of treatment—in which treatment includes the efforts of trained families in private homes so that treatment takes place in a more normalized setting. Crisis and emergency services are provided when acute episodes occur.

Residential services include psychiatric hospitalization and residential treatment centers. Inpatient services are reserved for extreme situations such as acute disturbances or difficult, perplexing problems. Included will be individual, family, and group therapy, pharmacotherapy, milieu therapy, and behavioral modification. Residential treatment centers range from highly to less structured setting similar to group homes or halfway houses. Some centers provide a full-range of services while others are strictly custodial.

Families are viewed as partners in the treatment plan for their children and services are provided to support and assist families. When a child is ill, there are disruptions in family communication patterns, family roles and patterns of daily living are disrupted, the child's cognitive and emotional development is unpredictable, and there is a sense of loss as the expectations for achievement in all spheres and abilities of the child to cope with life may be seriously threatened. In addition to management of family stress in the present situation, parents and siblings may have concerns about the long-term care and support of the child.

Case management—connecting patients with community support resources and assuring service, helping to develop needed services, and coordinating patient-centered support systems[19]—serves to link and coordinate services to ensure the most comprehensive program required to meet the patient's needs for care actually are delivered. Case management includes assessment of the situation and persons involved, service planning, implementation, coordination, monitoring and evaluation, and advocacy where needed.[20]

Policy Choices. Claims are made that insufficient sums are devoted to the treatment of mental disorders among children and youth. However, preventive interventions have been found to reduce the impact of risk factors for mental disorders by providing—for example—educational programs for young children, parent-education programs, and systematic nurse and other mental health practitioner home visits.

Primary care and the schools are strategic settings for the potential recognition of mental disorders in children and adolescents; even so, the number of trained personnel is limited, and the options for referral to specialty care are also limited.

The multiple problems associated with serious emotional disturbance in children and adolescents are best addressed with a system approach in which multiple service sectors work collaboratively in an organized fashion. Positive results for children (functional outcomes) when systems of care are instituted have been reported but the relationship between changes at the system level and clinical outcomes remains unclear. Nevertheless, the attention of mental health services has shifted somewhat to pay attention to concrete societal issues such as employment, housing, nutrition,etc.

Cultural differences are a growing phenomenon in American society that exacerbate the problems of access to appropriate mental health services (when they exist). Culturally appropriate services have been designed but are not widely available for people. According to Surgeon General David Satcher members of minority groups suffer disproportionately from mental illness because they often lack access to services, receive lower quality care, and are less likely to seek help when in distress.[21]

Social Work Roles. Social workers play important roles at every point in the delivery of mental health services from prevention services to identification of those in need of service to treatment for children and youth and their families. Social workers may be able to play significant roles in working toward (1) Attainment of improved funding for mental health services for young people; (2) greater coordination of services among the mental health, health, social welfare, educational, juvenile justice, and employment and training systems. (3) Advocacy on behalf of adequately funded, staffed, and accessible community-based systems that serve young people is another role which social workers play. (4) Enhancement of the multi-cultural approach to the delivery of mental health services is an aspect to which social work brings much experience and knowledge. (5) Lobbying and advocacy for jobs at decent pay, income security, broader health care services, a greater stress on prevention services and early intervention with individuals and their families, and appropriate housing, education, and job training, all are aspects to which social workers can make contributions. (6) As direct service practitioners, as case managers, as supervisors, administrators, team members and team leaders, social workers bring unique perspectives to mental health treatment.

A Second Welfare System: Corporate and Taxpayer Welfare

In the earlier sections of this chapter, we examined some of the social welfare issues related to poor single-parent women and their children and later will do so for persons with disabilities in the context of American society. We turn now to another welfare system, one which remains beneath the "radar" for most Americans. The second welfare system is seldom publicly acknowledged by people and the media place much more emphasis upon the poor, especially poor women. During the debates about re-making "welfare," it was clear that many American families believe that the value of family self-sufficiency outweighs the value of a parent's care for children. In fact, while the 1996 welfare reform law allowed states to exempt new mothers from work requirements until their children reach one year old, many states adopted stricter requirements.[22]

Many people are "familiar" with welfare mothers and have feelings about their presumed dependency. They have been viewed—in general—as taking advantage of the welfare system, having many children, not sustaining their families, living loose lives, remaining overlong on the welfare rolls, and in general not being good citizens. While assistance for poor women is viewed as a drag on the economy and frivolous spending, subsidies of great magnitude for corporations and others are viewed as necessary for the good of the nation, unconnected to dependency, and the due of "good citizens" and "good citizen" corporations. Calls for reform of social programs designed to help poorer individuals are forceful; calls to reduce corporate and other welfare through the tax system are muted.

Tax Expenditures

Tax expenditures are revenue losses attributable to provisions of the federal tax laws that allow special exclusions, exemptions or deductions from gross income or that provide special credits, preferential tax rates, or deferral of tax liabilities. They are, therefore, any reductions in *individual* and *corporate* tax liabilities that result in special tax provisions or regulations that provide tax benefits to particular taxpayers. These tax provisions are referred to as tax expenditures because they are analogous to direct spending programs, both of which may have similar budget policy objectives. Tax expenditures are most similar to direct spending programs that have no spending limits and are available as entitlements to those who meet the established statutory criteria. There is a wide array of programs to assist businesses through direct services, cash grants, subsidized credit, tax credits and tax deductions.

Many expenditures are to encourage business, trade, development of natural resources, and other economic developments. One way in which government supports corporations is through research grants and subsidies. Even where no business will reap large profits, it may be necessary for the federal government to fund basic research in areas that have potential for enriching society. One never knows the potential of basic research or the possibilities of programs such as NASA, materials science, biotechnology, or other investigations. So one can assume there ought to be a federal role in which industry is subsidized, but questions can be raised about the aims, dimensions, and efficacy of such subsidies. Some subsidies provide housing or health care but others may be little more than political payoffs to constituents or business expenditures that businesses might be expected to pay themselves.

To gain a sense of the dimensions of tax expenditures, estimates were prepared by the Office of Management and Budget (part of the White House) for the fiscal years 2002–2006. The anticipated total is $3.8 trillion dollars. Among the larger expenditures are capital gains treatment of certain income, accelerated depreciation of machinery and equipment, exclusion of employer contributions for medical insurance premiums and medical care, enhanced oil recovery credit, and mortgage interest on owner-occupied homes.[23]

Corporate income tax revenue decreased as a percentage of the gross domestic product (GDP) fifty percent from the mid-1960s until 1999. The percentage of Federal revenues derived from individuals in 1965 was 41.8 percent; in 1999, the percentage was just over 48 percent, *a fifteen percent increase.* During the same time period, the percentage of revenues derived from corporate income taxes was reduced from 21.8 percent in 1965 to 10.1 percent in 1999, *a fifty four percent decrease.*[24]

Individual and corporate welfare costs taxpayers more than means-tested assistance programs such as Temporary Assistance to Needy Families, Food Stamps, housing assistance, and child nutrition. Much attention was paid by the public and legislators to ending "welfare as we know it." But, scarce attention has been paid to calls to end *corporate* welfare as we know it. Individual welfare for the poor is perceived as undeserved "handouts" but corporate welfare and tax expenditures for the middle class and wealthy are viewed as serving the public interest by promoting economic growth. Traditional welfare is seen as unwarranted because it redistributes wealth but corporate welfare or tax benefits for the middle and wealthier classes is not understood as serving the same function.

Policy Options (Low). Tax expenditures are designed to accomplish social and/or economic goals. If the government, that is the legislature, wants to subsidize wages for low-income workers, there are several options: (1) It could regulate wages by requiring businesses to pay a minimum hourly wage; (2) a federal department, perhaps the Department of Labor, could provide direct wage subsidies to workers or to their employers; (3) Or, the Internal Revenue Service could administer tax expenditures by reducing income taxes or providing tax "refunds" for those who were low earners and owed no income taxes. The minimum wage is an example of the first case. Salaries are subsidized for some persons through payments to employers. The Earned Income Tax Credit for low-and moderate income working families is an example of the third type of policy.

Two Welfare Systems.   The two welfare systems differ in a number of ways and can be compared on different dimensions.[25] Among others, the following dimensions generally are used in public discussions to differentiate the two systems:

Corporate and "Better Off" Welfare	*Low Income Individual Welfare*
Incentives to produce	Handouts
Benefits society	Drains society
Investment	Redistribution
Creates Jobs	Disincentive to work
Generates income	Tax burden
A source of growth	Source of poverty

According to this schema, corporate welfare is viewed as a part of and contributing to the economy, is productive, efficient, and generates prosperity. Individual welfare, on the other hand, is not viewed as either a part or contributing to the economy, is unproductive, inefficient, and constrains economic growth.

Evaluation Criteria.   Citizens for Tax Justice suggests a series of questions to consider when evaluating tax expenditures:

1. Is the subsidy designed to serve an important public purpose?
2. Is the subsidy actually helping to achieve its goals?
3. Are the benefits from the subsidy, if any, commensurate with its cost?
4. Are the benefits of the subsidy fairly distributed, or are they disproportionately targeted to those who do not need or deserve government assistance?
5. Is the subsidy well-administered?[26]

As you read the next several paragraphs, consider the above criteria and come to a decision about each of the programs described below.

President Bush and Corporate Welfare.   President George W. Bush proposed during his campaign for the presidency and again early in his administration advocated that many subsidies to business be ended. Because of his general ties and biases toward corporate America, it was possible that this agenda item might find some success without damaging his political base but previous efforts had achieved very limited success. An example of the corporate welfare "pork barrel" is the case of shipbuilding in Mississippi. The last time a passenger cruise ship was built in the United States was in 1958. But, two 1,900 passenger ships costing together more than $1 billion dollars are being constructed in that state.

According to one view, there is no justification for the subsidized loans (government guaranteed loans so shipbuilders can borrow from investors at low cost and with little risk). The absence of a shipbuilding industry would not threaten national security since war with all three of the world's ship builders, Europe, Japan, and South Korea, at the same time is highly unlikely. Shipbuilding could be rejuvenated quickly if needed in a national emergency that required massive mobilization. From an economic perspective, support for the shipbuilding also falls short because the costs of production in Mississippi are twice what they would be at the other shipbuilders. The program props up an uncompetitive industry. If it is a question of employment in poor urban areas, other forms of grants such as enterprise grants or other targeted programs could be more attractive. The difficulty of cutting back on corporate welfare becomes clear when the suggestion to end the subsidy program was countered immediately by almost 40 senators (including Trent Lott of Mississippi who had been Senate Republican Majority leader and whose wife is from the city in which the ships are built).[27]

It is not just major corporations that profit from corporate welfare. Many farmers receive checks from the government whether they have good crops or bad, high yields or low. They are paid subsidies when market conditions result in their failure to make money and they are paid subsidies when they take land out of production. Some farmers can make almost $300,000 by having a year of failure.[28]

The conservative "think tank" the CATO Institute is also critical of corporate welfare. They suggest the following program. Congress should * terminate programs that provide direct grants to businesses; *eliminate programs that provide research and other services for industries; * end programs that provide subsidized loans or insurance for businesses; * eliminate trade barriers designed to protect U.S. firms in specific industries from foreign competition at the expense of higher prices for American consumers; * base defense procurement contract decisions on national security needs, not on the number of jobs created in key members' districts; * and eliminate the income tax loopholes carved out solely for the specific companies or industries and substantially lower the tax rate so that there is no net revenue increase. To their credit, their program is an honest, conservative free-enterprise agenda.[29]

Policy Options (High).   Earlier, we suggested there are lower level policy decisions. By lower level policy we mean that once it is decided to utilize tax expenditures, there are technical methods for operating them. These choices reflect the philosophy behind the overall direction—the technical methods reflect value choices and philosophies, for example, use of government, use of the private sector. But today there are a series of policy decisions being made which result in broader, higher level policy results about basic societal directions. Implied in the use of the panoply of tax expenditures is a culture of dependency, but a culture of dependency for corporations instead of individuals. Corporations cannot be expected to risk, to invest, to provide jobs, and to produce without government assistance. These actions are inconsistent with the widely proclaimed virtues of the free market philosophy.

Furthermore, when corporate welfare is included in the welfare state, there is a shift away from "social" welfare to "corporate" welfare. The shift is presented as necessary for the overall public good. These actions end in shifting "welfare" overall from those who are poor as well as others who also need help in various ways to private decisions and private gain by businesses and industries. At the highest level, this privatization of welfare to the benefit of corporations drains potential resources for helping individuals and families with a wide array of human needs. Thus, there are social and economic *opportunity costs:* programs, energy, and dollars directed to corporate welfare are unavailable for use by the middle and lower classes.

Persons with Disabilities

For many persons in American society, "people with severe or multiple disabilities are invisible,"[30] and their daily frustrations and struggles with everyday activities go unremarked. Nevertheless, the number of persons with disabilities is large. In 1997, almost 4 million 6-to-14-year old young people had disabilities, of these 1.7 million had severe disabilities. There were over 30 million persons 15 years and older with severe disabilities. Of those 30 million persons, more than half (16.9 million persons) had disabilities which interfered with there ability to work. Almost 5 million were disabled workers receiving Social Security Disability and there were 6.5 million other persons whose disabilities made them eligible for receipt of Supplemental Security Income (SSI) payments and still others received General Assistance. Furthermore, over 166,000 military veterans were totally disabled. Of those with work disabilities, 21.6 percent were poor in 1994. So those with disabilities may not be on the public's radar screen, but there are many of them, as well as their dependents, and they have economic difficulties.

When we speak of persons with disabilities, we include a vast array of people with differing abilities, types of disabilities, and different numbers and degrees of disability, ranging from minor to severe impairments. Among those with disabilities, there are a variety of physically functional limitations such as hearing, seeing, and speaking, as well as developmental and mental problems.

Furthermore, persons with disabilities differ in other ways as well. Varying sociocultural factors shape the experience of the disability, that is, persons with disabilities have diverse social and cultural identities. They differ by *social class.* Being disabled can be expensive. Access to technical aids and personal assistance can ease the effects of and overcome some social barriers. Persons differ by *race* and the effects of racism and discrimination. *Age* is important because children have far less control over their lives than adults. They are subject to greater restrictions. Views of male and female *genders* also influence how persons with disabilities will be perceived and responded to. Finally, *sexuality* alters the experience of disabled persons as well. Both male and female disabled persons are often viewed as asexual; sexual activity and orientations are more closely regulated in people who have less control over their lives.[31]

There are definitional problems regarding disabilities. What is viewed as a physical or health condition by many persons may not be understood as a limitation by others. Nevertheless, definitions are important in many ways. Definitions and assessments are used to make decisions about health care, eligibility for educational and training services, Social Security disability, SSI, and other programs and services. In general, a disability refers to any long- or short-term reduction of a person's activity that results from an acute or chronic condition that interferes with the ability to perform the activity in the manner and range considered normal.

It is not possible here to review all disabling limitations, nor the specific histories of the ways in which our society has dealt with each of them. Although there have been improvements, in general, community members are uncomfortable with and about persons with disabilities. This discomfort ranges from mild reactions to stigmatization, stereotyping, and avoidance. Several social policies have been enacted as legislation and have moved our society toward the goal of normalization for the greatest number possible of those with disabilities. Many of those concerned with the disabled have an additional goal their empowerment to obtain their rights, access, and services as needed.

Civil Rights. During the past 30 years, the United States gradually reduced legal barriers based on race, religion, sex, and national origin. The Americans with Disabilities Act (ADA) removed barriers that deny equal opportunities to individuals with disabilities. Sponsored by Senator Lowell Weicker (R-Conn.) and Representative Tony Coelho (D-Calif.), the legislation became law in July 1990.

The act, amalgamating the Civil Rights Act (1964) and the Rehabilitation Act (1973), provides civil rights protections for persons with disabilities parallel to those established by the federal government for women and minorities. One provision of the act prohibits discrimination against individuals with disabilities in public- and private-sector employment. This part of the act requires employers to make reasonable accommodations to the known physical or mental limitations of a qualified applicant or employee, unless the accommodation would impose an undue hardship on the employer.

Several Supreme Court cases were heard in 1999 (nine years after enactment of the legislation) and early on were identified as the equivalent to *Brown v. Board of Education* for the disability rights movement. Hearing the cases forced the Court to conduct an extensive review of the Americans with Disabilities Act. The Supreme Court ruled that people with physical impairments who can function normally when they wear their glasses or take their medicine generally cannot be considered disabled, and therefore do not come within the law's protection against employment discrimination. (*Sutton et al v. United Airlines*, 1999; *Albertson's, Inc., v. Kirkingburg*, 1999; and *Murphy v. United Parcel Service*, 1999).

The cases involved two nearsighted women, twins with vision correctable to 20/20, who were turned down by United Airlines for jobs as pilots; a truck driver with functional vision in only one eye who saw normally for many situations but who was dismissed for not meeting the Federal standard for driving commercial vehicles; and a hypertensive automobile mechanic whose blood pressure kept him from meeting Federal standards for driving a truck but, when kept under control by medication, left him able to hold mechanics' jobs.

The Court took a restrictive view of the definition of disability under the Americans with Disabilities Act. Employers greeted the ruling with relief because they thought the ruling would prevent an expansion of the law and an explosion of court cases. Advocates for the disabled thought the Court's decision would remove the law's protection from millions of persons who needed such protection and undermined the intent of the law to eliminate discrimination against every person with a disability.

In a separate case, the Court ruled in *Olmstead*, Commissioner, Georgia Department of Human Resources *v. L. C. and E. W. by Zimring*, guardian ad litem and next friend, et al, 1999 that states are obliged to care for people with mental and other disabilities in group homes or other non-institutionalized settings when medically appropriate and not an unreasonable burden on the state's resources. In this case, two women whose disabilities included mental retardation, mental illness, and brain damage sought a life outside a large state hospital institution. The women had waited many months in the hospital for placement in a more home-like environment that their physicians said would be medically and socially appropriate but for which there were long waiting lists.[32]

In yet another case, the Supreme Court created a zone of immunity for the states beyond the reach of the civil rights law when they ruled in *Alabama v. Garrett* (2001) that state employees cannot sue for damages for violations of the Americans with Disabilities Act. Essentially, the ruling constricted the power of Congress and expanded the sphere of state immunity. The decision immediately impacted on state workers but also suggested future problems might occur in other types of cases under the disabilities and civil rights laws. Some advocates for those with disabilities feared the ruling might eventually affect the Fair Housing Act, special education, and the rights of persons with disabilities to live in noninstitutional, community-based settings.

During January 2002, the Supreme Court in a unanimous ruling continued its interpretations generally narrowing the terms of the Americans with Disabilities Act (1990). The original law obligated employers to make reasonable accommodations for disabled workers. As a result of the Court's trend, plaintiffs are finding it more difficult to win or even to get a court hearing.

In *Ella Williams v. Toyota, Motor Manufacturing, Kentucky, Inc.* (2002) the Court overruled a U.S. Appeals Court decision when it stated the lower Court used the wrong standard in the case and suggested that the person's impairments must have substantial limitations on abilities that are central to daily life, preventing that person from performing important daily tasks. Justice Sandra Day O'Connor writing for the Court and returning the case to the lower Court said the proper test involved whether the impairments prevented or restricted an individual from performing tasks of central importance to most peoples' lives. Furthermore, the ruling suggested it was applicable to other provisions of the law dealing with public transportation and public accommodations for persons with disabilities. The case might still be won by Ella Williams when it returns to the United States Court of Appeals in Cincinnati, but advocates for business called the decision a major victory.[33]

A second provision of the act seeks to ensure that individuals with disabilities have access to transportation. Still another provision provides that public accommodations ensure access and includes business establishments, educational institutions, recreational facilities, and social service centers. The act, however, exempts religious organizations from the public accommodations requirements.

The act amended the Communications Act (1934) to require that telephone companies provide telecommunications relay services to permit speech- or hearing-impaired persons to have opportunities for communication equivalent to those provided by other customers.

Malinda Orlin reviewed the ADA in order to identify the act's implications for providers of social services. Agencies are required to make reasonable modifications of their policies and procedures in order to attain the act's aims. These aims include making architectural and communication changes that remove barriers to the service for persons with disabilities. Also, the goal is full participation by people with disabilities, so agencies need to examine their operations to identify barriers that reduce the participation of those with disabilities. Those who serve persons with disabilities need to be certain they review all facets of their agencies to best achieve the aims of the act and also empower them to the highest extent possible.[34]

A large percentage of persons with disabilities are poor. More than one in six (17.8 percent) of persons 15 to 69 years of age with a work disability is poor.[35] There are several income security programs that assist persons with disabilities. Social Security Disability Insurance and Supplemental Security Income were discussed in chapter 9. Their importance is reflected in the total number of their beneficiaries, including disabled workers, spouses, children, the aging, and those who may be ineligible for Social Security, including those who are blind and otherwise disabled.

Family and Medical Leave Act.   The Family and Medical Leave Act (1993) is designed to balance the demands of the workplace with the needs of families through entitling employees to take reasonable leave for medical reasons or for the care of a child, spouse, or parent. This program is only available for workers in businesses with 50 or more employees.

The poverty of some persons with disabilities is a result of difficulties finding employment because of discrimination and other barriers. Title I of the ADA prohibits employers with 15 or more employees from discriminating against qualified individuals with disabilities—just because they have disabilities—in job application procedures, hiring, advancement, compensation, job training, and other conditions of employment. Employers must make reasonable accommodation to employees with disabilities who can perform the essential functions of the job unless to do so would impose an undue hardship that causes significant difficulty and/or expense.[36] In fact, the Supreme Court found unanimously that disabled state prisoners are covered against discrimination by the ADA.[37]

The ADA was passed by a Democratic Congress and signed into law by a Republican President, George Bush. There are people who see the law as positive and those who find fault with it. As a result of the act, persons with disabilities have attained a greater ability to find employment, travel, enjoy recreation with their children, and participate in life more fully. Some point to the benefits to businesses that hire those with disabilities, seek to sell goods or services to them, and to the utility for the general population of technologies intended originally to help the disabled such as computer speech-recognition programs. Others complain about unnecessary expenses attributable to a national building code that requires building access even where sparsely used.

Children, Learning, and Social Participation.   Federal laws require that every student has a right to free and appropriate public education. The landmark Education for All Handicapped Children Act (1975) first opened the doors for children with disabilities to free and appropriate education in the public schools by providing funds to enable local school districts to provide such education without cost to the students' parents and regardless of the severity or type of disability. No child was to be denied an education because of perceived educability. Prior to this legislation, many students with disabilities were either excluded from public schools or, if in the public system, were educated in segregated and separate facilities. Educational programs, where they existed, were viewed as custodial rather than educational.

The Rehabilitation Act (1973) required that all children—those with and without disabilities—be treated equally whether in regular or special education settings. Also, the ADA (1990) required state and local governments to make their programs and services accessible to qualified persons with disabilities.

The Individuals with Disabilities Education Act (1990) requires that children with disabilities be mainstreamed in educational institutions unless the severity of their disability or the need for special services and supports precludes satisfactory progress in regular classrooms. Among the children considered disabled are those with mental retardation; hearing, visual, orthopedic, and other chronic or acute health impairments; the speech-impaired; seriously emotionally disturbed; as well as those with specific learning disabilities. This type of legislation is based on the assumption that children with disabilities will benefit both educationally and in social interaction when they are included in the ordinary educational classroom setting and not placed in what many consider to be isolating and stigmatizing settings.

In another Supreme Court case, the Court ruled that public school districts must pay for full-time nursing care for disabled students who require that service to attend classes. At the time of the ruling, there were estimates that nationwide there were 17 thousand students who would qualify for the service. The Court held that such services were needed in order to guarantee that students with disabilities are integrated into the public schools. The Court ruled that schools have no duty to provide physicians' services but one-on-one nursing throughout the school day must be financed by the school district. Since individual circumstances differ, the decision's impact has to be worked out in negotiations for each disabled student who needs special support to attend a regular public school.[38]

The services to be provided to a particular child are determined on a case-by-case basis following a school evaluation process, which must be consented to in writing by the parents. Within 30 days of the completion of the evaluation process, an individualized education program (IEP) must be prepared and presented in a meeting that includes one or both parents and the team of professional educators.

The results of several studies suggest that mainstreaming has not improved the social relations and interactions of children with disabilities. These studies have shown that nondisabled children are less accepting and direct more negative behaviors toward children with disabilities. In addition, children with disabilities are frequently ignored or excluded from activities. Furthermore, the nondisabled children often assume adult roles in relation to children with developmental disabilities, in this way undermining the potential of child-to-child interactions. These findings suggest that mainstreaming children with disabilities requires support systems and social skills programs as part of the provision of opportunities for the development of friendships.[39]

General Social Services for Persons with Disabilities.   The chief goals of social services for this varied group of persons are normalization and empowerment so they can participate as fully as possible in society—educationally, vocationally, as well as socially. Basic to all services is the concept of empowerment so that persons with disabilities will know the rights to which they are entitled and have access to assistance when needed for advocacy of their rights. There is a special role for social workers to advance understanding of ADA rights by individuals with disabilities and/or other significant persons, while recognizing the difference between social work advocacy and legal advocacy. One result of education and advocacy for the pursuit of legal rights should be greater employment and other rewards, greater financial and pyschological resources, and more options regarding lifestyles.[40] Associated services are efforts aimed at overcoming community rejection and stereotyping of those with disabilities, a major force that supports resistance to mainstreaming and other normalization efforts. During the 1980s, attempts were made to remove Social Security benefits from persons with disabilities. During the 1990s, efforts were made to deny SSI to children with disabilities and to deny benefits to *legal* immigrants with disabilities. Efforts such as these are influenced by the cultural representation of persons with disabilities and suggest social workers have an important role in overcoming such cultural representations.[41]

Among other social services provided are, as appropriate, education, employment, and a variety of work opportunities, including sheltered workshops. Vocational rehabilitation is of assistance for those who are in need of this service. Other services include group homes, nursing homes, residential treatment facilities, day-care centers, hospitals and health care, Meals-on-Wheels, home health services, homemaker services, transportation, improved access to buildings and other resources, and counseling for both individuals and families.

Alternatives Facing the Practitioner

Policy choices are not just made at the macro level, although as one reads about social programs the policy choices are most often discussed at this high level. But social workers at the "line" level and in supervisory positions also influence policy choices that affect services.

For example, the staff at a community center meets to set fees for a day camp service. There are serious policy decisions to be weighed. If no fee is charged, there will be insufficient funds to fully support the program and fewer children will be served. Also, the day camp may take on a "charity" flavor in the locality, and those children who do attend may be stigmatized. If a high fee is charged, perhaps based on the full cost of the program, only 20 or 30 percent of the families can pay this full fee. As a result, there will have to be a means test for the other 70 or 80 percent of families to use the service. Stigma usually accompanies such tests, and some people will probably pay less than they should; others will forego the service rather than submit to a test.

Thus do problems of universal versus selective service touch every level. In the case cited, the staff may decide on a low fee for all. This gives clients the dignity of contributing to a service, brings in some income, and minimizes the number who cannot pay and need a means test. Or the decision may be for a higher fee to maximize income, with a low fee available on a simple declaration of need. But the choices are not simple. If the service is made universally available, this decision will reduce the question of stigma but also will reduce the possibility of aiming the program specifically at a group of children who may need the program and its services most. On the other hand, if the day camp is aimed at those children who are most needy, one sacrifices inclusivity for serving the needs of a special group, thus running the risk of demeaning the quality of the service and perhaps fostering divisive feelings in the community. Serving the poor, the middle class, or the wealthy in such situations may be a question of balance, not a question of either/or. But this too depends on the goals that one has in a community for the service provided. The population served and the needs to be met determine, finally, what the choices and the shadings of choices will be.

Suppose a staff member of a community mental health center is seeking apartments for people who have been hospitalized for mental illness. Because of community resistance to this kind of program, in spite of all the community education that has been attempted, she is having great difficulty in locating apartments for people waiting to be discharged from hospitals. An urban university has space in its dormitories for a few groups of three or four mental patients. For a variety of reasons the worker is reluctant. The dormitory community is less of a natural community than the surrounding neighborhood. It will be harder for the patients to integrate. There will be times when the dormitories are vacant, and the patients will be living in a kind of a ghost town. Here the worker is struggling with the dilemma of vertical versus horizontal adequacy. If she maintains her principles about getting the best possible service, she will have fewer group homes available; or the ones she finds will be closer to the desirable pattern but more people will be left behind in the mental institution. If she sacrifices vertical adequacy for horizontal adequacy, more patients can be discharged to halfway houses and can have a chance at integration, but in a less-desirable setting. One has to weigh the gains and losses in each case in making this kind of decision.

As another example, suppose the parents who use a day-care center are dismayed by the cost. The worker attempts to move them toward social action to pressure the state office to provide more adequate funding for the day-care center. However, the parents, in part despairing of that kind of change, volunteer to do supplementary fund-raising and to provide all the amenities missing in the day-care center. Is this step to be encouraged? It could provide the improvement in services needed, but it is not equitably financed. What should be done?

All these cases are attempts to illustrate that the "line" worker in day-to-day practice is faced with social welfare decisions not unlike those described on the macro level throughout this book. This is not a text on practice methodology, and therefore we will not get into a description of how a worker effects social change and social policy. But it is important to know that workers are involved in social policy on the micro level at least and that they need to be armed with analytic tools to help them decide on the directions in which they will press, using the skills learned in other courses and from other texts. How important this can be is perhaps best illustrated in the earlier example of how guideline writers in the War on Poverty may have shaped the whole "maximum feasible participation" component of the effort in ways never anticipated by the legislators. It is clear from this that what each social worker does in each situation makes a difference. Perhaps the point of this entire book has been that what each citizen and what each social worker knows can make a difference, and what that citizen or social worker does can contribute to the general welfare. In the following section, we introduce how technological tools can be used in social action to attain important goals.

Technology and Social Action

The United States has a rich history of community organizing, social action, lobbying, and community development as individuals, groups, and communities work to improve their world. Jack Rothman and John E. Tropman identified methods for changing systems above the level of the individual, group, and family, that is organizations, neighborhoods and communities, regions and states, and national systems. A major model for community organization practice is *social action* that attempts to shift power relationships and resources and seeks basic institutional change to improve conditions for disadvantaged populations, enhance social justice, minimize deprivations, and reduce inequities.[42]

Community organization involves active, voluntary engagement of citizens as individuals and groups to change problematic conditions and to influence policies and programs that affect the quality of their lives or the lives of others.[43]

For generations, community organizers used meetings, phones, mailings, telegrams, and other means to organize and affect problematic conditions, using various strategies. Recently technologies have expanded and powerful new tools are available to serve community and political groups.

Although basic organizing methods and strategies do not differ from those used in the past, the significant difference today is speed and efficiency. On a local level, new means of organizing can enhance organizing efforts of working people, women, ethnic and cultural minorities, the poor, and the disadvantaged.[44] Today, there is almost no group that does not have access themselves or through others to new technologies for communication, organization, and influence. Similarly, political action at regional, state, and federal levels may follow the same organizing principles as earlier, but the speed and ability to target decision makers have been enhanced.

New technologies can play a part in every stage of community organization and social action. Here is an abbreviated outline of such methods:

1. Problem identification and data/information gathering;
2. Identifying relevant persons and institutions by interest and/or involvement in the problem at local, state, region, national, and international level;
3. Selecting appropriate strategies and objectives to resolve or at least reduce the problem;
4. Targets to achieve change;
5. Involving persons, groups, and organizations in the organizing and advocacy effort;
6. Implementing the strategy; and
7. Monitoring and evaluating the results, identifying additional problems, and making on-course corrections.

New technologies that can be used at each of the preceding stages are computers (email, the Internet, World Wide Web, conferencing and message disks), teleconferencing, faxes, videoconferencing, and videotapes. In addition, it is possible to use the mass media as aids to organizing efforts. Use of the media requires skill at reaching them and getting them to enhance in appropriate ways the community organization and social action efforts. Organizers can obtain information: governmental statistics and reports, input from organizations concerned with the problem area, and finding and obtaining reports from persons with the same concerns. They can track problems though community bulletin boards, teleconferencing, and email.

Technology can be used, for example, to obtain demographic and census data, for voter registration; voter targeting; analysis of voter turnout; voting patterns; lobbying efforts; tenant, environmental, and other organizing; identifying "swing" election districts; obtaining profiles of voters; testing messages; and making personal appeals. Evidence supportive of the organizing effort can be obtained from relevant sources, including official documents, legislation, court rulings, administrative regulations, statistical data. One can obtain information as to who would be an active ally, an opponent, or be uninvolved, or who sits "on the fence" and might be open to involvement. As with all organizing, the message can be individualized and the delivery of the message can be specifically aimed and delivered as needed. Furthermore, technology can enhance "getting one's message across," an organizing campaign's fund-raising ability, and the way an organizing effort markets its program.

These technologies can be used for coalition building and also as a means for targeting influentials, contacting local, state, and national legislatures, government officials, courts, and those who administer policy and programs. Not only can one send messages, but the fact that the message was received can be confirmed. Use of the computer and other technologies does not rule out the use of traditional means to organize and advocate, such as one-on-one meeting with influentials; establishing a power base through individuals, groups, and coalitions; group visits; letters; telephone drives; debates; community meetings; written and oral testimony; and *amicus* briefs for courts. Preparation of computer disks or videotapes also hold promise as being useful at various stages of an organizing effort.[45]

Mass media can also play a part in community organizing and social action. Among the potential tools are network television, national and local newspapers, journals, and cable television. Among the organizing aims are educating the public and influential segments regarding the needs and/or problem; providing accurate information; interpreting the organizing effort's goals, characteristics, and activities; and educating regarding the desirability of change. Use of the media requires the skillful development of contacts, including reporters; obtaining opportunities for interviews; news releases; letters to editors; radio and TV appearances.[46]

Where We Are

Until recent years, the creation of the modern world brought with it the welfare state. The evolution of modern society is accompanied by problems that seek solutions. Whatever their economic or political system, whatever the ideologies of elites or masses, the more economically developed countries over the past century have converged in types of health and welfare programs, in increasingly comprehensive coverage, and, to a lesser extent, in methods of financing. The fraction of national resources devoted to these programs climbed, eventually at a decelerating rate.

However, the entire thrust of social welfare in the United States since the Great Depression is being challenged. One agenda focuses on private, personal solutions to problems. Many persons doubt the efficacy of government intervention and, in some instances, view such actions as destructive of individual and family values. This individualistic philosophy is based on the "can-do" American myth, which suggests that those who work hard enough can succeed, regardless of the nature of the job market and the economy. Others argue that governmental intervention is necessary to shore up the economy of the United States and other nations whose economies influence that of the United States.

Joel Blau places this debate in the context of rights and suggests the right to an entitlement is not a right accepted by all persons. The issue is the conflict between property rights and personal rights and between two political traditions. In one tradition, property serves as an economic and political counter to the state's power. Those who have a financial stake in the society can be expected to behave responsibly. This leads to civil liberties. The second tradition—the radical democratic tradition—holds that people need protection from the power of both government and private property. According to this latter tradition, such resources as medical care and affordable housing are natural rights. Some conservatives support the rights of property over the rights of persons; social welfare for them is a form of charity delivered by the state but not a right or an absolute entitlement.[47]

There is a continuing shift in national involvement between public purpose and private interest, an oscillation between the maximization of profit, the cult of the free market, the survival of the fittest, and equality, freedom, social responsibility, and general welfare. Furthermore, as Daniel Bell suggested, the state increasingly has the double problem of aiding capital formation and growth and meeting the rising claims of citizens for income security, social services, social amenities, and the like.[48] Both liberals and conservatives intend to balance the budget but differ in their priorities and the rate of changes. Conservatives desire cuts in domestic programs and seek to diminish the size of the federal government by reducing taxes and devolving federal functions to the state level. Conservative critics charge that social welfare is too expensive, undermines the traditional family, encourages the growth of single-parent families and children born out of wedlock, has failed to reduce the number of poor persons, and encourages dependence.

To what extent can a capitalist society provide for a cooperative morality *and* for individualism, the enhancement of all individuals as opposed to the autonomy of some individuals? How can we achieve a proper relationship between individuals and society, freedom and planning, pluralism and shared values? What should and can be done to eliminate poverty or to deal with other social problems depends on the ideologies and values of those who make legislative decisions. A backlash has grown against social welfare provision in quite different societies. Individual responsibility is touted as the answer to economic and social problems. The advocacy of individual responsibility is emphasized in a society in which the Federal Reserve system uses unemployment to offset possible inflation, and there is a shortage of jobs at a living wage for those who are unskilled.

Some persons attribute the successes of the pro-market and anti-social welfare position to the fact that many social welfare supports are in place buffering the shock and burden of unemployment. A number of social insurance and public assistance programs are counter-cyclical in nature and come into play when recession forces begin to appear. Even so, various events have caused nations with highly developed social welfare systems to reevaluate their efforts.

These issues grow out of ideological and political values and perspectives on the nature of social welfare in a capitalist society. From one point of view, social welfare serves to repair, contain, and suppress the negative effects of the capitalist system. There are always casualties of this kind of economy as businesses enlarge, move, and lay off workers. Furthermore, the culture of capitalism leads to and depends on an individualistic ideology and morality. These then call forth the need for a second set of social welfare measures to restore social morale and a sense of community. The worldwide collapse of communism encouraged a turn to capitalist solutions to social problems. No viable political or economic alternative to democratic capitalism appears on the horizon.

The strength of the U.S. economy is critically influenced by its relationship to other nations. We live in an interdependent world in which U.S. social welfare is closely interrelated with other parts of U.S. society and, in turn, U.S. society and social welfare are influenced by developments in other nations. Perhaps we have reached a stage of recognized interdependence in which the nations of the world need to share the risks through cooperative efforts to provide for the welfare of all people.

The market and a "thousand points of light" cannot rectify injustices in a modern state or allow socially more or less unfettered forces to determine the life chances and quality of life of its members. Aside from altruistic ideas, a society such as ours requires healthy persons involved in the life of the society with high morale. Robert Heilbroner and Lester Thurow argue that when problems arise from the market process itself there is no way of coping with those problems other than by government. "…Therefore, all market economies must have public sectors. It is impossible to have an economic system in which government would play no role whatever in the allocation of resources, where the dollar would decide everything and the voting rights of individuals would decide nothing. What is at stake is where to draw the line, not whether to draw the line."[49]

Where the state is unable for whatever reasons to adequately confront the social problems of the day, the path leads to policy failure and is perceived as unfairness. One result is a loss of popular support for social programs. The suggestion has been made that:

> from the point of view of progressive reform, the failure of a too-small welfare state to meet people's needs has created the worst of worlds because it has convinced many that government cannot work for them and paved the way for a symbolic politics of blame rather than a sustained effort to restructure government to make it more effective.[50]

Two Scenarios

As suggested earlier, future developments hold the key to the nature of social welfare. Essentially, there are two scenarios, both developed on the basis of technological innovations, one pessimistic and the other optimistic. The *pessimistic* perspective describes today's global unemployment as having reached a level higher than any time since the Great Depression. There are predictions that the reorganizing of the global economy and technology will lead to unemployment, underemployment, and relatively lower wages. High technology will destroy more jobs than it creates. Fewer people will produce more. There will be a withering away of comfortable full-time jobs, deteriorating employment opportunities and lost benefits, all threats to health care and economic security. According to this scenario, comparatively few people will be able to enjoy life without the constant stress of economic worries. Most people will be buried in work without end, anxious about getting or sustaining livelihoods. Even today both private and public employers demand "give backs." Those who envision this future claim it can be offset only by reduced working hours for workers, regulation of capital so that jobs do not float around the world seeking the lowest employee costs, and a guaranteed income is needed.[51]

Computer and communication technologies are replacing humans with machines. Their impact is being felt more and more on workplaces and communities as the world traverses a great revolution. Even fewer workers will be needed to produce goods and services. In the past, when employment needs were reduced in one area of the economy, another area took up the slack. In turn, manufacturing took up the slack from agriculture, and services took up the slack from a drop in manufacturing employment. Today, all three sectors are experiencing the same technological displacement. The results of these factors are both liberating for some and destabilizing for many others.[52]

The more *optimistic* view predicts an American renaissance, a long-term economic resurgence. According to this view, the United States reinvented its economy at the end of the Cold War with new technologies. The United States has ample room for expansion, favorable demographics, and a dynamic labor market. Information technology and information will grow cheaper, to the benefit of all those who have access to them. The United States with available capital will be able to control networks and high-tech information systems. With a large and diverse population, the United States is poised to take advantage of the electronic cultural revolution, and it will be both a market and a source for new cultural ideas—music, video, and writing. With technological advantages and the ability to create and use new technologies, optimists expect the United States for the foreseeable future to lead the world into the next millenium.[53]

Our Proposal

In our view, the amelioration of poverty cannot be left to the vagaries of the marketplace. The current situation requires governmental intervention. Basic to the general welfare is the growth of the economy and improved economic conditions for individuals and families. Economic growth along with a reduction of the federal debt and deficits are essential prerequisites for combating poverty. Governmental actions are needed to redistribute wealth through income transfers, education and training, and job creation. Our aim is not equality of incomes but equal access for all Americans to basic necessities such as food, education, appropriate housing, and health care to sustain life at a decent level as well as fair opportunities to pursue a range of opportunities in a healthy environment. Continual encouragement of employment in the private sector is needed along with the public sector's serving as the employer or work subsidizer of last resort. This is necessary so that as many people as possible can work, especially low-skilled workers and those who have sought work but have been unable to find employment. This requires enlarged labor markets, both private and public, forming a work-based safety net. In addition, the minimum wage needs to be adjusted upward to keep pace with inflation.

The use of a family or children's allowance combined with enhanced use of the Earned Income Tax Credit and enhancement of TANF, child support assurance, and an increased use of "living wages" will better protect poor children and their parents. Income security, training and education, affordable and decent housing, food, health care, personal social services, day care, and family planning are basic programs. In addition, the child tax credits and dependent care tax credits can be made refundable. These fundamental programs—joined with inclusion, antidiscrimination laws, and investment in human capital—add up to a strategy that could enable the United States to move toward the minimization of poverty.

Summary

Throughout this book, we have examined the impact of values and of social and economic structures on social welfare and on peoples' lives. We recognized the importance of both social and economic structures *and* individual responsibility. We believe people are responsible for their actions and behavior, if not their fates, within the boundaries of opportunity available to them. We have seen that private troubles and public issues are interrelated and people with unequal capacities encounter different obstacles (including for many people oppressive social forces) and opportunities. Illustrative of this is the finding that greater inequality in the distribution of income contributes to higher overall mortality rates and deaths from heart disease, cancer, and homicide.[54]

The elimination and diminishment of life-sustaining basic guarantees for food, housing, and other necessities is regressive and injurious to many children and adults. Such regressive actions are not consonant with the American dream of "general welfare" and will decrease the quality of life of those who need help but also diminish the rest of us as well.

Questions for Consideration

1. Select one social problem that interests you (and is not discussed in this chapter). Why is it a problem?

2. How has the United States (your state or community) dealt historically with the problem?

3. Can you identify any theories about the causation of the problem? Can you identify the social and economic costs of the problem? Can you identify the relevant policies, legislation, and services currently provided?

4. If the necessary resources were available, what would you suggest an ideal set of services to deal with the problem would include?

Notes

1. Sheila B. Kamerman and Alfred J. Kahn, "Family Change and Family Policies: United States," *Family Change and Family Policies in Great Britain, Canada, New Zealand, and the United States,* *Sheila Kamerman and Alfred Kahn,* eds. Oxford: Clarendon Press, 1997, pp. 305–417.

2. Joseph Dalaker, *Poverty in the United States: 2000,* Current Population Reports, P60-214, U.S.

Department of Commerce, U.S. Census Bureau, Washington, D.C.: September 2001and Carmen De-Navas-Walt, Robert W. Cleveland, and Marc L. Roemer, *Money Income in the United States: 2000,* Current Population Reports, P60-213, U.S. Department of Commerce, U.S. Census Bureau, Washington, D.C. September 2001, www.census.gov, October 31, 2001.

3. Children's Defense Fund, *The State of America's Children.* Boston: Beacon Press, 2000, pp. xi, xiii, xiv.

4. Aletha C. Huston, Vonnie C. McLoyd, and Cynthia G. Coll, "Children and Poverty: Issues in Contemporary Research," *Child Development,* Vol. 65, 1994, pp. 275–282.

5. Jason DeParle, "Child Poverty Twice as Likely After Family Split, Study Says," *New York Times,* March 2, 1991, p. 8.

6. Arloc Sherman, *Wasting America's Future: The Children's Defense Fund Report on the Costs of Child Poverty,* Boston: Beacon Press, 1994, pp. 13–15.

7. Keith Bradsher, "Low Ranking for Poor American Children," *New York Times,* August 14, 1995, p. A9.

8. Sheila B. Kamerman, "Gender Role and Family Structure Changes in the Advanced Industrialized West: Implications for Social Policy," in *Poverty, Inequality, and the Future of Social Policy,* Katharine McFate, Roger Lawson, and William J. Wilson, Eds., New York: Russell Sage Foundation, 1995, pp. 244–245.

9. Victor R. Fuchs and Diane M. Reklis, "America's Children: Economic Perspectives and Policy Options," *Science,* Vol. 255, January 3, 1992, pp. 41–46.

10. Barbara P. Noble, "Women Seeking a Working Agenda," *New York Times,* February 5, 1995, p. F23.

11. Greg J. Duncan and Jeanne Brooks-Gunn, Eds., *Consequences of Growing Up Poor,* New York: Russell Sage Foundation, 1997.

12. Children's Defense Fund, *The State of America's Children,* p. xx.

13. National Institute of Mental Health, "Brief Notes on the Mental Health of Children and Adolescents," www.nimh.nih.gov/publicat/childnotes.cfm, August 8, 2001.

14. Department of Health and Human Services, *Report of the Surgeon General's Conference on Children's Mental Health,* www.surgeongeneral.gov/cmh/childreport.htm, August 28, 2001.

15. National Institute for Mental Health, *Blueprint for Change: Research on Child and Adolescent Mental Health,* August, 2001.

16. Paula Allen-Meares, "Children: Mental Health," *Encyclopedia of Social Work,* ed. Richard L.. Edwards, Washington, D.C.: National Association of Social Workers, 1995, pp. 460–465.

17. J. H. Williams, Robert Pierce, Nioka S. Young, and Richard A. Van Dorn, "Service Utilization in High Crime Communities: Consumer Views on Supports and Barriers, *Families in Society: The Journal of Contemporary Human Services,* 82 (4), July–August, 2001, pp. 409–417.

18. Nicholas S. Ialongo, Gail Edelsohn, Sheppard G. Kellam, "A Further Look at the Prognostic Power of Young Children's Reports of depressed Mood and Feelings," *Child Development,* 72 (3), May–June, 2001, pp. 736–747.

19. Jack Rothman and Jon Simon Sager, *Case Management,* 2nd edition, Boston: Allyn and Bacon, 1998, pp. 12–13.

20. Krista Kutash and Vestena R. Rivera, *What Works in Children's Mental Health Services?* Baltimore: Paul H. Brookes Publishing Co., 1996

21. Erica Goode, "Disparities Seen In Mental Care for Minorities," *New York Times,* August 27, 2001, pp. 1, 12.

22. Gretchen Rowe, *State TANF Policies as of July 1999, Assessing the New Federalism, Welfare Rules Databook,* Urban Institute, November 2000, www.urban.org, October 31, 2001.

23. The White House, Office of Management and Budget, "Tax Expenditures by Function, www.whitehouse.gov/omb/budget/fy2002/bud22-4html, June 11, 2001.

24. *2000 Green Book,* p. 1346.

25. Paulette Olson and Dell Champlin, "Ending Corporate Welfare As We Know It: An Institutional Analysis of the Dual Structure of Welfare," *Journal of Economic Issues,* 32 (3) September, 1998, pp. 759–771.

26. Citizens for Tax Justice, "The Hidden Entitlements," www.ctj.org/hid_ent/part1.htm, September 6, 2001.

27. Leslie Wayne, "Bush 'Corporate Welfare' Attack Faces a Strong Challenge by Lott," *New York Times,* June 25, 2001, p. 1 and A12.

28. Timothy Egan, "Failing Farmers Learn to profit From Wealth of U.S. Subsidies," New York Times, December 24, 2000, pp. 1 and A16.

29. Cato Institute, *Cato Handbook for Congress, Corporate Welfare,* www.cato.org/pubs/handbook/hb105-9.html, September 6, 2001.

30. Stanley L. Witkin, "Chronicity and Invisibility," Editorial, *Social Work,* Vol. 43, No. 4, July 1998, p. 293.

31. Deborah Marks, *Disability: Controversial Debates and Psychosocial Perspectives,* London: Routledge, 1999.

32. Linda Greenhouse, "High Court Limits Who is Protected By Disability law," *New York Times,* June 23, 1999, pp. 1, A16 and Linda Greenhouse, "States

Limited on Institutionalization," *New York Times*, June 23, 1999, p. A16.

33. Lyle Denniston, "Court Limits Right to Sue By Disabled," *Baltimore Sun*, June 23, 1999, pp. 1,9A; *Toyota Motor Manufacturing, Kentucky, Inc.* v. *Williams*, Legal Information Institute, http://supct.law.cornell.edu/supct/html/00-1089.ZO.html, March 24, 2002.

34. Malinda Orlin, "The Americans with Disabilities Act: Implications for Social Services," *Social Work*, Vol. 40, No. 2, March 1995, pp. 233–239.

35. U.S. Bureau of the Census, *Statistical Abstract of the United States: 1995*, Table 751, "Monthly Measures of Poverty Status, by Selected Characteristics: 1990–91 Period," p. 483.

36. Felice D. Perlmutter, Darlyne Bailey, and F. Ellen Netting, *Managing Human Resources in the Human Services*, New York: Oxford University Press, 2001.

37. Linda Greenhouse, "Disabled State Inmates Protected by U.S. Law Barring Discrimination," *New York Times*, June 16, 1998, p. A18.

38. Lyle Denniston, "U.S. Schools to Pay Costs for Disabled," *Baltimore Sun*, March 4, 1999, pp. 1, 5a.

39. Juanita B. Hepler, "Mainstreaming Children with Learning Disabilities: Have We Improved Their Social Environment?" *Social Work in Education*, Vol. 16, No. 3, July 1994, pp. 143–154.

40. Robert H. Woody, "Americans with Disabilities Act: Implications for Family Therapy," *American Journal of Family Therapy*, Vol. 21, No. 1, 1993, pp. 71–78.

41. Michael Berube, "The Cultural Representation of People with Disabilities Affects Us All," *The Chronicle of Higher Education*, May 30, 1997, pp. B4–5.

42. Jack Rothman and John E. Tropman, "Models of Community Organization and Macro Practice Perspectives: Their Mixing and Phasing," *Strategies of Community Organization*, 4th Edition, Fred M. Cox, John L. Ehrlich, Jack Rothman, and John E. Tropman, Eds., Itasca, Ill.: F. E. Peacock Publishers, Inc., 1987, pp. 3–26.

43. Dorothy N. Gamble and Marie O. Weil, "Citizen Participation," *Encyclopedia of Social Work*, 19th Edition, Richard L. Edwards, ed., Washington, D.C.: National Association of Social Workers, 1995, pp. 483–494.

44. Gary Chapman and Lodis Rhodes, "Nurturing Neighborhood Nets," *Technology Review*, October 1997, http://www.techreview.com, October 1, 1998.

45. Willard C. Richan, *Lobbying for Social Change*, New York: Haworth Press, 1996; John Downing, et al, Eds., *Computers for Social Change*, New York: Haworth Press, 1991.

46. Edward A. Brawley, *Human Services and the Media*, Newbury Park, Calif.: Harwood Academic Publishers, 1995.

47. Joel Blau, "Theories of the Welfare State," *Social Service Review*, Vol. 63, No. 1, March 1989, pp. 35–36.

48. Daniel Bell, "The Future World Disorder," *The Winding Passage*, Cambridge, Mass.: Abt Books, 1980, p. 215.

49. Robert L. Heilbroner and Lester C. Thurow, *Five Economic Challenges*, Englewood Cliffs, N.J.: Prentice Hall, 1981, pp. 55, 77.

50. Charles Noble, *Welfare As We Knew It*, New York: Oxford University Press, 1997, p. 156.

51. Stanley Aronowitz, *The Last Good Job in America*, Lanham, MD.: Rowman & Littlefield Publishers, 2001.

52. Jeremy Rifkin, *The End of Work: The Decline of the Global Labor Force and the Dawn of the Post-Market Era*, New York: G. P. Putnam's Sons, 1995, pp. xv–xviii.

53. Michael Moynihan, *The Coming American Renaissance*, New York: Simon & Schuster, 1996, *passim* and pp. 285–289.

54. M. Harvey Brenner, "Political Economy and Health," in *Society and Health*, Eds. Benjamin C. Amick, III, Sol Levine, Alvin R. Tarlov, Diana Chapman Walsh, New York: Oxford University Press, 1995, pp. 211–246.

Appendix

Sources of Information

The following are some leads for beginning research. The first task is to be as clear as possible as to the subject you want to study, the key words (for example, employment, minimum wage) associated with the subject or other words or concepts that define the same subject (voluntarism, volunteerism, volunteers, and so on). The more specific your search, the greater the possibility the search can be useful. Bibliographical searches can be done by computer in most libraries, which lead you to books and journals, magazines, newspapers, and so on. In many cases, governmental documents will also be listed. Remember too as you read publications that their bibliographies also can supply you with additional leads.

Electronic information sources are becoming a dominant mode of exchanging information. Here are several leads. Some access is through universities and colleges. Other access is through commercial ventures.

Web Sites on the Internet

For a comprehensive review of governmental sites, see Bruce Maxwell, *How to Access the Federal Government on the Internet, 1998*, Washington: Congressional Quarterly, 1997.

To connect directly to sites for specific *government* agencies, go to these sites:

Bureau of Labor Statistics   http://stats.bls.gov/blshome.html

U.S. Census Bureau   http://www.census.gov/

Catalog of Federal Domestic Assistance   http://www.gsa.gov/fdac/default.htm

Census State Data Centers   http://www.census.gov/ftp/pub/sdc/www/

Centers for Disease Control   www.cdcnac.org

Congressional Budget Office Studies & Reports   http://www.cbo.gov/reports.cfm

Department of Health and Human Services, Administration for Children and Families   http://www.acf.dhhs.gov

Department of Health and Human Services, Research, Policy and Administration   http://www.os.dhhs.gov:80/policy/index.html

Department of Health and Human Services: Childhood and Youth Policy http://aspe.os.dhhs.gov/hsp/cyphome.htm

Department of Housing and Urban Development   www.hud.gov

Department of Veterans Affairs   www.va.gov

Federal Budget   http://www.access.gpo.gov/su_docs/budget98/maindown.html

FEDSTATS   http://www.fedstats.gov

Fedworld Information Network   http://www.fedworld.gov

Health Care Financing Administration (HCFA)   http://www.hcfa.gov/

Library of Congress   http://lcweb.loc.gov/

Medicare   www.medicare.gov

National Data Archive on Child Abuse and Neglect   www.ndacan.cornell.edu/

National Institutes of Health   http://www.nih.gov

National Institute on Alcohol Abuse and Alcoholism   www.niaaa.nih.gov/

National Institute of Mental Health   http://www.nimh.nih.gov/

Nonprofit Gateway   http://www.nonprofit.gov/

Social Security Online   http://www.ssa.gov/

State and Local Government on the Net   http://www.piperinfo.com/state/states.html

Statistical Abstract of the U.S.   http://www.census. gov/statab/www/

THOMAS: Legislative Information   http://thomas.loc.gov/

U.S. House of Representatives   http://www.house.gov/

U.S. Senate   http://www.senate.gov/

White House   http://www.whitehouse.gov/

Nongovernment Sites

AIDS   www.hopkins-aids.edu

American Association of Retired Persons   www.aarp.org

American Public Human Services Association   www.aphsa.org

Cato Institute   www.cato.org

Center on Budget and Policy Priorities   www.cbpp.org

Center for Law and Social Policy   www.clasp.org

Center for the Study of Issues in Public Mental Health   www.rfmah.org/csipmh/

Center for Substance Abuse Prevention   www.covesoft.com/csap.html

Children Now   www.childrennow.org

Child Welfare League of America   http://cwla.org/

Child Welfare Resource Center   http://www.child welfare.ca

Children's Defense Fund   cdfupdate@childrensdefense.org

Citizens Budget Committee   www.epn.org/cbc/

Citizens for Tax Justice   www.ctj.org

Council on State Governments   www.csg.org

The Electronic Policy Network   www.epn.org

Mental Health Net   http://cmhc.com/   http://cmhc.com??

National Aging Information Center   http://www.aoa.dhhs.gov/naic/

National Alliance for the Mentally Ill   www.nami.org.

National Association of Developmental Disabilities
Councils   www.igc.apc.org/NADDC/

National Association of Social Workers   http://www.naswdc.org

National Clearinghouse for Alcohol and Drug
Information   www.health.org/ index.htm

National Federation of the Blind   www.nfb.org

Social Work and Social Services Web Sites   http://gwbweb.wustl.edu/web-
sites.html

The National Governors' Association   www.nga.org

The Society for Prevention Research   http://www.oslc.org/spr/sprhome.
html

The Urban Institute   www.urban.org

The Welfare Information Network   www.welfareinfo.org

Welfare Law Center   http://www.welfarelaw.org

Encyclopedia/Handbooks

Encyclopedia of Social Work
Statistical Abstract of the United States
Social Work Dictionary
Social Work Almanac

Indexes/Abstracts

The following sources are available in both computerized and print formats:

Social Work Research and Abstracts
PAIS International
Psychological Abstracts

Monthly Catalog of U.S. Government Publications
New York Times Index
Washington Post Index

Serial Publications

Brookings Review
Child Welfare
Congressional Quarterly Weekly Report
Journal of Health and Social Policy
Journal of Policy Analysis and Management
Journal of Sociology and Social Welfare
Monthly Labor Review
New York Times
OECD in Figures: Statistics on the Member Countries (Organization for Economic Co-Operation and Development)
Policy Studies Journal
Policy Studies Review
Population Bulletin
Public Welfare
Social Security Bulletin
Social Security Bulletin, Annual Statistical Supplement
Social Security Throughout the World
Social Service Review
Social Work
Washington Post

Other Sources of Information

Federal Information Center (800-688-9889) for information about taxes, Social Security benefits, governmental publications, federal programs, agencies, and services, and so on.

Government Documents

Here are the Superintendent of Documents classification codes of some useful sources in a Government Documents section. (Note some libraries may classify these materials with their regular collection.)

Bureau of the Census: C3.612:IN 2/ 5/994
Joint Economic Committee of the Congress: Y4.EC 7:D 36/14

Joint Committee on Taxation: Y4.T 1914-10:995-99

House of Representatives Committee on Education and Labor: Y4.ED 8/1:103-77

Senate Committee on Labor and Human Resources: Y4.L 11/4:S.HRG

House of Representatives Committee on Ways and Means: Y4.W 36:10-7/994

Department of Health and Human Services: HE 1.1/2:993-94

Department of Labor: L1.1:993

Bureau of Labor Statistics: L2.2:OC1/53

National Center for Health Statistics: HE 20.6202:H 34/15

National Institute of Mental Health: HE 20.8102:AN 9

National Institute on Aging: HE 20.3852:AL 9/5

National Institute on Drug Abuse: HE 20.8202:EP 4/3/992

President of the United States: PR 42.2:   P 31

Social Security Administration: HE 3.1:994

Substance Abuse and Mental Health Services Administration: HE 20.8008:AL 1/11

Women's Bureau: L36.114/3:94-1

Index